The LEGAL ADVISOR
for LIBRARIANS,
EDUCATORS, &
INFORMATION
PROFESSIONALS

THE
COMPLETE
COPYRIGHT
LIABILITY
HANDBOOK
FOR LIBRARIANS
AND EDUCATORS

Tomas A. Lipinski

Neal-Schuman Publishers, Inc.
New York   London

**The Legal Advisor for Librarians, Educators, and
Information Professionals**

No. 1—*The Complete Copyright Liability Handbook for Librarians and Educators.* By Tomas A. Lipinski

Published by Neal-Schuman Publishers, Inc.
100 William St., Suite 2004
New York, NY 10038

Printed and bound in the United States of America.

The paper used in this publication meets the minimum requirements of American National Standard for Information Sciences—Permanence of Paper for Printed Library Materials, ANSI Z39.48-1992.

PLEASE READ THIS:
"This publication is designed to provide accurate and authoritative information in regard to the subject matter covered. It is sold with the understanding that the publisher is not engaged in rendering legal, accounting, or other professional service. If legal or other expert assistance is required, the services of a competent professional person should be sought." *From a Declaration of Principles adopted jointly by a Committee of the American Bar Association and a committee of Publishers.*

Library of Congress Cataloging-in-Publication Data

Lipinski, Tomas A., 1958-
   The complete copyright liability handbook for librarians and educators / Tomas A. Lipinski.
        p. cm. — (The legal advisor for librarians, educators & information professionals ; no. 1)
   Includes index.
   ISBN 1-55570-532-4 (alk. paper)
   1. Copyright infringement—United States. 2. Fair use (Copyright)—United States. I. Title. II. Series.
   KF3080.L57 2006
   346.7304'82—dc22
                                                        2005033387

▶Dedication

I dedicate this book to all of my students, and to other members of the copyright audience to whom I speak, past, present, and future.

It is often through your enthusiastic questions that I am encouraged to seek further understanding of the law.

►Contents

►PART I
THREE TYPES OF COPYRIGHT LIABILITY

▶ PART II
PENALTIES AND IMMUNITIES IN
COPYRIGHT LAW FOR LIBRARIES AND SCHOOLS

▶ PART III
THE IMPACT OF THE DIGITAL MILLENNIUM
COPYRIGHT ACT ON LIBRARY AND EDUCATIONAL ENVIRONMENTS

▶PART IV
THREE WAYS LIBRARIES AND
SCHOOLS CAN LIMIT THEIR EXPOSURE

▶ PART V
COMPLIANCE TOOLS FOR SCHOOLS AND LIBRARIES

▶Series Editor's Introduction

This series, "The Legal Advisor for Librarians, Educators, and Information Professionals," offers sound legal scholarship aimed at non-lawyers. This first book, *The Complete Copyright Liability Handbook for Librarians and Educators*, like others in the series, provides answers to the essential "what" and "how" questions:

▶ What is the law?

▶ How does it affect us?

▶ How do we comply with it to our advantage?

This series presents a variety of legal topics—ranging from licensing to liability, from the American with Disabilities Act (ADA) to privacy, from copyright to protected speech, and many more. The subjects will interest a wide variety of information organizations in both the private and public sectors: libraries, schools, archives, manuscript and special collections, and museum collections.

Each monograph in the series follows a similar structure: presentation of the law, followed by the application of the law through discussion of examples. Each substantive chapter includes case studies and bullet-point summaries. Each volume constains a Compliance Tools section that includes a legal audit or Q & A that can be used as both a professional teaching device and as a compliance and risk management tool. In addition, there are model policy statements that can be incorporated into your existing policy structures. Where appropriate, a third appendix will feature sample language of use in contracts or licenses, signs or notices, or other appropriate contexts.

"The Legal Advisor for Librarians, Educators, and Information Professionals" presents—in a readable format, drawn from sound legal analysis—practical information on a variety of specific topics. Each title, written by a leading expert in the field, puts forward legal scholarship and offers practitioners a useful tool for compliance.

As the editor of the series, I have enlisted an array of contacts in the legal-library information community to solicit submissions and interest from perspective authors. Future topics include licensing, use of public library spaces, gifts, information liability, privacy, and confidentiality. Neal-Schuman Publishers and I are committed to featuring only the highest quality work from contributors who have strong research foundations as well as experience in both law and libraries or related information settings.

We hope you enjoy and find useful our efforts.

Tomas A. Lipinski
Associate Professor
Co-Director, Center for Information Policy Research
School of Information Studies
University of Wisconsin—Milwaukee

►Foreword

As someone who conducts copyright workshops for librarians, I am often asked by non-librarians, including lawyers, why librarians need to know anything about copyright. I think they are stunned when I answer that librarians confront copyright issues every single day in their work as librarians. Whether photocopying for library users, posting copyrighted materials on the Internet, or answering reference questions by providing copies of materials, librarians are involved with copyright. That is not to say that all of these activities are infringement, but rather that copyright principles are in play and librarians need to be familiar with the law in order to make the best possible decisions. Teachers face copyright issues when they distribute photocopies of copyrighted works to their students, reproduce portions of sound recordings for listening, and post copyrighted materials into course management software. The general public seems to understand why teachers need to know about copyright law, but not so with librarians.

For both librarians and teachers the digital environment has made understanding copyright law even more difficult—the temptation to reproduce copyrighted works grows as technology makes it increasingly easy to do. A common shared misunderstanding is that if what teachers and librarians do is for educational purposes, there must be an exception that permits them to reproduce and distribute copyrighted works to students and library patrons in whatever format they choose. This book helps refute this misunderstanding and offers assistance on how to accomplish one's purpose and still comply with the law.

Many librarians have mastered the basics of copyright law or at least have some familiarity with it. In my experience, educators generally are less knowledgeable about copyright than are librarians, but there are exceptions, of course. High-profile cases, such as the recent U.S. Supreme Court *Grokster* decision that deals with peer-to-peer file sharing, have raised awareness about copyright and the difficulties copyright owners face in the digital world. Still, some librarians and educators remain unaware how these cases affect them in their daily work.

The Complete Copyright Liability Handbook for Librarians and Educators starts with the premise that the reader has a basic knowledge of copyright and builds on this fundamental knowledge to examine liability for infringing activities in libraries and educational institutions. Thus, this should not be a reader's first book about copyright—instead, it is an important second one.

Tom Lipinski has produced a well-written and well-researched guide that fills an important gap in the copyright literature for librarians and educators. Individuals assess risk on a daily basis (for example, whether to exceed the speed limit when driving one's car), but seldom are librarians and educators directed to balance the potential for liability against the benefits of conducting certain types of activities. The more important the activity is to the organization, the more risk one may be willing to take. However, it is not just individual liability that is at issue but also institutional liability. Lipinski does an excellent job in discussing risk assessment for copyright infringement.

The book is organized into five parts, covering (1) types of copyright infringement, (2) penalties and immunities, (3) the impact of the Digital Millennium Copyright Act, (4) how to limit exposure to infringement claims, and (5) compliance tools. Each part consists of several chapters that explain the law very well in lay terms without sacrificing either legal accuracy or nuance. Part I examines direct infringement, contributory infringement, and vicarious liability. Part II looks at damages and what libraries and educational institutions can do to limit damages, and examines whether any immunity is possible, and, if so, how to obtain it. Part III, the impact of the DMCA, focuses on the impact of this 1998 amendment on libraries and schools, particularly online service provider liability and the so-called "anti-circumvention" provision. Part IV reviews three specific limitations on liability: the requirements libraries must meet in order to reproduce copyrighted materials for patrons, circulation of software, and compliance for distance education programs. Each chapter has an excellent section of real-world examples that help illustrate the law in that area. Additionally, each chapter concludes with a section that lists key points for institutional policy and practice, a very innovative and useful addition.

The final part, Part V, contains three very useful compliance tools. The first two are a copyright compliance audit tool and an implementation checklist for section 512 registered agents. Both of these tools are very helpful and they will do much to assist libraries and educational institutions to limit their liability for copyright infringement. The most important tool, however, is the third: a collection of sixteen sample copyright policies. Two of the limitations on liability, section 110(2) (the distance education exception) and section 512 (the online service provider liability provision), require educational institutions to have copyright policies. Many institutions are currently engaged in drafting such policies, and these models serve as excellent guides for institutions that want to take advantage of these important provisions.

Tom Lipinski has done a masterful job in demystifying the law and creating a very readable and usable handbook. It is an important addition to the literature and will quickly become a standard reference tool for librarians and educators.

Laura N. Gasaway
Director of the Law Library and Professor of Law
University of North Carolina

▶ Preface

WHY READ THIS BOOK?

The Complete Copyright Liability Handbook for Librarians and Educators helps librarians, educators, network administrators, and other knowledge workers understand what copyright law requires them to do as stewards of information. In general, this is referred to as "copyright awareness." In day-to-day work, it encompasses enforcement of copyright notices; the development of appropriate policies; informational outreach; the use of technological controls, including password protection and user authentication; and, in some instances, removing infringing materials or disabling access to content deemed in violation.

Under the copyright law, an individual or institution can enjoy the advantages of specific "use" provisions only when it complies with the full scope of the law. By not undertaking proper efforts, many librarians and educators put their institutions, themselves, and their colleagues at risk of not only losing any educational "fair use" and "safe harbor" provisions, but also of being successfully sued.

The Complete Copyright Liability Handbook provides readers with a framework for developing a copyright compliant environment-including understanding what must be done, when actions should be taken, and what tools librarians, educators, and administrators should employ in their quest to stay on the right side of the law.

WHY WORRY ABOUT COPYRIGHT COMPLIANCE?

While new laws like the Digital Millennium Copyright Act (DMCA) and the Technology, Education and Copyright Harmonization (TEACH) Act give libraries and schools new use rights, they also increase the ability of copyright owners to enforce their rights. As a result, users of copyrighted materials as well as the institutions that provide or facilitate access to those works face an unprecedented—and growing—legal infrastructure.

The Sonny Bono Copyright Term Extension Act,[1] the Digital Millennium Copyright Act,[2] and the Technology, Education and Copyright Harmonization Act[3] constitute the latest additions to the arsenal of weapons copyright holders bear. Perhaps in response to recent industry initiatives (read "lawsuits"[4]) regarding illegal file sharing, and in spite of a recent study that students and other institutional clients are getting the industry message,[5] Congress does not plan to slow down new legislation. After holding hearings in 2003 on the P2P rampage and other copyright abuses among student Internet users,[6] legislation was introduced that would offer plaintiffs the opportunity to sue those who aid or abet another's infringement,[7] as well as legislation that would criminalize unlawful file sharing under certain circumstances.[8] As providers of access (those who aid or abet another's infringement), schools and libraries are at legal risk. Moreover, copyright liability is strongest in the digital environment,[9] a medium that dominates the technology-infused environment of the modern library, school, college, or university.

At the same time that new laws strengthen the holder's rights, new technologies make it easier to identify infringing patrons and, where applicable, the institutional locus of their infringement. Copyright owners are becoming far less patient and far more belligerent. The massive subpoena attack launched by the RIAA in the summer and early fall of 2003 indicates that the copyright owners are becoming aggressive in their search for infringing practices.[10] College students were early targets, but as abusers become younger, the average age of defendants may decrease. Congress is also becoming frustrated and appears, at the writing of this book, poised to respond as well.[11]

Schools and libraries are, paradoxically, at risk because they inform and teach. Librarians and educators have done a superb job instructing their charges in the uses of high technology, integrating computer technology into the information-seeking and educational process, and creating a generation of savvy, digitally oriented, cut-and-paste users. The problem is that these librarians and educators forgot, or perhaps deliberately neglected, to tell patrons and students that just because technology allows one to do something, that does not mean one should do it; legality and ability or possibility do not necessarily operate on the same margin. Educators, regardless of institutional setting, should have a pedagogical concern and professional responsibility to educate their charges or constituents on the legal responsibilities that come with new technologies—just as they have with other forms of unacceptable behavior and socialization.

What is the proper response and measure? Should educational institutions begin offering courses or course components in copyright law?[12] Some schools and universities now require incoming freshmen to attend copyright education programs before granting them access to the university computer networks.[13] Many states have, in fact, established minimum assessment standards requiring that students be educated about various aspects of intellectual property rights as part of a technology education template.[14]

Even if not required by law, compliance efforts might represent an inexpensive hedge or insurance of sorts. Preventing copyright abuse in library and educational settings from ever occurring is a simple impossibility. A strong compliance program can, however, reduce the instances of abuse as well as minimize the risk of exposure to liability, not only on the part of the individual patron, student, teacher, or staff member, but, more important, on the institution as "host" or employer, should those instances occur.

COPYRIGHT APPROACHES

The adage that the law giveth and the law taketh away is alive and well in copyright law. Section 106 establishes the exclusive rights of the copyright owner[15] (giveth), while subsequent provisions, some of which are the focus of this book, operate as a limitation (taketh away) on those exclusive rights. For educators and librarians, these provisions focus on our professional activities—the reproduction of materials for distribution to patrons or students, the performance and display of materials in the distance education classroom (or the broader context of networked environments), the use of copyrighted material by faculty, staff, or even students. Some provisions are the result of the new TEACH Act,[16] while others, such as section 108, have been around for quite some time.

Fair use, if applicable, is a defense to a claim of copyright infringement, but, short of that, there are other provisions of the law that operate to minimize the impact of liability, should it arise. Built within the copyright law are a variety of so-called damage limitation provisions. These provisions may reduce the bottom-line liability—damages—to "actual" damages or loss of profits and offer the remission of the often more exorbitant "statutory" damages. Understanding damage remission and knowing when it is available can help maximize the availability of such refuge in your institutional setting. While this book does not review in detail the basic provisions of the copyright law, an explanation of the background and context precedes the presentation of each compliance-oriented provision discussed. Sample language is offered, either as required by law or in the author's best guess of what would likely satisfy the statutory and legislative intent of the provision. A useful appendix collects these for quick review. As always, legal interpretations, sample language, and suggestions are provided for informational purposes only and they are not a substitute for legal advice.

Violate any of the copyright owner's exclusive rights listed in section 106 (reproduce the work or prepare derivative of it, distribute the work to the public, perform the copyrighted work publicly, display the work publicly, perform a sound recording publicly by means of a digital audio transmission[17]) and you have infringed copyright. In theory, the individual responsible for that violation is considered the "direct" infringer, e.g., the librarian that made the infringing copies or the educator that played the movie for the class. A direct infringement is distinguished from what can be called an indirect infringement. The terms "primary" for direct and "secondary" for indirect can also be used. Though not codified, courts have developed two indirect or secondary ways (and perhaps for the library as institution or intermediary, more important ways) to be liable: contributory and vicarious copyright infringement.

Understanding the relationships among the three sorts of copyright infringement is important. It is through concepts of secondary liability that the institution can be liable. However, before this can occur, there must be an act of direct infringement; without it secondary liability cannot attach. Of course the law contains many "limitations" on these exclusive rights. One example of importance to libraries is section 108, which indicates that, under certain conditions, reproductions or distributions by qualifying libraries are not considered infringement. Section 107 also labels fair use as a "limitation," though in practice (case law) it is often discussed as a defense to a claim of infringement.

HOW TO USE THIS BOOK

Most books on this subject for our profession feature a general introduction to the copyright law—what it is or how long it lasts—or to general use concepts, such as fair use. *The Complete Copyright Liability Handbook for Librarians and Educators* moves beyond these basics. Accordingly, some knowledge of the essential concepts of copyright law may be helpful in the following chapters. Where applicable, there is reference and brief discussion of sections of copyright law not covered in detail here, especially where it furthers the main objectives. If you do not have knowledge of these fundamental theories, do not despair! Simply understand that there may be some gaps in your knowledge base as you move through the chapters. Moreover, it goes without comment that the author assumes that this is not the only copyright book you will ever purchase or read.

Remember as you read that the focus of this text is on those provisions and concepts that limit the amount of damages a plaintiff can recover, that preclude the recovery of any monetary damages, or that offer complete immunity from liability, as well as on those provisions that condition a limitation on the copyright owner's exclusive right on what might be deemed a "compliance" effort or activity. Sometimes this might mean the use of copyright warning notices or the adoption of a copyright policy. These requirements will generally be referred to as compliance-oriented provisions. These provisions are often targeted at libraries, or, in the case of section 512, a broader category of online service providers that can include libraries and schools. It should be clear, many of the matters discussed in this book have repercussions for information-oriented institutions of all types. In order to obtain the benefits of the use privilege, the intermediary-institution must "do" something to help other users comply with the law. Explaining the particularities of that "something" is the guide's fundamental drive. Indeed, the handbook's purpose is to move you beyond basic considerations toward practical and informed action.

The Complete Copyright Liability Handbook for Librarians and Educators begins with a "Glossary of Essential Terms Used in This Book." It may be helpful to read through this glossary before beginning any of the chapters, to familiarize yourself with the terms that will be used. The glossary also serves as an essential reference as you read the text and implement the tools.

Part I, "Three Types of Copyright Liability," details the nuances of infringement by both the institutions and individuals.

▶ Chapter 1, "What Is Direct Copyright Infringement?" presents the overt violation of the copyright protections on a work.

▶ Chapter 2, "What Is Contributory Copyright Infringement?" discusses when one party somehow abets the infringing activities of another.

▶ Chapter 3, "What Is Vicarious Infringement?" deals with occasions when individuals and institutions can be held accountable for the actions of those under their supervision.

Part II, "Penalties and Immunities in Copyright Law for Libraries and Schools," moves on to examine the basics of how institutions can obtain and maintain protection from the various forms of liability described in Part I.

▶ Chapter 4, "What Are Damages and How Can They Be Limited?" looks at both the awarding of damages in copyright cases and the ways institutions can ensure that those damages are either reduced or negated outright.

▶ Chapter 5, "How Can Libraries and Schools Obtain Immunity?" opens with a more specific look at the way libraries can guarantee immunity from prosecution for patron misuse of some technologies that facilitate copying. This chapter also examines the legal provisions allowing for the production of temporary digital copies, such as those stored in an Internet browser's cache or a computer's RAM.

▶ Chapter 6, "What Is the Section 512 Safe Harbor?" works to explain the part of the act that provides immunity from damages to "service providers"—those organizations or entities that provide some form of Internet access to others—so long as they follow very stringent compliance measures.

Part III, "The Impact of the Digital Millennium Copyright Act on Library and Educational Environments," deals in depth with some of the thornier elements of the DMCA.

▶ Chapter 7, "How Should Libraries and Schools Respond to Claims of Infringement?" makes sense of section 512(c)—the registered agent requirement—and offers strategies for responding to subpoenas.

▶ Chapter 8, "What Is Different About Section 512 in Higher Education?" looks at the unique compliance issues for academic institutions.

▶ Chapter 9, "What About Technological Protections on Copyright Under Section 1201?" works through section 1201 of copyright law, a series of provisions protecting the technological measures that control access to copyrighted works in new digital media.

Part IV, "Three Ways Libraries and Schools Can Limit Their Exposure," attempts to make compliance easier for libraries and educational institutions by describing the warning notices they should post and the actions they can take to ensure immunity.

▶ Chapter 10, "What Must Be Done to Legally Reproduce and Distribute Copyrighted Materials in the Library?" discusses warning notices for both interlibrary loan and library reproduction services.

▶ Chapter 11, "What About the Circulation of Copyrighted Software?" looks at the legal regulations governing the circulation of software by libraries.

▶ Chapter 12, "What's Different About Copyright Compliance for Distance Education Programs?" works through the ways institutions can limit their exposure when transmitting copyrighted materials in distance learning.

▶ Chapter 13, "Afterword: Final Thoughts About Liability, Immunity, and Risk Assessment in Copyright Law," attempts to bring together and finalize much of the information shared in the preceding chapters.

The Complete Copyright Liability Handbook for Librarians and Educators concludes with Part V, "Compliance Tools for Schools and Libraries," three compliance tools to help institutions conform to the complex mesh of obligations created by copyright law.

▶ Tool 1, "A Copyright Compliance Audit," presents in chart form the various warning notices an institution might need to display, along with some brief information about the situations to which such notices are applicable.

▶ Tool 2, "Implementation Checklist for Section 512 Registered Agents," is a thorough checklist of conditions to which institutions must comply to ensure full immunity and protection under existing copyright law.

▶ Tool 3, "Sixteen Sample Copyright Policies," provides 16 proven models for implementing copyright compliance provisions.

Tool 2 and Part III of this book cover two recent provisions of the DMCA—section 512 and section 1201, respectively given the somewhat ominous, or at least confusing, names "Limitations on Liability Relating to Material Online" and "Circumvention of Copyright Protection Systems." These provisions are often overlooked in the literature and rarely receive even moderately detailed analysis. Related to the scope of *The Complete Copyright Liability Handbook for Librarians and Educators* and reflected in its title, section 512 is really about how the conditions under which intermediaries that provide access to online copyright content, like libraries and schools (including primary, secondary, and tertiary institutions), can reduce their liability, or, more accurately, limit the remedies that may be available to copyright plaintiffs.

This section of the copyright law contains the notable and somewhat controversial subsection 512(h), by which a copyright owner may request the "clerk of any United States district court to issue a subpoena to" that online intermediary library, school or any other "service provider for identification of an alleged infringer." With growing concern, for example, of infringement by students (and staff) in schools, colleges, and universities, understanding this provision and the so-called "safe harbor" that section 512 offers is critical. In addition, subsection

512(e) is designed specifically for institutions of higher education—and, with the close support that libraries and related technology and computing organizations play in providing access to copyrighted materials online, understanding the protections (and at what cost to the institution) that subsection 512(e) can offer is paramount within any compliance efforts the institution undertakes. Needless to say, understanding these new and rarely studied laws is an urgent need for all information sciences professionals, a need this book helps fulfill.

So, too, section 1201, also known as the anti-circumvention and anti-trafficking rules, contains a specific exception for libraries with respect to collection development and assessment activities. A companion section (section 1203) covers damage limitation, again for so-called innocent infringement. Most important (and controversial), section 1201 creates liability for offenses separate from that of the copyright law, with the result that, even if an ultimate use of the copyrighted material is deemed fair or otherwise lawful under the copyright law, circumventing a technological access protection to "get at it" or making an access or use technology available (trafficking) may still be punishable under the anti-circumvention and anti-trafficking rules. Understanding the trap or fair use catch-22 that section 1201 can create is important in the technologically infused world of most libraries today.

Many of the concepts and legal provisions discussed in *The Complete Copyright Liability Handbook for Librarians and Educators* are undeniably complicated, but every attempt has been made to ensure that even the most obtuse material presented should be accessible to the legal novice. A thorough glossary of legal terms and concepts has been placed at the front of the book. Further, each chapter concludes with a series of Real-World scenarios from which the reader should get some sense of how copyright liability law works in practice. Also included at the end of every chapter is a list of the key points covered in the preceding pages; the reader should refer to these key points if and when the body of the text grows confusing. Be forewarned, however, that these summary statements may not capture the nuances of the law and are not meant as definitive statements of it. Instead, they are offered for purposes of quick review. It is the author's hope that they will facilitate understanding, but they should never be the sole source of it. In particular, do not rely on these statements for purposes of institutional decision making. Instead, use them as a guide when referring to the text where the concepts are discussed and referenced in detail.

The author's years of experience in conducting dozens (likely well over 100) of copyright lectures, workshops, and in-service training sessions at conferences, libraries, schools, colleges, universities, and other educational entities reveal that the issues of copyright liability remain obscure, often impenetrable and misunderstood. It is thus hoped that the glossary, and the real-world examples and key points in each chapter will facilitate comprehension by librarians and educators.

A word about the nature of developing case law is also called for here. As observed above, some of the law discussed is so new that there is little or no case law interpreting these provisions; nor, for that matter, is there case law interpreting sections 108 or 110, for example, in the context of our target institutional context, the library or educational entity (though there is limited case law interpreting section 109 in the context of the nonprofit library). However, as anyone trained in the law will observe, it is quite a tenuous position to base a conclusion of law upon one, two, or a handful of cases alone; thus, for most of the libraries and educational entities in this country, most of that case law remains persuasive precedent alone. Particular cases discussed do not necessarily represent "the law" of the entire country, as only a decision of the United States Supreme Court can do that. In legal practice, a given case only represents the law in the jurisdiction to which it applies, though a case may represent the start of a trend, or at least could serve as persuasive precedent if a similar case arose in another jurisdiction. If your institution faced legal challenge under a similar set of facts, opposing counsel would likely cite that decision in an attempt to "persuade" the court to reach a similar result in your case. As a result, these cases should not be ignored. With these limitations in mind, knowledge of the developing law in other jurisdictions as well as your own is desirable and may place you and your legal counsel ahead of the legal curve, so to speak.

The lack of case law, or at least the lack of Supreme Court decisions in particular areas of the copyright relevant to this book, also makes the few cases that do arise all the more important. Further, the legislative history, especially of recent sections from the DMCA or TEACH, may take on additional significance. As a result, one can turn to the words of the statute and the legislative history in order to discern legislative intent, i.e., legal meaning and the way the statute should be applied and work in practice. Now, it should be mentioned that using legislative history to interpret the text of a statute has its limitations. Some judges, for example, do not like to rely upon legislative history, Supreme Court Justice Scalia being the most famous example. However, in the author's experiences, courts do often use the legislative history of the copyright law more often than not when it appears on point. Furthermore, with respect to the new distance education law discussed herein, the legislative history is extensive and offers explanation and context not offered by a reading of the text of the statute alone. With the DMCA and TEACH, it is often contradictory, or appears at times to add additional meaning to the text of the statute as written. As one appellate court recently observed, "there is no Rosetta stone for the interpretation of the copyright statute" [*Bridgeport Music, Inc. v. Dimension Films*, 383 F.3d 390, 401 (6th Cir. 2004)]; thus, we are all to an extent in the same proverbial boat. However, the author has some experience researching and writing on copyright issues in library and educational settings, and he brings that humble insight to bear when interpreting and applying the legislative history to the preset task.

I must once again note that while I use the words library and librarian or educator, the principles here would be of assistance to archivists and curators, educators, and related institutional support or administrative personnel, such as Webmasters, network administrators, chief information officers, etc. Of course, some of the provisions covered here apply to librarians or educators alone, but others will be significant for any category of information professional.

My intent for *The Complete Copyright Liability Handbook for Librarians and Educators* is simple: to have you read and understand the law surrounding liability and its avoidance or at least its management (insofar as the copyright law statutorily provides structure to that avoidance). But more than that, I would like for you to understand the practical relationship between the law and its application in the practical library or education setting. Students pursuing an MBA or a graduate degree in administrative leadership are often required to take a course in business law or education law, yet such information is rarely covered (much less required) in our library, archive, museum, or teacher training programs. This book will help you overcome that lack of training and help increase your professional competence. I hope it also serves to empower you by providing a thorough discussion of the context, the law, and application of that law to your information compliance practices.

ENDNOTES

[1] Pub. L. No. 105-298, 112 Stat. 2827 (1998). The constitutionality of CTEA was upheld in *Eldred v. Ashcroft*, 537 U.S. 186, 193 (2003) ("In accord with the District Court and the Court of Appeals, we reject petitioners' challenges to the CTEA. In that 1998 legislation, as in all previous copyright term extensions, Congress placed existing and future copyrights in parity. In prescribing that alignment, we hold, Congress acted within its authority and did not transgress constitutional limitations.").

[2] Pub. L. No. 105-304, 112 Stat. 2860 (1998).

[3] Pub. L. No. 107-273, 116 Stat. 1758, tit. III, subtitle C, sec. 13301 (21st Century Department of Justice Appropriations Authorization Act).

[4] See, e.g., *BMG Music et al. v. Does 1-203*, No. 2:04-CV-00650 (E.D. Pa., filed Feb 17, 2004); *Elektra Entertainment Group, Inc. et al. v. Does 1-7*, No. 04-607 (D.N.J., filed Feb 17, 2004); *Interscope Records et al. v. Does 1-25*, No. 6:040CV-197 (M.D. Fla., filed Feb 17, 2004). "Our campaign against illegal file shares is not missing a beat. The message to illegal file shares should be as clear as ever—we will continue to bring lawsuits on a regular basis against those who illegally distribute copyrighted music."—Cary Sherman, President, RIAA, quoted in THE ENTERTAINMENT LITIGATION REPORTER, February 29, 2004. See also, Press Release: RIAA, Copyright Infringement Lawsuits Brought Against 753 Additional Illegal File Sharers, February 28, 2005 ("The Recording Industry Association of America (RIAA), on behalf of the major record companies, today announced a new wave of copyright infringement lawsuits against illegal file sharers, including individual network users at 11 different colleges. . . . Among those sued today are users of computer networks

at 11 universities and colleges, including: Hamilton College; Louisiana State University; Louisiana Tech. University; Loyola University Chicago; Ohio University; Old Dominion University; Rennselaer Polytechnic Institute; Texas A&M University; University of Southern California; Vanderbilt University; and Wright State University."), available at www.riaa.com/news/newsletter/022805.asp.

[5] PEW Internet Project and COMSCORE Media Matrix Data Memo: The Impact of Recording Industry Suits Against Music File Swappers, January, 2004 (available at www.pewinternet.org) ("A new nationwide phone survey of 1,358 Internet users from November 18–December 14, by the Pew Internet & American Life Project showed that the percentage of music file downloaders had fallen to 14% (about 18 million users) from 29% (about 35 million) when the project last reported on downloading from a survey conducted during March 12–19 and April 29–May 20." In specific the report found that: "Steep drops in downloading were recorded among students, broadband users, young adults (those ages 18-29) and Internet veterans.").

[6] Hearing, U.S. House of Representatives, Judiciary Committee, Subcommittee on Courts, the Internet, and Intellectual Property, Committee on the Judiciary, U.S. House of Representatives, February 26, 2003, on Peer-to-Peer Piracy on University Campuses (available at commdocs.house.gov/committees/judiciary/hju85286.000/hju85286_0.htm); and Hearing, U.S. Senate, Committee on Governmental Affairs, Permanent Subcommittee on Investigations, September 30, 2003, on Privacy and Piracy: The Paradox of Illegal File Sharing on Peer-to-Peer Networks and the Impact of Technology on the Entertainment (Senate Hearing 108-275) (available at hsgac.senate.gov/index.cfm?Fuseaction=Hearings.Detail&HearingID=120).

[7] S. 2560, 108th Cong., 2nd Sess. (2004) (Inducing Infringement of Copyright Act of 2004). Section 2 of S. 2560 amends 17 U.S.C. § 501 by adding subsection (g) and creates a new form of copyright infringement: anyone who "intentionally induces any violation identified in subsection (a) [of section 501] shall be liable as an infringer."

[8] H.R. 4077, 108th Cong., 1st Sess. (2004) (Piracy Deterrence and Education Act of 2004). Section 10 of the bill amends section 506 of the copyright law governing criminal copyright infringement to include as a crime, within any 180-day period, the "knowing distribution, including by the offering for distribution to the public by electronic means, with reckless disregard of the risk of further infringement . . . 1 or more copies or phonorecords of 1 or more copyrighted pre-release works.")

[9] Tomas A. Lipinski, The Myth of Technological Neutrality in Copyright and the Rights of Institutional Users, 54 JOURNAL OF THE AMERICAN SOCIETY FOR INFORMATION SCIENCE AND TECHNOLOGY 824 (2003).

[10] See, Paying to Play: Industry Spreads Subpoenas and Fear over Music Copying, THE NATIONAL LAW JOURNAL, August 11, 2003, at A1.

[11] See, Hearing, U.S. House of Representatives, Judiciary Committee, Subcommittee on Courts, the Internet, and Intellectual Property, February 26, 2003, on Peer-to-Peer Piracy on University Campuses (available at commdocs.house.gov/committees/judiciary/

hju85286.000/hju85286_0.htm); Congressional Developments: Hearing, U.S. Senate, Committee on Governmental Affairs, Permanent Subcommittee on Investigations, September 30, 2003, on Privacy and Piracy: The Paradox of Illegal File Sharing on Peer-to-Peer Networks and the Impact of Technology on the Entertainment Industry (Senate Hearing 108-275) (available at hsgac.senate.gov/index.cfm?Fuseaction=Hearings.Detail& HearingID=120).

[12] Vistoria Slind-Flor, Students Flunk IP Rights 101, THE NATIONAL LAW JOURNAL, March 13, 2000, at B6. See also, Marc Lindsey, World File Sharing War, THE COPYRIGHT & NEW MEDIA LAW NEWSLETTER, No. 4, 2004, at 9, 10, discussing a program at Washington State University where students whose bandwidth and port activity suggest excessive or infringing use of copyrighted material are denied further network access, are referred to a course in basic copyright law, and have their network access restored only after passing the class.

[13] 150 CONGRESSIONAL RECORD H 7654-01, June 25, 2004 (Statement of Representative Sensenbrenner).

[14] See, e.g., CALIFORNIA DEPARTMENT OF EDUCATION, EDUCATION TECHNOLOGY PLANNING: A GUIDE FOR SCHOOL DISTRICTS 87 (2001) ("Planning, Designing, and Implementing Learning Experiences . . . Factors to Consider . . . Demonstrates knowledge and understanding of the legal and ethical issues concerned with the use of computer-based technology . . . Personal Profile . . . Demonstrates and advocates legal and ethical behaviors for students and colleagues regarding the use of technology and information . . . Performance Indicators . . . Models, teaches, and reinforces intellectual property rights and acceptable-use policies . . . Evidence of lessons that include copyright and policy citations . . . copyright and plagiarism in classroom . . ."); CONNECTICUT STATE DEPARTMENT OF EDUCATION, LEARNING RESOURCES AND INFORMATION TECHNOLOGY FRAMEWORK 83 (1998) ("Educational experiences in Grades K–4 will assure that students: . . . observe the legal and ethical limitations for using or copying print, nonprint or electronic information sources ... Educational experiences in Grades 5-8 will assure that students: observe educational 'fair use' guidelines . . . differentiate among various types of ownership or protection of intellectual property (e.g., copyright, patent). . . . Educational experiences in Grades 9–12 will assure that students: . . . observe all legal and ethical restraints in copying or using material from any print, nonprint or electronic information sources."); WISCONSIN DEPARTMENT OF PUBLIC INSTRUCTION, WISCONSIN'S MODEL ACADEMIC STANDARDS FOR INFORMATION AND TECHNOLOGY LITERACY 14–15 (1998) (A series of performance standards are presented that suggest the given level of knowledge a member of a K–12 learning community should possess: "By the end of grade 4 students will . . . Use information, media, and technology in a responsible manner, by the ability to demonstrate use consistent with the school's acceptable use policy, understand concepts such as etiquette, defamation, privacy, etc. in the context of online communication . . . Respect the concept of intellectual property rights, by the ability to explain the concept of intellectual property rights, describe

how copyright protects the right of an author or producer to control the distribution, performance, display, or copying of original works . . . [and] identify violations of copyright law as a crime . . . By the end of grade 8 students will . . . use information, media, and technology in a responsible manner by the ability to describe and explain the applicable rules governing the use of technology in the student's environment, demonstrate the responsible use of technology, recognize the need for privacy and protection of personal information . . . Respect intellectual property rights by the ability to explain the concept of fair use, and that the application of the concept may differ depending on the media format, relate examples of copyright violations, explain and differentiate the purposes of a patent, trademark, and logo. . . . By the end of grade 12 students will . . . use information, media, and technology in a responsible manner by the ability to assess the need for different informational polices and user agreements, understand concepts such as misrepresentation and the need for privacy of certain data files or documents . . . Respect intellectual property rights by the ability to explain why fair use is permitted for educational purposes but not in for profit situations, and the conditions under which permission must be obtained for the use of copyrighted materials.").

[15] The exclusive rights listed in section 106 are as follows: to reproduce the work, to prepare derivative works, to distribute copies of the work to the public, to perform or display the work publicly, and in the case of sound recordings to perform the work publicly by means of a digital audio transmissions. 17 U.S.C. § 106. Understanding the nuances of these rights and the terms the law uses to define the parameters of the rights, e.g., public performances versus private performances is important but beyond the scope of this book. An explanation in the context of the library is found in, KENNETH D. CREWS, COPYRIGHT LAW FOR LIBRARIANS AND EDUCATORS 28-36 (2006).

[16] TEACH, the Technology, Education and Copyright Harmonization Act of 2002, introduced as S. 487, 107th Congress, 1st Sess. (2001) was incorporated into H.R. 2215, the 21st Century Department of Justice Appropriations Authorization Act, later enacted into law as Pub. L. No. 107-273, 116 Stat. 1758, tit. III, subtitle C, sec. 13301. A detailed discussion of TEACH is found in, TOMAS A. LIPINSKI, COPYRIGHT LAW AND THE DISTANCE EDUCATION CLASSROOM (2005).

[17] See, 17 U.S.C. § 106.

►Acknowledgments

I would like to offer special thanks to the great folks at West Librarian Relations for their continued support of Westlaw and other research tools. This collaboration has made legal information available to me and many other grateful, like-minded seekers in the LIS field!

► Glossary of Essential Terms Used in This Book

Please note: the following do *not* necessarily represent legal definitions, but the concepts have been simplified to make understanding easier.

► **Actual Damages**—Actual damages consist of the fiscal damages suffered by the plaintiff as a result of an infringement and the illicit profits of the infringer.

► **Audiovisual Work**—As defined in section 101 of the copyright law, audiovisual work is a work consisting of a series of related images, possibly accompanied by sounds, typically shown by the use of a machine like a VCR. Examples would be a motion picture or a slide show with recorded narration.

► **Berne Convention**—Short title for the Convention for the Protection of Literary and Artistic Works, an international copyright treaty first drafted in Berne on September 9, 1886, and subsequently revised in Berlin in 1908, including all acts, protocols, and revisions. The treaty provides that works created in one country are protected in another without the need for registration and publication formalities, assuming both countries are signatories. The United States finally ratified the treaty 1989.

► **Caching**—Temporary storage of data in a computer, occurring through an automatic technical process for the purpose of making the material available to users of the system or network. The concept is codified in section 512(b).

► **Case Law**—The law developed by the courts that builds upon prior decisions. In the case of copyright, this process is generated by the federal court system, comprised of district courts, appellate courts (known as circuit courts), and the Supreme Court, all of which create case law by interpreting the copyright statutes. Compare, Statute.

► **Circumvention**—In colloquial terms, to hack or otherwise break a technological barrier or other mechanism designed to regulate access to copyrighted works. An example is the CSS code on a DVD. Statutorily defined in section 1201(a)(3)(A): "descramble a scrambled work, to decrypt an encrypted work, or otherwise to avoid, bypass, remove, deactivate, or impair a technological measure, without the authority of the copyright owner."

► **Codify**—In the context of this monograph, to enact through legislation a concept into the copyright law, Title 17 of the United States Code. See, Statute.

► **Common Law**—The law developed by the courts that builds upon prior decisions. The concept often is used to distinguish court-made law from codified law (or statutes) made by legislators. For example, the concept of infringement by inducement was first created by the courts in the patent law, then codified by

Congress in the patent law, then applied by the Supreme Court once again, this time in the copyright law with the *Grokster* decision.

▶ **Conduit Service Provider**—Defined in section 512(k)(1)(A), and based on a definition of common carrier used in telecommunications law, such as a long distance phone company. The legislative history indicates that the definition is designed to include entities that offer transmission or routing, or that provide connections for online communications of digital content. Digital satellite television would not be included, as it is not online, but an Internet service provider, such as America Online, would be included.

▶ **Contributory Infringement**—According to the case law, this is the concept that recognizes that although a person or entity such as a library or school may not itself be misusing the copyrighted work, it should nonetheless be legally held responsible when one with knowledge of the infringing activity induces or causes or materially contributes to the infringement of another. See also, Vicarious Infringement and Innocent Infringement.

▶ **Copy**—The reproduction of a work in fixed form and from which the work can be perceived, reproduced, or otherwise communicated; it can be analog or digital. The copyright law speaks of making copies or phonorecords often depending on the nature of the work and nature of the reproduction or recording that is made. See, Phonorecords.

▶ **Copyright**—Though without actual statutory definition, a copyright is a congressional grant of a limited monopoly right. There are three requirements: the work must be original; it must be a work of authorship (including literary, musical, dramatic, choreographic, pictorial, graphic, sculptural, and architectural works, motion pictures and other audiovisual works, and sound recordings); and it must be fixed in a tangible medium. A grant of the right entitles the copyright owner to exclusive control over reproduction, public distribution, display and performance, and derivative creations.

▶ **Copyright Act of 1976**—While there have been amendments to the law in the past several years, the last major overhaul of the copyright law, Title 17 of the United States Code, known as the Copyright Act of 1976, took place in 1976 and became effective as of January 1, 1978.

▶ **Damage Reduction or Remission**—The statutory mechanism whereby a defendant's monetary penalty is reduced or, in the case of remission, eliminated completely.

▶ **Damages**—In the copyright law, damages are monetary penalties typically awarded to the copyright owner (but see section 512(f)). They can take the form of actual damages or statutory damages.

▶ **Derivative Work**—A work based on one or more preexisting works, such as a translation, sequel, or a movie version of a book, or any other form in which a work may be recast, transformed, or adapted.

▶ **Digital Millennium Copyright Act of 1998 (DMCA)**—Enacted by Congress in 1998, the DMCA amended section 108, and created provisions dealing with service providers (section 512) and circumvention and trafficking (section 1201).

▶ **Direct Financial Benefit**—A fiscal gain generated by infringing activity. In the context of service providers and section 512, a service provider conducting a legitimate business would not be considered to receive a "financial benefit directly attributable to the infringing activity" where the infringer makes the same kind of payment as noninfringing users of the provider's service. Variable fee structures, such as where the more infringing activity that occurs results in higher revenue generated, are suspect.

▶ **Direct Infringement**—In the context of copyright, the conduct of the person who made a use of the work that interferes with the copyright owner's exercise of exclusive right over the work. See, Infringement.

▶ **Direct Liability**—Also referred to as primary liability and distinguished from secondary liability, direct liability is the liability assigned to the person who made a use of the work that interferes with the copyright owner's exercise of exclusive right over the work.

▶ **Display**—Display means to show a copy of a copyrighted work, either directly or by means of a film, slide, television image, or any other device or process, or, in the case of a motion picture or other audiovisual work, to show individual images nonsequentially. Defined in section 101.

▶ **Fair Use**—Codified in section 107, fair use is a defense against charges of copyright infringement determined through the application of four factors: nature of use, nature of work, amount of work used, and impact of use on market.

▶ **File Sharing**—Participating in network communications whereby individuals upload and download copyrighted material; the process can occur automatically as with certain P2P or peer-to-peer systems, such as Napster, Aimster, and Grokster.

▶ **First Sale Doctrine**—Codified in section 109, the statutory right of users to transfer or otherwise dispose (make a public distribution) of a lawfully made copy or phonorecord of a work in their possession without the permission of the copyright owner.

▶ **Infringement (also "Direct Infringement")**—To violate the exclusive rights of a copyright owner under the Copyright Act by making use of a protected work without permission of the copyright owner where such use does not constitute an exemption. See also, Contributory Infringement, Vicarious Infringement, and Innocent Infringement.

▶ **Injunctive Relief or Remedy**—A form of nonmonetary remedy, such as preliminary or permanent injunction, requesting that the infringing practice be discontinued, e.g., that the material be removed from the Web site, a subscriber's access be terminated, or the entire Web site or network be shut down.

▶ **Intellectual Property**—Refers to a cluster of assets protected by federal or state law, including copyrights, patents, trademarks, and trade secrets.

▶ **ISP**—Acronym for Internet service provider, typically a business or public institution, that offers access to the Internet.

▶ **Liability**—In the context of this book, legal responsibility for the infringement of the copyright law, Title 17, United States Code.

▶ **Licensing**—A contract and, in the context of this book, a right—governed not by the law of copyright, but by the terms and conditions of the agreement, the license—to use copyrighted material.

▶ **Linking**—In the context of the Internet, an active locator mechanism that when clicked opens a page of another Web site. The concept is codified in section 512(d) to include the broader activity of referring or linking users to an online location containing infringing material or infringing activity, by using information location tools, including a directory, index, reference, pointer, or hypertext link.

▶ **MP3**—A popular digital audio compression algorithm designed to limit the size or bandwidth of files when transferred or stored. More formally known as MPEG-1 Audio Layer 3.

▶ **Musical Work**—A category of copyrighted work (work of authorship) representing the expression of music, such as the score of a symphony or the sheet music of a song. Compare, Sound Recording.

▶ **Notice**—A notice required by the copyright law that informs members of the public that the work used is subject to copyright protection.

▶ **Open Collections**—In the context of sections 108 or 1201, access to the physical collection of the library, archives, or school by members of the public or persons not directly affiliated with the institution doing research in a specialized field.

▶ **P2P**—Acronym for peer-to-peer systems that allow users to share files via computing networks, often through the execution of automatic commands.

▶ **Peer-to-Peer Network**—A network of linked computers that allows individuals to copy using P2P technology, such as Napster, Aimster, and Grokster.

▶ **Perform**—To recite, render, play, dance, or act a work, either directly or by means of any device or process, or, in the case of a motion picture or other audiovisual work, to show its images in any sequence or to make the sounds accompanying it audible. Defined in section 101.

▶ **Phonorecords**—Material objects in which sounds, other than those accompanying a motion picture or other audiovisual work, are fixed and from which the sounds can be perceived, reproduced, or otherwise communicated. Defined in section 101.

▶ **Piracy**—In the context of copyright, piracy is the unlawful reproduction and distribution of copyrighted material. While accomplished in analog environments through the use of sale or trade in so-called bootleg copies, on the Internet it can occur through the use of P2P networks.

▶ **Posting**—In the context of the copyright law, reproducing material on a bulletin board, Web site, or similar electronic location. The concept is codified in section 512(c) to include storage, at the direction of a user of material, that resides on a system or network controlled or operated by or for the service provider.

▶ **Premise Liability**—The concept that an owner of physical property is legally responsible for the harm that occurs there, even if committed by others. Compare, Vicarious Liability.

▶ **Prima Facie**—In the context of copyright law, asserting facts that, if true, would establish the elements of claim of copyright infringement or establish grounds for injunctive relief.

▶ **Public Domain**—In the context of copyright, those works not subject to protection, because the material either by definition is not the subject of copyright protection (see, Copyright) or by statutory designation is not protected, such as works of the federal government, or because, though once protected, it is no longer subject to protection because the copyright has expired.

▶ **Publication**—Defined in section 101, the distribution of copies or phonorecords of a work to the public by sale or other transfer of ownership, or by rental, lease, or lending. The offer to distribute copies or phonorecords to a group of persons for purposes of further distribution, public performance, or public display constitutes publication. A public performance or display of a work does not of itself constitute publication.

▶ **Publicly**—To perform or display a work publicly is to do so (1) at a place open to the public or at any place where a substantial number of persons outside of the normal circle of a family and its social acquaintances is gathered; or (2) to transmit or otherwise communicate a performance or display of a work to such a place, or to the public, by means of any device or process, whether the members of the public capable of receiving the performance or display receive it in the same place or in separate places or whether they receive it at the same time or at different times. Defined in section 101.

▶ **RAM**—Acronym for random access memory, the transient or temporary storage in a computer.

▶ **Red Flag**—In the context of contributory infringement or section 512, the knowledge or awareness from which infringing activity is apparent, thus imposing responsibility on the intermediary to take action or face legal responsibility. The "red flag" test has both a subjective and an objective element. In determining whether the service provider was aware of a "red flag," the service provider's subjective awareness of the facts or circumstances must be determined.

▶ **Registered Agent**—In the context of section 512(c), the person designated to receive and respond to notice from the copyright owner to remove or disable access to alleged infringing material. The service provider must publicize the identification of its registered agent to the public and through registration with the U.S. Copyright Office.

▶ **Repeat Infringer Policy**—It is a requirement of qualification of section 512(i) (1)(A) that service providers adopt and reasonably implement a policy that provides for the termination, in appropriate circumstances, of system or network subscribers and account holders who are repeat infringers. Subscribers and account holders must be informed of the policy.

▶ **RIAA**—Acronym for the Recording Industry Association of America, the RIAA is the trade association charged with legal representation of copyright owners of musical works.

▶ **Safe Harbor**—In common or codified law, the conditions that, if met, result in relief from liability; in the context of copyright law, section 512 defines such a safe harbor for service providers.

▶ **Secondary Liability**—In the copyright law, in addition to direct infringement, there are two forms of secondary liability by which third parties may be legally responsible: contributory liability based on the conduct of the third party, and vicarious liability based on the relationship of the third party to the direct infringer.

▶ **Section 512**—Enacted by the DMCA in 1998, this section codifies the circumstances under which service providers may obtain remission from all monetary relief. Section 512 is broader than other remission statutes in the copyright law, as it includes relief from costs and attorney's fees as well.

▶ **Service Provider**—In the context of the section 512 safe harbor, this could be any provider of access to the Internet, such as schools, colleges, universities, or public libraries. See, ISP.

▶ **Sonny Bono Act**—The Sonny Bono Copyright Term Extension Act of 1998, upheld as constitutional by the Supreme Court, extended the term of copyright by 20 years. See, Term of Copyright.

▶ **Statute**—The resulting law created through the process of codification; in the copyright law, this would be a section of Title 17, United States Code. Compare, Case Law.

▶ **Statutory Damages**—In the case of copyright law, statutory damages are assigned by court or jury and can range from $750 up to $30,000 per work that is infringed.

▶ **Strict Liability Law**—Law that imposes liability on the defendant irrespective of whether the defendant knew the conduct was unlawful. Direct liability and vicarious copyright liability are subject to a standard of strict liability as are the circumvention and trafficking rules; however, damage reduction or remission may be available for so-called innocent infringement.

▶ **Subpoena**—A request to appear in court, provide response, or produce documents. Subpoenas may be issued by a court or may issue from an investigatory or administrative agency.

▶ **Subscriber**—In the context of section 512, the user of a service provider's service, such as a customer, library patron, or student.

▶ **TEACH Act**—Technology, Education, and Copyright Harmonization Act of 2002; exempts from copyright protection certain public performances and displays made in the course of providing distance education.

▶ **Technological Measure**—As used in the Copyright Act, a technological control used in conjunction with copyrighted material to control access and use of the work. Also known as Standard Technical Measures in section 512.

▶ **Term of Copyright**—The duration of copyright protection for published works is the author's life plus 70 years, or, if corporate, anonymous, pseudonymous, the lesser of 95 years from publication or 120 from creation; in the case of unpublished works, protection is the life of the author plus 70 years, or 120 years from creation for corporate, anonymous, pseudonymous materials. When the death date of an author is unknown, the duration of protection is 120 years from creation.

▶ **Trafficking**—In the context of this monograph, the manufacture, importation, offer to the public, provision, or other exchange of any technology, product, service, device, component, or part thereof that allows a user to circumvent a technological measure designed to prevent the reproduction of or illegitimate access to copyrighted materials. Defined in section 1201(a)(2) and (b)(1).

▶ **Transformative Use**—The use of copyrighted material in such a way that the use is not a substitute for the original but offers new expression, meaning, or message. Assessing whether a use is transformative is a factor in a fair use analysis. The Supreme Court indicates that parody is an example of transformative use.

▶ **Unsupervised Use**—In the context of section 108, a use of reproducing equipment that is not assisted or performed by employees of an institution.

▶ **Vicarious Infringement**—According to case law, the concept recognizes that although a person or entity such as a library should be held legally responsible for the infringing activity of others when it has the "right and ability to supervise the infringing activity" and also has a direct financial interest in such activities. See also, Contributory Infringement and Innocent Infringement.

▶ **Virtual Premises**—A digital space, such as a Web site, over which the owner or operator should be able to exhibit control over the conduct of visitors, patrons, or users, such that legal liability could be imposed on the proprietors for the unlawful activity of those under their supervision.

▶ **Willful Infringement**—Conduct that shows reckless disregard for the possibility that one's actions might be in violation of the exclusive rights of a copyright holder, or the knowing violation of those rights.

►Part I

THREE TYPES OF COPYRIGHT LIABILITY

1

WHAT IS DIRECT COPYRIGHT INFRINGEMENT?

Read this chapter to find out the legality of copyright situations like:
▶ Whether a library can make a copy of a whole book.
▶ Whether a library can show clips from a DVD in a public program.

For a copyright plaintiff, making an initial case of infringement appears rather straightforward, at least in theory. In general, as well as in copyright law, this is referred to as a prima facie case. In cases of infringing copying (violating the exclusive right of reproduction)—the sort most likely to occur in library settings (and the type of infringement along with the preparation of unauthorized derivative works that is most often litigated)—the plaintiff must establish four elements:

1. provide proof of ownership of the copyright
2. establish that the defendant had access to the work
3. introduce evidence that copying took place
4. argue that the copying is indeed unlawful.[1]

Access is an important part of establishing a claim of copyright infringement because direct evidence of the infringement is often not available. So, too, access can contribute to evidence that copying in fact took place, as again such evidence is often unobtainable.[2] Courts often compare the similarity of works here in what one expert has called "probative similarity."[3] Finally, courts compare the similarity of two works in determining whether the copying that did occur is unlawful. "This test proceeds on the simple question of whether the ordinary observer would find that, in comparing the two works, there is a similarity substantial enough to conclude that illicit copying has taken place."[4] This is also why courts rely on a test of substantial similarity, as the infringing reproduction may not have been made by means of a direct copy. In library and educational settings, however, evidence of such copies, analog or digital, would likely exist (for example, the closet full of off-the-air-recordings, the shelf of photocopied workbooks, or files of scanned standardized tests). Thus the case against an infringing library that had in its collection unlawfully made copies of protected material would be a relatively simple one to prove, the discussion of fair use or other limitations on the exclusive rights notwithstanding, as the infringing item would be listed in the library's catalog,[5] appear on its shelves, or be posted on its intranet.[6]

The term direct infringement is used to distinguish it from two forms of indirect or secondary liability discussed in detail in Chapters 2 and 3, contributory and vicarious liability. Here the focus is on the person, instructor, student, staff member (such as a librarian), or other constituent whose conduct violated one of the exclusive rights of the copyright owner:

1. to reproduce the copyrighted work in copies or phonorecords
2. to prepare derivative works based upon the copyrighted work
3. to distribute copies or phonorecords of the copyrighted work to the public by sale or other transfer of ownership, or by rental, lease, or lending, in the case of literary, musical, dramatic, and choreographic works, pantomimes, and motion pictures and other audiovisual works
4. to perform the copyrighted work publicly, in the case of literary, musical, dramatic, and choreographic works, pantomimes, and pictorial, graphic, or sculptural works, including the individual images of a motion picture or other audiovisual work
5. to display the copyrighted work publicly, and, in the case of sound recordings, to perform the copyrighted work publicly by means of a digital audio transmission.[7]

In an institutional setting such as education, secondary liability concepts must also be considered and these are discussed next. However, under the copyright law, there can be no secondary liability unless a direct or primary liability has first been established. While this book is not a comprehensive explanation of the copyright law, it will introduce a few concepts here and in the next chapter so the reader can fully appreciate the subsequent remission, reduction, and immunity mechanisms of copyright law.

The connection between understanding the interrelationship between liability concepts and compliance concepts is critical. If the library or educational entity has a successful compliance program in place, then the likelihood of direct infringement either by third-party patrons, students, or employees is significantly reduced or eliminated. A finding of direct infringement is a required element of both. Thus by eliminating or reducing significantly the risk of direct infringement, the institution also eliminates or reduces the risk of contributor or vicarious infringement. Once the risk of direct infringement is minimized, there can be no contributory or vicarious infringement, or at least the likelihood is far reduced; a finding of direct infringement is a required element of both types of infringement.[8]

As stated earlier, discussing how much copying, distribution, and display is too much copying, distribution, and display, and determining whether fair use or some other provision of the copyright law, such as section 108, would "authorize" the copying is not the purpose of this book. It is enough for the purpose at hand to understand that each of the following individuals would be considered a potential "direct" infringer:

▶ the interlibrary loan librarian who scanned an entire workbook (reproduced the work)

▶ the teacher who adapted the children's novel for the eighth-grade regional play competition (prepared the derivative work)

▶ the service-counter aid who circulated the unlawful copy of the workbook (distributed the work to the public)

▶ the librarian who ran the video equipment at the travel night (performed the copyrighted work publicly)

▶ the instructor who displayed multiple images of copyrighted material to every terminal in the computing lab (displayed the work publicly)

▶ the music reserve librarian who broadcast a music CD over a distance education Web site (performed a sound recording publicly by means of a digital audio transmission).

Once the reader is familiar with the basic concept of direct liability, understanding the potential for liability on the part of the institution should be apparent. Understanding the concept of direct infringement is necessary, but this is not an end, rather a means to understanding more advanced concepts of institutional liability. These advance concepts include the secondary liability and the operation of more complex provisions of the copyright, such as the service provider damage limitations provided by section 512, i.e., limiting to injunctive relief the legal remedy available to copyright plaintiffs.

INTRODUCING THE NUANCES AND SIGNIFICANCE OF DIRECT INFRINGEMENT

First, a few words can be said about the nature of direct copyright infringement. Subsequent chapters will discuss how these concepts relate to the potential for liability on the part of either staff or the institution as a contributory infringer or the institution as a vicarious infringer. Recent and popular examples can demonstrate these concepts. Direct copyright infringement is a strict liability law, in that the person who engages in the infringement does not need to intend to infringe or have awareness that his or her conduct is infringing. While the knowledge or awareness of infringement is not an element of a claim of direct copyright infringement, as discussed in Chapter 2, it is an element in a claim of contributory infringement. However, the lack of knowledge is a necessary element in a designation of what is often called "innocent" infringer status, which results in the remission of statutory damages, but more on this concept in Chapters 5 and 8. The adage about ignorance of the law being no excuse is alive and well in the copyright law!

As long as the plaintiff can demonstrate that the claimed infringement is of a work protected by copyright of which he or she is the owner, and that the defendant violated one of the exclusive rights of the copyright holder, a basic case of infringement is made. Of course, it is a bit more complicated than that, as some defenses (or, more accurately, privileges), such as fair use, or specific statutory allowances are granted to particular sorts of users, to certain types of uses, and to particular categories of copyrighted works. (The title or heading of sections 108 through 123 of the copyright law, title 17 of the United States Code, all begin with the phrase "Limitations on exclusive rights: . . .") The point for library administrators to remember here is that the infringing conduct of an employee or patron can serve to position the library to exposure under two concepts of secondary liability— even if the employee or patron does not know that the behavior is infringing.

While courts cases involving educational institutions are rare, such cases are not without any precedent.[9] There are also several cases involving the creation of course packs and other classroom copying,[10] publication of standardized tests in an educational newsletter,[11] related library photocopying in for-profit settings,[12] as well as a recent circuit decision involving nonprofit library reproduction and distribution.[13] There have also been a handful of recent cases in the digital environment testing the rights of copyright owners and their new enforcement tools in digital mediums—mediums of relevance to libraries and especially to providers of distance education. These cases may signal the winds of change, so to speak. As Congress, with the support of the courts, appears to be sending a consistent message, there is less toleration of copyright infringement, even in educational settings. Moreover, libraries and other institutions must begin to take a more noticeable role in compliance, not necessarily by active monitoring and policing but by helping to create—through awareness, example, and response mechanisms—a kinder, gentler, more compliant copyright environment, which in turn is less likely to spawn the next generation of infringers.

UNDERSTANDING COPYRIGHT INFRINGEMENT IN LIGHT OF NEW TECHNOLOGIES

Consider the comment made by one court in an early, pre-P2P case involving the use of a bulletin board system to exchange illegal software, characterizing the conduct of the intermediary, the bulletin board operator: "If the indictment is to be believed, one might at best describe his actions as heedlessly irresponsible, and at worst nihilistic, self-indulgent, and lacking in any fundamental sense of values."[14] In a more recent example from litigation involving MP3 technology:

> Here, although defendant recites that My.MP3.com provides a transformative 'space shift' by which subscribers can enjoy the sound recordings contained on their CDs without

lugging around the physical discs themselves, this is simply another way of saying that the unauthorized copies are being retransmitted in another medium—an insufficient basis for any legitimate claim of transformation."[15]

Finally, the section 1201 anti-circumvention and anti-trafficking cases have not gone well for defendants either: courts appear to have had enough, especially in cases of systematic (repeated and widespread) infringement.

Of more relevance perhaps, the courts that have discussed direct infringement in the context of either P2P file sharing or other digital technology cases, such as the anti-circumvention and anti-trafficking rules of section 1201 (discussed in detail in Chapter 9), and made comment on the state of compliance or lack thereof, appear nearly as frustrated as some members of Congress. One federal district court wryly observed: "Congress certainly could have approached the problem by targeting the infringers, rather than those who traffic in the tools that enable the infringement to occur. However, it is already unlawful to infringe, yet piracy of intellectual property has reached epidemic proportions. Pirates are world-wide, and locating and prosecuting each could be both impossible and ineffective, as new pirates arrive on the scene. But, pirates and other infringers require tools in order to bypass the technological measures that protect against unlawful copying. Thus, targeting the tool sellers is a reasoned, and reasonably tailored, approach to 'remedying the evil' targeted by Congress."[16] The comment reflects two important points. First, previous DMCA statutory structures have proved less than successful in curbing copyright infringement by direct infringers in online environments. Second, Congress is more often turning to intermediaries (that is, those who provide technologies that can be used to infringe or traffic, in the case of the section 1201 cases), circumventing technologies, and crafting a larger role for those intermediaries in the copyright compliance matrix. As a result, Congress envisions an increased role for intermediaries such as libraries and educational entities: that of partner or link in the copyright compliance chain. The courts appear willing to enforce this shift in enforcement strategy.

In a significant post-Napster case evaluating the liability of the creators and promoters of the Aimster P2P technology, the Seventh Circuit expressed little patience for the conduct of those who use P2P technology to infringe the copyrights of others: "The swappers, who are ignorant or more commonly disdainful of copyright and in any event discount the likelihood of being sued or prosecuted for copyright infringement, are the direct infringers."[17] One lesson demonstrated by these cases is that courts have little trouble in concluding that those who use Internet technologies to copy (upload and download) and distribute copyrighted works are liable for direct copyright infringement. Courts have shown little sympathy for infringing P2P or related behavior. Second, courts are also willing to conclude that those actors (intermediaries) who contribute to or benefit from this direct infringement may also be liable under the two theories of secondary liability. As a result, in the library or school setting, paying close attention to the potentially infringing behavior of patrons, students, and employees (the direct infringers) is prudent, if not recommended, especially in the climate of today's Internet-based infringement, as this direct infringement is a necessary perquisite for the occurrence of any secondary liability.

Curb infringing practices by patrons, students, or staff in the library or school, and the institution has effectively curbed or greatly reduced the likelihood of exposure from secondary liability. Eliminate the possibility of direct infringement by patrons, students, and staff, and the institution has eliminated its liability based on a claim of contributory or vicarious infringement. Of course the efficacy of achieving 100 percent compliance is a myth. The copyright law "understands" this, and built within its structures are provisions that establish a certain amount of what might be called copyright-compliance-breathing room, that accept less than 100 percent compliance by patrons and students and perhaps by staff at times as well. Often the availability of this breathing room is conditional, based on some other measure of conduct by the intermediary institution, i.e., the library or school. Understanding these provisions and the conduct required is a major focus of this book.

The point here is not to spread the fear among readers of an omnipotent and omnipresent copyright god. Rather it is to suggest that, for a library or educational entity that ignores copyright issues or has a lax compliance program in place, the likelihood that it would be embroiled in a future copyright dispute increases with each passing year. Moreover, the conduct needed to secure this so-called breathing room does not come with impossible requirements, though it does require some effort. In addition, such discussions may lead librarians, educators, and their constituents to acknowledge a lack of satisfaction with the current state of the law, vis-à-vis institutional liability and compliance matrix, and to advocate change.

REAL-WORLD EXAMPLES

▶ **Real-World Example I**

Situation: An employee of a public library decides to photocopy several cover-to-cover copies of a monograph in its collection to place in the reference collections of its branch libraries.

Legal Analysis: The school media specialist would be considered the "direct" infringer here. As discussed in subsequent chapters, the administrator and district may be subject to a claim of infringement as well, under theories of secondary copyright liability. This conclusion would be consistent with *Marcus v. Rowly*, 695

F.2d 1171 (9th Cir. 1983), where a teacher and district were sued for reproduction (of about half of the book *Cake Decorating Made Easy*) and repeat (term-to-term) distribution in excess of the "classroom" guidelines.

▶ **Real-world Example II**

Situation: A Young Adult Librarian at the local public library is organizing a series of events as part of its annual summer reading program. As part of a talk-back session on relationships, the librarian plans to show several episodes from the television series *The Gilmore Girls*. The first season is out on DVD and the library owns a copy of it.

Legal Analysis: The performance of the episodes in the library's public meeting room as part of the talk-back sessions constitutes a public performance, as either clause of the first paragraph of the section 101 definition of public performance is met: "perform or display it at *a place open to the public or at any place where a substantial number of persons outside of a normal circle of a family and its social acquaintances is gathered.*" The meeting room is a place "open to the public" and the teenagers gathered constitute a "substantial number of persons outside of a normal circle of a family and its social acquaintances." Since each episode is a copyrighted work, showing an episode is a complete taking of a creative (so-called thick copyright) work and arguably impacts both the primary (sales of the first season on DVD) and secondary (license fees from authorized public performances such as the library makes) authorized market for the work, thus its performance is not a fair use. Nor is the performance authorized under section 110(1) which covers performance of such works—but only in a classroom setting, not to members of the general public. The librarian in this example would be subject to direct infringement.

KEY POINTS FOR YOUR INSTITUTION'S POLICY AND PRACTICE

▶ Direct or primary copyright infringement occurs whenever the use of copyrighted material violates one of the exclusive rights of the copyright owner and the use does not fall within one of the limitations on the exclusive rights provided by the copyright law such as fair use. See pp. 3–5.

▶ Knowledge of the infringing nature of the activity is not needed to establish a claim of copyrighted infringement; a librarian does not need to know that a particular use of copyrighted material is infringing to be liable. Direct or primary copyright infringement is a strict liability law. See pp. 5–6.

▶ A claim of direct infringement must be established before the library, school, or other institution can be subject to a charge of indirect or secondary (contributory or vicarious) copyright infringement. See pp. 4–5.

ENDNOTES

[1] See, *Feist Publications, Inc. v. Rural Telephone Service Co., Inc.*, 499 U.S. 340, 361 ("To establish infringement, two elements must be proven: (1) ownership of a valid copyright, and (2) copying of constituent elements of the work that are original.").

[2] JOHN W. HAZARD JR., COPYRIGHT LAW IN BUSINESS AND PRACTICE § 7:12, at 7-22 (2004) ("The sheer necessity of the theory of access in proving copying acknowledges that a plaintiff will rarely have direct proof of copying (as would exist, for example, where a plaintiff or witness actually *saw the defendant put the work into the automatic feed of a photocopying machine.*" (emphasis added).

[3] Alan Latman, "Probative Similarity" as Proof of Copying: Toward Dispelling Some Myths in Copyright Infringement, 90 COLUMBIA LAW REVIEW 1187, 1204–1206 (1990).

[4] JOHN W. HAZARD JR., COPYRIGHT LAW IN BUSINESS AND PRACTICE § 7:3, at 7-6 (2002).

[5] *Hotaling v. Church of Latter Day Saints*, 118 F.3d 199 (4th Cir. 1997).

[6] See, *Lowry's Reports, Inc. v. Legg Mason, Inc.*, 271 F. Supp. 2d 737 (D. Md. 2003).

[7] 17 U.S.C. § 106.

[8] *Metro-Goldwin Studios, Inc. v Grokster, Ltd.*, 380 F.3d 1154, 1164 (9th Cir. 2004) ("Three elements are required to prove a defendant vicariously liable for copyright infringement: (1) direct infringement by a primary party, (2) a direct financial benefit to the defendant, and (3) the right and ability to supervise the infringers." (citation omitted)), vacated and remanded 125 S. Ct. 2764 (2005).

[9] Textual material: *Marcus v. Rowley*, 695 F.2d 1171 (9th Cir. 1983), teacher and district sued for reproduction, about half of the book *Cake Decorating Made Easy*: "Rowley admits copying eleven of the twenty-four pages in her LAP from plaintiff's booklet. The eleven pages copied consisted of the supply list, icing recipes, three sheets dealing with color flow and mixing colors, four pages showing how to make and use a decorating bag, and two pages explaining how to make flowers and sugar molds." Id. at 1173. The court concluded that this repeat reproduction (term to term) was not a fair use and observed in addition that the use was in excess of the "classroom" guidelines. Id. at 1178. Textual materials: *Bridge Publications, Inc. v. Vien*, 827 F. Supp. 629 (S.D. Cal. 1993) ("The undisputed evidence shows that defendant copied or directed her students to copy plaintiffs' copyrighted materials as part of a 'Dynamism' course which she offered for sale." Id. at 632. Four-factor fair use test: First factor weighs against fair use as the material was an "integral part of the Dynamism course she [the defendant] sells to her students . . . she uses the copyrighted works for the same intrinsic purpose as plaintiffs." Id. at 635. Second factor also weighs against fair use as the work is creative. Third factor weighs against fair use as the defendant "substantially copied each work at issue, and in some cases the whole work." Id. at 636. Fourth factor weighs against fair use as well as the copied material fulfills the demand for the original and reduces potential sale. "Finally, the court finds defendant's use does not fit within the special guidelines approved by Congress as to fair use in the educational

context. *See* Notes of Committee on the Judiciary, House Rep. No. 94-1476, *reprinted in* 17 U.S.C.A. pp. 113–14. Defendant's copying and use of the works was not restricted to one copy for her own use in teaching. Additionally, the undisputed evidence shows defendant's copying was not limited and spontaneous, but was extensive and methodical, and consisted of copying from the same author, time after time. *This is clearly not within the letter or spirit of the Congressional guidelines.*" Id. at 636 (emphasis added). Audiovisual works: *Encyclopedia Britannica Educational Corp. v. Crooks*, 447 F. Supp. 243 (W.D.N.Y. 1978) (Board of Cooperative Educational Services of Erie County sued for reproduction and distribution of off-air tapes.). Moreover, in the author's experience, by the time a school district, for example, is actually sued, there may be little left to litigate as the facts raise few, if any, questions of law and the evidence demonstrates unquestionable infringement and the best that can be hoped for are favorable settlement terms.

[10] *Princeton University Press v. Michigan Document Services*, 99 F.3d 1381 (6th Cir. 1996), cert. denied 529 U.S. 1156 (1997).; *Basic Books, Inc. v. Kinko's Graphics Corp.*, 758 F. Supp. 1522 (S.D.N.Y. 1983); *Addison-Wesley Publishing v. New York University*, Copyright L. Rptr. (CCH) ¶ 25,544 (S.D.N.Y. 1983); *Harper & Row, Publishers, Inc. v. Tyco Copy Service*, Copyright L. Rptr. (CCH) ¶ 25,230 (D. Conn. 1981); *Basic Books, Inc. v. Gnomon Corp.*, Copyright L. Rptr. (CCH) ¶ 25,145 (D. Conn. 1981).

[11] *Chicago School Reform Board of Trustees v. Substance, Inc.*, 354 F.3d 624 (7th Cir. 2003), cert. denied 125 S.Ct. 54 (2004) ("[T]ests are expressive works that are not costlessly created . . . no analytical difference . . . destroying the subsequent years' market for a standardized test by blowing its cover." Id. at 627.). *Accord, Educational Testing Service v. Katzman*, 793 F.2d 533 (3rd Cir. 1986).

[12] *American Geophysical Union v. Texaco [Texaco I]*, 37 F.3d 881 (2nd Cir. 1994); *American Geophysical Union v. Texaco [Texaco II]*, 60 F.3d 913 (2nd Cir. 1994); *Lowry's Reports, Inc. v. Legg Mason, Inc.*, 271 F. Supp. 2d 737 (D. Md. 2003) (posting the newsletter *Lowry's New York Stock Exchange Market Trend Analysis* on nationwide intranet ["Hundreds of Legg Mason brokers and other employees, at over a hundred Legg Mason offices, accessed or downloaded the intranet-posted *Reports* over 16,000 times." Id. at 745.] as well as more limited paper and e-mail copying for members of central research department determined not to be a fair use.) "Legg Mason does not argue that the posting and massive downloading of complete copies of the *Reports* via its intranet constitute fair use. Nor would such an argument prevail." Id. at 748. However the research department multiple copying ("six or more members") and the alleged single e-mail copy were discussed. The fair use analysis of the multiple copying was as follows: First factor "weighs heavily against" as the copying was not personal but served the "commercial benefit" of Legg Mason. Id. at 748. The second factor "weighs against Legg Mason, albeit less heavily" being only four pages of "nonfiction, replete with uncopyrightable facts," yet the court noted the legislative history relating to the vulnerability of newsletters. Id. at 748. The third factor "weighs more heavily against Legg Mason" as the copying was in the entirety to advance the business of Legg Mason. Id. at 748-749. The fourth factor "weighs heavily against Legg Mason." Here the

court posed two questions: whether the use would "materially impair the marketability" and whether the use would "act as a market substitute for the original." Id. at 749.); *Pasha Publications v. Enmark Gas Corp.*, 19 Media L. Rptr. (BNA) ¶ 2062 (N.D. Texas 1992) (Photocopied and faxed cover-to-cover copies of newsletter not a fair use according to the four-part test. Nature of the use: Enmark is a commercial enterprise; nature of the work: the work is a newsletter subject to "broad protection"; the amount copied: entire newsletters were reproduced; and the impact on the market: the copying "rendered unnecessary the purchase of additional subscriptions to the newsletter and therefore has an obvious detrimental effect on the potential market for 'Gas Daily.'" Id. at 2063.). Other cases in the corporate environment have arisen but settled out of court: *Washington Business Information, Inc. v. Collier, Shannon & Scott, S.C.*, No. 91-0305A (E.D. Va. 1991); *Harper & Row, Publishers, Inc. v. American Cyanimid Co.*, No. 81-7813 (S.D.N.Y 1981); *Harper & Row, Publishers, Inc. v. Squibb, Co.*, No. 82-2363 (S.D.N.Y 1982).

[13] *Hotaling v. Church of Latter Day Saints*, 118 F.3d 199 (4th Cir. 1997) (Library was liable for the use (distribution) of unlawful copies of copyrighted works found in its collection).

[14] *United States v. LaMacchia*, 871 F. Supp. 535, 545 (D. Mass. 1994).

[15] *UMG Recordings v. MP3.com, Inc.*, 92 F. Supp. 2 d 349, 351 (S.D.N.Y. 2000).

[16] *United States v. Elcom, Ltd.*, 203 F. Supp. 2d 1111, 1132 (N.D. Cal. 2002).

[17] *In Re Aimster Copyright Litigation*, 334 F.3d 643, 645 (7th Cir. 2003).

▶2

WHAT IS CONTRIBUTORY COPYRIGHT INFRINGEMENT?

Read this chapter to learn about copyright situations like:
▶ Whether an instructor can place a consumable workbook on reserve and tell students to make copies of it instead of buying their own copies.
▶ Whether a librarian or instructor can be sued for suggesting that students visit Web sites where they can illegally download copies of copyrighted material.
▶ Whether a school can be held accountable for illegal downloading by students.
▶ Whether a library can get in trouble if an employee advocates the use of a program that facilitates piracy.

◀

The concept of what might be called indirect or secondary liability was introduced in Chapter 1. In copyright law, secondary liability comes in two forms: contributory and vicarious liability. Neither form is defined in the text of the copyright law, the statute. Rather secondary liability is a concept developed by the courts. The focus of this chapter is to discuss the first sort of secondary liability, contributory infringement. Contributory copyright infringement occurs when "one who, with knowledge of the infringing activity, induces or causes, or materially contributes to the infringement of another."[1] Liability for contributory infringement is not a strict liability law. Rather, it is based on the conduct of the second party, the "contributing" infringer. As a result, a claim of contributory infringement contains an element of scienter, that is, the contributing or contributory infringer must know or have reason to know of the infringing behavior. A contributory infringer must engage in conduct that "contributes" to the direct infringement of another person and know or have reason to know that the subsequent use of the copyrighted material by the other person would be infringing. As with vicarious liability, if there is no direct infringement there can be no contributory liability. This means that if the behavior to which a person or entity "contributes" is not infringing, then that person or entity, such as a library or school, cannot be liable for contributory infringement.

In examining the decision of the Ninth Circuit in *Napster* the reader would discover that the court first discussed whether individual file sharing in the circumstances of the case was infringing or not. This was a discussion prior to any court considering either form of secondary liability. The court concluded that the individual file sharers indeed engaged in direct infringement of the copyrighted music uploaded and downloaded through Napster. Even though the individual Napster users did not sell the music but freely exchanged the music, the court concluded that this was a commercial use:

> Direct economic benefit is not required to demonstrate a commercial use. Rather, repeated and exploitative copying of copyrighted works, even if the copies are not offered for sale, may constitute a commercial use. [citations omitted] In the record before us, commercial use is demonstrated by a showing that repeated and exploitative unauthorized copies of copyrighted works were made to save the expense of purchasing authorized copies.[2]

Thus tipping the scale against fair use on the one fair use factor, the Napster users had a chance on which to prevail. The remaining three factors were likely to impact negatively against fair use: the works were created (nature of the work), the uploading and downloading involved the entire song (the portion of the work used), and the "deleterious effect on the present and future digital download market" impact negatively on the market for the work, the fourth fair use factor. As a result, the court proceeded to the concepts of secondary liability.

TAKING PRECAUTIONS WITH TECHNOLOGIES THAT FACILITATE CONTRIBUTORY INFRINGEMENT

As the concept of contributory infringement is based on the *conduct* of one person toward another and the effect that the *conduct* can have on another, this concept can be contrasted with vicarious liability, another secondary liability concept. As discussed in Chapter 3, vicarious liability is based upon the *relationship* between the two parties, i.e., the direct or primary infringer and the secondary infringer. The cases suggest two ways that a person might induce or cause, or materially contribute to the infringement of another. First, one could create a technology that allows another to infringe. An example is the seminal case involving the Betamax machine, where Sony, the makers of the Beta machine were sued, not because Sony employees were making off-air recordings of movies or other programming broadcast on network television but because it created a technology that allowed others—you, me, library staff, or teachers—to do so. However, the Supreme Court, in that case,[3] concluded that recording of a television program for later viewing at a more convenient time, the so-called "time shifting" of a program was a fair use.[4] As the "privilege" of fair use applied to the recording activities of home-tapers, and, more important for the discussion of secondary liability, because there was no direct infringement there could be no contributory infringement. Sony was not liable for contributory copyright infringement.

In addition to Napster, another P2P system, Grokster, has been the subject of recent litigation. While educational institutions are not engaging in the creation of P2P or other contributory infringing technologies, or it is hoped that such institutions are not engaging in this behavior, the lessons of these contributory infringement cases are well learned, especially when the institution engages in other facilitating conduct that might expose it to liability, short of actual technology creation. Of course under the *Sony* standard, an institution could be involved, as many are in the development of technology that could be put to infringing use, but the institution would not be liable as long as the technology would be capable of substantial noninfringing use. Moreover, in a somewhat clairvoyant and telling footnote, the *Sony* dissent observed that "[t]his case involves only the home recording for home use of television programs broadcast free over the airwaves. No issue is raised concerning cable or pay television, or the sharing or trading of tapes."[5] In other words, *Sony's* substantial safeharbor for noninfringing uses arguably only protects the use of copyrighted content obtained through various mass media, such as radio and broadcast television (as opposed to cable or satellite), or some modes of Internet communication. Such is not the source of most P2P content, e.g., as recorded music (CD) or movies (DVD).

The *Sony* court discussed the nature of the alleged contributory technology: Some uses to which the technology, the Beta machine, could be put were conceivably infringing, so-called "library building," for example, but others were fair, e.g., a consumer might buy or rent a video or watch a home movie of family outings. In other words, a substantial number of noninfringing uses were possible. Therefore the Beta machine is not a contributory technology.[6] The Court used this distinction to develop a test that courts use to determine whether a certain technology "contributes" to the infringement of others to such an extent that its producers should be deemed to have engaged in contributory conduct and be liable for contributory copyright infringement.

In a recent decision the appellate court in Grokster summarized this test and the shifting burden of proof it requires:

> If the product at issue *is not* capable of substantial or commercially significant non-infringing uses, then the copyright owner need only show that the defendant had constructive knowledge of the infringement. On the other hand, if the article *is* capable of substantial or commercially significant non-infringing uses, then the copyright owner must demonstrate that the defendant had reasonable knowledge of specific infringing files and failed to act on the knowledge to prevent infringement.[7]

Even though the Supreme Court rejected such a narrow reading of *Sony* (that once substantial noninfringing uses are established liability can arise only with knowledge of specific unlawful uses[8]), the principle of some safe harbor for distribution of technologies with substantial noninfringing uses remains the standard by which to assess the initial copyright dangers of such conduct. Thus *Sony* remains established law.[9] Since a significant number of technologies fall into the latter category the preventative measures that the court suggests intermediaries take is instructive for the technology infused environment of the modern library or school. As the Internet is surely a technology capable of substantial noninfringing uses, therefore access to it alone should not raise a question of liability for the library or educational institution.[10] More than constructive knowledge is needed.

Applying Liability Principles to Institutional Settings

As discussed below, short of actual knowledge, circumstances exist where a library or educational institution would have reason to know of the infringing nature of the use of its Internet or other computing facilities. The appellate court agreed with the district court when it concluded that the Grokster P2P system was capable of substantial noninfringing uses; therefore the higher standard of reasonable knowledge of specific infringement plus failure to act was needed. This might be characterized as a "knowledge-plus an act" concept,[11] where the "act" could be a failure to intercede and halt the infringing uses to which the technology (the Internet in our example) is put. On the other hand, when distributing a technology with no substantial or significant noninfringing uses (in other words, a technology designed for the purpose of infringement), such infringing uses should be expected. Suppose a technology called "The RIP-Burner" is created, where RIP stands for "requisite infringing purpose" and the technology is designed for the sole purpose of ripping content (i.e., in spite of any copyrighted control protections in place), from a DVD or CD-ROM and copying it on to a blank disk. This might be characterized as an "act plus-knowledge" concept. In either situation, both the latter act of producing and distributing technology one would expect would be put to infringing uses (the act plus knowledge) as well as the former failure to stop the infringing uses of legitimate technology put to an illicit use once aware of that infringing use (knowledge plus act) results in the sort of material contribution to the infringing activity of others that courts conclude warrants the imposition of legal liability. In a comment predating the significant P2P litigation, Alfred C. Yen observes:

> An ISP may investigate why a particular page was generating enough traffic to crash the ISP's computers. Such an investigation may reveal that people were flocking to the site for free access to copyrighted works. . . . The only remaining question concerning liability would be whether continued provision of Internet service to the infringing subscriber would constitute material contribution. Existing case law indicates that this question would be answered affirmatively.[12]

In these circumstances the law has little trouble in establishing liability: but for the distribution of the infringing technology or the failure to prevent obvious infringing uses of other technology, the infringement would not occur.

In *Grokster*, the appellate court further concluded that there was no material contribution toward the infringement either. Though the Supreme Court found ample evidence of inducement to infringe,[13] what remains significant is the appellate court's tripartite hypothesis of how an entity might make a material contribution to the infringement of another that can be instructive for the library or educational entity in similar network settings:

> Material contribution can be established through the provision of site and facilities for infringement, followed by a *failure to stop specific instances of infringement* once knowledge of those infringements is acquired. . . . If the Software Distributors were true access providers, *failure to disable that access* after acquiring specific knowledge of user's infringement might be material contribution [citing *Religious Technology Center v. Netcom On-Line Communications Services*, 907 F. Supp. 1361, 1375 (N.D. Cal. 1995)]. . . . *Failure to delete the offending files or offending index listings* might be material contribution [citing *A&M Records, Inc. v. Napster, Inc.*, 239 F. 3d 1004, 1022 (9th Cir. 2001)].[14]

The obligation of the intermediary, i.e., the alleged contributory infringer, to take corrective measures is limited to those computing facilities under the control of the intermediary: "'Failure' to alter software located on another's computer is simply not akin to the failure to *delete* a filename from one's own computer, to the failure to *cancel* their registration name and password of a particular user from one's user list, or to the failure to *make modification* to software on one's own computer."[15] Courts apply the substantial noninfringing use test when plaintiffs challenge defendant behavior in conjunction with the production and distribution of infringing technology. This is a logical legal requirement. If a technology with a lack of substantial noninfringing uses is available and if constructive knowledge is sufficient, one should expect that the technology would likely be put to infringing uses. By the same token, it would not be proper to hold a manufacturer liable for selling a technology simply because someone else discovered an infringing use for it and at his or her own instigation undertook that infringing use.

Cases have suggested that where the intermediary, once notified of the infringing nature of material on its facilities, bulletin board, Web site, or DE course site, fails to remove the material, this failure does not per se rise to a level of contributory infringement. However, "failure effectively to remove infringing photographs and dissuade infringers at some point began to comprise inducement or material contribution."[16] The two elements, knowledge and contributing conduct, can both shift and work together, as the amount of contribution required may depend on the level of knowledge, actual or constructive. As one district court put it:

> There is a critical interplay between the level of knowledge possessed by LoopNet as a result of CoStar's notices [of infringing material] and the amount of policing, deterrence and removal demanded of LoopNet to avoid being liable for contributory

infringement. If CoStar's notice to LoopNet gave LoopNet a broad scope of knowledge that infringements were occurring, then it creates a high level of policing necessary by LoopNet to avoid inducing infringement.[17]

Likewise, as the Seventh Circuit pointed out, after reflecting on the *Sony* decision, "the ability of a service provider to prevent its customers from infringing is a factor to be considered in determining whether the provider is a contributory infringer."[18]

Divergence in the Federal Circuits?

The Ninth Circuit said as much in *Napster:* "We are bound to follow Sony, and will not impute the requisite level of knowledge to Napster merely because peer-to-peer file sharing technology may be used to infringe plaintiffs' copyrights."[19] However, what sunk Napster is the application of this knowledge-plus an act contributory infringement concept—an aspect incorporated into the section 512 rules for service provider liability limitation discussed more fully in Chapter 13—actual knowledge plus failure to act to prevent continuing infringement equates to the requisite knowledge plus conduct (induce or cause, or materially contribute): "We agree that if a computer system operator learns of specific infringing material available on his system and fails to purge such material from the system, the operator knows of and contributes to direct infringement."[20]

Here is an important point for educational entities. If one is aware of the infringement and fails to intercede and prevent future infringement (by students for example)—even if that technology is not normally associated with infringement, or more accurately, can be put to substantial noninfringing uses—by disabling access to or deleting infringing materials, for example, a claim of contributory infringement can result. This was the issue in suits filed in the wake of *Napster* against several high-profile universities,[21] and in more recent disputes.[22]

The Seventh Circuit Standard

In the recent *Aimster* litigation, the Seventh Circuit may also be suggesting a variation of the application of contributory infringement concepts where technologies are involved:

> What is true is that when a supplier is offering a product or service that has noninfringing as well as infringing uses, some estimate of the respective magnitudes of these is necessary for a finding of contributory infringement. . . . The balancing of costs and benefits is necessary only in a case in which substantial noninfringing uses, present or prospective, are demonstrated.[23]

Under this "relative" standard of cost (e.g., policing network users or checking the content of linked sites) and benefit (prevention of infringement) a potential contributory infringer such a library, school, college, or university is liable only when it would not be efficient for it to cease its contributory conduct relative to the amount of infringement it would prevent, sort of like the old adage applied to the copyright law "an ounce of prevention (policing, monitoring, etc.) to a pound of cure (compliance)."

> Even when there are noninfringing uses of an Internet file-sharing service, moreover, *if the infringing uses are substantial* then to *avoid liability* as a contributory infringer the provider of the services must show that it would have been *disproportionately costly for him to eliminate or at least reduce substantially the infringing uses.*[24]

How this factor is to be applied is not further elucidated by the court.

> In context it appears that a service provider's ability to prevent infringement is a threshold question to determine whether or not the activity is subject to *Sony's* protection. Rather than accepting the recording industry's argument that *Sony* is inapplicable to services, the [*Aimster*] court found *Sony* to apply only in those cases where preventing infringement would be "highly burdensome." In short, the service provider's ability to prevent infringement is relevant in determining the preliminary question of which test to apply) *Sony's* staple article of commerce test or the traditional test for contributory infringement) but not to the ultimate question of infringement.[25]

At least in the Seventh Circuit, including federal courts in Wisconsin, Illinois, and Indiana, this statement may suggest that even where the network technology is subject to substantial infringing uses, an intermediary (i.e., the potential contributory infringer) could find refuge in the argument that it would have been disproportionately costly to eliminate or at least reduce substantially the infringing uses. Of course this argument would need support from credible evidence. A simple network maintenance program that monitors bandwidth and port activities for excessive file sharing is likely not the sort of disproportionately costly mechanism to which the Seventh Circuit is referring.

The Ninth Circuit Retort

The Ninth Circuit issued its decision in *Grokster* after the *Aimster* case was decided, thus it had the benefit of reflection on Judge Posner's "law and economics" influenced opinion. As is typical, such analysis reflects a cost-benefit approach to legal decision making, not necessarily weighing the right or wrong, but determining which result is the most efficient and cost effective. However, the Ninth Circuit was not convinced of Judge Posner's treatment of P2P providers in light of both Supreme Court precedent, such as *Sony*, and its own, such as *Napster*.

> We are mindful that the Seventh Circuit has read *Sony's* substantial noninfringing use standard differently. . . . However, *Aimster* is premised specifically on a fundamental disagreement with *Napster I's* [*Napster, Inc.*, 239 F. 3d 1004 (9th Cir. 2001).] reading of

Sony-Betamax. . . . Even if we were free to do so [entailing an overrule of *Napster*] we do not read *Sony-Betamax's* holding as narrowly as does the Seventh Circuit. . . . Implicit in the *Aimster* analysis is that a finding of substantial noninfringing use, including potential use, would be fatal to a contributory infringement claim, regardless of the level of knowledge possessed by the defendant.[26]

The Supreme Court Steps In

In June of 2005, the United States Supreme Court in a unanimous decision authored by Justice Souter, held "that one who distributes a device with the object of promoting its use to infringe copyright, as shown by clear expression or other affirmative steps taken to foster infringement, is liable for the resulting acts of infringement by third parties."[27]

The question before the Court was "under what circumstances the distributor of a product capable of both lawful and unlawful use is liable for acts of copyright infringement by third parties using the product."[28]

According to Justice Souter, "one infringes contributorily by intentionally inducing or encouraging direct infringement."[29] In a like-minded legal articulation reminiscent of the sole Supreme Court decision involving the distribution of technology that may be put to infringing uses—the *Sony* decision in which the Court adopted the "staple-article of commerce" doctrine from the patent law—the Supreme Court in 2005 adopted the "inducement" rule, also from the patent law.[30] In the common law copyright now, as in the codified patent law, "[l]iability under our jurisprudence may be predicated on actively encouraging (or inducing) infringement through specific acts (as the Court's opinion develops) or on distributing a product distributees use to infringe copyrights, if the product is not capable of 'substantial' or 'commercially significant' noninfringing uses."[31] The intended impact will be to "deter them [entrepreneurs] from distributing products that have no other real function than—or that are specifically intended for—copyright infringement, deterrence that the Court's holding today reinforces (by adding a weapon to the copyright holder's legal arsenal)."[32]

As a result of its opinion, the Ninth Circuit decision in the *Grokster* was vacated and remanded for further proceedings. The immediate significance is that Grokster, Streamcast (the two defendants in the case) as well as other similarly situated defendants may be subject to secondary liability for copyright infringement if those defendants "distribute[] a device with the object of promoting its use to infringe copyright, as shown by clear expression or other affirmative steps taken to foster infringement [if supported by the evidence, the defendant] is liable for the resulting acts of infringement by third parties."[33]

The Grokster Decision: A Closer Look

The copyright infringement issues surrounding Napster, Grokster, and Aimster, and whatever subsequent "next-ster" did not arise by accident. In fact, the Court found significant the use of a too-oft sounding name, along with program attributes; in short it attempted to ride the coattails of Napster's, albeit illegal, but successful customer base and activities.[34] Unlike the lower courts, the Supreme Court found ample evidence of the defendants' unsavory conduct in the hundreds and hundreds of pages of the record which both Souter and Ginsberg quoted from and referred to liberally.[35] "But MGM's evidence gives reason to think that the vast majority of users' downloads are acts of infringement, and because well over 100 million copies of the software in question are known to have been downloaded, and billions of files are shared across the FastTrack and Gnutella networks each month, the probable scope of copyright infringement is staggering."[36]

In commentary similar to recent lower court opinions, the Court was not persuaded by arguments that Grokster, Streamcast, and similar P2P systems are widely put to legitimate uses and recognized, as have lower courts, the scale of piracy facilitated through digital and Internet technologies. While the court based its theory of liability on a concept heretofore foreign to the copyright law, i.e., under the *Sony* rule a safe harbor could be sought if the device is capable of substantial noninfringing uses, the Court nonetheless displayed disdain for the argument that such capabilities are realistic in the case before it: Morpheus "[u]sers seeking Top 40 songs, for example, or the latest release by Modest Mouse, are certain to be far more numerous than those seeking a free Decameron, and Grokster and Stream-Cast translated that demand into dollars."[37] Justice Ginsburg offered additional criticism of the lower court's reliance on such evidence as tentative at best: "Here, there has been no finding of any fair use and little beyond anecdotal evidence of noninfringing uses. In finding the Grokster and StreamCast software products capable of substantial noninfringing uses, the District Court and the Court of Appeals appear to have relied largely on declarations submitted by the defendants. These declarations include assertions (some of them hearsay) that a number of copyright owners authorize distribution of their works on the Internet and that some public domain material is available through peer-to-peer networks including those accessed through Grokster's and StreamCast's software."[38]

Will the rule created by the Supreme Court in *Grokster* stifle development of Internet technology, or any copyright-related technologies for that matter? Is the *Grokster* inducement rule more restrictive than the *Sony* substantial noninfringing uses rule? Perhaps future events alone will tell. In the aftermath of *Sony*, the VCR did not sink the movie industry; in fact, such technology opened new legitimate markets or revenue streams to copyright owners, e.g., video rentals of television series and motion pictures, television series anthologies, restored, anniversary, director's or other special cuts of feature films, and direct to video feature films. These markets either offered additional opportunities for revenue to copyright owners or allowed additional works to enter the market place because the limited television, cable, or theatrical markets, etc. alone would have offered an insufficient market base on which to make such endeavors profitable.

The *Sony* safe harbor allowed "breathing room for innovation and a vigorous commerce"[39] because "where an article is 'good for nothing else' but infringement, *Canada v. Michigan Malleable Iron Co., supra* [124 F. 486 (6th Cir. 1903)], at 489, there is no legitimate public interest in its unlicensed availability, and there is no injustice in presuming or imputing an intent to infringe."[40] Likewise the inducement rule only seeks to penalize entrepreneurs that demonstrate a desire to have their devices put to infringing uses through affirmative acts expressive of that desire, i.e., encouragement of infringement. "The inducement rule, instead, premises liability on purposeful, culpable expression and conduct, and thus does nothing to compromise legitimate commerce or discourage innovation having a lawful promise."[41] Developers without any ill will should have little to fear under this new rule. It would be unlikely for lower courts to find such inducement by mistake, for example.

However, even here the Court commented on the misapplication of the *Sony* precedent by the Ninth Circuit: "Because the [Ninth] Circuit found the Stream-Cast and Grokster software capable of substantial lawful use, it concluded on the basis of its reading of *Sony* that neither company could be held liable, since there was no showing that their software, being without any central server, afforded them knowledge of specific unlawful uses. This view of *Sony*, however, was in error, converting the case from one about liability resting on imputed intent to one about liability on any theory."[42] The *Sony* rule still is law, but the analysis does not end their blind faith analysis, i.e., if there are substantial noninfringing uses but the entrepreneur encourages (induces) only infringing ones, as the evidence indicated Grokster did ("clear expression or other affirmative steps to foster infringement"), then *Sony* will not bar a finding of secondary liability. Second, the Court rejected the copyright owner's request to "add a more quantified description of the point of balance between protection and commerce when liability rests solely on distribution with knowledge that unlawful use will occur. It is enough to note that the Ninth Circuit's judgment rested on an erroneous understanding of *Sony* and to leave further consideration of the *Sony* rule for a day when that may be required."[43] Finally, the Court did not reach the question of whether the defendants could be found vicariously[44] liable.[45]

Looking most favorably on the Supreme Court decision one could conclude that the rule created in *Grokster* is a rather sanguine approach to the wink-wink reality of many P2P environments: *while this technology could be put to good use, we trust it won't!* The Court was simply unwilling to let such entrepreneurs survive legal review in instances where the *Sony* rule had evolved from safe harbor for legitimate developers into loophole for low-minded ones. "Thus, where evidence goes beyond a product's characteristics or the knowledge that it may be put to infringing uses, and shows statements or actions directed to promoting infringement, *Sony's* staple-article rule will not preclude liability."[46] So, too, if the lower court decisions since *Sony* are any indication, the adoption of any new form of copyright liability would suggest that courts would tread carefully in determining inducement, separating the true cases of culpable behavior from the innocent. The Court reviewed the communications made by the defendants and concluded the inducing message was clear from the Internet-based advertisements, e-newsletter, etc.[47] Additional circumstances in the wake of *Napster* in the design and operation of the defendants' technology supported the conclusion of intent: an aim to "satisfy a known source of demand for copyright infringement," similarity of product name, offering of similar program and function and attempts to divert queries for Napster onto its own site, the lack of any attempt to "develop filtering tools or other mechanisms to diminish the infringing activity using their software," and the positive relationship between infringing use and advertising revenue, a main source of income for Grokster.[48] The lesson should be clear for libraries, schools, colleges and universities—do not induce or encourage infringement in any statements, publications, etc. or "other affirmative steps to foster infringement."

The impacts of the decision are many. In general, the case stands for the proposition that the members of the Court are cognizant of the "gigantic scale" of infringement online and elsewhere as well perhaps and are not reluctant to fashion a new basis for liability in response to a new mode of infringement. The decision stands as a victory for copyright owners against infringers and especially targets intermediaries as part of the enforcement equation. This may embolden copyright owners to challenge the other practices of intermediaries relating to copyright in other contexts of relevance to libraries, schools, colleges, and universities, e.g., e-reserve practices of universities; considering the number of courses in which e-reserves are used, the number of items placed on reserve for each class and the number of institutions employing such mechanisms across the country, the number of copyrighted works placed is likely also staggering. However, unlike *Grokster*, there is a higher percentage of use that is likely fair.

The decision also signals that the court will not hesitate to fashion a remedy when faced with new technology environments. That is exactly what the Court did with VCR technology in the 1980's in *Sony* and that is what the Court did in 2005 with P2P systems. If there is any criticism here, it is that borrowing from patent law might not be the best strategy overall as the nature of patent versus copyright laws while both based on the grant of monopolistic rights is different in that the latter is thought to be a limited monopoly. The copyright statutes are populated with numerous exceptions or limitations on the exclusive rights of copyright owners, while the patent law is far less forgiving. In specific, it lends judicial support for any related legislation, such as the S. 2560, 108th Cong., 2nd Sess. (2004) (Inducing Infringement of Copyright Act of 2004) discussed below. Beyond the pundits, the true impact will have to wait with the passages of time, or at least the first few lower court decisions applying these concepts. What is certain is that if a copyright safe harbor is still sought by an intermediary, the *Grokster* decision offers another underwater obstacle that must also be avoided.

AVOIDING ENCOURAGEMENT AND FACILITATION OF INFRINGEMENT

What sort of conduct (besides providing a contributory technology or service and offering the capability of substantial or commercially significant noninfringing uses to network users) would induce, cause, or materially contribute to the infringement of another? Consider the following instructive case. A person can contribute to the infringement of another through more immediate or connected practice: by encouraging conduct that infringes. For example, in *Intellectual Reserve, Inc. vs. Utah Lighthouse Ministry, Inc.*[49] the defendants posted directions on their Web site where an unpublished church handbook could be obtained on three other Web sites. The defendants had previously received a temporary restraining order to cease display of infringing material. Subsequent to removing the infringing material from their Web site, the defendants located several other Web sites where the infringing material resided. The defendants proceeded to announce on their Web site that the material, unpublished and proprietary documentation relating to the Mormon Church, was back on the Web, and encouraged visitors to their site to seek out the material and further distribute it across the Web. Thus the defendants knew that when visitors to their site followed their directions and visited the other Web sites a copy would be made in the RAM of their computers and thus an infringing reproduction would be made. This infringing copy was the necessary direct infringement required before a claim of contributory copyright infringement could be made. Further the defendants knew these copies were infringing because, like the versions of the church documentation posted on their site earlier, all versions were posted without permission and in excess of fair use, thus infringing.

The question before the *Intellectual Reserve, Inc. vs. Utah Lighthouse Ministry, Inc.* court was whether the conduct of the defendants was sufficient to meet the "induce, cause, or materially contribute" to the direct infringement. On their site, the defendants also included admonitions that encouraged subsequent browsing of the handbook by site visitors and implored their viewers to copy and send the handbook to others. The court found this behavior and other antics designed to encourage proliferation of the infringing copies significant. For example, "in response to an e-mail stating that the sender had unsuccessfully tried to browse a Web site that contained the Handbook, defendants gave further instructions on how to browse the material."[50] The court concluded that the defendants materially contributed (contributory infringement) to the infringement of others, those visitors to their site who then proceeded from their site to the three other Web sites where the church's work was posted (direct infringement). It should be observed that while the defendant's Web site did list the URL of the other Web sites where the infringing Church materials were posted, it did not contain an active or hypertext link to the material.

The Element of Knowledge

What is the meaning of the concept "have reason to know"? In tort law for example, "reason to know" is contrasted with a "should have known" concept.

> The words "reason to know" are used throughout the Restatement of this Subject [Restatement of Torts 2d] to denote the fact that the actor has information from which a person of reasonable intelligence or of the superior intelligence of the actor would infer that the fact in question exists, or that such person would govern his conduct upon the assumption that such fact exists.[51]

It does not require that one is under a duty to use reasonable diligence to ascertain the existence or nonexistence of the fact in question, as this would represent the higher, "should know" standard.[52]

> Where the defendant's activities are relatively close to the directly infringing acts, the plaintiff may meet the knowledge requirement by showing that, although the defendant lacked actual knowledge of the infringement, he knew of facts that would have prompted a reasonable person to inquire into whether an infringement was occurring.[53]

The comments made by courts in recent P2P and other secondary liability cases can serve to demonstrate when the "reason to know" standard has been met.

In the *Intellectual Reserve, Inc. vs. Utah Lighthouse Ministry, Inc.* court focused on the encouragement of the infringing activities offered by the defendants to visitors of their site, i.e., promoting the access, retrieval, and forwarding of the handbook from other sites where it was unlawfully posted.[54] The lesson for the library or educational institution and its constituents is one of common sense. While educators need not review every Web site to which students are linked or referred for potential infringing material, this would be a "should know" standard, i.e., determine whether the site is infringing. So, too, common sense should prompt the librarian to question the logic of linking, bookmarking, or referring patrons or students to sites with offerings such as "a thousand textbooks or workbooks downloadable for free" or having a URL such as bootlegbookstore.com! Common sense suggests a reasonable person would have cause to suspect the legitimacy of such sites; thus, to refer patrons to the site without further review or to encourage students to download or distribute material located on that site would not be prudent.

Once this "reason to know" is established, a court might conclude that your referral or similar reader's advisory commendation of the Web site to a patron or student is sufficient inducement, cause, or material contribution to the subsequent infringement that occurs when that patron or student seeks out the infringing material on that Web site. Consider the assistance that one district court concluded could support a finding of material contribution:

> However, there is sufficient evidence from which a factfinder could determine that MP3Board engaged in an overall course of conduct which materially contributed to copyright infringement. . . . MP3Board offered new users "getting started" information and a tutorial containing instructions on how to locate and download audio files via MP3Board—actually using one of the record companies' copyrighted recordings as an example. The site also contained a message board which allowed users to post questions to be answered by other users or MP3Board staff. Significantly, when individual users posted messages on the message board requesting particular songs which they could not find links to on the MP3Board site, MP3Board personnel personally searched for links to the requested song files and posted the links on the message board. When one MP3Board employee could not find any links to one particular work, he solicited users to provide the work.[55]

Perhaps the best way to test whether the "reason to know" standard has been met is the very unlegal but practical "gut" or "red flag" test. What is the nature or circumstances surrounding the material to which you are referring a patron or student? What does your gut tell you? Does a red flag go up? Are you referring to a Web site that boasts downloadable popular music or movies for free? Does it have a dubious URL, like deathtocopyrightowners.org or piratedmusic.com? Moreover, why are you referring patrons to the material? Is it, for example, to save the cost of students having to purchase supplementary course materials or to acquire material for library reserves or fill patron requests that the library would otherwise have to obtain permission to use or license? Often times answers to these questions may indicate the suspicious nature of the site. There is a sound adage that is also useful here: if it sounds too good to be true, it probably is.

An educator or librarian serving as an educator, such as a school media specialist, can be in a position to influence the behavior of those in their charge (induce, cause, or materially contribute), more perhaps than in other library or information environments. As a result, school librarians and educators at all levels should therefore be sensitive to the potential for contributory liability by referral and more important by command, such as when students are told to seek out copyrighted content from an infringing source and bring a copy of it to class or are otherwise told to make an infringing use of copyrighted material. An example of the latter would occur when the faculty advisor to a foreign language club tells (commands) students to devise a segment for an upcoming meeting that includes the viewing of a foreign language film to club members with a follow-up discussion. Using the film in this way is a public performance beyond the scope of either section 110(1) or fair use (section 107). Its performance is most assuredly infringing. The teacher's role in procuring the infringing performance is precisely the sort of contributory conduct the concept of secondary liability is intended to dissuade. As the Seventh Circuit commented in the peer-to-peer file-sharing case involving the *Aimster* system: "The law allows a copyright holder to sue a contributor to the infringement instead, in effect as an aider and abettor. Another analogy is to the tort of intentional interference with contract, that is, inducing a breach of contract."[56] A sense of fairness underlies the concept of contributory infringement in copyright law in that it may be an unfair result that someone (in the above examples, the librarian or teacher), who though not executor of the direct infringement is still its instigator. This instigator might nonetheless have undertaken conduct such that he or she should also share some responsibility for the subsequent infringement, or, as is often the case in online settings, the continued infringement undertaken by others, the librarian, teacher, or student. A practical issue also exists in that courts have recognized the "impracticability or futility of a copyright owner's suing a multitude of individual infringers."[57] The concept of contributory infringement serves then as a leveraged and more efficient form of liability. Like an ounce of prevention for a pound of cure, suing a contributor to infringement can curtail the infringement of numerous direct infringers, e.g., shutting down Napster prevented, at least for a time, hundreds or perhaps thousands of file-share from subsequent infringing behavior.

How to Avoid Inducing Infringement

The ninth circuit concluded that the distributors of P2P sharing software Grokster and StreamCast were **not** found liable for contributory infringement because their conduct did not amount to the sort of active inducement or goading as was present in the *Intellectual Reserve, Inc. vs. Utah Lighthouse Ministry, Inc.* case. The district court characterized the technical assistance rendered to Grokster users differently: the assistance occurred after the specific act of direct infringement, was routine, and nonspecific.[58] Patterning classroom, library, or network assistance that mirrors the generally passive or otherwise "removed" assistance of the *Grokster* defendants is prudent and less unlikely to constitute contributory conduct than assistance that targets or facilitates infringement of specific infringing conduct. However, as discussed above, the Supreme Court found sufficient evidence of secondary liability based on a theory of intentional inducement not necessarily related to general technical issues related to use of its system but in the promotion of the system generally for specific acts of infringement.[59]

The Ninth Circuit, the same court that decided *Napster*, though by a different panel of three judges, observed:

The Copyright Owners have not provided evidence that defendants materially contribute in any other manner. StreamCast maintains an XML file from which user software periodically retrieves parameters. These values may include the addresses of websites where lists of active users are maintained. The owner of the FastTrack software, Sharman, maintains root nodes containing lists of currently active supernodes to which users can connect. Both defendants also communicate with users incidentally, but not to facilitate infringement. All of these activities are too incidental to any direct copyright infringement to constitute material contribution. No infringing files or lists of infringing files are hosted by defendants, and the defendants do not regulate or provide access."[60]

Unlike Groskter, Aimster engaged in conduct that evidenced its contribution to the infringement of others. For example, the Aimster tutorials were limited to examples of copyrighted music alone,[61] thus the examples were based on infringing activity and as such instructed others how to infringe. Second, the creation of Club Aimster, whereby a single click would download the most popular 40 shared songs for a "monthly fee [wa]s the sole means by which Aimster [wa]s financed and so the club [read, infringing activity] cannot be separated from the provision of the free software."[62] Finally, there was no evidence to suggest the all-important substantial noninfringing uses, or at least the potential for substantial noninfringing uses. As the Aimster court observed, the potential must be real, not some strained hypothetical possibility: "*Absent is any indication* from real-life Aimster users that their *primary use* of the system *is to transfer non-copyrighted files* to their friends or identify users of similar interest and share information."[63] If there were such evidence, it might be a sign that there were substantial noninfringing uses for the P2P software.

Ignorance Cannot Be Feigned

Nor can a potential contributory infringer, such as a library or school, look the other way, either literally or technologically through the use of protections measures that obfuscate the discovery of infringing activity in order to claim in defense that it had no knowledge or reason to know of the infringing behavior of patrons, students, or other users of its networks. Rather, having a copyright compliance program in place that identifies obvious or highly likely infringement by patrons, students, or other users and that requires remedial responses when such suspicion is raised is the more sound policy. Even if the educational entity is not a contributory infringer, another benefit of an active compliance program is that it might reduce the likelihood of receiving one of those nasty subpoenas from the copyright owner should the copyright owner desire to pursue legal action against the patron or student file sharer, as direct infringer.[64] Also, such efforts work to reduce the likelihood that any infringement that does occur will not be pervasive or lingering, thus reducing the exposure of the institution to risk.

Of course the *Aimster* decision, like the other cases discussed here, is controlling only in the jurisdiction in which it is decided. Here is an example of a case setting a legal standard that per se is "the law" only in the Seventh Circuit (i.e., the states of Wisconsin, Illinois, and Indiana), yet its lessons are well learned by any library or educational institution. To be sure, in the educational setting, an ounce of prevention is worth a pound of cure, and another district or circuit court might see it that way as well. The case remains instructive nonetheless: looking the other way is an insufficient response! "Willful blindness is knowledge, in copyright law (where indeed it may be enough that the defendant should have known of the direct infringement [citation omitted], as it is in the law generally."[65] Infringement can occur even when, as in the Aimster case, that knowledge is blocked through the use of encryption technology: "Our point is only that a service provider that would otherwise be a contributory infringer does not obtain immunity by using encryption to shield itself from actual knowledge of the unlawful purposes for which the service is being used."[66] Moreover, the encryption software that Aimster used in order to protect the privacy of its users, and which in the court's opinion was also a subterfuge in inhibiting its ability to police its system, only complicated its claim of innocence: "Aimster hampered its search for evidence by providing encryption. It must take responsibility for that self-inflicted wound."[67] A similar comment from a district court involved a defendant that changed its contact e-mail address without notifying the U.S. Copyright Office and without instituting any e-mail forwarding program. As a result, it was near impossible for copyright owners to make it aware of the infringing nature of material on its network:

> If AOL could avoid the knowledge requirement through this oversight or deliberate action, then it would encourage other ISPs to remain willfully ignorant in order to avoid contributory copyright infringement liability. Based on the record before the court a reasonable tier of fact could certainly find that AOL had reason to know that infringing copies of Ellison's work were stored on their Usenet servers.[68]

Again the question, even in the Seventh Circuit, would be what is a reasonable response for an intermediary, a provider of potentially infringing technology or computing facilities, to make? Courts, believe it or not, are pretty savvy in trudging through the muck of excessive rationalization or other mental smoke screening. "[N]o more can Deep by using encryption software prevent himself from learning what surely he strongly suspects to be the case: that the users of his services—maybe all the users of his service—are copyright infringers."[69] Unfortunately, the inability of some library or educational institutions to curtail infringement in the past may have contributed to Congress' enactment of statutory requirements that conditions the safe-harbor damage limitation of section 512 on a remedial response mechanism (disable or delete) or similarly posits a new distance education law the amended section 110(2) that now requires a qualifying entity (accredited nonprofit educational organization) to engage in numerous prevention measures. When the provisions of those sections apply, such action is no longer merely prudent, it **is** *required!* These sections are covered in detail in chapters 6, 7, 8 and 12.

UNDERSTANDING HOW LEGISLATIVE INITIATIVES AFFECT THE CONCEPT OF FACILITATION

One final development is worth comment here. Senate bill 2560, the Inducing Infringement of Copyright Act of 2004,[70] would create a new form of direct copyright infringement. The Supreme Court decision in *Grokster*[71] adopting the intentional inducement rule lends judicial support for such mechanisms; however legislative remedy would elevate the offense to one of direct infringement and not merely a subset of secondary liability. However, its structure parallels concepts of "assisted" infringement, and so it is logical that discussion occurs in the present Chapter.[72] Section 2 of S. 2560 amends 17 U.S.C. § 501 by adding subsection (g) and creates a new form of copyright infringement: anyone who "intentionally induces any violation identified in subsection (a) [of section 501] shall be liable as an infringer." Section 501(a) indicates that "[a]nyone who violates any of the exclusive rights of the copyright owner as provided by section 106 through 121 . . . is an infringer of the copyright . . ."[73] This is akin to an aiding and abetting provision, with the additional element of intent. While S. 2560 creates a concept of direct infringement it is nonetheless predicated on the occurrence of another's infringement and in this way operates in sequence as if it were a concept of secondary liability. However, Section 2 makes clear that "[n]othing in this subsection shall enlarge the doctrines of vicarious and contributory liability for copyright infringement or require any court to unjustly withhold or impose any secondary liability for copyright infringement."[74] Introduced the year before the Supreme Court decision in *Grokster,* the bill sponsor's accuracy in reading into the future remains uncanny: In *Sony,* the Supreme Court borrowed the concept of "substantial non-infringing use test from the patent law.[75] According to Senator Hatch, S. 2560 codifies the importation of another concept from the patent laws: "active inducement."[76]

New section 501(g)(1) would define the term "intentionally induces" to mean "intentionally aids, abets, induces, or promotes." Thus, in an odd twist, it appears to turn an intentional contributory infringer of sorts into a direct infringer, except that there is no explicit knowledge requirement as in a claim of contributory infringement; it may be implicit, as one would conceive it difficult to intend the infringement of another if one does not know the induced activity would indeed be infringing. However, it could be argued that all that is required is an intent to induce some conduct and that the conduct so induced results in infringement—not that you as a section 501(g) infringer know the result is infringing nor intend it to be, only that you intended to induce ("aid, abet, induce or procure") some conduct. This is the potential danger of a broad interpretation of the provision.

According to the new law, intent could be demonstrated by "acts from which a reasonable person would find intent to induce infringement upon all relevant information about such acts then reasonably available to the actor."[77] However, this reasonableness standard also suggests an implicit scienter, actual or constructive ("reason to know"): are there facts present that suggest that the intended result, the induced conduct would in fact be infringing? Even if this is a sound reading of the provision, new section 501(g) does not infuse a knowledge requirement into the subsequent act of direct infringement. Intentionally induce an unsuspecting person into infringing the copyright of another, even if the unwitting actor does know that his or her actions would constitute infringement and you could still be liable as a section 501(g) infringer.

In this way the provision is designed to reach the actions of some P2P software designers. While it may be possible to put their technologies to noninfringing uses, the intent of their conduct was to create, with full knowledge, a technology that would in fact be used to infringe the copyrights of others and would induce others to use that technology in just such a fashion:

> By preserving the general rule of liability for knowing inducement and its DMCA and *Sony* limitations, S. 2560 thus affects only [sic] of distributors of copying devices who intend to induce infringing uses of their devices. In the *Napster* and *Grokster* cases, such distributors distracted courts by raising issues of non-infringing uses that should have been as irrelevant as they were to the defendants' business plans. S. 2560 will end the confusion caused by these flawed analyses.[78]

Senator Hatch also explained what the bill would not do: "

> [It] is our expectation that most defendants will never be affected by S. 2560 because they already face broader liability for inducing copyright infringement. . . . [T]he prevailing rule for contributory infringement imposes liability upon anyone who knows or has reason to know of infringing activity and induces, causes or materially contributes to the infringing conduct of another. For the overwhelming majority of defendants governed by this rule of liability for knowing inducement, no additional liability results from liability for intentional inducement.[79]

Referring to the safe harbor provisions of section 512 discussed in Chapter 6, Senator Hatch commented: "Nor do we intend to affect defendants for whom Congress or courts have narrowed the general rule of secondary liability for knowing inducement. . . . It is also not our intent to affect distributors of copying devices who merely know that their devices can be or are being used by others to make infringing copies."[80] As a result, only distributors who make available copying or other technologies capable of infringing uses *and* engage in activity that induces others to use such technology in that unlawful way would be subject to this provision. This measure did not pass in the 108th Congress, but it or a similar measure may be reintroduced in the 109th Congress in 2005–2006.[81] Whether such measures are introduced in the future may depend on how successful copyright plaintiffs are in the lower courts armed with the new weapon of contributory infringement by intentional inducement. One advantage for copyright owners with follow-up legislation to the *Grokster* standard is that it would allow Congress to also establish or target a specific damage amount to the conduct.

KEEPING UP WITH RECENT ENFORCEMENT INITIATIVES

In late summer 2004 the Attorney General announced the first use of the criminal laws against a P2P infringer in the execution of six search warrants at five different residences and to one Internet service provider in Texas, New York, and Wisconsin belonging to a group of P2P users known as The Underground Network.[82] The seizure resulted in the confiscation of more 40 terabytes of illegally distributed materials, about 60,000 movies or 10.5 million songs.[83] Attorney General Ashcroft observed:

> The execution of today's warrants disrupted an extensive peer-to-peer network suspected of enabling users to traffic illegally in music, films, software and published works. The Department of Justice is committed to enforcing intellectual property laws, and we will pursue those who steal copyrighted materials even when they try to hide behind the false anonymity of peer-to-peer networks.[84]

The enforcement initiatives are part of Operation Digital Gridlock, a joint investigation conducted by the FBI, the Office of the U.S. Attorney for the District of Columbia, and the Justice Department's Computer Crime and Intellectual Property Section.

In fall 2004 the Justice Department's Computer Crime and Intellectual Property Section issued a report[85] on the use of available enforcement mechanisms against those who abuse the intellectual property rights of others. The Report of the Department of Justice's Task Force on Intellectual Property forwarded several principles on which its recommendations are based and which have relevance here: (1) enforcement, (2) government responsibility vis-à-vis enforcement, in specific, (3) "a leading role in the prosecution of the most serious violations," most relevant to the present discussion of P2P, (4) the "federal government should punish those who misuse innovative technologies rather than innovation itself," and (5) international enforcement.[86] As a result, the prosecution of intellectual property offenses is a "high priority" at the Justice Department.[87]

Moreover, S. 2237,[88] also proposed in the 108th Congress, would give the Attorney General the authority to "commence a civil action in the appropriate United

States district court against any person who engages in conduct constituting an offense under section 506." In other words, the government will have the persuasive powers of copyright owners (civil remedies), in cases that rise to the level of criminal copyright infringement as well, i.e., under section 506, uncharacteristically placing the government in the role of copyright prosecutor and now victim (copyright plaintiff). The measure passed in the Senate on June 25, 2004.[89] As explained in the Report of the Department of Justice's Task Force on Intellectual Property, this additional tool is needed as "these violators are difficult to prosecute criminally for a variety of reasons. . . . [E]nforcement is thus generally left to owners of the intellectual property to locate offenders and file civil lawsuits against them. Private civil enforcement, however, is not always effective."[90] As a result, the Justice Department supports civil enforcement of intellectual property laws. Though not all members of Congress would agree the Justice Department is doing enough,[91] and as a result such legislative initiatives are sure to be reintroduced until Congress believes the "law and order" of the copyright law has been restored.

REAL-WORLD EXAMPLES

▶ Real-World Example I

Situation: An instructor has just received the new edition of a workbook companion to a current textbook as a desk copy with an order form for additional classroom copies. The instructor places her only copy on the library reserve and tells students to copy all of the exercises at the back of each chapter and bring them to class to work on throughout the upcoming semester.

Legal Analysis: While each student who follows the instructions would be considered the direct infringer of the workbook photocopied, a claim could also be made against the teacher who ordered her students to make the copies. Certainly the teacher is in a position of authority over her charges such that it is reasonable to expect that students would follow any direction or similar instruction that is given. A court could conclude that this is sufficient inducement, cause, or material contribution to the direct infringement by her students. While no notice of the infringement has been provided to the teacher from the publisher, the likely copyright owner, it is reasonable to conclude, and a court would also likely conclude, that the teacher would know or have reason to know that making a complete copy of each test in the companion workbook under the circumstances would be infringing.

▶ Real-World Example II

Situation: A public library patron is seeking information on language courses for travelers. All of the relevant library books and audio sets are in circulation at the moment. The librarian, an avid traveler himself, knows of several personal Web sites where users have scanned and posted several titles from the Rick Steves series of pocket language guides and where others have converted into MP3 format and posted audio files of several titles in the Michelle Thomas learn-by-listening foreign language instruction as well. The reference librarian refers the patron to these sites and encourages the patron to download the titles for use in preparation of her upcoming travels.

Legal Analysis: Given the widespread coverage in the press that recent P2P controversies have generated, the librarian would have reason to know that the Rick Steves and Michelle Thomas titles appear on the Web sites of individual Web users without the permission of the copyright owners. So, too, the referral and active encouragement to download this material would likely constitute sufficient inducement, cause, or material contribution to subject the librarian to a claim of contributory infringement.

▶ **Real-World Example III**

Situation: Suppose that a foreign language student downloads several of the text and audio files from the Web site in Real-world Example II into his folders on the school's computing network. Sometime thereafter, school officials receive a letter from the publishers indicating that students at their school have been downloading the various language titles from unauthorized Web sites. The school responds that it does not monitor student use of computing facilities and that it can do nothing to prevent excessive downloading by either students or staff.

Legal Analysis: The refusal by school administrators to take any remedial action and either delete the infringing files or disable access to the student's network folders where the infringing files reside would be considered sufficient inducement, cause, or material contribution to the continued infringement. In this case the actual notice received from the publishers would constitute sufficient notice for purposes of the knowledge element in a claim of contributory infringement.

▶ **Real-World Example IV**

Situation: Suppose the substitute computer science teacher, quite savvy with technology, designs a program called "Grab-IT" that allows users to enter the title of any copyrighted publication into the search box, and locate and download a copy of it quickly from the Internet. The Grab-IT search parameters can be set to screen out or bypass those sites subject to any sort of authorization or payment system, and to search for sites where copies reside without permission of the copyright owner. The teacher posts the free program on his Web site where other programs he developed are also advertised and available for sale. In addition, the teacher contributes to numerous student-oriented blog and chat sites where the abilities of the Grab-IT program to locate and download recent copyrighted articles, textbooks, and workbooks is constantly praised and promoted. In his blog and chat postings the teacher includes links to his Web site where interested students may obtain the program for their own use.

Legal Analysis: Students who use the Grab-IT program to locate and download copyrighted articles, textbooks, and workbooks would be viewed as direct infringers. (Of course the assumption, likely true, is that the copyrighted articles, textbooks, and workbooks posted at the "free" sites are infringing.) However, the teacher may share in liability for inducing the infringement of the students who use the Grab-IT program. Under recent Supreme Court precedent, "one who distributes a device with the object of promoting its use to infringe copyright, as shown by clear expression or other affirmative steps taken to foster infringement, is liable for the resulting acts of infringement by third parties." *Metro-Goldwyn-Mayer Studios Inc. v. Grokster, Ltd.*, 125 S.Ct. 2764 (2005). Depending on the facts, it could be argued that, like the defendants in *Grokster*, the teacher is promoting infringement by targeting a known source of demand for such products, failing to incorporate any safeguards (in fact specifically designing the program to avoid legitimate sites of the sought-after material), and establishing a potential connection between the distribution of the device and a personal revenue stream. *Metro-Goldwyn-Mayer Studios Inc. v. Grokster, Ltd.*, 125 S.Ct. 2764, 2781-2782 (2005).

KEY POINTS FOR YOUR INSTITUTION'S POLICY AND PRACTICE

▶ Contributory infringement occurs when "one who, with knowledge of the infringing activity, induces or causes, or materially contributes to the infringement of another." See pp. 13–15, 24–25.

▶ Before the conduct of a librarian or other defendant could be found contributory, the underlying activity must first be found infringing. For example, the use the patron made of the material must be infringing before the librarian's material contribution could be found contributory. See pp. 13–14.

▶ Developing case law suggests that if a library or other information intermediary such as a school, college, or university has reasonable knowledge of specific infringing activity occurring through its site or facilities or that if infringing files or links are posted or linked on its computing network, the library must act to stop the activity, deny access to or disable the link, or delete the infringing material. See pp. 17–17, 27–29.

▶ Developing case law suggests that library employees should not encourage others to engage in infringing conduct and should not refer patrons to obvious sources of infringing material by link or bookmark or other affirmative conduct. See pp. 24–26.

ENDNOTES

[1] *Gershwin Publishing Corp. v. Columbia Artists Management, Inc.*, 443 F.2d 1159, 1162 (2d Cir. 1971).

[2] *A & M Records, Inc. v. Napster, Inc.*, 239 F. 3d 1004, 1015 (9th Cir. 2001).

[3] *Sony Corp. of America, Inc. v. Universal City Studios*, 464 U.S. 417 (1984).

[4] According to Judge Posner of the Seventh Circuit in *In Re Aimster Copyright Litigation*, 334 F.3d 643 (7th Cir. 2003), implicit in *Sony* is the conclusion that the remaining two uses of off-air recordings proposed by the defendants were not a fair use: "library building" or making copies of programs to retain permanently, and "skipping" or editing, as "skipping a commercials by taping a program before watching it and then, while watching the tape, using the fast-forward button on the recorder to skip over the commercials . . . [c]ommercial skipping amounted to creating an unauthorized derivative work." Id. F.3d at 647. This is a significant finding and implications for a library or educational institution that undertook the same activity. According to Judge Posner (and based on the Supreme Court in *Sony*) a school or library that created a permanent library of copied copyrighted audiovisual programs or perhaps other material for that matter, for use in reserves for example (library building) is not engaging in a fair use. Likewise when the school or library later uses that off-air tape in the classroom or school media center and fast-forwards through the recorded commercials would also not be engaging in a fair use. However, an educational use, as is hypothesized here, is specifically listed in section 107; the fair use provision uses the term "teaching," as a possible fair use. Scholars, in contrast, have not read *Sony* quite the same way: "In *Sony*, the Court touched upon the use of a VCR to fast forward through commercials but did not issue a direct opinion on the matter, and instead held that personal 'time-shifting' of commercial network television programs was permissible under fair use." Derek J. Schaffner, The Digital Millennium Copyright Act: Overextension of Copyright, 14 CORNELL JOURNAL OF LAW AND PUBLIC POLICY 145, 166 (2004).

[5] *Sony Corp. of America, Inc. v. Universal City Studios*, 464 U.S. 417, 459, n.2 (1984) (J. Blackmun, dissenting) (another member of the dissent is still on the Court, J. Rehnquist) (of the majority, Justice Stevens remains on the current court).

[6] *Sony Corp. of America, Inc. v. Universal City Studios*, 464 U.S. 417, 442 (1984) ("Accordingly, the sale of copying equipment, like the sale of other articles of commerce, does not constitute contributory infringement if the product is widely used to legitimate, unobjectionable purpose. Indeed, it need merely be capable of substantial noninfringing uses.").

[7] *Metro-Goldwin Studios, Inc. v Grokster, Ltd.*, 380 F.3d 1154, 1161 (9th Cir. 2004) (first emphasis added, second emphasis original), reversed 125 S. Ct 2764 (2005).

[8] *Metro-Goldwyn-Mayer Studios Inc. v. Grokster, Ltd.*, 125 S. Ct. 2764, 2778 (2005).

[9] *Metro-Goldwyn-Mayer Studios Inc. v. Grokster, Ltd.*, 125 S. Ct. 2764, 2778-2779 (2005) (U.S.), ("Because *Sony* did not displace other theories of secondary liability . . . we do not revisit

Sony further. . . . It is enough to note that the Ninth Circuit's judgment rested on an erroneous understanding of Sony and to leave further consideration of the Sony rule for a day when that may be required.").

10 Alfred C. Yen, Internet Service Provider Liability for Subscriber Copyright Infringement, Enterprise Liability, and the First Amendment, 88 GEORGETOWN LAW JOURNAL 1833, 1874 (2000) ("The requisite level of knowledge, therefore, makes the imposition of contributory liability for the simple provision of Internet services highly unlikely.").

11 Metro-Goldwin Studios, Inc. v Grokster, Ltd., 380 F.3d 1154, 1161-1162 (9th Cir. 2004) ("In short, from the evidence presented, the district court quite correctly concluded that the software was capable of substantial noninfringing uses and, therefore, that the Sony-Betamax doctrine applied."), vacated and remanded 125 S. Ct. 2764 (2005).

12 Alfred C. Yen, Internet Service Provider Liability for Subscriber Copyright Infringement, Enterprise Liability, and the First Amendment, 88 GEORGETOWN LAW JOURNAL 1833, 1874 (2000).

13 Metro-Goldwyn-Mayer Studios Inc. v. Grokster, Ltd., 125 S. Ct. 2764, 2782 (2005). ("MGM's evidence in this case most obviously addresses a different basis of liability for distributing a product open to alternative uses. Here, evidence of the distributors' words and deeds going beyond distribution as such shows a purpose to cause and profit from third-party acts of copyright infringement. If liability for inducing infringement is ultimately found, it will not be on the basis of presuming or imputing fault, but from inferring a patently illegal objective from statements and actions showing what that objective was. There is substantial evidence in MGM's favor on all elements of inducement, and summary judgment in favor of Grokster and StreamCast was in error. On remand, reconsideration of MGM's motion for summary judgment will be in order.").

14 Metro-Goldwin Studios, Inc. v Grokster, Ltd., 380 F.3d 1154, 1163 (9th Cir. 2004) (all emphasis added), vacated and remanded 125 S. Ct 2764 (2005).

15 Metro-Goldwin Studios, Inc. v Grokster, Ltd., 380 F.3d 1154, 1163-1164 (9th Cir. 2004), vacated and remanded 125 S. Ct 2764 (2005).

16 Costar Group Inc. v. LoopNet, Inc., 164 F. Supp. 2d 688, 707 (D. Md. 2001), affirmed Costar Group Inc. v. LoopNet, Inc., 373 F.3d 544 (4th Cir. 2004).

17 Costar Group Inc. v. LoopNet, Inc., 164 F. Supp. 2d 688, 706 (D. Md. 2001), affirmed Costar Group Inc. v. LoopNet, Inc., 373 F.3d 544 (4th Cir. 2004).

18 In Re Aimster Copyright Litigation, 334 F.3d 643, 648 (7th Cir. 2003).

19 A&M Records, Inc. v. Napster, Inc., 239 F.3d 1004, 1020-1021 (9th Cir. 2001).

20 A&M Records, Inc. v. Napster, Inc., 239 F.3d 1004, 1121 (9th Cir. 2001) ("We nevertheless conclude that sufficient knowledge exists to impose contributory liability when linked to demonstrated infringing use of the Napster system." Id.).

21 Metallica v. Napster, Inc., No. 00-0391 (C.D. Cal. April 13, 2000) (UCS, Yale, Indiana University joined as defendants on a theory of contributory infringement, later dismissed

when campuses agreed to police their networks.). See also, THE NATIONAL LAW JOURNAL, November 1, 2004, at 3 ("The recording industry last week filed another round of copyright infringement lawsuits against people it said were illegally distributing songs over the Internet. This latest wave of federal litigation targeted 750 computer users across the nation, including 25 students at 13 universities, according to the Recording Industry Association of America. . . . The association claims that the defendants used university computer networks to distribute recordings on unauthorized peer-to-peer services, including eDonkey, Kazaa, LimeWire and Grokster. Among the universities attended by students named in the lawsuits were Indiana State, Iowa State, Ohio State and Southern Mississippi.").

[22] Press Release: RIAA, Copyright Infringement Lawsuits Brought Against 753 Additional Illegal File Sharers, February 28, 2005 ("The Recording Industry Association of America (RIAA), on behalf of the major record companies, today announced a new wave of copyright infringement lawsuits against illegal file sharers, including individual network users at 11 different colleges. . . . Among those sued today are users of computer networks at 11 universities and colleges, including: Hamilton College; Louisiana State University; Louisiana Tech. University; Loyola University Chicago; Ohio University; Old Dominion University; Rennselaer Polytechnic Institute; Texas A&M University; University of Southern California; Vanderbilt University; and Wright State University."), available at *www.riaa.com/news/newsletter/022805.asp.*

[23] *In Re Aimster Copyright Litigation,* 334 F.3d 643, 650 (7th Cir. 2003).

[24] *In Re Aimster Copyright Litigation,* 334 F.3d 643, 653 (7th Cir. 2003) (all emphasis added).

[25] Jesse M. Feder, Is Betamax Obsolete?: *Sony Corp. of America v. Universal City Studios, Inc.* in the Age of Napster, 37 CREIGHTON LAW REVIEW 859, 886-887 (2004).

[26] *Metro-Goldwin Studios, Inc. v Grokster, Ltd.,* 380 F.3d 1154, 1162, at n. 9 (9th Cir. 2004), reversed and remanded 125 S. Ct 2764 (2005).

[27] *Metro-Goldwyn-Mayer Studios Inc. v. Grokster, Ltd.,*125 S. Ct. 2764, 2770 (2005).

[28] *Metro-Goldwyn-Mayer Studios Inc. v. Grokster, Ltd.,* 125 S. Ct. 2764, 2770 (2005).

[29] *Metro-Goldwyn-Mayer Studios Inc. v. Grokster, Ltd.,* 125 S. Ct. 2764, 2776 (2005).

[30] *Metro-Goldwyn-Mayer Studios Inc. v. Grokster, Ltd.,* 125 S. Ct. 2764, 2780 (2005). (For the same reasons that *Sony* took the staple-article doctrine of patent law as a model for its copyright safe-harbor rule, the inducement rule, too, is a sensible one for copyright.")

[31] *Metro-Goldwyn-Mayer Studios Inc. v. Grokster, Ltd.,* 125 S. Ct. 2764, 2783 (2005). (Ginsburg, J., Concurring).

[32] *Metro-Goldwyn-Mayer Studios Inc. v. Grokster, Ltd.,* 125 S. Ct. 2764, 2790 (2005). (Bryer, J., Concurring).

[33] *Metro-Goldwyn-Mayer Studios Inc. v. Grokster, Ltd.,* 125 S. Ct. 2764, 2770 (2005).

[34] *Metro-Goldwyn-Mayer Studios Inc. v. Grokster, Ltd.,* 125 S. Ct. 2764, 2781 (2005). ("Grokster's name is apparently derived from Napster; it, too, initially offered an OpenNap program; its software's function is likewise comparable to Napster's, and it attempted to divert queries for Napster onto its own Web site.").

[35] *Metro-Goldwyn-Mayer Studios Inc. v. Grokster, Ltd.*, 125 S. Ct. 2764, 2766-2767 (2005). ("The record is replete with evidence that from the moment Grokster and StreamCast began to distribute their free software, each one clearly voiced the objective that recipients use it to download copyrighted works, and each took active steps to encourage infringement."). "In sum, when the record in this case was developed, there was evidence that Grokster's and StreamCast's products were, and had been for some time, overwhelmingly used to infringe, and that this infringement was the overwhelming source of revenue from the products. Fairly appraised, the evidence was insufficient to demonstrate, beyond genuine debate, a reasonable prospect that substantial or commercially significant noninfringing uses were likely to develop over time," at *19 (citations omitted) (Ginsburg, J., Concurring).

[36] *Metro-Goldwyn-Mayer Studios Inc. v. Grokster, Ltd.*, 125 S. Ct. 2764, 2772 (2005). ("The argument for imposing indirect liability in this case is, however, a powerful one, given the number of infringing downloads that occur every day using StreamCast's and Grokster's software." Id. at 2776.).

[37] *Metro-Goldwyn-Mayer Studios Inc. v. Grokster, Ltd.*, 125 S. Ct. 2764, 2774 (2005).

[38] *Metro-Goldwyn-Mayer Studios Inc. v. Grokster, Ltd.*, 125 S. Ct. 2764, 2785 (2005) (citations omitted) (Ginsburg, J., Concurring). However, Justice Breyer recounted a litany of legitimate noninfringing uses: research information, public domain films, historical recordings and digital educational materials, digital photos, shareware and freeware, secured licensed music and movie files, news broadcast past and present, user-created audio and video files, and all manner of free open content works collected by Creative Commons. Id. at 2788-2790 (section IB of the opinion) (Breyer, J., Concurring).

[39] *Metro-Goldwyn-Mayer Studios Inc. v. Grokster, Ltd.*, 125 S. Ct. 2764, 2778 (2005).

[40] *Metro-Goldwyn-Mayer Studios Inc. v. Grokster, Ltd.*, 125 S. Ct. 2764, 2777 (2005).

[41] *Metro-Goldwyn-Mayer Studios Inc. v. Grokster, Ltd.*, 125 S. Ct. 2764, 2780 (2005).

[42] *Metro-Goldwyn-Mayer Studios Inc. v. Grokster, Ltd.*, 125 S. Ct. 2764, 2778 (2005).

[43] *Metro-Goldwyn-Mayer Studios Inc. v. Grokster, Ltd.*, 125 S. Ct. 2764, 2778 (2005).

[44] *Metro-Goldwyn-Mayer Studios Inc. v. Grokster, Ltd.*, 125 S. Ct. 2764, 2776 (2005) ("One infringes . . . vicariously by profiting from direct infringement while declining to exercise a right to stop or limit it.").

[45] *Metro-Goldwyn-Mayer Studios Inc. v. Grokster, Ltd.*, 125 S. Ct. 2764, 2778 (2005). ("Because we resolve the case based on an inducement theory, there is no need to analyze separately MGM's vicarious liability theory.").

[46] *Metro-Goldwyn-Mayer Studios Inc. v. Grokster, Ltd.*, 125 S. Ct. 2764, 2779 (2005).

[47] *Metro-Goldwyn-Mayer Studios Inc. v. Grokster, Ltd.*, 125 S. Ct. 2764, 2773-2774 (2005).

[48] *Metro-Goldwyn-Mayer Studios Inc. v. Grokster, Ltd.*, 125 S. Ct. 2764, 2781-2782 (2005). ("Grokster and StreamCast's efforts to supply services to former Napster users, deprived of a mechanism to copy and distribute what were overwhelmingly infringing files, indicate a principal, if not exclusive, intent on the part of each to bring about infringement." 2781.).

[49] *Intellectual Reserve, Inc. v. Utah Lighthouse Ministry, Inc.*, 75 F. Supp. 2d 1290 (D. Utah 1999).

[50] *Intellectual Reserve, Inc. v. Utah Lighthouse Ministry, Inc.*, 75 F. Supp. 2d 1290, 1295 (D. Utah 1999) ("The following evidence establishes that defendants have actively encouraged the infringement of plaintiff's copyright. After being ordered to remove the Handbook from their website, defendants posted on their website: 'Church Handbook of Instructions is back online!' and listed the three website addresses. . . . Defendants also posted e-mail suggesting that the lawsuit against defendants would be affected by people logging onto one of the websites and downloading the complete handbook. One of the e-mails posted by the defendants mentioned sending a copy of the copyrighted material to the media. In response to an e-mail stating that the sender had unsuccessfully tried to browse a website that contained the Handbook, defendants gave further instruction on how to browse the material. At least one of the three websites encourages the copying and posting of copies of the allegedly infringing material on either websites. ('Please mirror these files. . . . It will be a LOT quicker for you to download the compressed version. . . . Needless to say, we need a LOT of mirror sites, as absolutely soon as possible.')." (Citations to internal court documents omitted.).

[51] RESTATEMENT OF TORTS 2d § 12.

[52] RESTATEMENT OF TORTS 2d § 12, comment a.

[53] Alfred C. Yen, Internet Service Provider Liability for Subscriber Copyright Infringement, Enterprise Liability, and the First Amendment, 88 GEORGETOWN LAW JOURNAL 1833, 1878-1879 (2000).

[54] *Intellectual Reserve, Inc. v. Utah Lighthouse Ministry, Inc.*, 75 F. Supp. 2d 1290, 1294-1295 (D. Utah 1999).

[55] *Arista Records, Inc. v. MP3Board, Inc.*, 2002 WL 1997918, ¶ 5 (S.D.N.Y. 2002).

[56] *In Re Aimster Copyright Litigation*, 334 F.3d 643, 645 (7th Cir. 2003).

[57] *In Re Aimster Copyright Litigation*, 334 F.3d 643, 645 (7th Cir. 2003).

[58] *Metro-Goldwin Studios, Inc. v Grokster, Ltd.*, 259 F. Supp. 2d 1029 (C.D. Calif. 2003) (P2P sharing software distributors Grokster and StreamCast not liable for contributory infringement: Here, the technical assistance was rendered after the alleged infringement took place, was routine and nonspecific in nature, and, in most cases, related to use of other companies' software (e.g., third-party media player software). Id. at 1042. Grokster not liable for contributory infringement: "Defendants argue principally that they do not have the ability to control the infringement as did these other defendants. Because they have no ability to supervise or control the file-sharing networks, or to restrict access to them, Defendants maintain that they cannot police what is being traded as Napster could." Id. at 1045. District court distinguished the circumstances of the distribution from those of Napster, more akin to premise liability, i.e., use of its system: "In a virtual sense, the 'premises' of the infringement were the Napster network itself, and Napster had a duty to exercise its reserved right and ability to police those

premises to the fullest extent possible. The client software was an essential component of the integrated Napster system, and Napster's obligation to police necessarily extended to the client software itself. Such is not the case here. Defendants provide software that communicates across networks that are entirely outside Defendants control. In the case of Grokster, the network is the propriety FastTrack network, which is clearly not controlled by Defendant Grokster. In the case of StreamCast, the network is Gnutella, the open-source nature of which apparently places it outside the control of any single entity." Id. at 1045.), affirmed, 380 F.3d 1154 (9th Cir. 2004), vacated and remanded 125 S. Ct. 2764 (2005).

[59] *Metro-Goldwyn-Mayer Studios Inc. v. Grokster, Ltd.*, 125 S. Ct. 2764 (2005). ("The inducement rule, instead, premises liability on purposeful, culpable expression and conduct, and thus does nothing to compromise legitimate commerce or discourage innovation having a lawful promise.").

[60] *Metro-Goldwin Studios, Inc. v Grokster, Ltd.*, 380 F.3d 1154, 1164 (9th Cir. 2004), vacated and remanded 125 S. Ct 2764 (2005).

[61] *In Re Aimster Copyright Litigation*, 334 F.3d 643, 651 (7th Cir. 2003) ("The tutorial is the invitation to infringement that the Supreme Court found was missing in *Sony*.").

[62] *In Re Aimster Copyright Litigation*, 334 F.3d 643, 652 (7th Cir. 2003).

[63] *In Re Aimster Copyright Litigation*, 334 F.3d 643, 653 (7th Cir. 2003) (emphasis added) ("Absent is any indication that even a single business without a network administrator uses Aimster to exchange business records as Deep suggests." Id.).

[64] See, *In re Verizon Internet Services, Inc.*, 257 F. Supp. 2d 244 (D.D.C. 2003) (Stay denied, subpoena issued pending appeal, under § 512(h) of anonymous Verizon customer who used facilitated infringement of over 600 songs through P2P software. "Verizon's customers should have little expectation of privacy (or anonymity) in infringing copyrights." Id. at 267.), reversed, 351 F.3d 1229, 1236-1237 (D.C. Cir 2003), cert. denied 125 S. Ct. 309 (2004). The D.C. circuit concluded that the subpoena power of section 512(h) does not apply to online intermediaries as conduit under section 512(a). This is based on a reading of the statute, as the subsection (h) subpoena coordinates notice with the subsection 512(c)(3) requirements that apply the ability of intermediaries to disable access to infringing material, versus disabling access to the Internet, a section 512(a) conduit intermediary can only disable access to the Internet not to content, thus the subpoena power of section of section 512(h) cannot apply. Thus, when an educational entity acts in the capacity of a conduit alone, the subpoena power of section 512(h) could not apply. However, in the store and forward, post and link roles (subsection (b), (c), and (d), section 512(h) can apply, as the remedy of disabling access to infringing content would be possible. Moreover, even in pure conduit scenarios, a subpoena could still issue, though it would not issue under section 512(h). For example, the courts have been evolving standards under which subpoenas will issue to Internet access (conduit) service providers to uncover the identity of anonymous tortfeasors and posters of other harms for several years. See cases and criteria discussed in Tomas A. Lipinski, To Speak or Not to Speak:

Developing Legal Standards for Anonymous Speech on the Internet, 5 INFORMING SCI-
ENCE 95 (2002) 95-111.

[65] *In Re Aimster Copyright Litigation*, 334 F.3d 643, 650 (7th Cir. 2003).

[66] *In Re Aimster Copyright Litigation*, 334 F.3d 643, 650 (7th Cir. 2003).

[67] *In Re Aimster Copyright Litigation*, 334 F.3d 643, 654 (7th Cir. 2003).

[68] *Ellison v. Robertson*, 189 F. Supp. 2d 1051, 1058 (C.D. Cal. 2002), affirmed in part and reversed in part and remanded, *Ellison v. Robertson*, 357 F.3d 1072 (9th Cir. 2004) ("AOL
changed its contact e-mail address from 'copyright@aol.com' to 'aolcopyright@aol.com'
in the fall of 1999, but waited until April 2000 to register the change with the U.S. Copyright Office. Moreover, AOL failed to configure the old e-mail address so that it would
either forward messages to the new address or return new messages to their senders. In
the meantime, complaints such as Ellison's went unheeded, and complainants were not
notified that their messages had not been delivered. . . . Because there is evidence indicating that AOL changed its e-mail address in an unreasonable manner and that AOL should
have been on notice of infringing activity we conclude that a reasonable trier of fact could
find that AOL had reason to know of potentially infringing activity occurring within its
USENET network." Id. at 1077).

[69] *In Re Aimster Copyright Litigation*, 334 F.3d 643, 650 (7th Cir. 2003).

[70] S. 2560, 108th Cong., 2nd Sess. (2004) (Inducing Infringement of Copyright Act of
2004).

[71] *Metro-Goldwyn-Mayer Studios Inc. v. Grokster, Ltd.*, 125 S. Ct. 2764 (2005).

[72] See, Protecting Innovation and Art while Preventing Art. Hearing on 5.2560 before the
Senate Committee on the Judiciary, U.S. Senate, 108th Congress, 2nd Sess, July 22, 2004
on Efforts to Curb Illegal Downloading Copyrighted Music (Opening Statement of Chair,
Orrin Hatch) ("The Act provides that the courts can impose secondary liability upon
those who intend to induce copyright infringement."), available at *http://judiciary.senate.
gov/print_member_statement.cfm?id=1276&wit_id=51.*

[73] 17 U.S.C. § 501.

[74] S. 2560, 108th Cong., 2nd Sess. (2004) (Inducing Infringement of Copyright Act of 2004).

[75] *Sony Corp. of America, Inc. v. Universal City Studios*, 464 U.S. 417, 441-442 (1984).

[76] Hearing, Committee on the Judiciary, U.S. Senate, 108th Congress, 2nd Sess., July 22,
2004 on Efforts to Curb Illegal Downloading Copyrighted Music (Opening Statement of
Chair, Orrin Hatch) ("Second, S. 2560 uses a proven model for structuring secondary liability. The substantial-noninfringing-use rule that Sony imported from the Patent Act
coexists there alongside liability for intent to induce infringement—a concept that the
Patent Act calls active inducement. This proven model can address cases of intent to
induce infringement that were explicitly not covered or addressed by the Supreme
Court in Sony."), available at *http://judiciary.senate.gov/print_member_statement.cfm?id=
1276&wit_id=51.*

[77] S. 2560, 108th Cong., 2nd Sess. (2004) (Inducing Infringement of Copyright Act of
2004).

[78] Hearing, Committee on the Judiciary, U.S. Senate, 108th Congress, 2nd Sess., July 22, 2004 on Efforts to Curb Illegal Downloading Copyrighted Music (Opening Statement of Chair, Orrin Hatch), available at *http://judiciary.senate.gov/print_member_statement.cfm?id=1276&wit_id=51.*

[79] Hearing, Committee on the Judiciary, U.S. Senate, 108th Congress, 2nd Sess., July 22, 2004 on Efforts to Curb Illegal Downloading Copyrighted Music (Opening Statement of Chair, Orrin Hatch), available at *http://judiciary.senate.gov/print_member_statement.cfm?id=1276&wit_id=51.*

[80] Hearing, Committee on the Judiciary, U.S. Senate, 108th Congress, 2nd Sess., July 22, 2004 on Efforts to Curb Illegal Downloading Copyrighted Music (Opening Statement of Chair, Orrin Hatch), available at *http://judiciary.senate.gov/print_member_statement.cfm?id=1276&wit_id=51.*

[81] Tony Roda, Copyright Forecast for the 109th Congress, THE COPYRIGHT & NEW MEDIA LAW NEWSLETTER FOR LIBRARIANS & INFORMATION SPECIALISTS, No. 9, 2005, at 4, 6. ("Congressional decisions on major copyright legislation will not be made until the Supreme Court issues a ruling in the *Grokster* case.").

[82] News Release: Attorney General Ashcroft Announces First Criminal Enforcement Action Against Peer-to-Peer Copyright Piracy, DOJ 04-578, 2004 WL 1904321 (D.O.J.) (August 25, 2004).

[83] UNITED STATES DEPARTMENT OF JUSTICE, REPORT OF THE DEPARTMENT OF JUSTICE'S TASK FORCE ON INTELLECTUAL PROPERTY 16 (2004).

[84] News Release: Attorney General Ashcroft Announces First Criminal Enforcement Action Against Peer-to-Peer Copyright Piracy, DOJ 04-578, 2004 WL 1904321 (D.O.J.) (August 25, 2004).

[85] UNITED STATES DEPARTMENT OF JUSTICE, REPORT OF THE DEPARTMENT OF JUSTICE'S TASK FORCE ON INTELLECTUAL PROPERTY (2004).

[86] UNITED STATES DEPARTMENT OF JUSTICE, REPORT OF THE DEPARTMENT OF JUSTICE'S TASK FORCE ON INTELLECTUAL PROPERTY 11-12 (2004).

[87] UNITED STATES DEPARTMENT OF JUSTICE, REPORT OF THE DEPARTMENT OF JUSTICE'S TASK FORCE ON INTELLECTUAL PROPERTY 19 (2004).

[88] S. 2237, 108th Cong., 2nd Sess. (2004) (Protecting Intellectual Property Against Theft and Expropriation Act of 2004).

[89] 2003 CONGRESSIONAL RECORD S 2237, June 25, 2004.

[90] UNITED STATES DEPARTMENT OF JUSTICE, REPORT OF THE DEPARTMENT OF JUSTICE'S TASK FORCE ON INTELLECTUAL PROPERTY 39 (2004).

[91] 150 CONGRESSIONAL RECORD S10822-02 (October 8, 2004) (Comments of Senator Leahy: "For some unimaginable reason, the Justice Department, which cannot issue enough press releases about its newly-minted Intellectual Property Task Force, has taken no interest in or action on this legislation. Apparently, the Ashcroft Justice Department rejects having the law enforcement authority to stop large-scale infringers and protect America's intellectual property from piracy. A Justice Department that has reinterpreted

treaties and contorted the law to claim vast and unfettered authorities for this executive has little interest in assembling legislatively enacted tools for copyright protection and to stop piracy.").

►3

WHAT IS VICARIOUS INFRINGEMENT?

Read this chapter to find out about copyright situations like:
► Whether a public library system can place photocopies of a monograph in its branch libraries.
► Whether a friends of the library group can show copyrighted films as a fundraiser.
► Whether a school can get in trouble if a teacher makes copies of a workbook for students.

While contributory infringement is based on *conduct* of the secondary infringer towards the direct infringer, the touchstone of vicarious liability is the nature of *relationship* between the vicarious infringer and the direct infringer. The Ninth Circuit articulated a leading standard for vicarious infringement in *Fonovisa, Inc. vs. Cherry Auction, Inc.*, stating that vicarious infringement is found when one has the "right and ability to supervise the infringing activity and also has a direct financial interest in such activities."[1] The law attaches liability to the failure of the vicarious infringer vis-à-vis his or her relationship with the direct infringer to exercise the responsibility incumbent upon him or her and prevent the infringing activity. "A company may be found vicariously liable for copyright infringement if it has the right and ability to supervise infringing activity and also has a direct financial interest in that activity."[2]

Likewise "[a]n officer or director of a corporation who knowingly participates in the infringement can be held personally liable, jointly and severally, with the corporate defendant."[3]

Employers of course benefit financially from the infringement of employees, as there is, for example, one less handbook to purchase, subscription to order, or site or performance license to obtain. Moreover, employers are thought to have the ability to control the actions of their employees even if not subject them to constant, over-the-shoulder monitoring or supervision. Since the vicarious infringer benefits financially from the infringement, has the right and ability to control the infringing acts of the direct infringer, and fails to do so, the law concludes that he or should also share some liability for the infringement. Vicarious infringement also is applicable in independent contractor settings, that is, the acts of the independent contractor are likewise imputed to the contracting institution.[4]

This is not to say that everyone who is in a position to stop or control the infringement of another is liable for vicarious infringement, as the second element requires that the vicarious infringer have some direct financial interest in allowing the contemplated infringing conduct to proceed.

The more infringement occurs, the greater the financial benefit for the vicarious infringer. Consider the dance hall operator[5] or tavern owner[6] or similar concessionaire[7] who hires a Beatles cover-band for a weekend gig. If the band neglected to obtain a performance right for the songs it performs, each rendering of a copyrighted Lennon-McCartney or George Harrison composition would be an infringement. From the dance hall or tavern owner's perspective, the more infringement that occurs, the more songs that are performed, the longer the sets are, the more people can eat and drink, or the more sets there are, the greater the number of people who can enter and pay a cover charge, and the greater the take at the door. Thus there a positive relationship between the amount of infringement that the dance hall operator or tavern owner allows to occur and the financial benefit it generates to the operator or owner, i.e., the more money he or she makes from the infringing event. The owner or operator has a financial stake in seeing the infringement occur. This is a direct financial interest. Moreover, the dance hall operator or tavern owner in the Beatles tribute scenario could have stopped the infringement. Short of shutting down the power, the dance hall operator or tavern owner could simply require cover bands to have evidence of the requisite performance rights in the form of a license before booking the band or at least before taking the stage.[8]

RECOGNIZING INSTITUTIONAL LIABILITY FOR EMPLOYEE ACTIONS

The concept of vicarious copyright liability is based on the general concept of vicarious liability in tort law where the principal is responsible for the act of his or her agents—not necessarily because the principal participates in the harm agents cause but because, through the relationship of principal to agent, the principal is in the best position to prevent the agent from committing harm. Moreover, "one of the principle rationales of vicarious liability [is] the difficulty of obtaining effective relief against an agent, who is likely to be impecunious."[9] A typical vicarious relationship is one of employment. Thus under a theory of vicarious liability, public libraries or educational institutions are responsible for the copyright infringement in which their librarians, faculty, and other staff engage. Vicarious liability is imputed from employee to employer, that is, the employer is charged responsible for the acts of its employees, but not vice versa. Vicarious liability is grounded in the tort concept of *respondeat superior*, which means "let the superior answer."[10]

Applying the theory of vicarious liability in copyright law, the employer "answers" for the infringing acts of its employees. Vicarious infringement is founded in the tort concept of enterprise liability: "Benefit and control are the signposts of vicarious liability, [whereas] knowledge and participation [are] the touchstones of contributory infringement."[11] Vicarious liability, like direct infringement is a strict liability concept, thus in employment settings the concept does not require knowledge of the infringement by the vicarious defendant.[12] The imposition of strict liability fulfills a risk-shifting as well as a benefit-inducing function:

> The enterprise and the person profiting from it are better able than either the innocent injured plaintiff or the person whose act caused the loss to distribute the costs and to shift them to others who have profited from the enterprise. In addition, placing responsibility for the loss on the enterprise has the added benefit of creating a greater incentive for the enterprise to police its operations carefully to avoid unnecessary losses.[13]

This is a critical point for administrators of the library or educational entity as employer to understand, as the institution, represented by its administrators, need not be aware (know or reason to know) of the infringement committed by employees to be liable as a vicarious infringer.

While it may never be possible, short of looking over every employee's shoulder at every moment, to monitor and control the behavior of each employee, a compliance program that minimizes the risk of liability can ensure that when infringement does in fact occur it is identified and remedied in due course, thus decreasing the likelihood of suspicion and discovery by others including the copyright owner, and thus reducing the opportunity of exposure to litigation or the threat of litigation by the copyright owner. Furthermore the imposition of intermediary liability even in networked environments is consistent with the enterprise liability concept:

> Enterprises that create risk should bear the burden of that risk as a cost of doing business. Such cost internalization is more than just fair. It encourages risk creators to take precautions against loss. It provides compensation for victims, and it spreads the costs among all who benefit from the risk-creating activity. These principles are easily marshaled to make a case for ISP vicarious copyright liability.[14]

Even more so, the "enterprise" of the library or educational institution (i.e., the risk that it creates) is arguably greater than a high-level ISP; such an entity has an immediate connection to the locus of the infringement in its ability to control either the infringing activity or access to the infringing material and the financial benefit it might reap from such behavior. Thus it is logical to cast the net of liability in its direction.

AVOIDING STRICT LIABILITY IN EMPLOYMENT SETTINGS

A copyright risk management or compliance program that includes notice to employees of their individual responsibility and, more important, the repercussions of deviating from that responsibility will minimize risk of having the infringement perpetuate and permeate the organization. Unfortunately for the organization, even the strongest words are no insurance, either in a practical sense (i.e., that employees will heed such admonitions, warnings, policies) or in a legal sense (i.e., such efforts have no bearing whatsoever on the determination of vicarious liability as it is a strict liability).[15] Employers as well as employees may be committed to the principles of copyright compliance but ignorance or confusion about the law may be the largest impediment.[16]

A recent case involving the reproduction of a newsletter in a corporate setting is instructive. Because vicarious liability is a strict liability law, an institution with the most stringent copyright policy cannot be shielded from the infringing acts of its employees.

> There can be no doubt that Legg Mason had the right and ability to supervise its own employees, who infringed Lowry's copyrights at Legg Mason offices, using company equipment, on company time. Nor can there be any doubt that Legg Mason had an obvious and direct financial interest in the widespread copying: at the very least, its employees' infringement saved it the cost of additional subscriptions to the Reports.[17]

If a situation in which employees who ignore the organization's copyright policy can still trigger liability on the part of the organization, is the adoption of a copyright policy worth the bother?[18] Of course, some provisions of the copyright law that will be discussed in subsequent chapters require the adoption and use of copyright policies. One benefit of a copyright policy, assuming there is the reality of its enforcement coupled with genuine threat of repercussions for behavior deviating from its standards, is that it might actually be effective and reduce the liability of the organization. More important is the fact that while an ignored policy cannot impact liability, compliance efforts, even if failed, can impact the assessment of damages!

> Legg Mason's reliance on company policies and orders is misplaced. The law of copyright liability takes no cognizance of a defendant's knowledge or intent. . . . The fact that Legg Mason's employees infringed Lowry's copyrights in contravention of policy or order bears not on Legg Mason's liability, but rather on the amount of statutory and punitive damages and the award of attorneys' fees. Accordingly, unless Legg Mason can establish an affirmative defense, it is liable for the infringing conduct of its employees.[19]

The strict nature of vicarious liability underscores the comment of the Ninth Circuit in *Napster*: "Turning a blind eye to detectable acts of infringement for the sake of profit gives rise to liability."[20] Thus the concept of vicarious liability does not accommodate the employer or administrator who would rather "look the other way" instead of confronting the noncompliant behavior of his or her employees. By the same token, because the direct infringement of an employee is also measured under a strict liability standard, an employee need not know that his or her conduct is infringing before triggering a chain of liability that links the infringing conduct to his or her "also-in-the-dark" employer. However, like the other form of secondary copyright liability, contributory infringement, in order for the employer to be liable for vicarious liability, an act of direct infringement by an employee, librarian, instructor, or staff member (such as a network supervisor or distance education coordinator) must underlie the vicarious liability. There can be no vicarious liability without a finding of direct liability to which it relates.

As both direct and vicarious copyright infringement are strict liability concepts, it is critical for employers and other individuals or entities that could potentially satisfy the requirements of a claim for vicarious infringement to institute a copyright risk-management program in an attempt to minimize the occurrence of infringement by employees or others similarly situated (i.e., third parties such as patrons or students under the control of the library or school and whose infringing activity generates a direct financial benefit to the library or school). Subsequent chapters discuss the components of a risk-management program. Examples include general network monitoring (but not necessarily the monitoring of specific individuals), development and implementation of policies, use of notices, production of signage and other awareness materials, and copyright outreach services such as informal lectures or formal training sessions.

UNDERSTANDING PREMISE LIABILITY

An employment setting is not the only place where vicarious infringement can be found. While it could be argued that students would meet the control element (the first prong of the legal test for vicarious liability) because educators and administrators in K–12 environments are said to act *in loco-parentis*,[21] patrons in most library scenarios would not fall into that category. However unlikely it would be for either library patron or school student to meet the financial benefit test, it is not inconceivable. Since vicarious copyright liability is court-made law, a review of several cases can demonstrate the principles underlying the concept and indicate the circumstances under which a third party in a library or school setting might satisfy these two requirements.

The nature of the relationship between the second party and the premise where the direct infringement occurs can create the requisite "control" and "benefit" required of vicarious infringers. This concept is demonstrated in *Fonovisa, Inc. v. Cherry Auction, Inc.*,[22] where a swap-meet purveyor was liable for infringing acts of booth renters who bought and sold bootleg tapes, and in *Columbia Pictures Industries v. Redd Horne, Inc.*,[23] where a shop owner who allowed customers to view copyrighted videocassettes was liable for the infringing acts of it customers, i.e., the unauthorized public performance of audiovisual works.

Contrast these results with *Artists Music, Inc. v. Reed Publishing, Inc.*,[24] where a trade-show organizer was not liable for the vendors that played ambient music in their booths. In the trade-show case the court found any ability to control the infringing activity impractical at best: "Reed would have had to hire several investigators with the expertise to identify music, to determine whether it was copyrighted, to determine whether the use was licensed, and finally to determine whether the use was a 'fair use'."[25] The court also found that the revenue of the trade-show organizers was in no way dependent upon the infringement of the booth operators, as attendees did come to the trade show expecting to have copyrighted works performed for their benefit.[26]

One commentator believes that these case findings demonstrate inconsistency.[27] However, the trade-show case is different from either the traditional dance hall cases or the more recent swap-meet purveyor case, as attendees expect to come to either of the latter locales because of the precise nature of the event, i.e., patrons enter a dance hall to hear music performed and customers enter a swap meet to trade tapes, discs, and other items of prerecorded music, some of which one would expect might be bootlegged. However, folks do not attend a trade show with a similar expectation. For example, one would not attend a farm machinery show in the hopes that the Harvester or John Deere booth might be playing the music of the Amanda Smith Band. As the court in *Artists Music, Inc. v. Reed Publishing, Inc.*, observed:

> Plaintiffs finally argue that the music created an ambiance necessary to the success of the Show. This Court only notes that had music been necessary to the success of the Show, Reed probably would have undertaken to provide music itself, which it did not do. This Court finds that plaintiffs have failed to establish that defendant derived any financial benefit, direct or otherwise, from the exhibitor's performances of copyrighted songs.[28]

Another trade-show case decided the same year, *Polygram International Publishing, Inc. v. Nevada/TIG, Inc.*,[29] reached the opposite result. Yet it is distinguishable by evidence that the trade-show proprietor did in fact attempt to exercise control over booth vendors through the terms of the lease, various trade-show "Rules and Regulations" which the trade-show proprietor enforced through the use of aisle monitors.[30] Arguably the district court may have engaged in a strained analysis when it found a direct financial benefit between the use of copyrighted music and the draw of attendees, i.e., that the ambiance created by the performance of prerecorded music results in higher attendance figures,[31] the precise argument rejected in *Artists Music, Inc. v. Reed Publishing, Inc.*[32] However, given the facts of a particular case, the trade-show environment generally appears more like the landlord precedent than the swap-meet cases where the attraction may be indeed the precise reason for fluctuation in at-the-door revenues. For example, attendees at a video-gaming trade show would expect to hear copyrighted music performed when the games are demonstrated as the industry trend is toward the incorporation of prerecorded music of well-known artists into its products. Likewise, at an electronics trade show featuring the latest in iPOD and other communication technologies, attendees would expect to hear music, in fact might look forward to hearing the latest titles by U2 performed on the latest in audio and visual technology. Similarly, in *Polygram International Publishing, Inc. v. Nevada/TIG, Inc.*, the computer-industry trade show was a likely venue for the performance of copyrighted music. The court made clear, however, that the decisive factor was not related to expectation, but to the actual control that the trade-show organizer exhibited, thus pushing its event from the landlord-type cases where there is no liability for lack of control into the dance hall cases where liability exists.

Vicarious Liability in Nonemployment, Networked Environments

Recent P2P and related online scenarios such as bulletin boards and Web site operators have given courts the opportunity to discuss the concept of vicarious liability in network environments. For example, one district court concluded that the ability of an online intermediary to block an infringer's access to a particular Web site or computer network constitutes proof of its right and ability to supervise and control the infringing activity.[33] Does the library or school intermediary have the right and ability to control the actions of the direct infringer to the same extent as the dance hall operator or swap-meet purveyor, or does the relationship while perhaps including financial benefit lack the requisite "right and ability to control" the conduct of the primary party? In contrast, is the relationship to the primary actor, the direct infringer, more like that of a landlord (where vicarious liability is generally absent), who once the lease is signed has little ability to control what goes on behind the doors of the tenant's abode?

> Although landlords could arguably require lease provisions that prohibit copyright infringement, allow themselves the right to enter premises for inspection, and penalize noncompliance, they lack sufficient ability to supervise their tenants. In addition, landlords do not have the same financial interest in their tenants' copyright infringement as dance hall proprietors have in their performers' infringements. The fixed monthly rental that characterizes ordinary leases means that the tenant's infringement does not directly affect the landlord's profitability.[34]

The private nature of the tenants premise was an underlying factor in a case involving a hotel that allowed guests to rent videos for viewing in the privacy of their rooms. Hotel guest rooms are considered private places, thus no public performance occurred when guests viewed rented videos in their rooms. In cases involving video viewing in video stores, courts held that although the viewings were in individual booths, such uses were nonetheless public performances, because the stores where the booths were located were "public."[35] Compare this to the case of the playing of a video in a hotel room with a videotape system designed for remote operation by hotel guests, whereby the transmission of selected videotapes to the TVs in hotel rooms was found to be a public performance requiring copyright license.[37] This conclusion is consistent, not because hotel rooms are deemed "open to the public,"[38] the first genus of public performance,[39] but rather because of the transmission of protected materials to the public, satisfying the second genus of public performance.[40]

Control in Virtual Premises

Analogizing the circumstances of the historical precedent to the online environment, the Ninth Circuit characterized the defendants in *Grokster* less like the swap-meet purveyor of old and more like the intermediary landlord with limited ability to control infringing behavior use of its P2P technology:

> Moreover, the alleged ability to shut down operations altogether is more akin to the ability to close down an entire swap meet or stop distributing software altogether, rather than the ability to exclude individual participants, a practice of policing aisles, an ability to block individual users directly at the point of log-in, or an ability to delete individual filenames from one's own computer.[41]

In *Grokster*, the court concluded this right and ability to control specific infringing conduct was absent: "The sort of monitoring and supervisory relationship that has supported vicarious liability in the past is completely absent in this case."[42] Recall, however, and as discussed earlier, the Supreme Court of course found liability based upon other conduct of Grokster; the intentional inducement of infringing conduct by the way Grokster promoted its product as essentially the next Napster![43]

To what extent is the requisite right and ability to control infringing activity in the digital environment similar to that of the swap-meet organizer who physically patrols, controls, or monitors the booth vendors to ensure conformity with the conditions of compliant use? The absence of this right and ability to control infringing network users distinguished the defendants in *Grokster* from the *Napster* defendants who, the Ninth Circuit concluded, did have the right and ability to control infringing conduct on its P2P network: "Napster, however, has the ability to locate infringing material listed on its search indices, and the right to terminate users' access to the system. The file name indices, therefore, are within the 'premises' that Napster has the ability to police."[44] Unlike the landlord who has no control over what a tenant may do behind the closed doors of his or her apartment or flat, the swap-meet purveyor can control the conduct of the vendors who line the aisles of swap booths to which it and public has access:

By contrast, landlords exercise far less control over rented premises than dance hall proprietors do over their halls. Although landlords could arguably require lease provisions that prohibit copyright infringement, allow themselves the right to enter premises for inspections, and penalize noncompliance, they lack sufficient ability to supervise their tenants. In addition landlords do not have the same financial interest in their tenants' copyright infringement as dance hall proprietors have in their performers' infringements. The fixed monthly rental that characterizes ordinary leases means that the tenant's infringement does not directly affect the landlord's profitability.[45]

Control of premise, whether consisting of traditional or virtual space, is the gravemen [*BLOCK'S LAW DICTIONARY* (8th ed. 2004) defines *graveman* as "[t]he substantial point or essence of a claim, grievance, or complaint." Id. at 721] of vicarious liability. As a result, vicarious liability is sometimes referred to as "premise" liability.[46]

It would appear that a library or educational institution is more like the swap-meet purveyor than the landlord. Early Internet cases held high-level service providers to be more like landlords than dance hall proprietors.[47] However, it can be argued that access level providers such as libraries and schools exercise more control than do providers such as AOL or EarthLink. A library or school certainly has the right and ability to control uses of its computing facilities and other potentially infringing technologies, such as scanners, samplers, or photocopiers. The library or school administrator can monitor network traffic and account activity, regulate access to various network components and services through password controls, and otherwise restrict or even terminate access to the computing network altogether. Moreover, many libraries and schools routinely develop and promote so-called AUPs (acceptable-use policies) designed to govern the use of such technologies on the premises. Such mechanisms surely demonstrate a decided position of "right and ability to control" on the part of the entity itself, i.e., that the library or school has the right and ability to control the conduct of users by articulating standards of acceptable use and to impose a penalty against those whose conduct deviates from those standards. This practice is certainly as watchful as the trade-show organizers in *Polygram International Publishing, inc. v. Nevada/TIG, Inc.*, or the swap-meet cases also discussed above.

The court in *Napster* likewise concluded:

> Napster may be vicariously liable when it fails to affirmatively use its ability to patrol its system and preclude access to potentially infringing files listed in its search index. Napster has both the ability to use its search function to identify infringing musical recordings and the right to bar participation of users who engage in the transmission of infringing files.[48]

As Professor Dratler observes, "most litigation likely will focus on their practical ability to terminate users' access after receiving warnings, or to terminate users;

infringing activities while leaving innocent activities in place."[49] This ability was missing in the *Grokster* litigation, i.e., between Grokster and its file sharers there was no right to terminate, no control over access to the system, and no ability to patrol or police. The district court distinguished the circumstances of the Grokster distribution from those present in *Napster* where the latter was found more akin to premise liability, i.e., use of the Napster system over which the defendants maintained control.[50]

Given a library or educational institution's ability to control which patrons or students (non-employees) have access to its computing network or other potentially infringing technologies, and viewing the library or campus computing network or other facilities as the institution's virtual or actual premises over which it can exercise control of patron or student conduct, a court would likely conclude that the institution indeed has the requisite right and ability to control behavior either on its computing network, its virtual premises, or on its physical premises (e.g., a computing lab, library stacks, meeting room, classroom, or other physical location). In the library or school setting, the control is more likely to consist of the ability to exclude individual participants from computing labs, police actual specific terminals or banks of terminals (akin to "policing aisles"), block individual access at the point of log-in through password limitations, or delete infringing patron or student files from library or school server space or folders. The library or educational entity is arguably more like the swap-meet purveyor than a mere landlord (at least as far as the "control" element is concerned) and as a result would satisfy the first "right and ability to control" element of a claim of vicarious infringement.

Direct Financial Benefit and Premise Liability

What of the second element, requiring a direct financial interest on the part of a library or educational entity for acts of nonemployee third parties such as patrons or students? While a fixed-fee arrangement (in return for access to premise) might not provide the requisite direct financial interest, case law suggests that if a Web site acts as a draw for customers it can be sufficient to establish the second element.[51] "However, it may not take much additional financial interest to push a fixed monthly fee over the threshold of a 'direct financial interest' in infringement."[52] Moreover, it need not be a substantial proportion of a defendant's income; the Ninth Circuit rejected this standard.[53] Consider a Web site of infringing material. If the existence of that infringing material acts as a draw for customers to that site, then a court could conclude that the requisite financial benefit exists.[54] Even a di minimus amount could be sufficient: "The essential aspect of the 'direct financial benefit' inquiry is whether there is a causal relationship between the infringing activity and *any* financial benefit a defendant reaps, regardless of *how substantial* the benefit is in proportion to a defendant's overall profits."[55] Based on the early dance hall cases, one can conceive of translation to the Web-based environment of current online computing.

Suppose Entity A runs a network service and allows Person B to operate a Web site on its service. In return for space on Entity A's server, Person B pays rent to Entity A. The amount of rent is based on the monthly number of hits to B's Web site; the more hits, the more rent.[56] A and B have an agreement that defines the parameters of the use that B can make of A's Web space. Now suppose that B loads and allows others to download copyrighted materials without the permission of the copyright owner. The site gains some notoriety and so visits to the site increase over time as net-surfers discover all the cool stuff one can download from the Web site. The increase in A's rent is in direct correlation to the infringing activity occurring on B's site, and on A's network: the more infringing activity B conducts on its site, the more Web surfers visit the site and the greater A's rent becomes. A direct financial interest is present in the primary infringement of B. Moreover, Entity A had the right (it is his or her server space) and ability (A could have made clear by the terms of the Web server rental agreement that there could be no uploading of copyrighted material unless the permission of the copyright owner was first obtained) to control the behavior of B. Thus, the two elements for vicarious copyright infringement would be established. (In employment settings, the fact that the employer saves money when its employs infringe is assumed to establish the direct financial relationship, e.g., making software available on the network without paying the proper license fee, or reproducing 20 copies of a workbook instead of purchasing the needed copies, saves the employer from a financial outlay it would otherwise need to make.)

As there is no employment relationship between the library patron or student and library educational or other information entity, infringing patron, student, or customer conduct would typically not trigger the imposition of vicarious liability. Of course if the student were employed as a research assistant, teaching assistant, or lecturer, that would be another matter, or if the library patron committed acts of copyright infringement related to his or her service as a library docent, that, too, might place the relationship within the employee-employer continuum for purposes of both the control and financial benefit analyses (even though a docent is not paid, the relationship maintains certain control and potential benefit factors present with normal employees).

In relationships other than employee, independent contractor, or docent, a direct financial relationship could nonetheless be established, i.e., the more infringement in which the institution allows patrons or students to engage, the more patrons or students view it as a great place to go to infringe. Sort of like getting the "Best Library to Exploit Technology for Infringing Purposes" or "Best Campus to Engage in P2P Infringement" ranking, however remote that might be, it serves as an example nonetheless. In a more realistic sequence, could a similar "great-place-to-go-to-infringe" reality establish the requisite direct financial benefit? Some library patrons might pay for additional levels of service, like database access, and students certainly pay tuition.[57] Could these payments establish the direct financial benefit necessary? The more infringement that is allowed, the more the infringement acts as a draw for patrons and students, and the more circulation or service fees or tuition revenues rise. Not that any library or educational institution would engage in such thinking and planning outright, but given the proper circumstances a court might conclude similarly. Of course the challenge for the copyright plaintiff would be to prove the dynamics of this relationship, a sort of copyright cause and effect.[58]

An argument could be made, however, that unlike the dance hall cases upon which vicarious liability is based, there needs to be a positive correlation between revenue and customers and a single premise event, i.e., the greater the number of customers who come in to hear the orchestra on a particular night, the greater "the take" (cover charge) at the door. A library fee for annual computing access or tuition for a course or term is not the specific premise-event that the cases suggest triggers liability, although this would not prevent a court from developing such an additional standard in the future. This is the distinction behind the conclusion of one district court that a defendant that charged a flat quarterly fee of $67.50 did not meet the requisite direct financial interest; the fees never changed to reflect the number of times users requested access to infringing files or visited the Web site.[59] Thus an annual service or tuition fee, regardless of the number of times a patron or student might obtain infringing materials from library or wider campus computing facilities in a given year or semester of use, appears more akin to the insufficient flat fee arrangement.

However, one could conceive of a scenario in a library or school that did in fact tie infringing behavior of a third party to a scheme of shifting revenue. Suppose a library Friends group or other third party held a fund-raising event in the library meeting room at which copyright infringement occurred, say through the public performance of a copyrighted audiovisual work such as motion picture or musical works similar to the dance hall cases. Patrons were asked to make a donation at the door and the proceeds were "donated" to the library's collection development fund or used to fund its summer reading program. The more patrons that attended the event, the greater the revenue generated for the library. Library administrators have the right and ability to control uses of its meeting room space. Second, there is a positive correlation between the infringing conduct and the revenue received by the library from it, thus a direct financial relationship could be found to exist and the two elements of a vicarious infringement claim proved. As a result, the library or school should make careful review of the circumstances anytime revenue is generated through potentially infringing conduct of patrons.

A library or school that rents audiovisual equipment for patron or student personal use could face a similar claim if, for example, patrons are allowed to view copyrighted VHS or DVD movies on the premises of the library or school. Performance of VHS or DVD movies in a public library or school would constitute a public performance of the work,[60] thus patrons and students would infringe copyright when the movies are watched (the works are performed) as a reward in the library or school (performance outside the scope of section 110, the educator exception)[61] or otherwise governed by a license. The more infringing uses patrons and students make of the VHS and DVD tapes, the more revenue is generated from rental fees of videocassette and DVD players. The library and school certainly has the right and ability to control the uses of such equipment and could adopt and enforce a rental policy that says the premise use of such technologies is limited to classroom viewings consistent with section 110(1). While a claim of vicarious infringement against a library or school based on the infringing conduct of third parties would be improbable; as discussed above it is not impossible given the proper facts. Moreover, a claim of vicarious infringement is also likely to be successful where a copyright identifies library or school employees as the instigators of direct copyright infringement.

REAL-WORLD EXAMPLES

▶ Real-World Example I

Situation: An employee of a public library decides to photocopy several cover-to-cover copies of a monograph in its collection to place in the reference collections of its branch libraries.

Legal Analysis: While the librarian who made the copies would be the direct infringer, the library would be liable as well under the theory of vicarious liability. The employee is under the control of library administrators. Second, the direct financial interest is established because the library can now forego the cost of having to purchase a copy of the monograph for each branch library.

▶ Real-World Example II

Situation: A public library Friends group decides to have an "Italian Night" as part of its travel series. It plans to show the movies *Dinner Rush* and *Big Night*. In conjunction, the Friends group offers finger food, such as bruschetta, before the viewing, as a fund-raiser. Similarly themed events in the past have proved quite successful. The event takes place in the library's public meeting room. Patrons pay an entrance fee at the door as well as make donations for the finger food and beverages.

Legal Analysis: While there is no employment relationship between the Friends group and the library, there is a direct financial relationship between the infringing performance and the revenue it generates for the library. The event could be said to act as a draw for patrons. Furthermore, the library has the right and ability to control the use of its public meeting room and to institute and enforce a policy whereby performances and displays of copyrighted material must first be reviewed by library administration to ensure that the required permissions or performance and display rights are obtained or otherwise are within fair use. In the absence of such permissions the showing of the entire movies is sure to be infringing, thus the library may also be subject to vicarious liability as well.

▶ **Real-World Example III**

Situation: Similar to the Real-World Example I from Chapter 2 (see p. 33), a teacher member has just received the new edition of a workbook companion to a current textbook as a desk copy, with an order form for additional classroom copies. The school typically purchases supplemental materials for student use at the beginning of each year, but due to budget cuts the additional supplements cannot be ordered until next year. The teacher makes a copy of new workbook for every student in the class.

Legal Analysis: While the teacher would be considered the direct infringer, the school district is also liable as it has both the right and ability to control the conduct of its teachers, and it also receives direct financial benefit from not having to purchase a copy of the workbook for each student.

▶ **Real-World Example IV**

Situation: As in Real-World Example IV from Chapter 2 (see pp. 34–35), the computer science teacher, quite savvy with technology, designs a program called "Grab-IT." This program allows users to enter the title of any copyrighted publication into the search box, and locate and download a copy of it quickly from the Internet. In addition, the teacher is now a full-time employee of the school district, and includes suggestions to use Grab-IT on syllabi and other documentation in every class he teaches.

Legal Analysis: In addition to student liability for direct infringement, teacher liability for contributory infringement by inducement, the school district as the employer would likely be subject to vicarious liability for the acts of the teacher, and perhaps for the acts of students, depending on the circumstances. The institution would have the right and ability to control the infringing conduct of students on its systems and networks; if evidence of "profiting from the direct infringement" exists, such as a situation where the institution, because of the infringing copies, foregoes the cost of purchasing articles (for use in course packs), textbooks, and workbooks, it might also share in vicarious liability as a result of the students' actions. The Supreme Court in *Metro-Goldwyn-Mayer Studios Inc. v. Grokster, Ltd.*, 125 S.Ct. 2764, 2776, at n. 9 (2005) left undecided whether the teacher could be held vicariously liable as well: "Because we resolve the case based on an inducement theory, there is no need to analyze separately MGM's vicarious liability theory."

KEY POINTS FOR YOUR INSTITUTION'S POLICY AND PRACTICE

▶ A claim for vicarious infringement is established when an individual or institution possesses the right and ability to supervise infringing activity and also has a direct financial interest in that activity. See pp. 45–46.

▶ Like primary or direct copyright infringement, vicarious liability is a strict liability concept. A vicarious infringer does not need to be aware of the direct infringement to be found liable, thus neither party need know or have reason to know that the underlying conduct is infringing. See pp. 46–47.

▶ Employers such as a library or school, college, or university are vicariously liable for the infringement committed by employees. Because of the strict nature of vicarious liability, employers are responsible in situations where the employee takes action contrary to or in clear violation of the organization's operating rules, such as copyright policy. See pp. 48–49.

▶ The library can also be responsible (as a vicarious infringer) for the infringement of third parties such as patrons, however this is far less likely. Public libraries have control over the stacks, meeting rooms, and other public spaces, including networked "spaces." Establishing a direct financial benefit from the infringing activity may be more difficult in the public library setting but may exist where revenue-generating mechanisms are tied to the infringing activity and a financial benefit is derived from it, e.g., fund-raising, rental, or service fee scenarios. See pp. 51–57.

ENDNOTES

[1] *Fonovisa, Inc. v. Cherry Auction, Inc.*, 76 F.3d 259, 262 (9th Cir. 1996).

[2] *Arista Records, Inc. v. MP3Board, Inc.*, 2002 WL 1997918, ¶ 8 (S.D.N.Y. 2002).

[3] *Columbia Pictures Industries v. Redd Horne, Inc.*, 749 F.2d 154, 160 (3rd Cir. 1984) (citations omitted).

[4] *Southern Bell Telephone and Telegraph v. Associated Telephone Directory*, 756 F.2d 801, 811 (11th Cir. 1985) ("Maurice Lewis and ATD-TX, and subsequently A.L. Cunningham and ATD, employed the services of C.A. Lewis [the independent contractor]. They all had a financial interest in the infringing activity and the right to supervise Lewis's activities.").

[5] *Dreamland Ball Room, Inc. v. Shapiro, Bernstein & Co.*, 36 F.2d 354 (7th Cir. 1929) ("An orchestra of several persons was engaged, through a contract with its leader, to furnish music. . . . Appellants assert they had no voice in the selection of the musicians . . . no control over the players, nor . . . the musical selections to be rendered during an evening's engagement. They did not direct the playing . . . and did not know that any musical selection played by the orchestra was copyrighted. Neither did they know the orchestra was without consent from appellees to play the copyrighted musical selections "Mississippi Mud,' 'My Ohio Home,' and 'Dream Kisses.' . . . The authorities are, we believe, unanimous in holding that the owner of a dance hall at whose place copyrighted musical compositions are played in violation of the rights of the copyright holder is liable, if the playing be for the profit of the proprietor of the dance hall. And this is so even though the orchestra be employed under a contract that would ordinarily make it an independent contractor." Id. at 355 (citations omitted)).

[6] See, *Blendingwell Music, Inc. v. Moor-Law, Inc.*, 612 F. Supp. 474 (D. Del. 1985) ("There can be no issue as to Moor-Law's liability as a direct or contributory infringer. Moor-Law, as proprietor of the Triple Nickel, hired live bands and operated the jukeboxes. Thus, Moor-Law is responsible under the normal agency rule of respondeat superior." Id. at 481 (citation omitted). "As discussed earlier, Moor may not have been present at the Triple Nickel at the time of the acts of infringement, and thus, this Court must assume for purposes of summary judgment that he was not. Moreover, Moor's deposition clearly indicates that he delegated some authority with respect to the selection of bands to his general manager. . . . While these factors bear on whether liability should be imposed on Moor, they do not preclude as a matter of law a finding of vicarious liability against Moor. Vicarious liability may be predicated on the right and ability of an individual to supervise activities that may lead to infringement coupled with that individual's direct financial interest in those activities." Id. at 481-482 (citations omitted); *KECA Music, Inc. v. Dingus McGee's Co.*, 432 F. Supp. 72 (W.D. Mo. 1977) ("A person who has promoted or induced the infringing acts of a performer is jointly and severally liable as a 'vicarious' infringer even though he has no actual knowledge that a copyright is being infringed by the performer. Further, the owner of an establishment who hires a performer who gives an unlicensed performance of a musical composition is liable as an infringer *even if the performer acted in specific derogation of directions by the owner not to play copyrighted compositions.*" Id. at 74 (emphasis added, citations omitted).).

[7] *Shapiro, Bernstein & Company v. H. L. Green Company*, 316 F.2d 304 (2d Cir. 1964) (record store).

[8] *In Re Aimster Copyright Litigation*, 334 F.3d 643, 654 (7th Cir. 2003) ("The canonical illustration is the owner of a dance hall who hires bands that sometimes play copyrighted music without authorization. The bands are not the dance hall agents, but it may be impossible as a practical matter for the copyright holders to identify and obtain legal remedy against the infringing bands yet quite feasible for the dance hall to prevent or at least limit infringing performances.").

[9] *In Re Aimster Copyright Litigation*, 334 F.3d 643, 654 (7th Cir. 2003).

[10] BLACK'S LAW DICTIONARY (8th ed. 2004) defines *respondeat superior:* "The doctrine holding an employer or principal liable for the employee's or agent's wrongful act committed within the scope of the employment of agency." Id. at 1338.

[11] *Demetriades v. Kaufmann* 690 F. Supp. 289, 293 (S.D.N.Y. 1988).

[12] JOHN W. HAZARD JR., COPYRIGHT LAW IN BUSINESS AND PRACTICE § 7:60, at 7-126 (2004) ("Courts have been quite willing to find liability for officers, directors, and employees in copyright-infringement cases. In so doing, the courts have relied on the 'related defendants' doctrine, which exceeds the traditional scope of the employer-employee relationship and quite literally knows few bounds.").

[13] *Polygram International Publishing, Inc. v. Nevada/TIG, Inc.*, 855 F. Supp. 1314, 1325 (D. Mass. 1994) ("Taking into consideration this body of case law, I find, as a fact-finder engaged in adjudicative fact finding, that Interface had a right and ability to control and supervise its exhibitors, as those terms are used in the context of vicarious liability in copyright cases. I base this finding in part on my evaluation of the weight and materiality of the stipulated facts that (1) Interface exercised authority and control over its exhibitors through its Rules and Regulations and (2) the exhibitors were bound to follow these rules. Also, I base this finding in part on my evaluation of the weight and materiality of the following facts drawn from submitted affidavits and depositions. First, the vice-president of Interface, Richard Schwab, acknowledged in his deposition that Interface could have altered its Rules and Regulations to prohibit music at COMDEX/Fall, but it did not. (Dep. at 66). Instead, Interface chose only to prohibit music at levels that were intrusive to other exhibitors, and advised exhibitors to obtain proper licenses for any music they did play." Id. at 1328.).

[14] Alfred C. Yen, Internet Service Provider Liability for Subscriber Copyright Infringement, Enterprise Liability, and the First Amendment, 88 GEORGETOWN LAW JOURNAL 1833, 1856 (2000).

[15] See, e.g., *KECA Music, Inc. v. Dingus McGee's Co.*, 432 F. Supp. 72 (W.D. Mo. 1977) ("A person who has promoted or induced the infringing acts of a performer is jointly and severally liable as a 'vicarious' infringer even though he has no actual knowledge that a copyright is being infringed by the performer. Further, the owner of an establishment who hires a performer who gives an unlicensed performance of a musical composition is liable as an infringer even if the performer acted in specific derogation of directions by the owner not to play copyrighted compositions." Id. at 74 (citations omitted).

[16] See, e.g., COPYRIGHT CLEARANCE CENTER, COPYRIGHT IN THE DIGITAL WORKSPACE: CONTENT USE AND ATTITUDES TOWARD COPYRIGHT IN CORPORATE AMERICA 3-4 (2004).

[17] *Lowry's Reports, Inc. v. Legg Mason, Inc.*, 271 F. Supp. 2d 737, 746 (D. Md. 2003).

[18] *Lowry's Reports, Inc. v. Legg Mason, Inc.*, 271 F. Supp. 2d 737, 746 (D. Md. 2003) ("Legg Mason asserts, however, that the copying contravened express company policy. It offers in evidence several memoranda from its legal and compliance department. *See, e.g.*, Defs.' Mot., Ex. 10 (undated) ('[I]nformation published within financial periodicals, newspapers,

etc. are copyrighted and owned either by the author or the publication and are not available for reproduction or unauthorized use or distribution.'); *id.*, Ex. 11 (dated December 9, 1999) ('*[A]ny* material published by an independent third party is subject to copyright laws and requires appropriate authorization and approval prior to being used. . . . It is extremely important that these procedures be followed to avoid violating applicable regulatory and Firm standards as well as copyright laws.'). Legg Mason further asserts that the copying that occurred after the intranet posting ceased violated its direct order not to 'mak[e] or distribut[e] any copies, in any fashion, of *Lowry's New York Stock Exchange [Market] Trend Analysis.*' *Id.*, Ex. 18 (dated August 3, 2001).").

[19] *Lowry's Reports, Inc. v. Legg Mason, Inc.*, 271 F. Supp. 2d 737, 746 (D. Md. 2003).

[20] *A and M Record Inc. v. Napster, Inc.*, 239 F.3d 1004, 1023 (9th Cir. 2001).

[21] BLACK'S LAW DICTIONARY (8th ed. 2004) defines *in loco parentis*, literally "in the place of a parent": "Of, relating to, or acting as a temporary guardian or caretaker of a child, taking on all or some of the responsibilities of a parent." Id. at 1338.

[22] *Fonovisa, Inc. v. Cherry Auction, Inc.*, 76 F.3d 259 (9th Cir. 1996) ("This analogy to absentee landlord is not in accord with the facts as alleged in the district court and which we, for purposes of appeal, must accept. The allegations below were that vendors occupied small booths within premises that Cherry Auction controlled and patrolled. According to the complaint, Cherry Auction had the right to terminate vendors for any reason whatsoever and through that right had the ability to control the activities of vendors on the premises. In addition, Cherry Auction promoted the swap meet and controlled the access of customers to the swap meet area." Id. at 362.).

[23] *Columbia Pictures Industries v. Redd Horne, Inc.*, 749 F.2d 154 (3rd Cir. 1984) ("Robert Zeny is the president and the sole shareholder of Maxwell's Video Showcase, Ltd. He knowingly initiated and participated in the infringing activity, and ignored repeated requests from the plaintiffs that he cease and desist the activity. He too, therefore, is clearly liable as a co-infringer. . . . Glenn W. Zeny, Robert's brother, is not a stockholder or officer, nor does he have a direct financial interest in Maxwell's Video Showcase, Ltd. . . . Glenn W. Zeny, like his brother, participated knowingly and significantly in the infringing activity and ignored the plaintiffs' persistent requests that the activity cease." Id. at 160. "In addition, Glenn W. Zeny's knowledge of, and substantial participation in, the infringing activities may be imputed to his employer, Redd Horne, Inc." Id. at 161.) (citations omitted.)

[24] *Artists Music, Inc. v. Reed Publishing, Inc.*, 31 U.S.P.Q. 2d 1623, 1994 WL 191643 (S.D.N.Y. 1994).

[25] *Artists Music, Inc. v. Reed Publishing, Inc.*, 31 U.S.P.Q. 2d 1623, 1994 WL 191643, *6 (S.D.N.Y. 1994).

[26] *Artists Music, Inc. v. Reed Publishing, Inc.*, 31 U.S.P.Q. 2d 1623, 1994 WL 191643, *6 (S.D.N.Y. 1994) ("Reed's revenues from the show did not in any way depend on whether or not the exhibitors played any music whatsoever.").

[27] Alfred C. Yen, Internet Service Provider Liability for Subscriber Copyright Infringement, Enterprise Liability, and the First Amendment, 88 GEORGETOWN LAW JOURNAL 1833,

1849 (2000) ("Moreover, their contrasting attitudes towards vicarious liability represent a general disagreement that can be found throughout the relevant case law.") (footnotes to various cases omitted)).

[28] *Artists Music, Inc. v. Reed Publishing, Inc.*, 31 U.S.P.Q. 2d 1623, 1994 WL 191643, *6 (S.D.N.Y. 1994).

[29] *Polygram International Publishing, Inc. v. Nevada/TIG, Inc.*, 855 F. Supp. 1314 (D. Mass. 1994).

[30] *Polygram International Publishing, Inc. v. Nevada/TIG, Inc.*, 855 F. Supp. 1314 1328-1329 (D. Mass. 1994) ("Mr. Schwab states in his affidavit that during the COMDEX/Fall show, 10 to 12 Interface employees walked the aisles to ensure 'rules compliance.' (Aff. ¶ 8). Although Mr. Schwab believes it would be impractical to police the show for *all* rules violations, it is clear from Mr. Schwab's statement that Interface was actively involved in managing the show and did not function as an absentee landlord. For example, Interface employees were available during the show to address exhibitor needs and to answer exhibitor complaints, including complaints about exhibitors encroaching on other space or blocking aisles during the show. (Aff. ¶¶ 8-9.)" (emphasis added)).

[31] *Polygram International Publishing, Inc. v. Nevada/TIG, Inc.*, 855 F. Supp. 1314 (D. Mass. 1994).

[32] *Artists Music, Inc. v. Reed Publishing, Inc.*, 31 U.S.P.Q. 2d 1623 (S.D.N.Y. 1994).

[33] *Arista Records, Inc. v. MP3Board, Inc.*, 2002 WL 1997918, ¶ 9 (S.D.N.Y. 2002) ("Thus, there is evidence that MP3Board had the right and ability to remove links to infringing works and bar the participation of users who transmitted those infringing files.").

[34] Alfred C. Yen, Internet Service Provider Liability for Subscriber Copyright Infringement, Enterprise Liability, and the First Amendment, 88 GEORGETOWN LAW JOURNAL 1833, 1845 (2000) (footnotes to various cases omitted).

[35] *Columbia Pictures Industries, Inc. v. Aveco, Inc.*, 800 F.2d 59 (3d Cir. 1986), *Columbia Pictures Industries, Inc. v. Redd Horne, Inc.*, 749 F2d 154 (3rd Cir. 1984). The *Columbia Pictures Industries, Inc. v. Aveco, Inc.* court saw no distinction in either set of facts: "Unlike Maxwell's employees located in the public lobby, Aveco's customers are in private screening rooms. Aveco argues that while these viewing rooms are available to anyone for rent, they are private during each rental period, and therefore, not 'open to the public.' The performance—the playing of the video cassette—thus occurs not in the public lobby, but in the private viewing rooms. We disagree. The necessary implication of Aveco's analysis is that Redd Horne would have been decided differently had Maxwell's located its video cassette players in a locked closet in the back of the stores. We do not read Redd Horne to adopt such an analysis. The Copyright Act speaks of performances at a place open to the public." 800 F.2d at 63.

[36] *Columbia Pictures Industries, Inc. v. Professional Real Estate Investors, Inc.*, 866 F.2d 278 (9th Cir. 1989). In distinguishing this case with *Columbia Pictures Industries, Inc. v. Aveco, Inc.* and *Columbia Pictures Industries, Inc. v. Redd Horne, Inc.* decisions, the court observed: "La Mancha's operation differs from those in Aveco and Redd Horne because its 'nature' is the providing of living accommodations and general hotel services, which may incidentally include the

rental of videodiscs to interested guests for viewing in guest rooms. While the hotel may indeed be 'open to the public,' a guest's hotel room, once rented, is not." Id. at 281.).

[37] *On Command Video Corp. v. Columbia Picture Industries,* 777 F. Supp 787 (N.D. Cal. 1991).

[38] *On Command Video Corp. v. Columbia Picture Industries,* 777 F. Supp 787, 789 (N.D. Cal. 1991) ("A movie video is thus performed only when it is visible and audible. In On Command's system, this viewing and hearing occurs only in an individual guest room. That can be the only relevant place of performance for public place analysis. Since hotel guest rooms are indisputably not public places for copyright purposes, On Command's system results in no public performances under the public place clause.").

[39] See, 17 U.S.C. § 101. Under the first genus, the "place" clause, a performance is public if it occurs "at a place open to the public or at any place where a substantial number of persons outside of a normal circle of a family and its social acquaintances is gathered." Under the second genus, the "transmission" clause, a performance is public if someone "transmit[s] or otherwise communicate[s] a performance or display of the work to a place specified by clause (1) or to the public, by means of any device or process, whether the members of the public capable of receiving the performance or display receive it in the same place or in separate places and at the same time or at different times." Id.

[40] *On Command Video Corp. v. Columbia Picture Industries,* 777 F. Supp 787, 790 (N.D. Cal. 1991) ("Thus, whether the number of hotel guests viewing an On Command transmission is one or one hundred, and whether these guests view the transmission simultaneously or sequentially, the transmission is still a public performance since it goes to members of the public.") (citation omitted.).

[41] *Metro-Goldwin Studios, Inc. v. Grokster, Ltd.,* 380 F.3d 1154, 1165 (9th Cir. 2004), vacated and remanded __ U.S. __, 2005 WL 1499402 (2005).

[42] *Metro-Goldwin Studios, Inc. v. Grokster, Ltd.,* 380 F.3d 1154, 1165 (9th Cir. 2004), vacated and remanded 125 S. Ct. 2764 (2005).

[43] *Metro-Goldwyn-Mayer Studios, Inc. v. Grokster, Ltd.,* __ U.S. __, 2005 WL 1499402 (2005), at *14-*15.

[44] *A&M Records, Inc. v. Napster, Inc.,* 239 F. 3d 1004, 1024 (9th Cir. 2001).

[45] Alfred C. Yen, Internet Service Provider Liability for Subscriber Copyright Infringement, Enterprise Liability, and the First Amendment, 88 GEORGETOWN LAW JOURNAL 1833, 1845 (2000) (footnotes omitted).

[46] *BLOCK'S LAW DICTIONARY* (8th ed. 2004)

[47] See, *Religious Technology Center v. Netcom On-Line Communication Services, Inc.,* 907 F. Supp. 1361, 1373 (N.D. Cal. 1995) ("Unlike a landlord, Netcom retains some control over the use of its system.").

[48] *A&M Records, Inc. v. Napster, Inc.,* 239 F.3d 1004, 1027 (9th Cir. 2001).

[49] Jay Dratler, Jr. Cyberlaw: Intellectual Property in the Digital Millennium, n. 19.12, § 6.01[2], 6-12, 6-13 (2004).

[50] *Metro-Goldwin Studios, Inc. v Grokster, Ltd.,* 259 F. Supp. 2d 1029, 1041 (C.D. Calif. 2003) ("Plaintiffs appear reluctant to acknowledge a seminal distinction between Grokster/

StreamCast and Napster: neither Grokster nor StreamCast provides the "site and facilities" for direct infringement."), affirmed, 380 F.3d 1154 (9th Cir. 2004), vacated and remanded 125 S. Ct. 2764 (2005).

[51] *Religious Technology Center v. Netcom On-line Communications Services, Inc.*, 907 F. Supp. 1361, 1376-1377 (N.D. Cal. 1995). See also, JAY DRATLER, JR. CYBERLAW: INTELLECTUAL PROPERTY IN THE DIGITAL MILLENIUM, n. 19.12, § 6.01[2], at 6-12 (2004) reaching a similar conclusion and citing cases in a circuit by circuit review, including *A&M Reecords v. Napster, Arista Records, Inc. v. MP3Board, Inc., In re Aimster Copyright Litigation.* See also, *Fonivisa, Inc. v. Cherry Auction, Inc.*, 76 F.3d 259, 263-264 (9th Cir. 1996) (where "the sale of pirated recordings at the Cherry Auction swap meet is a 'draw' for customers.").

[52] JAY DRATLER, JR. CYBERLAW: INTELLECTUAL PROPERTY IN THE DIGITAL MILLE-NIUM, n. 19.12, § 6.01[2], 6-12, 6-13 (2004).

[53] *Ellison v. Robertson*, 357 F.3d 1072, 1078 (9th Cir. 2004) ("The district court interprets Fono-visa [Fonivisa, Inc. v. Cherry Auction, Inc., 76 F.3d 259 (9th Cir. 1996)] and 'direct financial benefit' to require a 'substantial' proportion of a defendant's income to be directly linked to infringing activities for the purpose of vicarious liability analysis. [citation omitted] We *disagree* with the addition of this quantification requirement." (emphasis added).

[54] *A&M Records v. Napster, Inc.*, 239 F.3d 1004, 1023 (9th Cir. 2001) ("Financial benefit exists where the availability of infringing material 'acts as a "draw" for customers . . . Ample evi-dence supports the district court's finding that Napster's future revenue is directly depen-dent upon 'increases in userbase.'"). See also, *Arista Records, Inc. v. MP3Board, Inc.*, 2002 WL 1997918, ¶ 10 (S.D.N.Y. 2002) ("The record companies have also introduced evidence indicating that MP3Board possessed a direct financial interest in the exchange of infring-ing files. Infringement which increases a defendant's user base or otherwise acts a draw for customers constitutes a direct financial interest.").

[55] *Ellison v. Robertson*, 357 F.3d 1072, 1079 (9th Cir. 2004) (first emphasis added, second em-phasis original).

[56] *Ellison v. Robertson*, 357 F.3d 1072, 1079 (9th Cir. 2004) ("There is no requirement that the draw be 'substantial.' AOL offers access to USENET groups as part of its service for a reason: it helps to encourage overall subscription to its services. Here, AOL's future rev-enue is directly dependent upon increases in its userbase. Certainly, the fact that AOL pro-vides its subscribers access to certain USENET groups constitutes a small 'draw' in proportion to its overall profits, but AOL's status as a behemoth online service provider, by itself, does not insulate it categorically from vicarious liability. Regardless of what *frac-tion* of AOL's earnings are considered a direct result of providing its subscribers access to the USENET groups that contained infringing material—indeed, almost any aspect of AOL's services would appear *relatively* minuscule because of its sheer size— they would be earnings nonetheless. The essential aspect of the 'direct financial benefit' inquiry is whether there is a causal relationship between the infringing activity and any financial benefit a defendant reaps, regardless of *how substantial* the benefit is in proportion to a de-fendant's overall profits." (all emphasis original)).

[57] It could be argued that like the student-as-employee relationship the student-as-student relationship alone might also represent a vicarious relationship: one might argue that by transfer of tuition payments from student to institution, a contract is formed between student and school with the terms and conditions contained in the student handbook or course syllabus. While there is some case law to support this contention, it has yet to be applied in the copyright arena. See e.g., *Mangla v. Brown*, 135 F.3d 80 (1st Cir. 1998) (contract terms and conditions may include statements in student manuals and registration material). See, Terrence Leas, The Course Syllabus: Legal Status and Implications for Practitioners, 177 EDUCATION LAW REPORTER [771] (August 14, 2003), observing that there were no reported cases regarding the legal status of course syllabus but that "judges have generally recognized written materials available to students as part of the contract between the student and the institution." (Footnote and citations to cases omitted). See also, Michael Zolandz, Note: Storming the Ivory Tower: Renewing the Breach of Contract Claim by Students Against Universities, 69 George Washington Law Review 91 (2000).

[58] Such evidence would likely be demonstrated by expert testimony in the way that similar testimony in Napster demonstrated that use of P2P technology produced a negative market effect in record shops surrounding college campuses where the P2P technology was in extensive use: "We, therefore, conclude that the district court made sound findings related to Napster's deleterious effect on the present and future digital download markets." *A&M Records, Inc. v. Napster, Inc.*, 239 F.3d 1004, 1017 (9th Cir. 2001) ("Plaintiffs also offered a study conducted by Michael Fine, Chief Executive Officer of Soundscan, (the 'Fine Report') to determine the effect of online sharing of MP3 files in order to show irreparable harm [the standard for issuing an injunction]. Fine found that online file sharing has resulted in a loss of 'album' sales within college markets." Id. at 1016-1017).

[59] *Marobie-FL, Inc. v. National Association of Firefighting Equipment Dealers*, 983 F. Supp. 1167, 1179 (N.D. Ill. 1997) ("As mentioned above, the degree to which Northwest monitored, controlled, or had the ability to monitor or control the contents of NAFED's Web Page is unclear. However, it is undisputed that NAFED paid Northwest a one-time set-up fee of $20 and that since that time NAFED has paid Northwest a flat fee of $67.50 each quarter. It is also undisputed that the fee Northwest receives has never changed based on how many people visit NAFED's Web Page or what is accessed. In other words, NAFED's infringement did not financially benefit Northwest. Accordingly, Northwest cannot be held vicariously liable for NAFED's infringement."). See also, *Religious Technology Center v. Netcom On-Line Communication Services, Inc.*, 907 F. Supp. 1361, 1376 (N.D. Cal. 1995) ("For example, a landlord who has the right and ability to supervise the tenant's activities is vicariously liable for the infringements of the tenant where the rental amount is proportional to the proceeds of the tenant's sales. However, where a defendant rents space or services on a fixed rental fee that does not depend on the nature of the activity of the lessee, courts usually find no vicarious liability because there is no direct financial benefit from the infringement." (citations omitted)).

[60] 17 U.S.C. § 101, defines a public performance of a work as one made "at a place open to the public or at any place where a substantial number of persons outside of a normal circle of a family and its social acquaintances is gathered." See also, Kenneth D. Crews, Distance Education and Copyright Law: The Limits and Meaning of Copyright Policy, 27 JOURNAL OF COLLEGE AND UNIVERSITY LAW 15, 23-24 (2000) ("The live, face-to-face classroom could arguably be a place open to the public. Even if entrance is limited to enrolled students, the assembled students in any particular course are likely beyond the customary circle of family and friends. Similarly, when the performances and displays are transmitted to other locations in the name of distance education, they may also be received by similar groups of students constituting the 'public.' Moreover, in the case of a transmission of the educational content, received by students at their own time and place as distance education, the activity can be 'public' even though the students are receiving the content in 'separate places' and 'at different times.'").

[61] For section 110(1): H. R.Rep. No. 94-1476, 94th Cong., 2d Sess. 81 (1976) (conf. Rep.) U.S.C.C.A.N. reprinted in 5 United States Code Congressional and Administrative News 5659, 5695 (1976) ("The 'teaching activities' exempted by the clause encompass systematic instruction of a very wide variety of subjects, but they do not include performances or displays, whatever their cultural value or intellectual appeal, that are given for the recreational or entertainment of any part of their audience."). For section 110(2): The Conference Report, H. R.Rep. No. 107-685, 107th Cong., 2nd Sess. 230 (2002) (Conf. Rep.) ("this test of relevance and materiality connects the copyrighted work to the curriculum, and it means that the portion performed or displayed may not be performed or displayed for the mere entertainment of the students, or as unrelated background material.").

►Part II

PENALTIES AND IMMUNITIES IN COPYRIGHT LAW FOR LIBRARIES AND SCHOOLS

▶4

WHAT ARE DAMAGES AND HOW CAN THEY BE LIMITED?

Read this chapter to find out about copyright situations like:
- ▶ Whether a public school can perform a copyrighted musical without permission.
- ▶ How non-profit schools and libraries can avoid some damages in copyright law.

Once liability is established, a variety of remedies are available to the plaintiff-copyright owner. While it is beyond the scope of this book to discuss these remedies in thorough detail, a review is helpful before reading the following discussion on damage limitation. Many of the reported copyright cases are actually requests for injunctive relief,[1] either in the form of a preliminary or permanent injunction requesting that the infringing practice discontinue, e.g., that the material be removed from the Web site, a subscriber's access discontinued, or the entire Web site or network be shut down. The injunction would be enforceable by proceedings in contempt.[2] In the copyright law, additional injunctive relief as well as damage limitation is found in section 512[3] and is discussed in detail in Chapter 6.

Another nonmonetary remedy is section 503, which allows for the impoundment and final disposition ("destruction or other reasonable disposition"[4]) of infringing articles. An example in the school setting would be an order requesting the erasure or destruction of the closet full of off-air tapes an instructor has been collecting over the years, somewhat similar to the facts of *Encyclopedia Britannica Educational Corp. v. Crooks*,[5] or in a library setting an order for the destruction of any additional copies of a monograph reproduced without permission and still available for patron use.[6] A more likely order occurs in a case where the bootleg copies were made with the intention of later sale or other commercial distribution; here an impoundment and destruction order ensures that no further bootleg copies make it into the marketplace.[7]

INTRODUCING MONETARY DAMAGES

Regarding monetary remedies, there are two broad categories: first, damages, and second, costs and attorney's fees. Damages come in two species: actual and statutory.[8]

Plaintiffs have the right to request one form of damage or the other: "the copyright owner may elect, at any time before final judgment is rendered, to recover, instead of actual damages and profits, an award of statutory damages for all infringements involved in the action with respect to any one work."[9] The phrase "with respect to any one work" means that the court may assign a statutory damage amount for each work that is infringed. The phrase "for all infringements involved" means that if one work is infringed in multiple ways as part of the same general incident, the damages are *not* multiplied by each incident of infringement. Suppose a particular work is reproduced by the defendant, then distributed or displayed or performed without permission as well. If all such uses are later found to be infringing, violating the exclusive right or reproduction and distribution (or display or performance), for example, are damages awarded for each exclusive right that is violated? No. This is practical result of the "for all infringements involved in the action" proviso. If multiple infringements occur of any one work, the award of statutory damages is linked to the single work but not the multiple infringements of that work. Of course, in cases with multiple infringements of multiple works, damages can nonetheless be considerable.

The Realm and Range of Statutory Damages

Statutory damages can range from $750 up to $30,000 per work "as the court considers just."[10] Except in cases of specific statutory remission discussed below, the court may not reduce statutory damages to less than the minimum $750. "Because damages are often difficult to prove in an infringement case, statutory or automatic damages are rather important and can be an important leverage tool in settling a dispute quickly."[11] Congress has increased the amount of statutory damages over the years, from the initial 1976 Copyright Act range of $100 to $10,000 to the current amounts, with the most recent change to the present range made in 1999.[12] The reason for this raising of the stakes:

> It has been well over a decade since we last adjusted statutory damages for inflation. Our purpose must be to provide meaningful disincentives for infringement, and to accomplish that, the cost of infringement must substantially exceed the cost of the compliance so that those who use or distribute intellectual property have incentive to comply with the law.[13]

Another downside for defendants in copyright actions is the understanding that "[b]ecause statutory damages are an alternate to actual damages, there has never been a requirement that statutory damages must be strictly related to actual injury."[14] In cases of infringement of multiple works, from the defendant's perspective the so-called "damage meter" can run quite high, quite fast. In one case involving the music site My.MP3.com,[15] the court established a per work amount of

$25,000; with over 4,700 songs unlawfully available on its servers the court observed that statutory damages could be as high as $118 million![16]

Types of Actual Damages

Actual damages consist of two components. First are the actual damages suffered as a result of the infringement, such as a loss of plaintiff's sales revenues or rental or license fees as well as loss of other profits. Second, the illicit profits of the infringer are also recoverable, i.e., "any profits of the infringer that are attributable to the infringement and are not taken into account in computing the actual damages."[17] Including defendant profits resulting from the infringement is a logical addition as these profits represent a "fruit of the poisonous 'copyright' tree" of sorts, to borrow a perhaps more familiar legal imagery from the search and seizure law.[18] Including the profits of the defendant in the mix of damage calculations provides copyright plaintiffs the ability to prevent defendants from unfairly benefiting from the wrongful act, the infringement. Moreover, there is a presumption that all profits of infringer are tainted. "In establishing the infringer's profits, the copyright owner is required to present proof *only* of the infringer's gross revenue," then the burden shifts to the defendant-infringer "to prove his or her deductible expenses and the elements of profit attributable to factors other than the copyrighted work [i.e., the item infringed]."[19]

The plaintiff cannot double-recover for the same profit damages, i.e., when the loss of plaintiff revenues or profits and the gain of the defendant (in profits) is the same. This restriction gives practical meaning to the phrase relating to the limitation on actual damages when it occurs in the form of profits: "and any profits of the infringer that are attributable to the infringement and are not taken into account in computing the actual damages." For example, Plaintiff A might have a loss of $50,000 resulting from the decreased licensing revenue (actual damages) earned from Client B because of Defendant C's infringement (as Defendant C usurped Plaintiff A's legitimate market with pirated copies). Attributable to the actual infringement, A suffers lost profits of another $50,000 and C gained profits of $75,000. (Not only does Defendant C infringe, he may overcharge as well! More likely he has no product development costs to recover, as a privateer his illicit revenue is pure profit!). Plaintiff A cannot recover both the second 50K and 75K amounts (the lost profits of A and the gained profits of C that are attributable to the same act of infringement) but is limited to $75,000, representing $50,000 of the plaintiff's lost profits and representing another $25,000 of the defendant's illicit gain in profit that were "not taken into account in computing the actual damages." Plaintiff A can recover an award of $50,000 (for actual damages) and another $75,000 (actual damages and profits of the infringer) in lost profits, for a total of $125,000 in actual damages.

Of course the task for copyright plaintiffs is to prove the loss. In some cases this may be quite easy: 100 copies of the workbook reproduced without permission, retailing at $49.95 would equate to lost sales of $4,995. In other cases, calculating the lost sales from repeated and insidious file sharing would be an exercise in futility. Thus, the copyright statute allows plaintiffs to elect statutory damages, with the court assigning an amount per infringing work.[20] In cases where a defendant requests a jury trial, the jury must also calculate the appropriate statutory damage amount.[21]

The use of a jury trial to determine damages also impacts the timing of the election by the plaintiff-copyright owner. If the plaintiff-copyright owner is not satisfied with the amount of the jury's actual damages award, can the plaintiff-copyright owner now opt for statutory damages? The Supreme Court found that unlikely or at least impractical:

> The parties agree, and we have found no indication to the contrary, that election may occur even after a jury has returned a verdict on liability and an award of actual damages. It is at least unlikely that Congress intended that a jury, having already made a determination of actual damages, should be reconvened to make a determination of statutory damages.[22]

At least one lower court decision offered this interpretation as a result of the comment by the Court:[23] "Absent the ability to reconvene the jury or to empanel a new one, it would seem that, in those circumstances in which the defendant has requested a trial by jury, the plaintiff's last opportunity to elect statutory damages effectively matures when the case is submitted to the jury for deliberation."[24] This in effect rewrites wording of the phrase "at any time before final judgment is rendered" in a jury trial to mean not before the final judgment is entered by the court but rather to mean a time before the jury verdict on damages is rendered.

As observed earlier, statutory damages are subject to election by the plaintiff-copyright owner, but not the defendant-infringer under section 504(c), and can range from "a sum not less than $750 or more than $30,000 as the court considers just." However, it is the court (or jury, as the case may be) in its "just" consideration that establishes the amount of the statutory damage per work. The court or jury may select an amount toward the maximum of the range when it determines that a "punitive" award is warranted or may be set at a token $750 in less egregious cases.[25] However, the evidence considered by either trier may vary, e.g., the jury may not have the jurisprudential "memory" that a federal district court judge might have regarding the copyright law. In the workbook example, and notwithstanding the discussion of damage remission below, in a case where the plaintiff-publisher-copyright owner opted for statutory damages under section 504(c)(1), circumstances may warrant a token $750 (somewhat less than the $4,995 in actual damages as a result of lost sales) or it may bring the wrath of the law upon the defendant and establish statutory damages at the maximum of $30,000. If the 100 workbooks consisted of a series of 4 subtitles (25 copies made of each), where each title in the series is considered an individual work, the statutory damages could quickly reach $120,000, again underscoring the danger of being on the receiving end of an award of statutory damages where the infringement of multiple works is involved.

AVOIDING DAMAGE ENHANCEMENT FOR WILLFUL INFRINGEMENT

Recall that intent is not an element of a claim of direct copyright infringement. However, if the infringement is proved—the burden of proof is on the plaintiff-copyright owner—to be "willful," the court may increase damages further: "In a case where the copyright owner sustains the burden of proving, and the court finds, that infringement was committed willfully, the court in its discretion may increase the award of statutory damages to sum of not more than $150,000."[26] The plaintiff-copyright owner must convince the court as well ("and the court finds"). However, recent Supreme Court precedent suggests that the "court" that makes a determination of willfulness as in any determination of damages can also be the jury, as an increase due to willfulness under section 504(c)(2), is a subset of statutory damages, and thus is subject to the same conditions in jury trials.[27] Likewise, this means that a damage enhancement due to willfulness cannot exist in an infringement action where the plaintiff-copyright owner elects actual damages: "Insofar as the question of willfulness is inextricably bound up with determining the amount of statutory damages, it would seem to lie beyond the judge's competence to determine that question independently."[28] This bifurcated statutory structure within section 504 is another factor encouraging a plaintiff to make the statutory damage election.

Understanding the Concept of Willfulness

In the context of general (not necessarily copyright) criminal cases, the Supreme Court indicates that willfulness exists where the defendant "either knows or acts in reckless disregard of its prohibition of the depravation of a defined constitutional or other federal right."[29] In copyright cases, the standard is somewhat different,[30] though the notion of knowledgeable as well as recklessness is retained: "Willfulness in this context [discussing section 504] means that the defendant 'recklessly disregarded' the possibility that 'its conduct represented infringement,'"[31] or, in an earlier configuration, "The standard is simply whether the defendant had knowledge that its conduct represented infringement or perhaps recklessly disregarded the possibility.[32]

In copyright law, willfulness "exists where there is a deliberate act of infringement, knowledge that an act constitutes infringement, or intentionally disregards of warnings that infringement is taking place."[33] The standard "connotes wantonness,"[34] a belief so unsupportable in law that a court would in fact consider it unreasonable. In vacating and remanding a district court's determination of willfulness in the Michigan Document Services copy-shop litigation, an en banc Sixth Circuit observed: "[w]e cannot say that the defendants' belief that their copying constituted fair use was so unreasonable as to bespeak willfulness."[35] Likewise, in a case where there is evidence of customary knowledge of a plaintiff's copyright, such as in the television industry, the Ninth Circuit observed that a defendant "who nonetheless continued to air the series in question until well into the course of this litigation is sufficient to support a finding of willfulness."[36] One way to look at the knowledge factor is to recall that direct copyright infringement is a strict liability statute where knowledge is not an element. However, if the infringement does occur with some scienter[37] then it may be considered willful and subject to enhancement, assuming statutory damages are elected:

> It seems clear that here, "willfully" means with knowledge that the defendant's conduct constitutes copyright infringement. Otherwise, there would be no point in providing specifically for the reduction of minimum awards in the case of innocent infringement, as any infringement that was nonwillful would necessarily be innocent.[38]

Though the relationship may not be as inopposite as Nimmer contends. Add a "purpose[] of commercial advantage or private financial gain" to willful infringement and a defendant may be facing prosecution for criminal copyright infringement as well.[39]

A Few Words About Criminal Copyright Infringement

In 1997 the criminal copyright law was amended to indicate that the "private financial gain" standard could be present in the absence of a commercial transaction.[40] The copyright law now defines financial gain to mean the "receipt, or expectation of receipt, of anything of value, including the receipt of other copyrighted works."[41] Thus, exchange, barter, or similar arrangements, even if not the result of a formal negotiation or transaction, could qualify. The change was made to rectify the result of *United States v. LaMacchia*,[42] where defendants, though receiving no direct benefits (direct payment), nonetheless benefited financially from the infringing activity of trading (now covered by the "private financial gain" clause[43]) or sharing (covered by a "bootleg" clause: "reproduction or distribution, including by electronic means, during any 180-day period, of 1 or more copies or phonorecords of 1 or more copyrighted works, which have a total retail value of more than $1,000"[44]) illegal software, computer and video games, and other copyrighted works through online bulletin boards and similar exchange mechanisms.[45] "De minimus infringement (e.g., a child copying a software program for a friend or brother or sister) would not be pursued or punished."[46] As the Committee report observed, the target is that willful behavior that causes harm to another's interest:

> In effect, H.R. 2265 does just that: it criminalizes computer theft of copyrighted works, whether or not the defendant derives a direct financial benefit from the act(s) of misappropriation, thereby preventing such willful conduct from destroying businesses, especially small businesses, that depend on licensing agreements and royalties for survival.[47]

Pending legislation, H.R. 4077, the Piracy Deterrence and Education Act of 2004 would also subject to criminal penalty the "knowing distribution, including by . . . electronic means, with reckless disregard of the risk of further infringement . . . 1 or more copies or phonorecords of 1 or more copyrighted pre-release works."[48] This provision is designed to reach the controversy over the release of Oscar-nominated works to members of the academy in VHS or DVD format that often, shortly thereafter appeared in various black markets, as well as address problems related to other pirated works. The amendment would "clarify that it may be a violation merely to offer copyrighted works in digital format for others to copy."[49]

Factors in the Award of Costs and Attorney's Fees

A final set of monetary remedies may take the form of costs and attorney's fees.[50] Similarly these amounts can be significant[51] and disproportional to the damage award.[52] It should be observed that costs and attorney's fees are awarded to the prevailing party,[53] which could be a defendant, whereas the injunctive and other monetary remedies are available obviously only to plaintiffs if prevailing. The award is made at the discretion of the court in the instance of both "recovery of full costs by or against any party" and "a reasonable attorney's fee to the prevailing party."[54]

The Supreme Court approved of the following factors in determining whether to award costs and attorney's fees: "frivolousness, motivation, objective reasonableness (both in the factual and in the legal components of the case) and the need in particular circumstances to advance considerations of compensation and deterrence."[55] A recent district court relied, as did the Supreme Court, on factors similar to those articulated in *Lieb*.[56] In observing that the defendant "obstructed discovery, made material representations to the Court, and destroyed evidence,"[57] the court favored award of fees. However, the court observed that the second[58] and third factors[59] did not. As a result the court declined to award the requested $108,025.99 and $1,573,178.38 in costs and attorney's fees, respectively.[60] The $19,725,270 in damages awarded by the jury for breach of contract and willful copyright infringement was allowed to stand. (There was disagreement on the amount of actual damages as the plaintiff argued an amount in excess of $6 million, the defendant a more conservative $59,000.) The case, involving the infringement in a corporate setting of the plaintiff's newsletter underscores the concept of damage meter in cases of willful infringement, where a total of $36,000,000 in willful statutory damages was possible.[61]

The Impact of the DMCA and the Willfulness Standard

An unanswered question is whether, in light of the notice mechanism created by section 512 (discussed in detail in Chapter 6), a failure to act expeditiously and remove infringing material, thus allowing infringement to continue, would not only deny the service provider recourse to the section 512(c) safe harbor, but it would also open the defendant to an increase in damages as a willful infringer because the defendant acted with intentional disregard of warnings of infringement. In brief, and for purposes of the immediate discussion, section 512 contains a mechanism whereby a copyright owner may contact a service provider (for example, a public library or educational institution)and provide "a notification of claimed infringement . . . [in the form of] a written communication provided to the designated agent of a service provider"[62] that infringing material that results from either "storage at the direction of a user of material that resides on a system or network controlled or operated by or for the service provider"[63] (the so-called "post" functions) or the "referring or linking users to an online location containing infringing material or infringing activity, by using information location tools, including a directory, index, reference, pointer, or hypertext link,"[64] (the so-called "link" functions). The service provider must then "upon notification of claimed infringement as described . . . respond[] expeditiously to remove, or disable access to, the material that is claimed to be infringing or to be the subject of infringing activity."[65] If this is done then the only remedy available to the plaintiff-copyright owner is injunctive relief. When operative, the section 512 safe-harbor works to eliminate all monetary damages and awards, including costs and attorney's fees.

The section 512(c)(3)(A) statutory notice includes a written statement identifying the copyrighted work, or if multiple works are involved a representative list of works claimed to have been infringed and the identification of the material claimed to be the source of infringing that is residing on the defendant's network. In short, the notice is sufficient to alert the defendant and prompt action through removal or disabling under common law standards, the section 512 safe-harbor notwithstanding. The concepts of contributory liability discussed thus far dictate that institutional, organizational, or corporate intermediaries ignore such notice at great peril. A pre-section 512 example of notice disregard is found in *Rodgers v. Eighty Four Lumber Company*,[66] where the district court found the infringement willful when a nationwide chain, after numerous phone calls and letters from copyright representatives, refused to enter into a licensing arrangement regarding the playing of music over its store's loudspeaker systems. In a similar result, the Seventh Circuit found willfulness in the infringement of a defendant who received a letter from the plaintiff-copyright owner stating that it could "not broadcast radio music over the loudspeakers in its clubs without first obtaining an appropriate license."[67]

The point is that section 512 may in the future naturally create circumstances of awareness or notice that if not acted upon may actually increase the risk of liability under common law concepts of secondary liability, not to mention loss of the section 512 safe harbor, as well as the potential for increased damage exposure should liability be established and its character determined to meet the willfulness standard. A saving measure was added to section 512, which may operate to ensure that such interpretation is not made: "The failure of a service provider's conduct to qualify for limitation of liability under this section shall not bear adversely upon the consideration of a defense by the service provider that the service provider's conduct is not infringing under this title or any other defense."[68] The Conference Report further explains: "As provided in subsection (l), Section 512 is not intended to imply that a service provider is or is not liable as an infringer whether for conduct that qualifies for a limitation on liability or for conduct that fails to so qualify. Rather, the limitations of liability apply if the provider is found to be liable under existing principles of law."[69] However, the issue remains a valid one, conduct that might underlie a failure to comply with the expeditious "remove" or "disable" proviso of either section 512(c)(1)(C) for the posted material or section 512(d)(3) for linked material (formal notice) or the section 512(c)(1)(A)(i) and (ii) ("notice" through actual knowledge or other awareness) might also under common law standards indicate the "willful" wanton, reckless disregard of such notice. The Senate Report implies as much: "liability in these circumstances would be adjudicated based on the doctrines of direct, vicarious or contributory liability for infringement as they are articulated in the Copyright Act and in the court decisions interpreting and applying that statute, which are unchanged by section 512."[70]

Conduct of a defendant-institutional service provider like that of any other service provider under section 512, is a two-way street. While a failure to qualify for the safe harbor by not undertaking section 512 remedial measures ("expeditiously to remove, or disable access to, the material") does not necessarily mean that a case for secondary infringement is established, section 512(l) states as much, but by the same token, the facts disqualifying section 512 protection can also work to establish secondary liability and, as hypothesized above, even willful behavior.[71] The point is that section 512 places greater emphasis on compliance mechanisms in two ways. First, as a result of the formal notice requirements introduced in the present discussion. Second and more informally through the inherent attention that section 512 draws to the conduct of service providers contained in its other subsections (and discussed in greater detail in Part III) to the conduct of service providers. This organizational re-direction of efforts may in turn unwittingly increase also the attention directed to the concept of "notice" or other awareness (reason to know), i.e., a failure to respond to such knowledge may suggest the sort of wanton, reckless disregard that would support a finding of willfulness.

The Statute of Limitations in Copyright

The statute of limitations for copyright infringement is three years for civil actions[72] and five years for criminal actions.[73] The short duration of the period in which a civil action, the most likely suit against a library or school, can be brought is deceptive. In a case involving the use of an off-air recording or use of photocopied or scanned material, consider the cluster of rights a copyright owner maintains. The right to reproduce the work is just one of several exclusive rights of the copyright owner. Suppose the off-air recording or photocopy or scan was made several years ago, now comfortably beyond the period of limitations. Can the library or school now look the other way? Is the library or school off the liability hook, so to speak, if it continues to use the tape in instructional or event programming or to make it available for private at-home use by students or patrons? (Liability aside, there are other negative repercussions of such an attitude, i.e., the creation of an environment where disdain for the copyright encourages such behavior among staff and patrons or students in the hope that if enough time passes no legal harm could befall the library or school.) This would not be a wise approach to take, as this proverbial sigh of relief would be rather short-lived if the library or school continued to use the off-air tape, photocopy, or scanned item, as this use might constitute public performance (in library meetings rooms or school classrooms) or public display of the work (on the library or school Web site), or a continued distribution (by placement of the item in the collection or through its circulation). For example, as discussed in Chapter 11, library rights of distribution under Section 109 require that the public distribution be tied to lawfully made copies of the work, and, as discussed in Chapter 12, educator rights of performance and display are likewise linked to lawfully made copies. In distance education environments, a related requirement exists under section 110(2) for audiovisual works, akin to the one governing the use of off-air tape in face-to-face instruction under section 110(1).

Thus, while a claim against the library or school for an unauthorized reproduction may be barred by the copyright statute of limitations under section 507 when three years have passed after the making of the copy, a claim may not be barred based on the exclusive right to make a public distribution, performance, or display of the work or to make a derivative work under section 106, as the statute of limitations would begin to toll anew each time the item is placed on reserve, circulated, played in the classroom or meeting room, or displayed on the Web site. This was the result of the circumstances in *Hotaling v. Church of Latter Day Saints*.[74] Although the statute of limitations for infringement based on unauthorized reproduction had passed, plaintiffs claimed distribution was on-going as the work was available to members of the public in the holdings of the library. "When a public library adds a work to its collection, lists the work in its index or catalog system, and makes the work available to the borrowing or browsing public, it has completed all the steps necessary for distribution to the public."[75]

The dissent argued that distribution (lending) should not be equated with the mere access to materials via a library's in-house collections. However, the dissent remained silent on whether the check-out (actual lending under 17 U.S.C. § 106(3)) of reproduced (unauthorized) materials would be an illegal distribution. Arguably, if this were the case, both the majority and the dissent might have agreed that the circulation of unauthorized or illegal reproductions would be an infringement.

The lessons of the *Hotaling v. Church of Latter Day Saints* decision are several: First, lending of unlawfully made copies by a library or handing out to students unlawfully made copies of a workbook is an illegal distribution. Second, use of a particular copyrighted work may implicate various exclusive rights of the copyright owner in addition to the right of reproduction. Third, there are implications for library or school in-house collections such as photocopied vertical file or media resource material. For the library or school to retain its first sale distribution rights under section 109, or its classroom performance rights under section 110(2), the material must be lawfully made, otherwise those distribution or performance and display rights do not exist and the exclusive right of the copyright owner to distribute and perform the work may be violated. Fourth, possession alone of an unlawful copy by a library (or school) in its library or resource collection may or may not be a public distribution, as the majority and dissent opinions in *Hotaling v. Church of Latter Day Saints* disagree on this point. Finally, this case is law only in the Fourth Circuit, but would likely be cited by plaintiff's counsel if similar facts arose in another jurisdiction.

UNDERSTANDING STATUTORY DAMAGE REDUCTION AND REMISSION

Circumstances exist that can prompt a court (or jury) to reduce the award of statutory damages as well. One provision is a general statutory damage reduction provision. A second statutory damage remission provision is specific to the "nonprofit educational institution, library or archives" and is discussed below. Both provisions, like the willfulness (increase) provision, operate with respect to statutory damages alone; neither can apply to a claim for actual damages (or profits of the infringer). The general damage reduction provision is available to all defendants and is known as an "innocent infringer" provision, though as the discussion below indicates, this is a rather limited option. This term is used to describe several provisions of the copyright law where the lack of knowledge, while not affecting the analysis of initial liability (recall that copyright is a strict liability law) can nonetheless mitigate the damages. As another district court put it:

> In copyright cases, an innocent infringer is likewise liable for infringement, as intent is not an element of a §501(a) violation. It is relevant, however, for the determination of the remedy, since the remedy is equitable in nature. Therefore, as to the issue of liability, defendant's claim that he innocently infringed plaintiffs' rights affords him no solace. His defense lacking merit, the axe must be allowed to fall.[76]

In addition to section 504, discussed here, section 405, discussed below, contains an innocent infringer provision that mitigates both actual and statutory damages. Unlike section 405, section 504 offers mitigation (reduction and remission) of statutory damages alone.

As with the potential for an increase in damages under the willfulness provision, the burden here is on the party that would benefit most, in the instance of general statutory damage reduction, the defendant-infringer. Likewise the burden must be proved to the court as well (or to the jury, as the case may be). Thus the burden of proof is on the defendant ("the infringer sustains the burden of proving") to demonstrate to the court ("and the court finds") that "such infringer was not aware and had no reason to believe that his or her acts constituted an infringement of copyright."[77] If this burden is met, the court may under section 504(c)(2), but is not required to, "reduce the award of statutory damages to a sum of not less than $200." In its discretion there can be a reduction in statutory damages, a court or jury could still award either the minimum[78] or maximum in statutory damages.[79] "It is well-established that district courts have broad discretion in setting the amount of statutory damages within the minimum and maximum amounts prescribed by the Copyright Act."[80] Thus a somewhat "token" damage amount (the minimum $750 under section 504(c)(1)) can be reduced further to $200 where the infringement is found to be innocent. In our workbook example, this further-reduced-to $200 amount would be far less than the actual damages of $4,995 in lost sales or the minimum statutory damage award of $750.

Between Innocence and Willful Infringement

There is a subtle relationship between conduct that is not willful but nonetheless is beyond the realm of innocence. As a recent district court observed: "The Court's independent research has not turned up any case where a defendant who knew of the plaintiff's copyright claim but disagreed with the claim was held an 'innocent' infringer. Such a defendant may not be a willful infringer . . . [citation omitted], but is not an 'innocent' infringer."[81] Recall that direct copyright infringement is assessed under a strict liability standard where ignorance of the law, true to the adage, is no defense.

In a case where the defendant's behavior is not willful it does not mean that the conduct is necessarily innocent: "'Innocent' intent, however, is more than just the absence of willfullness."[82] The one concept is not the converse of the other. "It is plain that 'willfully' infringing and 'innocent intent' are not the converse of one another. Thus, it is possible in the same action for a plaintiff not to be able to prove a defendant's willfullness, and, at the same time, for the defendant to be unable to show that it acted innocently."[83]

However, "ignorance" if reasonable can operate to reduce the bottom-line liability, i.e., damages. As the statute indicates, the burden would be on the defendant library or educational institution or any other innocent infringer to prove that its lack of awareness of copyright infringement was reasonable.[84] Not only does the defendant need to possess that belief but the court (or jury) must be convinced as well. This is an objective standard.[85] In other words a "rationalized" belief by the infringer will not suffice, rather the belief so "analyzed" must be reasonable in the opinion of the trier of fact, i.e., the court or jury.

In the words of one court: "[a]s a practical matter, the problems of proof inherent in a rule that would permit innocent intent as a defense to copyright infringement substantially undermine the protection Congress intended to afford to copyright holders."[86] As with an award enhancement under the willfulness provision, reduction under the innocent infringer provision is likewise the exception to the rule:

> Predictably, the parties approach these limits from opposite poles, the plaintiff typically seeking heightened damages for willful infringement at the same time the defendant proclaims itself to have behaved innocently and, hence, to be entitled to a downward remittitur. In most cases, the court is unmoved by those contrary pleas, and makes an award within the normal range for knowing infringement.[87]

Professor Nimmer characterizes the infringement as "knowing" because it falls within the boundaries of the infringement-continuum, i.e., the defendant's conduct could be said to be neither innocent nor willful.

The Impact of Copyright Notices on Damages

In the era of post–Berne Convention copyright law,[88] use of a copyright notice is permissible,[89] but many copyright owners continue the practice of placing a notice on all published copies that are distributed to the public. With the passage of the 1976 Copyright Act,[90] the effective date of which was January 1, 1978, notice was still required upon the publication of the work. However, its harsh effect was lessened.[91] Under prior law, a work published without proper notice of copyright fell into the public domain upon that publication.[92] "Even though the 1976 Act, as amended by the Berne Act, makes notice voluntary rather than mandatory, it is still encouraged under the amended act because the innocent-infringement defense *is not available where notice has been given.*"[93] However, a "super" innocent infringer provision of sorts was added in 1988 to absolve defendants of both actual and statutory damages, but applicable in very limited situations tied to that time period.

Under section 405(b), a person who "innocently infringes" an authorized copy of a work

> from which the copyright notice has been omitted and which was publicly distributed by the copyright owner before the effective date of the Berne Convention Implementation Act of 1988 [March 1, 1989], incurs *no liability for actual or statutory damages* under section 504 for any infringing acts committed before receiving actual notice that registration for the work has been made under section 408, *if such person proves that he or she was misled by the omission of notice.*[94]

The period between the post 1976 Copyright Act effective date of January 1, 1978, and March 1, 1989, the effective date of the Berne Convention Implementation Act of 1988 is known as the decennial era.[95] Since that time, notice is permissible. Again the burden is on the defendant to prove reliance on the omission. Observe, however, that this relief from both actual and statutory damages applies only to works distributed before the effective date of the Berne Convention Implementation Act of 1988, or March 1, 1989.

Since that time, notice is permissible; thus it is assumed all works are protected whether or not accompanied by notice. In that instance a lack of notice would be one factor in considering a claim of innocent infringement ("not aware and had no reason to believe").[96] However the use of a notice will preclude a claim of innocent infringement:

> If a notice of copyright in the form and position specified in this section appears on the *published* copy or copies to which a defendant in a copyright infringement suit had access, then *no weight shall be given* to such a defendant's interposition of a *defense based on innocent infringement* in mitigation of actual statutory damages, except as provided in the last sentence of section 504(c)(2).[97]

A parallel provision relates a similar evidentiary result on the innocent infringer defense in cases where notice is also present on published phonorecords.[98] In other words, in the post-Berne era, since March 1, 1989, the appearance of a copyright notice on a published work will preclude any defendant from claiming that his or her infringement was innocent under the general remission clause of section 504. However, as discussed below, there remains a specific innocent remission clause in section 504 in which qualifying libraries and educational entities may still seek refuge.

In brief summary:

► Before the effective date of the Berne Convention Implementation Act of 1988, March 1, 1989, works published without proper notice generally fell into the public domain upon that publication.

▶ If a published work bears notice of its copyright, section 401(d) operates as a statutory bar to a claim of innocent infringement under the general statutory damage reduction provision of section 504(c)(2).

▶ However, as discussed below, innocent infringer status is preserved for the specific statutory damage remission provision under section 504(c)(2), this is a significant impact of the clause "except as provided in the last sentence of section 504(c)(2)."

The Impact of Copyright Registration on Damages

So, too, registration is no longer a prerequisite to copyright protection but it is also permissive.[99] However, preservation of the statutory damage election (as well as the ability to recover attorney's fees) requires that registration be made before the infringement of an unpublished work occurs, or if the work is published, registration must occur within three months of the date of publication.[100] Moreover, registration of a work within five years of publication is considered prima facie evidence of its validity in copyright.[101] In any event, registration must occur before an action for copyright infringement is begun.[102] Failure to comply with these requirements can result in sanction against the plaintiff-copyright owner or his or her attorney.[103]

As a result of sections 401(d) and a similar provision for phonorecords in 402(d), "[t]he upshot is that . . . even an innocent defendant generally cannot remit statutory damages . . . unless the subject work was unpublished, bore an invalid notice or was inaccessible to the defendant."[104] In sections 401 and 402, access is not equated with possession alone, rather a marketplace accessibility is contemplated: "Assuming that published copies of the plaintiff's work bore the requisite copyright notice, it is unlikely that such work would be inaccessible to the defendant."[105]

In brief summary:

▶ Registration must occur before an action for infringement may be commenced.

▶ If the work is unpublished, registration must occur before infringement, or in the instance of a published work, within three months of the publication. Otherwise, ability of the plaintiff-copyright owner to obtain statutory damages and costs and attorney's fees is foreclosed.

▶ The lack of notice in a work published before March 1, 1989, operated to preclude the imposition of both actual and statutory damages for infringement committed before receiving actual notice of registration.

▶ Use of notice precludes the reduction of statutory damages, but not its remission if the defendant qualifies for the special innocent infringer provision relating to the "nonprofit educational institution, library or archives," representing a smaller subset of potential defendant-innocent infringers.

Most works obtained for library collections or curricular use are published—and very likely were registered before publication occurred and were then published with notice. In the age of the Internet, when does publication occur? If a material is posted on the Internet, is it considered unpublished, such that a plaintiff-copyright owner would need to register that work (or Web site) before any infringements occurred or be precluded from award of statutory damages or attorney's fees per section 412(1). One district court has addressed this issue and concluded that posting material on the Internet constitutes publication.[106] An argument to the contrary is possible, however.[107] First-year law students come to know well the old adage: "tough cases make bad law" and perhaps this represents one of those cases. Other courts may not be so inclined to reach the same conclusion. Moreover this case may represent the court's reaction to the specific facts of the case in which a Web site went live in June, with infringement after that date and registration occurring sometime later that summer but within the three-month post-publication registration window. Without a finding that the Web site material was published, the plaintiff-copyright owner would have been precluded from an award of statutory damages or attorney's fees under operation of section 412.

Damage Reduction

Assuming a work is unpublished, or otherwise did not trigger the innocent infringer foreclosure provision of sections 401(d) or 402(d) (i.e., improper notice), what are the circumstances in which a defendant could demonstrate that there was no "reason to believe that his or her acts constituted an infringement of copyright"?

Given the increased awareness of copyright law among libraries and educational institutions as well as the statutory structures, discussed in subsequent chapters, that promote that awareness, it may become more and more difficult for a library or educational institution to convince the court ("and the court finds") that ignorance was indeed, as the saying goes, bliss, i.e., that the infringer was neither aware nor had any awareness that his or her acts constituted an infringement and that the lack of awareness was reasonable. So, too, increased awareness of the copyright law within the library and educational institution can work to increase the likelihood that conduct undertaken is in fact undertaken with a reasonable belief in its lawfulness, i.e. that it would not be infringing ("was not aware and had no reason to believe that his or her acts constituted an infringement of copyright") but in spite of that belief was later determined to be so.

Suppose a library purchases a number of used computers or other items such as videotapes, CDs, or DVDs. Various software programs are on the hard drives of the computers but without any documentation of license agreement, manuals, etc., and none of the CDs or DVDs are accompanied by the original cases or cover-jackets. (Assume that the items are all one-of-kind, i.e., unpublished, or that, for some odd reason, if published did not contain proper notice. In other words the section 401(d) proviso does not preclude innocent infringer status. If it is later found that the software and items are infringing, could the library claim innocent infringer status in a lawsuit charging unlawful distribution of copyrighted material?[108] Likely not, since the facts suggest that the library, in light of common practice, should have suspected something. A similar result was reached in a case involving a company that took over another's jukebox distribution business and the machines it "inherited" did not have the proper ASCAP license documentation attached.[109]

On the other hand, a library or educational institution misled by the alteration of the copyright notice (changed date of publication) or by misleading license documentation (clause allowing successive licensee) would arguably have a claim of innocent infringement, although it would not serve as a defense to a claim of infringement in the first instance. "Innocent infringement is relevant to statutory damages, but not to the issue of infringement."[110] This is indicative of the importance of understanding that reliance on a general innocent infringer status here or the specific innocent infringer status discussed below is not a panacea. Lack of knowledge or ignorance goes only to the concept of contributory infringement. However, a reasonable lack of knowledge ("was not aware and had no reason to believe") can, in limited circumstances, result in a reduction in the statutory damages under the "general" reduction provision. A far more likely scenario relevant to the readership of this book is the "special" or specific damage remission provision.

Damage Remission in a Nonprofit Educational Institution, Library, or Archive

There is a second and specific statutory damage alteration provision. This provision, unlike a reduction provision (which includes a discretionary "may" and reduces damages to no less than $200), is mandatory when it applies and reduces statutory damages to zero. It is specific in the sense that it applies to a specific set of defendants in a specific set of circumstances. After the sentence referencing general discretionary statutory damage reduction, Section 504(c)(2) continues:

> The Court *shall remit* statutory damages in any case where an infringer believed and had reasonable grounds for believing that his or her use of the copyrighted work was a fair use under section 107, if the infringer was: (i) an employee or agent of a nonprofit educational institution, library, or archives acting within the scope of his or her employment who, or such institution, library, or archives itself, which infringed by reproducing the work in copies or phonorecords.[111]

Several considerations are of importance here. The most significant advantage of the specific statutory damage remission provision is that it can still operate in cases where the work is published with proper notice. Recall that under Section

401 use of proper notice precludes a claim of innocent infringement, yet the statute preserves precisely that defense for "an employee or agent of a nonprofit educational institution, library, or archives acting within the scope of his or her employment who, or such institution, library, or archives itself," as this provision is found in the last sentence of section 504(c)(2):

> If a notice of copyright in the form and position specified in this section appears on the published copy or copies to which a defendant in a copyright infringement suit had access, then no weight shall be given to such a defendant's interposition of a defense based on innocent infringement in mitigation of actual statutory damages, *exempt as provided in the last sentence of section 504(c)(2).*[112]

A similar proviso exists for published phonorecords.[113] In sequence then, observe that the willfulness provision is found in the first sentence of Section 504(c)(2). The general statutory damage reduction provision discussed above is found in the subsection's second sentence, but the specific statutory damage remission provision is found in the last sentence of Section 504(c)(2)! Thus the "specific employee or agent of a nonprofit educational institution, library, or archives acting within the scope of his or her employment who, or such institution, library, or archives itself" can avail itself of damage remission, even in those instances that would otherwise fail to qualify for the general innocent infringement status and damage reduction. This is an important statutory "gift" Congress has given to the nonprofit education, library, and archive community. Understanding how it can benefit those in the school, library, or archive is part of a sound risk-management program.

Second, the provision applies either to a person or an institution: "an employee or agent of a nonprofit educational institution, library, or archives acting within the scope of his or her employment who, *or* such institution, library, or archives itself." An institution is a practical and legal fiction, i.e., an institution does not stand at the photocopier, press "start," and reproduce a copyrighted workbook. Rather its liability would arise through secondary liability, contributory or vicarious, e.g., through the acts of an employee, and perhaps at the direction of a supervisor. This means that Section 504 applies to both direct (employee) and secondary (institutional) liability. However, the statutory damages subject to remission employee-direct or the institutional-indirect or secondary liability must be the result of infringement that is work related, not just committed by an employee, done by "an employee or agent . . . acting within the scope of his or her employment." Thus, if a public library employee used the city-employer's photocopying equipment to make infringing copies of sheet music for distribution to her church choir, it would not be subject to specific statutory damage remission under section 504(c)(2). However, it could still qualify for general innocent infringer statutory damage reduction under the previous sentence of the same subsection, subject of course to the unlikely qualification of that subsection. In this example, published religious sheet music would likely have a notice of copyright on it and so under the statutory bar of section 401(d) would be precluded from making the assertion. Yet, as section 401(d) states, if the photocopies were made for work-related purposes, even if the music contains notice of copyright, the statutory damage remission provision still operates per the "except as provided in the last sentence of section 504(c)(2)" proviso.

A third element is significant. An obvious difference between the general statutory damage reduction and the specific statutory damage remission targeting "an employee or agent of a nonprofit educational institution, library, or archives acting within the scope of his or her employment who, or such institution, library, or archives itself" is that the latter is more limited, applying only to infringement resulting from reproduction that exceeds fair use ("his or her use of the copyrighted work was a fair use under section 107 . . . which infringed by reproducing the work in copies or phonorecords"). As the section 504(c)(2) statutory damage remission is limited to reproductions under fair use alone, it does not apply to other "reproduction" provisions, such as a belief that a reproduction is not infringing under Section 108, discussed in Chapter 12, or Section 112, ephemeral recordings, often used in distance education environments. (Of course fair use can apply in any reproducing scenario, but the damage remission language does require the recipient to allege that connection when claiming remission.)

So, too, Section 504(c)(2) offers the possibility of statutory damage remission only in those situations where infringements occurred by (fair use) reproduction, not to infringements of any of the other exclusive rights of the copyright owner, under fair use or otherwise, such as derivative works (section 107, making a score of a complex piece of music easier to play for a student orchestra), performance (section 110, showing a DVD as a reward to a class for a productive semester as part of a library travel night), or distribution (section 109, placing the copies of the infringing workbooks in the circulating collection or on reserve for check-out and use by students).

Thus failing to qualify for the specific damage remission would still offer the "employee or agent of a nonprofit educational institution, library, or archives acting within the scope of his or her employment who, or such institution, library, or archives itself" the opportunity to qualify for the more widely applicable though less rewarding general damage reduction, but the court need not remit in that circumstance ("may reduce the award of statutory damages"), and even if the court does reduce the damage amount it may not remit, the amount entirely, there must be at least a token $200 per work ("may reduce . . . to a sum of not less that $200"). Moreover, as discussed above, when notice appears on the work, section 401(d) and section 402(d) operate as a statutory bar to general damage reduction under the previous proviso of section 504(c)(2). This stipulation presents another significant advantage to the damage remission provision. When applicable, it commands the court ("shall remit") to reduce the statutory damage award to zero.

Third, consider the shift in evidence that would be necessary in the specific statutory damage remission provision as opposed to the general damage reduction provision. In the latter, general damage reduction provision, the existence of a *negative* must be proved: the defendant must prove that he or she was "not aware and had no reason to believe that his or her acts constituted an infringement of copyright." It could further be argued that even an after-the-act "awareness" would negate the necessary lack of awareness, thus general damage reduction would not be available. The specific damage remission provision requires that a person or institution "*believed* and had reasonable grounds for believing that his or her use of the copyrighted work was a fair use under section 107." This is a *positive* state of mind, and further, like the general damage reduction provision ("such infringer was not aware and had no reason to believe that his or her acts constituted an infringement of copyright"), that state of mind is set in the past as well.

The Burden of Proof in Statutory Damage Remission

While the specific statutory damage remission provision does not contain any "in a case where the infringer sustains the burden of proving, and the court finds" language as exists in the previous general statutory reduction provision, it is logical to conclude that at least some measure of evidence would need be made to the trier of fact (i.e., the jury) as to the reasonableness of this belief as well. Although the statute is silent as to with whom that burden should rest, it seems logical to propose that it is incumbent on the defendant to furnish evidence ("employee or agent of a nonprofit educational institution, library, or archives . . . or such institution, library, or archives"). However, the Conference Report states, "the burden of proof with respect to the defendant's good faith *should rest on the plaintiff.*"[114] This evidentiary design is in contrast to the burden placed on the defendant in circumstances of general discretionary damage reduction.[115] In spite of this language it would seem rather illogical for a plaintiff to prove the reasonableness of a damage remission "defense." (Though one could conceive of a rule whereby the plaintiff would be required to prove the absence of it!) However, the House Report may be suggesting that once the mere assertion of fair use reproduction ("believed") is made by the employee or institution, the burden shifts to the plaintiff-copyright owner to make an evidentiary showing that there were no reasonable grounds for that belief. Thus, the specific statutory damage remission may operate as a rebuttable presumption.[116] This is indeed a profound statutory expression of the deference of Congress toward the integrity of nonprofit educational, library, and archive institutions, a presumption (assuming that some initial showing is made of reasonableness) that reproduction of copyrighted material conforms to the requirements of the copyright law.

The defendant here need possess and demonstrate (offer some evidence) of a state of mind in the past, i.e., during the act of alleged infringement: "*believed and had reasonable grounds for believing* that his or her use of the copyrighted work was a fair use under section 107 . . . which *infringed* by reproducing the work in copies or phonorecords." In the alternative under the House Report formulation, the plaintiff needs to disprove this existence. Still, the claim must be founded upon a reasonable grounds for believing the use was fair, merely having that belief alone will not help either, though it is a prerequisite, i.e., the defendant must have believed the use was fair and acted upon it, not just come to that reasonable belief now that he or she has been sued. Further, the belief must be a reasonable one or, to use the word of the legislative history, it must be an "honest" belief.[117] Though courts have never interpreted this section, it would likely be an objective standard, as with the willfulness increase in damages or innocent reduction in damages under earlier section 504(c)(2) provisions, not a subjective one, as most of those who infringe can rationalize (an unreasonable belief) their behavior as fair.

The most important difference between the general statutory damage reduction provision and the "specific employee or agent of a nonprofit educational institution, library, or archives acting within the scope of his or her employment who, or such institution, library, or archives itself" statutory damage remission provisions is that in the latter instance there need only be a "reasonable belie[f] and reasonable grounds for believing that his or her use of a copyrighted work was a fair use under section 107" versus proof that the "infringer was not aware and had no reason to believe that his or her acts constituted an infringement of copyright." It is one thing to prove a belief that the reproduction was indeed fair, quite another to demonstrate to the court that one did not realize the work was protected by copyright and thus was "not aware and had no reason to believe that his or her acts constituted an infringement of copyright" when in fact it appeared just like every other work (book, videocassette, CD) obtained by the educational, library, or archive institution, save for its appearance sans notice. The specific statutory damage remission provision makes inquiry into the defendant's positive state of mind, while the general statutory damage reduction provision requires the defendant to prove the absence of certain circumstances ("not aware and had no reason to believe"). This is a negative. Moreover, the burden of the general statutory damage reduction is on the defendant (to show the absence of a condition), while the burden in an instance of specific statutory damage remission is on the plaintiff (to challenge the existence of a condition), or at least if the legislative history is determinative, once infringement is asserted by the defendant it must be disproved by the plaintiff.

Perhaps it is a judgment call here, but the author would forward that in law as in life, it is much easier to prove the existence of a fact (a positive) than to prove the absence of a fact (a negative). However, the positive proof would consist of two elements. A defendant would need show not only that the belief that a "fair use" reproduction was reasonable ("had reasonable grounds for believing"), but that the defendant acted on that belief as well ("believed"). Again the trier of fact, the judge or jury, would decide the reasonableness of that belief. Thus a library that could later articulate a fair use defense for a particular reproduction (but that at the time of the alleged infringement had no such belief) would not be able to trigger the requisite knowledge. In other words, a library that did not believe its use (reproduction) of copyrighted material was fair but later found, after the commencement of legal proceedings, that its actions had reasonable defense in the law (fair use) could not avail itself of the remission provision. This position is forwarded because while there are "reasonable grounds" for believing its use fair, that belief was not extant at the time the use was actually made. This is the evidentiary impact of the first element in the phrase "*believed* and had reasonable grounds for believing."

Once the conduct qualifies for remission, however, the court must remit all statutory damages; the court does not have the discretion to do so. This is a mandatory damage remission, not reduction. If the nonprofit educational institution, library, or archives qualifies, the court has no choice but to eliminate from consideration the imposition of the variable and deadly statutory damages and is limited to awarding actual damages alone. In the hypothetical workbook scenario, remitting statutory damages, reducing damages to zero, would be substantially less than potential statutory damages that might reach $30,000 per infringed work, or in our four-part workbook scenario, $120,000, and even less than the actual damages of $4,995.

In summary, then:

▶ Statutory damage remission applies even when the work contains proper notice of copyright per the "except as provided in the last sentence of section 504(c)(2)" proviso of section 401(d) or 402(d), relating to phonorecords.

▶ The section 504(c)(2) statutory damage remission is limited to reproductions under fair use (section 107). It does not apply to other "reproduction" provisions such as a belief that a reproduction is not infringing under section 108 or section 112, ephemeral recordings, often used in distance education environments, or to other uses of copyrighted material in excess of fair use that impinge on some other exclusive right of the copyright owner, such as public performance, display, distribution, or the right to make derivative works.

▶ According to the 1976 House Conference Report "the burden of proof with respect to the defendant's good faith should rest on the plaintiff"[118] in instances of the mandatory statutory damage remission. This is in contrast to the burden placed on the defendant in circumstances of general discretionary damage reduction.

▶ Once it is determined that the conduct qualifies for remission, however, the court must remit all statutory damages; the court does not have the discretion to do so.

The Monetary Impact of Remission

What is the impact of jury trials to determine statutory damages in copyright law? "The *Feltner* decision . . . perhaps weakens to a certain extent the potency of statutory damages in the process. If jury trials had been disallowed by the Feltner case, the swiftness of the remedy provided by these damages would still exist. Now, because of the cumbersome nature of jury trials, the threat of statutory damages may be counted by a defendant's threat to make the plaintiff go through the expensive process of picking a jury and convincing it (through all of the risk and uncertainty inherent in this procedure) of his or her right to prevail."[119] To the chagrin of defendants all is not lost for plaintiffs. Prevailing party plaintiffs can still claim attorneys' fees under section 504. In fact the imposition of such fees can represent more severe 'punishment' against a defendant than would the award of damages, statutory or otherwise. Recall that deterrence is a factor for a court to consider in making an award of attorneys' fees.[120] Moreover, the standard of review of an award of attorney's fees once granted by the district court is based upon the highest standard of review, abuse of discretion, thus it is highly deferential to the district court.[121]

As a result, in a case in which statutory damages are remitted to zero or reduced to the minimum $200 the defendant (e.g., librarian, teacher, or institution) could still be subject to an award of attorney's fees under section 505. Of course attorney's fees are always discretionary, but even in a jury trial are nonetheless awarded by the court. Moreover awards of attorney's fees are an equitable consideration. Perhaps in a jury trial where complete remission occurs, the judge believes that the equities of the situation (the defendant convinced the jury but the judge was less so convinced) dictate that an award of attorney's fees should still be awarded to the plaintiff. The statute does not prohibit this result. There is nothing in the language of section 505 authorizing the imposition of attorney's fees but linking the award to the section 504 damage remission provisions, i.e., predicating one on the imposition of the other or precluding the award in the absence of the other. In contrast, and as discussed in Part III, those qualifying for the safe harbor of section 512 are protected from the imposition of "monetary relief," and section 512(k)(2) specifically includes "damages, costs, attorney's fees and any other form of monetary payment."[122] The point here is that if Congress desired to foreclose the award of attorney's fees in cases where damages are remitted to zero, it could have amended section 505 governing costs and attorney's fees in 1998 when it enacted section 512 and its remission provision, a provision that specifically addressed all monetary awards including costs and attorney's fees.

CONSIDERING STATE IMMUNITY IN COPYRIGHT LAW

Section 501 indicates that "anyone" who violates one of the exclusive rights of the copyright identified in Section 106 can be sued for copyright infringement. Section 501 continues to clarify that fact:

> As used in this subsection, the term "anyone" includes any State, any instrumentality of a State, and any officer or employee of a State or instrumentality of a State acting in his or her official capacity. Any State, and any such instrumentality, officer, or employee, shall be subject to the provisions of this title in the same manner and to the same extent as any nongovernmental entity.[123]

Moreover, section 511, added by the Copyright Remedy Clarification Act of 1990,[124] states that

> any State, any instrumentality of a State, and any officer or employee of a State or instrumentality of a State acting in his or her official capacity, shall not be immune, under the Eleventh Amendment of the Constitution of the United States or under any other doctrine of sovereign immunity, from suit in Federal court by any person, including any governmental or nongovernmental entity, for a violation of any of the exclusive rights of a copyright owner provided by section 106 through 121, for importing copies or phonorecords in violation of 602, or for any other violation under this title.[125]

In spite of the clarity of these provisions, the law in this area is under some cloud as a result of recent case developments. First, the United States Supreme Court ruled in *Seminole Tribe of Florida v. Florida*,[126] that Congress does not have the authority under the Indian Commerce clause to abrogate a state's sovereign immunity under the Eleventh Amendment. Next, in *Florida Prepaid Postsecondary Education Expense Board v. College Savings Bank*[127] and *College Savings Bank v. Florida Prepaid Postsecondary Education Expense Board*[128] the United States Supreme Court ruled that states cannot be sued in federal court for patent or trademark infringement, as Congress overstepped its bounds by passing legislation making states subject to such lawsuits. While "[t]he Copyright Remedy Clarification Act and § 511 of the 1976 Act were not ruled unconstitutional in the *Seminole Tribe* case, yet the decision has created questions regarding state immunity under § 511 in one subsequent federal circuit."[129]

The Fifth Circuit expanded the concept to include claims of copyright infringement.[130] However, a strong dissent by Justice Wisdom concluded that Congress does indeed have the authority under section 5 of the Fourteenth Amendment to abrogate state sovereign immunity in copyright infringement cases. This position would be consistent with opinion in Congress and is based on the view that if states (i.e., and their systemwide library or educational institutions) can benefit from the intellectual property laws such as copyright, and if such institutions are developing and exploiting such assets through new technology transfer initiatives, such institutions should also respect the intellectual property rights of others and be subject to intellectual property laws when they deviate from that respect.

Of course an institution can waive its right to sovereign immunity. In a recent dispute involving patent dispute between two faculty members and the University of New Mexico, the Eleventh Circuit concluded that because the institution initiated the litigation against the faculty members, it was not immune to counterclaims from the faculty; this evidenced the institution's desire to voluntarily waive its right to sovereign immunity.[131] Such waiver could be contained within a license agreement as well. In further developments, a federal district has also held that Eleventh Amendment immunity applies to misappropriation claims.[132]

Even if immunity does exist, the immunity would in theory apply to a state law library, state archive or historical society, state university library, or other state actor and so on, but may not apply to municipalities, counties, and other political subdivisions, such as a public school district, which do not partake in a state's Eleventh Amendment immunity.[133] Thus a local public library or county library system or K–12 school district remains liable for copyright infringement. Some states may designate such political subdivisions as instrumentalities of the state, and so preserve immunity.[134] Court may nonetheless consider the circumstances and conclude that the local school district is not an instrumentality of the state.[135] For primary and secondary schools and their libraries and for public libraries a check should be made of state law to determine whether state immunity encompasses the institution. Second, all contracts, those that are new and those already in force, should be reviewed to determine the existence of clauses waiving such immunity, and depending on the results, insurance policies should be reviewed to determine the appropriate level of coverage.[136]

The Illusion of State Immunity: Practical and Professional Realities

The developing precedent or other condition of immunity does not mean that state libraries or educational entities should infringe copyright with reckless abandon, as Senator Leahy and others in Congress have vowed to close the gap created by the *College Savings Bank* cases.[137] Even without this legislation,[138] states may still find themselves liable as immunity can always be waived, by the terms of a license agreement, for example.[139] In this circumstance the waiver would apply to the licensed content, such as the publications available in an online database.

Notwithstanding these concerns, even in the jurisdiction of the Fifth Circuit, pedagogical responsibilities (i.e., the professional-ethical implications of "teaching" copyright infringement), by example, may dictate that a compliant course of conduct by the public library or educational entity and its library is the more prudent course of action. What would be a rational risk-management response? Should state institutions of higher education ignore copyright with impunity? That would be an unwise course of action. First and most obvious, the Fifth Circuit decision is not the law of land; it is binding precedent only in the states of Texas, Louisiana, and Mississippi. Though it represents persuasive precedent in other jurisdictions, it might nonetheless be indicative of the trend lower courts are taking.

A more important reason is that

> if the immunity applies, it is not complete. In particular, the law is clear that full immunity does not extend to employees sued in their individual capacities for money damages. . . . Moreover, the immunity of the individuals and the institution is limited. It may bar claims for dollar damages, but not preclude equitable remedies, such as declaratory judgments or injunctions.[140]

As a result, the immunity, even if it applies, does not mean the library or educational institution is free from the threat of litigation, as a suit for injunctive relief may still be forwarded. So, too, it is unclear that in such litigation whether the immunity forecloses the award of costs and attorney's fees under section 505. If it does not, the bottom-line financial outlay by the institution can still be great, i.e., an award of costs and attorney's fees as well as the "costs" of compliance with the injunctive relief that is ordered. Moreover, "Eleventh Amendment immunity protection does not extend to suits against public officials as individuals."[141]

While perpetuating an environment of copyright infringement may ultimately result in no loss of monetary damages by the institution, it does disservice to employees by leaving a false impression of immunity and yet a reality, if recent litigation by the RIAA is any indication,[142] that the employee is still liable and likely to be sued for infringement. In fact it could be argued that, immunity notwithstanding, the section 512 mechanisms of damage reduction, whereby the service provider is released from all monetary awards, naturally forces the plaintiff-copyright owner to pursue individual claims for monetary relief against the remaining defendants who are not damage-proof, i.e., the individual employees. The specter of possible Eleventh Amendment institutional immunity would only appear to promote that litigation strategy.

Moreover, the institution would still have the legal cost and practical cost of defending nonmonetary claims for injunctive relief, such as for removal of infringing content on its computing facilities. The practical cost could be greater, as current and prospective employees may be less willing to work in such a Russian-roulette, noncompliant environment. Second, the negative publicity may tarnish the good name and reputation of the institution (nothing spends good will faster than a high-profile court case). More immediate, content providers might be reluctant to sell or license copyrighted material (e.g., textbooks, databases, or software) if aware of these noncompliant institutional attitudes. Third, ignoring copyright within the institution can have a progressive and debilitating effect. For example, should state immunity be foreclosed by legislative remedy, the task of restoring the "copyright law and order" within the institution will be made all the more difficult.

So, too, an institution adopting a lax attitude with respect to copyright, may find it all the more difficult to enforce its other legal obligations. For example, employees may be confused as to why there exists little concern for the legal standards of copyright or trademark, compared to such other legal standards as disability or discrimination. As result, such inconsistency may also undermine the confidence employees have in the overall administration of the campus.

Finally, most license agreements contain terms and conditions that restrict the use of copyrighted content to that which conforms to the boundaries of copyright law. Some terms and conditions may limit use of content within the boundaries of the copyright as well, e.g., eliminating some interlibrary loan rights granted by section 108. The practical result is that the institution as part of its obligations under the terms and conditions of the license agreement would also need to comply with the copyright law, at least as far as use of the licensed content is concerned. The remedy in law for such violations of the license would be for breach of contract, a claim not foreclosed by the supposed Eleventh Amendment immunity: "An improper use of the work may be copyright infringement, but it may also be a breach of contract, perhaps an unfair trade practice, or some other legal violation."[143] Thus, Eleventh Amendment immunity would not foreclose litigation that results from infringement of a work that is the subject of a license agreement as such an "infringement" would be a claim based on contract law, not copyright law.

Achieving copyright compliance in spite of the potential for immunity is problematic for a reason related to the theme of this monograph. Waiting to see if the law changes before complying makes reversing bad copyright habits of employees even more difficult. Moreover, it is also inconsistent with creating the climate of compliance very much of concern to Congress, expressed in the legislative structure and history of the DMCA discussed in Part III, TEACH discussed in Chapter 12, and recent P2P hearings and proposed legislation discussed thus far. Finally the immunity is not complete and may lead to more serious litigation issues:

> Any such decision would be a serious mistake. It would first be a gross misreading of [*sic*] the law. If for no other reason, faculty librarians, and others who engage in uncontrolled copying could be charged with "willful infringement." Willful infringement can be grounds for criminal prosecution [to which the immunity would not apply].[144]

Furthermore, such wanton behavior, short of constituting criminal conduct or triggering the statutory damage enhancement for willfulness, would in the least foreclose any statutory damage remission, for individual actors, who as noted above remain liable.

The discussion thus far is dominated by talk of liability. This focus was deliberate: to impress upon the reader the seriousness of the law and, more important, the seriousness of the recent conviction of the copyright owners to pursue legal satisfaction. Now for some additional good news! Two sections of the copyright law immunize the qualifying educational entity or its related organ, the library. These two provisions are the focus of the next chapter. In addition, additional damage reduction or remission provisions exist within two significant provisions of the DMCA and are the focus of Part III.

REAL-WORLD EXAMPLES

▶ **Real-World Example I**

Situation: A midsized school district performs *Bat Boy: The Musical* without the permission of Dramatists Play Service, the holder of the rights to this copyrighted work. This public performance is unauthorized. The performance rights would have cost $1,200. The school also makes a videotape of the performance to sell as a fund-raiser. Sales of the tape, a distribution of an unauthorized derivative work, total $2,500. Dramatists Play Service typically licenses nonexclusive derivative rights for an additional $800.

Legal Analysis: Actual damages would be as follows: Attributable to the actual infringement, the public performance, the copyright owner suffers lost "sales" of $1,200 resulting from the decreased licensing revenue (actual damages). Second, there is a loss of another $800 in licensing fees and $2,500 sales (profits) earned from the sales of the tapes. The copyright owner cannot recover both the $800 and $2,500 amounts, but rather only his lost profits and "any profits of the infringer that are attributable to the infringement and are not taken into account in computing the actual damages." This would be his lost $800 in additional fees and the school's additional "any profits . . . not taken in account" of $1,700. Furthermore, in calculating the infringer's profits, the "infringer [school district] is required to prove his or her [or its] deductible expense." The total actual damages would be $1,200 + $800 + $1,700 = $3,700.

▶ **Real-World Example II**

Situation: The facts are the same as Real-World Example I, except the copyright owner, in lieu of actual damages, elects to have statutory damages awarded and requests a jury trial.

Legal Analysis: Statutory damages are set at the discretion of the trier of fact, which could be the judge or could be the jury (the choice is the plaintiff's to make). Here the plaintiff has elected for a jury trial, so it will be up to the jury to set damages per infringing within the range allowed by statute, i.e., from $750 to $30,000. Suppose the jury decides to award statutory damages of $20,000 per work. Even though the exclusive rights to make a public performance and derivative work were violated, statutory damages are awarded "for all infringements involved in the action, with respect to any one work." The damages would not be $40,000, i.e., $20,000 per infringement (for the performance and the derivative recording), but for each work infringed. Since both infringements relate to the same work, the amount remains $20,000. (Arguably the right to make a public distribution of that derivative work is an infringement of a second work!) However, at the request of the plaintiff, judges may also award costs and attorney's fees under the statute as well, often as a punitive measure. Suppose here, too, the judge enters an additional award of costs and attorney's fees in the amount of $12,500 as requested by the copyright owner against the school. The school would owe a total of $32,500 in damages, costs, and attorney's fees. The lesson is that statutory damages, costs, and fees are often more devastating for the copyright defendant. Here note the $32,500 decision as opposed to the $3,700 in actual damages awarded to the plaintiffs in Real-World Example I.

▶ **Real-World Example III**

Situation: A large urban public library with a significant archive publishes on its Web site (constituting both a reproduction as well as a display) an anthology of 60 letters from its collection. The publication is later found to be infringing in a case where the copyright owner of the letters, in this case the descendents of the original author, elects statutory damages. At trial the jury sets statutory damages at $2,000 for "any one work," i.e., for each letter reproduced.

Legal Analysis: Statutory damages would total $120,000 (60 × $2,000 = $120,000). The library may be able to convince the trier of fact (judge or jury) that its infringement was innocent, i.e., that it "was not aware and had no reason to believe that" the publication of the collected letters was an infringement. If successful, the court or jury may reduce the statutory damages to as little as $200.00 per work, i.e., for each letter so published, or $12,000 (60 × $200 = $12,000). The second mandatory remission provision of section 504(c)(2) will not bar imposition of damages as remedy for the infringing display as that remission provision operates with respect to "reproductions" alone and would not extend to displays that are infringing.

▶ **Real-World Example IV**

Situation: Consider the same situation as Real-World Example III except that the plaintiff-copyright owner previously published the letters with proper notice and the publication involves an in-house paper reproduction of various sets of the anthology. The defendant is a special library within a corporation with a significant archive collection as well.

Legal Analysis: While the infringing reproduction is not barred by the section 510(c)(2) "by reproducing the work in copies" proviso, by operation of the statutory bar in section 401(d), the corporate archive is precluded from claiming innocent infringer status for purposes of statutory damage reduction.

▶ Real-World Example V

Situation: Consider the same situation as Real-World Example IV, except that plaintiff-copyright owner previously published the letters with proper notice and the defendant is once again a large urban public library with a significant archive.

Legal Analysis: By operation of section 401(d), the large urban public library qualifies for the "except as provided in the last sentence of section 504(c)(2)" proviso and is not precluded from claiming innocent infringer status for purposes of damage mitigation. As a result, if the mitigation is successful, the court (or jury) must remit all statutory damages under the section 504(c)(2) statutory damage remission proviso.

▶ Real-World Example VI

Situation: A school district was involved in disputes with copyright owners over repeated use of off-air recordings in the library building. In the past, the district has settled its differences and agreed to compensate the copyright owners after destroying the alleged infringing recordings. This year a new set of approximately 100 off-air recordings was made of copyrighted audiovisual works and used in various classrooms throughout the school year. The copyright owners have filed a lawsuit and requested a bench trial and have opted for imposition of statutory damages; at the damage phase of the trial the plaintiffs requested that additional damages be imposed for the willful violation of the copyright law.

Legal Analysis: Willfulness in copyright can be established where the defendant "had knowledge that its conduct represented infringement or perhaps recklessly disregarded the possibility." As a result of the previous disputes, the school district administrators and employees should realize the impropriety of continuing its off-air recording practices and uses. The facts suggest a reckless disregard for the copyright law and as a result the court in its discretion may increase the statutory damages to a sum of not more that $150,000. The court sets the enhanced statutory damages award for willfulness at $50,000 per work or $500,000 ($100 \times \$50,000 = \$500,000$). Without the willfulness penalty the statutory damages might have been as low as $75,000 ($100 \times \$750 = \$75,000$) or as high as $300,0000 ($100 \times \$30,000 = \$300,000$). Damages under the willfulness enhancement might have been as high as $1,500,000 ($10 \times \$150,000 = \$1,500,000$).

KEY POINTS FOR YOUR INSTITUTION'S POLICY AND PRACTICE

▶ Damages in a copyright infringement action can consist of monetary remedies (i.e., damages and court costs and attorney's fees) and nonmonetary remedies (such as preliminary and permanent injunctive relief and orders for impoundment and destruction of infringing copies). See pp. 71–75.

▶ Damages can consist of actual damages including the profits derived from the infringement and statutory damages. The plaintiff-copyright owner elects either actual or statutory damages. See pp. 72–73.

▶ The amount of statutory damages is determined by the judge or jury and can range from a minimum of $750 to a maximum of $30,000 for each work infringed, but not per infringement. If the plaintiff-copyright owner proves willful infringement, the court may increase the award of statutory damages to $150,000 for each work infringed. See pp. 72–75.

▶ The statute of limitations for a copyright infringement claim is three years, five years for criminal proceedings. See pp. 80–81.

▶ Developing precedent suggests that state actors, such as a university system, are immune from monetary damages awards for violations of the copyright law unless that state voluntarily waives its right to immunity. The immunity does not apply to injunctive relief, nor would it apply to an action arising in contract (i.e., license agreement) nor would it preclude a court from awarding costs and attorney's fees if the plaintiff prevails. Most important the immunity does not extend to employees of the state institution. See pp. 94–98.

▶ The trier of fact (court or jury) may reduce the statutory damages award to a minimum of $200 if the defendant can prove that he or she was "not aware and had no reason to believe that his or her act constituted an infringement of copyright." This is so-called "innocent infringer" status. However, notice on a published work forecloses a defense of innocent infringement for most defendants. See pp. 81–87.

▶ The right of a nonprofit educational institution, library, or archives to claim innocent infringer status under section 504(c)(2) ("believed and had reasonable grounds for believing") is preserved even if the work was published with proper notice. The special innocent infringer status is available to the employee as direct infringer and the institution as secondary infringer. See pp. 87–90.

▶ As a result of the innocent infringer status for the nonprofit educational institution, library, or archives statutory, monetary damages are remitted. The remission of damages is mandatory. However, remission applies only to instances of reproduction thought to be a fair use under section 107, not to all infringing conduct. See pp. 87–93.

ENDNOTES

[1] 17 U.S.C. § 502(a) ("Any court having jurisdiction of a civil action arising under this title may . . . grant temporary and final injunctions on such terms as it may deem reasonable to prevent or restrain infringement of a copyright.").

[2] 17 U.S.C. § 502(b) (The injunction "shall be operative throughout the United States, and shall be enforceable, by proceedings in contempt or otherwise, by any Untied States court having jurisdiction of that person").

[3] 17 U.S.C § 512(j).

[4] 17 U.S.C. § 503(b).

[5] *Encyclopedia Britannica Educational Corp. v. Crooks*, 447 F. Supp. 243, 245 (W.D.N.Y. 1978) ("The plaintiffs demand that the defendants be enjoined from videotaping copyrighted films and they seek both actual and statutory damages for past infringement. They also request an award of costs and fees, and the surrender or destruction of all infringing copies of the films. At the time of filing the complaint, the plaintiffs moved for a temporary restraining order to prevent the destruction of the existing videotapes and records pertaining to the tapes in BOCES' possession pending a final decision in the case, and also to obtain accelerated discovery privileges.").

[6] See, *Hotaling v. Church of Latter Day Saints*, 118 F.3d 199 (4th Cir. 1997) ("In July, 1991, Donna Hotaling learned that the Church was making copies and placing them in its branch libraries. She contacted the Church and demanded that it stop this activity. After receiving her complaint, the Church recalled and destroyed many of the copies that it had made. According to the affidavits submitted by the Church, it did not make any copies after 1991, and there is no evidence to contradict that assertion." Id. at 201-202.).

[7] See, *Hart v. Sampley*, 24 U.S.P.Q.2d 1223, 1992 WL 336496, at *2 (D.D.C. 1992) (court ordered destruction of t-shirts and photographs containing images of the copyrighted "Three Serviceman Statue" of the Vietnam War Veterans).

[8] 17 U.S.C. § 504(a) ("an infringer of copyright is liable for either (1) the copyright owner's actual damages and any additional profits of the infringer, as provided by subsection (b); or (2) statutory damages, as provided by subsection (c).").

[9] 17 U.S.C. § 504(c)(1).

[10] 17 U.S.C. § 504(c)(1).

[11] JOHN W. HAZARD, JR., COPYRIGHT LAW IN BUSINESS AND PRACTICE § 5:21, at 5-19 (2004).

[12] Pub. L. No. 106-160, 113 Stat. 1774 (1999) (Digital Theft Deterrence and Copyright Damages Improvement Act of 1999).

[13] 145 Cong. Rec. H12884 (daily edition November 18, 1999) (Comments of Representative Berman) ("It makes significant improvements in the ability of the Copyright Act to deter copyright infringement by amending it to increase the statutory penalties for infringement" Comments of Representative Coble.).

[14] *Lowry's Reports, Inc. v. Legg Mason, Inc.*, 302 F. Supp. 2d 455, 459 (D. Md. 2004), citing *F.W. Woolworth Co. v. Contemporary Arts*, 344 U.S. 228, 233 (1952) ("Even for uninjurious and unprofitable invasions of copyright the court may, if it deems just, impose a liability within statutory limits to sanction and vindicate the statutory policy").

[15] *UMG Recordings v. MP3.com, Inc.*, 92 F. Supp. 2d 349 (S.D.N.Y. 2000).

16 *UMG Recordings, Inc. v. MP3.com, Inc.*, 2000 WL 1262568, at *6 (S.D.N.Y. 2000) ("Weighing not only the foregoing factors but all the other relevant factors put before the Court, the Court concludes, and hereby determines, that the appropriate measure of damages is $25,000 per CD. If defendant is right that there are no more than 4,700 CDs for which plaintiffs qualify for statutory damages, the total award will be approximately $118,000,000; but, of course, it could be considerably more or less depending on the number of qualifying CDs determined at the final phase of the trial scheduled for November of this year."). Judgment was later entered in the amount of $53,400,000; the amount included costs and attorney's fees.

17 17 U.S.C. § 504(b).

18 BLACK'S LAW DICTIONARY (8th ed. 2004), defines the *fruit-of-the-poisonous-tree doctrine* as "[t]he rule that evidence derived from an illegal search, arrest, or interrogation is inadmissible because the evidence (the 'fruit') was tainted by the illegality (the 'poisonous tree')." Id. at 693.

19 17 U.S.C. § 504(b) (emphasis added).

20 17 U.S.C. § 504(c)(1) ("the copyright owner may elect, at any time before final judgment is rendered, to recover, instead of actual damages and profits, an award of statutory damages for all infringements involved in the action with respect to any one work.").

21 *Feltner v. Columbia Pictures Television, Inc.*, 523 U.S. 340, 355 (1998) (The "Seventh Amendment provides a right to a jury trial on all issues pertinent to an award of statutory damages under § 504(a) of the Copyright Act, including the amount itself.").

22 *Feltner v. Columbia Pictures Television, Inc.*, 523 U.S. 340, 347, at n. 5 (1998).

23 *Alexander v. Chesapeake, Potomac, and Tidewater Books, Inc.*, 60 F. Supp. 2d 544, 546 (E.D. Va. 1999) ("Alexander did not elect statutory damages before the case was submitted to the jury. Therefore, only actual damages are available to Alexander, which he now requests.").

24 NIMMER ON COPYRIGHT § 14.04[A] (2004). Though Nimmer also comments: "One expedient might be to instruct the jury on both statutory and actual damages, and allow plaintiff to elect the greater figure following return of the verdict." Id. at n. 6.5.

25 *Peer International Corp. v. Pausa Records, Inc.*, 909 F.2d 1332, 1337 (9th Cir. 1990) ("The Supreme Court has stated that '[e]ven for injurious and unprofitable invasions of copyright, the court may, if it deems just, impose a liability within [the] statutory limits to sanction and vindicate the statutory policy' of discouraging infringement." quoting *F.W. Woolworth Co. v. Contemprary Arts*, 344 U.S. 228, 233 (1952)).

26 17 U.S.C. § 504(c)(2).

27 *Feltner v. Columbia Pictures Television, Inc.*, 523 U.S. 340, 355 (1998) (The "Seventh Amendment provides a right to a jury trial on all issues pertinent to an award of statutory damages under § 504(a) of the Copyright Act, including the amount itself.").

28 NIMMER ON COPYRIGHT § 14.04c[B][3] (2004).

29 *Screws v. United States*, 325 U.S. 91, 105 (1945).

30 See, JOHN W. HAZARD, JR., COPYRIGHT LAW IN BUSINESS AND PRACTICE § 7:49, at 7-118 (2004) and the cases cited in n. 14.

[31] *Yurman Design, Inc. v. PAJ, Inc.*, 262 F.3d 101 (2d Cir 2001), citing *Hamil America Inc. v. GFI,* 193 F.3d 92, 97 (2d Cir 1999).

[32] *Hamil America Inc. v. GFI*, 193 F.3d 92, 97 (2d Cir 1999).

[33] JOHN W. HAZARD, JR., COPYRIGHT LAW IN BUSINESS AND PRACTICE § 7:49, at 7-115 (2004).

[34] NIMMER ON COPYRIGHT § 14.04c[B][3] (2004).

[35] *Princeton University Press v. Michigan Document Services*, 99 F. 3d 1381, 1392 (6th Cir. 1996), cert. denied 529 U.S. 1156 (1997).

[36] *Columbia Pictures Television, Inc. v. Krypton Broadcasting of Birmingham, Inc.*, 259 F.3d 1186, 1195 (9th Cir. 2001), cert. denied 534 U.S. 1127 (2002).

[37] BLACK'S LAW DICTIONARY (8th ed. 2004) defines *scienter:* "A degree of knowledge that makes a person legally responsible for the consequences of his or her act or omission; the fact of an act's having been done knowingly, especially as a ground for civil damages or criminal punishment." Id. at 1373.

[38] NIMMER ON COPYRIGHT § 14.04c[B][3] (2004) (footnotes omitted).

[39] 17 U.S.C. § 506(a), referencing, 18 U.S.C. § 2319 (criminal penalties up to $250,000 and imprisonment up to five years for any person who infringes a copyright willfully and for purposes of commercial advantage or private financial gain).

[40] Pub. L. No. 105-147, 111 Stat. 2678 (1997) (The NET [No Electronic Theft] Act).

[41] 17 U.S.C. § 101 ("The term 'financial gain' includes receipt, or expectation of receipt, of anything of value, including the receipt of other copyrighted works.").

[42] *United States v. LaMacchia*, 871 F. Supp. 535 (D. Mass. 1994).

[43] 17 U.S.C. § 506(a)(1).

[44] 17 U.S.C. § 506(a)(2).

[45] H.R. Rep. No 105-339, 105th Cong., 1st Sess., 3 (1997) ("The purpose of H.R. 2265, as amended, is to reverse the practical consequences of *United States v. LaMacchia*, 871 F. Supp. 535 (D. Mass. 1994) [hereinafter LaMacchia], which held, inter alia, that electronic piracy of copyrighted works may not be prosecuted under the federal wire fraud statute; and that criminal sanctions available under Titles 17 and 18 of the U.S. Code for copyright infringement do not apply in instances in which a defendant does not realize a commercial advantage or private financial gain.").

[46] JOHN W. HAZARD, JR., COPYRIGHT LAW IN BUSINESS AND PRACTICE § 7:52, at 7-121 (2004).

[47] H.R. Rep. No 105-339, 105th Cong. 1st Sess., 6 (1997).

[48] H.R. 4077, 108th Cong., 1st Sess. (2004).

[49] UNITED STATES DEPARTMENT OF JUSTICE, REPORT OF THE DEPARTMENT OF JUSTICE'S TASK FORCE ON INTELLECTUAL PROPERTY 46 (2004).

[50] 17 U.S.C. § 505.

[51] In *Columbia Pictures Television, Inc. v. Krypton Broadcasting of Birmingham, Inc.*, 106 F.3d 284 (9th Cir. 2001), reversed 523 U.S. 340 (2002), the district court awarded $8.8 million in statutory damages and $750,000 in "reasonable attorney's fees to the prevailing party," which the circuit later remanded. Id. at 288 and 296.

[52] *Branch v. Ogilvy & Mather, Inc.*, 772 F. Supp. 1359 (S.D.N.Y. 1991) (awarding $10,000 in statutory damages and $116,729 in attorney's fees, reduced from the initial request made by the plaintiff for $233,458).

[53] *Fogerty v. Fantasy, Inc.*, 510 U.S. 517 (1994).

[54] 17 U.S.C. § 505.

[55] *Fogerty v. Fantasy, Inc.*, 510 U.S. 517, 535, at n. 19 (1994) (citing *Lieb v. Topstone Industries, Inc.*, 788 F.2d 151, 156 (3d Cir. 1986)) ("Some courts following the evenhanded standard have suggested several nonexclusive factors to guide courts' discretion. For example, the Third Circuit has listed several nonexclusive factors that courts should consider in making awards of attorneys' fees to any prevailing party. These factors include 'frivolousness, motivation, objective reasonableness (both in the factual and in the legal components of the case) and the need in particular circumstances to advance considerations of compensation and deterrence.' [citation to *Lieb* omitted]. We agree that such factors may be used to guide courts' discretion, so long as such factors are faithful to the purposes of the Copyright Act and are applied to prevailing plaintiffs and defendants in an evenhanded manner.").

[56] "[T]he Court must consider and make findings on: (1) the motivation of the defendant; (2) the reasonableness of its positions; (3) the need for deterrence and compensation; and (4) other relevant factors." *Lowry's Reports, Inc. v. Legg Mason, Inc.*, 302 F. Supp. 2d 455, 463 (D. Md. 2004), citing, *Rosciszewski v. Arete Associates, Inc.*, 1 F.3d 225, 234 (4th Cir. 1993) (the *Rosciszewski* decision relied on and cited *Lieb* at 156).

[57] *Lowry's Reports, Inc. v. Legg Mason, Inc.*, 302 F. Supp. 2d 455, 463 (D. Md. 2004).

[58] *Lowry's Reports, Inc. v. Legg Mason, Inc.*, 302 F. Supp. 2d 455, 463 (D. Md. 2004). "Although Legg Mason has made some incredible arguments, this litigation is likely to clarify the law in some respects and, therefore, was not of absolute insignificance."

[59] *Lowry's Reports, Inc. v. Legg Mason, Inc.*, 302 F. Supp. 2d 455, 463 (D. Md. 2004). "The third consideration . . . was adequately provided for by the jury's award. [footnote omitted] Although attorneys' fees are appropriate when a plaintiff successfully litigates an important right but receives only nominal damages, Lowry's vindicated the public's interest and secured a significant damages award. . . . Accordingly, no further incentive is needed in this case."

[60] *Lowry's Reports, Inc. v. Legg Mason, Inc.*, 302 F. Supp. 2d 455, 463-464 (D. Md. 2004) ("An award of attorneys' fees would provide little benefit in this case. The jury award will compensate Lowry's and allow it to pay its attorneys' fees. The size of the award also serves the deterrent purposes of the Copyright Act. Accordingly, the Court will exercise its discretion and decline to award attorneys' fees.").

[61] *Lowry's Reports, Inc. v. Legg Mason, Inc.*, 302 F. Supp. 2d 455, 458, n.3 (D. Md. 2004) ("Legg Mason's maximum liability in this case, for the willful infringement of 240 registered copyrights, was $36 million." 240 × $150,000 = $36,000,000).

[62] 17 U.S.C. § 512(c)(3)(A).

[63] 17 U.S.C. § 512(c)(1).

[64] 17 U.S.C. § 512(d).

[65] 17 U.S.C. § 512(c)(1)(C) and (d)(3).

[66] *Rodgers v. Eighty Four Lumber Company*, 623 F. Supp. 889, 892 (W.D. Pa. 1985) ("We find the evidence supports the conclusions that the infringements were deliberate and willful; they continued after many warnings and showings of specific proofs; they continued after specific denials that any music was currently being played. Finally, we find that defendant avoided responses to many notices and did not negotiate for a license in good faith.").

[67] *Chi-Boy Music v. Charlie Club, Inc.*, 930 F.2d 1224, 1228-1229 (7th Cir. 1991).

[68] 17 U.S.C. § 512(l).

[69] H.R. Rep. No. 105-796, 105th Cong., 2d Sess. 73 (1998). (Conf. Rep.)

[70] S.Rep. No. 105-190, 105th Cong., 2d Sess. 55 (1998). Identical language is found in the H.R. Rep. No 551 (Part 2), 105th Cong., 2d Sess. 64 (1998).

[71] Professor Dratler admits as much: "Indeed, the same underlying facts advanced in an unsuccessful effort to claim a limitation on remedies under Section 512 may justify a court's limiting or modifying [increasing as well as decreasing] remedies for copyright infringement under the law governing those remedies, as if Section 512 had never been adopted." JAY DRATLER JR., CYBERLAW: INTELLECTUAL PROPERTY IN THE DIGITAL MILLENNIUM § 6.07[2], at 6-155 (2004).

[72] 17 U.S.C. § 507(b) ("No civil action shall be maintained under the provisions of this title [Title 17 of the United States Code] unless it is commenced within three yeas after the claim accrued.").

[73] 17 U.S.C. § 507(a) ("[N]o criminal proceeding shall be maintained under the provisions of this title [Title 17 of the United States Code] unless it is commenced within 5 years after the cause of action arose.").

[74] *Hotaling v. Church of Latter Day Saints*, 118 F.3d 199 (4th Cir. 1997).

[75] *Hotaling v. Church of Latter Day Saints*, 118 F.3d 199, 203 (4th Cir. 1997).

[76] *Columbia Pictures Industries, Inc. v. Pacheco*, 15 U.S.P.Q.2d 1668, 1990 WL 29787, at *2 (D. Puerto Rico).

[77] 17 U.S.C. § 504(c)(2).

[78] See, *Columbia Pictures Indus, Inc. v. Pacheco*, 15 U.S.P.Q.2d 1668, 1990 WL 29787 (D. Puerto Rico) (awarding a total of $21,750 after assigned $250 for each innocent infringement, then the minimum amount during the "decennial" period, i.e., the ten-year period between the effective date of the 1976 Copyright Act, January 1, 1978, and March 1, 1989, the effective date of the Berne Convention Implementation Act of 1988, after which time, notice was optional; thus it was far more difficult to claim innocent infringement, as the presumption that every work, irrespective of notice, was protected by copyright: "Finally, we must also take into account defendant's claim of innocent infringement, a claim which, having remained uncontested, we accept as true and weigh favorably for defendant in our calculation. All facts considered, and as requested in their motion for summary judgment, we award plaintiffs the minimum amount of $250.00 for each of 87 of the incidents of infringement for a total of $21, 750.00 in statutory 'in lieu' damages." Id. at *3.).

[79] *National Football League v. PrimeTime 24 Joint Venture*, 131 F. Supp. 2d 458, 481 (S.D.N.Y. 2000) ("PrimeTime having made the decision to take the risk and again 'proceed with

business as usual' despite two decisions by Judge McKenna finding its conduct to constitute copyright infringement, and considering all other appropriate factors and evidence, the Court finds that statutory damages of $10,000 per infringement is appropriate for this period."); *Los Angeles News Service v. Tullo*, 973 F.2d 791 (9th Cir. 1992) ("The district court did not find AVRS 'had no reason to believe' its acts did not constitute infringement. Even if the court had so found, § 504(c)(2) does not mandate a nominal award. On this record, the district court did not abuse its discretion by declining to reduce the award." Id. at 800. In fact, timing, it seems, is everything, as "the statutory maximum for the infringement of the copyright to the plane crash footage was $20,000. The court found the infringement occurred on March 1, 1989, the date the statutory maximum increased from $10,000 to $20,000 under the Berne Convention." Id. at n. 10.).

[80] *National Football League v. PrimeTime 24 Joint Venture*, 131 F. Supp. 2d 458, 472 (S.D.N.Y. 2000), citing among others, *Feltner v. Columbia Pictures Television, Inc.*, 523 U.S. 340, 345-346 (1998) ("'the court in its discretion' may, within limits, increase or decrease the amount of the statutory damages").

[81] *National Football League v. PrimeTime 24 Joint Venture*, 131 F. Supp. 2d 458, 472 (S.D.N.Y. 2001).

[82] *National Football League v. PrimeTime 24 Joint Venture*, 131 F. Supp. 2d 458, 476 (S.D.N.Y. 2000).

[83] *Fitzgerald Publishing Co. v. Baylor Publishing Co.*, 807 F.2d 1110, 1115 (2d Cir. 1986).

[84] In questioning the decision in *Broadcast Music, Inc. v. Coco's Development Corp.*, 212 U.S.P.Q. 714 (N.D.N.Y. 1991), one commentator observed: "Defendant's innocence may have been in good faith, but as the proprietor of a restaurant where music was publicly performed without a license, it is submitted that his innocence was not reasonable." NIMMER ON COPYRIGHT § 14.04c[B][1][b], at n. 60 (2004) (emphasis added).

[85] Case law on innocent infringer and reasonableness standard.

[86] *Abkco music, Inc. v. Harrisongs Music, Inc.*, 722 F.2d 988, 999 (2d Cir. 1983).

[87] NIMMER ON COPYRIGHT § 14.04c[B][1][a] (2004).

[88] See, Berne Convention Implementation Act of 1988, Pub. L. No. 100-568, 102 Stat. 2858 (1988).

[89] 17 U.S.C. § 401 ("a notice of copyright as provided by this section may be placed on publicly distributed copies from which the work can be visually perceived, either directly or with the aid of a machine or device." (emphasis added)).

[90] Pub. L. No. 94-553, 90 Stat. 2478 (1976).

[91] In section 405(a)(1)–(3) several narrow exceptions to the notice upon publication rule are listed: "(1) the notice has been omitted from no more than a relatively small number of copies or phonorecords distributed to the public; or (2) registration for the work has been made before or is made within five years after the publication without notice, and a reasonable effort is made to add notice to all copies or phonorecords that are distributed to the public in the United States after the omission has been discovered; or (3) the notice has been omitted in violation of an express requirement in writing that, as a condition of

the copyright owner's authorization of the public distribution of copies or phonorecords, they bear the prescribed notice."

[92] See, S. Rep. No. 100-352, at 13 (1988), or as reprinted in 1988 U.S.C.C.A.N. 3706, 3718 (1988) ("Under the present law [referring to the post 1976 copyright law, but pre-1989 Berne implementation law], omission or mistakes amounting to an omission of the notice can result in the work being placed in the public domain in this country if prescribed corrective measures are not taken within the statutorily specified timeframe.").

[93] JOHN W. HAZARD, JR., COPYRIGHT LAW IN BUSINESS AND PRACTICE § 5:15, at 5-15 (2004) (emphasis added). "Nevertheless, notice is still the best way to protect a work, and it should be included on all published works." Id. § 5:1, at 5-4.

[94] 17 U.S.C. § 405(b). ("emphasis added")

[95] See, *Bryce & Palazzola Architects and Associates, Inc. v. A.M.E. Group, Inc.*, 865 F.Supp. 401, 404-405 (E.D. Mich.1994) ("During the Decennial Era, which immediately preceded the Berne Era, former § 405 of the Act provided the basis for an innocent infringement defense which reduced, but did not eliminate, liability under the Act when proved by the infringer . . . . Thus, the statute now limits the innocent infringement defense to claims asserted during the Berne Era for which there was public distribution upon authority of the copyright owner *prior* to March 1, 1989. Defendants' argument that publication has occurred in this case is predicated upon their receipt of the spec sheet on the Cottingham dwelling when they viewed the premises in 1991. Therefore, Defendants are barred from asserting an innocent infringer defense on that basis.").

[96] See, *D.C. Comics, Inc. v. Mini Gift Shop*, 912 F.2d 29, 32 (2d Cir. 1990) ("All of the defendants were recent immigrants from Asia who spoke little or no English.") ("In this regard, the district court was presented with evidence that there were no copyright notices on the infringing goods and that a layman would not be able to distinguish between licensed and unlicensed goods based on the style or quality of the art work. This evidence tends to establish that defendants' infringement was innocent. . . . The court determined that the defendants who appeared at the hearing and trial lacked 'the sophistication or level of understanding' to prompt an inquiry into the source of the unmarked goods. The court had a short colloquy with each pro se defendant at the start of the hearing. Plaintiffs' own evidence also established that the defendants were unsophisticated merchants." Id. at 35.).

[97] 17 U.S.C. § 401(d) (all emphasis added).

[98] 17 U.S.C. § 402(d) ("If a notice of copyright in the form and position specified in this section appears on the published phonorecord or phonorecords to which a defendant in a copyright infringement suit had access, then *no weight shall be given* to such a defendant's interposition of a *defense based on innocent infringement* in mitigation of actual statutory damages, except as provided in the last sentence of section 504(c)(2).") (all emphasis added).

[99] 17 U.S.C. § 408 ("[T]he owner of copyright or of any exclusive right in the work may obtain registration of the copyright claim by delivering to the Copyright Office the deposit specified by this section, together with the application and fee specified by sections 409 and 708.").

[100] 17 U.S.C. § 412 ("[N]o award of statutory damages or of attorney's fees, as provided by section 504 and 505, shall be made for (1) any infringement of copyright in an unpublished work commenced before the effective date of its registration; or (2) any infringement of the copyright commenced after first publication of the work and before the effective date of its registration, unless such registration is made within three months after the first publication of the work.").

[101] 17 U.S.C. § 410(c) ("In any judicial proceedings the certificate of registration made before or within five years after first publication of the work shall constitute prima facie evidence of the validity of the copyright and of the facts stated in the certificate. The evidentiary weight to be accorded the certificate of registration made thereafter shall be within the discretion of the court.").

[102] 17 U.S.C. § 411 ("[N]o action for infringement of the copyright in any United States work shall be instituted until registration of the copyright claim has been made in accordance with this title.").

[103] See *Lloyd v. Schlag*, 884 F.2d 409, 412 (9th Cir. 1989) ("Had Lloyd's attorney conducted a reasonable inquiry into the facts, he would have discovered his client's innocent misapprehension of copyright transfer requirements, and been able to remedy the error *prior* to filing suit. . . . We hold that a reasonable attorney admitted to practice before the district court would have discovered that a copyright infringement suit cannot be brought unless and until the copyright transfer has been properly recorded, and ascertained that the recordation has been accomplished.").

[104] NIMMER ON COPYRIGHT § 14.04c[B][2][a] (2004) (footnotes omitted).

[105] NIMMER ON COPYRIGHT § 14.04c[B][2][a] (2004), at n.71.

[106] *Getaped.com v. Cangemi*, 188 F. Supp. 2d 398 (S.D.N.Y. 2002).

[107] In an article predating the decision, one commentator argued that an Internet transmission cannot constitute publication: R. Anthony Reese, The Public Display Right: The Copyright Act's Neglected Solution to the Controversy Over Ram "Copies," 2001 UNIVERSITY OF ILLINOIS LAW REVIEW 83, 131-132 (2001).

[108] *Hotaling v. Church of Latter Day Saints*, 118 F.3d 199 (4th Cir. 1997) (Library was liable for the use (distribution) of unlawful copies of copyrighted works found in its collection.).

[109] *Little Mole Music v. Spike Inventory, Inc.*, 720 F. Supp. 751 (W.D. Missouri 1989).

[110] JOHN W. HAZARD, JR., COPYRIGHT LAW IN BUSINESS AND PRACTICE § 7:48, at 7-113 (2004).

[111] 17 U.S.C. § 504(c)(2). (emphasis added).

[112] 17 U.S.C. § 401(d). (emphasis added).

[113] 17 U.S.C. § 402(d) ("If a notice of copyright in the form and position specified in this section appears on the published copy or copies to which a defendant in a copyright infringement suit had access, then no weight shall be given to such a defendant's interposition of a defense based on innocent infringement in mitigation of actual statutory damages, *exempt as provided in the last sentence of section 504(c)(2)*.").

[114] R. Rep. No. 94-1476, 94th Cong., 2d Sess. 163 (1976), reprinted in 5 U.S.C.C.A.N. 5659, 5779 (1976) (emphasis added).

[115] This distinction is also observed in NIMMER ON COPYRIGHT § 14.04c[B][2][b] (2004), at n.79 ("Contrast this with the burden of proof on the defendant, in connection with the general innocent infringement exception.").

[116] BLACK'S LAW DICTIONARY (8th ed. 2004) defines a rebuttable presumption as "[a] inference drawn from certain facts that establish a prima facie case, which may be overcome by the introduction of contrary evidence." Id. at 1224.

[117] R. Rep. No. 94-1476, 94th Cong., 2d Sess. 163 (1976), reprinted in 5 U.S.C.C.A.N. 5659, 5779 (1976) ("Section 504(c)(2) provides that, where such a person or institution infringed copyrighted material in the honest belief that what they were doing constituted fair use, the court is precluded from awarding any statutory damages.").

[118] R. Rep. No. 94-1476, 94th Cong., 2d Sess. 163 (1976) (conf. Rep.), reprinted in 5 U.S.C.C.A.N. 5659, 5779 (1976).

[119] JOHN W. HAZARD, JR., COPYRIGHT LAW IN BUSINESS AND PRACTICE § 9:22, at 9-27 (2004)

[120] *Fogerty v. Fantasy, Inc.*, 510 U.S. 517, 535, at n. 19 (1994). See also, *Lowry's Reports, Inc. v. Legg Mason, Inc.*, 302 F. Supp. 2d 455, 463-464 (D. Md. 2004). ("An award of attorneys' fees would provide little benefit in this case. The jury award will compensate Lowry's and allow it to pay its attorneys' fees. The size of the award also serves the deterrent purposes of the Copyright Act. Accordingly, the Court will exercise its discretion and decline to award attorneys' fees.").

[121] *Matthew Bender & Co., Inc. v. West Pub. Co.*, 240 F.3d 116, 121 (2d Cir. 2001). See also, *In re Bolar Pharmaceutical Co., Inc., Securities Litigation*, 66 F.2d 731, 732 (2d Cir. 1992) (per curiam) ("'Abuse of discretion' is one of the most deferential standards of review; it recognizes that the district court, which is intimately familiar with the nuances of the case, is in a far better position to make certain decisions than is an appellate court, which must work from a cold record.").

[122] 17 U.S.C. § 512(k)(2).

[123] 17 U.S.C. § 501.

[124] Pub. L. No. 101-553, 104 Stat. 2749 (1990).

[125] 17 U.S.C. § 511.

[126] *Seminole Tribe of Florida v. Florida*, 517 U.S. 44, 47 (1996) ("We hold that notwithstanding Congress' clear intent to abrogate the States' sovereign immunity, the Indian Commerce Clause does not grant Congress that power, and therefore § 2710(d)(7) cannot grant jurisdiction over a State that does not consent to be sued. We further hold that the doctrine of *Ex Parte Young*, 209 U.S. 123 (1908), may not be used to enforce § 2710(d)(3) against a state official.").

[127] *Florida Prepaid Postsecondary Education Expense Board v. College Savings Bank*, 527 U.S. 627 (1999).

[128] *College Savings Bank v. Florida Prepaid Postsecondary Education Expense Board*, 527 U.S. 666 (1999).

[129] JOHN W. HAZARD, JR., COPYRIGHT LAW IN BUSINESS AND PRACTICE § 7:62, at 7-135 (2004).

[130] *Chavez v. Arte Publico Press*, 204 F.3d 601 (5th Cir. 2000).

[131] *Regents of the University of New Mexico v. Knight and Scallen*, 321 F.3d 1111, 1126 (11th Cir. 2003) ("We thus hold that when a state files suit in federal court to enforce its claims to certain patents, the state shall be considered to have consented to have litigated in the same forum all compulsory counterclaims, i.e., those arising from the same transaction or occurrence that gave rise to the state's asserted claims. Accordingly, we conclude that by filing suit for a declaration of patent ownership and inventorship based on certain contracts and conduct, UNM waived its Eleventh Amendment immunity with respect to all compulsory counterclaims arising from those contracts and conduct.").

[132] *Boyd v. University of Illinois*, 1999 U.S. Dist. LEXIS 15348 (S.D.N.Y. 1999).

[133] *Mt. Healthy School District Board of Education v. Doyle*, 429 U.S. 274, 280-281 (1977) ("On balance, the record before us indicates that a local school board such as petitioner is more like a county or city than it is like an arm of the State. We therefore hold that it was not entitled to assert any Eleventh Amendment immunity from suit in the federal courts.").

[134] *Mt. Healthy School District Board of Education v. Doyle*, 429 U.S. 274, 280 (1977) ("The issue here thus turns on whether the Mt. Healthy Board of Education is to be treated as an arm of the State partaking of the States Eleventh Amendment immunity, or is instead to be treated as a municipal corporation or other political subdivision to which the Eleventh Amendment does not extend. The answer depends, at least in part, upon the nature of the entity created by state law. Under Ohio law the 'State' does not include 'political subdivisions,' and 'political subdivisions' do include local school districts.").

[135] See, e.g., *Clark v. Tarrant County, Texas*, 798 F.2d 736, 743-745 (5th Cir. 1986) ("The relevant factors include: (1) whether state statutes and case law characterize the agency as an arm of the state; (2) the source of funds for the entity; (3) the degree of local autonomy the entity enjoys; (4) whether the entity is concerned primarily with local, as opposed to statewide, problems; (5) whether the entity has authority to sue and be sued in its own name; and (6) whether the entity has the right to hold and use property."); *Ambus v. Granite Bd. of Education*, 995 F.2d 992, 994 (10th Cir. 1993) ("The [*Mt. Healthy School District Board of Education v. Doyle*] Court ruled four factors to be relevant: (1) the characterization of the district under state law; (2) the guidance and control exercised by the state over the local school board; (3) the degree of state funding received by the district; and (4) the local board's ability to issue bonds and levy taxes on its own behalf." Concluding: "Because Utah school districts are considered 'political subdivisions' under Utah law, there is significant local board authority over school district operations, and Utah school districts obtain funding at least in part through locally administered property taxes, we conclude that they are not arms of the state for purposes of the Eleventh Amendment. Therefore they are not entitled to immunity from § 1983 suits in federal court." Id. at 997.).

[136] Jason Lane, Robert M. Hedrickson, and M. Christopher Brown, Sovereign Immunity and Public Education, 182 EDUCATION LAW INTO PRACTICE [7], 13 (December 18, 2003).

[137] See also, Peter Bray, Note: After *College Savings v. Florida Prepaid*, Are States Subject to Suit for Copyright Infringement?: The Copyright Remedy Clarification Act and *Chavez v. Arte Publico Press*, 36 HOUSTON LAW REVIEW 1531 (1999). See also, Brenda Sandburg, Universities May Lose IP Immunity, THE LEGAL INTELLIGENCER, September 13, 2000, at 4.

[138] See, e.g., S. 1191, 108th Cong., 1st Sess. (2003) (Intellectual Property Protection Restoration Act of 2003) (Section states that a purpose is to "abrogate State sovereign immunity in cases where States or their instrumentalities, officers, or employees violate the United States Constitution by infringing Federal intellectual property"); companion legislation is H.R. 2344, 108th Cong., 1st Sess. (2003) (Intellectual Property Protection Restoration Act of 2003).

[139] Michael J. Mehrman, IP Decisions: Strip Owners of Claims Against States, THE NATIONAL LAW JOURNAL, Oct. 25, 1999, at C10 (also indicating that a private suit or other legal remedies are available); see also, Molly Buch Richard, Developments in the Substantive Law: No Ticket to Infringe, TEXAS LAWYER, December 20, 1999 (no pagination, available in the LEXIS LegNew Library).

[140] Kenneth D. Crews and Georgia K. Harper, The Immunity Dilemma: Are State Colleges and Universities Still Liable for Copyright Infringement? 50 JOURNAL OF THE AMERICAN SOCIETY FOR INFORMATION SCIENCE 1350, 1351 (1999).

[141] Kern Alexander and M. David Alexander, AMERICAN PUBLIC SCHOOL LAW 80 (6th ed. 2005).

[142] "The recording industry last week filed another round of copyright infringement lawsuits against people it said were illegally distributing songs over the Internet. This latest wave of federal litigation targeted 750 computer users across the nation, including 25 students at 13 universities, according to the Recording Industry Association of America. . . .The association claims that the defendants used university computer networks to distribute recordings on unauthorized peer-to-peer services, including eDonkey, Kazaa, LimeWire and Grokster. Among the universities attended by students named in the lawsuits were Indiana State, Iowa State, Ohio State and Southern Mississippi." THE NATIONAL LAW JOURNAL, November 1, 2004, at 3.

[143] Kenneth D. Crews and Georgia K. Harper, The Immunity Dilemma: Are State Colleges and Universities Still Liable for Copyright Infringement? 50 JOURNAL OF THE AMERICAN SOCIETY FOR INFORMATION SCIENCE 1350, 1351-1352 (1999).

[144] Kenneth D. Crews and Georgia K. Harper, The Immunity Dilemma: Are State Colleges and Universities Still Liable for Copyright Infringement? 50 JOURNAL OF THE AMERICAN SOCIETY FOR INFORMATION SCIENCE 1350, 1352 (1999).

▶5

HOW CAN LIBRARIES AND SCHOOLS OBTAIN IMMUNITY?

Read this chapter to learn about copyright situations like:
▶ Whether a library can avoid liability from patron misuse of photocopiers.
▶ Whether a library can get in more trouble when an employee directly aids a patron's infringing activities.
▶ Whether an institution can get in trouble for copies of protected material stored in a computer's temporary memory.

◀

Unlike the statutory damages reduction or remission of section 504, discussed above and the additional damages reduction and remission provisions in sections 512 and 1203, enacted by the DMCA, discussed in Part III, section 108(f)(1) is a true immunity provision in that it eliminates all liability. However, in return for this broad sweep of protection, section 108 poses this monograph's first introduction to what can be called a compliance-oriented provision, requiring the institution to post a copyright warning notice on "reproducing equipment." More important, section 108 does not apply to all copyrighted users but to a narrow category of qualifying nonprofit libraries and archives. The immunity would likely apply to a library or archive within an educational institution, but not to the institution at large. This an important limitation and the distinction should be well noted in any institutional risk-management plan, e.g., explaining why such third-party (e.g., student) copying is "acceptable" (creates little risk) when done in the library but not when done in the lunch or dorm room. Moreover, unlike the section 504(c)(2) damages remission, section 108 does not include reproductions or distributions in the classroom. Thus classroom copying is not subject to the section 108(f)(1) immunity but still may be subject to the section 504(c)(2) remission provision.

ENSURING IMMUNITY UNDER SECTION 108

Qualifying for section 108 status is important for the library or archive because it allows the library or archive, in addition to the immunity clause introduced above and discussed in detail below, to take advantage of additional reproduction and distribution rights under subsections 108(b) and (c) for copies of phonorecords of unpublished and published works made for its collection, respectively, or for subsection (d) and (e) for copies or phonorecords of works made for patrons. While it is beyond the scope of this monograph to discuss the provision of section 108 in detail,[1] the initial qualifying conditions are discussed for two reasons of relevance here. First, section 108(a)(iii) contains a notice provision, which does fit within the "compliance" scope of this book. Second, securing the benefit of the immunity and other use rights of section 108 is dependant upon compliance with the initial qualifying conditions.

Qualifying for Section 108 Status

When a library or archives engages in reproductions or distributions under the provisions of section 108 it must meet three requirements contained in section 108(a):

> (1) the reproduction or distribution is made without any purpose of direct or indirect commercial advantage, (2) the collections of the library or archives are (i) open to the public, or (ii) available not only to researchers affiliated with the library or archives or with the institution of which it is a part, but also to other persons doing research in a specialized field, and (3) the reproduction or distribution of the work includes a notice of copyright that appears on the copy or phonorecord that is reproduced under the provisions of this section, or includes a legend stating that the work may be protected by copyright if no such notice can be found on the copy or phonorecord that is reproduced under the provisions of this section.[2]

Since the second and third requirements are somewhat straightforward and the first is somewhat less so, the requirements are discussed below in reverse order. Second, the immunity of section 108(f)(1), like the operation of any other privilege conferred by subsection of section 108, is limited to libraries or archives and the employees of either when performing actions within the scope of their employment. This is the impact of the section 108(a) proviso indicating that the section is intended to benefit a "library or archives, or any of its employees acting within the scope of their employment."[3] Personal copying is not covered by section 108, but would be subject to the fair use provisions of section 107.

The Notice Requirement

Taking the section 108(a)(3) requirement first, if the library is reproducing copyrighted material under section 108, the library should locate the copyright notice on the work from which the copy is being made. It is typically in the front pages of a book, or at the beginning or end of an article. This notice, e.g. "Copyright © 2005 Tomas A. Lipinski" must be added to the copy that the library makes. If a copyright notice does not appear, a "legend" can be stamped on the copy, saying that the work may be under copyright protection, for example: "NOTICE: This material may be protected by Copyright Law (Title 17 U.S.C.)"

"Open" and "Available" Collections

Second, section 108(a)(2) requires that "the collections of the library or archives are (i) open to the public, or (ii) available not only to researchers affiliated with the library or archives or with the institution of which it is a part, but also to other persons doing research in a specialized field." Notice that the statute references the "collections" of the library or archives; the statute does not state that the *library* be "open to the public" or "available not only to researchers affiliated with" but that the *collections* be so "open" or "available." The 1976 legislative history, the House, Senate, and Conference Report are silent on this subsection, or for any other provision of section 108(a) for that matter. Does this mean that a closed-stack library where collections are actually not open for patron browsing is disqualified? It would appear so, as the literal interpretation of the statute suggests that the collections must in fact be open to the public. Is this a common occurrence? It may be at major research institutions with varying levels of access.

The author recalls that, when he was a doctoral student, while a member of the public could enter the graduate library at the University of Illinois at Urbana-Champaign (UIUC), its main stacks were closed to the public and open to faculty and graduate students alone, i.e., not all of its collections were open to the public (though numerous smaller subject collections were indeed accessible and open to the public). What if the entire collection, or a large majority of it save for a small reference collection in the main reading room, were in these closed-stack areas? If this were the case, then the requirement of the section 108(a)(2)(i) proviso would not be met by this library—its collections are closed or have some other restriction preventing the free roam of members of the public to its collections. What if some of its collections were closed to the public, such as a special collection, but the rest of the library were open to the public? Does restricted public access to some of its collections disqualify the entire library? Notice that section 108(a)(i) does not offer that "some of the collections" be "open to the public," it merely states the suggestive and all-inclusive "collections" be so open. Such interpretation can be the result from a strict reading of the statute.

Does the second (a)(ii) "available" proviso offer some assistance? It could be argued that the materials in the closed stacks were at least made available to the public, i.e., staff retrieved books for undergraduates or other members of public with borrowing privileges? However, this is not the requirement of the section 108(a)(2)(ii) proviso, as it does **not** read "collections of the library or archives [be available] to the public." Rather "the collections of the library or archives" must be "available not only to researchers affiliated with the library or archives or with the institution of which it is a part [i.e., the undergraduates or local citizens with guest privileges, for example], but also to other persons doing research in a specialized field." Members of the public certainly could be "persons doing research in a specialized field" but they are not so necessarily. Thus if the UIUC library or other library in the example were to allow researchers from other "Big Ten" campuses to use the library collections, they would nonetheless qualify for section 108 status by meeting the section 108(a)(2)(ii) "available to" proviso. A library or archives would not need to have its collections "open" to the "other persons doing research in a specialized field"; it could merely make the collections available to those "other persons" but still retain its present closed-stack modus operandi. However, making its collections "available" to the public would not qualify, as this is not what the statute demands. Thus it is important to conform library and archives access policies in such a way that use triggers either the open-collections "to the public" proviso of section 108(a)(2)(i) or the available-collections "to other persons doing research in a specialized field" proviso of section 108(a)(2)(ii).

A K–12 school library that allows parents to access the collection would be "open to the public," but would not otherwise be "open to the public" simply because instructors, staff, and students come from the community at large. Also, such instructor, staff, and student access alone would fail to meet the "available proviso of section 108(a)(2)(ii) as it would indeed be "available . . . only to researchers affiliated with the library or archives or with the institution of which it is a part." However, if the library granted access to outside researchers after the receipt of a formal letter of introduction from the researcher's home institution, such as another school district or a graduate student in a library and information science or school media certification program, though still closed to public, it would meet the requirements of the second qualifying access proviso in clause (2)(ii) in section 108(a).

Likewise, a corporate library that allows some access (recall that in clause (ii), availability is the standard) to outside researchers from industry (a competing corporation), as unlikely as it might be, may also qualify. The most likely scenario in which the "available" proviso triggers qualification is one where a library is *not* open to public, such as a corporate archives, but would allow "other persons doing research in a specialized field" to have access to the collection, such as an academic or investigative journalist or other party studying the history of the industry of which the corporation is a part.

In the end it may not make much difference whether a library qualifies under either the "open" or "available" proviso of section 108(a)(i) or (ii), respectively, but it might. In other words, as long as a library makes it collections "available" to "other persons doing research in a specialized field" it would at least qualify for the (ii) proviso, though "researchers affiliated with the library or archives or with the institution of which it is a part" cannot be counted in that subset. This appears an odd result, to turn the applicability of section 108 on variation or nuance in institutional access policy. Perhaps it is poor drafting, but the literal interpretation suggests a decided focus on "collections" as well as a difference between being "open" and being "available." Hopefully, a court would see the closed-stack library in the author's example as the sort nonetheless consistent with the spirit of the statute, or in the alternative, qualifying for the "available" section 108(a)(2)(ii) proviso. This interpretive risk, however, underscores the need to have an access policy that is precise in its conformity to one of the two (a)(2) provisos to its letter, rather than rely on conformity based on the spirit of the subsection.

Avoiding Commercial Advantage

Finally, according to subsection (a), a third requirement for section 108 qualification is that any reproduction and distribution undertaken by the library or archive must be "made without any purpose of direct or indirect commercial advantage." There is no case law interpreting the "direct or indirect commercial advantage" proviso, but it is suggested that charging on a cost recovery basis for reproducing material would be acceptable. Furthermore, the use of the word "purpose" suggests that motive is a factor. So as long as the library or archive is not seeking to generate revenue (direct advantage) from the exercise of its section 108 rights or otherwise placing itself in a position of advantage vis-à-vis those rights, such as a decrease in subscription or licensing fees (arguably an indirect advantage),[4] or contributing to some overall commercial advantage of the entity, the library should continue to qualify for section 108. A general user fee would also appear to be acceptable, as the "purpose of direct or indirect commercial advantage" would not be tied to the "reproduction or distribution" but to general access to the library or archive collection or facility. This conclusion is made based on the interpretation given to the concept of "direct financial benefit" by courts regarding the second prong of vicarious liability (see the discussion in Chapter 3) where there needs to be some variable revenue generation scheme, such that the revenue is positively correlated to the intended reproduction and distribution of materials.

Section 108 clearly states that reproduction or distribution must be made without any purpose of direct or indirect commercial advantage.[5] Unlike the evolving standard of "commercial" versus noncommercial in fair use, the section 108 standard appears to be more rigid. The district court in *American Geophysical Union v. Texaco, Inc.* concluded that because the defendant used the copies as part of its overall commercial enterprise it could not qualify for section 108(1) status:

> Section 108 authorizes library photocopying under narrowly specified circumstances. The circumstances do not apply. Section 108 is made applicable only "if the reproduction . . . is made without any purpose of direct or indirect commercial advantage." [Citation omitted]

As noted above, Texaco makes the photocopies solely for commercial advantage. Texaco's $80 million annual budget for scientific research, of which its photocopying represents a microscopic part, is not expended as an exercise in philanthropy. *It is done for profit.* Articles are photocopied to help Texaco's scientists *in their profit-motivated research.*[6]

A recent corporate newsletter case produced a similar comment:

> None of the members of the research department had any personal interest in the *Reports.* All of them used the copies they received solely to prepare for the "morning call" and to field daily inquiries from Legg Mason brokers about market conditions. Olszewski Deposition at 84; Thayer Deposition at 96-97, 109-10. Their use thus exploited the *Reports* for the commercial benefit of Legg Mason, at the price of a single subscription.[7]

While the House, Senate, and Conference Report each made comment on the "direct or indirect commercial advantage" proviso, none appeared to distinguish between a "direct commercial advantage" and an "indirect commercial advantage." The House Report observed that "the 'advantage' referred to in this clause must attach to immediate commercial motivation behind the reproduction or distribution itself, rather than to the *ultimate profit-making motivation behind the enterprise* in which the library is located."[8] The *Texaco* commentary appears to contradict this, suggesting that advantage can accrue to the overall purpose of the research conducted by the oil conglomerate's scientists: "profit." However the comment of the *Lowry's Reports, Inc. is* consistent with this legislative comment as the newsletter was reproduced ("exploited") to save the outlay of additional subscription or license fees.

The comment in *Texaco* and the result in *Lowry's* appears consistent with the Senate Report that suggests that Section 108 is limited to libraries or archives in nonprofit organizations. According to the Senate Report it is "*intended to preclude a library in a profit-making organization* from providing photocopies of copyrighted materials to employees engaged in furtherance of the organization's commercial enterprise, unless such copying qualifies as a fair use, or the organization has obtained the necessary copyright licenses."[9] The House Conference Report appears to strike a balance:

> As long *as the library or archives meets the criteria* in section 108(a) and the other requirements of the section including the prohibitions against multiple and systematic copying in subsection (g), the conferees consider that the *isolated, spontaneous making of single photocopies by a library or archives in a for-profit organization without any commercial motivation,* or participation by such a library or archives in interlibrary arrangements, *would come within the scope of section 108.*[10]

Unfortunately the repeated infringement undertaken by the defendants in *Lowry's Reports, Inc. v. Legg Mason, Inc.,* not only nixed any hope of meeting such a standard (note, however, that the defendants did not argue section 108 as a defense), but it also triggered imposition of enhanced damages for willful infringement:

> The jury was not required to believe Legg Mason's assertions that the repeated infringement was due to its oversights and set its damages award accordingly. Further, the evidence indicated that Legg Mason was a sophisticated entity that repeatedly infringed Lowry's copyrights, even when asked to stop. In light of this evidence, the Court will not modify the jury's award or order a new trial because of its size.[11]

The Conference Report use of the word motivation also supports an earlier observation that a court might attempt to consider the motivation behind the reproduction, i.e., is it done with intent to avoid subscription or otherwise "paying" (through license, for example) for the item, or is it more accidental or incidental? Further, as in *Lowry's Reports, Inc. v. Legg Mason, Inc.*, was there attempt made after the fact to cover the tracks of the infringement?[12]

The Scope of Section 108(f)(1) Immunity

Section 108(f)(1) states that nothing in section 108 "shall be construed to impose liability for copyright infringement upon a library or archives or its employees *for* the unsupervised use of reproducing equipment located on its premises: Provided, That such equipment displays a notice that making of a copy may be subject to the copyright law."[13] This is the provision responsible for the now ubiquitous copyright warning notices that populate the photocopying area of many libraries. This provision, enacted as part of the Copyright Act of 1976, uses the phrase "reproducing equipment" and was written with 1970s technology in mind. However, the copyright law is intended to be technology neutral and so reproducing equipment in the first decade of the 21st century would logically include computers, scanners, samplers, and the like, as these items would constitute "reproducing equipment." As long as a notice is placed on the equipment and the use is unsupervised, no infringement that might occur on the premises of the library or archives though use of that reproducing equipment by students or other third parties will impose any liability for a neglectful librarian (under a contributory liability standard, i.e., knowledge of and failure to stop continued infringement) nor will an infringement be imputed to the institution ("library or archives or its employees") otherwise under vicarious standards. Notice that the statute does **not** state the notice can be on or near the equipment, rather the notice must be on the equipment itself, the "equipment displays." Thus general signage would appear inadequate, such as posted on the wall or hanging down from the ceiling near the photocopiers or Internet terminals. Again no case law has applied this provision of the law. The legislative history is little help as well, as the Senate and Conference Reports do not mention the provision, and the House Report merely repeats the words of the statute.[14]

Working with the text of the section (f)(1) alone, but in light of the principles of direct and secondary liability discussed in Chapters 1, 2, and 3, several comments can be made nonetheless. While the immunity ("Nothing in this section shall be construed to impose liability for copyright infringement upon a library or archives or its employees") provided by section 108(f)(1) applies to the entity or its employees, the "use" is not similarly limited but could apply to any user of the "reproducing equipment." However, its application *is* restricted by the practical operation of the provision in conjunction with section (f)(2) and the concepts of secondary liability.

Understanding "Unsupervised" Infringement

First, section 108(f)(2) reminds us that "nothing in this section . . . excuses a person who uses such reproducing equipment or who requests a copy or phonorecord under subsection (d) from liability for copyright infringement for any such act, or for any later use of such copy or phonorecord, if it exceeds fair use as provided by section 107."[15] Thus the immunity applies not to the user but to the entity or its employee. Next, the use must be "unsupervised." Normally employees are supervised, even if not subject to constant over-the-shoulder monitoring, so the provision arguably would not provide protection from an employee engaging in direct copyright infringement. Since employees are in fact the targets of some measure of supervision, section 108(f)(1) cannot by law apply to use of reproducing equipment by employees. Again the application of the concepts *respondeat superior* and "right and ability to control" by courts in analysis of the vicarious liability, discussed in Chapter 3, supports this conclusion. As the *Lowry's Reports, Inc. v. Legg Mason, Inc.* case demonstrates, employees are considered supervised and under the control of the employer even if the employee engages in conduct contrary to policy.[16]

One might reasonably ask to which "users" section 108(f)(1) applies if it does not offer immunity to the employees of qualifying libraries or archives as users of copying equipment? The answer is that the provision targets third-party infringers such as public library patrons, students, or members of the public who might use the institution's library reproducing equipment where their acts of direct infringement would otherwise predicate the secondary liability of employees or the institution. This is logical as section 108(f)(2) states that nothing in section 108 "excuses a person who uses such reproducing equipment . . . from liability for copyright infringement for any such act, or for later use of such copy or phonorecord, if it exceeds fair use provided by section 107." Liability is preserved for the initial direct infringer. In other words, while a student might use the library photocopiers to copy an entire textbook, or a public library patron might use library computers to infringe copyright by uploading and downloading dozens of

MP3 files, the librarian on duty at the reference desk when the infringement occurred ("or its employees") or the institution ("a library or archives") could not under the (f)(1) proviso be sued for infringement under either a primary or secondary theory of liability; however, under the (f)(2) initial infringer proviso, the possibility of litigation against the school, student, or library patron is preserved. That is the practical impact and relationship of subsections (f)(1) and (f)(2) of section 108.

More important, this immunity applies only to the library and its employees, for on-library-premises infringements. It does not protect the teacher in the classroom from secondary liability for requiring each student to make a copy of the assigned out-of-print text and bring it to class even if students chose to make their copies in the library. It does not insulate the institution from secondary liability for students who use general university computing facilities to upload and download infringing MP3 files or other copyrighted works from their dorm rooms. However, in the former example, the school media specialist on reference duty when the students made the copies would be protected by subsection (f)(1), assuming that the school library qualified for section 108 status as discussed above, and further assuming that the school media specialist did not assist the student in the illicit endeavor (or the use would no longer be "unsupervised").

This immunity is nonetheless a great privilege granted to qualifying libraries and archives for infringements arising out of the availability of "reproducing equipment located on its the premises." The authors of the infamous "white paper" on intellectual property perhaps offered the most telling observation on the significance of section 108(f)(1) when the report noted: "A library is exempted from liability for the unsupervised use of reproducing equipment located on its premises provided that the equipment displays a copyright law notice. [citation omitted] This exemption does not apply to the user of such equipment, and no other provider of equipment enjoys any statutory immunity."[17] When section 108(f)(1) applies, it offers complete immunity against direct (primary) or indirect (secondary) liability on the part of employees or the institution *for* the infringing uses of reproducing equipment by third parties, i.e., nonemployees. While the sort of immunity would most likely be for contributory infringement, it could be for direct infringement or vicarious infringement.

Circumstances could exist where the librarian could be said to supervise the use of the reproducing equipment and thus disqualify the use for the immunity offered by section 108(f)(1). However, routine equipment or network monitoring should not be equated with "supervision." For example, if an employee interrupted patron photocopying to replace a toner cartridge, add paper, or clear a jam, such conduct would not appear by logic to be the sort that would disqualify the library; use of the equipment could be said to remain "unsupervised." It is argued that even the sort of network signals ("red flags") as discussed in Chapter 2, that might trigger the requisite knowledge in a contributory infringement analysis, such as port or bandwidth or file server problems due to excessive uploading and downloading, should not disqualify the employee or library. Again maintenance of the library's computing network would not appear to be the sort of "supervision" that would disqualify use of reproducing equipment under the statute, i.e., in this case the computers and printers connected to the network. In fact, this is the logical set of circumstances for which section 108(f)(2) was designed, i.e., the insulation of employees and libraries from potential contributory activity. Again, qualifying library or archives "reproducing equipment" is limited to that which is physically "located on its premises." Section 108(f)(1) would not insulate the institution (or other employees) from others who at locations around campus retrieve and reproduce infringing materials from the library's network at their workstations, computers, and printers through the broader campus computing facilities.

Moreover, the inquiry into whether use is unsupervised or supervised does not equate with the broader concept of control in a vicarious liability analysis as discussed in Chapter 3. The section 108(f)(1) "unsupervised" test does not fail if the employee or library had the "right and ability to control," rather the section 108(f)(1) test fails if the employee or library exercised actual control, i.e., supervised the use of the reproducing equipment located on its premises. However, other such infringing uses of reproducing equipment could in fact be supervised.

Consider an example where a patron asks the reference librarian to offer assistance in locating and downloading material from a Web site. Being a good service-oriented professional the librarian jumps at the opportunity to assist a patron. The librarian then proceeds to stand over the shoulder of the patron walking the patron step by step through the process of locating and downloading or printing material later found to be infringing. Is the librarian liable for copyright infringement under section 108? No. Section 108 does not impose liability. Rather, under section 108 the supervised use of the reproducing equipment (the computer and printer) fails to qualify for the subsection (f)(1) immunity. The question of liability would then proceed to a consideration of whether the requisite knowledge was present, though it would seem that such supervision would meet the "induces or causes, or materially contributes" element in an analysis of contributory infringement, as discussed in Chapter 2. In a more accurate procedural-legal sequence, if the patron and library were sued, the court or jury would first decide if the downloading by the patron constituted direct infringement, as there can be no secondary liability without primary liability. Then the liability of the employee and library would be assessed under contributory infringement standards. Third, if found liable, the employee and library would attempt to assert a section 108(f)(1) defense (i.e., claim immunity for the secondary liability), but it would fail here as the use was indeed supervised. Consider asking the question another way: is the librarian assisting the patron in such a way and to such an extent that without such assistance the infringement could not occur, or is the librarian otherwise oversee-ing patrons in such a way that the intervention of deviating (infringing) conduct could be made (for example during an Internet skills or computer literacy train-ing session when patrons begin to use new-found skills through an illicit P2P site)?

Another question that arises is whether the over-the-shoulder assistance given to patrons who are unable or incapable of using reproducing equipment qualifies as unsupervised, such as with children or disabled patrons. First, over-the-shoulder as-sistance whereby the librarian or other staff actually punches the keys and clicks the mouse would not appear to be within the section 108(f)(1) construct as this is not patron use of the reproducing equipment; the librarian or staff *is* making the copies, not the patron. A second scenario, whereby the librarian or staff member is talking the patron through the process and not actually commanding the tech-nology but commanding the process of its use, would not also seem to fall within section 108(f)(1) as the copying is surely supervised. This might appear a harsh result, but, by the same token, diminished capacity (whether physical, mental, or intellectual) should not in and of itself create a subset of patron infringement that the statute does not contain. In practice it may merely require that assisted copy-ing done with children or the disabled comply with reasonable interpretations of fair use and other provisions of the copyright law.

No court has addressed the application of the concept in the context of a copy-right dispute. Moreover only one court has defined unsupervised at all, then rely-ing on a dictionary definition of the term, i.e., as not being under constant supervision.[18] However, a scenario where the librarian instructs the patron in the use of the technology and then walks away to return to the reference desk and the child or disabled patron proceeds to use the reproducing equipment to make a copy or phonorecord would fall within section 108(f)(1) context of unsupervised.

Liability Avoidance with Reproduction Technologies

A limitation on the operation of section 108(f)(1) to immunize the liability that may result from the initial infringement of third parties derives from the nature of the underlying conduct to which the immunity applies: use of reproducing equip-ment. Consider a public performance of an audiovisual work (VHS or DVD) made by a patron or student in a library. If that performance is infringing, section 108(f)(1) does nothing to insulate the library or archive, only infringement relat-ing to the copyright owner's exclusive right of reproduction is mitigated.

Second, that mitigation when it is operative does nothing to transform the nature of the work so reproduced. The 1976 legislative history suggests as much:

> Clause (2) of subsection (f) makes clear that this exemption of the library or archives
> does not extend to the person using such equipment or requesting such copy if the use

exceeds fair use. Insofar as such person in concerned *the copy or phonorecord made is not considered 'lawfully' made* for purposes of section 109, 110, or other provisions of the title.[19]

In another example, consider a student in a qualifying (meets the requirements of section 108(a)(1)–(3)) school library who uses reproducing equipment to make a copy of a VHS movie obtained through interlibrary from another school district. Section 108(f)(1) would insulate the library from any liability as a direct or indirect infringer as to the student's infringing conduct. However, since the copy of the movie is unlawfully made, a teacher could not use the tape later in the classroom as part of a presentation as section 110(1) includes the use "in the case of a motion picture or other audiovisual work [where] the performance, or the display of individual images, is given by means of a copy that was not lawfully made under this title, and that the person responsible for the performance knew or had reason to believe was not lawfully made."[20]

A final limitation is that any reproductions to which the immunity applies must be tied to the physical premises of the library ("unsupervised use of reproducing equipment located on its premises"). In other words, a library could still in theory be responsible for the infringement generated by a patron with remote access who uses the virtual premises of the library (its computing network) to infringe copyright by reproducing material at his or her home or office. However, in this scenario this is not the end of the discussion, as immunity, or more properly damages reduction, is offered to service providers under section 512, discussed in great detail in the next chapter.

By the same token, section 108(f)(1) does not demand that the material reproduced with the "unsupervised use of reproducing equipment" be physically "located on its [the library's] premises," only that the reproducing equipment be so located. In other words, the source of the material copied could be an item the patron brought into the library, took from library shelves, obtained from an online database to which the library subscribed, or obtained from a Web site. Any infringement the patron committed by reproducing any of these items by photocopying, scanning, downloading, or the like would be the subject of the section 108(f)(1) immunity.

The conclusion that section 108 does *not* apply to virtual spaces is also supported by the legislative history of the DMCA that amended other subsections of section 108 allowing for digital reproductions and up to three copies or phonorecords in subsections (b) and (c). Why the distinction between real or physical and virtual library spaces? Congress expressed its concern with application of the section 108 rights of libraries and archives to the digital environment. Balance between owners and users[21] is the intended benchmark of copyright legislation. Offering libraries and archives too many rights would jeopardize that delicate balance. As a result, the DMCA Senate Report was unwilling to embrace the concept of the digital library and drew a distinction between the physical premises of the library and virtual spaces:

> Although online interactive digital networks have since given birth to online digital "libraries" and "archives" that exist only in the virtual (rather than physical) sense on Web sites, bulletin boards and home pages across the Internet, it is not the Committee's intent that section 108 as revised apply to such collections of information. . . . The extension of the application of Section 108 to all such sites is tantamount to creating an exception to the exclusive rights of copyright holders that would permit any person who has an online Web site, bulletin boards, or a home page to freely reproduce and distribute copyrighted works. Such an exemption would swallow the general rule and severely impair the copyright owner's right and ability to commercially exploit their copyrighted works.[22]

The message is clear, right or wrong: digital information is different, both in terms of the embodiment of the copyrighted material and in the use patrons can make of that material.[23]

The final requirement of section 108(f)(1) is that the library or archives is granted immunity on condition that "such [reproducing] equipment displays a notice that the making of a copy may be subject to the copyright law." As a result, the library or archives should place a copyright notice on all equipment that could be used to reproduce copyrighted material. The U.S. Copyright Office has not provided a model notice to fulfill the section 108(f)(1) posting obligation. However, use of the following notice, adapted from the text provided by the U.S. Copyright Office offered for use in for-patron reproductions under subsections 108(d) and (e), such as interlibrary loan[24] is possible:

> NOTICE WARNING CONCERNING COPYRIGHT RESTRICTIONS. The copyright law of the United States (Title 17, United States Code) governs the making of photocopies or other reproductions of copyrighted material. Libraries and archives furnish unsupervised photocopy or other reproduction equipment for the convenience of and use by patrons. Under 17 U.S.C. § 108(f)(2) the provision of unsupervised photocopy or reproduction equipment for use by patrons does not excuse the person who uses the reproduction equipment from liability for copyright infringement for any such act, or for any later use of such copy or phonorecord, if it exceeds fair use as provided by section 107 or any other provision of the copyright law. This institution reserves the right to refuse to make available or provide access to photocopy or other reproduction equipment if, in its judgment, use of such equipment would involve violation of copyright law. Repeat violation of the copyright law may result in the termination of network access and use privileges.

The last sentence also fulfills the section 512(i) repeat infringer policy ("adopted and reasonably implemented, and informs subscribers and account holders" of that policy) requirement, discussed in detail in the next chapter. Again the notice must be placed on the reproducing equipment ("the equipment displays"), not just near it!

Ongoing Developments: The Section 108 Study Group

Should section 108 be amended again to increase the immunity of a library and its employees in, for example, Internet or other virtual library or digital archive scenarios? If the experience of recent years is any predictor, a study would likely be undertaken first. A recent Section 108 Study Group of stakeholders, coordinated by copyright guru Laura Gasaway and Richard Rudick (former vice president and general counsel of John Wiley and Sons) may be just such a first step. In a way, however, this is an odd development, because, other than the changes brought by the DMCA to section 108, there has been no amendment since the provision was enacted in 1976 but for one, and it is of relevance to the general mission of the Section 108 Study Group. The purpose of the initiative is to foster dialogue between library and copyright holder interests regarding the library provisions of the copyright act in the hopes of accommodating evolving library practices in the digital environment.[25] The focus would likely be on expanding the digital preservation provisions of section 108 and well as those relating to distribution of materials in digital form. It may be that amendment of section 108 in this light will serve as an end-run or alternative strategy to the roadblock the U.S. Copyright Office placed in the path of reform advocates when it recommended not amending section 109 (the first sale right of libraries) to include allowance for "circulation" of collections in digital form (e.g., an e-book), as such distribution is ultimately both a distribution and a reproduction, the latter right not the subject of section 109.[26] Section 109 of course pertains to both distributions and reproductions. However, bringing such library transactions into the purview of section 108 may not be within the design of that provision. In either case, most digital content is licensed rather than purchased by libraries and schools, so the terms and conditions of any such license agreement might override any new statutory right created by legislative amendment.[27]

Oddly, the Copyright Amendments Act of 1992[28] deleted the original subsection (i) requiring that

> [f]ive years from the effective date of this Act, and at five-year intervals thereafter, the Register of Copyrights, after consulting with representatives of authors, book and periodical publishers, and other owners of copyrighted materials, and with representatives of library users and librarians, shall submit to the Congress a report setting forth the extent to which this section has achieved the intended statutory balancing of the rights of creators, and the needs of users. The report should also describe any problems that may have arisen, and present legislative or other recommendations, if warranted.

Two such reports were filed.[29] Oddly enough in repealing the reporting requirement, the House Report observed that the 1993 law "simply deletes paragraph (i) of section 108, thereby eliminating this recurring reporting requirement, whose purpose has been fulfilled by the reports already filed."[30] At the time, Congress considered that the 12 years and two reports filed since enactment were enough to demonstrate that "Congress struck a fair balance between the public and proprietary interests."[31] Furthermore, the committee observed that the third report, due in 1993, would not be necessary; thus impact on the Copyright Office would be great: "a cost saving of approximately $500,000 will be achieved. The Copyright Office will be able to devote these resources elsewhere."[32] Considering the continued questions the discussion herein raises as well the recent work of the Section 108 Study Group, the repeal of the five-year reporting requirement might have been somewhat premature.

OBTAINING IMMUNITY FOR THE PRODUCTION OF TEMPORARY COPIES

As amended by the TEACH Act,[33] three new undesignated paragraphs have been added to section 110(2).[34] The first two are statements of definition. One defining mediated instructional activities and the other defining accreditation are of course a critical component to understanding the distance education copyright law, but they are less important to the present discussion. However, a third and final paragraph is an immunity provision, and discussion of that paragraph is relevant to and consistent with the topic of this monograph. In short, the paragraph confers immunity on nonprofit educational institutions for the transient or temporary storage of copyrighted material in the course of a distance education class session qualifying under section 110(2), or in the words of the statute, during "an authorized transmission." An accredited nonprofit educational institution must comply with numerous requirements before it can qualify for the section 110(2) privilege, i.e., the right to display or perform copyrighted material in distance education transmissions. These requirements are reviewed at the beginning of Chapter 12, however the operation of the immunity provision itself is discussed here as it falls within the scope the present chapter.

Distance Education and the Transmission of Copyrighted Materials

An on-campus class that uses the Web or computing facilities to connect students from around campus to course materials could be said to constitute a "transmission" for purposes of the copyright law, thus be a "distance education" classroom and fall under the section 110(2) rules as opposed to the section 110(1) rules, the latter rules applying to face-to-face teaching encounters. Under section 110(1) qualifying performances and displays occur within the context "of face-to-face teaching activities of a nonprofit educational institution, in a classroom or similar place devoted to instruction."[35] However, the section 110(1) "concept does not require that the teacher and the students be able to see each other, although it does require their simultaneous presence in the same general place."[36] As long as the instructor and pupil are in the same building or general area, even though the performance might be "broadcast" via in-house, closed-circuit television, the exemption applies, i.e., would *not* be considered a "transmission" qualifying it as a distance education transaction, but still remain governed by the less burdensome and more generous (to copyright users) rules of section 110(1).

Under section 101, "[t]o 'transmit' a performance or display is to communicate it by any device or process whereby images or sounds are received beyond the place from which they are sent."[37] As a result, many class encounters in the modern technology-infused instructional environment might under the copyright fall into the section 110(2) "distance education" rules. Moreover, many circumstances exist whereby faculty, staff, or student access to copyrighted course content as a result of such transmission would also entail the automatic making of a copy of that material somewhere in the system. Multiple copies might even result from copies made at numerous points in the system (such as computers and servers). Are these copies of concern (remember the exclusive right of the copyright owner to reproduce the work)? If so, it would greatly limit the performance and display right granted to educators under section 110(2). Never fear, the copyright law provides special immunity for these so-called "transient or temporary storage" copies made in the course of qualifying section 110(2) transmissions.

Temporary Copies Defined

Section 110(2) concludes by offering immunity to educational institutions:

> For purposes of paragraph (2) [i.e., section 110(2)], no governmental body or accredited nonprofit educational institution *shall be liable* for infringement by reason of the transient or temporary storage of material carried out through the automatic technical process of digital transmission of the performance or display of that material as authorized under paragraph (2) [i.e., section 110(2)]. No such material stored on the system or network controlled or operated by the transmitting body or institution under this paragraph shall be maintained on such system or network in a manner ordinarily accessible to anyone other than anticipated recipients. No such copy shall be maintained on the system or network in a manner ordinarily accessible to such anticipated recipients for a longer period than is reasonably necessary to facilitate the transmission for which it was made.

What are the sorts of transient or temporary storage copies and why is the immunity offered? Examples include the scenario where a copy of work is made in the RAM of a computer in the instructor's office as he or she performs or displays the work and a second copy made in the buffer file of the student receiving the section 110(2) transmission. In any case the copy is "transient or temporary." According to the legislative history the concept is akin to the "conduit" function of service providers embodied in the section 512(a) damage limitation discussed in the next chapter: "The paragraph refers to 'transient' and 'temporary' copies consistent with the terminology used in section 512, including transient copies made in the transmission path by conduits and temporary copies, such as caches, made by the originating institution, by service providers or by recipients."[38] The section 110(2) "carried out through the automatic technical process" is repeated as a condition of the subsection (a) conduit requirements for liability limitation under section 512. Furthermore, the section 512(a)(4) reequirement[39] is repeated nearly word for word in the section 110(2) proviso:

> No such material stored on the system or network controlled or operated by the transmitting body or institution under this paragraph shall be maintained on such system or network in a manner ordinarily accessible to anyone other than anticipated recipients. No such copy shall be maintained on the system or network in a manner ordinarily accessible to such anticipated recipients for a longer period than is reasonably necessary to facilitate the transmission for which it was made.

However, unlike the characterization of section 110(2) by the TEACH legislative history, section 512 offers protection to intermediaries such as institutions or service providers, **not** to recipients. For example, additional copies of works may be created as material is accessed from storage on external or internal servers and loaded onto an institutional distance education server,[40] or a copy may be made in the hard drive or RAM of an instructor's or student's computer as part of the perception of a section 110(2) transmission[41] or by a similar buffering that occurs during transmissions of material loaded by instructors and students from their own computers onto the distance education network at the educational institution.[42] In spite of the section 110(2) language of the statute stating that "no governmental body or accredited nonprofit educational institution *shall be liable*," the examples provided by the legislative history include both sender ("governmental body or accredited nonprofit educational institution") and recipient.

In each of these examples, and assuming the work performed or displayed is protected, a copy of a copyrighted work has been made. This paragraph is designed to offer immunity to the educational institution for any infringement that could be said to occur as a result of those transient or temporary copies. Unlike the section 108(f)(1) immunity, which did not apply to the educational institution as a whole, but only to its library, section 110 *is* an educator's provision, though the concept is broad enough to include staff and students. It does not include any transient copy made on the institution's servers or computers, but only those copies made in conjunction with a distance education transmission. For example, the copy of an infringing work that the assistant to the provost accessed from an illicit P2P Web site and which is now residing in the transient space (e.g., buffer, cache, or RAM) of the assistant's computer would not be covered by the section 110(2) immunity.

The general requirements of section 110(2) must be met—and there are many. The major limitation is that the material must be used in conjunction with actual online instruction. The nature of the content in the online instruction can however be analog or digital under section 110(2). In its simplest form, section 110(2) pertains to material that is part of the actual teaching session, synchronous or asynchronous, and not background resources such as e-reserves.[43] However, the immunity here only applies to copies of that material that exist in digital form. Suffice it to say that the transient or temporary storage copies offered immunity here are those linked to a section 110(2) performance or display: "of the performance or display of that material as authorized under paragraph (2) [i.e., section 110(2)]." These are transient copies that are used in an actual online instructional encounter, not just any material the institution might make available in online environments, transient or otherwise, such as in its e-reserve system.

Without engaging in a detailed discussion of section 110(2), but perhaps anticipating an obvious question, this transient or temporary storage immunity does not address copies that are purposely made by instructors or students in anticipation of a section 110(2) online teaching encounter. In these circumstances where a copy is purposefully made, it cannot be said to be incidental, "temporary or transient storage"; rather it is of a more permanent nature, retained for a subsequent section 110(2) use. Is the making of those "permanent" copies authorized here? No, copies for storage for periods beyond transient or temporary are the purview of section 112, the ephemeral recording provision.[44] In some circumstances, section 112 authorizes the making of copies, either in anticipation of a qualifying section 110(2) performance or display of that material under section 112(f) (a before-the-fact-of-teaching copy) or as a qualifying section 110(2) performance or display that has already occurred under section 112(b) (an after-the-fact-of-teaching copy). In the latter case, the teacher would like a copy of his or her instructional transmission to use for review or critique and that copy would necessarily include copies of material he or she performed or displayed during that (now recorded) session. In the former case, section 112(f) authorizes the institution to make so-called ephemeral copies of copyrighted materials as a precursor to a section 110(2) transmission, e.g., load the material on its distance education server to facilitate 24/7 access by students. However, in either example, the ephemeral recording that results must be in conjunct with a bona fide section 110(2) performance or display.

In the process of using those authorized before-and-after-the-fact copies, additional and successive copies may be made by instructors and students as the material is legitimately accessed and used; it is these transient or temporary storage RAM, buffer, server, and similar copies that are the subject of the transient or temporary storage immunity provision of section 110. As a result of the inability to police the making of these transient or temporary copies, the provision "recognizes that transmitting organizations should not be responsible for copies or phonorecords made by third parties, beyond the control of the transmitting organizations."[45]

Requirements and Limitations of Temporary Copy Immunity

In addition to the nuances of section 110(2) qualification, two other requirements are contained in the immunity paragraph, one related to who may access the transient or temporary storage material, and a second related to how long that access may exist. In short, the only persons with access to the material should be enrolled students, i.e., the "anticipated recipients." This is the meaning of the sentence: "No such material stored on the system or network controlled or operated by the transmitting body or institution under this paragraph shall be maintained on such system or network in a manner ordinarily accessible to anyone other than anticipated recipients." Second, the duration of the access of the anticipated recipients can be for a period no longer than the class session, i.e., no "longer period than is reasonably necessary to facilitate the transmission for which it was made." Echoing the Register's Report,[46] the Conference Report indicates that these two conditions address the "concern that the exemption should not be transformed into a mechanism for obtaining copies."[47]

The purpose of the provision is to immunize the nonprofit educational institution against any potential liability for transient or temporary storage of material carried out through the automatic processes of making a bona fide section 110(2) transmission. As a result of the inability to police the making of these transient or temporary copies, the provision "recognizes that transmitting organizations should not be responsible for copies or phonorecords made by third parties, beyond the control of the transmitting organizations."[48] This provision provides immunity from secondary liability, contributory and vicarious, that might otherwise result from the direct infringement caused by an employee or student as he or she uses copyrighted material in conjunction with a section 110(2) online instructional encounter.

While the statute uses the language "no governmental body or accredited nonprofit educational institution shall be liable for *infringement*" without qualifying the targeted "infringement" as either primary or secondary, as observed in the previous discussions of secondary liability and reduction, remission, and immunity, a "governmental body or accredited nonprofit educational institution" is a legal fiction; it can do nothing of its own accord but acts through its employees or permits others (third parties such as students) to work through it. Thus the provision, similar to section 108(f)(1), in practice protects the institution from the contributory infringement of third parties such as students. However, the good news is that unlike section 108(f)(1), it is argued here that the section 110 proviso offers immunity to the educational institution from the vicarious infringement that might result from the acts (direct infringement, i.e., the making of transient copies) of its employees, though arguably in rather limited circumstances: "by reason of the transient or temporary storage of material carried out through the automatic technical process of digital transmission of the performance or display of that material as authorized under paragraph (2)." Thus the transient or temporary storage immunity applies to circumstances of potential vicarious employee-based liability as well.

Institutional Immunity and the Individual Infringer

The language of the statute confers immunity on the "accredited nonprofit educational institution." As discussed in Chapters 1 through 4, under statutory and common-law liability and statutory immunity concepts there is a legal difference between employees or third parties (such as patrons or students) and intermediaries (such as an institution or an employer). According to the plain language of the transient and temporary storage immunity provision and unlike section 108(f)(1) ("library or archives *or its employees*"), the immunity here is *not* conferred upon the employee as potential secondary infringer. However, the legislative history supports a broad sweep of protection that could be interpreted to apply to the initial actor, the student, or employee as well as the intermediary institution, assuming the other qualifying circumstances are present:

> The third paragraph added to the amended exemption by section 1(b)(2) of the TEACH Act is intended to make clear that *those authorized to participate* in digitally transmitted performances and displays as authorized under section 110(2) are *not liable for infringement* as a result of such *copies created as part of the automatic technical process of the transmission* if the requirements of that language are met.[49]

An officially enrolled student would be one of "those authorized to participate" as well as a more obvious group of "those authorized to participate," the instructional staff.

Is the legislative history in conflict with the statute? To an extent it is. Which prevails? The plain language of the statute suggests that the transient or temporary storage immunity applies only to the institution and not to third parties such as students or the public or employees. If it were meant to so apply, this immunity amendment, added in 2002, could have been drafted to clearly include those actors. Something along these lines was done in the reproducing equipment immunity provision of section 108(f)(1), which was enacted in 1976, and with respect to which it is assumed the 107th Congress in 2002 had full knowledge.[50] Furthermore, interpreting a more limited (and literal) application would be consistent with section 110(2), the focus of which is on activities of the educational intermediary (i.e., the school, college, university) and not necessarily on individuals such as teachers, staff, and students. On the other hand, the Conference Report consistently uses examples of "recipients" when offering examples of the application of the provision: "such as caches, made by the originating institution, by service providers or by *recipients*... or in the computer of the *recipient* of the transmission ... the *recipient's* browser may create a cache copy of an encrypted file on the *recipient's* random access memory at the time the content is perceived."[51] Nonetheless, faced with a possible claim of infringement, an employee or student could point to this legislative history and hope a court would likewise come to a broader application of the immunity. However, it should be pointed out that courts are not required to accept the interpretation offered in the legislative history.

Consider several concluding observations regarding the nature of the section 110(2) transient or temporary storage copies in contrast with the section 108(f)(1) reproducing equipment copies. Section 110 offers immunity only with respect to transient or temporary storage of copies or phonorecords, whereas section 108(f)(1) offers immunity for copies or phonorecords made with some permanency, i.e. those made by the patrons for extended and repeated use. The section 110(2) immunity applies to material used in qualifying online instructional performances and displays that by the plain language of the statute is limited for certain categories of copyrighted works to certain portion limitations (see Chapter 12), whereas the section 108(f)(1) immunity applies to material reproduced by the patron for any use. The text of section 110(2) indicates two circumstances of the immunity: "carried out through the automatic technical process of a digital transmission." The content copied must be digital and would apply to transient copies made by either the sender or receiver and could further result from either on-site or off-site transmission. This is the meaning of the word "process" (as the statute could have used the word "result of a digital transmission" to indicate only received content). Second the copied material must be the result of an automatic technical process such as copies. In contrast, a section 108 "reproducing equipment" copy anticipates either analog or digital but decidedly restricts the qualifying reproductions to those made on its premises, i.e., "any reproducing equipment *located on its premises*." Section 110 contains no such digital "premises" requirement, and in fact the "anytime, anywhere" characteristic of modern distance education is supported by section 110 as revised by TEACH.[52]

REAL-WORLD EXAMPLES

▶ Real-World Example I

Situation: A public library makes photocopiers and computers available for patron use. A patron uses the photocopier to reproduce an entire series of romance novels, while another patron uses the computer to download numerous files of infringing music from a music-sharing site. A copyright warning notice is posted on all library photocopiers and computers.

Legal Analysis: Under section 108(f)(1), a qualifying library shares no liability for the unsupervised use of reproducing equipment. As long as circumstances do not exist that would suggest supervision of the reproducing activity, and since a warning notice is posted, section 108(f)(1) operates to immunize the employees and library for any liability arising out of the infringing activity of either patron. However, according to section 108(f)(2), the possibility of patron liability is preserved.

▶ **Real-World Example II**

Situation: The situation is similar to Real-World Example II, except that in the case of the photocopier, an employee makes the copies as a back-up for use in an upcoming library book club discussion series, and in the case of the computer, the librarian assists the patron by guiding the patron through the entire search-and-download session.

Legal Analysis: The section 108(f)(1) immunity will not operate to shelter the library from potential secondary liability here, as the use of the reproducing technology is not "unsupervised." The librarian is under the supervision of his or her employer even if not subject to constant real-time, visual monitoring. Likewise, the over-the-shoulder assistance from search to download is also a supervised use by the patron of the reproducing equipment.

▶ **Real-World Example III**

Situation: This is similar to the previous examples, except that the setting is a public school library that makes available for patrons and staff use of the photocopies and computers. While all visitors must register at the front office before entering the building, parents and other interested members of the community may use the resources of the library at any time during the school day.

Legal Analysis: In order to qualify for the section 108(f)(1) immunity, or any other subsection of section 108, the "collections of the library or archives" must be either "open to the public, or available not only to researchers affiliated with the library or archives or with the institution of which it is a part, but also to other persons doing research in a specialized field." The mere fact that patrons-students come from the community does not necessary cause the collections to be "open to the public" but since parents and others may also use the collections of the library, the school library would be considered "open to the public" and qualify for the section 108(f)(1) immunity.

▶ **Real-world Example IV**

Situation: As part of a distance education class session that otherwise complies with the copyright statute relating to distance education (Section 110(2)), numerous copies of course materials are made on the computers of faculty and students, such as in the RAM or buffers, and on the file servers of various network links on campus.

Legal Analysis: Under the "transient or temporary storage" provision of section 110, an accredited nonprofit educational institution is immunized from liability for copyright infringement that may result from the "transient or temporary storage of material carried out through the automatic technical process of digital transmission of the performance or display of that material as authorized under paragraph (2)." This provision assumes that the material is used in support of a qualifying performance or display under section 110(2). If that is the case, then the institution is immune from any infringement resulting from the successive copies that are made ("transient or temporary storage of material"); this includes copies made by students as well as faculty or other employees.

KEY POINTS FOR YOUR INSTITUTION'S POLICY AND PRACTICE

▶ A qualifying nonprofit library or archives or its employees is immune from copyright liability for copies made by patrons, students, or other third parties through "the unsupervised use of reproducing equipment located on its premises." See pp. 120–123.

▶ In order to qualify for this protection, the library or archive should place a suitable warning notice "that the making of a copy may be subject to the copyright law" on all equipment capable of reproducing copyrighted material, such as a photocopier, scanner, sampler, computer, or printer. See pp. 123–126.

▶ Section 108 of the copyright law grants qualifying libraries and archives additional reproduction and distribution rights beyond that of fair use. However, the library or archives must ensure that the reproduction or distribution is made "without any purpose of direct or indirect commercial advantage; the "collections" of the library or archives must be "open to the public" or "available . . . to other persons doing research in a specialized field; and any copies or phonorecords made must include either the original notice of copyrighted material or, if no notice appears on the work, "a legend stating that the work may be protected by copyright." See pp. 113–119.

▶ In instances where the immunity applies, the statute makes clear that the immunity does not extend to the initial party making use of the unsupervised reproducing equipment, e.g., the patron or student. Furthermore, if the copy so made is found to be infringing, the immunity extended to the library or archive does nothing to otherwise validate the infringing nature of the copy. In other words, such copy could not satisfy any of the so-called "lawfully made" requirements that exist elsewhere in the copyright law, such as the right to distribute (circulate) materials under section 109, or to perform audiovisual works under section 110(1), or to perform or display materials under section 110(2). See pp. 123–124.

▶ Finally, the section 108(f)(1) immunity applies only to copies made with reproducing equipment *located on the premises* of the library or archives. It does not apply to copies made through reproducing equipment located elsewhere throughout the institution in the case of a school, college, or university or by library patrons off-site, i.e., by remote access. See pp. 124–126.

▶ In distance education environments, immunity also exists for successive and infringing copies that may result from the "transient or temporary storage of copyrighted material carried out by the automatic technical process of a digital transmission of the performance or display of that material as authorized under paragraph (2) [of section 110]." Examples would be copies in the RAM, file buffers, program caches, or servers of computing networks and facilities used in distance education. See pp. 127–130.

▶ This immunity applies only if the transient or temporary storage copies are made in conjunction with a digital distance education performance or display that otherwise complies with the copyright relating to distance education, discussed in Chapter 12. See pp. 130–132.

ENDNOTES

[1] See, generally, KEN CREWS, COPYRIGHT LAW FOR LIBRARIANS 81-90 (2000); MARY MINOW AND TOMAS A. LIPINSKI, THE LIBRARY'S LEGAL ANSWER BOOK 40-53 (2003) (Q24-Q55).

[2] 17 U.S.C. § 108(a).

[3] 17 U.S.C. § 108(a) begins: "Except as otherwise provided in this title and notwithstanding the provisions of section 106, it is not an infringement of copyright for a library or archives, *or any of its employees acting within the scope of their employment,* to reproduce no more than one copy or phonorecord of a work, except as provided in subsections (b) and (c), or to distribute such copy or phonorecord, under the conditions specified by this section."

[4] This is not to suggest that all scenarios that might reduce subscription or license fees, for example that might result from the creation of coursepacks, would be disqualifying. First, the "law" of coursepacks is section 107, fair use law, not section 108. However, if the library invites through signage or other statements in school or campus newsletter, Web notices, etc., that students are "encouraged to save money, forego the purchase of course packs and come to library and photocopy the semester's worth of reading," this might well constitute

a "reproduction or distribution [] made with . . . [a] purpose of direct or indirect commercial advantage," especially if some arm of the campus, say its bookstore, would typically be the device of the coursepack preparation and distribution.

[5] 17 U.S.C. §108(a).

[6] *American Geophysical Union v. Texaco, Inc.*, 802 F. Supp. 1, 27 (S.D.N.Y. 1992), *aff'd*, 60 F.3d 913, 917 (2nd Cir. 1993) (emphasis added).

[7] *Lowry's Reports, Inc. v. Legg Mason, Inc.*, 271 F. Supp. 2d 737, 748 (D. Md. 2003).

[8] R. No. 94-1476, 94th Cong., 2nd Sess. 75 (1976) (conf. rep.), reprinted in 5 United States Code Congressional and Administrative News 5659, 5689 (1976) (emphasis added).

[9] S. Rep. No. 94-473, 94th Cong., 2nd Sess. 67 (1976).

[10] H. Rpt. No. 94-1733, 94th Cong., 2nd Sess. 74 (1976) (Conference Report), reprinted in 5 U.S.C.C.A.N. 5810, 5815 (1976) (all emphasis added).

[11] *Lowry's Reports, Inc. v. Legg Mason, Inc.*, 302 F. Supp. 2d 455, 459 (D. Md. 2004).

[12] *Lowry's Reports, Inc. v. Legg Mason, Inc.*, 302 F. Supp. 2d 455, 463 (D. Md. 2004) ("However, Lowry's has also provided evidence that Legg Mason obstructed discovery, made material misrepresentations to the Court, and destroyed evidence.").

[13] 17 U.S.C. §108(f)(1).

[14] H. R. No. 94-1476, 94th Cong., 2nd Sess. 76 (1976) (conf. rep.), reprinted in 5 U.S.C.C.A.N. 5659, 5690 (1976) ("Clause (1) of subsection (f) specifically exempts a library or archives or its employees from liability for the unsupervised use of reproducing equipment located on its premises, provided that reproducing equipment displays a notice that the making of a copy may be subject to the copyright law.").

[15] 17 U.S.C. § 108(f)(2).

[16] *Lowry's Reports, Inc. v. Legg Mason, Inc.*, 271 F. Supp. 2d 737, 745-746 (D. Md. 2003) ("There can be no doubt that Legg Mason had the right and ability to supervise its own employees, who infringed Lowry's copyrights at Legg Mason offices, using company equipment, on company time.").

[17] INFORMATION INFRASTRUCTURE TASK FORCE, INTELLECTUAL PROPERTY AND THE NATIONAL INFORMATION INFRASTRUCTURE: THE REPORT OF THE WORKING GROUP ON INTELLECTUAL PROPERTY RIGHTS 111, n. 357 (1995) ("A contributory infringer may be liable based on the provision of services or equipment related to the direct infringement." Id. at 111.).

[18] *People v. Saucier*, 221 Ill. App. 3d 287, 293, 581 N.E.2d 852, 856 (1991) ("The order required that defendant have no unsupervised contact with any minors whatsoever. While it is arguable that defendant had at least visual contact from a distance, and while we sympathize with the victim in her extreme discomfort in seeing defendant, unfortunately, the term 'unsupervised' is not defined in any way. The word has been defined to mean: 'not under constant observation.' (WEBSTER'S THIRD NEW INTERNATIONAL DICTIONARY 2512 (1986).) It is undisputed there was at least one adult present at all times who observed the drive-by incident. Regarding his harassment of the victim, defendant's conduct may have been less than honorable. However, it was not a violation of the probation order.").

[19] R. No. Rep. 94-1476, 94th Cong., 2nd Sess. 76 (1976) (conf. rep.), reprinted in 5 U.S.C.C.A.N. 5659, 5690 (1976).

[20] 17 U.S.C. § 110(1).

[21] The DMCA Senate Report cautioned: "this proviso is necessary to ensure that the amendment strikes the appropriate balance, permitting the use of digital technology by libraries and archives while guarding against the potential harm to the copyright owners' market from patrons obtaining unlimited access to digital copies from any location." S. Rpt. 105-190, 105th Cong., 2d Session 61-62 (1998).

[22] S. Rpt. No. 105-190, 105th Cong., 2d Session 62 (1998).

[23] Tomas A. Lipinski, The Myth of Technological Neutrality in Copyright Law and the Rights of Institutional Users, 54 JOURNAL OF THE AMERICAN SOCIETY FOR INFORMATION SCIENCE AND TECHNOLOGY 824 (2003).

[24] 37 C.F.R. § 201.14.

[25] The U.S. Copyright Office and the National Digital Information Infrastructure and Preservation Program is sponsoring the Section 108 Study Group. The timeline includes the preparation of findings and recommendations by mid-year 2006, followed by a U.S. Copyright Office round of public hearings, with final recommendations to Congress sometime thereafter. "This effort will seek to strike the appropriate balance between copyright holders and libraries and archives in a manner that best serves the public interest." See, Press Release, Section 108 Study Group Convenes to Discuss Exceptions to Copyright Law for Libraries and Archives, May 13, 2005. Compare to mission statement of the Section 108 Study Group: "The group will provide findings and recommendations on how to revise the copyright law in order to ensure an appropriate balance among the interests of creators and other copyright holders, libraries and archives in a manner that best serves the *national* interest." Id. (note addition of creators and shift from public interest to national interest, i.e., a broader range of stakeholders and interests).

[26] DMCA: SECTION 104 REPORT, U.S. COPYRIGHT OFFICE (A REPORT OF THE REGISTER OF COPYRIGHTS PURSUANT TO §104 OF THE DIGITAL MILLENNIUM COPYRIGHT ACT), p. xx (2001) ("We are concerned that these proposals for a digital first sale doctrine endeavor to fit the exploitation of works on line into a distribution model—the sale of copies—that was developed within the confines of pre-digital technology. If the sale model is to continue as the dominant method of distribution, it should be the choice of the market, not due to legislative fiat"). See also, Tomas A. Lipinski (in progress), The Emerging Paradigm of Ownership Rights in Digital Media and Its Impact on the Future of the E-Book and the Virtual Library: Is the Legal Infrastructure a Help or Hindrance? (2005). Part 1: From Gutenberg to the Global Information Infrastructure . . .

[27] *See* Lee S. Strickland, Copyright's Digital Dilemma Today: Fair Use or Unfair Constraints? Part 2: The DMCA, The TEACH Act and Other E-Copying Considerations, BULLETIN OF THE AMERICAN SOCIETY FOR INFORMATION SCIENCE AND TECHNOLOGY, December/January, 2004, at 18, 19 ("Without UCITA, one has a broader right to contest legally many onerous provisions of a license or the license in its entirety if it was presented in a manner that did not achieve the users consent.").

[28] Pub. L. No. 102-307, 106 Stat. 264, title III, section 301 (1992).

[29] LIBRARY REPRODUCTION OF COPYRIGHTED WORKS (17 U.S.C. 108): REPORT OF THE REGISTER OF COPYRIGHT (1983); AND LIBRARY REPRODUCTION OF COPY-RIGHTED WORKS (17 U.S.C. 108): REPORT OF THE REGISTER OF COPYRIGHT (1988).

[30] H.R. Rpt. 102-379, 1 (1991).

[31] H.R. Rpt. 102-379, 2 (1991), quoting the 1988 Register's Report indicating the agreement of major library associations (LIBRARY REPRODUCTION OF COPYRIGHTED WORKS (17 U.S.C. 108): REPORT OF THE REGISTER OF COPYRIGHT 118 (1983)).

[32] H.R. Rpt. 102-379, 3 (1991).

[33] TEACH, the Technology, Education and Copyright Harmonization Act of 2002, introduced as S. 487, 107th Cong., 1st Sess. (2001) was incorporated into H.R. 2215, the 21st Century Department of Justice Appropriations Authorization Act, later enacted into law as Pub. L. No. 107-273, 116 Stat. 1758, tit. III, subtitle C, sec. 13301 (2002).

[34] Section 110(2) is the main provision of the copyright law dealing with distance education. A brief overview is presented in Chapter 12.

[35] 17 U.S.C. § 110(1).

[36] H. Rep. No. 94-1476, 94th Cong., 2d Sess. 81 (1976) (conf. rep.), reprinted in 5 U.S.C.C.A.N. 5659, 5695 (1976).

[37] 17 U.S.C. § 101.

[38] Conference Report, H. R. Rep. No. 107-685, 107th Cong., 2nd Sess. 233 (2002). (conf. rep.)

[39] 17 U.S.C. § 512(a)(4) ("no copy of the material made by the service provider in the course of such intermediate or transient storage is maintained on the system or network in a manner ordinarily accessible to anyone other than anticipated recipients, and no such copy is maintained on the system or network in a manner ordinarily accessible to such anticipated recipients for a longer period than is reasonably necessary for the transmission, routing, or provision of connections").

[40] H. R. Rep. No. 107-685, 107th Cong., 2nd Sess. 233 (2002) (conf. rep.) ("Organizations providing digital distance education will, in many cases, provide material from source servers that create additional temporary or transient copies or phonorecords of the material in storage known as 'caches' in other servers in order to facilitate the transmission.").

[41] H. R. Rep. No. 107-685, 107th Cong., 2nd Sess. 233 (2002) (conf. rep.) ("Thus, by way of example, where content is protected by a digital rights management system, the recipient's browser may create a cache copy of an encrypted file on the recipient's hard disk, and another copy may be created in the recipient's random access memory at the time the content is perceived.").

[42] H. R. Rep. No. 107-685, 107th Cong., 2nd Sess. 233 (2002) (conf. rep.) ("In addition, transient or temporary copies or phonorecords may occur in the transmission stream, or in the computer of the recipient of the transmission").

[43] A thorough review of section 110(2) is found in TOMAS A. LIPINSKI, COPYRIGHT LAW AND THE DISTANCE EDUCATION CLASSROOM 35-114 (2005).

[44] Though the making of these copies may be allowed by section 112(f), also added by the TEACH Act. For a discussion of section 112(f) and the so-called ephemeral recording right see, TOMAS A. LIPINSKI, COPYRIGHT LAW AND THE DISTANCE EDUCATION CLASSROOM 115-154 (2005).

[45] H. R. Rep.. No. 107-685, 107th Cong., 2nd Sess. 233 (2002) (conf. rep.).

[46] U.S. COPYRIGHT OFFICE, REPORT ON COPYRIGHT AND DIGITAL DISTANCE EDUCATION 151 (1999) ("First, any transient copies permitted under the exemption should be retained for no longer than reasonably necessary to complete the transmission. [footnote omitted] This ensures that the partial coverage of the reproduction right is not broadened beyond its technological necessity in enabling performances and displays, and does not transform the limited purpose of this exemption into a mechanism for obtaining copies.").

[47] H. R. Rep. No. 107-685, 107th Cong., 2nd Sess. 233 (2002) (conf. rep.).

[48] H. R. Rep. No. 107-685, 107th Cong., 2nd Sess. 233 (2002) (conf. rep.).

[49] H. R. Rep. No. 107-685, 107th Cong., 2nd Sess. 233 (2002) (emphasis added).

[50] NORMAN J. SINGER, SUTHERLAND STATUTORY CONSTRUCTION § 22:29 (2002) (Construction of amendatory acts.) ("In ascertaining the meaning of amendatory language, a court must look to prior law, matters deemed to require correction and the remedy enacted. The legislature is presumed to be aware of existing statutes when it amends state or enacts a new one.") (footnotes omitted).

[51] H. R. Rep. No. 107-685, 107th Cong., 2nd Sess. 233 (2002) (conf. rep.) (all emphasis added).

[52] See, H. R. Rep. No. 107-685, 107th Cong., 2nd Sess. 230 (2002) (conf. rep.) ("One of the great potential benefits of digital distance education is its ability to reach beyond the physical classroom, to provide quality educational experiences to all students of all income levels, in cities and rural settings, in schools and on campuses, in the workplaces, at home, and at times selected by students to meet their needs.").

6

WHAT IS THE SECTION 512 SAFE HARBOR?

Read this chapter to learn about copyright situations like:
▶ Whether a library or school can be held accountable for illegal copies uploaded by patrons to the institution's Website.
▶ Whether an institution can receive immunity for adopting a repeat copyright infringer policy after the fact of initial infringements.

For over a decade, sections 108 and 109 remained the only provisions requiring nonprofit organizations to do much of anything in the way of copyright compliance efforts, and then through the use of copyright warning notices alone. (Section 108 was enacted as part of the Copyright Act of 1976,[1] while the notice provision of section 109 became law as a result of amendment in 1990.[2]) Section 108, as discussed in Chapter 5, applies to qualifying nonprofit libraries and archives, and is further discussed in Chapter 12. For the purposes of this monograph, section 109 applies to qualifying nonprofit libraries and educational institutions and is discussed in Chapter 11. Requiring the use of warning notices is but one way the copyright law can "encourage" that a compliant environment be created within the library or educational institution. The word "encourage" is used as the law typically does not require that such notices be used, but conditions the availability of an additional benefit (in copyright parlance, a limitation on one or more of the exclusive rights of the copyright owner) upon some compliance effort, in this case the use of a warning notice. In the case of section 108, use of the warning notice offers immunity to qualifying libraries and archives for any liability arising from the infringing acts of patrons, while section 109 provides qualifying libraries and educational entities with the right to distribute software. Copyright warning notices are but one tool of compliance. In fact as Parts III and IV of this monograph demonstrate, Congress is expanding its array of compliance measures with each new piece of copyright legislation it enacts. Examples of compliance measures include adopting copyright policies, engaging in informational outreach (which could take the form of in-service or other training sessions, signs, and newsletters or other written documentation), incorporating technological protection measures into a network environment, and offering the appropriate response when notified of infringing conduct.

In contrast to these heretofore rather basic "compliance-as-notice provisions," section 512, enacted as part of the DMCA,[3] represents a significant departure and new trend within the copyright law, as it requires entities to take the next logical and more active compliance step. "The DMCA, therefore, encourages ISPs to co-operate with content providers by offering insulation from potential copyright liability."[4] Recent changes to the law such as section 512 move intermediaries such as libraries and educational institutions beyond the simple first step—requiring the posting of copyright notices. The copyright law now directs, as a second step, those entities desiring the protection of the section 512 so-called safe harbor to establish a copyright policy,[5] and in certain circumstances to designate a registered agent,[6] to make appropriate responses (take-down or disable[7] and copyright owner notification[8] as well as subscriber notification[9]). In addition, for an institution of higher education desiring additional protection under the safe harbor, it must also have an informational compliance program in place.[10]

UNDERSTANDING THE CONCEPT OF SAFE HARBOR

Section 512 provides a so-called "safe harbor" for service providers or other online intermediaries. Consider the following: By seeking the benefit of a secure port ("safe harbor") in a storm, a captain and crew can rest assured that their efforts to properly moor their ship will result in little or no damage to the vessel. Translating the analogy to the copyright law, the storm is copyright liability, the damage to the vessel is the plaintiff's monetary remedy including cost and attorney's fees, and the mooring efforts represent the compliance-oriented provisions required of the intermediary-service provider. Of course the harbormaster may establish a set of basic rules governing vessels that enter and travel within the harbor. The statute operates as a harbormaster of sorts, articulating the conditions and circumstances under which a ship (a library or educational institution) may seek the safety of its waters. Qualifying for entry into the confines of the safe harbor requires a series of extensive compliance-oriented measures. These rules of comportment are the basic requirements of qualification under section 512. The safe harbor rules are rather complex[11] though an overview is provided here. In its simplest terms, section 512 provides this safe harbor when the intermediary-service provider engages in one of four functions, corresponding to subsections (a)-(d), conduit, caching, posting, and linking. Section 512 is not a liability provision, it does not in any of its subsections create any additional liability for copyright infringement. As explained by Dratler: "Section 512 is thus like a one-way valve. It admits any defendant that meets the conditions for its limitations on remedies, but it bars any plaintiff who seeks to 'bootstrap' failure to meet its precise and narrow terms into reason for imposing copyright liability. It is a shield, not a sword."[12]

Functions Covered by the Safe Harbor: "Conduit" Functions

First, in section 512 parlance, it is most accurate to speak of a "service provider," as that is the term the statute uses. However, the author often inserts the word "intermediary" or "online intermediary" into the discussion, as this concept is a bit more descriptive of the broad scope of the statute's application. This "service provider" or online intermediary could be a public library, school, college, university, or its library or any unit within such organization—any entity that offers computing facilities that provide conduit, cache, post, or link functions. The definition of service provider for the conduit (also referred to as the "transitory digital network communications" (the words of the statute) or store and forward function (Professor Dratler's words) provision, subsection 512(a), is contained in section 512(k)(1)(A): "(A) As used in subsection (a), the term 'service provider' means an entity offering the transmission, routing, or providing of connections for digital online communications, between or among points specified by a user, of material of the user's choosing, without modification to the content of the material as sent or received."[13] When the subsection "(A)" conduit definition applies to a particular service provider, the safe harbor protects the service provider from any monetary damages due to copyright infringement "by reason of the provider's transmitting, routing, or providing connections for, material through a system or network controlled or operated by or for the service provider, or by reason of the intermediate and transient storage of that material in the course of such transmitting, routing, or providing connections,"[14] provided other conditions are met, as discussed below.

This "transmission, routing, or providing of connections" is not a new concept in the law, as the legislative history explains: "This free-standing definition is derived from the definition of 'telecommunications' found in the Communications Act of 1934 (47 U.S.C. § 153(48)) in recognition of the fact that the functions covered by new subsection (a) are essentially conduit-only functions."[15] This is the online equivalent of the phone company, and it is unlikely that a library or educational institution with even the most elaborate computing facilities would qualify. However, in a critical difference between the copyright law (section 512) and the telecommunications law (Title 47), section 512 applies only to digital content and only to that digital content in Internet or other "online" environments:

> The Committee, however, has tweaked the definition . . . to ensure that it captures offerings over the Internet and other on-line media. Thus, the new definition . . . not only includes "the offering of transmission, routing or providing of connections," but also requires that the service provider be providing such services for communications that are both "digital" *and* "on-line." By "on-line" communications, the Committee means communications over interactive computer networks, such as the Internet."[16]

As a result, even if it is digital, "over-the-air broadcasting," cable, satellite, and the like would be excluded from obtaining the protection of the safe harbor as these are not "communications over interactive computer networks."[17] Of course such technologies could be designed to provide connectivity to "interactive computer networks," thus falling within the definition.

Furthermore it does not matter if the original *form* of the information was altered, i.e., converted from analog to digital so that the transmission, routing, or provision of connections is now Internet-based; it qualifies. Alteration of form is allowed, but alteration of *content* is not.[18] For example, providing access to a Web site would qualify, but hosting one would not as the latter implies the ability to alter content, store content, post content, link to content, and so forth. These are functions of the section 512(b)–(d) provisos and the other definitional provision that that relate to activities: "[h]osting a web site *does not* fall within the new subsection (j)(1)(A) definition [at the time Part 2 of the House Report was issued, the definitions were contained in section 512(j)], whereas the mere provision of connectivity to a web site *does* fall within that definition."[19] In a further distinction, only the functions of the service provider that fall within a particular definition (the conduit or the cache-post-link) are given the protection of the safe harbor.[20] By the same token, simply because some functions of a service provider do not fall within the definition, it does not mean that the service provider is excluded from qualifying for the safe harbor with regard to those functions that do qualify; it just means that the protection does not extend beyond the limits of the definition.[21]

Functions Covered by the Safe Harbor: Caching, Posting, and Linking

For the remaining subsections, (b) through (d), the cache, post, and link functions respectively, or "any other new subsection of new Section 512" for that matter,[22] the definition is as follows: "As used in this section, other than subsection (a), the term 'service provider' means a provider of online services or network access, or the operator of facilities therefor [*sic*], and includes an entity described in subparagraph (A)."[23] The legislative history offers numerous examples of the sorts of service providers that are included in the subsection "(B)" definition governing the cache, post, and link functions: "This definition is broader than the first, covering providers of on-line services or network access, or the operator of facilities therefor. [*sic*] This definition includes, for example, services such as providing Internet access, e-mail, chat room and web page hosting services."[24] Of course a section 512(a) conduit service provider could also offer "online services or network access." "The new definition also specifically includes any entity that falls within the first definition of service provider. A broadcaster or cable television system or satellite television service would not qualify, except to the extent it performs functions covered by (j)(1)(B) [as enacted (j)(1)(B) became section 512(k)(1)(B)]."[25] In other words, a service provider could qualify for both definitions, depending on how the copyrighted material came to be associated with its service.

The example provided by the legislative history above is the more likely (i.e., that a section 512(a) service provider, "offering the transmission, routing, or providing of connections for digital online communications," would also offer "online services or network access") rather than the other way around (i.e., that a public library or university, clearly a section 512(k)(1)(B) service provider, would also be a high-level communications service provider under section 512(k)(1)(A), "offering the transmission, routing, or providing of connections for digital online communications"). The sorts of institutions where these functions occur is made clear to include those relevant to the focus of this monograph: "The new subsection (j)(1)(B) definition of service provider, for example, *includes universities and schools* to the extent that they perform the functions identified in new subsection (j)(1)(B)."[26] For example, a federal district court concluded that eBay met the section 512(k)(1)(B) definition of service provider and that, even though copies of the item at issue, pirated reproductions of the documentary film *Manson*, were not posted on the eBay Web site, an "infringing activity" occurred (i.e., using the eBay service to sell and distribute unauthorized copies), and this act nonetheless met the "post" function of subsection (c).[27]

Appreciating the Value of the Safe Harbor

When the safe-harbor protection is triggered it provides a limitation on the imposition of all monetary relief available to copyright plaintiffs, including the dark cloud of attorney's fees! Subsections (a)–(d) begin with the same generous grant of refuge: "A service provider shall *not be liable for monetary relief,* or, except as provided in subsection (j), for injunctive or other equitable relief, for infringement of copyright." Section 512(k)(2) defines monetary relief to include "damages, costs, attorneys' fees, and any other form of monetary payment."[28] The Conference Report offers a sentiment of broad protection: "The limitations in subsections (a) through (d) protect qualifying service providers from liability for *all monetary relief for direct, vicarious and contributory infringement.*"[29] This protection would apply to claims for monetary damages arising not only from copyright owners but from a subscriber (i.e., the direct infringer), as would be the case where a claim is made that alleged infringing material was removed in error under subsection (g) discussed below.[30]

Moreover, any injunctive relief is limited to that provided in section 512(j) ("except as provided in subsection (j), for injunctive or other equitable relief"), and as discussed below, this is a narrower range of nonmonetary relief than is otherwise provided in the copyright law as discussed in Chapter 4. Because the safe harbor eliminates monetary damages, it can best be described consistent with the Chapter 4 nomenclature as a remission provision rather than an immunity provision. However, it is broader than damage remission under section 504 as it eliminates all monetary awards, either for damages (actual or statutory) or costs and attorney's fees. So, too, once it applies, it is mandatory, not discretionary. When the safe harbor applies, the best that section 512 can offer to plaintiffs is the injunctive relief rigidly prescribed under statute.[31] Section 512(j) replaces the injunctive relief that would otherwise be forthcoming under section 502. Section 512(j) divides its injunctive remedies into two groups based on the same two categories of service providers: conduit and cache-post-link.

It should be obvious that this limitation on monetary remedy would make a plaintiff think carefully before charging ahead into litigation. In fact, that is the precise design of section 512—to force the copyright owner and the service provider (e.g., library, school, college, or university) to work together to stop the misuse of its facilities in perpetuating the infringement. As a result, online intermediaries are less likely to be sued in the future. But do not sleep better at night and do not stop reading this book, as the mechanisms built into section 512 make it more likely that the intermediary will become a more active participant in the copyright compliance dance. The decision makers at your institution may decide that the cost of compliance with section 512 is not worth its benefit, as section 512 does not alter the conditions of liability in copyright; rather this section established conditions under which its sting is mitigated. In other words, a library or school in a low-risk-of-copyright infringement environs might conclude that it gains little by additional compliance with section 512. A second likely result, also promoted by section 512 mechanisms such as the section 512(h) subpoena provision, is that copyright owners are more likely to sue individual staff such as faculty, or patrons and students-the primary infringers-as monetary relief against the intermediary institution is now foreclosed by section 512.

FURTHER ADVANTAGES OF THE SAFE HARBOR

In cache, post, and link scenarios, relief can take the form of an "order restraining the service provider from providing *access* to infringing material or activity residing at a particular online site on the provider's system or network,"[32] or an "order restraining the service provider from providing access to a subscriber or account holder of the service provider's system or network who is engaging in infringing activity and is identified in the order, by *terminating the accounts* of the subscriber or account holder that are specified in the order."[33] The former would be an order "for the removal or blocking of infringing material or activity that is residing at a specific location on the provider's system or network."[34] The reference to subscriber is elaborated in a footnote in both the House Report and Senate Report by reference to a previous footnote:

> By "subscribers," the Committee intends to include account holders who are parties with a business relationship to the service provider that justifies treating them as subscribers,

for the purposes of section 512, even if no formal subscription agreement exists. Examples include *students who are granted access to a university's system or network;* or household members with access to a consumer online service by virtue of a subscription agreement between the service provider and another member of that household."[35]

The reference to "students" in the example is revealing because it indicates that by design the statute anticipates that any injunctive measures imposed upon the library or school as intermediary ultimately impact its constituents.

In the alternative, the court may fashion any other injunctive relief as it may consider it "necessary to prevent or restrain infringement of copyrighted material specified in the order of the court at a particular online location, if such relief is the *least burdensome* to the service provider among the forms of relief comparably effective for that purpose."[36] The legislative history makes clear that the section 512(j)(1)(A)(i) and (ii) denial of access to material and termination of account are the preferred remedies; if another is fashioned by the court, "it must determine that the injunctive relief is the least burdensome to the service provider among those forms of relief that are comparably effective."[37] Thus, in a choice of injunctive options where one remedy would impose a harsh result on the third-party student (enroll and pay for a workshop on information ethics or copyright law) but be easy to comply with on the part of the library or school (its school of library or information science or education offers such courses on a regular basis) versus a remedy that in the alternative might preserve as much access for patrons or students but be enormously difficult for the institution to execute (such as real-time monitoring of accounts), the court should side with the intermediary. As presented in subsequent discussion, the legislative history and commentators suggest that such training is preferred while monitoring is not; education not subjugation is the key.

Understanding the Limits of Injunctive Relief Under the Safe Harbor

In conduit service provider scenarios under section 512(a), injunctive remedy is limited to one or both of two statutorily prescribed options: termination[38] and blocking (but blocking is an option only if the source of the infringing material is outside the jurisdiction of the United States,[39] where for obvious reasons, a removal order is unenforceable).[40] When the infringing activity is on a Web site within the United States, the preferred remedy directed to a conduit service provider is to terminate the account of its subscriber rather than block network access to the Web site. Again, implicit in the remedy is that which is easiest for the service provider to accomplish. In other words, if subscribers are accessing infringing material from a foreign Web site, the court may order the service provider either to terminate the subscriber account or undertake a less harsh remedy in terms of the subscriber (the subscriber may be unaware for example that the specific site has been blocked by Internet filtering technology for example though nonetheless no longer has access to it) but arguably more burdensome in terms of the service provider's (as the service provider must undertake the effort to affect the actual block) effort to block access to the "off-shore" material. If the material is "on-shore" so to speak, the remedy is simple, terminate the subscriber's access to the network altogether![41]

Finally, when fashioning section 512(j) injunctive relief, courts "shall" consider:
- ▶ whether the injunction "either alone or in combination with other such injunctions issued against the same service provider would significantly burden either the provider or the operation of the provider's system or network"
- ▶ the "magnitude of the harm likely to be suffered by the copyright owner in the digital network environment" if no action is ordered
- ▶ if the relief ordered is technically feasible and effective, and would not interfere with access to noninfringing material at other online locations"
- ▶ if "less burdensome and comparably effective means of preventing or restraining access to the infringing material are available."[42]

Accommodating Injunctive Relief

The institutional service provider shall receive notice and have an opportunity to appear before the court, and argue, for example, for the imposition of less burdensome relief: "Injunctive relief under this subsection shall be available only after notice to the service provider and an opportunity for the service provider to appear are provided, *except* for orders ensuring the preservation of evidence or other orders having no material adverse effect on the operation of the service provider's communications network."[43] Notice that under section 512(j)(3) an injunctive remedy might have one of three characteristics: burdensome to the intermediary, nonburdensome to the intermediary (the "no material adverse effect" proviso in the "*except*" clause), and ordering the intermediary to preserve evidence.

The latter order would likely occur in a scenario where monetary remedy against the intermediary is foreclosed by the statute but the copyright owner is pursuing action against the direct infringer staff member or patron or student. The records of the intermediary library or educational entity would be vital in that litigation, and so the copyright owner seeks as one of its remedies the preservation of the necessary evidence. Remember that because injunctive relief is the only remedy to copyright plaintiffs, when secondary infringement is subject to section 512 finding defendants to obtain monetary relief will become more difficult. This means suits against direct infringers will likely increase. Of the three scenarios, the service provider can only object to orders that will have adverse material effect upon it; by exclusion of the statute, evidentiary orders or foreclosed from this objection. This is another example of the mechanisms built within the statute to protect the service provider while leaving third parties—staff such as teachers, librarians, patrons, students, clients, and customers—open to litigation. Moreover, the mechanisms limit the ability to interfere in that process ("opportunity for the service provider to appear" are foreclosed "for orders ensuring the preservation of evidence"), and in fact require the intermediary to help it along (i.e., compliance with "orders ensuring the preservation of evidence"). As a result, service providers such as libraries and schools, colleges, and universities may be placed in an uncomfortable choice between self-preservation and undermining the trust of their patrons or charges.

Accommodating Injunctive Relief in Higher Education

A practical result, the quid pro quo mechanism (expansion of safe harbor in return for additional compliance measures), built into section 512(e) discussed below suggests[44] that section 512(j) injunctive relief aimed at an infringing nonprofit educational institution might go "beyond disabling access to particular material on a specified site . . . [and i]n a proper case, the nonprofit educational institution might even be subject to structural relief designed to correct a chronic or persistent tendency to infringe copyrights."[45] In other words, section 512(e)(2) commands that the injunctive relief of section 512(j)(1) relating to subsection (a) conduit service providers is not available to section 512(e) service providers. Section 512(e) service providers are "nonprofit institution[s] of higher education." Such structural relief might, in keeping with the spirit of section 512(e), include specific evidence of remedy. Short of having the faculty or graduate student write "I must not infringe copyright" 1,000 times, the institution might include a more practical solution of having the faculty and graduate students responsible for the infraction demonstrate their knowledge of the law through attendance at copyright seminars or similar remedial sessions perhaps followed by the successful completion of a brief test of proficiency,[46] in the same way that sensitivity or diversity training might be ordered as part of the remedy in a hostile work environment in a discrimination case or a campus speech violation against a faculty member.

Limits of the Safe Harbor: "Initial" Employee Infringements Excluded

As the language from the legislative history quoted earlier indicates, the remission mechanism of section 512 can relate to damages arising from direct, contributory, or vicarious infringement. The most common subject-actor of a direct infringement would be the one responsible for the initial act of infringement (e.g., the person who made the copy or performed the song). This individual could be a third party, such as a public library patron, or it could be a student, but it might also be an employee. The language of the statute in the opening proviso of subsections (a)–(d) as well of the legislative history does not distinguish between employees and other sorts of third parties. Are employees included within the safe harbor? In other words, does section 512 operate when employees are the cause of the initial infringement?

Professor Dratler observes: "When the safe harbor applies, it limits both *direct and secondary* liability for copyright infringement, *including the liability of employees as such*; when it does not, the federal common law applies as if section 512 had not been enacted."[47] Dratler bases his opinion on an early section 512 case concluding that section 512 does indeed include employees:

> To hold that the safe harbor provision of the DMCA protects the company but not its employees for the same alleged bad acts would produce an absurd result. Congress could not have intended to shift the target of infringement actions from the Internet service providers to their employees when it enacted the safe harbor provisions. Accordingly, the Court holds that [the individual defendants] are also entitled to summary judgment in their favor.[48]

However, the Dratler comment as well as the court conclusion should not be read too broadly if the facts of the *Hendrickson v. eBay, Inc.* decision are considered. It was not on the basis of an initial-direct infringement that eBay president, Senior Intellectual Property Counsel, and other employees were sued and that extension of the section 512 protection remission was made.

The phrase "initial-direct" infringement is used to distinguish that infringement from direct infringement because should a court label eBay a direct infringer under the facts, section 512 should still offer a safe harbor. The point is that the infringement that section 512 shielded eBay and its employees from arose from the acts of third parties, those who offered allegedly infringing (pirated) copies of the documentary film *Manson* for sale and distribution through eBay. The liability of eBay and its employees arose because "they wrongfully continued to allow the sale of unauthorized copies of the film *Manson* by eBay users.[49]

A compounding factor here is that an occasional court concluded that an intermediary was responsible as a direct infringer, for engaging in behavior that should have been more properly characterized as secondary infringement of some sort. Thus the legislative history states that "[t]he limitations in subsections (a) through (d) protect qualifying service providers from liability for all monetary relief for *direct*, vicarious and contributory infringement."[50] The reference is to the fact that while employees share in the refuge of the safe harbor, in our maritime analogy both the vessel owner and its crew remain safe from the storm; that protection, that refuge, does not exist where the employee is the source of the harm, however. Rather, the comments suggest that in cases where both employees and employer share some liability (regardless of its misnomer by a court) as a result of the infringing conduct of system, network, facilities, users, or students, it is not only the employer-service provider that may seek the refuge of the safe harbor, but the employee as well.

Consider a case where the employee might otherwise be viewed as a contributory infringer and the employer the vicarious infringer in relationship to the direct infringement a library patron or student commits when he or she, at the insistence of the reference librarian follows a link from the library Web site to a Web site of infringing material. This set of circumstances is similar to the *Intellectual Reserve, Inc. vs Utah Lighthouse Ministry, Inc.* case. In the absence of section 512, the reference librarian could be found liable as a contributory infringer and the employer vicariously liable for the librarian's infringement, assuming of course that the patron's use of the material at the referred Web site is infringing. Depending on the additional circumstances, i.e., meeting the other requirements of the statute, the section 512 safe harbor may exist; if it does, then both the reference librarian and the library would be protected and injunctive relief would be the most a copyright owner could achieve against those two parties. This is the logical operation of the statute, but can section 512 be expanded to reach employees in other circumstances?

Rationale for Employee Exclusions

Does the safe harbor include remission of all monetary remedies that might arise from the initial infringing acts of employees, i.e., acts of a character that might more properly be described as direct infringement and rather than be given the misnomer or misapplication some courts have offered? An argument can be made that it does not. In fact, it is argued that when the source of the initial, direct, or secondary infringement is the employee, section 512 operates neither to protect the employee from liability nor is the safe harbor available to the employer-service provider. Several reasons are offered for this conclusion: legislative history, overall purpose, and rules of statutory construction avoiding superfluous provisions.

Legislative History of Employee Exclusions

First, consider the language of the earlier House Report quoted above, to which the House Conference Report defers the majority of its discussion regarding section 512 except for 512(e),[51] discussing the post function of subsection (c) for example. (This example is also significant because section 512(e) was crafted specifically to indicate the conditions under which acts of employees of institutions of higher education in limited circumstances should not be imputed to the employee-service provider, i.e., rare cases in which the safe harbor would indeed continue to apply.) The additional safe harbor provided by subsection (e) can help to achieve an understanding of the circumstances that fall outside of the safe harbor initially. This in turn assists in resolving the issue of whether the safe harbor provided by the other 512 subsections applies to the initial infringing acts of employees, thus an employer from seeking the refuge of the safe harbor as well: "Information that resides on the system or network operated by or for the service provider *through its own acts or decisions* and not at the direction of a user *does not fall within* the liability limitation of subsection (c)."[52] The first clause ("resides on the system or network operated by or for the service provider") is the activity that is granted safe harbor protection and is found in the text of section 512(c). The point is that an "institution" can logically never *act or decide* anything, or in this instance under subsection (c), *act or decide* to post anything; rather the people that staff and administer its programs do, its employees. Service providers under section 512, as in the discussion of liability concepts in Chapters 2 and 3 indicates, are legal fictions. It is typically as a result of the direct infringement of employees that an employer (an educational institution, for example) incurs secondary liability.

Incorporating these concepts into the legislative history might result in the following modification to the that statement: Information that resides on the system or network operated by or for the service provider, through its *employee's* own acts or decisions and not at the direction of a user does not fall within the liability limitation of subsection (c). The italics has added the word "employees" to indicate that 'its own acts or decisions' is in reality the acts or decisions of its employees. This change does not alter the statement's meaning, but merely reveals the fact that a service provider is, in typical circumstances, a legal fiction. (Of course a service provider could be an individual, such as a bulletin board operator, but then the initial actor and the service provider would be one and the same and the discussion of employee versus employer-service provider becomes moot! This construct is anticipated by the section 512(k)(2) definition of service provider: "a provider of online services or network access, *or the operator of facilities therefore* [sic].") The phrase "and not at the direction of a user" is the precise sort of activity from which the safe harbor was designed to offer refuge: infringing material that is posted on the service provider's facilities by third parties such as patrons or students. Of course, other third parties such as students (or, in the case of commercial entity, customers) populate a service provider's or other online intermediary's system in addition to employees, and can trigger the chain of events that lead to service provider or other online intermediary liability.

Rationale for Employee Exclusions: Overall Purpose of the Safe Harbor

Second, this interpretation is best consistent with the overall purpose of section 512:

> Title II preserves the strong incentives for service providers and copyright owners to cooperate to detect and deal with copyright infringements that take place in the digital networked environments. At the same time, it provides greater certainty to service providers concerning their legal exposure for infringements that may occur in the course of their activities.[53]

But what of the later Conference Report regarding the section 512 damage limitation applying to acts of "direct" infringement, not just contributory and vicarious infringement? The service provider's or other online intermediary's individual employees, and of course third-party users such as students, would be the individuals committing the acts of direct infringement, which would then trigger potential secondary liability on the part of the service provider or other online intermediary.

That distinction of users into two groups is critical for understanding section 512, in order to give practical meaning to the Conference and House statements, and conclude that acts of employees must be excluded from its safe harbors, subsection (e), discussed below, notwithstanding. The target of the post provision, section (c), like other subsections of 512, is arguably the acts of third parties,[54] or to a lesser extent those odd circumstances where a service provider or other online intermediary would be deemed a direct infringer for what would traditionally be viewed as acts of secondary liability. It was this occurrence in the developing case law that mobilized the industry to petition Congress for relief, and that is the "direct" infringement safe harbor to which the legislative history refers.

It is arguable, in light of the Congressional response to the developing case law, that the legislative history, e.g., the Conference Report, was referring to the those instances of direct infringement where, consistent with the developing law, the intermediary-service provider had been held on occasion to be a direct infringer.[55] It is suggested that, unlike the typical scenario of employee or other user conduct as direct infringement, it is the intermediary-service provider as direct infringer to which the legislative history refers.

This interpretation is further supported by the fact, as pointed out earlier, that an online intermediary cannot typically do anything itself (for example, engage in direct copyright infringement)—its employees engage in those acts. So there are few if any acts of direct infringement in which an institutional or organizational online intermediary could engage. As noted above, however, some courts have concluded that certain conduct in conjunction with the operation of online services constituted direct infringement. In the odd case where a court would arrive at that conclusion, the legislative history makes clear that section 512 can still operate as a safe harbor for its acts (at least in the eyes of the court) of "direct" infringement. What the House Report makes clear is that if an infringement, regardless of how it is classified by a subsequent court, results from *its own acts or decisions* in instances of an service provider as a person, it is not protected within the safe harbor of section 512. This remains true under the rephrasing of the statement, "through *its own employees*" in instances where the service provider is an institution.

Further, this interpretation is consistent with that of Dratler quoted above, as long as the reference to the damage limitation of employees still relates to acts of third parties, and not to the employees' acts of direct infringement, i.e. where the party responsible for the initial infringement is still a third party, external to the institutional service provider, but the employee, under a court's articulation of liability would be considered the direct infringer. If section 512 provided a damage limitation for acts of infringement engaged in by employees, it would appear to offer carte blanche to online intermediaries and their staff to engage in copyright infringement—the exact opposite of intent of the legislation, which was to discourage online intermediaries from facilitating copyright infringement by users of its facilities.

Rationale for Employee Exclusions: Subsection (e)

A conclusion that subsections (a)–(d) do not protect the service provider-library or educational institution or any organizational service provider for that matter from the acts of its employees is also consistent with section 512(e) discussed in detail below. Section 512(e) extends the protection of the safe harbor to some instances of infringement that teaching faculty, staff, and students of tertiary educational institutions might commit. The default is that these employees are not included in the safe harbor. Section 512(e) offers some circumstances in which this may not be so. If this were not the result, then section 512(e) would be superfluous. Under the basic operation of section 512, liability, however labeled, arising from the acts of employees would already be covered. Statutes are interpreted to avoid superfluous language.

In short, section 512(e) allows institutions of higher education to treat faculty and graduate students engaged in teaching and research functions as third parties, because without subsection (e) under the operation of section 512, subsections (a)–(d), there is little to insulate the service provider or other online intermediary, such as a college or university, from the acts of its own employees. If the basic damage limitation of section 512, subsections (a)–(d), protected the educational institution against the acts of its employees in addition to those of third parties, then section 512(e) would be redundant at best, as protection from the infringing acts of teaching and researching faculty and graduate students would already be included. Refuge from such liability would already be included in the basic safe harbor of subsections (a)–(d). Statutory provisions are not to be interpreted as superfluous.[56] As discussed in detail below, Congress felt that because of the unique environment of tertiary education, circumstances warranted treating teaching and researching functions of faculty and graduate students as emanating from third parties, thus expanding the reach of the safe harbor for those qualifying tertiary institutions. As a basic tenant, employees remain liable under section 512, and the service provider or online intermediary, depending on the circumstances, might share secondary liability and might also qualify for the section 512 safe harbor, and limit its "bottom line" liability to injunctive relief alone under section 512.

RECOGNIZING THE RELATIONSHIP BETWEEN COPYRIGHT LAW AND THE SAFE HARBOR

The provisions of section 512 are complex, though a thorough discussion is offered here.[57] In section 512 Congress articulates the conditions and circumstances under which an online intermediary's copyright "liability" for monetary remedy (e.g., actual or statutory damages, costs, and attorney's fees) arising from the use of its facilities will be remitted. In addition, the remaining injunctive relief is limited to those forms authorized by the statute. In institutional library or educational settings, caching and linking at the direction of staff and patrons and students may occur in many ways. For example, servers may cache copyrighted material, routinely making multiple copies of the work on the institution's computing facilities; patrons or students may download copyrighted material into their network accounts. In terms of linking, librarians or educators may link to Web sites containing apparent or less-than-obvious infringing material as part of a resources Web site, or students may create volatile documents with hypertext links embedded within their assignment serving as online footnotes. If the subject of the cache, post, or link is infringing material, is the institution liable for these potential third-party infringements? Under the pre-DMCA developing law[58] or post-1998 cases not decided under the DMCA rules,[59] and the circumstances of each case, some courts answered in the affirmative. As discussed in Chapters 2 and 3, copyright liability can arise from the conduct of others through concepts of contributory liability and from the relationship with others through concepts of vicarious liability. The most important point to remember is that section 512 does not change the law of copyright liability per se, that part of the common law is left free to develop. But section 512 does appear to codify the law of secondary liability, at least as it existed in 1998 when enacted.

Codifying the rule with respect to contributory infringement: "This exemption codifies the result of *Religious Technology Center v. Netcom On-Line Communications Services, Inc.*, 907 F. Supp. 1361 (N.D. Cal. 1995) ('*Netcom*'), with respect to liability of providers for direct infringement."[60] Further contrasting the rule with respect to the knowledge requirement of the post and link functions:

> The knowledge standard in subparagraph (A) [referring to the original House bill, H.R. 2281, this language essentially became adopted in section 512(c)(1)(A)(i) and (ii) and section 512(d)(1)(A) and (B)[61]], in addition to actual knowledge, includes "facts or circumstances from which infringing activity is apparent." This would include a notice or any other "red flag"—information of any kind that a reasonable person would rely upon. . . . As subsection (b) makes clear, the bill imposes no obligation on a provider to seek out such red flags. Once a provider becomes aware of a red flag, however, it ceases to qualify for the exemption. This standard *differs from existing law*, under which a defendant may be liable for contributory infringement if it knows or *should have known* that material was infringing.[62]

The first comment suggests a codification of an existing legal standard, while the next page of the same legislative report suggests an opposite intent. This observation is puzzling to say the least and, as discussed in Chapter 2, for another reason.

The knowledge element in contributory liability is best described as a "know or reason to know" standard, whereas a "should have known" standard suggests an affirmative responsibility to determine whether facts or circumstances exist from which such infringement is, for example, apparent, likely, or probable.

Codifying the rule of vicarious liability:

> The financial benefit standard in subparagraph (b) [again referring to the House bill, H.R. 2281, this language essentially became adopted in section 512(c)(1)(B) and section 512(d)(1)(C)[63]] is intended to codify and clarify the direct financial benefit element of vicarious liability as it has been interpreted in cases such as *Marobie-FL, Inc. v. National Association of Firefighting Equipment Dealers*, 983 F. Supp. 1167 (N.D. Ill. 1997).[64]

Perhaps the best that can be offered is to recall that section 512 did not codify the common law of secondary copyright liability, though there is some evidence to suggest that it "essentially codifies" it.[65]

What section 512 does codify however, is a test for remission of monetary remedy (the safe harbor) that is indeed based on the existing concepts of that liability, at least as those concepts existed in 1998 when section 512 was enacted. The legislative history reflects this perspective: "Rather than embarking upon a wholesale clarification of these doctrines, the Committee decided to leave current law in its evolving state and, instead, to create a series of 'safe harbors,' for certain common activities of service providers."[66] As a result, the common law of copyright liability is left free to develop, while the section 512 safe harbor remains more or less stuck (less if Congress decides to periodically amend the statute, more if it does nothing) in 1998 standards.[67] The problems inherent in such a scheme should be immediately apparent even to the casual or legally untrained observer, as the common law will continue to develop while the statute may not. Recall section 512 is not mandatory, thus courts may find that discussion in section 512 is not necessary in every case, but only in those where the defendant is claiming refuge in its provisions.

A true appreciation of this illogic, as well as of how section 512 is designed to operate and how it differs from the common law, can only be maximized if one understands the basic concepts of liability presented in Chapters 1, 2, and 3. Moreover, the significance of the safe harbor's monetary remedy remission is best appreciated if the reader also understands the basic concepts of damages, and the damages reduction and remission covered in Chapter 4. If the reader skipped ahead to the present discussion and remains ignorant of those concepts, now might be a good time to review those chapters.

Understanding the Copyright Law and the Safe Harbor in Practice

Though Congress made clear that section 512 does not replace copyright liability concepts as defined by the common law with a new set of standards, the new law attempts to define the space of the playing field. This "definition" offers predictability. Legal predictability offers safety and is thus part of a sound risk-management program within the institution. This is the reason why an institution would undertake the myriad of compliance protocols section 512 requires. Of course, an institution might weigh the compliance costs and benefits and conclude that the cost is not worth the benefit, and would rather take its "legal chances" under the common law as it continues to develop. In fact, that common law is left free to develop a stance more favorable to intermediaries, altering the assessment of the cost and benefit of section 512 compliance. Of course, courts may move the law in the other direction as well.

The beauty of this statutory structure lies in its determinability, save at least variation in its interpretation by the courts. As one court summarized: "Either Loop-Net [or any other service provider] could comply with the 'take-down' provisions of the DMCA and remain in the safe harbor or refuse to remove the allegedly infringing material and expose itself to the choppier waters of contributory infringement liability."[68] Risk aversion is accomplished through statutory certainty, but as observed above, reliance on statuary standards can also prove to be the ultimate source of downfall, increasing risk where the statute is poorly crafted. So, too, legal predictability is a function of how clearly and precisely a statute is written. The author leaves that determination up to each reader's perspective, but as observed in previous discussion, commentators have used less than glowing terms to describe section 512!

As a result, the interplay between the common law of copyright liability and section 512 relates to the process and burden of proof. In its simplest sequence, a service provider attempts to conform its practices to the requirements of section 512, in the likelihood that it might be sued. While section 512 does not require a service provider to do anything, as will be observed in subsequent discussion, logic suggests that attempts to meet its requirements and secure the safe harbor must be in place before infringement occurs.

As with the other compliance provisions discussed thus far, the statute in practice is not remedial but preemptory. For example, under section 108(f)(1), a qualifying library or archives could not expect to qualify for the immunity by posting a warning notice on its reproducing equipment after it is sued for contributory infringement for excessive patron photocopying. Likewise, once the service provider is sued and found liable, section 512 is used as a defense to the imposition of monetary remedy. If found not liable, there is no need to seek the protection of the section 512 safe harbor!

Previous discussion indicated that remedy under the statute is limited to injunctive relief alone. This means that the best a copyright owner can hope to accomplish is a restraining order against the service provider to deny access to infringing material,[69] block access to material residing off-shore,[70] terminate a subscriber account,[71] or preserve evidence,[72] for example. Even if the copyright owner prevails in the liability phase under section 512, there can be no cost recovery of litigation expenses, costs, and attorney's fees, much less any form of damages. This makes litigation a rather costly venture for the plaintiff. The reader might be prompted to ask what incentive is this for the plaintiff? Not much? But in return, and by the same token, the requirements placed on the service provider are great. In this way, much of the impact of section 512 occurs outside of the courts. And that *is* the distinct design and the success of section 512; it forces service providers and copyright owners to work together to end the perpetuation of copyright infringement.

Sequencing of the Safe Harbor

This discussion suggests that when a determination of direct, contributory, or vicarious infringement is made and then section 512 consulted, if the requirements of the safe harbors have been met, then the limitation on "liability"—or to be more precise, remission of monetary award—occurs through offering a lesser array of injunctive remedies to copyright plaintiffs, i.e., relief limited to that injunctive relief prescribed in section 512(j): "Section 512 is not intended to imply that a service provider is or is not liable as an infringer either for conduct that qualifies for a limitation of liability or for conduct that fails to so qualify. Rather, the limitations of liability apply *if the provider is found to be liable under existing principles of law.*"[73] Once this limitation occurs, then the burden shifts to the defendant-service provider to demonstrate that compliance with the safe harbor conformed to the letter of the law as laid out in section 512: "While the burden of proving the elements of direct or contributory infringement, or vicarious liability, rests with the copyright owner in a suit brought for copyright infringement, a defendant asserting this exemption or limitation as an affirmative defense in such a suit bears the burden of establishing its entitlement."[74] In other words, the burden of proof shifts as it does in any copyright litigation, and like the section 108(f)(1) immunity, the monetary remedy remission of section 512, the safe harbor, operates as a privilege asserted after the plaintiff has succeeded in establishing initial liability.

The Ninth Circuit summarized the sequence in this way: "We thus agree with the district court that '[t]he DMCA did not simply rewrite copyright law for the online world.' [citation omitted] Congress would have done so if it so desired. Claims against service providers for direct, contributory, or vicarious copyright infringement, therefore, are generally evaluated just as they would be in the non-online world."[75] However, one district court appears to suggest that the safe harbor is applied first then contributory legal analysis undertaken:

> The existence of the safe harbor convolutes the analysis of copyright infringement which, theoretically, should proceed in a straight line. Ideally, CoStar would have to

make a prima facie showing that LoopNet was liable of contributory infringement and then the court would turn to the question of whether the "safe harbor" provided a defense. However, because the parameters of the liability protection provided by the "safe harbor" are not contiguous with the bounds of liability for contributory infringement, the analysis may proceed more efficiently if issues are decided a bit out of order.[76]

It is important to note that the safe harbor, like insurance, must be obtained before the acts of infringement occur. Regardless of litigation sequence, what is clear is that compliance with section 512 must occur first, before the infringement triggering flight to the safe harbor. The safe harbors are undertaken as anticipatory measures, like the markings of safe passage on a nautical chart, the route is marked ahead of time, and, like insurance, is not purchased after the harm or injury has occurred. Likewise, nothing in section 512 requires a service provider or other online intermediary to do anything per se—section 512 is an optional provision—but in that case the refuge of the safe harbor cannot be sought. As with the other specific provisions of the copyright law, fair use again remains available as a defense to any instance of infringement.[77] The only protection available would be a conclusion that the service provider or other online intermediary was not liable in the first instance, a decision that is made by recourse to existing (and developing) principles of the copyright law. Yet the terms and conditions of the safe harbor are set, at least until Congress amends the statute! In summary, with the safe harbors in force, the common law is still consulted to determine if liability exists. If it does exist, and if the safe harbor applies as well, then the court is limited to granting the injunctive relief articulated in the statute, i.e., a disabling, blocking or termination order being the most likely remedy.

IDENTIFYING THE BASIC REQUIREMENTS OF SECTION 512

Once a library or educational institution meets the definition of service provider in section 512(k)(1), two additional threshold requirements must be met. In addition, depending on the function involved—conduit, cache, post, link—additional qualifications must be met relevant to that function, i.e., the requirements of subsection (a) through (d). However, before these are consulted, one of two threshold requirements represents a landmark in the compliance quid pro quo that Congress chose to incorporate into the copyright law. Instead of the mere posting of warning notices, for the first time Congress requires the adoption and enforcement of a copyright policy, in specific one addressing repeat infringers.[78] As a second threshold requirement, the online intermediary must be a passive participant ("accommodate and not interfere") in the use of any technological protection measures the copyright owner may employ to protect his or her material.[79]

Repeat Infringer Policy

While each subsection of 512 (the conduit, cache, post, and link provisions) has various requirements, there is an important requirement that applies to all safe harbor subsections. Section 512(i)(1)(A) requires that, as a general condition of eligibility, a service provider "adopt and reasonably implement, and inform subscribers and account holders of the service provider's system or network of, a policy that provides for the termination in appropriate circumstances of subscribers and account holders of the service provider's system or network who are repeat infringers." Believe it or not, common sense often rules the day in copyright law, at least among most judges. The language of the statute, as well as the few cases to interpret this provision, suggests that merely writing a few words into the institution's policy and procedure manual or into a network acceptable-use policy (that users agree to but likely never read or care about) or designing a log-on screen (that users routinely click-by) to prompt system users of their responsibilities (but then turning a blind eye to such correction, enforcement, or discipline when employee, student, patron, client, or customer behavior deviates from such policy), would be an insufficient response to the statute's command.

While neither the statute nor the legislative history offers much guidance as to either the content or application of the repeat infringer policy, logic would dictate that "reasonable implementation" means enforcement of the policy consistent with the ways and means with which other policies and procedures are enforced within a given institutional structure. So, too, within any organization there is a margin for error built into the statutory language, as Professor Dratler observes: "All the statute requires is reasonableness, not effectiveness, and certainly not effectiveness in every case. . . . To hold otherwise would render Section 512 a virtual dead letter in providing any comfort to service providers seeking relief from the uncertainties of copyright infringement liability."[80] In other words, the statute uses the words "reasonably implemented." The statute does not require that the service provider ensure that infringement never occurs:

> The Committee recognizes that there are different degrees of online copyright infringement, from the inadvertent to the noncommercial, to the willful and commercial. In addition, the Committee does not intend this provision to undermine the principles of subsection (l) or the knowledge standard of subsection (c) by suggesting that a provider must investigate possible infringements, monitor its service, or make difficult judgments as to whether conduct is or is not infringing.[81]

Rather the House report and Senate reports suggest that "willful," "flagrant," or otherwise obvious cases demand action, close calls are at the discretion of the service provider. In fact, the entire point of section 512 is not to prevent copyright infringement from ever occurring, but rather to govern the behavior of service providers after the infringement by users is discovered or alleged, as discussed below.

Case Law and the Repeat Infringer Policy

One district court that suggested the head-in-the-sand approach of having a policy without any likelihood of effective enforcement or threat of termination is adequate was rejected on appeal: "[S]ubsection (i) does not require [service providers] to actually terminate repeat infringers, or even to investigate infringement in order to determine if [their] users are behind it. . . . Subsection (i) only requires an [ISP] to put its users on notice that they face a realistic threat of having their Internet access terminated if they repeatedly violate intellectual property rights."[82] It is argued that this statement is contrary to the statute and moreover defies logic; why command a service provider to adopt a policy but not assume that the service provider should also enforce it? The court's statement itself is contradictory; if the service provider need never enforce its policy ("to actually terminate repeat infringers") then how would those repeat infringers ever "face a realistic threat of having their Internet access terminated"? Moreover, the statement of the district court is contrary to the logic and practice of policy implementation and enforcement and litigation in other institutional contexts such as public libraries.[83]

The Ninth Circuit disagreed with the interpretation made by the district court:

> We hold that the district court erred in concluding on summary judgment that AOL satisfied the requirements of § 512(i). . . . There is ample evidence in the record that suggests that AOL did not have an effective notification procedure in place at the time the alleged infringing activities were taking place. Although AOL did notify the Copyright Office of its correct email address before Ellison's attorney attempted to contact AOL and did post its correct email address on the AOL website with a brief summary of its policy as to repeat infringers. . . . AOL allowed notices of potential copyright infringement to fall into a vacuum and to go unheeded; that fact is sufficient for a reasonable jury to conclude that AOL had not reasonably implemented its policy against repeat infringers.[84]

It would be logical to conclude that a repeat infringer policy that had little chance of being enforced, such as the one AOL employed in *Ellison v. Robertson*, was not "reasonably implemented" under the section 512(i)(1)(A) requirement.

The legislative history indicates that the threat of termination should indeed be real. For example, would there be an institutional memory of past enforcement of the same or similar policy? Were other provisions of an acceptable-use policy enforced while the provision regarding copyright and repeat infringement was ignored, or are rogue users, once identified, subject to proper discipline consistent with that particular institutional climate? Both the House and Senate Reports offer the same admonition: "However, those who repeatedly or flagrantly abuse their access to the Internet through disrespect for the intellectual property rights of others should know that there is a realistic threat of losing that access."[85] So, too, anyone who has been involved in institutional risk management would attest to the fact that promulgating a policy but never bothering to enforce it is the legal equivalent of "open season" on the policies and procedures of the institution, as would choosing to enforce some policies while ignoring violations of others. Abuse of the policy would soon be rampant within the institution, especially in an area such as digital copyright.

The statute:

▶ commands that a policy be adopted: "The limitations on liability established by this section shall apply to a service provider only if the service provider— (A) has adopted . . ."

▶ indicates the content of that policy: "a policy that provides for the termination in appropriate circumstances of subscribers and account holders of the service provider's system or network who are repeat infringers"

▶ requires that users be informed of the policy: "and informs subscribers and account holders of the service provider's system or network"

▶ suggests a gauge or measure of successful enforcement or level of operation: "reasonably implements."

The statute does not state: "the service provider has adopted . . . and informs subscribers and account holders of the service provider's system or network of, a policy that provides for the [*reasonable implementation and*] termination in appropriate circumstances of subscribers and account holders of the service provider's system or network who are repeat infringers." Rather, the statute's command is clear, the service provider must adopt a termination policy, and inform users that it will execute its provisions.

Policies are not to be taken lightly in any institutional context. Practice must be consistent with policy; practice must adhere to the principles of policy. Professor Dratler's comment above is well taken, the statute does not require perfect efficacy. One-hundred percent compliance in section 512 is a myth as it is in the rest of the copyright law. What is a reasonable implementation in a particular library or educational institution will vary under the circumstances, but the above standard proposed by the author would hold the best hope of convincing a court that the service provider library or educational institution has a policy, informs its users of it, and reasonably implements it in conformity with other policies the institution has adopted. Copyright is no different from, say, discrimination law in this regard, and Congress and the courts appear to be tired of library and educational institutions looking the other way when it comes to copyright, giving the copyright law short shrift when compared to other issues. Section 512 simply reflects that maintaining a proper demeanor and taking reasonable action in response to statutory triggering events is both logical and consistent with the statute. Logic and consistency are benchmarks of a sound legal risk management program, copyright or otherwise.

The point is that the burden of demonstrating that the service provider has adopted, informed its users of, and reasonably implemented the repeat infringer policy, consistent with the structure of section 512 as an affirmative defense, will rest with the service provider. Can the provider offer evidence that it has such a policy that complies with the stature? What evidence of dissemination can it offer? Has the policy ever been enforced?

Designing the Repeat Infringer Policy

Does the policy contain language indicating that "termination in appropriate circumstances of subscribers and account holders of the service provider's system or network" will occur if a user is "repeat infringer"? Including this or similar language in the policy and referencing the statute would appear a sound measure. As discussed below, the statute does not define what "repeat" means, and until courts provide clarification a conservative approach appears in order. As with the section 108 copyright warning notice ("This institution reserves the right to refuse to accept a copying order if, in its judgment, fulfillment of the order would involve violation of copyright law."[86]), that determination can rest with the service provider. The following language could be adopted into the library or school, college, university, etc. acceptable-use policy:

> As a patron [student or other as the case may be] your ability to post (including storage) or link to copyrighted material is also governed by United States copyright law. This institution or its staff reserves the right to delete or disable access to any post or link if, in its judgment, the post or link would involve violation of copyright law. In accordance with 17 U.S.C. § 512(i)(1)(A), the institution adopts and shall make all reasonable effort to enforce a policy whereby the institution or staff reserves the right to terminate in appropriate circumstances the access to the system or network of patrons who disrespect the intellectual property rights of others and are repeat infringers.

The service provider is still left to wonder, however, how many infringements represent a "repeat" infringer. A dictionary definition, a not uncommon resort of courts, suggests the obvious: "of, relating to, or being one that repeats an offense, achievement, or action."[87] Make no mistake, a court would be within the text of the statute to interpret repeat as *more than once*, and to interpret terminate not mere "suspension" but termination *with no chance of return to service*. This interpretation would also be consistent with the expanded safe harbor offered institutions of higher education in section 512(e) and discussed below, which uses the concept of repeat to mean twice, but again consistent with the purpose of subsection (e) offering additional legal breathing space to extend situations beyond a single repeat and limiting the tolling period to three years, i.e., excluding from the additional safe harbor instances "within the preceding 3-year period, received *more than two* notifications described in subsection (c)(3) of claimed infringement."[88] The number two is significant in both sections 512(i) and 512(e).

Implementing the Repeat Infringer Policy

Moreover, the statute does not indicate by what standard the infringer is to be judged. Must the copyright owner commence litigation, or is a notice from the copyright in conformity with the notice and is the take-down mechanism, described below and built into section 512, the proper standard? How does a service provider determine that "subscribers and account holders" are repeat infringers?

> As a result, service providers are left to determine such things as what number of infringements qualifies as repeated infringement. . . . [I]t may be relatively safe to simply arrive at an arbitrary number such as three or four; at the same time, because the provision is relatively untested in court, and because in practice the policy may be difficult to implement meaningfully in the first place, it may make sense to avoid doubt by simply establishing that infringements beyond a single occurrence amount to repeat infringements.[89]

The legislative history offers little guidance as to the form and content of the policy or what would constitute appropriate circumstances of implementation.[90] As a result, "[t]o ensure that they have adopted and implemented an appropriate policy and, thus, are not denied the benefits of the act's limitations on liability, service providers should document and maintain records of all attempts to implement their policies reasonably."[91] Short of receiving an actual notice under the section 512 mechanisms, what sort of conduct must the library or educational institution engage in to meet the reasonable implementation standard? Must the service provider engage in active monitoring, what level of policing is appropriate?

Comments throughout the legislative history indicate that Congress did not desire active monitoring. As the later House Report and Senate Report observed, this does not require a "should know" standard[92] of active monitoring and investigation: "the Committee does not intend this provision to undermine the principles of new subsection (l) or the knowledge standard of new subsection (c) by suggesting that a provider must investigate possible infringements, monitor its service, or make difficult judgments as to whether conduct is or is not infringing."[93] But by the same token, a service provider is not prohibited from monitoring, and it should not be held to some higher standard if infringement occurs in spite of monitoring: "This legislation is not intended to discourage the service provider from monitoring its service for infringing material. Courts should not conclude that the service provider loses eligibility for limitations on liability under section 512 solely because it engaged in a monitoring program."[94] In fact, such self-monitoring can work to the advantage of the institution:

When students download or share music or movies, the amount of bandwidth used along with other factors flags the activity. No content is monitored, only bandwidth and port activities. When suspected viruses or file sharing is detected, access to the Internet outside the campus network is temporarily terminated. The students are then referred to a copyright class emphasizing Internet copyright issues. When students pass the course, Internet services are restored. . . . While the file sharing war promises to endure indefinitely, bandwidth monitoring and copyright education may prove to be an effective bomb shelter for both students and universities.[95]

Whether monitoring is implemented or not, the repeat infringer policy must be in place before the occurrence of infringement from which the safe harbor is sought, or at least must be in place before the copyright owner contacts the service provider under the statute's notification provision.

Case Law and the Implementation of the Repeat Infringer Policy

The district court discussion in *Napster* is instructive here. Napster attempted to argue that it met the requirements of section 512, including the adoption of a repeat infringer policy under Section 512(i) ("has adopted and reasonably implemented, and informs subscribers and account holders of the service provider's system or network of *a policy* that provides for the termination in appropriate circumstances of subscribers and account holders of the service provider's system or network who are repeat infringers"). As observed earlier, Section 512(i) does not require active monitoring of users or that a service provider "investigate possible infringements, [or] monitor its service to make difficult judgements as to whether conduct is or is not infringing," rather the policy is designed to ensure "a realistic threat of losing access."[96] Unfortunately, Napster had created its policy only after the recording industry began legal proceedings against it, some two months after the fact![97]

To be sure, Napster "adopted" a policy, but the question remained as to whether this after-the-fact policy adoption met the "reasonably implemented" standard required by the statute. Napster's fruitless response was to answer that question in the affirmative. However the rationale (or "irrationale" as the case may be) involved a bit of legal illogic: the statute did not indicate when the repeat infringer policy should be in place, vis-à-vis an act of infringement only that the service provider have such a policy in place before it asserts protection of the safe harbor.[98] The court was not convinced and responded that such *rationalization* "defies the logic of making formal notification to users or subscribers a prerequisite to exemption from monetary liability."[99] More important, the district court's discussion suggests that merely disabling a password is insufficient. Cuing the denial of access to IP address is a more effective method for ensuring that a particular individual will not obtain access under a different password. The nuance of this response reveals a perceptive awareness of computing behavior in the net-worked world. An Internet user is far more likely to change passwords or identity than change locations from which the false identities emanate:

> If Napster is formally notified of infringing activity, it blocks the infringer's password so she cannot log on to the Napster service using that password. Napster does not block the IP address of infringing users, however, and the parties dispute whether it would be feasible or effective to do so. Plaintiffs aver that Napster willfully turns a blind eye to the identity of its users—that is, their real names and *physical addresses*—because their anonymity allows Napster to disclaim responsibility for copyright infringement.[100]

Is focus on IP address a more effective means of monitoring and preventing access? The district court appeared to think so: "Farmer also cast doubt on Nap-ster's contention that blocking IP addresses is not a reasonable means of terminat-ing infringers."[101] What is clear is that an after-the-fact policy is not an effective means of enforcing that policy and so does *not* meet the requirements of section 512(i): "Hence, plaintiffs raised genuine issues of material fact about whether Nap-ster has reasonably implemented a policy of terminating repeat infringers. They have produced evidence that Napster's copyright compliance policy is neither timely nor reasonable within the meaning of subparagraph 512(i)(A)."[102] The goal of section 512 is to have service providers promote a climate of copyright compli-ance, not to test whether the boundaries of minimum compliance with a literal-il-logical reading and application of the text of the statute will satisfy its requirements. Again the purpose of section 512 should be kept in mind: "In short, ISPs presently do not know if they are in fact liable for the behavior of their sub-scribers, but they do know that they can escape liability by cooperating with con-tent providers who complain of copyright infringement."[103] The message is clear: the section 512(i) repeat infringer policy should be adopted now, before potential infringements occur.

Responding to a Breech of Policy in the Library or Educational Setting

While the educational institution does need not to monitor network traffic or system use,[104] at least not yet,[105] it must be responsive to its network or system when such traffic or use raises the all-critical "red flag." At a minimum, the educa-tional institution, after adopting a copyright compliance policy, should make every effort to publicize the copyright policy and provide patrons, employees, students, and so on with a basic education in copyright law. Sham policies will not shield contributory infringing intermediaries under the common law,[106] and it is likely not to shield service providers under section 512 either. This effort might include postings on all institutional Web pages, distribution of relevant documentation, orientation and training programs, inclusion of such information in employee and student handbooks, and some acknowledgment by patrons, teachers, staff, and students of their awareness of and compliance responsibility with the copyright law. This acknowledgment, in the guise of a signature or online click-on "I agree," at least in form fulfills the statutory requirement that the service provider indeed "informs subscribers and account holders" of the existence of the policy and circumstances under which it will be enforced, i.e., termination of service for repeat infringement. Moreover, intermediaries need to "think outside the box" of infringing user behavior. Based on the likely nature of infringing activity on its system, is denial of service cued to password alone effective? What about IP address or another more effective protocol?

An unanswered question is whether the termination must be permanent. In a commercial "subscriber" scenario, permanent termination would appear logical. However in library and school, college, university settings, the patron or student would face a harsh future if he or she once terminated could never regain the privileges of service. To be sure, termination should occur, and it should hold for some significant period. Perhaps it would be appropriate to delay reactivation or restoration until the patron or student demonstrates a knowledge of the copyright law, much in the same way a careless driver takes a remedial driver safety or education course. Requiring patrons or students to successfully complete a copyright education course or other responsible use of network technology course would be a sound strategy. In fact, one could argue that such training should be required of all users before an account is initially activated. If the goal is to minimize risk, requiring this sequence appears prudent, however unpopular.[107] This suggestion may also appear harsh, but it is an opportunity to send a clear message to Congress and the industry and other copyright-owner proponents that libraries and educational institutions are indeed serious about copyright compliance.

Hopefully the injunctive relief crafted by a court would reflect a termination-as-suspension-until-education approach, as it would appear reasonable. However, it would also be reasonable to conclude that if such suspension occurred, followed by remedial education and restoration of service, any subsequent offense should properly be met with permanent suspension, i.e., termination as termination! While unfortunate, the reality is that some abusive users simply do not deserve network access to the facilities of a particular service provider (library, school, college, or university, for example).

Avoiding Interference with "Standard Technical Measures"

Like the repeat infringer policy, a second qualifying requirement extends to either definition of service provider (applicable to the conduit function or applicable to the cache, post, and link functions) and operates as an antiinterference provision of sorts: the service provider must ensure that it "accommodates and does not interfere with standard technical measures."[108] Standard technical measures are defined as those measures "used by copyright owners to identify or protect copyrighted works."[109] The statutory definition of standard technological measure suggests some sort of marketplace determination of what those measures might be. Section 512(i)(2)(A)-(C) offers a three-part test to determine what qualifies as a technological measure: industry consensus, availability, and absence of burdensome cost. Section 512(i)(2)(A) indicates that a standard technological measure is one that has "been developed pursuant to a broad consensus of copyright owners and service providers in an open, fair, voluntary, multi-industry standards process." This clause suggests that technical solutions will cross industry lines, i.e., music, film, etc. However, unlike the familiar CONTU[110] and CONFU[111] mechanisms and the guidelines each process produced, there is no suggestion here that such measures be developed in light of content users' concerns or with a broad range of input from other stakeholders such as unhappy librarians and academics.

The legislative history offers a plea for acceptance nonetheless by the excluded service provider representative: "The Committee strongly urges all of the affected parties expeditiously to commence voluntary, inter-industry discussion to agree upon and implement the best technological solutions available to achieve these goals."[112] The focus here is on the industry, the content owner or provider alone. Availability occurs when the technology is available to any person on "reasonable and nondiscriminatory terms."[113] This phrasing coupled with the section 512(i)(1)(B) "accommodates" suggests at least that any affirmative duty to accept and adopt ("accommodates") such measures is first conditioned on the technology (the "standard technical measures") being available ("reasonable and nondiscriminatory terms").

Finally the technological measure must be affordable; it must "not impose substantial costs on service providers or substantial burdens on their systems or networks."[114] Of course the statute says nothing of the imposition such technologies might impose on users! So, too, the cost to service providers need only be less than substantial to still require its burden be imposed on the service provider statutorily. In other words, as long as the cost would not be substantial, it is acceptable under the statute and the statute requires that the service provider accommodate and not interfere with its use, even though its adoption would not occur without some cost. Of course the concept of "cost" or "burden" is relative, to both service provider and to its network. Actual dollars and cents as well as time could be considered in determining the cost. However, considering that service providers continually outlay for improvements in service (that is the nature of the technological beast), the author is at a loss to suggest what percent beyond these normal costs of doing business would "impose substantial costs." Regarding the burden to system or network, it is suggested that measures that pose a significant impediment to operability would in fact "impose substantial burden." Here a cue from the online "trespass" cases might offer some hope.[115] Where the technological measure so slow system performance that it drives constituents away or otherwise negatively impact service, such as by periodically crashing the system could indeed be imposing a substantial burden.

While technology is the bane of copyright owners, Congress views technology as the solution as well. The legislative history reflects this attitude: "The Committee believes that technology is likely to be the solution to many of the issues facing copyright owner and service providers in this digital age. For that reason, the Committee has included new subsection (h)(1)(B) [(i)(1)(B) as enacted], which is intended to encourage appropriate technological solutions to protect copyrighted works."[116] The comment indicates Congress's continued belief that technology can be both surreptitious and savior. What are the sorts of technical measures Congress hopes will be developed? They could be "those designed to protect works from unauthorized access and use and those designed to associate copyright management information with copyrighted works,"[117] such as tracking technologies.

Who will develop these measures?

> The Committee anticipates that these provisions could be developed both in recognized open standards bodies or in ad hoc groups as long as the process used is open, fair, voluntary, and multi-industry and the measures developed otherwise conform to the requirements of the definition of standard technical measures set forth in paragraph (h)(2) [enacted as (i)(2)]. . . . The Committee also notes that an ad hoc approach has been successful in developing standards in other contexts, such as the process that has developed copy protection technology for use in connections with DVD.[118]

However, if the track record of CSS protection technology and DeCSS litigation is any predictor, the level of success of such mechanisms remains in doubt. True, the industry is sure to develop new and improved technological protection measures, but "hackers" are sure to respond in like force, and so perpetuate the copyright protection arms race.

Most important, this legislative comment supported by Dratler suggests that if a service provider violates any of the section 1201 rules, prohibiting circumvention of access controls or trafficking in access or use controls, the section 512 safe harbor would not be available to it. The Committee reference to the DVD is a clear link to the CSS controls the movie industry employs and circumventing DeCSS code which has been the focus of several cases under section 1201. The section 1201 rules, discussed in detail in Chapter 9, prohibit the circumvention and trafficking in such controls. Moreover, the section 512(i)(B) command of noninterference with standard technical measures potentially reaches a far broader range of activities than the anti-circumvention and anti-trafficking rules of section 1201, as those rules only prohibit circumventing access controls and the trafficking of either circumventing access or use control technologies. Any sort of protection is covered by section 512(i)(2): "the term 'standard technical measures' means technical measures that are used by copyright owners to identify or protect copy-righted works." However, the reach of the section 512 standard technical measures concept is narrowed somewhat by its three-part definition as discussed above.

The section 512(i)(B) prohibition reaches all "technological solutions [designed] to protect copyrighted works."[119] The only limitation comes from the definition of "standard technical measures" which better applies to how the technology is created and implemented and not to the sort of activities (circumventions or trafficking as in section 1201) the technology targets. Under section 512(i)(2)(A)–(C) the tech-nology need only be the result of "broad consensus" in its development, be avail-able under fair terms ("reasonable and nondiscriminatory"), and not impose substantial cost on providers or otherwise impact its network. While the word "ac-commodates" does not suggest a posture as aggressive as "promote," its juxtaposition with the phrase prohibiting actual interference ("does not interfere with") sug-gests something more than merely refrain from circumvention or trafficking (as, for example, under the section 1201 rules), which would be covered by the inter-ference clause alone. Perhaps the language suggests that a service provider, given a choice of options, would be required to configure its system or network in such a way as to make the standard technical measures the most effective. Until a case occurs in which the copyright owner claims that the section 512(i)(1)(A) accommo-date proviso has been violated and a court evaluates the claim in light of the given facts, conjecture, however informed, is the best that can be offered at this point.

REAL-WORLD EXAMPLES

▶ Real-World Example I

Situation: A student used the library photocopier to reproduce an entire book. Later the student scanned the book and loaded the copy onto his personal student Web page on the institution's servers.

Legal Analysis: Assuming the library follows the proper procedures it may be insu-lated from any liability by operation of section 108 for any infringing conduct that results from the student's photocopying (see Chapter 12). Section 512 offers no as-sistance with respect to the photocopying, as section 512 deals with digital and online content alone. A public library or educational institution is the sort of entity the legislative history indicates would be protected by the safe harbor of section 512. "The new subsection (j)(1)(B) definition of service provider, for example, in-cludes universities and schools to the extent that they perform the functions identi-fied in new subsection (j)(1)(B)." H.R. Rep. No 551 (Part 2), 105th Cong., 2d Sess. 64 (1998); Senate Report 105-190, 105th Cong., 2d Sess. 54-55 (1998). As a result, the infringing copy posted by the student would qualify for the section 512(c) safe harbor. This assumes that, in addition to the other requirements of section 512, the educational institution possesses no knowledge of infringing material residing on its Web server and is not aware of facts or circumstances exist from which such infringing activity is apparent, or once the staff (e.g., administrators, teachers, or network staff) possess such knowledge or become aware of facts or circumstances, act expeditiously to remove the scanned book from its server file or disable the student's access to his or her Web page. See Chapter 7 for further discussion.

▶ **Real-World Example II**

Situation: As part of a travelogue initiative, a public library allows patrons to maintain personal Web pages of their recent travels. After a recent trip to Italy, one patron digitizes a significant portion of the film *Under the Tuscan Sun* and then loads it on to her personal page on the library's "World Traveler" area. After receiving a notice from the copyright holder that includes the necessary statutory requirements, the library makes all the statutorily appropriate responses. Nevertheless, the copyright owner commences litigation against the library, alleging that the library had not adopted and reasonably implemented a repeat infringer policy as required by the statute. In response, the library buys this book, and locates and adapts the sample suggested policy language into its copyright policy.

Legal Analysis: Early precedent interpreting the repeat infringer policy provision of section 512(i)(1)(A) suggests that the policy must be adopted as a prerequisite to having the safe harbor apply to particular infringing conduct—the policy may not be adopted remedially. Napster "adopted" a policy, to be sure, but the question remained as to whether this after-the-fact policy adoption was nonetheless "reasonably implemented." Napter's fruitless response to this bit of illogic was that the statute did not indicate when the repeat infringer policy should be in place. *A&M Records, Inc. v. Napster, Inc.*, 2000 WL 573136, at *9 (N.D. Cal. 2000). The court was not convinced and responded that such *rationalization* "defies the logic of making formal notification to users or subscribers a prerequisite to exemption from monetary liability." *Id.*

▶ **Real-World Example III**

Situation: The situation is similar to that of Real-World Example II, except the library had implemented a repeat infringer policy, and every patron who desired a personal Web page first needed to click on "I Agree" after reading the online terms and conditions of use, which specify that a patron's Web account may be terminated in instances of repeat infringement.

Legal Analysis: The adoption of the repeat infringer policy would meet the requirements of section 512(i)(1)(A), and the safe harbor would apply, assuming the other requirements of section 512 were met.

KEY POINTS FOR YOUR INSTITUTION'S POLICY AND PRACTICE

▶ The copyright law creates a so-called "safe harbor," protecting service providers from liability. The safe harbor applies to four functions of service providers: conduit, caching, posting, and linking. If the requirements of the "safe harbor" are met, then the statute operates to remit all monetary relief. Monetary relief includes damages, costs, attorneys' fees, and any other form of monetary payment. See pp. 141–146.

▶ Under the statute, the definition of service provider includes universities and schools to the extent that they offer the identified functions to patrons, i.e., caching, posting, and linking. See pp. 146–147.

▶ If a service provider fails to qualify for the safe harbor offered by the statute, then no additional liability is created. Section 512 is not a liability provision, rather without it, the liability of the service provider is determined and damages are assessed as if section 512 were never enacted, i.e., under the law of secondary liability as developed by the courts and discussed in earlier chapters. See pp. 154–159.

▶ When the safe harbor applies, the only available remedy is injunctive relief. This relief is further limited by statute and depends on categories of service provider function: conduit, cache, post, and link. For the cache, post, and link scenarios, a court may order a service provider to prevent subscriber *access* to infringing material or activity or to terminate the subscriber's account. For conduit service providers, termination and blocking are also possible, but if the source of the infringing material is located within the jurisdiction of the United States, then a blocking order is not possible. See pp. 146–149.

▶ While the safe harbor can protect the library or educational institution from liability arising from the infringing acts of third parties, such as patrons and students, the safe harbor does not offer protection from the acts of infringing employees. See pp. 149–154.

▶ Section 512 does not codify existing concepts of copyright liability, rather those concepts are left free to develop under the common law. In a given copyright case, a determination of liability is first made under those common law concepts. When applicable (if the requirements of the safe harbor are met), the statute then operates to limit the remedy of the copyright owner to the injunctive relief alone. See pp. 156–159.

▶ All service providers (conduit, cache, post, and link) are required by section 512(i)(1)(A) to "adopt and reasonably implement [] . . . a policy that provides for the termination in appropriate circumstances of subscribers and account holders of the service provider's system or network who are repeat infringers." Subscribers must also be informed of the policy through appropriate institutional mechanisms as proscribed by the statute. See pp. 160–167.

▶ In a second qualifying requirement, service providers must accommodate and must not interfere with standard technical measures. Standard technical measures are defined as those measures "used by copyright owners to identify or protect copyrighted works." See pp. 167–170.

ENDNOTES

[1] Pub. L. No. 94-553, 90 Stat. 2478 (1976).

[2] Pub. L. No. 101-650 (Title VIII), § 802 and § 803, 104 Stat. 5134, 5135 (1990) (Computer Software Rental Amendments Act of 1990).

[3] Pub. L. No. 105-304 (Title II), § 202, 112 Stat. 2860, 2877-2886 (1998) (codified at 17 U.S.C. § 512).

[4] Alfred C. Yen, Internet Service Provider Liability for Subscriber Copyright Infringement, Enterprise Liability, and the First Amendment, 88 GEORGETOWN LAW JOURNAL 1833, 1881 (2000).

[5] 17 U.S.C § 512(i)(1)(A).

[6] 17 U.S.C § 512(c)(2).

[7] 17 U.S.C § 512(b)(2)(E), (c)(3), and (d)(3), the cache, post, and link provision, requires that "service provider[s] respond[] expeditiously to remove, or disable access to, the material that is claimed to be infringing upon notification of claimed infringement." Oddly, and as discussed in detail later, the registered agent is only required for section 512(c) post scenarios. (This is one of many examples of inconsistent and otherwise poor drafting found within section 512.) A second takedown and disable provision, contained in (c)(2)(a)(iii) and (d)(1)(C), applies only to the post and link provisions and requires that the service provider or other online intermediary "act [] expeditiously to remove, or disable access to, the material" upon actual knowledge or awareness of "facts or circumstances from which infringing activity is apparent" upon obtaining such knowledge. The former "notice and take-down" scenario anticipates notice conforming to precise standards prescribed in the statute and derives from the copyright owner or representative, in the latter form of the knowledge is not elucidated and need not come from the copyright owner.

[8] 17 U.S.C § 512(c)(3)(B)(ii) and 17 U.S.C § 512(g)(2)(B).

[9] 17 U.S.C § 512(g)(2)(A).

[10] 17 U.S.C § 512(e)(1)(C).

[11] Other commentators have been less kind: "the DMCA's cumbersome and disorganized structure makes its provisions difficult to untangle." Alfred C. Yen, Internet Service Provider Liability for Subscriber Copyright Infringement, Enterprise Liability, and the First Amendment, 88 GEORGETOWN LAW JOURNAL 1833, 1881 (2000). See also, JAY DRATLER JR., CYBERLAW: INTELLECTUAL PROPERTY IN THE DIGITAL MILLENNIUM § 6.02[1], at

6-42 (2004) ("What was upon introduction a relatively simple, straightforward bill became, by the time of adoption, an over-lawyered nine-page monstrosity that mocks the first law of statutory drafting ('simplicity and certainty are inversely proportional to the number of words').").

[12] JAY DRATLER JR., CYBERLAW: INTELLECTUAL PROPERTY IN THE DIGITAL MIL-LENNIUM § 6.0[3]1, at 6-20.11 (2004) ("It leaves courts free to develop other defenses or exceptions to copyright liability, as the Netcom [*Religious Technology Center v. Netcom On-line Communications Services, Inc.*, 907 F. Supp. 1361 (N.D. Cal. 1995)] court did, as a matter of federal common law." Id. (footnote omitted).

[13] 17 U.S.C. § 512 (k)(1)(A).

[14] 17 U.S.C. § 512 (a).

[15] H.R. Rep. No. 551 (Part 2), 105th Cong., 2d Sess. 63 (1998); S. Rep. No. 105-190, 105th Cong., 2d Sess. 54 (1998).

[16] Ibid.

[17] H.R. Rep. No. 551 (Part 2), 105th Cong., 2d Sess. 63 (1998); S. Rep. No. 105-190, 105th Cong., 2d Sess. 54 (1998) ("Thus, over-the-air broadcasting, whether in analog or digital form, or a cable television system. A satellite television service, would not qualify, except to the extent it provides users with on-line access to a digital network such as the Internet, or it provides transmission, routing or connections to connect material to such a network, and then only with respect to those functions.").

[18] See also, 17 U.S.C. § 512 (a)(5) ("the material is transmitted through the system or network without modification of its content."). See also, H.R. Rep. No 551 (Part 2), 105th Cong., 2d Sess. 63 (1998) ("An entity is not disqualified from being a 'service provider' because it alters the form of the material, so long as it does not alter the content of the material"); S. Rep. No. 105-190, 105th Cong., 2d Sess. 54 (1998) ("An entity is not disqualified from being a 'service provider' because it alters the form of the material, so long as it does not alter the content of the material").

[19] H.R. Rep. No. 551 (Part 2), 105th Cong., 2d Sess. 63-64 (1998); S. Rep. No. 105-190, 105th Cong., 2d Sess. 54 (1998) (all emphasis added).

[20] H.R. Rep. No. 551 (Part 2), 105th Cong., 2d Sess. 64 (1998); S. Rep. No. 105-190, 105th Cong., 2d Sess. 54 (1998) ("the fact that a service provider performs some functions that fall within the definition of new paragraph (A) does not imply that its other functions that do not fall within the definition of new subparagraph (A) qualify for the limitation of liability under new subsection (a).").

[21] H.R. Rep. No. 551 (Part 2), 105th Cong., 2d Sess. 64 (1998); S. Rep. No. 105-190, 105th Cong., 2d Sess. 54 (1998) ("The new subsection (j)(1)(A) definition is not intended to exclude providers that perform additional functions, including the functions identified in new subsection (j)(1)(B).").

[22] H.R. Rep. No. 551 (Part 2), 105th Cong., 2d Sess. 64 (1998); S. Rep. No. 105-190, 105th Cong., 2d Sess. 54 (1998).

[23] 17 U.S.C. § 512(k)(1)(B).

[24] H.R. Rep. No. 551 (Part 2), 105th Cong., 2d Sess. 64 (1998); S. Rep. No. 105-190, 105th Cong., 2d Sess. 54 (1998).

[25] H.R. Rep. No. 551 (Part 2), 105th Cong., 2d Sess. 64 (1998); S. Rep. No. 105-190, 105th Cong., 2d Sess. 54 (1998).

[26] H.R. Rep. No. 551 (Part 2), 105th Cong., 2d Sess. 64 (1998); S. Rep. No. 105-190, 105th Cong., 2d Sess. 54-55 (1998) (emphasis added).

[27] *Hendrickson v. eBay, Inc.*, 165 F. Supp. 2d 1082, 1088 (C.D. Cal. 2001) ("Here, because the focus of the copyright claims against eBay concerns infringing activity—the sale and distribution of pirated copies of 'Manson'-using 'materials' posted [sic] eBay's website, Section 512(c) would provide eBay a safe harbor from liability if eBay meets the conditions set forth therein.").

[28] 17 U.S.C. § 512(k)(2) (emphasis added).

[29] H.R. Rep. No. 105-796, 105th Cong., 2d Sess. 73 (1998) (Conf. Rep.) (bold and italics added).

[30] Alfred C. Yen, Internet Service Provider Liability for Subscriber Copyright Infringement, Enterprise Liability, and the First Amendment, 88 GEORGETOWN LAW JOURNAL 1833, 1887 (2000) ("ISPs, therefore, have reason to use the DMCAs safe harbor to gain certain protection against suit from all quarters by disabling access to alleged infringing materials and then going through the process of notifying their subscribers, allowing an opportunity for response, restoring the material, and allowing a counter-response from the content provider.").

[31] 17 U.S.C § 512(j).

[32] 17 U.S.C § 512(j)(1)(A)(i) (emphasis added).

[33] 17 U.S.C § 512(j)(1)(A)(ii) (emphasis added).

[34] H.R. Rep. No. 551 (Part 2), 105th Cong., 2d Sess. 62 (1998); S. Rep. No. 105-190, 105th Cong., 2d Sess. 53 (1998).

[35] H.R. Rep. No. 551 (Part 2), 105th Cong., 2d Sess. 61, n. 3 (1998) (emphasis added); S. Rep. No. 105-190, 105th Cong., 2d Sess. 52, n. 24 (1998) (emphasis added).

[36] 17 U.S.C § 512(j)(1)(A)(iii) (emphasis added).

[37] H.R. Rep. No. 551 (Part 2), 105th Cong., 2d Sess. 62 (1998); S. Rep. No. 105-190, 105th Cong., 2d Sess. 53 (1998).

[38] 17 U.S.C § 512(j)(1)(B)(i) ("An order restraining the service provider from providing access to a subscriber or account holder of the service provider's system or network who is using the provider's service to engage in infringing activity and is identified in the order, by terminating the accounts of the subscriber or account holder that are specified in the order.").

[39] 17 U.S.C § 512(j)(1)(B)(ii) ("An order restraining the service provider from providing access, by taking reasonable steps specified in the order to block access, to a specific, identified, online location outside the United States.").

[40] The difficulty of pursuing off-shore defendants is demonstrated in the litigation against Kazaa. In, *Metro-Goldwyn-Mayer Studios Inc. v. Grokster, Ltd.*, 243 F. Supp. 2d 1073 (C.D. Cal. 2003), the district court determined that jurisdiction was proper over Kazaa BV, a

Netherlands corporation that transferred ownership of key assets to the newly formed Sharman Networks, Ltd., a company organized under the laws of the island-nation Vanuatu and doing business principally in Australia. "First, Sharman essentially does not dispute that a significant number of its users—perhaps as many as two million—are California residents. . . . Second, Sharman does not dispute that the distribution of its software is an essentially commercial act. . . . In sum, Sharman engages in a significant quantum of commercial contract with California residents constituting a but for cause of Plaintiffs' claims Jurisdiction is therefore presumptively reasonable." Id. at 1087-1088. Jurisdiction was proper in this claim of contributory and vicarious infringement: "[A]nd thus that it is, at a minimum, constructively aware of continuous and substantial interaction with residents of this forum. Further, Sharman is well aware that California is the heart of the entertainment industry, and that the brunt of the injuries described in these case is likely to be felt here." Id. at 1092. However, the court concluded that jurisdiction was reasonable for an additional reason: Sharman's effective predecessor, Kazaa BVm was engaged in this very litigation when Sharman was formed. . . . If Sharman wished to 'structure [its] primary conduct with some minimum assurance' that it would not be haled into court in this forum, it simply could have avoided taking over the business of a company already enmeshed in litigation here." Id. at 1092. As a result, while Kazaa and its progeny could be sued in California, enforcing that order in Vanuatu could be legally impossible and at least practically improbable.

[41] H.R. Rep. No. 551 (Part 2), 105th Cong., 2d Sess. 63 (1998); S. Rep. No. 105-190, 105th Cong., 2d Sess. 53 (1998) ("Such blocking orders are not available against a service provider qualifying under new subsection (a) in the case of infringing activity on a site within the United States or its territories.").

[42] 17 U.S.C § 512(j)(2)(A)–(D).

[43] 17 U.S.C § 512(j)(3) (emphasis added).

[44] 17 U.S.C § 512(e)(2) provides: "For the purposes of this subsection, the limitations on injunctive relief contained in subsections (j)(2) and (j)(3), but not those in (j)(1), shall apply."

[45] JAY DRATLER JR., CYBERLAW: INTELLECTUAL PROPERTY IN THE DIGITAL MILLENNIUM § 6.06, at 6-146 (2004).

[46] According to Dratler, this is a legitimate quid pro quo for the expanded liability limitation section 512(e) provides: "Thus, injunctive relief against a nonprofit educational institution successfully claiming a limitation on monetary remedies by virtue of the special attribution rules of subsection (e) can expect orders for relief that go beyond disabling access to particular material on a specified site, or other 'least burdensome' relief." JAY DRATLER JR., CYBERLAW: INTELLECTUAL PROPERTY IN THE DIGITAL MILLENNIUM §6.06, at 6-145-1-146 (2004) (footnote omitted).

[47] JAY DRATLER JR., CYBERLAW: INTELLECTUAL PROPERTY IN THE DIGITAL MILLENNIUM § 6.01[3], at 6-20.9–6-20.10 (2004) (first emphasis original, second emphasis added) (footnotes omitted).

[48] *Hendrickson v. eBay, Inc.*, 165 F. Supp. 2d 1082, 1094-1095 (C.D. Cal. 2001).

[49] *Hendrickson v. eBay, Inc.*, 165 F. Supp. 2d 1082, 1086 (C.D. Cal. 2001).

[50] H.R. Rep. No. 105-796, 105th Cong., 2d Sess. 73 (1998) (Conf. Rep.)(bold and italics added).

[51] H. R. Rep. No. 105-796, 105th Cong., 2d Sess. 73 (1998) ("The Senate recedes to House Section 202 with modifications.").

[52] H.R. Rep. No. 551 (Part 2), 105th Cong., 2d Sess. 53 (1998) (all emphasis added). The House Report contains similar language regarding the cache provision of subsection (b) that also would appear to target its application to third parties, i.e., nonemployees: "For subsection (b) to apply, the material must be made available on an originating site, transmitted *at the direction of another person through the system or network* operated by or for the service provider *to a different person*, and stored through an automatic technical process so that users of the system or network who subsequently request access to the material from the originating site may obtain access to the material from the system or network." Id., at 52 (emphasis added). Similarly, the target of the link provisions of subsection (d) emanates from other parties as well: "The intended objective of this standard is to exclude from the safe harbor sophisticated 'pirate' directories-which refer Internet users to other selected Internet sites where pirate software, books, movies, and music can be downloaded or transmitted. Such pirate directories refer Internet users to sites that are obviously infringing because they typically use words such as 'pirate,' 'bootleg,' or slang terms in the URL and header information to make their illegal purpose obvious, in the first place, to the pirate directories as well as other Internet users. Because the infringing nature of such sites would be apparent from even a brief and casual viewing, *safe harbor status for a provider that views such site and then establishes a link to it would not be appropriate.*" Id., at 59 (emphasis added).

[53] H.R. Rep. No. 105-796, 72 (1998) (Conf. Rep.).

[54] See, e.g., H.R. Rep. No 551 (Part 2), 105th Cong., 2d Sess. 53 (1998) ("New section 512(c) limits the liability of qualifying service providers for claims of direct, vicarious and contributory infringement for storage at the direction *of a user* of material that resides on a system or network controlled or operated by or for the service provider. Examples of such storage include providing server space for user's web site, for a chatroom, or other forum in which material may be posted *at the direction of users.*") (emphasis added).

[55] See, S. Rep. No. 105-190, 105th Cong., 2d Sess. 19 (1998) ("There have been several cases relevant to service provider liability for copyright infringement. Most have approached the issue from the standpoint of contributory and vicarious liability." (footnote to developing case law including *Playboy Enterprises, Inc. v. Frena*, 839 F. Supp. 1552 (M.D. Fla. 1993), a case discussing the liability of the intermediary for acts of direct infringement, omitted).). H.R. Rep. No. 551 (Part 1), 105th Cong., 2d Sess. 11 (1998) ("As to direct infringement, liability is ruled out for passive, automatic acts engaged in through a technological process initiated by another. Thus, the bill essentially codifies the result in the leading and most thoughtful judicial decision to date: *Religious Technology Center v. Netcom On-Line Communications Services, Inc.*, 907 F. Supp. 1361 (N.D. Cal. 1995). In doing so, it overrules those

aspects of *Playboy Enterprises, Inc. v. Frena,* 839 F. Supp. (M.D. Fla 1993), insofar as that case suggests that such acts by service providers could constitute direct infringement, and provides certainty that Netcom and its progeny, so far only a few district court cases, will be the law of the land.").

[56] NORMAN J. SINGER, SUTHERLAND STATUTORY CONSTRUCTION § 46:6 (2002) (Each word given effect.) ("A statute should be construed so that effect is given to all its provisions, so that no part will be inoperative or superfluous, void or insignificant, and so that one section will not destroy another unless the provision is the result of obvious mistake or error. No clause sentence or word shall be construed as superfluous, void or insignificant if the construction can be found which will give force to and preserve all the words of the statute. . . Likewise, the courts do not construe different terms within a statute to embody the same meaning. However, it is possible to interpret an imprecise term differently in two separate sections of a statute which have different purposes. . . The use of different terms within related statutes generally implies that different meanings were intended.") (Numerous footnotes to supporting case law excluded.)

[57] The best analysis is found in JAY DRATLER, JR., CYBERLAW: INTELLECTUAL PROPERTY IN THE DIGITAL MILLENNIUM (2004), a legal treatise focusing exclusively on two sections of the copyright law: 512 and 1201 (the so-called anti-circumvention and anti-trafficking rules, both enacted by the DMCA). The treatise emphasizes section 1201 and also focuses on general service provider application as opposed to library or educational institutions.

[58] *Playboy Enterprises, Inc. v. Frena,* 839 F. Supp. 1552 (M.D. Fla. 1993); *Playboy Enterprises, Inc. v. Webbworld, Inc.,* 991 F. Supp. 543 (N.D. Tex. 1997).

[59] *Intellectual Reserve, Inc. v. Utah Lighthouse Ministry, Inc.,* 75 F. Supp. 2d 1290 (Dist. Utah 1999) (No actual link, referral only, is sufficient to establish liability for contributory infringement, direct infringement by viewers of material.). See also, *Universal City Studios v. Reimerdes,* 82 F. Supp. 2d 211 (S.D.N.Y. 2000); 111 F. Supp. 2d 294 (S.D.N.Y. 2000) (permanent injunction) (Leave to amend, contributory infringement for third party, first case to apply the anti-trafficking and anti-circumvention rules of Section 1201.), affirmed sub. nom. UNIVERSALCITY STUDIOS v. CORELY, 273 F3d429 (23nd Cir 2001).

[60] H.R. Rep. No 551 (Part 1), 105th Cong., 2d Sess. 24 (1998).

[61] Compare the language from H.R. 2281 as reported in H.R. Rep. No 551 (Part 1), 105th Cong., 2d Sess. 28 (1998), "does not have actual knowledge that the material is infringing or circumstances from which infringing activity is apparent," with the eventual section 512(c)(1)(A)(i) language, "does not have actual knowledge that the material *or an activity* **using the material on the system or network** is infringing; (ii) in the absence of such actual knowledge, is not aware of facts or circumstances from which infringing activity is apparent," and the eventual section 512(d)(1)(A) language, "does not have actual knowledge that the material *or activity* is infringing; (B) *in the absence of such actual knowledge, is not aware of facts or* circumstances from which infringing activity is apparent." The italics phrasing is different from the original House bill, and the bold-italics is different between

subsections 512 (c) and (d). The difference can be due to the fact that section 512, as enacted, split the provisions into separate functions of posting and linking, while the House bill treated them together in instances of contributory infringement or vicarious liability.

[62] H.R. Rep. No. 551 (Part 1), 105th Cong., 2d Sess. 25 (1998) (first emphasis added, second emphasis original).

[63] Compare the language from H.R. 2281 as reported in H.R. Rep. No. 551 (Part 1), 105th Cong., 2d Sess. 28 (1998), "does not receive a financial benefit directly attributable to the infringing activity, **if** the service provider has the right and ability to control such activity." This is essentially the same as eventual 512(c)(1)(B) language, "does not receive a financial benefit directly attributable to the infringing activity, *in a case in which the* service provider has the right and ability to control such activity," and the eventual section 512(d)(2) language, "does not receive a financial benefit directly attributable to the infringing activity, *in a case in which the* service provider has the right and ability to control such activity."

[64] H.R. Rep. No. 551 (Part 1), 105th Cong., 2d Sess. 25 (1998).

[65] See, H.R. Rep. No. 551 (Part 1), 105th Cong. 2d Sess. 11 (1998) and discussed in JAY DRATLER, JR., CYBERLAW: INTELLECTUAL PROPERTY IN THE DIGITAL MILLENNIUM § 6.01[3], at 6-20.8– 6-33 (2004). See also, Alfred C. Yen, Internet Service Provider Liability for Subscriber Copyright Infringement, Enterprise Liability, and the First Amendment, 88 GEORGETOWN LAW JOURNAL 1833, 1882 (2000) ("If the ISP gains such knowledge or awareness, no liability attaches as long as the ISP removes or disables access to the alleged infringement. This approximates contributory liability's requirement that an ISP have actual knowledge or knowledge of facts which clearly establish infringement.").

[66] S. Rep. No. 105-190, 105th Cong., 2d Sess. 19 (1998).

[67] *Costar Group Inc. v. LoopNet, Inc.*, 373 F.3d 544, 552 (4th Cir. 2004) ("We conclude that in enacting the DMCA, Congress did not preempt the decision in *Netcom* [*Religious Technology Center v. Netcom On-Line Communications Services, Inc.*, 907 F. Supp. 1361 (N.D. Cal. 1995)] nor foreclose the continuing development of liability through court decisions interpreting §§ 106 and 501 of the Copyright Act.")

[68] *Costar Group Inc. v. LoopNet, Inc.*, 164 F. Supp. 2d 688, 707 (D. Md. 2001), affirmed *Costar Group Inc. v. LoopNet, Inc.*, 373 F.3d 544 (4th Cir. 2004).

[69] 17 U.S.C § 512(j)(1)(A)(i).

[70] 17 U.S.C § 512(j)(1)(B)(ii).

[71] 17 U.S.C § 512(j)(1)(A)(ii) and (B)(i).

[72] 17 U.S.C § 512(j)(3).

[73] See, H.R. Rep. No. 105-796, 105th Cong., 2d Sess. 73 (1998) (Conf. Rep.) (emphasis added).

[74] H.R. Rep. No. 551 (Part 1), 105th Cong., 2d Sess. 26 (1998).

[75] *Ellison v. Robertson*, 357 F.3d 1072, 1077 (9th Cir. 2004).

[76] *Costar Group Inc. v. LoopNet, Inc.*, 164 F. Supp. 2d 688, 699 (D. Md. 2001), affirmed *Costar Group Inc. v. LoopNet, Inc.*, 373 F.3d 544 (4th Cir. 2004).

[77] 17 U.S.C § 512(l) provides: "The failure of a service provider's conduct to qualify for limitation of liability under this section shall not bear adversely upon the consideration of a defense by the service provider that the service provider's conduct is not infringing under this title or any other defense." The educational institution might in fact have a broader range of choices, if it chose not to take action which insures refuge of the safe harbor; fair use of course may be more readily available in the educational environment. See, H.R. Rep. No. 551 (Part 1), 105th Cong., 2d Sess. 11 (1998) ("For example, an educational institution which receives notice infringement and determines that the material may be subject to a fair use defense would still be able to assert such a defense whether or not it chose to block access to the material.").

[78] U.S.C. § 512(i)(1)(A) ("has adopted and reasonably implemented, and informs subscribers and account holders of the service provider's system or network of, a policy that provides for the termination in appropriate circumstances of subscribers and account holders of the service provider's system or network who are repeat infringers").

[79] U.S.C. § 512(i)(1)(B) ("accommodates and does not interfere with standard technical measures").

[80] See, JAY DRATLER, JR., CYBERLAW: INTELLECTUAL PROPERTY IN THE DIGITAL MILLENNIUM § 6.02[2][a], at 6-44.11 (2004) (suggesting a standard of "commercial reasonableness" throughout the discussion at § 6.02[2][a], at 6-44.10–6-44.15).

[81] H.R. Rep. No. 551 (Part 2), 105th Cong., 2d Sess. 61 (1998); S. Rep. No. 105-190, 105th Cong., 2d Sess. 52 (1998).

[82] *Ellison v. Robertson*, 189 F. Supp. 2d 1051, 1065 (C.D. Cal. 2002), affirmed in part and reversed in part and remanded, ELLISON V. ROBERTSON, 357 F.3d 1072 (9th Cir. 2004).

[83] See, e.g., *Kreimer v. Bureau of Police for Town of Morristown*, 958 F.2d 1242 (3d Cir. 1992) (patron code of conduct policy); *Mainstream Loudoun v. Board of Trustees of the Loudoun County Library*, 2 F. Supp. 2d 783 (*Loudoun I*), 24 F. Supp. 2d 552 (*Loudoun II*) (E.D. Va. 1998) (Internet acceptable use policy); *Sund v. City of Wichita Falls, Texas*, 121 F. Supp. 2d 530 (N.D. Texas 2000) (collection development policy); *Pfeifer v. City of West Allis*, 91 F. Supp. 2d 1253 (E.D. Wis. 2000) (meeting room use policy); and *Case v. Unified School District No. 233*, 908 F. Supp. 864 (D. Kan. 1995) (school library gift policy). See also, Claire Weber, Designing, Drafting, and Implementing New Policies, in LIBRARIES, MUSEUMS AND ARCHIVES: LEGAL ISSUES AND CHALLENGES IN THE NEW INFORMATION ERA 303-319 (Tomas A. Lipinski, ed. 2002); and Donna L. Ferullo, STRUGGLING WITH YOUR COPYRIGHT POLICY, THE COPYRIGHT & NEW MEDIA LAW NEWSLETTER FOR LIBRARIANS & INFORMATION SPECIALISTS, No. 8, 2004, at 3,3.

[84] *Ellison v. Robertson*, 357 F.3d 1072, 1080 (9th Cir. 2004). See also, *Corbis Corp. v. Amazon.com, Inc.*, 351 F. Supp. 2d 1090 (W.D.Wash. 2004). ("A service provider must: 1) adopt a policy that provides for the termination of service access for repeat copyright infringers in appropriate circumstances; 2) inform users of the service policy; and 3) implement the policy in a reasonable manner. *See id.* As discussed below, Amazon has satisfied each of the three *Ellison* prongs." Id. at 1100. "[W]hat constitutes reasonable implementation of

an infringement policy. Cases that have addressed this issue generally raise two questions. The first is whether the service provider adopted a procedure for receiving complaints and conveying those complaints to users. [Citation omitted] If such a procedure has been adopted, then the second question is whether the service provider nonetheless still tolerates flagrant or blatant copyright infringement by its users." Id. at 1102 (Citation omitted); *Perfect 10, Inc. v. Cybernet Ventures, Inc.*, 213 F. Supp. 2d 1146 (C.D. Cal. 2002) ("When confronted with "appropriate circumstances," however, such service providers should reasonably implement termination. [Citation omitted] These circumstances would appear to cover, at a minimum, instances where a service provider is given sufficient evidence to create actual knowledge of blatant, repeat infringement by particular users, particularly infringement of a willful and commercial nature." Id. at 1177).

[85] H.R. Rep. No. 551 (Part 2), 105th Cong., 2d Sess. 61 (1998); S. Rep. No. 105-190, 105th Cong., 2d Sess. 52 (1998).

[86] 37 C.F.R. § 201.14(b).

[87] MERRIAM-WEBSTER'S COLLEGIATE DICTIONARY 1055 (11th 2003).

[88] 17 U.S.C. § 512(e)(1)(B) (emphasis added).

[89] JOHN W. HAZARD JR., COPYRIGHT LAW IN BUSINESS AND PRACTICE § 7:36, at 75 (2003 Cumulative Supplement No. 2) (footnote omitted).

[90] This lack of detail, in light of the complexity of the remainder of section 512 is perplexing. See, JAY DRATLER, JR., CYBERLAW: INTELLECTUAL PROPERTY IN THE DIGITAL MILLENNIUM § 6.02[2], at 6-44.8 (2004) ("Unless interpreted flexibly, the language of subsection (i) provides little reason to hope that the average service provider can get to that gate with relative certainty" for a discussion of this problem and the additional unanswered questions he poses.)

[91] Keith Kupferschmind, Something for Everyone, INTELLECTUAL PROPERTY MAGAZINE, February, 1999, no pagination (available in the LEXIS-NEXIS LEGNEW Library).

[92] But see, H.R. Rep. No. 551 (Part 1), 105th Cong., 2d Sess. 25 (1998) ("As subsection (b) makes clear, the bill imposes no obligation on a provider to seek out such red flags. Once a provider becomes aware of a red flag, however, it ceases to qualify for the exemption. This standard *differs from existing law*, under which a defendant may be liable for contributory infringement if it knows or *should have known* that material was infringing." (first emphasis added, second emphasis original).

[93] H.R. Rep. No. 551 (Part 2), 105th Cong., 2d Sess. 61 (1998); S. Rep. No. 105-190, 105th Cong., 2d Sess. 52 (1998).

[94] House (Conference) Report 105-796, 105th Cong., 2d Sess. 73 (1998).

[95] Marc Lindsey, World File Sharing War, THE COPYRIGHT & NEW MEDIA LAW NEWSLETTER, No. 4, 2004, at 9, 10 (noting that once the program was instituted at the author's university complaints under the DMCA dropped from four a week to four a year).

[96] H.R. Rep. No 551 (Part 2), 105th Cong., 2d Sess. 61 (1998), as cited in *A&M Records, Inc. v. Napster, Inc.*, 2000 WL 573136, at * 9 (N.D. Cal. 2000).

[97] *A&M Records, Inc. v. Napster, Inc.*, 2000 WL 573136, at * 9 (N.D. Cal. 2000).

[98] *A&M Records, Inc. v. Napster, Inc.*, 2000 WL 573136, at * 9 (N.D. Cal. 2000) ("Napster attempts to refute plaintiffs' argument by noting that subsection 512(i) does not specify when the copyright compliance policy must be in place. Although this characterization of subsection 512(i) is facially accurate, it defies the logic of making formal notification to users or subscribers a prerequisite to exemption from monetary liability.").

[99] *A&M Records, Inc. v. Napster, Inc.*, 2000 WL 573136, at * 9 (N.D. Cal. 2000).

[100] *A&M Records, Inc. v. Napster, Inc.*, 2000 WL 573136, at * 9 (N.D. Cal. 2000) (emphasis added) (citations to internal court documents omitted).

[101] *A&M Records, Inc. v. Napster, Inc.*, 2000 WL 573136, at * 9 (N.D. Cal. 2000).

[102] *A&M Records, Inc. v. Napster, Inc.*, 2000 WL 573136, at * 9 (N.D. Cal. 2000).

[103] Alfred C. Yen, Internet Service Provider Liability for Subscriber Copyright Infringement, Enterprise Liability, and the First Amendment, 88 GEORGETOWN LAW JOURNAL 1833, 1837 (2000) (footnote omitted).

[104] H.R. Rep. No. 551 (Part 1), 105th Cong., 2d Sess. 26 (1998) ("[T]he knowledge standard in subsection (a) shall not be construed to condition the limitation contained in that subsection on monitoring a network for infringement or searching out suspicious information.").

[105] See. e.g., Peer-to-Peer Piracy on University Campuses, Hearing, Subcommittee on Courts, the Internet, and Intellectual Property, Committee on the Judiciary, U.S. House of Representatives, 108th Congress, 1st Session, February 26, 2003 ("88% of Residence Hall networks at the University of Indiana were at one time consumed with P2P file-trafficking. When Texas Christian University blocked Napster, it freed up 70% of its bandwidth. . . . Kansas State estimated that it saved more than $100,000, or a quarter of its bandwidth costs."), at p. 17 (Statement of Representative Smith); Id. ("More than 2.6 million music files are illegally downloaded every month on unauthorized P2P systems. Of this number, a significant percentage of the transfers occur over campus networks."), at p. 33 (Prepared Statement of Hilary Rosen, RIAA) (available at *http://commdocs.house.gov/committees/judiciary/hju85286.000/hju85286_0.htm*).

[106] See, e.g., *In Re Aimster Copyright Litigation*, 334 F.3d 643, 653 (7th Cir. 2003) (grant of preliminary injunction to shut down Aimster upheld) ("Aimster has failed to produce any evidence that its service has ever been used for a noninfringing use, let alone evidence concerning the frequency of such uses. . . . Aimster blinded itself in the hope that by so it might come within the rule of the *Sony* decision. . . . Aimster hampered its search for evidence by providing encryption. It must take responsibility for that self inflicted wound."). The district court observed: "Aimster has adopted a repeat infringer policy. . . . Finally, the notice provides that 'uses who are found to repeatedly violate copyright rights of others may have their access to all services terminated.'. . . These facts support a finding that Aimster has adopted a repeat infringer policy." Id. at (footnotes omitted). However, the court also noted that the policy "is, as we shall see, an absolute mirage, but it is a stated policy nonetheless." Id. at 659, n. 18.

[107] See, e.g., Marc Lindsey, World File Sharing War, THE COPYRIGHT & NEW MEDIA LAW NEWSLETTER, No. 4, 2004, at 9, 10, discussing a program at Washington State University

where students whose bandwidth and port activity suggest excessive or infringing use of copyrighted material are denied further network access, referred to a course in basic copyright law, and have their network access restored only after passing the class.

[108] 17 U.S.C. § 512(i)(1)(B).

[109] 17 U.S.C. § 512(i)(2).

[110] For example, CONTU (National Commission of New Technological Uses of Copyrighted Works) developed the widely adopted Guidelines on Photocopying and Interlibrary Arrangements, reprinted, H.R. Rep. No. 94-1476, 94th Cong. 2d Sess. 163 (1976) (Conf. Rep.), reprinted in 5 U.S.C.C.A.N. 5659, 5779 (1976).

[111] For example, CONFU (Conference on Fair Use) developed the somewhat less widely adopted Fair Use Guidelines for Educational Multimedia, reprinted in ARLENE BIELE-FIELD AND LAWRENCE CHEESEMAN, TECHNOLOGY AND COPYRIGHT LAW: A GUIDEBOOK FOR THE LIBRARY, RESEARCH, AND TEACHING PROFESSIONS, 92-102 (1997).

[112] H.R. Rep. No. 551 (Part 2), 105th Cong., 2d Sess. 61 (1998); S. Rep. No. 105-190, 105th Cong., 2d Sess. 52 (1998).

[113] 17 U.S.C. § 512(i)(2)(B).

[114] 17 U.S.C. § 512(i)(2)(C).

[115] *eBay, Inc. v. Bidder's Edge, Inc.*, 100 F. Supp. 2d 1058, 1066 (N.D. Cal. 2000) (If BE's activity is allowed to continue unchecked, it would encourage other auction aggregators to engage in similar recursive searching of the eBay system such that eBay would suffer irreparable harm from reduced system performance, system unavailability, or data losses. (*See* Spafford Decl. ¶ 32; Parker Decl. ¶ 19; Johnson-Laird Decl. ¶ 85.) BE does not appear to seriously contest that reduced system performance, system unavailability or data loss would inflict irreparable harm on eBay consisting of lost profits and lost customer goodwill. Harm resulting from lost profits and lost customer goodwill is irreparable because it is neither easily calculable, nor easily compensable and is therefore an appropriate basis for injunctive relief.); *Register.com v. Verio, Inc.*, 126 F. Supp. 2d 238, 250 (S.D.N.Y. 2000) ("Furthermore, Gardos also noted in his declaration 'if the strain on Register.com's resources generated by Verio's searches becomes large enough, it could cause Register.com's computer systems to malfunction or crash' and 'I believe that if Verio's searching of Register.com's WHOIS database were determined to be lawful, then every purveyor of Internet-based services would engage in similar conduct.' (Gardos Decl. ¶¶ 33, 34). Gardos' concerns are supported by Verio's testimony that it sees no need to place a limit on the number of other companies that should be allowed to harvest data from Register.com's computers. (*See* Ayers Depo. at 71). Furthermore, Verio's own internal documents reveal that Verio was aware that its robotic queries could slow the response times of the registrars' databases and even overload them. (*See* Ex. 29 & to Pl.'s Sept. 8, 2000 Motion). Because of that possibility, Verio contemplated cloaking the origin of its queries by using a process called IP aliasing. (*See id.; see also* Ex. 64 to Pl.'s Sept. 8, 2000 Motion). Accordingly, Register.com's evidence that Verio's search robots have presented

and will continue to present an unwelcome interference with, and a risk of interruption to, its computer system and servers is sufficient to demonstrate a likelihood of success on the merits of its trespass to chattels claim."). See also, *Ticketmaster, Corp. v. Tickets.com*, 2000 U.S. Dist. LEXIS 12987 (C.D. Calif. 2000) (tacit acceptance of digital trespass, but no evidence of harm demonstrated).

[116] H.R. Rep. No. 551 (Part 2), 105th Cong., 2d Sess. 61 (1998); S. Rep. No. 105-190, 105th Cong., 2d Sess. 52 (1998).

[117] JAY DRATLER JR., CYBERLAW: INTELLECTUAL PROPERTY IN THE DIGITAL MIL-LENNIUM § 6.02[2], at 6-44.7 (2004) (citation to footnote 40, referencing earlier discussion of section 1201, omitted).

[118] H.R. Rep. No. 551 (Part 2), 105th Cong., 2d Sess. 61 (1998); S. Rep. No. 105-190, 105th Cong., 2d Sess. 52 (1998).

[119] H.R. Rep. No. 551 (Part 2), 105th Cong., 2d Sess. 61 (1998); S. Rep. No. 105-190, 105th Cong., 2d Sess. 52 (1998).

▶Part III

THE IMPACT OF THE DIGITAL MILLENNIUM COPYRIGHT ACT ON LIBRARY AND EDUCATIONAL ENVIRONMENTS

▶7

HOW SHOULD LIBRARIES AND SCHOOLS RESPOND TO CLAIMS OF INFRINGEMENT?

Read this chapter to learn about copyright situations like:

▶ Whether a professor can direct his or her students to Web pages that have excellent information but appear to contain pirated files.

▶ Whether an institution can ignore a notice of infringement from a copyright owner if it does not meet the statutory notice requirements.

▶ Whether a copyright holder can demand information about patrons who have engaged in some infringing activity using the library's resources.

MAKING SENSE OF THE REGISTERED AGENT REQUIREMENT OF SECTION 512(C)

As discussed in the previous chapter, the purpose of section 512 is to articulate circumstances under which service providers can rest easy, having recourse to the safe harbor rules. The "insurance" that these rules offer from the potential monetary liability that might result from acts of service provider's users such as library patrons or students, is all the more important considering the increased and recent interest by Congress in curbing rampant copyright infringement on college campuses and other network environments.[1] In light of these developments, section 512(c) is most important as it targets the posting by users of infringing material on the service provider's network: "storage at the direction of a user of material that resides on a system or network controlled or operated by or for the service provider."[2] Promoting use of the section 512(c) mechanisms and its "cooperative"[3] spirit, then, is in the best interest of the institutional intermediary, lest Congress tinker with the law again and increase the "quid" in the quid pro quo of the compliance-monetary remission mix.

The mechanism is designed to work in this way: suppose a student downloads infringing material into his or her account on the institution's server (caches), uploads (posts) other infringing content to his or her student Web page, or creates an online directory to the infringing material (information locations tool) or places a URL (link) on that page to a source of infringing material.[4] The institution now has infringing material somewhere on its network or, through the link on its network, provides access to a source of infringing material. Subsections (b), (c), and (d) of section 512 command the agitated copyright plaintiff to first contact the institution, identify the material,[5] and request that it be taken down or that access to it be disabled "expeditiously."

Appointing a Registered Agent

Recall that the grant of the liability limitation, or more accurately monetary remission for the posting function, is found in section 512(c)(1): "A service provider shall not be liable for monetary relief, or, except as provided in subsection (j), for injunctive or other equitable relief, for infringement of copyright by reason of the storage at the direction of a user of material that resides on a system or network controlled or operated by or for the service provider."[6] However in order to receive this benefit the service provider must meet several conditions in section 512(c)(1)(A) through (C). Subsections (c)(1)(A) and (B) are discussed later, Subsection (c)(1)(C) is relevant to this discussion. Three related provisions with subsection (c) are at play here.

Section 512(c)(1)(C) provides that the service provider, "upon notification of claimed infringement as described in paragraph (3), responds expeditiously to remove, or disable access to, the material that is claimed to be infringing or to be the subject of infringing activity." Section 512(c)(3) discussed below details the requirements of the notice the copyright owner sends to the service provider to trigger this removal or disabling.

Section 512(c)(2) requires that service providers designate a registered agent to receive such section 512(c)(3) notices. Thus there is a statutory link between the contents of the notice the copyright owner provides to the service provider, the person designated to receive that notice (the registered agent), and what the service provider must do upon receipt of the notice. This section of Chapter 7 discusses these mechanisms. The service provider should weigh and evaluate the costs of the commitment required under section 512 against the risk of litigation.[7] Of course, an alternative would be to have a compliance program in place that accomplishes the same goals, minimizes the risk of litigation, but does not need to comply with the statutory burdens of section 512.

Use of the Agent in Other Scenarios: Caching and Linking

Unlike the two qualifying compliance-oriented provisions discussed earlier—the repeat infringer policy and the accommodation and noninterference admonition—

which apply to all service providers, the registered agent provision applies only to section 512(c), i.e., the post functions of service providers ("storage at the direction of a user"). However, as discussed below, because the notice and removal or disabling requirement of section 512(c)(1)(C) is also found in section 512(b)(2)(D) and section 512(d)(3), the notice given by the copyright owner to a subsection (b) or (d) service provider must likewise conform by statutory reference in those two sections to the section 512(c)(3) notice, the designation and use of a registered agent for subsections (b) and (d) is also recommended, if not implicit in the statute. In other words, designate a registered agent in cache and link scenarios as well!

The appointment of an agent registered with the U.S. Copyright Office is required by 512(c)(2). The registered agent designation is not required of the conduit or store and forward provisions of section 512(a). Though optional under section 512(b) and (d), cache and link, incorporating the "registered agent" provision into the link provisions of section 512(d) increases the administrative oversight the institution must perform. Is this absence intended or is it the result of poor drafting and lack of adequate legislative oversight?

At least one commentator recommends the appointment of a registered agent to receive notices in instances of alleged caching and linking: "It [expeditious removal or disabling requirement] is not a precondition to the limitation on remedies for 'store and forward' activities under subsection (a). Thus, service providers engaged in caching [subsection (b)] or linking [subsection (d)] activities *are best advised to designate such an agent,* as both a precaution and a good business practice, but those engaged only in routing or 'store and forward' activities need not do so."[8] This is a logical recommendation as those two subsections, (b) and (d), in addition to subsection (c), also contains a notice and removal or disabling provision. Designating a registered agent to receive complaints can facilitate the notice and expeditious removal or disabling provisions present in subsections (b)(2)(E), (d)(3), then as well as (c)(1)(C).

Moreover, the notice and takedown provisos of section 512(b)(2)(E) ("the service provider responds expeditiously to remove, or disable access to, the material that is claimed to be infringing upon notification of claimed infringement as described in subsection (c)(3)") and section 512(d)(3) ("upon notification of claimed infringement as described in subsection (c)(3), responds expeditiously to remove, or disable access to, the material that is claimed to be infringing or to be the subject of infringing activity") both reference the section 512(c)(3) notification provision (which, of course, is in place to give purpose to the designation of a registered agent per section 512(c)(2) to in fact receive such notices). Thus it is perfectly logical to use the registered agent mechanism as the starting point for a section 512(b)(2)(E) and section 512(d)(3) notice and expeditious removal or disabling as well.

The Registered Agent in Practice

How does section 512(c) work in practice? Must the service provider do anything under section 512? No, remember, like other compliance provisions of the law, section 512 creates no affirmative duty, but then of course the limitation on liability will not be available. The legislative history reaffirms this concept: "On the other hand, the service provider is free to refuse to 'take-down' the material or site— even after receiving a notification of claimed infringement for the copyright owners. In such a situation, the service provider's liability, if any, will be decided without reference to new Section 512(c)."[9]

Section 512(c)(2) requires the designation of a registered agent with the U.S. Copyright Office: "The limitations on liability established in this subsection apply to a service provider only if the service provider has designated an agent to receive notifications of claimed infringement described in paragraph (3)."[10] The purpose of the agent is to receive complaints as part of the notice and "takedown," to use Professor Dratler's formulation, i.e., the expeditious removal or disabling mechanism of section 512(c)(1)(C): "upon notification of claimed infringement as described in paragraph (3), responds expeditiously to remove, or disable access to, the material that is claimed to be infringing or to be the subject of infringing activity."[11] The designation of the agent must include "substantially the following information: the name, address, phone number, and electronic mail address of the agent, and other contact information which the Register of Copyrights may deem appropriate."[12]

Publicizing the Registered Agent

Section 512(c)(2) facilitates this process by requiring the appointment of a registered agent: "The limitations on liability established in this subsection apply to a service provider only if the service provider has designated an agent to receive notifications of claimed infringement described in paragraph (3), by making available through its service, including on its website in a location accessible to the public, and by providing to the Copyright Office."[13] The statute suggests three locations where the registered agent information should appear or modes whereby the registered agent information is disseminated: somewhere through its service ("by making available through its service"), on its Web site if it has one ("including on its website in a location accessible to the public"), and to the U.S. Copyright Office's Agent registry ("and by providing to the Copyright Office"). Examples of the first "through its service" mechanism might be as part of a log-on sequence or bulletin board. If the service provider maintains a Web site, a part of which is password protected, encrypted, or otherwise not available to the public (such as an e-reserve system), the service provider must make the information available on the part of the Web site that is "accessible to the public," such as its home page.

To facilitate the process of removal or disabling, certain information must be made available to copyright owners regarding the registered agent: "(A) the name, address, phone number, and electronic mail address of the agent [and] (B) other contact information which the Register of Copyrights may deem appropriate."[14] Finally, "[t]he Register of Copyrights shall maintain a current directory of agents available to the public for inspection, including through the Internet, in both electronic and hard copy formats, and may require payment of a fee by service providers to cover the costs of maintaining the directory."[15] While the Register of Copyrights is to maintain a hard copy of the listing, the registry will not be distributed in that format. Rather the legislative history indicates:

> The Register of Copyrights is directed to maintain a directory of designated agents available for inspection by the public, both on the web site of the Library of Congress, and in hard copy format on file at the Copyright Office. The Committee does *not* intend or anticipate that the Register will publish hard copies of directory. The directory shall have entries for the name, address, telephone number, and electronic mail address of an agent designated by service providers.[16]

It makes sense to maintain an online directory; a service provider will by definition be online, so having the access point of registry information be also online is consistent. Moreover, it allows the most up-to-date information to be maintained by the Register of Copyrights, as a print list of online contacts would be likely out of date the moment it is so published.

Registering the Agent with the U.S. Copyright Office

The U.S. Copyright Office regulations indicate the contents of the registered agent filing ("Interim Designation of Agent to Receive Notification of Claimed Infringement"),[17] though no particular form is provided.[18] There is a $30 filing fee and "[d]esignations and amendments will be posted online on the Copyright Offices' website (http://www.loc.gov.copyright)."[19] Should contact information change or the service provider cease operations, the service provider must notify the Copyright Office.[20]

The use of a registered agent is pivotal in facilitating a rapid response to claimed violations of the copyright law occurring on the service provider's network or through its facilities. This important role suggests that the registered agent should have the institutional authority to order the removal or disabling of access to the identified material or at least know from whom such authority must be obtained, as the removal or disabling must be done "expeditiously"! Thus an institution having a cumbersome decision-making structure, whereby decisions are continually passed up the chain of command or where administrators are sometimes reluctant to respond decisively, is unlikely to be in a position to take advantage of the section 512 safe harbor, since such responses are unlikely to be made "expeditiously" as required by statute. Consider the following scenario: a disabling or take-down request received by the registered agent is reported to the agent's supervisor. The supervisor then relays the request notice to the network manager, and the university CIO to whom both the registered agent's supervisor and the network manager report. Upon receipt of the notice, the CIO alerts the provost and the general counsel with whom the provost consults on all legal matters. Here, each person along the chain of institutional descision making individually questions whether the material should be removed. Such a decision-making process might well jeopardize the institution's ability to seek the safe harbor, as the communication processing time alone would not meet the "expeditious" requirement. Appoint a person with authority within the institution, have that person versed in section 512 and the copyright law, and encourage him or her to be ready to execute immediate decisions regarding removal or disabling requests from copyright owners.

As discussed below, this process is more than technical, e.g., searching for and deleting a file, disabling a link, or turning on or off a switch. There is also an elaborate counter-contact and counter-notice process, of which the service provider may be a part, as well as other responsibilities that logically include the registered agent, such as a subpoena request for subscriber identity. Subpoenas received under section 512(h) must also be responded to "expeditiously." Regardless of where the agent sits on the institutional food-chain of command, if authority to act is not given for all mechanisms within section 512, there should be established procedures for immediate response from the proper decision maker.

Copyright Owner Obligations: Designing the Notice

Whether a service provider designates a registered agent to receive complaints under subsection 512(b) and (d)—recall, such designation is not required under those subsections—or only designates an agent for section 512(c) functions, the notice that a copyright owner or its agent must give to the service provider or agent *must* in all three instances meet the same requirements of section 512(c)(3): "To be effective under this subsection, a notification of claimed infringement must be a written communication provided to the designated agent of a service provider that includes substantially the following."[21] A telephone call, no matter how emphatic, is insufficient.[22]

Possessing an understanding of the required notice content is important for two reasons. First, a service provider might make use of this provision because it might be a copyright owner itself. Second, while a failed subsection (c)(3)(A) notice might not be sufficient to trigger the required notice and removal or disabling response, it could still trigger a general "knowledge" or "awareness" and removal or disabling under section 512(c)(1)(A) or section 512(d)(1). This possibility is discussed below.

The first condition of proper notice includes "[a] physical or electronic signature of a person authorized to act on behalf of the owner of an exclusive right that is allegedly infringed."[23] While the communication must be written, the first proviso suggests that its form can be electronic. What is inadequate is a telephone call, even if during the conversation, the copyright owner detailed the information required by section 512(c)(3)(A)(i)-(vi). Moreover, "[t]he requirement for signature, either physical or electronic, relates to the verification requirements of new subsections (c)(3)(A)(v) and (vi)."[24]

Identifying the Work Infringed and the Infringing Material

Second and third, the work that is infringed must be identified as well as the material that it is claimed infringes upon it:

> (ii) Identification of the copyrighted work claimed to have been infringed, or, if multiple copyrighted works at a single online site are covered by a single notification, a representative list of such works at that site. (iii) Identification of the material that is claimed to be infringing or to be the subject of infringing activity and that is to be removed or access to which is to be disabled, and information reasonably sufficient to permit the service provider to locate the material.[25]

These are two related but obviously separate pieces of information.

In situations where the notice is issued under the section 512(d)(3) link function, then a slight variation is made to the contents of the notice relating to identification: "[t]he information described in subsection (c)(3)(A)(iii) shall be identification of the reference or link, to material or activity claimed to be infringing, that is to be removed or access to which is to be disabled, and information reasonably sufficient to permit the service provider to locate that reference or link."[26] This variation is logical because, in link scenarios, it is the link or other "information location tools" that is the target of the removal or disabling obligation.

Observe also that, in situations where numerous works are infringed, only a "representative list" need be provided. The notice requirements are not intended to place the copyright owner in the legal equivalent of a straitjacket but to offer a mechanism whereby service providers may do their part to curb infringement.[27] As a result, a representative list is acceptable:

> Thus, for example, where a party is operating an unauthorized Internet jukebox from a particular site, it is not necessary that the notification list every musical composition or sound recording that has been, may have been, or could be infringed at that site. Instead it is sufficient for the copyright owner to provide the service provider with a representative list of those compositions or recordings in order that the service provider can understand the nature and scope of the infringement being claimed.[28]

Suppose that a number of copyrighted works are being infringed, the copyright owner need only provide a "representative list"; each work need not be identified according to section 512(c)(3)(A)(ii). However, the location or locations would need to be specified in detail "reasonably sufficient to permit the service provider to locate the material." An example would be a URL where the infringing material is located.[29]

Professor Dratler points out that "a defendant should not have to receive a certified copy of a registration certificate in order to be charged with knowledge that material is copyrighted; to hold otherwise would be to require actual, not constructive, notice. A copyright notice that later proves proper should be enough to put a defendant on inquiry."[30] Moreover, as recent case law supports,[31] the statute imposes this burden even in the absence of identification of every copyrighted work; it is sufficient if a "representative" list is provided: "Identification of the copyrighted work claimed to have been infringed, or, if multiple copyrighted works at a single online site are covered by a single notification, a representative list of such works at that site."[32] Again a reticent response by the library or other institutional intermediary that the list is incomplete or otherwise less than helpful is unlikely to convince a court that an expeditious response was made. The burden here is clearly upon the service provider to do what it can once suspicion has been raised that infringing works might reside on its system: "The language of the statute eschews an interpretation of slavish adherence to form as opposed to substantial notice designed to inform the owner of an internet site about infringing materials and copyright ownership of them."[33]

Making Use of Contact Information

Next, proper contact information must be provided from the copyright owner to the registered agent. This is important, as discussed below, because an incomplete or inadequate notice places a duty on the service provider to contact the copyright owner and ask for clarification—in order to offer the copyright owner a chance to perfect notice. If this counter contact is not undertaken, then according to section 512(c)(3)(b) the incomplete (c)(3) notice may be used to trigger a similar removal or disabling requirement, as it might provide sufficient "general" knowledge or awareness under either (c)(1)(A)(i) and (ii) or (d)(1)(A) and (B). Proper contact information should convey "[i]nformation reasonably sufficient to permit the service provider to contact the complaining party, such as an address, telephone number, and, if available, an electronic mail address at which the complaining party may be contacted."[34]

One of the earliest appellate cases regarding section 512 involved a dispute over the sufficiency of the (c)(3) notice. The Fourth Circuit concluded that compliance with the notice provisions of 512(c)(3) and (d)(3) is satisfied if the identification of the infringing material is "substantial," though it need not detail every item in

specific, before the take-down or disable trigger is activated.[35] The notice requirement is adequate if copyright owner "substantially" complied with requirements;
specificity is not required for collections of multiple infringing works. Rather section 512(c)(3)(A)(ii) requires the

> identification of the copyrighted work claimed to have been infringed, or, if multiple
> works at a single online site are covered by a single notification, a representative list of
> such works at that site. . . . [T]he requirements are written so as to reduce the burden
> of holders of multiple works who face extensive infringement of their works. Thus,
> when a letter provides notice equivalent to a list of representative works that can be
> easily identified by the service provider, the notice substantially complies with the noti-
> fication requirements.[36]

The point is that the section (c)(3)(A)(i)–(vi) list of notice components does not
require 100 percent compliance by the copyright owner, the list need only include
"substantially the following." However, no such statutory slack is built into section
512(c) or other subsections for service providers, e.g., a service provider would be
required to remove or disable all works, at the infringing site as indicated by its
URL, even if only a representative list of works was provided by the copyright
owner. Moreover, a service provider in receipt of a proper section 512(c)(3) notice
cannot remove or disable most or substantially all of the alleged infringing material—the service provider has no such flexibility.

Moreover, the notice and removal or disabling provision of section 512 does not
anticipate that the alleged infringement be proved in a court of law. However, to
prevent copyright owners from willy-nilly erring on the side of caution and accusa-
tion, thus forcing removal or disabling of copyrighted material unnecessarily, section 512(c)(3)(A)(v) requires that the copyright include "[a] statement that the
complaining party has a good faith belief that use of the material in the manner
complained of is not authorized by the copyright owner, its agent, or the law."[37]
So, too, section 512(f), discussed below, also creates separate liability for misrepresentations that are "knowingly materially" made. However, there is a bit of legal
wiggle room between a copyright owner that in good faith believes his or her
works are being infringed and one who "knowingly materially misrepresents" that
it is so infringed.

Including Statements of Accuracy and Authorization

Of course the inconsistency of such mechanisms should be clear to anyone who
has followed the debate in the literature over the lawfulness of e-reserve systems in
libraries or P2P file sharing (before the courts began deciding these cases). Copyright owners and copyright users generally disagree over the legality of such
processes, especially in noncommercial settings like public libraries or schools. However, resolving such disputes is not part of the section 512 response mechanism.

Here all that is needed is that the copyright owner possess a good-faith belief that the material is not authorized, not that it is infringing as well, but it is logical that this is what the statute intends to be the standard. The point is supported by the legislative history which suggests: "the notification from complaining parties must contain a statement that the complaining party has a good faith belief that the *allegedly* infringing use is not authorized by the copyright owner, or it agent, or the law."[38] Of course, good-faith allegation of infringement can, nevertheless, be erroneous under the law. The statement of infringement made in good-faith by the copyright owner as part of the notice mechanism goes only to its allegation and in the absence of any authorization from the copyright owner not to its eventual adjudication as infringement. While the ultimate accuracy of the allegation through adjudication may be desired by the service provider, it is not a requirement of the statute triggering the service provider's obligation to respond accordingly.

In fact, the only portion of the section 512(c)(3) notice that is made under penalty of perjury is the authorization of the notice issuer's authority to act on behalf of the owner; the general accuracy of the notice (the good-faith belief proviso of (c)(3)(A)(V), for example) is not: "A statement that the information in the notification is accurate, and under penalty of perjury, that the complaining party is authorized to act on behalf of the owner of an exclusive right that is allegedly infringed."[39] The legislative history indicates that "[t]he term 'perjury' is used in the sense found elsewhere in the United States Code. See, e.g., 28 U.S.C. § 1746. 18 U.S.C. § 1621."[40] Yet the statute does not read: "A statement *under penalty of perjury* that the information in the notification is accurate, and, that the complaining party is authorized to act on behalf of the owner of an exclusive right that is allegedly infringed" with the effect being that the accuracy and authority to act are both covered by the threat of perjury. The statute only requires that the statement "that the complaining party is authorized to act on behalf of the owner of an exclusive right that is allegedly infringed" be subject to a penalty of perjury. The legislative history appears to confirm the difference between the statement of accuracy and authority, with the latter being subject to the perjurious assertion and not the former.[41]

As discussed below, blatantly false ("knowingly materially misrepresents") assertions are subject to civil remedy (including damages, costs, and attorney's fees) under section 512(f). However, assertions that are inaccurate may not in all necessarily meet the higher "knowingly materially misrepresents." Moreover, assertions that are false and meet this standard will result in recovery for harm only if the person aggrieved undertakes legal proceedings and the "cost" such litigation naturally entails. Requiring that section 512(c)(3)(A) notice be subject to an accuracy standard under penalty of perjury as well might go a long way to ensure that such notices are proper in the first instance. In the author's opinion, this is yet another example of the favoritism section 512 offers to copyright owners at the expense of intermediaries.

Obligations of the Copyright Owner in Caching Scenarios

Section 512(b)(2)(E) cues the notice and takedown in caching scenarios to the notice requirements of section 512(c)(3). Triggering of the notice and takedown mechanism under section 512 requires an additional prerequisite, however. According to the statute, (c)(3) applies only if

> (i) the material has previously been removed from the originating site or access to it has been disabled, or a court has ordered that the material be removed from the originating site or that access to the material on the originating site be disabled; and (ii) the party giving the notification includes in the notification a statement confirming that the material has been removed from the originating site or access to it has been disabled or that a court has ordered that the material be removed from the originating site or that access to the material on the originating site be disabled.[42]

Why add a requirement before the notice to the service provider can be considered effective? And why require that the material be made unavailable at the originating and infringing site? The answer has to do with the nature of the caching function: "This proviso has been added to subsection (b)(5) [enacted as (b)(2)(E)] because storage under subsection (b) occurs automatically, and unless infringing material has been removed from the originating site, the infringing material would ordinarily simply be re-cached."[43] In other words, it would be rather pointless to require a service provider to remove or disable access to material that is still available (or, at least in the case of an impending execution of a court order, that is unlikely to be available much longer) and accessible through automatic computing functions.

The Impact of a Failed Specific Notice

Both section 512(c) and section 512(d) also contain an obligation to expeditiously remove or disable if the service provider possesses actual knowledge of infringement or if facts or circumstances exist from which infringing activity is apparent. These two mechanisms, specific notice (discussed above) and knowledge or awareness (discussed in a later section), are distinct. Section 512(c)(3)(B)(i) indicates that a failed notice and takedown attempt—failed in the sense of not meeting the (c)(3) notice requirements—cannot constitute the triggering knowledge or awareness that would otherwise require response by the service provider under the general knowledge or awareness and removal or disabling proviso of section 512(c)(1)(A) or possibly section 512(d)(1):

> Subject to clause (ii), a notification from a copyright owner or from a person authorized to act on behalf of the copyright owner that fails to comply substantially with the provisions of subparagraph (A) [referring to section 512(c)(3)(A)(i)–(vi) list of notice

elements] *shall not be considered* under paragraph (1)(A) [referring to section 512(c)(1)(A)] in determining whether a service provider has actual knowledge or is aware of facts or circumstances from which infringing activity is apparent.[44]

If a notice fails to substantially comply with contents under 512(c)(3)(A)(i)–(vi), it cannot operate as sufficient notice under the general knowledge or awareness proviso (i.e., the section 512(c)(1)(A) trigger, discussed in a later section of this chapter), as this lack of notice compliance "*shall not be considered* under paragraph (1)(A) in determining whether a service provider has actual knowledge or is aware of facts or circumstance from which infringing activity is apparent."

Obligations to Follow Up a Failed Specific Notice

However, and there is routinely a "however" in the copyright law, if the failed notice complies with subprovisos (ii), (iii), and (iv) of the 512(c)(3)(A)(i)–(vi) elements of the notice list (identification of the work, identification of infringing material, and contact information), then the defendant can find shelter in the 512(c)(3)(B)(i) language *only if* it "promptly attempts to contact the person making the notification or takes other reasonable steps to assist in the receipt of notification that substantially complies with all the provisions of subparagraph (A)."[45] To review, the standard to assess an incomplete subsection (c)(1)(C) notice (per the requirements in (c)(3)(A)) is nonetheless adequate to trigger a general and expeditious removal or disabling obligation under subsection (c)(1)(A) is whether the incomplete notice "substantially complies with clauses (ii), (iii), and (iv) of subparagraph (A)." In other words, if these three elements of the notice are substantially complied with, then, while such notice might not trigger the expeditious removal or disable provision of section 512(c)(1)(C), it may nonetheless trigger the expeditious removal and disabling under section 512(c)(1)(A)—*unless* the service provider contacts the sender of the failed notice or takes other steps to facilitate perfection of the notice. In other words there can be two ways in which the obligation to "expeditiously remove, or disable access to," alleged infringing material is triggered. The difference is that while a "formal" subsection (c)(1)(C) expeditious removal or disabling obligation can only proceed from a notice in accordance with the requirements in (c)(3)(A), an obligation to make the same expeditious removal or disabling can result from any source under subsection (c)(1)(A), as the latter obligation arises when a service provider possesses "actual knowledge that the material or an activity using the material on the system or network is infringing or, in the absence of such actual knowledge, is not aware of facts or circumstances from which infringing activity is apparent," including possibly a failed notice per the discussion below.

The statute does not say how soon the service provider must contact the sender for clarification. Though the legislative history suggests an attitude of function rather than form:

The Committee intends that the substantial compliance standard in new subsection (c)(2) and (c)(3) be applied so that technical errors (e.g., misspelling a name, supplying an outdated area code if the phone number is accompanied by an accurate address, supplying an outdated name if accompanied by an email address that remains valid for the successor of the prior designated agent or agent of a copyright owner) do *not* disqualify service providers and copyright owners from the protections afforded under subsection (c).[46]

Professor Dratler also observes that the statute requires an attempt to contact, not necessarily success at contact:

Although the statute requires only that a service provider attempt contact, not succeed, its [sic] does not say precisely to what extent the service provider must go before giving up an attempt to contact an ignorant, unavailable, busy, disinterested, hostile, or recalcitrant notifier. For these reasons, the preferred method of satisfying the "contact or assistance" condition would be to send a form of response, stating the requirements of the statue and in what respects the service provider deems the notification noncompliant.[47]

This interpretation is consistent with the mailbox rule in contract law that states that acceptance is valid once sent, even if never received.[48]

In *Hendrickson v. eBay, Inc.*, the plaintiff failed to substantially comply with the section 512(c)(3)(A) requirements, thus section 512(c)(3)(B)(i) operated to prevent the information that was provided from triggering the knowledge or awareness removal or disabling under section 512(c)(1)(A).[49] Further, because the sub (ii) identification was not substantially complied with, eBay was not obligated under section 512(c)(3)(B)(ii) to contact the plaintiff and offer the opportunity to perfect the failed (c)(3) notice.[50] The point is that a copyright owner must use the notice mechanism of section 512(c)(3)(A) anytime it desires to contact the service provider with legal effect, i.e., trigger the service provider's responsibility to expeditiously remove or disable. The notice mechanism can either comply with the statute triggering the notice and takedown proviso of (c)(1)(C) or it can fail to meet those standards but serve nonetheless as knowledge or awareness under (c)(1)(A). (Of course it can fail to do either, as was the case in *Hendrickson v. eBay, Inc.*).

If the notice still provides identification of the work, identification of the infringing material, and contact information, the service provider must further investigate: "the service provider promptly attempts to contact the person making the notification or takes other reasonable steps to assist in the receipt of notification that substantially complies" per section 512(c)(3)(B)(ii). After this required follow-up and attempt to perfect the defective notice, then the first notice and takedown proviso of subsection (c)(3)(B) applies: "If the service provider subsequently receives a substantially compliant notice, the provisions of new subsection (c)(1)(C) would apply upon receipt of such notice."[51] In these circumstances a failed specific notice cannot trigger the general expeditious removal or disabling obligation of subsection (c)(1)(A).]

A question remains whether section 512(c)(3)(B) applies to the link notice under section 512(d). While section 512(d) *does* contain a similar knowledge or awareness and removal or disabling sequence, i.e., section 512(d)(1)(A–C), the reference to the "paragraph (1)(A)" [referring to section 512(c)(1)(A)]in section 512(c)(3)(B) does not match up exactly, i.e., in subsection (d) it would be (1)(A)–(C) but not (1)(A) alone. In other words, when the subsection (c)(3) notice mechanism is incorporated by reference via subsection (d)(3) to apply to linking scenarios, then the inadequate notice and service provider follow-up language, in specific the numbering reference to an earlier paragraph, of subsection (c)(3)(B) does not align with the expeditious removal or disabling obligation in (d)(1) that the proviso it is trying to prevent from being triggered. This flaw is likely an oversight due to lack of adequate drafting, rather than a loophole for either the copyright owner or service provider.

IDENTIFYING THE TWO FORMS OF "NOTICE"

In addition to the notice and remove or disabling mechanism that might occur under the cache, post, or link provisions, a second "knowledge or awareness" provision in the post and link provisions, subsection (c) and (d), can also trigger a removal or disabling obligation. However, this obligation is not initiated by receipt of notice from the copyright owner; rather its trigger can originate from anywhere. As discussed above, under section 512(c)(3)(B), a failed (c)(3)(A) notice can trigger this obligation as well. However, more likely the knowledge or awareness ("aware of facts or circumstances from which infringing activity is apparent") will come from within the institutional service provider. The practical impact is a double whammy of sorts, with knowledge or awareness triggered either through formal process (subsection (c)(3) "notice" mechanism described above) or informal knowledge or awareness arising from the day-to-day operations of the institution. These other facts and circumstances can trigger an obligation to remove or disable.

As a result, not only can the copyright owner trigger a removal or disabling obligation but knowledge or awareness may arise in the normal course of the service provider's operations that would trigger the same obligations. Thus there are two removal or disable provisos, one under the notice mechanisms described earlier, and a second, discussed below. The former removal and disable provision might be referred to as a specific *notice* and removal or disabling provision. The latter is a general *knowledge* or awareness and removal or disabling. It should be obvious that a wider range of circumstances might trigger the latter obligation.

Considering the closer interaction that service providers such as public or academic libraries may have over their patrons and students, or that K–12 educational institutions may have over their charges as well, the likelihood of this general knowledge or awareness may be triggered quite frequently. For the post and link functions, this command is found in identical language in section 512(c)(1)(A) and section 512(d)(1). Understanding the sorts of circumstances that Congress desired to trigger the knowledge or awareness removal or disabling obligation is critical and somewhat difficult.

The Inclusion of Linking in the Safe Harbor

In the context of previous discussion regarding section 512(c)(1)(C), much has been said of the post function. A brief summary from the legislative history indicates the sorts of conduct that the safe harbor protects:

> New section 512(c) limits the liability of qualifying service providers for claims of direct, vicarious and contributory infringement for storage at the direction of a user of material that resides on a system or network controlled or operated by or for the service provider. Examples of such storage include providing server space for user's web site, for a chatroom, or other forum in which material may be posted at the direction of users.[52]

Section 512(d), however, concerns linking, the most common scenarios, or in the words of the statute: "information location tools." Section 512(d) offers a safe harbor for situations of infringement "by reason of the provider referring or linking users to an online location containing infringing material or infringing activity." The concept is broad and covers the use of "information location tools, including a directory, index, reference, pointer, or hypertext link."[53] The legislative history indicates the sorts of behavior that the safe harbor can reach:

> New Section 512(d) addresses instances where information location tools refer or link users to an on-line location containing infringing material or infringing activity. The term "infringing activities" means the wrongful activity that is occurring at the location to which the user is linked or referred by the information location tool, without regard to whether copyright infringement is technically deemed to have occurred at that location or at the location where the material is received. The term "information location tools" includes: a directory or index of on-line sites or material, such as a search engine that identifies pages by specified criteria; a reference to other on-line material, such as a list of recommended sites; a pointer that stands for an Internet location or address; and a hypertext link which allows users to access material without entering its address.[54]

Thus, the section 512(d) safe harbor would not protect a reference librarian who verbally informs a patron where infringing material resides in the course of a reference interview. The safe harbor would, however, protect a reference librarian who created an online reader's advisory of other Web sites (such as through books, click-activated frames, or lists of hypertext URLs) would be protected, if at some point the library receives a specific notice from the copyright owner per section 512(d)(3)[55] or otherwise obtains general knowledge or awareness per section 512(d)(1)[56] that the material is infringing and then expeditiously acts to remove or disable access to the material at the other Web sites.

Determining When "Red Flags" Occur Under the "Awareness" Standard

Both section 512(c)(1)(A)(ii) and section 512(d)(1)(B) contain the same triggering circumstance: "in the absence of such actual knowledge, is not aware of facts or circumstances from which infringing activity is apparent." In other words, a service provider may not have actual knowledge of infringing activity, but may have other information ("fact or circumstances") that would lead the service provider to conclude that such infringing activity is nonetheless apparent. For the conforming service provider the heart of this command is the ability to understand when the "awareness" concept is met and the statutory obligation to remove or disable is triggered.

The legislative history uses the phrase "red flag" extensively throughout the discussions relating to subsections (c) and (d) to underscore the concept of awareness:

> [A] service provider wishing to benefit from the limitation on liability under new subsection (c) must "take-down" or disable access to infringing material residing on its system or network in cases where it has actual knowledge or that the criteria for the "red flag" test are met—even if the copyright owner or its agent does not notify it of a claimed infringement.[57]

As demonstrated by the legislative history, these concepts operate in the both the post and link functions, subsections (c) and (d). Speaking of subsection (d) the House and Senate reports comments: "Like the information storage safe harbor in Section 512(c) . . . [u]nder this standard [the awareness concept], a service provider would have *no obligation to seek out copyright infringement*, but it would not qualify for the safe harbor if it had turned a blind eye to 'red flags' of obvious infringement."[58] A similar and consistent statement is made in the discussion of subsection (c):

> As stated in new subsection (c)(1), a service provider *need not monitor* its service or affirmatively seek facts indicating infringing activity (except to the extent consistent with a standard technical measure complying with new subsection (h) [and discussed above]), in order to claim this limitation on liability (or, indeed any other limitation provided by the legislation).[59]

Think of a continuum of behavior, on the one end is active monitoring or patrolling (not necessary) and on the other end is turning a blind eye or creating such firewall or other protections that one refuses to see or could never see what system users do (this should not be done). Somewhere in the middle, knowledge or awareness occurs. Determining when that red flag of knowledge or awareness exists is the challenge!

If the service provider expeditiously responds and the other qualifying conditions of section 512 are met, the safe harbor is reached, and the worse that follows for the defendant-institution is an order for injunctive relief, which might, in the library or educational environment, include a request to suspend the network access of the infringing patron or student. This represents the next major component of the compliance matrix established by section 512 and complements the registered agent provision; it establishes a *knowledge or awareness* obligation but applies only to the post and link functions of subsections (c) and (d), respectively. To remain within the boundaries of the safe harbor the service provider must "not have actual knowledge that the material or an activity using the material on the system or network is infringing, in the absence of such actual knowledge, is not aware of facts or circumstances from which infringing activity is apparent, or upon obtaining such knowledge or awareness, acts expeditiously to remove, or disable access to, the material."[60] While there is no obligation to seek out infringement, once knowledge is obtained or facts or circumstances exist from which infringing activity is apparent—perhaps a faculty member with an expertise in copyright law informs the distance education coordinator that students in a particular class are infringing copyright by posting material far in excess of fair use—then the service provider institution must act expeditiously to remove the material or disable access to it. Remember, the knowledge or awareness can come from anywhere, not necessarily the copyright owner, but from a student, staff member, or other third party.

Defining Expeditious Response

How fast is "expeditiously"? "Because the factual circumstances and technical parameters may vary from case to case, it is not possible to identify a uniform time limit for expeditious action."[61] However, since the purpose of the section 512 notice and knowledge and awareness mechanisms are to curtail further dissemination and infringement of copyrighted material, and given the ease with which such infringement can perpetuate in digital environments, it is suggested that an immediate or as-soon-as-possible standard be adopted. Deviation should be supportable with good reason and sound evidence.

Recall that the subsection (c)(1)(A)(iii) and (d)(1)(C) expeditious removal and disable requirement is triggered by knowledge (actual or constructive, i.e., a "red flag" to use the language of the legislative history, knowledge or awareness) of the infringing nature of the work, regardless of source, (i.e., it need not come from the copyright owner), but, as subsection (c)(1)(A)(ii) and (d)(1)(B) suggest, might derive from "facts or circumstances" that make the "infringing activity apparent, or, under (c)(1)(A)(iii) and (d)(1)(C), from some other source.[62] Such "facts and circumstances" would likely be judged on an objective standard: short of actual knowledge, could a reasonable and prudent person come to a conclusion that "infringing activity is apparent"? The legislative history offers little detail in the way of example for the post functions, perhaps because such material is readily observable; however, an extended discussion of the sort of red flags that might trigger a disable or removal obligation in the information location tools (link) scenarios is present.

Red Flags in Digital Library Practices

The House and Senate committees recognize the benefit of Internet indexing:

> Information location tools are essential to the operation of the Internet; without them, users would not be able to find the information they need. It is precisely the human judgment and editorial discretion exercised by these cataloguers which makes directories valuable. . . . The knowledge or awareness standard should not be applied in a manner which would create a disincentive to the development of directories which involve human intervention.[63]

There is a difference between a possibility of infringement and the probability of infringement: "In this way, the 'red-flag' test in section 512(d) strikes the right balance. The common-sense result of this 'red-flag' test is that online editors and catalogers would not be required to make discriminating judgments about potential copyright infringement. If, however, an Internet site is obviously pirate, then seeing it may be all that is needed for the service provider to encounter a 'red flag.'"[64] For example, in a information location tool scenario, "if the copyright owner could prove that the location was clearly, at the time the directory provider viewed it, a 'pirate' site of the type described below where sound recordings, software, movies or books were available for unauthorized downloading, public performance or public display,"[65] the red flag would be raised.

This distinction is critical for the sort of functional information access service libraries and other information intermediaries provide:

> [A] directory provider would not be similarly aware merely because it saw one or more well known photographs of a celebrity at a site devoted to that person. The provider could not be expected, during a brief cataloging visit, to determine whether the photograph was still protected by copyright or was in the public domain; if the photograph was still protected by copyright, whether the use was licensed; and if the use was not licensed, whether it was permitted under the fair use doctrine.[66]

The more obscure or clandestine file or URL tag would be in contrast to the obvious tip off, the red flag that would exist where "pirate directories refer Internet users to sites that are obviously infringing because they typically use words such as 'pirate,' 'bootleg,' or slang terms in their illegal purpose obvious to the pirate directories and other Internet users."[67] Consider the URLs mandymoorefanclub.org or mandmoorenudes.com or mandymorexxx.com—in light of Mandy Moore's squeaky clean persona, might the latter two sites be of questionable origin?[68] On the other hand, if the subject of the photograph is Paris Hilton and the site parishiltonxxx.com, the origin might indeed be a "legitimate," noninfringing site. In determining the red flag, context is everything!

Consider the sort of "monitoring" that LoopNet, "an Internet Service Provider whose website allows subscribers, generally real estate brokers, to post listings of commercial real estate on the Internet,"[69] performed. Some brokers using the LoopNet directory included photographs with the listings. As a precaution, when listings include a photograph

> [a] LoopNet employee then cursorily reviews the photograph (1) to determine whether the photograph in fact depicts commercial real estate, and (2) to identify any obvious evidence, such as a text message or copyright notice, that the photograph may have been copyrighted by another. If the photograph fails either one of these criteria, the employee deletes the photograph and notifies the subscriber.[70]

After LoopNet learned that some of photographs brokers submitted with listings were copyrighted (and that the brokers had no authority to post them) it added another layer to its review process: "In addition, LoopNet instituted and followed a policy of marking properties to which infringing photographs had been posted so that if other photographs were posted to that property, LoopNet could inspect the photographs side-by-side to make sure that the new photographs were not the infringing photographs."[71] The Fourth Circuit concluded that this "gatekeeping practice" did not transform LoopNet from a passive ISP into a direct infringer, as the process "does not amount to 'copyright,' nor does it add volition to LoopNet's involvement in storing the copy. . . . In performing this gatekeeping function, LoopNet does not attempt to search out or select photographs for duplication, it merely *prevents* users from duplicating certain photographs."[72]

The creation in the library or school setting of a "watch list" of troublesome accounts, while not required, appears a prudent measure. Of course in LoopNet, individuals were not flagged, but rather a work itself. Expanding this concept to individual accounts associated with particular users, while prudent from a risk-management perspective, might raise patron confidentiality issues. However, the author would argue that internal administrative measures targeting unlawful activity should not raise a confidentiality issue per se; moreover, making no response would appear to raise as many ethical obligations, if not legal obligations, e.g., failing to undertake any monitoring in any form. At least one court commented there is little expectation of privacy when engaging in unlawful acts.[73] Moreover, employees of public institutions may have additional due process rights where unlawful or even criminal activity is alleged. Again, consideration of the nature of the monitoring (targeting flagged or suspicious accounts as opposed to constant, real-time monitoring) coupled with the crafting of a commensurate response is critical.

As discussed earlier, an injunctive remedy under section 512(j) might mandate the use of such a "watch list" of repeat infringers for example. Consider an example of some repeat infringers at an institution that has, in compliance with section 512(i)(1)(A), adopted a repeat infringer policy. The institution has enforced the policy, and terminated the access of a number of subscribers, and perhaps it also has a restoration procedure whereby access is restored after remedial training in copyright law. These repeat infringers should be grateful at least that their access was not terminated indefinitely, as these subscribers in compliance with the court order subscribers then enter into a probationary period in which their use of the network is made part of a watch list.

While there is no command in the statute or legislative history, it is reasonable to expect that, as copyright pirates adopt new protocols for labeling and hiding pirated, bootlegged and otherwise infringing material and as those protocols become known, a concomitant range of realities that would send up a red flag would also be expected to impute to the service provider additional awareness.

> However, if the service provider becomes aware of a "red flag" from which infringing activity is apparent, it will lose the limitation of liability if it takes no action. The "red flag" test has both a *subjective* and an *objective* element. In determining whether the service provider was aware of a "red flag," the subjective awareness of the service provider of the facts or circumstances must be determined. However, in deciding whether those facts or circumstances constitute a "red flag"—in other words whether infringing activity would have been apparent to a reasonable person operating under the same or similar circumstances—an objective standard should be used.[74]

Once the red flag goes up do *not* link to that Web site: "Because the infringing nature of such sites would be apparent from even a brief and casual viewing, safe harbor status for a provider that views such a site and then establishes a link to it would not be appropriate."[75]

AVOIDING RECEIPT OF FINANCIAL BENEFIT IN POST AND LINK SCENARIOS

A final safe harbor requirement in the post and link functions states that a service provider-educational institution must "not receive a financial benefit directly attributable to the infringing activity, in a case in which the service provider has the right and ability to control such activity."[76] This statement might appear to codify the common law of contributory and vicarious liability.[77] However, as observed earlier, section 512 does not provide such codification. If it did, section 512 would be superfluous, as a service provider that is not liable would need no protection, one that was liable would seek a statutory refuge at odds with the common law.

Moreover, there are several ways to read a difference between the common law of secondary liability and the knowledge/awareness-takedown or disable and financial benefit control standard of subsections 512(c)(1)(A)-(B) and (d)(1)-(2), which might at first glance appear to codify the standards of contributory and vicarious liability. First, section 512 offers refuge from direct infringement as well. Second, it does not negate copyright liability; rather it lessens its sting by offering as a remedy only statutorily prescribed injunctive relief, if and only if the service provider or other online intermediary defendant has responded to the notice and knowledge or awareness removal or disable provisions.

Further, it should be pointed out that the common articulations of contributory liability and vicarious liability are not as uniform as perhaps the previous discussion intimates. Favoring breadth over depth, the discussion attempted to provide a basic grounding of these concepts so that the main focus of this monograph could be retained.

This approach may allow for cases in which the service provider library or educational institution might meet the four 512(c)(1)(A) and (B) or (d)(1) and (2) provisos (knowledge/awareness-takedown or disable financial benefit) but nonetheless satisfy a court's evolving notion of secondary liability. In that case the safe harbor would operate precisely as it was designed to operate, to limit liability to injunctive relief only. In this way another difference emerges between section 512 and the common law. Unless Congress amends section 512, these four standards are more or less set in time, subject to reasonable interpretation by the courts within concepts of statutory construction, whereas the courts are free to evolve the notions of secondary liability without such restraint within the common law of copyright.

Examples of the "Right and Ability to Control" in Institutional Settings

Envision a scenario where an administrator, an associate dean of a school or college, possessed the actual right and ability to control the behavior of a faculty member beyond that based on the mere relationship of faculty-employee and associate dean–employer. Such a situation might occur if the associate dean, while engaged in conversation with an instructor, observed another instructor using a computer workstation to cache a pirated copy of a workbook. The associate dean might have the ability to restrain or control the infringing behavior by turning off the machine or otherwise disabling its function, just as if the person copying the workbook were a student or other third party (i.e., "a person other than the institution" under control), but here that "right and ability to control" would indeed derive from the employment relationship and the control deans have over their faculty. A similar "right and ability" to control would result when the dean announces at the opening faculty meeting of the new academic year: "We've a new copyright policy on campus, I trust you will all read and follow it, and not infringe the copyright of others." These encounters would certainly appear to meet the right and ability to control test of section 512(c)(1)(C) and section 512(d)(2), but is there "financial benefit directly attributable to the infringing activity" as well?

One commentator argues that the "control" in the financial benefit standard of section 512(c)(1)(B) and (d)(2) should be interpreted as actual control not legal control, which would include the legal right to control even if not exercised, as some courts have previously interpreted it to mean.[78] In this way, both concepts, common and statutory law, can have legal and effective significance, each offering different rules—one for when liability exists (the common law) and another when that liability will be limited under section 512. Dratler, however, is less kind to Congress, and believes differing interpretations of the common law versus statutory law will be forced upon the courts in order to avoid a ludicrous result: "[T]he statute itself has an egregious logical flaw. . . . But if this condition applies [the lack of financial benefit and control], there is no vicarious liability under the chief cases that define the offense. In other words, that statute says there is a 'safe harbor' from vicarious liability for posting if there is no vicarious liability for posting."[79] Unfortunately, as Dratler indicates, interpreting the standards differently, as some courts are already doing,[80] further complicates the law obtusely rather than saves it.[81] Fortunately, there is much that is certain regarding section 512, especially the compliance-oriented provisions, as is demonstrated throughout this monograph. Other commentators have been less kind: "[T]he Act contains flaws. In particular Congress' decision to leave the underlying law of ISP liability unchanged creates a complicated scheme that goes too far in encouraging ISPs to advance the interest of content providers by removing alleged infringements from the Internet."[82]

Examples of Benefits that are "Directly Attributable to the Infringing Activity"

The legislative history offers this extended observation:

> In determining whether the financial benefit criterion is satisfied, courts should take a common-sense, fact-based approach, not a formalistic one. In general, a service provider conducting a legitimate business would not be considered to receive a "financial benefit directly attributable to the infringing activity" where the infringer makes the same kind of payment as non-infringing users of the provider's service. Thus, receiving a *one-time set-up fee and flat periodic* payments for service from a person engaging in infringing activity would *not* constitute receiving a "financial benefit directly attributable to the infringing activity." Nor is subsection (c)(1)(B) intended to cover fees based on the length of the message (e.g., per number of bytes) or by connect time. It would however, include any such fees *where the value of the service lies in providing access to infringing material.*[83]

This last comment suggests that a significant factor is whether the reason for establishing a relationship with a service provider is access to specific infringing material, not simply that such material might be obtained through the service. Otherwise, such a standard would foreclose safe harbor refuge from all but the most onerous of providers, as any subscriber with unrestricted access to the Internet could locate, access and thus infringe copyright material somewhere, sometime, somehow.

The sort of financial benefit that might still trigger a general concept of secondary liability is unclear. Recall the financial benefit required by House Report which again suggests a codification of existing law, this time *Marobie-FL, Inc. v. National Association of Firefighter Equipment Distributors*,[84] stressing that a "one-time set-up fee and flat periodic payments" or "fees based on the length of the message (per number of bytes, for example) or by connect time" intended to constitute the direct financial benefit do not trigger such direct benefit, but would "include any such fees where the value of the service lies in providing access to infringing material."[85] Consider a district revenue-sharing formula based on the number of student credit hours. The more students enrolled, the more the institution receives from its state funding source—regardless of whether the texts and other materials used in instruction are infringing or whether they derived from the acts of the particular faculty member (because use of infringing material allows more students to be enrolled in a given class). Here there is still a financial benefit directly attributable to the university, but it does not derive from the teaching or researching faculty member or graduate student status as employee alone. However, this financial benefit might be argued to be an indirect one.

Perhaps subscribing to a service on the basis of an expectation of having access to infringing material might also satisfy this standard; though the legislative history does suggest it, a court might find it nonetheless in keeping within the spirit of the admonition. The Ninth Circuit suggests, in a rephrasing by juxtaposition, that a flat fee could nonetheless constitute "direct financial benefit," thus preventing the safe harbor from applying:

> But "where the value of the service lies in providing access to infringing material," courts might find such "one-time set-up fee and flat periodic" fees to constitute a direct financial benefit. [citation to Senate Report 105-190 omitted] Thus, the central question of the "direct financial benefit" inquiry in this case is whether the infringing activity constitutes a draw for subscribers, not just an added benefit.[86]

To be sure, everyone can benefit from infringing material, it is generally available for free, and in the context of the Internet is often pernicious. The question is whether the infringing material acts as a draw to subscribers, patrons, students, customers, or other users to the system or network of the service provider.

What if two different faculty members each offer a section of a required course every semester? Section 101 is taught by teacher A and section 102 is taught by teacher B. Teacher B allows students to scan and place all the readings, including textbooks and workbooks, online for access by classmates. Students flock to section 102 because it widely known that there are no book bills associated with this class, at least not for those who waited until the illicit material was made available. What if this behavior occurs across the institution, and students flock to University X because most courses have extensive collections of course readings, including workbooks and textbooks? Could it not be said that enrollment, and the increased access to the institution's network it entails, was caused by the draw of free-but-infringing class resources? Again, the few courts thus far that have examined section 512 in light of the legislative history appear to focus on the "draw" standard. While unlikely in a library or educational setting, such circumstances are conceivable; thus awareness of this concept is important.

One district court intimated that a no-fee service never provides a direct benefit:

> Furthermore, LoopNet does not meet the other element for direct financial benefit. LoopNet does not charge a fee for any real estate listing, with or without photography. While CoStar correctly asserts that the legislative history of the DMCA supports the use of a common-sense rather than a formalistic approach, that same Senate Report stated that it would not be considered a direct financial benefit "where the infringer makes the same kind of payment as non-infringing users of the provider's service." [Citing H.R. Rep. No. 105-551, Part 2, at 54.] In this case, neither infringing or non-infringing users made any kind of payment.[87]

This finding would suggest that a public library scenario, where Internet and other services are likely free, or even where a flat annual fee is assessed equally upon all patrons, could not ever constitute a direct financial benefit

RESPONDING TO SECTION 512 SUBPOENAS

Due to the imprecise language of section 512, any time a service provider desires to be protected for its caching, posting, or linking functions, it should have a registered agent to receive complaints. The registered agent serves as a sort of point or front "man" and identifies the institutional contact with whom the copyright owner must initiate contact in order to fulfill the notice requirement of the notice and removal or disable provisions of the cache, post, and link subsections of 512(b), (c) and (d), respectively. The agent would also be the likely recipient of a section 512(h) subpoena to identify infringers, should the copyright owner desire to pursue legal action against the patron, student, or other subscriber, as direct infringer.[88] Pursuing remedy from direct infringers is a likely result of section 512, as copyright owners are foreclosed from obtaining any monetary remedy under the safe harbor. However, the direct infringer, in the institutional context most relevant to readers here, the library patron or student, may be unknown to the copyright owner; the infringer may be operating in cyberspace anonymously. "It is widely known in academic circles that virtually every university receives several—sometimes hundreds in the case of the biggest universities—formal DMCA copyright infringement claims because of student file sharing."[89] The subpoena may be an integral component of the enforcement mechanism after the specific notice process, i.e., a subpoena to identify the library patron or student. Section (h) contains a special provision to help copyright owners close this liability loophole, and, through the use of a subpoena, obtain the identification of an alleged infringer.

Existing Subpoena Powers

The use of the subpoena power under section 512 has received much attention in the press; it is the foundation of many suits against direct infringers.[90] Of course, the use of the subpoena power to identify unknown defendants was always available in federal court proceedings; however, enforcement typically required a court order. In related cases where the subpoena targeted confidential information in the possession of intermediaries or third parties, courts have developed a series of factors to use to evaluate whether the subpoena should be issued and the identity of the subscribers be revealed: jurisdiction; good faith, both as to party (internal) and as to claim (external); and necessity (basic and, in some cases, absolute).[91] In other words, the plaintiff seeking the identity of an anonymous poster must first demonstrate the legal merits of the action. "Legal merit" is established by showing that the court has jurisdiction over the defendant and that the claim would survive a motion for summary judgment (external good faith). The defendant must act in good faith as a party to the action (internal good faith). Courts would reject the subpoena requested as an exploratory device to identify unrelated anonymous persons, as this would be an abuse of the subpoena power. Internal good faith can also be demonstrated by showing that the plaintiff made fair attempts to determine the identity of the anonymous speaker without recourse to the subpoena process. There must also be some sense of urgency or necessity in that the information (the identity of the anonymous poster) is needed in order to proceed with the litigation (basic necessity) or absolute necessity, i.e., that there is no other source of the information.

Absolute necessity is often required in cases where the anonymous person is not a party to the action, e.g., is not the poster of a defamatory statement. This would arise in a case where a party to a lawsuit, based on the postings of an anonymous speaker, believes that the anonymous speaker has information that might exonerate or promote the case. That party needs to know who the anonymous poster is in order submit the poster to discovery proceedings, further subpoena, material witness order, and the like; however, the plaintiff is not suing the anonymous speaker. The theory behind the subpoena-anonymous speaker cases is that an aggrieved person should have a right to seek redress in a court by proper means. However, this right according to the case law should be balanced against a person's right to speak freely and anonymously if one so chooses—in any setting including the Internet.

Understanding the Section 512(h) Subpoena Power

The section 512(h) subpoena is different in several ways from subpoenas normally issued in conjunction with other sorts of federal litigation. First, the subpoena need not issue from a judge; rather, "[a] copyright owner or a person authorized to act on the owner's behalf may request the clerk of any United States district court to issue a subpoena to a service provider for identification of an alleged infringer in accordance with this subsection."[92] All the copyright owner or its designated agent need do is file three documents: (1) a copy of a notification described in subsection (c)(3)(A), (2) a proposed subpoena, and (3) a sworn declaration to the effect that the purpose for which the subpoena is sought is to obtain the identity of an alleged infringer and that such information will only be used for the purpose of protecting rights under this title.[93] (The contents of a section 512(c)(3)(A) notice was discussed in a previous section of this chapter.)

The section 512(h) authorization contains a harsh command to those in receipt of such subpoena: "The subpoena shall authorize and order the service provider receiving the notification and the subpoena to *expeditiously disclose* to the copyright owner or person authorized by the copyright owner *information sufficient* to identify the alleged infringer of the material described in the notification to the extent such information is available to the service provider."[94]

Two points are critical in understanding the power and reach of the section 512(h) subpoena. First, the "order for disclosure [should] be interpreted [by the receiving service provider] as requiring disclosure of information in the possession of the service provider, rather than obliging the service provider to conduct searches for information that is available from other systems or networks."[95] While the service provider need not seek out the user information from other sources, if such information is in its possession, it must provide it to the copyright owner or his or her agent.

The legislative history indicates that such "orders be expeditiously issued if the notification meets the provisions of new subsection (c)(3)(A) and the declaration is properly executed."[96] Review by the clerk of courts should not be evidentiary in nature but rather "should be a ministerial function performed quickly for this provision to have its intended effect."[97] If the procedural requirements are in order,[98] the clerk has no choice but to issue the order: "If the notification filed satisfies the provisions of subsection (c)(3)(A), the proposed subpoena is in proper form, and the accompanying declaration is properly executed, the *clerk shall expeditiously issue* and sign the proposed subpoena and return it to the requester for delivery to the service provider."[99]

Second, even if a service provider intends to refuse the removal or disabling command of its own notice-receipt, perhaps because it believes the material is not infringing, the service provider in receipt of a section (h) subpoena must nonetheless turn over the identifying information in its possession: "After receiving the order, the service provider shall expeditiously disclose to the copyright owner or its agent the information required by the order to the extent that the information is available to the service provider, regardless of whether the service provider responds to the notification of claimed infringement."[100] Moreover, this command is made irrespective of other law as well, such as a state library confidentiality statute, federal privacy law (such as FERPA),[101] or a contract provision in a service provider agreement ensuring the privacy of subscribers:

> Upon receipt of the issued subpoena, either accompanying or subsequent to the receipt of a notification described in subsection (c)(3)(A), the service provider shall expeditiously disclose to the copyright owner or person authorized by the copyright owner the information required by the subpoena, *notwithstanding any other provision of law* and regardless of whether the service provider responds to the notification.[102]

One federal appellate judge has interpreted the use of the word "notwithstanding" as indeed omnipresent: "The 'notwithstanding' provision in § 512(h) indicates that the DMCA subpoena power is intended to 'supercede [] other statutes that might interfere with or hinder the attainment of [its] objective.'"[103]

Both the clerk of court's issuance of the subpoena and the service provider's response must be 'expeditious': "expeditiously issue" and "expeditiously disclose."[104] However, since subpoenas are generally subject to pre-enforcement motions to quash, section 512(h)(6) suggests that such motion would be possible: "Unless otherwise provided by this section or by applicable rules of the court, the procedure for issuance and delivery of the subpoena, and the remedies for noncompliance with the subpoena, shall be governed to the greatest extent practicable by those provisions of the Federal Rules of Civil Procedure governing the issuance, service, and enforcement of a subpoena duces tecum."[105] However, considering the spurious nature of some anonymous online infringers, and the attitude expressed in the legislative history, time is of the essence and expediency the call of the day. Given the command of expeditiousness, any challenge or motion to quash must be done with the outmost urgency. Barring that action and given the time-sensitive circumstances of much online infringement, the release of subscriber (patron or student) identity must issue without delay. But how fast is expeditious? Notice the statute does not use the term "immediately," however, it is suggested that a response (i.e., request for more time to respond, notification of an intent to challenge, or refusal to comply) should be made within one or two business days.

Section 512(h) in the Courts

Several cases have challenged the use of the section 512(h) subpoena power resulting in appellate decisions from two different circuits. The district court in *In re Verizon Internet Services, Inc.*,[106] denied the service provider's motion to stay (suspend) enforcement of the subpoena and issued the order pending appeal against Verizon to obtain customer information regarding a subscriber who used the network to infringe over 600 songs through P2P software. The district court commented: "Verizon's customers should have little expectation of privacy (or anonymity) in infringing copyrights."[107] However, on appeal the appellate court vacated the order and remanded the matter for further proceedings.[108]

The appellate court drew a distinction between high-level service providers, the section 512(a) conduit or store and forward providers, and cache, post, and link service providers to which the section 512(c)(3) notice is tied through internal statutory reference with the subsections of section 512:

> The issue is whether § 512(h) applies to an ISP acting only as a conduit for data transferred between two internet users, such as person sending and receiving e-mail or, as in this case, sharing P2P files. . . . We conclude from the terms of § 512(h) and the overall structure of § 512 that, as Verizon contends, a subpoena may be issued *only* to an ISP engaged in storing on its servers material that is infringing or the subject of infringing activity.[109]

Because a high-level service provider can only deny service altogether, it cannot remove or disable access to actual material, a section 512(h) subpoena cannot properly issue to it:

> No matter what information the copyright owner may provide, the ISP can neither "remove" nor "disable access to" the infringing material because that material is not stored on the ISP's servers. . . . Congress considered disabling an individual's access to infringing material and disabling access to the internet to be different remedies for the protection of copyright owners, the former blocking access to the infringing material on the offender's computer, and the latter more broadly blocking the offender's access to the internet (at least via his chosen ISP).[110]

As a result, "[a]ny notice to an ISP concerning its activity as a mere conduit does not satisfy the condition of § 512(c)(3)(A)(iii) and is therefore ineffective."[111]

The Eighth Circuit came to a similar conclusion in *In re Charter Communication*,[112] reversing a lower court decision but only after it denied Charter's motion to stay enforcement of the subpoenas pending appeal. As a result, Charter released the subpoenaed information relating to about 200 customers[113] that the RIAA had tracked[114] and claimed were infringing music copyrights through various P2P networks. Ultimately the appellate court found that the subpoena was improperly issued because Charter, like Verizon was not able to remove or disable access to the allegedly infringing material: "Thus, where Charter acted solely as a conduit for the transmission of material by others (its subscribers using P2P file-sharing software to exchange files stored on their personal computers), Charter contends the subpoena was not properly issued. We agree."[115] A majority of the Eighth Circuit panel observed the same conduit versus cache-post-link distinction as did the *Verizon* court and concluded that a section 512(h) subpoena could not issue to such a high-level conduit service provider.[116] The appellate court vacated the district court order and remanded the case for further proceedings as necessary.[117] Such interpretation of section 512(h) offers some breathing space to conduit service providers; though a subpoena under the "general" rules of procedure could still issue, it would need to satisfy those requirements, i.e., section 45 of the Federal Rules of Civil Procedure. However, since the library or educational institution is likely to be a cache, post, or link provider, section 512(h) are proper within its environs and so it may continue to freely issue. Moreover, if the courts continue to apply this interpretation of the statute and Congress desires conduit providers also to be subject to subpoena, a clarifying amendment may arise in the future.

In what may be an alternative view, the dissent argued in *Charter Communication* for a broader reading of the statute for several reasons. First, conduit service providers are included in the statutory definition: "Section 512(h) authorizes a copyright owner or its representative to request a subpoena to a service provider in order to identify infringers, and the statutory definition of 'service provider' in § 512(k) specifically includes conduit service providers such as Charter."[118] This is true, but recall that the section 512(k) definition includes two separate definitions of service (one specifically for use in conduit scenarios), yet the second section 512(k)(1)(B) definition includes a (k)(1)(A) entity as well: "Although Charter contends that the subpoena power in the DMCA is limited by the function of the ISP, such a limitation is not to be found in a plain reading of the DMCA. . . . If Congress had wanted to limit the type of ISP subject to a statutory subpoena, it could have easily specified that in § 512(h), but it did not."[119] The dissent read the statutory notice in a way that does not disqualify an ISP merely because it does not have the ability to remove or disable, placing emphasis on the disjunctive.

Recall the pivotal clause in section 512(c)(3)(A), subsection (iii): "Identification of the material that is claimed to be infringing or to be the subject of infringing activity and that is to be removed or access to which is to be disabled, and information reasonably sufficient to permit the service provider to locate the material." Placing emphasis on the first "or" ("Identification of the material that is claimed to be infringing **or** to be the subject of infringing activity and that is to be removed or access to which is to be disabled") means that a section 512(h) subpoena can issue to an ISP if the moving party can at least identify material that is claimed to be infringing.

The *Charter Communications, Inc.*, dissent argued instead that the majority, and by implication the *Verizon* court, misread the statute as the appellate courts added the "and that is to be removed or access to which is to be disabled" proviso to each disjunctive (the "identification of the material that is claimed to be infringing" and the "*or* to be the subject of infringing activity") with the following interpretive result: "Identification of the material that is claimed to be infringing and that is to be removed or access to which is to be disabled, and information reasonably sufficient to permit the service provider to locate the material" **or** "to be the subject of infringing activity and that is to be removed or access to which is to be disabled, and information reasonably sufficient to permit the service provider to locate the material." According to the dissent: "That is not what Congress said, however."[120]

Moreover, the dissent argues that its interpretation is correct for several reasons. First, the subpoena power is a critical part of the section 512 redress mechanism available to copyright owners. Excluding conduit service providers from its reach would undermine that structure. The use of disjunctive indicates that the first clause merely duplicates the section 512(k) service provider characterizations. It is precisely because conduit cannot remove or disable access to content that the "[i]dentification of the material that is claimed to be infringing" phrasing is used: "The distinction with § 512(c)(3)(A) between material 'claimed to be infringing' and material that is 'the subject of infringing activity and that is to removed or access to which is to be disabled' appears to carry forward the initial distinction in the DMCA between § 512(a) conduit ISPs and §§ 512(b)–(d) storage ISPs."[121] Second, the subpoena does not require the service provider to remove and disable or do anything other than release the identifying information, section 512(h)(5) provides that "notwithstanding any other provision of law *and regardless of whether the service provider responds to the notification*" and "only references § 512(c)(3)(A) to indicate the kind of information which needs to be given to the clerk to request a subpoena."[122] The strongest argument in support of the dissent's position is that without the ability to reach anonymous users of conduit service providers through recourse to the section 512(h) subpoena, copyright owners would be left with the far more cumbersome John Doe subpoena processes of the existing law. This does appear to be what Congress intended by establishing the subpoena power in the first instance: "The suggestion that copyright holders should be left to file John Does lawsuits to protect themselves from infringement by subscribers of conduit ISPs like Charter, instead of availing themselves of the mechanism Congress provided in the DMCA, is impractical and contrary to legislative intent. John Doe actions are costly and time consuming."[123] Regardless of whether the position of the dissent becomes the majority view in other circuits, this issue will not be headed for adjudication before the U.S. Supreme Court in the foreseeable future, as writ of certiorari was denied in the *Verizon* case in fall 2004.[124]

REAL-WORLD EXAMPLES

▶ **Real-World Example I**

Situation: A professor in a school media specialist certification degree program required students to construct and post a list of Web resource related to teaching. While grading the assignment, the professor observed that many of the sites of teaching materials (e.g., textbooks, workbooks, exercises and tests) contain directory references with words such as "bootleg" and "pirate." The professor suspects that the linked site contains pirated (infringing) material, but the links lead to such great information that the links are nonetheless included and activated for other members of the class to use in the remaining weeks of the semester.

Legal Analysis: According to the legislative history, the "red flag" of awareness of the infringing nature of linked material (absence of infringing "facts or circumstances") is a prerequisite of section 512(d)(1)) by such sites: "pirate directories refer Internet users to sites that are obviously infringing because they typically use words such as 'pirate,' 'bootleg,' or slang terms in their illegal purpose obvious to the pirate directories and other Internet users." H.R. Rep. No 551 (Part 2), 105th Cong., 2d Sess. 58 (1998); Senate Report 105-190, 105th Cong., 2d Sess. 48 (1998).

▶ **Real-World Example II**

Situation: The public library in the "World Traveler" situation from Chapter 6, where the library allows patrons to maintain personal Web pages of their recent travels, receives a notice from the copyright holder, except that the notice does not "substantially" meet the requirements for proper notice. However, the notice does "substantially" contain sufficient contact information of the copyright owner, identifies the copyrighted work (a significant portion of the film *Under the Tuscan Sun*), and identifies the infringing material (the patron's personal page entitled "My Italian Tales"). Nevertheless, the registered agent, a stickler for protocol, decides to do nothing.

Legal Analysis: Generally, a failed notice should not be considered in determining whether a registered agent "has actual knowledge or is aware of facts or circumstances from which infringing activity is apparent." 17 U.S.C. § 512(c)(3)(B)(i). A failed notice under section 512(c)(3)(A) may nonetheless trigger an obligation to "expeditiously remove, or disable access to, the material." If the incomplete notice substantially complies with the three elements of identification of the copyrighted work, identification of the infringing material, and contact information (i.e., section 512(c)(3)(A)(ii)–(iv)), then this may be sufficient information to make the registered agent "aware of facts or circumstances from which infringing activity is apparent." The awareness may be prevented if the registered agent complies with section 512(c)(3)(A)(i)–(vi), requiring that the registered agent "promptly attempts to contact the person making the notification or takes other reasonable steps" in an attempt to receive a complete and proper (c)(3) notice.

▶ **Real-World Example III**

Situation: The registered agent of a large library system receives a proper (c)(3) notice and responds expeditiously to remove posts made by several patrons on the "Patron Information Exchange" page of its Web site. Because patrons must log on to the page, the library can determine which patrons made which posts. Not satisfied, and realizing that it would be pointless to sue the library as the safe harbor forecloses all monetary remedy, including attorney's fees, the copyright owner considers pursuing litigation against the library patrons, and obtains a subpoena requesting identification of those patrons from the federal clerk of courts to serve on the library.

Legal Analysis: Under section 512(h) a copyright owner may request the clerk of any United States district court to issue a subpoena to a service provider for identification of an alleged infringer. The request must contain a copy of a notification described in subsection (c)(3)(A), a proposed subpoena, and a sworn declaration to the effect that the purpose for which the subpoena is sought is to obtain the identity of an alleged infringer and that the information will only be used for the purpose of protecting copyright. Once the registered agent receives the subpoena, the library, acting through its registered agent, must expeditiously disclose the information required by the subpoena, i.e., the identity of the library patrons who posted the material. While many state statutes protect the identity of library patrons, many contain a subpoena exception. Regardless, the section 512(h) subpoena will override this protection, i.e., "notwithstanding any other provision of law." In theory, the library should be able to challenge the subpoena, as it would any other federal subpoena, as section 512(h)(6) indicates that the subpoena "shall be governed to the greatest extent practicable by those provisions of the Federal Rules of Civil Procedure governing the issuance, service, and enforcement of a subpoena duces tecum." Nonetheless, the library must disclose to the copyright owner the information requested by the subpoena (likely subscriber identity information) even in circumstances where it refuses to comply with the section 512(c)(3) notice: "regardless of whether the service provider responds to the notification."

KEY POINTS FOR YOUR INSTITUTION'S POLICY AND PRACTICE

▶ The three subsections of 512 relating to the cache, post, and link functions require that, once the service provider receives a formal notice of infringing material or activity on or through its system from the copyright owner, the service provider must act expeditiously to remove or disable access to the material. See pp. 187–188.

▶ The contents of the notice are listed in section 512(c)(3). The service provider's removal or disabling obligation is triggered when the notice substantially complies with the six requirements of statute: signature, identification of the work infringed, identification of the infringing material, copyright owner contact information, statement of good faith, and statement of accuracy and authorization. See pp. 192–196.

▶ Oddly, the post provision is the only subsection to require the appointment of a registerd agent to receive and respond to such notices, yet both the cache and link subsections reference the subsection (c)(3) notice and moreover require removal or disabling as well. As a result it is recommended for the cache and link subsections as well that a service provider appoint a registered agent. Registration of the designated agent is made with the U.S. Copyright Office. See pp. 182–192.

▶ Notices made by a copyright owner under the cache provision must also contain a statement that the material has been removed or access to it disabled, or a court has ordered such occurrence. 17 U.S.C. § 512(b)(E)(i) and (ii). This is to ensure that once the service provider removes or disables access to material cached on its system or network, the subscriber, patron, or student does not (through the automatic technical processes of his or her computer) simply re-cache the material from its original location. See p. 197.

▶ In addition to the notice and remove or disable that might occur under the cache, post, or link provisions, a second "knowledge or awareness" provision in the post and link provisions can also trigger a removal or disabling obligation. However, this obligation is not initiated by receipt of notice by the copyright owner, rather its trigger can originate from anywhere. This second obligation to expeditiously remove or disable applies only to the post and link functions. See pp. 200–201.

▶ A failed (c)(3) notice cannot generally trigger this second knowledge or awareness mechanism. However, if the failed (c)(3) notice substantially includes identification of the work, identification of infringing material, and contact information, then this partial notice can still trigger the removal or disabling obligation—unless the service provider "promptly attempts to contact the person making the notification or takes other reasonable steps to assist in the receipt of notification that substantially complies with all the provisions of subparagraph (A)." See pp. 197–200.

▶ The concept of awareness ("is not aware of facts or circumstances from which infringing activity is apparent") is designed to operate under a red flag concept.

The "red flag" test has both a subjective and an objective element. In determining whether the service provider was aware of a "red flag," the subjective awareness of the service provider of the facts or circumstances must be determined. However, in deciding whether those facts or circumstances constitute a "red flag"—in other words whether infringing activity would have been apparent to a reasonable person operating under the same or similar circumstances—an objective standard should be used. See pp. 202–206.

▶ Online editors and catalogers would not be required to make discriminating judgments about potential copyright infringement. If, however, an Internet site is obviously pirate, then seeing its URL or other file directory information may be all that is needed for the service provider to encounter a "red flag." See pp. 202–203.

> **No Red Flag:** "[A] directory provider would not be similarly aware merely because it saw one or more well known photographs of a celebrity at a site devoted to that person." H.R. Rep. No 551 (Part 2), 105th Cong., 2d Sess. 57-58 (1998); Senate Report 105-190, 105th Cong., 2d Sess. 48 (1998).

> **Red Flag!:** "[P]irate directories refer Internet users to sites that are obviously infringing because they typically use words such as 'pirate,' 'bootleg,' or slang terms in their illegal purpose obvious to the pirate directories and other Internet users." H.R. Rep. No 551 (Part 2), 105th Cong., 2d Sess. 58 (1998); Senate Report 105-190, 105th Cong., 2d Sess. 48 (1998).

▶ Before the safe harbor can apply in post and link scenarios, the service provider library or educational institution must "not receive a financial benefit directly attributable to the infringing activity, in a case in which the service provider has the right and ability to control such activity." Receiving a one-time set-up fee and flat periodic payments for service from a person engaging in infringing activity would not constitute receiving a financial benefit directly attributable to the infringing activity, nor would fees based on the length of the message (e.g., per number of bytes) or by connect time. It would, however, include fees based on the number of infringing uses or in providing access to infringing material in the first instance. See pp. 206–210.

▶ Under the statute, a copyright owner may request a subpoena from a clerk of the federal court "for identification of an alleged infringer." The subpoena requires the service provider library or educational entity in receipt of the subpoena to expeditiously disclose to the copyright owner information sufficient "to identify the alleged infringer of the material described in the notification to the extent such information is available to the service provider." See pp. 210–216.

▶ The issuance of the section 512(h) is designed to be ministerial in nature. Like all subpoenas, however, this subpoena may be challenged by a motion to quash. See pp. xxx–xxx.

ENDNOTES

[1] See, e.g., Peer-to-Peer Piracy on University Campuses, Hearing, Subcommittee on Courts, the Internet, and Intellectual Property, Committee on the Judiciary, U.S. House of Representatives, 108th Congress, 1st Session, February 26, 2003 ("FastTrack users trading from networks managed by U.S. educational institutions account for 10 percent of all users on FastTrack at any given moment. It's very unlikely that this amount of file-sharing activity is in furtherance of class assignments."), at p. 10 (Opening statement of Lamar Smith, Subcommittee Chair); ("It [prototype network traffic monitoring tool] monitored the activity of 54 users of only P2P network, Gnutella network, during the university's summer break. The results of the research showed that 89% of the files transferred to and from the university's network were infringing. Furthermore, those 54 monitored users uploaded 4,614 files."), at p. 106 (Prepared Statement of Representative Goodlatte, submitted into the record) (available at *http://commdocs.house.gov/committees/judiciary/hju85286.000/hju85286_0.htm*). See also, Hearing, U.S. Senate, Committee on Governmental Affairs, Permanent Subcommittee on Investigations, September 30, 2003, on Privacy and Piracy: The Paradox of Illegal File Sharing on Peer-to-Peer Networks and the Impact of Technology on the Entertainment (Senate Hearing 108-275) "Finally, we will end our hearing today with a discussion of the ethics of downloading and the potential need for business models. Have we inadvertently created a culture today that encourages the very behavior that today we feel needs to be corrected? . . . Many of these users are teenagers or younger. This generation of kids needs to be made aware that they are engaging in illegal behavior. . . . As a former prosecutor, I am troubled by a strategy that uses law to threaten people into submission. Yet, as a former prosecutor, I am also troubled by a prevailing attitude that says because technology makes it fee and easy, it is OK to do. . . . It is clear that the law, technology, and ethics are out of sync. They are woefully out of step with one another." (Opening statement of Chairman Coleman). (available at *http://www.senate.gov/~gov_affairs/index.cfm?Fuseaction=Hearings.Testimony&TestimonyID=324&HearingID=120*).

[2] 17 U.S.C. § 512(c)(1).

[3] H.R. Rep. No. 551 (Part 2), 105th Cong., 2d Sess. 54 (1998); S. Rep. No. 105-190, 105th Cong., 2d Sess. 45 (1998) ("This 'notice and takedown' procedure is a formalization and refinement of a cooperative process that has been employed to deal efficiently with network-based copyright infringement.").

[4] For example, identifying circumstances for which the post provisions might apply, the House Report observed: "New section 512(c) limits the liability of qualifying service providers for claims of direct, vicarious and contributory infringement for storage at the

direction of a user of material that resides on a system or network controlled or operated by or for the service provider. Examples of such storage include providing server space for user's web site, for a chatroom, or other forum in which material may be posted at the direction of users. H.R. Rep. No. 551 (Part 2), 105th Cong., 2d Sess. 53 (1998).

[5] The elements of the notification for instances of caching are found in 17 U.S.C. § 512(b)(2)(E) which reference the (c)(3) notice rules, for the post provisions the rules are found in 17 U.S.C. § 512(c)(3), the link provisions of 17 U.S.C. § 512(d)(3) also reference the (c)(3) rules.

[6] 17 U.S.C. § 512(c)(1).

[7] Professor Yen views the risk aversion as significant: "[T]his raises the further question of why any ISP would undergo the expense of complying with the DMCA's statutory requirements to shield itself from liability which does not exist. The answer, of course, is risk aversion. As noted earlier, the correct application of direct, vicarious, and contributory liability to ISPs is reasonably clear, but courts have not yet rendered enough decisions to establish the scope of the ISP liability beyond controversy." Alfred C. Yen, Internet Service Provider Liability for Subscriber Copyright Infringement, Enterprise Liability, and the First Amendment, 88 GEORGETOWN LAW JOURNAL 1833, 1883 (2000).

[8] JAY DRATLER JR., CYBERLAW: INTELLECTUAL PROPERTY IN THE DIGITAL MILLENNIUM § 6.03[2], at 6-78 (2004) (emphasis added).

[9] H.R. Rep. No. 551 (Part 2), 105th Cong., 2d Sess. 54 (1998); S. Rep. No. 105-190, 105th Cong., 2d Sess. 45 (1998).

[10] 17 U.S.C. § 512(c)(2).

[11] 17 U.S.C. § 512(c)(1)(C).

[12] 17 U.S.C. § 512(c)(2)(A) and (B).

[13] 17 U.S.C. § 512(c)(2).

[14] 17 U.S.C. § 512(c)(2)(A) and (B).

[15] 17 U.S.C. § 512(c)(2).

[16] H.R. Rep. No. 551 (Part 2), 105th Cong., 2d Sess. 55 (1998); S. Rep. No. 105-190, 105th Cong., 2d Sess. 46 (1998).

[17] 37 C.F.R. § 201.38(c) ("An 'Interim Designation of Agent to Receive Notification of Claimed Infringement' shall be identified as such by prominent caption or heading, and shall include the following information with respect to a single service provider: (1) The full legal name and address of the service provider; (2) All names under which the service provider is doing business; (3) The name of the agent designated to receive notification of claimed infringement; (4) The full address, including a specific number and street name or rural route, of the agent designated to receive notification of claimed infringement. A post office box or similar designation will not be sufficient except where it is the only address that can be used in that geographic location; (5) The telephone number, facsimile number, and electronic mail address of the agent designated to receive notification of claimed infringement.").

[18] 37 C.F.R. § 201.38(b) ("The Copyright Office does not provide printed forms for filing an Interim Designation of Agent to Receive Notification of Claimed Infringement.").

[19] 37 C.F.R. § 201.38(e) ("A service provider may file the Interim Designation of Agent to Receive Notification of Claimed Infringement with the Public Information Office of the Copyright Office, Room LM-401, James Madison Memorial Building, Library of Congress, 101 Independence Avenue, SE, Washington, DC, during normal business hours, 9 am to 5 pm. If mailed, the Interim Designation should be addressed to: Copyright GC/I & R, PO Box 70400, Southwest Station, Washington, DC 20024. Each designation shall be accompanied by a filing fee of $30. Designations and amendments will be posted online on the Copyright Office's website (*http://www.loc.gov/copyright*).").

[20] 37 C.F.R. § 201.38: "In the event of a change in the information . . . a service provider shall file . . . an amended Interim Designation of Agent to Receive Notification of Claimed Infringement," with updated information in conformity with subsection (c), signature and an additional $30 filing fee. Id. at § 201.38(f). "If a service provider terminates its operations, the entity shall notify the Copyright Office by certified or registered mail." Id. at § 201.38(g).

[21] 17 U.S.C. § 512(c)(3)(A).

[22] *Hendrickson v. eBay, Inc.*, 165 F. Supp. 2d 1082 (C.D. Cal. 2001) ("Plaintiff contends that during a January 2001 telephone conversation (shortly after he commenced suit), he told Richter that all copies of 'Manson' in DVD format infringe on his copyright because he has never authorized the release of this movie on DVD. . . . However, the dispute over the dates is immaterial. It is undisputed that Plaintiff has never provided this information in a written communications to eBay as required by Section 512(c)(3)." Id. at 1091, n. 8. "Plaintiff states that during a January 2001 telephone conversation, he informed Richter that all VHS tapes labeled 'new' had to be counterfeit. Because plaintiff did not provide this information to eBay in writing, the Court need not consider the deficient notice." Id. at 1091, n. 10.).

[23] 17 U.S.C. § 512(c)(3)(A)(i).

[24] H.R. Rep. No. 551 (Part 2), 105th Cong., 2d Sess. 55 (1998); S. Rep. No. 105-190, 105th Cong., 2d Sess. 46 (1998).

[25] 17 U.S.C. § 512(c)(3)(A)(ii) and (iii).

[26] 17 U.S.C. § 512(d)(3).

[27] H.R. Rep. No. 551 (Part 2), 105th Cong., 2d Sess. 55 (1998); S. Rep. No. 105-190, 105th Cong., 2d Sess. 45 (1998) ("The goal of this provision is to provide the service provider with adequate information to find and examine the allegedly infringing material expeditiously.")

[28] H.R. Rep. No. 551 (Part 2), 105th Cong., 2d Sess. 55 (1998); S. Rep. No. 105-190, 105th Cong., 2d Sess. 46 (1998).

[29] H.R. Rep. No. 551 (Part 2), 105th Cong., 2d Sess. 55 (1998); S. Rep. No. 105-190, 105th Cong., 2d Sess. 46 (1998).

[30] JAY DRATLER JR., CYBERLAW: INTELLECTUAL PROPERTY IN THE DIGITAL MILLENNIUM § 6.03[2], at 6-67 (2004).

[31] *ALS Scan, Inc. v. Remarq Communities*, 239 F.3d 619 (4th Cir. 2001).

[32] 17 U.S.C. § 512(c)(3)(A)(iii).

[33] JOHN W. HAZARD JR., COPYRIGHT LAW IN BUSINESS AND PRACTICE § 7:36, at 7-81 (2002).

[34] 17 U.S.C. § 512(c)(3)(A)(iv).

[35] *ALS Scan, Inc. v. Remarq Communities*, 239 F.3d 619 (4th Cir. 2001).

[36] *ALS Scan, Inc. v. Remarq Communities*, 239 F.3d 619, 625 (4th Cir. 2001) ("ALS Scan presses the contention that these two sites serve no other purpose than to distribute ALS Scan's copyrighted materials and therefore, by directing RemarQ to these sites, it has directed RemarQ to a representative list of infringing materials." Id. at 624-625.).

[37] 17 U.S.C. § 512(c)(3)(A)(v).

[38] H.R. Rep. No. 551 (Part 2), 105th Cong., 2d Sess. 55-56 (1998); S. Rep. No. 105-190, 105th Cong., 2d Sess. 46 (1998).

[39] 17 U.S.C. § 512(c)(3)(A)(vi).

[40] H.R. Rep. No. 551 (Part 2), 105th Cong., 2d Sess. 56 (1998); S. Rep. No. 105-190, 105th Cong., 2d Sess. 46 (1998).

[41] H.R. Rep. No. 551 (Part 2), 105th Cong., 2d Sess. 56 (1998); S. Rep. No. 105-190, 105th Cong., 2d Sess. 46 (1998) ("New subsection (c)(3)(A)(vi) specifies that the notification must contain a statement that the information contained therein is accurate. The complaining party—be it the copyright owner, or an authorized representative—also must confirm under penalty of perjury, that it has authority to act on behalf of the owner of the exclusive right that is allegedly being infringed.").

[42] 17 U.S.C. § (b)(2)(E)(i) and (ii).

[43] H.R. Rep. No. 551 (Part 2), 105th Cong., 2d Sess. 52-53 (1998); S. Rep. No. 105-190, 105th Cong., 2d Sess. 43 (1998).

[44] 17 U.S.C. § 512(c)(3)(B)(i) (emphasis added).

[45] 17 U.S.C. § 512(c)(3)(B)(ii).

[46] H.R. Rep. No. 551 (Part 2), 105th Cong., 2d Sess. 56 (1998); S. Rep. No. 105-190, 105th Cong., 2d Sess. 47 (1998).

[47] JAY DRATLER JR., CYBERLAW: INTELLECTUAL PROPERTY IN THE DIGITAL MILLENNIUM § 6.03[2], at 6-82.13 (2003) (footnotes omitted).

[48] BLACK'S LAW DICTIONARY (8th ed. 2004) defines the *mailbox rule* as "The principle that an acceptance becomes effective—and binds the offeror—once it has been properly mailed. The mailbox rule does not apply, however, if the offer provides that an acceptance is not effective until received." Id. at 972.

[49] *Hendrickson v. eBay, Inc.*, 165 F. Supp. 2d 1082, 1089-1090 (C.D. Cal. 2001) ("However when eBay requested that Plaintiff identify the alleged problematic listings by the eBay item numbers, Plaintiff refused." Id. at 1090.).

[50] *Hendrickson v. eBay, Inc.*, 165 F. Supp. 2d 1082, 1093 (C.D. Cal. 2001).

[51] H.R. Rep. No. 551 (Part 2), 105th Cong., 2d Sess. 56 (1998); S. Rep. No. 105-190, 105th Cong., 2d Sess. 47 (1998).

[52] H.R. Rep. No. 551 (Part 2), 105th Cong., 2d Sess. 53 (1998); S. Rep. No. 105-190, 105th Cong., 2d Sess. 43 (1998).

[53] 17 U.S.C. § 512(d).

[54] H.R. Rep. No. 551 (Part 2), 105th Cong., 2d Sess. 56-57 (1998); S. Rep. No. 105-190, 105th Cong., 2d Sess. 47 (1998).

[55] 17 U.S.C. § 512(d)(3) ("upon notification of claimed infringement as described in subsection (c)(3), responds expeditiously to remove, or disable access to, the material that is claimed to be infringing or to be the subject of infringing activity, except that, for purposes of this paragraph, the information described in subsection (c)(3)(A)(iii) shall be identification of the reference or link, to material or activity claimed to be infringing, that is to be removed or access to which is to be disabled, and information reasonably sufficient to permit the service provider to locate that reference or link.").

[56] 17 U.S.C. § 512(d)(1) ("(A) does not have actual knowledge that the material or activity is infringing; (B) in the absence of such actual knowledge, is not aware of facts or circumstances from which infringing activity is apparent; or (C) upon obtaining such knowledge or awareness, acts expeditiously to remove, or disable access to, the material.").

[57] H.R. Rep. No. 551 (Part 2), 105th Cong., 2d Sess. 54 (1998); S. Rep. No. 105-190, 105th Cong., 2d Sess. 45 (1998).

[58] H.R. Rep. No. 551 (Part 2), 105th Cong., 2d Sess. 57 (1998); S. Rep. No. 105-190, 105th Cong., 2d Sess. 48 (1998) (emphasis added).

[59] H.R. Rep. No. 551 (Part 2), 105th Cong., 2d Sess. 53 (1998); S. Rep. No. 105-190, 105th Cong., 2d Sess. 44 (1998) (emphasis added).

[60] 17 U.S.C. § 512(c)(1)(A)(i)–(iii) and 17 U.S.C. § 512(d)(1)(A)–(C).

[61] H.R. Rep. No. 551 (Part 2), 105th Cong., 2d Sess. 53-54 (1998); S. Rep. No. 105-190, 105th Cong., 2d Sess. 44 (1998).

[62] Both provisions include the following: "*upon obtaining such knowledge or awareness*, acts expeditiously to remove, or disable access to, the material." (emphasis added). 17 U.S.C. §§ (c)(1)(A)(iii) and (d)(1)(C).

[63] H.R. Rep. No. 551 (Part 2), 105th Cong., 2d Sess. 58 (1998); S. Rep. No. 105-190, 105th Cong., 2d Sess. 49 (1998).

[64] H.R. Rep. No. 551 (Part 2), 105th Cong., 2d Sess. 58 (1998); S. Rep. No. 105-190, 105th Cong., 2d Sess. 49 (1998).

[65] H.R. Rep. No. 551 (Part 2), 105th Cong., 2d Sess. 57 (1998); S. Rep. No. 105-190, 105th Cong., 2d Sess. 48 (1998).

[66] H.R. Rep. No. 551 (Part 2), 105th Cong., 2d Sess. 57-58 (1998); S. Rep. No. 105-190, 105th Cong., 2d Sess. 48 (1998).

[67] H.R. Rep. No. 551 (Part 2), 105th Cong., 2d Sess. 58 (1998); S. Rep. No. 105-190, 105th Cong., 2d Sess. 48 (1998).

[68] See, Walter A. Effross, Seamless Seaminess? Fake Nudes Are "Cropping" Up Online: Creators of Composites Most Likely Are Infringers, COMPUTER LAW STRATEGISTS, December, 1998, at 4 ("Such images, whether off line or online, clearly raise copyright

concerns. The creator of a composite or retouched fake nude image has likely infringed the rights of the copyright holders of the underlying photograph or photographs by making a 'derivative work' without permission." Id. at 4.), discussing examples of such Web sites involving images of actress Alyssa Milano and skater Nancy Kerrigan.

[69] *Costar Group Inc. v. LoopNet, Inc.*, 373 F.3d 544, 547 (4th Cir. 2004).

[70] *Costar Group Inc. v. LoopNet, Inc.*, 373 F.3d 544, 547 (4th Cir. 2004).

[71] *Costar Group Inc. v. LoopNet, Inc.*, 373 F.3d 544, 547 (4th Cir. 2004).

[72] *Costar Group Inc. v. LoopNet, Inc.*, 373 F.3d 544, 556 (4th Cir. 2004) (emphasis original). But see, *Costar Group Inc. v. LoopNet, Inc.*, 373 F.3d 544, 557 (4th Cir. 2004) (Gregory, J., dissenting) ("In so determining that LoopNet's 'gatekeeping function' does not expose it to direct infringement liability, I submit that the majority expands the non-volitional defense well beyond *Netcom* and subsequent holdings, and gives direct infringers in the commercial cybersphere far greater protections that they would be accorded in print and other more traditional media.").

[73] *In re Verizon Internet Services, Inc.*, 257 F. Supp. 2d 244, 267 (D.D.C. 2003), reversed 351 F.3d 1229 (D.C. Cir. 2003), cert. denied 125 S. Ct. 309 (2004).

[74] H.R. Rep. No. 551 (Part 2), 105th Cong., 2d Sess. 53 (1998); S. Rep. No. 105-190, 105th Cong., 2d Sess. 44 (1998). (emphasis added)

[75] H.R. Rep. No. 551 (Part 2), 105th Cong., 2d Sess. 58 (1998); S. Rep. No. 105-190, 105th Cong., 2d Sess. 48 (1998).

[76] 17 U.S.C. § 512(c)(1)(B) or (d)(2).

[77] Alfred C. Yen, Internet Service Provider Liability for Subscriber Copyright Infringement, Enterprise Liability, and the First Amendment, 88 GEORGETOWN LAW JOURNAL 1833, 1882 (2000) ("Subsection (B), therefore does no more than condition nonliability on the nonexistence of vicarious liability.").

[78] See, Charles S. Wright, Notes and Comments: Actual Versus Legal Control: Reading Vicarious Liability for Copyright Infringement into the Digital Millennium Copyright Act of 1998, 75 WASHINGTON LAW REVIEW 1005, 1026-1036 (2000). "A narrow construction of the codified control prong can both salvage protection for qualifying service providers and preserve the 'clean, well-lit place' where entities like eBay can monitor their sites without fear of losing safe-harbor protection." Id. at 1007 (footnotes omitted). Wright also argues that such an interpretation would increase the incentive of service providers to monitor (exercise 'actual control' under his framework) network activities of users more closely so as to qualify for the section 512(c)(1)(B) and (d)(2) "in a case in which the service provider has the right and ability to control such activity" proviso. Id. at 1033-1034. This is the overall goal of section 512, to, in short, have service providers and copyright owners "play nice" together, or, more formally, to have service providers minimize instead of exacerbate infringing environments in return for some statutory clarity of liability limitation. In the words of the Conference Report: "Title II preserves the strong incentives for service providers and copyright owners to cooperate to detect and deal with copyright infringements that take place in the digital networked environments. At the

same time, it provides greater certainty to service providers concerning their legal exposure for infringements that may occur in the course of their activities." H.R. Rep. No. 105-796, 105th Cong., 2d Sess. 72 (1998). (Conf. Rep.)

[79] Jay Dratler Jr., Cyberlaw: Intellectual Property in the Digital Millennium § 6.01[5], at 6-29 (2004) (footnotes omitted).

[80] *Costar Group, Inc. v. LoopNet, Inc.*, 164 F. Supp. 2d 688 (D. Md. 2001), affirmed *Costar Group Inc. v. LoopNet, Inc.*, 373 F.3d 544 (4th Cir. 2004) ("As will be seen, proof that [defendant] had knowledge of and induced the infringements are necessary elements of CoStar's LoopNet [the plaintiff's] contributory infringement claim. These elements are slightly different from those applicable to [defendant's] safe harbor defense and so require a separate determination if LoopNet [the defendant] fails to remain in the safe harbor." 164 F. Supp. 2d at 702-703.).

[81] JAY DRATLER JR., CYBERLAW: INTELLECTUAL PROPERTY IN THE DIGITAL MILLENNIUM § 6.01[5], at 6-31–6-32 (2004) ("The courts and litigants may be faced with defining, applying, and keeping track of *four* different standards of knowledge relating to contributory infringement liability (the three statutory standards [actual knowledge, constructive knowledge, and awareness] and the common-law one." (emphasis original)).

[82] Alfred C. Yen, Internet Service Provider Liability for Subscriber Copyright Infringement, Enterprise Liability, and the First Amendment, 88 GEORGETOWN LAW JOURNAL 1833, 1838 (2000).

[83] H.R. Rep. No. 551 (Part 2), 105th Cong., 2d Sess. 54 (1998); S. Rep. No. 105-190, 105th Cong., 2d Sess. 44-45 (1998) (emphases added).

[84] *Marobie-FL, Inc. v. National Association of Firefighter Equipment Distributors*, 983 F. Supp. 1167, 1179 (N.D. Ill. 1997) ("However, it is undisputed that NAFED paid Northwest a one-time set-up fee of $20 and that since that time NAFED has paid Northwest a flat fee of $67.50 each quarter. It is also undisputed that the fee Northwest receives has never changed based on how many people visit NAFED's Web Page or what is accessed. In other words, NAFED's infringement did not financially benefit Northwest. Accordingly, Northwest cannot be held vicariously liable for NAFED's infringement.").

[85] H.R. Rep. No 551 (Part 2), 105th Cong., 2d Sess. 54 (1998); see also, H.R. Rep No. 551 (Part 1), 105th Cong. 2d Sess. 25 (1998) ("As in *Marobie*, receiving one-time set-up fee and flat periodic payments for service from a person engaging in infringing activities would not constitute receiving 'a financial benefit directly attributable to the infringing activity.' Nor is subparagraph (B) intended to cover fees based on the length of the message (per number of bytes, for example) or by connect time. It would, however, include any such fees where the value of the service lies in providing access to infringing material."

[86] *Ellison v. Robertson*, 357 F.3d 1072, 1079 (9th Cir. 2004). Citation to Senate report 105-190 omitted.

[87] *Costar Group Inc. v. LoopNet, Inc.*, 164 F. Supp. 2d 688, 704-705 (D. Md. 2001), (citation to H.R. Rep. No. 105-551, part 2, at 54 omitted) affirmed *Costar Group Inc. v. LoopNet*, Inc., 373 F.3d 544 (4th Cir. 2004).

[88] See, *In re Verizon Internet Services, Inc.*, 240 F. Supp. 2d 24, 26 (D.D.C. 2003) ("Based on the language and structure of the statute, as confirmed by the purpose and history of the legislation, the Court concludes that the subpoena power in 17 U.S.C. § 512(h) applies to all Internet service providers within the scope of the DMCA, not just to those service providers storing information on a system or network at the direction of a user. Therefore, the Court grants RIAA's motion to enforce, and orders Verizon to comply with the properly issued and supported subpoena from RIAA seeking the identity of the alleged infringer."), reversed 351 F.3d 1229 (D.C. Cir 2003) (concluding that the subpoena power of section 512(h) does not apply to online intermediaries as conduit under section 512(a), as the subsection (h) subpoena coordinates notice with the subsection 512(c)(3) requirements that apply the ability of intermediaries to disable access to infringing material, versus disabling access to the Internet, a section 512(a) conduit intermediary can only disable access to the Internet not to content, thus the subpoena power of section of section 512(h) cannot apply. However, in the store and forward, post and link roles (subsection (b), (c), and (d), section 512(h) can apply, as the remedy of disabling access to infringing content would be possible.) A more likely subpoena would issue under section 45 of the Federal Rules of Civil Procedure.

[89] Marc Lindsey, World File Sharing War, THE COPYRIGHT & NEW MEDIA LAW NEWSLETTER, No. 4, 2004, at 9, 10 ("Since implementing this program [monitoring of bandwidth and port activity] at WSU [Washington State University], DMCA claims have dropped from a high volume of several claims a week to only four in 2004 as of September.

[90] *BMG Music et al. v. Does 1-203*, No. 2:04-CV-00650 (E.D. Pa., filed Feb 17, 2004); *Elektra Entertainment Group, Inc. et al. v. Does 1-7*, No. 04-607 (D.N.J., filed Feb 17, 2004); *Interscope Records et al. v. Does 1-25*, No. 6:040CV-197 (M.D. Fla., filed Feb 17, 2004). According to one industry spokesperson: "Our campaign against illegal file shares is not missing a beat. The message to illegal file shares should be as clear as ever—we will continue to bring lawsuits on a regular basis against those who illegally distribute copyrighted music." Cary Sherman, President, RIAA, quoted in THE ENTERTAINMENT LITIGATION REPORTER, February 29, 2004. "As of June 22, 2004, the RIAA had filed 3,047 such lawsuits." CBO Paper, Copyright Issues in Digital Media 19 (2004).

[91] See cases and criteria discussed in Tomas A. Lipinski, To Speak or Not to Speak: Developing Legal Standards for Anonymous Speech on the Internet, 5 INFORMING SCIENCE 95 (2002) (95-111).

[92] 17 U.S.C. § 512(h)(1).

[93] 17 U.S.C. § 512(h)(2)(A)–(C).

[94] 17 U.S.C. § 512(h)(3).

[95] H.R. Rep. No 551 (Part 2), 105th Cong., 2d Sess. 61 (1998); Senate Report 105-190, 105th Cong., 2d Sess. 51 (1998).

[96] H.R. Rep. No 551 (Part 2), 105th Cong., 2d Sess. 61 (1998); Senate Report 105-190, 105th Cong., 2d Sess. 51 (1998).

[97] H.R. Rep. No. 551 (Part 2), 105th Cong., 2d Sess. 61 (1998); S. Rep. No. 105-190, 105th Cong., 2d Sess. 51 (1998).

[98] The Eighth Circuit raised but did not address the issue of whether the grant of this authority by Congress to the clerk of courts was proper: "We comment without deciding that this provision *may* unconstitutionally invade the power of the judiciary by creating a statutory framework pursuant to which Congress, via statute, compels a clerk of a court to issue a subpoena, thereby invoking the court's powers. Further we believe Charter has at least a colorable argument that a judicial subpoena is a court order that must be supported by a case or controversy at the time of its issuance." *In re Charter Communication*, 393 F.3d 771, 777-778 (8th Cir. 2005). The dissent in *In re Charter Communication*, did reach both issued-sand concluded that ministerial nature of the subpoena did "not invoke the judicial power," therefore a statutory subpoena need not present a case or controversy. *In re Charter Communication*, 393 F.3d 771, 783 (8th Cir. 2005) (Murphy, J. dissenting).

[99] 17 U.S.C. § 512(h)(4).

[100] H.R. Rep. No. 551 (Part 2), 105th Cong., 2d Sess. 61 (1998); S. Rep. No. 105-190, 105th Cong., 2d Sess. 51 (1998).

[101] Family Educational Rights and Privacy Act, Pub. L. No. 93-380 (Title V), § 513a, 88 Stat. 571 (1974), as amended and codified at 20 U.S.C. 1232g(b)(1) ("No funds shall be made available under any applicable program to any educational agency or institution which has a policy or practice of permitting the release of education records (or personally identifiable information contained therein other than directory information, as defined in paragraph (5) of subsection (a) of this section) of students without the written consent of their parents.").

[102] 17 U.S.C. § 512(h)(5) (emphasis added).

[103] *In re Charter Communication*, 393 F.3d 771, 784-785 (8th Cir. 2005) (Murphy, J. dissenting) (quoting *Campbell v. Minneapolis Public Housing Authority ex rel City of Minneapolis*, 168 F.3d 1069, 1075 (8th Cir. 1999) and citing *Cisneros v. Alpine Ridge Group*, 508 U.S. 10 (1993)).

[104] See, 17 U.S.C. § 512(h)(4) and (5).

[105] 17 U.S.C. § 512(h)(6).

[106] *In re Internet Services, Inc.*, 257 (D.D.C. 2003), reversed F.supp.7d244 351 F.3d 1229 (D.C. Cir 2003), cert. denied 125 S.Ct. 309 (2004).

[107] *In re Verizon Internet Services, Inc.*, 257 F.Supp.2d 244, 267 (D.D.C. 2003), reversed 351 F.3d 1229 (D.C. Cir 2003), cert. denied 125 S.Ct. 309 (2004).

[108] *Recording Industry Association of America v. Verizon Internet Services, Inc.*, 351 F.3d 1229 (D.C. Cir. 2003), cert. denied 125 S.Ct. 309 (2004).

[109] *Recording Industry Association of America v. Verizon Internet Services, Inc.*, 351 F.3d 1229, 1234 (D.C. Cir. 2003) (emphasis added), cert. denied 125 S.Ct. 309 (2004).

[110] *Recording Industry Association of America v. Verizon Internet Services, Inc.*, 351 F.3d 1229, 1235 (D.C. Cir. 2003), cert. denied S.Ct. 309 (2004).

[111] *Recording Industry Association of America v. Verizon Internet Services, Inc.*, 351 F.3d 1229, 1236 (D.C. Cir. 2003), cert. denied S.Ct. 309 (2004).

[112] *In re Charter Communication, In re Charter Communication,* 393 F.3d 771 (8th Cir. 2005).

[113] *In re Charter Communication, In re Charter Communication,* 393 F.3d 771, 774 (8th Cir. 2005). (8th Cir. 2005) ("RIAA obtained subpoenas to produce the names, physical addresses, telephone numbers, and email addresses of approximately 200 of Charter's subscribers.").

[114] *In re Charter Communication, In re Charter Communication,* 393 F.3d 771, 780 (8th Cir. 2005) (Murphy, J. dissenting) (The RIAA used "a tracking program to discover that ninety-three of Charter Communication's internet subscribers were offering more than 100,000 copyrighted recordings of its members for downloading").

[115] *In re Charter Communication, In re Charter Communication,* 393 F.3d 771, 777 (8th Cir. 2005) ("Thus, because the parties do not dispute that Charter's function was limited to acting as a conduit for the allegedly copyright protected material, we agree § 512(h) does not authorize the subpoenas issued here." Id.).

[116] *In re Charter Communication, In re Charter Communication,* 393 F.3d 771, 777 (8th Cir. 2005) ("We agree with and adopt the reasoning of the United States Court of Appeals for the District of Columbia Circuit in *Verizon* as it pertains to this statutory issue [i.e., section 512(h) subpoenas do not issue under section 512(a) safe harbor-conduit scenarios]").

[117] *In re Charter Communication, In re Charter Communication,* 393 F.3d 771, 778 (8th Cir. 2005) ("This matter is hereby remanded so the district court may: (1) Order the RIAA to return to Charter any and all information obtained from the subpoenas; (2) Order the RIAA to maintain no record of information derived from the subpoenas; (3) Order the RIAA to make no further use of the subscriber data obtained via the subpoenas.").

[118] *In re Charter Communication, In re Charter Communication,* 393 F.3d 771, 780 (8th Cir. 2005) (Murphy, J. dissenting).

[119] *In re Charter Communication, In re Charter Communication,* 393 F.3d 771, 780 (8th Cir. 2005) (Murphy, J. dissenting).

[120] *In re Charter Communication, In re Charter Communication,* 393 F.3d 771, 782 (8th Cir. 2005) (Murphy, J. dissenting).

[121] *In re Charter Communication, In re Charter Communication,* 393 F.3d 771, 781 (8th Cir. 2005) (Murphy, J. dissenting).

[122] *In re Charter Communication, In re Charter Communication,* 393 F.3d 771, 781 (8th Cir. 2005) (Murphy, J. dissenting).

[123] *In re Charter Communication, In re Charter Communication,* 393 F.3d 771, 782 (8th Cir. 2005) (Murphy, J. dissenting).

[124] *In re Verizon Internet Services, Inc.,* 351 F.3d 1229, 1236 (D.C. Cir. 2003), cert. denied 125 S.Ct. 309 (2004).

►8

WHAT IS DIFFERENT ABOUT SECTION 512 IN HIGHER EDUCATION?

Read this chapter to learn about copyright situations like:

► Whether a school can be sued by a patron for taking down information that the patron uploaded illegally.

► Whether an institution can make public use of images that are not themselves protected but that are found on a copyrighted CD-ROM.

COMPLYING WITH SECTION 512 AT ACADEMIC INSTITUTIONS

Section 512(e) provides additional benefit to institutions of higher education if certain conditions exist. Why this special benefit? There are two interrelated reasons. First, faculties at tertiary educational institutions often have more autonomy than those in other educational environments. Second, by the same token, that autonomy decreases the ability of the institution to intervene in situations where risk may arise, such as copyright infringement. This risk impacts not only the common law standard for vicarious liability but section 512 as well: "[A] service provider may fail to qualify for the liability limitations in Title II simply because the knowledge or actions of one of its employees may be imputed to it under basic principles of respondeat superior."[1] The additional benefit conferred is twofold. First, the institution can treat faculty and teaching staff as third parties (and not as employees) with respect to the conduit and cache provisions, sections 512(a) and (b) ("such faculty member or graduate student shall be considered to be a person other than the institution"). Second, for purposes of the post and link provisions, sections 512(c) and (d), need not impute the knowledge of qualifying employees to the institutional mens rea[2] of the knowledge or "red flag" awareness of 512(c)(1)(A)(i)–(ii) and (d)(1)(A)–(B) ("such faculty member's or graduate student's knowledge or awareness of his or her infringing activities shall not be attributed to the institution").[3]

The provision applies only to institutions of higher education ("public or other nonprofit institution of higher education"), and only "when a faculty member or graduate student who is an employee of such institution is performing a teaching or research function." Thus not all employee duties, even if performed within the scope of employment are covered by section 512(e). Teaching and research are covered, but *not* administrative or service duties that faculty members or teaching or research assistants might perform within the scope of their duties.

Why is the tertiary educational environment different? Is Congress suggesting, recent testimony concerning P2P piracy on college campuses notwithstanding,[4] that teaching and researching faculty or graduate students are more likely to engage in copyright infringement? Not necessarily, but when and if they do, such activity is more likely to occur with less opportunity for risk-management intervention or prevention by the institution: "Since independence—freedom of thought, word and action—is at the core of academic freedom, the actions of university faculty and graduate student teachers and researchers warrant special consideration in the context of this legislation."[5] The uniqueness of the environment may suggest that employers have less control vis-à-vis concepts of academic freedom than does the average employer over its employees.[6] Thus for purposes of established refuge in the safe harbor the strict application of respondeat superior (vicarious liability) should not operate or at least the harness of the doctrine should be lessened. As a result, the institution of higher education should be less responsible for the acts of its employees. This is contrasted with the K–12 environment where the ebb and flow of the school day is more tightly structured, for both students and teachers.

Recognizing the Advantages of Section 512(e)

There are two main advantages once section 512(e) applies. First, for purposes of 512 (a) and (b) (transitory or conduit "store and forward" communication and system caching), section 512(e)(1) states that the "faculty member or graduate student shall be considered to be a person other than the institution." Thus an employee's infringing acts are not imputed to the employer, the educational institution. In other words, section 512(e) intercedes in the operation of vicarious liability principles. The Conference Report makes this clear as the underlying goal of section 512(e): "However, the conferees recognize that the university environment is unique. Ordinarily, a service provider may fail to qualify for the liability limitation in Title II simply because the knowledge or actions of one of its employees may be imputed to it under basic principles of respondent superior and agency law,"[7] those two legal concepts being the source of the vicarious liability in copyright.[8]

For purposes of 512 (c) and (d) (storage and information location tools), the knowledge of the infringement is not attributed to the institution: "such faculty member's or graduate student's knowledge or awareness of his or her infringing activities shall not be attributed to the institution." In other words, the knowledge or awareness of a post or link by a faculty member or graduate student is not imputed to the institution from that teaching or researching faculty member or graduate student. Second, knowledge or awareness of infringing activity could still impute to the institution, but it might instead come from the staff member or other employee working with the faculty or teaching graduate student, i.e., "that determination must be made on the basis of the knowledge or awareness of other employees of the institution, such as administrators and paid professional staff."[9] Moreover, the activity itself is not prevented from being imputed by virtue of the employment relationship, as it is for the conduit (store and forward) and cache functions under the earlier liability limitations proviso of section 512(e)(1), only the knowledge of infringement for post and link functions does not impute for purposes of determining whether the institution has satisfied subsections (c)(1)(A)(i) and (ii) and (d)(1)(B) and (C), the "actual knowledge" and constructive knowledge ("aware of facts or circumstances from which infringing activity is apparent") of the notice and takedown requirements for eligibility under section 512(c) and (d) respectively. Thus, "the rule is somewhat less protective."[10]

In order to give meaning to the subsection (e) language in spite of the legislative history, the logical application of the section 512(e)(1) intercession must then occur in a situation where the faculty member would have actual knowledge or awareness of infringing activity, e.g., the direct infringement of students, by directing them to use the Internet to download and view pirated course content. The institutional mens rea cannot derive from the teaching faculty or graduate student, under section 512(e)(1), but the institution might still be liable, might still have the requisite "knowledge" of a contributory infringer. However, it would need to derive from some other person, another employee, for example, associated with the institution and the contributory infringing conduct, such as a distance education coordinator or network administrator who is aware that the faculty has loaded an infringing copy of a workbook on its distance education server.

An oddity of the statute is found in the second advantage that 512(e) offers, i.e., that for "purposes of subsections (c) and (d) [the post and link functions, respectively] such faculty member's or graduate student's knowledge or awareness of his or her infringing activities shall not be attributed to the institution." This language targets and relaxes specific requirements of eligibility for the post and link subsections of 512(c) and (d), and that does actually appear in those subsections, in subsection 512(c)(1)(A)(i) and (ii) and 512(d)(1)(A) and (B): "does not have actual knowledge that the material or activity is infringing" or "in the absence of such actual knowledge, is not aware of facts or circumstances from which infringing activity is apparent," respectively. The discussion of this "knowledge" element or, mens rea, suggests in copyright parlance a contributory infringement concept, with which the 512(c) and (d)(1) language (specific eligibility) and 512(e)(1) language (a relaxing of that requirement) coincide. However, as discussed earlier, the legislative history suggests that the focus of 512(e) is relief from the operation of respondent superior and agency principles that are of course concepts of vicarious liability which, as also discussed earlier, have little if anything to do with a knowledge requirement. Is this suggestion intentional or is this another example of poor drafting or lack of adequate legislative oversight?

Section 512(e) should not be interpreted to mean that no circumstances exist where secondary liability cannot now be attributed to the tertiary educational institution, just that it cannot be derived from the employment relationship alone per se; subsection (e) prevents that occurrence. While it might be a rare circumstance indeed in which this could occur, it must remain a possibility under the logic of the statute. The point of subsection (e) is that secondary liability cannot derive from the mere status of the teaching or research faculty or graduate student, in and of itself.

Identifying Teaching and Research Functions of Employees

Before section 512(e) can be applied several requirements must be met. First, section 512(e) applies only to faculty or graduate students when "performing a teaching or research function."[11] This is a general requirement of eligibility. Persons included should be those educators without the title of faculty per se, such as non-tenure track or academic staff teachers or some similar category. By the words of the statute, students are within its purview, and by logic the statute should also include persons falling in between the range of the statutory terms "faculty" and "graduate student." While there is no logical reason to exclude teaching staff members who do not have either faculty or graduate student status, a court could nonetheless exclude them based on a strict reading of the statute. Congress could have clarified by adding *"or person employed to provide a similar function"* or similar clause to the end of "when a faculty member or graduate student who is an employee of such institution is performing a teaching or research function," but it did not. However, since the statute does indeed use the term "employee," a guest lecturer's infringing activity would not fall within the application of section 512(e), even if that person would be a qualifying faculty member or graduate student of another college or university, i.e., his or her home institution. On the other hand, the statute and legislative history are both silent as to whether the faculty member or graduate student must be employed full time. Again it would be logical to include both part-time and full-time faculty and graduate students, as they are common at many institutions.

Section 512(e) does not apply when that "faculty member or graduate student is performing a function other than teaching or research or when the faculty member or graduate student is exercising institutional administrative responsibilities, or is carrying out operational responsibilities that relate to the institution's function as a service provider."[12] Further, the research activity must be "genuine academic exercise," such as "a legitimate scholarly or scientific investigation or inquiry," as opposed to some activity that is claimed to be research but is "undertaken as a pretext for engaging in infringing activity."[13] Consider a faculty member who makes a complete copy of a Dutch-language tape and book series, claiming that it is part of the preparation for an upcoming scholarly conference in Amsterdam. In reality the faculty member is not serious about attending, or if the faculty member is indeed attending, learning Dutch is neither part of the conference requirement nor an experiential necessity of the event (since most everyone the scholar will likely encounter throughout the experience will speak English). This scenario might be the sort of somewhat-related-though-in-reality-subterfuge behavior or "pretext" to which the legislative history refers. So, too, in a case where a history professor also serves as department chair, infringing activities relating to curriculum preparation or library research would of course be protected, but infringing reproductions made in anticipation of a faculty meeting (e.g., posting copy or an article on strategic planning to the department intranet) would not be protected.

Three Qualifying Conditions: Online Instruction Excluded

Three specific requirements are contained in section 512(e)(1)(A)–C). After establishing that the section 512(e) applies only to teaching and research and not to other uses of copyrighted material by faculty or graduate students within the educational setting, the first specific requirement of section 512(e)(1)(A) excludes a significant portion of teaching activity from protection: "such faculty member's or graduate student's infringing activities do not involve the provision of online access to instructional materials that are or were required or recommended, within the preceding 3-year period, for a course taught at the institution by the faculty member or graduate student." In other words, section 512(e) will *not* shield the institution from liability for the infringing activity of teaching and research faculty and graduate students undertaken in conjunction with online education. Of course the basic safe harbor provisions of section 512 remain available to the institution, provisions which make no exclusion based on particular activity. However, if the material was "required or recommended" (e.g., listed in a syllabus,) the activity of the faculty member or graduate student will be imputed to the institution under the general concepts of copyright liability.[14]

Moreover, the legislative history suggests an expanded view of "online access" that includes not only online access through a distance education course Web site but also a scenario where the faculty member or graduate student e-mails students and references an attached article as additional reading (whether required or recommended) for an upcoming class. However, it is not intended "to refer to materials which, from time to time, the faculty member or graduate student may incidentally and informally bring to the attention of students for their consideration during the course of instruction."[15] The legislative history suggests that a passing reference would not trigger the disqualification, but a more directed comment, such as "you might want to take a look at this new article on strong and weak forces for the midterm," might. While both references might be "informally" presented, the connection to the impending midterm is not "incidental."

Less clear is whether educational activity that might occur outside the context of a particular course or curriculum, such as master's thesis advisement or comprehensive examination or doctoral preliminary examination preparation and assistance, would still fall within the teaching or research functions. Such an activity would appear to be within the concept of "teach" and "research," and not in the internal administrative activities excluded by the previous quoted legislative history; thus it would be included within the section 512(e)(1) purpose. In addition, such activity would not be specific to a particular class, so it would not be excluded by the section 512(e)(1)(A) "online access to instructional materials" proviso if, for example, that advisement or preparation and assistance were facilitated online, through an online master's or doctoral study group headed by the faculty member. Thus the activity would appear to qualify for the section 512(e) rules because it is within the concept of teaching, but it is not so specific as to be excluded as a result of the online proviso exclusion. Finally, observe that as with the (e)(1)(B) subproviso, the relevant time frame is the previous three years, counted not in calendar or academic years but from the date of the activity.

Three Qualifying Conditions: "Repeat" Infringers Excluded

Second, section 512(e)(1)(B) also excludes faculty and graduate students who are repeat infringers from the additional safe harbor of that subsection. However, and unlike the section 512(i)(1)(A) general repeat infinger policy, a time limit is established, again softening or limiting the harsh rule of subsection (i). Section 512(e)(1)(B) provides that within the preceding 3 years the institution must not have received three or more notices of infringement (according to the notice provisions of 512(c)(3)) from copyright owners regarding the teaching or research behavior of the specific faculty member or graduate student: "the institution has not, within the preceding 3-year period, received more than two notifications described in subsection (c)(3) of claimed infringement by such faculty member or graduate student, and such notifications of claimed infringement were not actionable under subsection (f)." Section 512(f), discussed below, creates a remedy against "any person who knowingly materially misrepresents . . . that material or activity is infringing."[16] In other words, the allegations made in a section (c)(3) notice, though not necessarily true (i.e., ultimately infringing), must have been made with a sincere belief! As subsection (f) indicates, a sincere notice is made in the absence of knowledge of material representation: "knowingly materially misrepresents."

Those administrators concerned about copyright compliance within their institutions might find it easier to recall this requirement by thinking of it as a 2-3 or full-count rule with respect to particular problematic faculty or graduate student behavior, i.e., there can be no more than two statutory notices of infringement within a three-year period. Why no more than two, why three strikes, why not more than one, why not more than three? Placing the disqualification at "no more than one" would make it equivalent to the general rule of section 512(i)(1)(A). This would be inconsistent with the structure of section 512(e), the purpose of which is to offer additional safe harbor "anchorages," so to speak, to certain service providers, institutions of higher education. By the same token, allowing too many repeat infringements would not be consistent with the general purpose of section 512, to increase copyright compliance in online environments: "If more than two such notifications have been received, the institution may be considered to be on notice of a pattern of infringing conduct by the faculty member or graduate student, and the limitation of subsection (e) does not apply with respect to the subsequent infringing actions of that faculty member of graduate student."[17] Three strikes and you're out!

In other words, if the institution has received, in a three-year period, three notices of a particular faculty member's infringing activity, then 512(e) will not operate to bar the imputation of that conduct to the institution, with the likely result that the liability limitation of section 512 will not operate, or that, at least, it would operate under the basic provisions per subsections 512(a)–(d) alone. Observe that the tolling period is three years, not three calendar years or academic years but actually three years from the date of the receipt of a (c)(3) notice. The benefit here is that a teaching or research faculty member or graduate student who has come to see the light of copyright salvation, has since repented, and now is a model citizen of the copyright law is not plagued by a dark past. A notice received in June of 2002 would not count when determining section 512(e) qualification in 2006, but a notice in June 2003 would count for the tolling purpose of a notice received in January 2006.

This time limit underscores the need for expanded record-keeping requirements in conjunction with the application of section 512. It may in turn create an environment of heightened scrutiny by the institution over its faculty and graduate students in an attempt to curb potential infringing conduct. A provision drafted to recognize and preserve concepts of intellectual freedom in the tertiary educational environment in the long run may result in less independence and more control of the teaching and research functions of faculty and graduate students.

Observe an important aspect of the criteria contained in the section 512(e)(1)(B) language. First, the institution counts notices as long as the notices were not actionable under subsection (f), i.e., as long as the notice did not constitute a "known and material misrepresentations of infringement." Second, common practice would suggest that a good-faith belief that such activity by a teaching or researching faculty member or graduate student was infringing,[18] even though it ultimately would not be deemed infringement, would still count for purposes of the 2-3 or full-count rule, and so still counts as a strike against the section 512(e)(1) benefit. In contrast, this (c)(3) notice as a "count" is different from the section 512(i)(1)(A) repeat infringer policy where the triggering event for purpose of the counting is actual "infringement" and not mere allegation of it as in subsection (e), i.e., the (c)(3) "notice" of infringement. This interpretation is consistent with the overall design of section 512, e.g., section 512(g)(1) no liability for good-faith removal or disabling "regardless of whether the material or activity is ultimately determined to be infringing." While the good-faith standard and statement of accuracy of the section 512(c)(3)(v) and (vi) notice requirements likely ensure that copyright owners will not engage in less-than-valid accusations, it is too early in practice to determine whether the counting of the "full count" could be problematic in practice. (See the discussion below of section 512(f) as well; this provision, too, offers some hope of curbing over-aggressive copyright owners from abusing the notice and removal or disabling mechanisms of section 512.)

The fact remains that by the plain language of section 512, a college or university could lose the additional protection offered by section 512(e) in situations where a faculty member did not actually engage in infringing activity but the institution was notified of more than two such good-faith beliefs of infringement in a three-year period. Such circumstances would foreclose application of section 512(e). Of course, if the conduct of the teaching or research faculty member or graduate student is not actually infringing, then in theory there is no need for the safe harbor in the first instance. But this argument portrays a circular (in terms of logic) safety net of sorts. By the same token, a finding of noninfringement, is not always determinable, at least not without the commencement of legal proceedings! This in turn undermines the effectiveness and purpose of section 512, which is to add a measure of definiteness to the determination of liability, as well as to remit the monetary damages that might result from such determination. Unfortunately section 512 errs on the side of the copyright owner in obtaining that definiteness.

Three Qualifying Conditions: Copyright Information Program Required

Section 512(e) contains a significant compliance-oriented measure—significant because, with the enactment of the DMCA, for the first time the copyright law commands that an institution, an information intermediary, in this case an educational tertiary entity, engage in a specific form of copyright outreach to its user community. Section 512(e)(1)(C) requires that "the institution provide[] to all users of its system or network informational materials that accurately describe, and promote compliance with the laws of the United States relating to copyright." The legislative history offers no further articulation of what sort of informational material should be provided, only to suggest what could be provided: "The legislation allows, but does not require, the institutions to use relevant informational materials published by the U.S. Copyright Office in satisfying the condition imposed by paragraph (C)."[19] This is reference to the various copyright circulars available from the Copyright Office Web site, but it could of course include other information in the form of posters, brochures, handouts, or brief articles in various institutional house organs, such as newsletters or magazines. In-services, workshops, and other methods of instruction might also satisfy this requirement. Moreover, it does not limit education to copyright issues related to section 512 alone, but all the laws relating to copyright, such as the section 1201 anti-circumvention and anti-trafficking rules discussed in Chapter 9. In addition, the "informational materials" must be provided to all users of its systems or network, such as students, other patrons, and staff—not just the section 512(c) targets, teaching and research faculty members and graduate students. In the technology-intensive and technology-connected world of higher education today, this stipulation effectively encompasses everyone associated with the campus. Such outreach must be institution-wide in scope.

Special Limitations on Injunctive Relief

Once it is concluded that the expanded protection of section 512(e)(1) applies, a major advantage of section 512(e), via subsection (e)(2), is that the range of injunctive relief is further limited to those "contained in subsection (j)(2) and (j)(3), but not those in (j)(1)." In other words, the only injunctive relief available to plaintiffs in a section 512(e) scenario is that described in the general injunctive relief guidelines and the ex parte order provisions of section 512(j)(2) and (3), and not the more restrictive disabling of access, account termination, and the least burdensome remedy proviso under section 512(j)(1)(A)(i), (ii), and (iii) or 512(j)(1)(B)(i) and (ii). This may be a blessing in disguise as Professor Dratler points out:

> Thus, injunctive relief against a nonprofit educational institution successfully claiming a limitation on monetary remedies by virtue of the special attribution rules of subsection (e) can expect orders for relief that go beyond disabling access to particular material on a specified site, or other "least burdensome" relief. [footnote omitted] In a proper case a nonprofit educational institution might even be subject to a structural relief to correct chronic or persistent tendency to infringe copyrights.[20]

It is logical for the range of injunctive remedies to be limited in section 512(e) scenarios—teaching and research faculty members or graduate student employee—

because if the subsection (j)(1) remedies were available, it would mean then a denial of access or termination could issue.

Considering the very close link between the mission of tertiary institutions and research and teaching, it could prove disastrous if the subsection (j)(1) remedies were available not only for the target of the order but for the institution itself as it would mean a denial of access or termination as a possible remedy. While it might be argued that teaching is a mission of the primary and secondary educational institution, research is not. Moreover, the process of replacing a K–12 instructor who can no longer access the school district's account because of such an order is far easier than the process of replacing a faculty member at a college or university—the author can attest that this process often takes months. However, this quid pro quo also suggests that section 512(j) injunctive relief aimed at an infringing nonprofit educational institution might also go "beyond disabling access to particular material on a specified site . . . [and i]n a proper case, the nonprofit educational institution might even be subject to structural relief designed to correct a chronic or persistent tendency to infringe copyrights."[21] Such a remedy would also be consistent with the emphasis in section 512(e) concerning additional compliance measures such as the "informational materials" proviso.

COMBATING OVER-ZEALOUS USE OF SECTION 512

Section 512(f) provides a monetary recourse against over-zealous use of the notice and removal or disabling provisos of subsections (c) and (d), the subsection (h) subpoena power, or any other subsection of 512, such as the "put-back" provisions of section 512(g), discussed below:

> Any person who knowingly materially misrepresents under this section—(1) that material or activity is infringing, or (2) that material or activity was removed or disabled by mistake or misidentification, shall be liable for any damages, including costs and attorney's fees, incurred by the alleged infringer, by any copyright owner or copyright owner's authorized licensee, or by a service provider, who is injured by such misrepresentation, as the result of the service provider relying upon such misrepresentation in removing or disabling access to the material or activity claimed to be infringing, or in replacing the removed material or ceasing to disable access to it.[22]

Any party in the chain of infringement may seek monetary remedy from misrepresentations that are material and made knowingly. This could be the copyright owner because the initial infringer falsely claimed the use was not infringing (and the subscriber posted defamatory messages about the aggressive behavior of the copyright owner), the service provider because it believed an initial infringer made a bogus claim of authorized use or ownership (and decided to its detriment not to remove or disable the material), or the alleged initial infringer who had his or her material removed by a service provider in response to a false claim of infringement by the copyright owner (perhaps a faculty member who believes his or her reputation has been harmed by insinuations of less-than-ethical behavior vis-à-vis another's copyrighted material).

All false claims must not only be incorrect, but such material representations must be knowingly made as well. It could be argued that any claim of infringement is material.[23] Again the concept of knowledge in copyright law relates to either actual knowledge or constructive knowledge, the reason to know concept as discussed in Chapter 2. A claim made with knowledge of its falsity triggers the damage restoration mechanism of section 512(f):

> New Section 512(e) [enacted as section 512(f)] establishes a right of action against any person who knowingly misrepresents that material or activity on-line is infringing, or that material or activity was removed or disabled by mistake or misidentification under the "put-back" procedure set forth in new subsection (f). [enacted as section 512 (g)] under new subsection (e) [enacted as subsection (f)] by any *copyright owner, a copyright owner's licensee, or by a service provider,* who is injured by such misrepresentation in either taking down material or putting material back on-line. Defendants who make such a knowing misrepresentation are liable for any damages, including costs and attorneys' fees, incurred by any of these parties as a result of the service provider's reliance upon the misrepresentation. This subsection is intended to deter knowingly false allegation to service providers in recognition that such misrepresentations are detrimental to *rights holders, service providers, and Internet users.*[24]

While the legislative history lists only two of the three parties to an online interaction involving copyrighted material—the copyright owner (the intermediary), the service provider (such as a library or educational entity), and, third, the subscriber, patron, or student—the statute is clear in including that the subscriber, the alleged infringer "shall be liable for any damages, including costs and attorneys' fees, incurred *by the alleged infringer, by any copyright owner or copyright owner's authorized licensee, or by a service provider,* who is injured by such misrepresentation."[25] This oversight example offered by the legislative history is in contrast to the clear words of the statute; moreover, as the legislative history reiterates that the purpose of the provision is to deter false allegations that can indeed be harmful to all three parties, i.e., "detrimental to rights holders, service providers, and *Internet users."*

Early Case Law

The *Online Policy Group v. Diebold, Inc.* litigation demonstrates the use (or abuse, depending on your perspective!) to which section 512 can be put by aggressive copyright owners (or in this case alleged owners), the value of section 512(f) fail-safe mechanism, and the role of the courts in applying this new law (recall the divergence of opinion in the application of the section 512(h) subpoena provision). In *Online Policy Group v. Diebold, Inc.*, Diebold, maker of electronic voting machines used in the controversial 2000 presidential election became the subject of criticism and commentary regarding the performance of its product. As in most cases of intrigue, there is always a memo, and true to form there was a document trail here as well: "It is undisputed that internal emails exchanged among Diebold employees (the 'email archive') contain evidence that some employees have acknowledged problems associated with the machines."[26] Enter section 512. Diebold attempted to use section 512 subpoena to quell public discussion of the issue—in specific, by sending cease and desist letters to many ISPs, including Swarthmore College, where two students, Nelson Chu Pavlosky and Luke Thomas Smith, had posted an e-mail archive of material related to the dispute. The letters sent to Swarthmore among others "advised that pursuant to these provisions [the safe harbor provisions of the DMCA] they would be shielded from a copyright infringement suit by Diebold if they disabled access to remove the allegedly infringing material."[27] Diebold contended that the memorandums and other documentation were subject to copyright protection. Diebold also contended its e-mail archive contained discussion of its proprietary election systems, trade secrets, and personal information of its employees.

Based in part on the protections embedded in section 512(f), the plaintiffs, those who disseminated the e-mails and other documentation, including Swarthmore (as a potential contributory), requested injunctive relief under the statute that included a ruling that the publication of the e-mail archive, hosting or providing collocation services to Web sites that link to it, and providing Internet service to those hosting sites that link are lawful activities. After the story hit the airwaves and net-waves, Diebold apparently discovered the error of its ways, realizing its copyright claim was tenuous at best: "Diebold has represented to the Court that it has withdrawn and in the future will not send a cease and desist letter pursuant to the DMCA to any ISP concerning the email archive."[28] However, the court did not let Diebold off with a legal mea culpa or the proverbial slap on the wrist. Rather in a legal reversal of fortune the court observed: "Plaintiffs' claims for an injunction and declaratory relief are moot. However, Plaintiffs' claims for damages, attorneys' fees, and cost relating to Diebold's past use of the DMCA's safe harbor provisions still require adjudication."[29] In other words, Diebold would face possible "sanction"[30] for its aggressive misuse of section 512.

Section 512(f) might be characterized as a sanction provision. However the statute does not indicate what standard should be applied in determining whether erroneous assertion is sufficient to meet the "knowingly materially misrepresents" standard. The court rejected the use of Rule 11 (the Federal Rules of Civil Procedure that govern attorney sanctions) i.e. a "frivolous" standard forwarded by

Diebold as well as a "likelihood of success"[31] standard typically applied by courts under preliminary injunction copyright precedent forwarded by Swarthmore.

The court, with reference to *Black's Law Dictionary*, chose the middle ground and concluded that "knowingly" means actual knowledge, should have known if acting with reasonable care or diligence, or would have had no substantial doubt had it been acting in good faith.[32] Based on this standard the court had little difficulty in determining that such a cease and desist letter would meet the materiality standard, as "material" means that the act has the intended effect on the ISP, i.e., that the ISP responds in the way that section 512 desires it to respond: remove or disable access to the alleged infringing material.

> Applying this standard and in light of the evidence in the record, the Court concludes as a matter of law that Diebold knowingly materially misrepresented that Plaintiffs infringed Diebolds' copyright interest, at least with respect to the portions of the email archive clearly subject to the fair use exception. No reasonable copyright holder could have believed that the portions of the email archive discussion of possible technical problems with Diebold's voting machines were protected by copyright, and there is no genuine issue of fact that Diebold knew—and indeed that it specifically intended—that its letter to OPG and Swarthmore would result in prevention of publication of that content.[33]

The section 512 notice mechanism, subpoena power, or other enforcement tools are to assist copyright owners in enforcing their copyright, not to prevent discussion about products or preserve sales of those same products: "The fact that Diebold never actually brought suit against any alleged infringer suggests strongly that Diebold sought to use the DMCA's safe harbor provisions—which were designed to protect ISPs, not copyright holders—as a sword to suppress publication of embarrassing content rather than as a shield to protect its intellectual property."[34] Moreover, the "goal of copyright law is to protect creative works in order to promote their creation"[35] not to protect the products that alleged copyrighted material might describe: "At most, Plaintiffs' activity might have reduced Diebold's profits because it helped inform potential customers of problems with the machines. However, copyright law is not designed to prevent such an outcome."[36] The court also saw little commercial value in the e-mail content, and characterized the use of it in public debate as "transformative: they used the email archive to support criticism that is in the public interest, not to develop electronic voting technology."[37] As a result, the court concluded that "the purpose, character, nature of the use, and the effect of the use upon the potential market for or value of the copyrighted work [i.e., the four factors of the fair use test] all indicate that at least part of the e-mail archive is not protected by copyright law."[38] Moreover, the court also appeared to characterize the e-mails as unworthy of copyright protection in a comment that underscored the court's disfavor with the use of the DMCA to suppress free inquiry: "Accordingly, there is no genuine issue of material fact that Diebold, through its use of the DMCA, sought to and did in fact suppress publication of content that is not subject to copyright protection."[39] While the Diebold controversy represents a single case,[40] it does stand for the proposition that section 512 as designed may not be used without limit. Working within the various mechanisms of section 512, whether copyright owner, service provider, or subscriber, advancing a position based on a belief that no reasonable person could maintain may result in the "sanction" of section 512(f). Monetary awards may be made under this subsection, suspending the benefit of the safe harbor when directed against service providers. However, service providers may likewise benefit from this provision when liability accrues "as the result of the service provider relying upon such misrepresentation in removing or disabling access to the material or activity claimed to be infringing, or in replacing the removed material or ceasing to disable access to it."

OBTAINING IMMUNITY FOR INFRINGEMENT CLAIMS NOT BASED IN COPYRIGHT

Once the service provider obligation arises to remove or disable access to infringing material, or once by either the (c)(1)(C) notice mechanism or the knowledge or awareness provision of (c)(1)(A) and (d)(1) discussed previously, and the service provider in fact decides to remove or disable (comply with the command of the safe harbor rules), that does not end the story nor, more important, the responsibilities that section 512 bestows on the service provider. The bit of good news is that section 512(g)(1) offers a service provider immunity against the ire of disgruntled users of its system or network whose access it disabled or whose posted material it removed: "Subject to paragraph (2), a service provider shall not be liable to any person for any claim based on the service provider's good faith disabling of access to, or removal of, material or activity claimed to be infringing or based on facts or circumstances from which infringing activity is apparent, regardless of whether the material or activity is ultimately determined to be infringing."[41] The immunity offered in section 512(g)(1) extends to instances of removal or disabling in error, i.e., "regardless of whether the material or activity is ultimately determined to be infringing." The immunity also operates in situations where the removal or disabling was not triggered by the section 512(c)(1)(C) notice mechanism, but rather was the result of the knowledge or awareness proviso of sections 512(c)(1)(A) and (d)(1).

The legislative history explains: "The purpose of this subsection is to protect service providers from liability to third parties whose material service providers take down in a good faith effort to comply with the requirements of new subsection (c)(1)."[42] If the requirements of section 512(g) are not met, the service provider does *not* lose the monetary remission safe harbor of section 512(a), (b), (c), or (d); rather it loses only the subsection (g) immunity, including immunity from injunctive relief to third parties. In this way, section 512(g) can be viewed as an additional or super-safe harbor, against all liability from third parties based on its behavior as a complying section 512 service provider. This potential liability would not rest in copyright but some other legal theory—(perhaps defamation or tortuous interference with contract or breach of subscriber agreement) for a removal or disabling that was made in error.

Triggering Mechanism: Subsection (c)(1)(C) Notice

Of course there is always a "but" in law, especially in the copyright law. The section 512(g) "but" is the "Subject to paragraph (2)" opening proviso indicating that section 512(g) contains an exception to immunity rule; moreover, section 512(g)(2) contains a rather large one.

> New Section 512(f) [enacted as subsection (g)] provides immunity to service providers for taking down infringing material, and establishes a "put back" procedure under which subscribers may contest a complaining party's notification of infringement provided under new subsection (c)(3). The put-back procedures were added to balance the incentives created in new Section 512 for service providers to take down material against third parties' interests in ensuring that material not be taken down.[43]

In order to obtain the immunity of section 512(g)(1) the service provider must take several additional steps in instances "with respect to material residing at the direction of a subscriber of the service provider on a system or network controlled or operated by or for the service provider that is removed, or to which access is disabled by the service provider, pursuant to a notice provided under subsection (c)(1)(C)."[44]

While the immunity applies in both removal and disabling scenarios under section 512 (notice and knowledge or awareness), the put-back sequence of subscriber contact, subscriber counter notification, copyright owner contact, and copyright owner counter-counter notification applies only to removal or disabling initiated by a section 512(c)(1)(C) notice. It does not apply to the same (c)(3) mechanism that might occur vis-à-vis subsection (b) or (d), in cache or link scenarios, but only "with respect to material residing at the direction of a subscriber of the service provider on a system or network controlled or operated by or for the service provider that is removed, or to which access is disabled by the service provider," i.e., posting scenarios. This conclusion is derived from the construction of the statute. It is true that the cache (subsection (b)) or link (subsection (d)) notice can result in subsection (c)(3) notice being received from the copyright owner. That notice is generated from the (b) and (d) subsections by reference to subsection (c)(3) directly, i.e., from language in subsection (b)(2)(E) ("upon notification of claimed infringement as described in subsection (c)(3)") or subsection (d)(3) ("upon notification of claimed infringement as described in subsection (c)(3)") and not via reference to subsection (c)(1)(C) first. Second section 512(g)(2) mechanism is specific in its reference to (c)(1)(C): "pursuant to a notice provided under subsection (c)(1)(C)." Again, this may be an oversight of legislative drafting, but the language of the legislative history supports the conclusion, that the statute intends the subsection (g) replacement to apply to post scenarios alone, using the phrase "take down" to describe the requirements of this second immunity provision.[45] A takedown applies by logic to a post, subsection (c), and not to a cache, subsection (b), or a link, subsection (d).

There are several steps to the subsection (g)(2)(A)–(C) replacement process (in response to a removal or disabling under the subsection (c)(1)(C) notice mechanism):

▶ The service provider receives **initial notice** from a copyright owner conforming to (c)(3)(A) (as discussed in chapter 7).

▶ The service provider (in the context of this monograph, that would be the library or educational entity) must "promptly" contact the "subscriber" (or patron or student) whose post was removed or whose access was disabled, offering the subscriber a chance to challenge the service provider's act of removal or disabling.

▶ A challenge may occur, a so-called **counter notification**, under (g)(2)(B) that conforms to (g)(3) (A)-(D).

▶ The service provider must in turn "promptly" contact the copyright owner or its designated representative (the "person" from whom it received the initial subsection (c)(1)(C) notice) informing that party that the service provider will replace the material or restore access.

▶ Such replacement of material and restoration of access does not occur, however, if the copyright owner or designated representative "has filed an action seeking a court order to restrain the subscriber from engaging in infringing activity relating to the material on the service provider's system or network" and notifies the subscriber that it has done so.

In other words, the copyright owner must put its proverbial legal money where its mouth is. Subscribers might be tempted to challenge, to force the legal hand of the copyright owner, as perhaps not all copyright owners will outlay the cost that such legal declaration entails. However, recall that subscribers like the over-aggressive copyright owners in the *Diebold* litigation can also be subject to legal sanction in the form of liability for all monetary damages including costs and attorney's fees. If a false "challenge" or counter notification meets the "known" material misrepresentation standard of section 512(f), the subscriber may be liable for any monetary damages that result from service provider reliance upon the subscriber's misrepresentation.

In review, the sequence for the service provider is as follows: service provider receives a section (c)(3) notice, per subsection (c)(1)(C) (i.e., under the post scenario), then "promptly" contacts the subscriber who made the allegedly infringing post, and waits to hear if such subscriber will challenge. If challenge ensues, then the service provider is under a second obligation to "promptly" contact the copyright owner and offer a final opportunity to assert its copyright authority (notice of court order); otherwise restoration will occur. Consider the role of the service provider in the sequence: initial notice *to service provider* from copyright owner, notice to subscriber *from service provider*, counter notice of challenge *to service provider* from subscriber, opportunity offered to copyright owner to verify or reassert claim of infringement, i.e., commencement of legal proceedings vis-à-vis injunction. This process, of course, places the service provider library or educational entity in the middle, as a sort of "can't we all just get along" copyright go-between.

Navigating the Statutory Processes

Again, this counter notification (opportunity for subscriber retort) and copyright owner reassertion of notice (in truth a second notice from the copyright owner to the designated agent indicating that the copyright owner or his or her designated representaive "has filed an action seeking a court order to restrain the subscriber from engaging in infringing activity relating to the material on the service provider's system or network") mechanism is required only in those cases where notice in conformity with the section 512(c)(3) mechanism occurs, and only when the service provider desires protection of subsection (g):

> New subsection (f)(2) [enacted as (g)(2)] establishes a "put back" procedure through an exception to the immunity set forth in new subsection (f)(1). The exception applies in a case in which the service provider, pursuant to a notification provided under new subsection (c)(1)(C) in accordance with new subsection (c)(3), takes down material that a subscriber has posted to the system or network. In such instances, to retain the immunity set forth in new subsection (f)(1) with respect to the subscriber whose content is taken down, the service provider must take three steps.[46]

There are several requirements at each step of the process. First, the "service provider [must] take[] reasonable steps *promptly* to notify the subscriber that it has removed or disabled access to the material." While no time frame is given, the attempt to notify must be made "promptly." The reasonable steps do not entail searching the Web for traces of the subscriber or other possible threads of contact but instead involve using the information apparent from the posting itself or documentation contained in the "subscriber" file such as a registration record or subscription agreement. In the words of both the House Report and Senate Report:

The Committee intends that "reasonable steps" include, for example, sending an e-mail notice to an e-mail address associated with a posting, or if only the subscriber's name is identified in the posting, sending an e-mail to an e-mail address that the subscriber submitted with its subscription. The Committee does not intend that this subsection impose any obligation on service providers to search beyond the four corners of a subscriber's posting or their own records for that subscriber in order to obtain contact information. Nor does the Committee intend to create any right on the part of subscribers who submit falsified information in their postings or subscriptions to complain if a service provider relies upon the information submitted by the subscriber.[47]

For a public library service provider, such information and "four corners" would likely be its registration and circulation records database and for an educational entity such as school, college or university, such information would be a similar databank of student files and records.

As Professor Dratler observes: "Thus, if a subscriber falsifies contact information in order to remain anonymous, the service provider will not lose its immunity from liability under subsection (g) if it uses that false information for purposes of the 'take-down' notification."[48] At this point, the subscriber, patron, customer, or student makes a decision—either to live with the removal or cessation of access to the material or offer a challenge. Given the short time within which restoration, as early as the 10th business day but no later than the 14th after receipt of a subscriber counter-notification, a 2-or-3-business days turn-around time appears prudent, as this would allow time for the next two procedures to occur within the ultimate 10-to-14-business-days limit of section 512(g)(2)(C), i.e., after receipt of a counter-notification from the subscriber, a second, prompt contact of the copyright owner offering a change to submit a second owner's notice must occur along with eventual restoration if no re-notice (counter-counter notification) from the copyright owner is forthcoming.

Receipt of a Counter Notice from a Subscriber

The requirements of a challenge, or counter notification, are prescribed by statute and must be written and must be provided to the designated agent, the same person established by the section 512(c)(2) mechanism. The same "substantially" standard that section 512(c)(3)(A) imposed on copyright owners when making removal or disabling notifications is also applied to the subscribers desiring that material be replaced or access restored.[49] "Second, pursuant to new subsection (f)(2)(B) [enacted as (g)(2)(B)], the subscriber may then file a counter notification, in accordance with the requirements of new subsection (f)(3) [enacted as (g)(3)], contesting the original take down on grounds of mistake or misidentification of the material and requesting 'put back' of the material that the service provider has taken down."[50] Notice that, under the sequence of notice, removal or disabling, contact, counter notice, potential restoration, the default is against access and to err on the side of caution vis-à-vis the copyright owner's rights. In other words, the service provider must respond expeditiously by removing the material or disabling access to it. The service provider cannot follow through this contact and counter-notice sequence and then wait to hear back from the subscriber before deciding that removal or disabling is indeed required. It must remove or disable first, then "promptly" offer the subscriber a chance to respond and offer (again "promptly") the copyright owner an opportunity to respond a second time before finally restoring access to the material.

The counter notification from the subscriber must "include[] substantially the following" information: (1) a physical or electronic signature of the subscriber, (2) identification and location of the material that has been removed or to which access has been disabled, (3) similar to the section 512(c)(3)(A)(v) and (vi) requirement, a statement under penalty of perjury that the subscriber has a good-faith belief that the material was removed or disabled as a result of mistake or misidentification, (4) contact information, a statement of consent to federal district court jurisdiction where the address is located, or if ex-territorial to any judicial district where the service provider is located, and a statement of consent to accept process from the same owner or agent who filed the subsection (c)(1)(C) notice.[51]

Unlike in section 512(c)(3)(B)(ii), there is no indication of what information less than the four section 512(g)(3)(A)–(D) provisos is substantial. Logic would suggest it is more than a majority of the factors, i.e., two of the four, but which three? Moreover, section 512(g)(4)(D) actually contains three separate though related requirements: contact information, consent to jurisdiction ("a statement of consent to federal district court jurisdiction where the address is located or if ex-territorial to any judicial district where the service provider is located") and consent to be served ("a statement of consent to accept process from the same owner or agent who filed the subsection (c)(1)(C) notice"). In the alternative, and parallel to section 512(c)(3)(B)(ii), the "substantially" requirement could be determined by looking the similar sort of information required for subsection (c)(3) compliance, a counter notification that substantially complies with (c)(3)(A)(ii)–(iv): identification of the infringing material and identification of contact information so that process can continue. This conclusion is also supported by the legislative history: "Subscriber counter notifications must *substantially comply* with defined requirements set forth in new subsection (f)(3). . . . The substantial compliance standard is the *same* as that set forth in new subsections (c)(2) and (3)."[52] Recall that the legislative history regarding that section urged service providers to look beyond "technical errors" and focus on the "functional requirements" ("such as providing sufficient information so that a designated agent or the complaining party submitting a notification may be contacted efficiently") in order that the "subsection [(c)] operate smoothly."[53] If this is the case, and the author argues it is a reasonable interpretation given the emphasis on service provider intervention obligations within section 512, then items 2 ("identification and location") and 4 (contact information, consent to jurisdiction, and consent to be served) alone might constitute substantial compliance, i.e., the section 512(g)(3)(B) and (D) provisos.

The purpose of the counter notification is not to embroil the parties in an argument over whether the "material that is claimed to be infringing or to be the subject of infringing activity" is or is not ultimately infringing. As Professor Dratler observes:

> The language of Subparagraph (C) restricts counter-notifications to assertions of mistake or misidentification of the material at issue. It does not permit counter-notifications based on disputes, whether or not in good faith, over ownership of copyright or copyright infringement (for example, based on a belief that an exception such as fair use applies). In addition, the statute restricts the class of persons who may file counter-notifications to the service provider's own subscribers. Presumably a service provider may ignore counter-notifications making assertions not contemplated by this language or sent by persons not eligible to do so.[54]

This would preclude third-party comments, such as "your subscriber got the material from our Web site which the copyright owner gave us permission to post" or similar interventions.

Waiting for a Second Response or Rebuttal from the Copyright Owner

Second, the service provider must then contact the copyright owner or its agent from whom the service provider received the initiating section 512(c)(1)(C) notice: "If a subscriber files a counter notification with the service provider's designated agent, new subsection (f)(2)(B) calls for the service provider to *promptly* forward a copy to the complaining party who submitted the take down request."[55] That contact must include two items: a copy of the subscriber's counter notification or challenge and a statement that the service provider will "replace the removed material or cease disabling access to it in 10 business days."[56] There is that ominous obligation again: "promptly." While no time limit is given, that contact must be made "promptly" as well. Given the short time (10 business days, i.e. restoration cannot occur before the tenth business day) within which restoration will occur, and the time it may take the copyright owner to respond, promptness might mean no more 1 or 2 business days, 3 at the most.

The next move is up to the copyright owner. Oddly enough, the statement need not include a list of options for the copyright owner, but the statute anticipates one of two options: do nothing and allow the restoration to occur, or file a second notice (a counter notice to the subscriber's counter notice) to preserve the effect of the initial notice, i.e., the removal of material or the disabling of access to it.

If the copyright owner or his or her agent, the person sending the section 512(c)(1)(C) notice to the service provider in the first instance, sends a second or counter-counter notice to the service provider, that "such person [i.e., 'the person who submitted the notification under subsection (c)(1)(C)'] has filed an action seeking a court order to restrain the subscriber from engaging in infringing activity relating to the material on the service provider's system or network,"[57] and then the subscriber does not proceed with restoration. In other words, if the copyright owner is serious about enforcing the copyright associated with the infringing material, and that seriousness is demonstrated by the commencement of legal proceedings seeking a restraining order against the subscriber, the owner can prevent restoration from occurring.

Determining the Timing and Restoration of the Material at Issue

If such second notice is not forthcoming from the copyright owner or agent of the copyright owner, then the service provider must "replace[] the removed material and cease[] disabling access to it not less than 10, nor more than 14, business days following receipt of the counter notice [the notice of challenge from a subscriber]."[58] Because the notification that the service provider sends to the copyright owner under section 512(g)(2)(B) must include a statement that restoration will occur within 10 business days ("informs that person that it will replace the removed material or cease disabling access to it in 10 business days"), and under section 512(g)(2)(C) that restoration will in fact occur "not less than 10, nor more than 14 business days following receipt of the counter notice," the copyright owner has little time to respond. In other words, unless the copyright owner files a second notice indicating the commencement of legal proceedings within the 10th business day, the service provider has, in fact, an affirmative duty under section 512(g)(2)(C) to replace the material or restore access to it with the 10–14 day window.

Notice that the copyright owner does **not** have ten business days from receipt of the documents from the service provider (copy of counter notice and statement of restoration time limit) in which to send a second notice to the service provider that legal proceedings have begun. Nor, in a far more likely scenario, does the copyright owner have ten business days to commence those proceedings and then relay that fact to the service provider in an attempt to stop the restoration from occurring. Rather the days are marked from day that the service provider received the *counter notification from the subscriber.*

Consider a scenario where the service provider receives a counter notification under section 512(g)(3), waits 9 business days, then contacts the copyright owner—on the 3rd business day—and informs the copyright owner of the impending restoration. Of course the service provider could wait until the maximum 14th business day, giving the copyright owner an additional 4 business days in which to prepare legal documentation and commence proceedings ("filed an action seeking a court order to restrain the subscriber from engaging in infringing activity relating to the material on the service provider's system or network"). In all fairness to potential copyright plaintiffs, this is not a very generous amount of time by which the courthouse gate must be entered!

Moreover, a delay such this by the service provider would not appear to be a prompt contact. In those instances where copyright owner contact did not occur on the same business day or within a business day, perhaps waiting until the last possible moment (i.e., the 14th business day from receipt of the subscriber's counter notice), before restoring the material or access to it, would not appear prudent.

If the service provider restores the material according to the sequence of section 512(g)(2), then section 512(g)(4) indicates that there should be no liability for restoration either: "A service provider's compliance with paragraph (2) shall not subject the service provider to liability for copyright infringement with respect to the material identified in the notice provided under subsection (c)(1)(C)."[59] The legislative history reiterates this position: "New subsection (f)(4) is included to make clear the obvious proposition that a service provider's compliance with the put-back procedure does not subject it to liability for copyright infringement or cause it to lose its liability limitation with respect to the replaced material."[60]

REAL-WORLD EXAMPLES

▶ Real-World Example I

Situation: The professor, in a situation from a previous chapter, reviews the list of Web resources related to teaching compiled by her school media certification students and cuts and pastes selected links from the student pages onto her own resource homepage. Many of the sites of teaching materials (textbooks, workbooks, exercises, and tests) contain directory references with such words as "bootleg" or "pirate." The list of resources is related to research and teaching at an institution of higher education, but not related to any specific course. The faculty member suspects that the linked sites contain pirated (infringing), material but because they contain such great information the links are nonetheless included and activated.

Legal Analysis: While the "function" of the activity falls within the "information location tools" of section 512(d), the infringing activity of employees are generally not covered by the safe harbor rules. However, section 512(e)(1) states that "for the purposes of subsections (c) and (d) such faculty member's or graduate student's knowledge or awareness of his or her infringing activities shall not be attributed to the institution." In other words, the knowledge or awareness of the infringing nature of the linked site will not trigger the section 512(d)(1)(A)–(C) provisos (knowledge, awareness, financial benefit) from excluding the conduct from the section 512(d) safe harbor. However, the university would also need to meet the three requirements of section 512(e)(1)(A)–(C): does not include access to online instructional material, does not run afoul of the 3–2 "full count," clean hands rule, i.e., that it received within the past three years no more than two notifications of infringement regarding the faculty member and has an informational compliance program in place that "provides to all users of its system or network informational materials that accurately describe, and promote compliance with, the laws of the United States relating to copyright."

▶ Real-World Example II

Situation: A public library meets all the conditions for securing the protection of the Section 512 safe harbor. Its registered agent eagerly awaits notification from copyright owners! The registered agent receives such a notice that material posted by a patron on the library's Web site is infringing. The notice appears in proper form. It removes the material but does nothing more. The person who posted the material on the library Web site sues the public library, claiming defamation of character as the patron would never violate the copyright law by posting infringing information.

Legal Analysis: Because the registered agent, or anyone else representing the service provider, failed to initiate the procedure of subscriber notice and opportunity for challenge under section 512(g)(2)(A)–(C), it cannot claim immunity from the patron for third-party claims arising from a good-faith takedown provided by section 512(g)(1). Under section 512(g)(2)(A), the service provider must first make a reasonable attempt to promptly notify the patron that his or her post was removed or disabled.

If the service provider makes this notice, then the patron would have an opportunity to offer a counter notice under section 512(g)(2)(B). The counter notice must conform to the requirements of section 512(g)(3)(A)–(D). If the registered agent of the library received a conforming counter notice, then under section 512(g)(2) it must promptly notify the copyright owner from whom it received the initial notice prompting the removal or disabling of the patron's post, including a copy of the subscriber patron's counter notice. The library must repost the material or reactivate access to it between 10 and 14 business days after receipt of the patron's counter notice—unless the public library receives a second notice from the copyright owner, indicating that the copyright owner has "filed an action seeking a court order to restrain the subscriber from engaging in infringing activity relating to the material on the service provider's system or network."[61]

▶ Real-World Example III

Situation: A large urban public library system maintains in its collection a CD-ROM of newspaper cartoon images from pre–World War I editions. Assume that the CD-ROM is governed by a license agreement prohibiting public display of any images. The public library creates a counting and ABC Web site for its Summer Reading Program Web site that uses some of the cartoon images. The copyright owner sends a cease and desist order, insisting that public display of the images on the library Web site is prohibited by copyright law. The library overreacts and cancels its Summer Reading Program!

Legal Analysis: Under *Online Policy Group v. Diebold, Inc.*, it could be argued that the use of the cease and desist letter meets the standard of section 512(f), i.e., that the copyright owner "knowingly materially misrepresents" that the material was infringing. While use of the images may nonetheless be prohibited under contract law (the license agreement), that prohibition does not rest in the copyright law as required by section 512 but in contract law, as works published before 1923 are in the public domain under the laws governing the duration of copyrights. The *Diebold* court concluded: "Accordingly, there is no genuine issue of material fact that Diebold, through its use of the DMCA, sought to and did in fact suppress publication of content that is not subject to copyright protection."[62] As a result, the library may be able to recover for any "damages, including costs and attorneys' fees . . . as a result of the service provider relying upon such misrepresentation in removing or disabling access to the material or activity claimed to be infringing." Of course, placing and proving a dollar value on the sequence of events might difficult (i.e., loss of good will for offering no reading program); however the library might have such evidence of it, after removal, reordered all of its print materials sans reference to the infringing material. This cost would arguably be recoverable.

KEY POINTS FOR YOUR INSTITUTION'S POLICY AND PRACTICE

▶ Section 512(e) offers additional benefit to public or nonprofit institutions of higher education. The institution is allowed to treat faculty and graduate students (when employed by the institution and performing teaching or research functions) as third parties (and not as employees) with respect to the conduit and cache provisions. For purposes of the post and link provisions, the knowledge of qualifying employees of their infringing conduct need not be imputed to the institution. See pp. 231–234.

▶ Section 512(e) does not apply to other duties of faculty or graduate students, such as administration. The statute does not shield the institution from liability for the infringing activity of teaching and research faculty and graduate students undertaken in conjunction with online education offered by such faculty members or students within the last three years. See pp. 234–235.

▶ There are several other requirements before section 512(e) can apply: there can be no more than two subsection (c)(3) statutory notices of infringement within a three-year period concerning the infringing conduct of that same faculty member. Recall this requirement by thinking of it as a 2-3 or full-count rule. See pp. 236–238.

▶ Finally, the statute requires that "the institution provide[] to all users of its system or network informational materials that accurately describe, and promote compliance with the laws of the United States relating to copyright." See pp. 238–239.

▶ Under section 512(f), any party may seek monetary remedy from misrepresentations that are material and made knowingly: the copyright owner, because the subscriber patron or student falsely claimed the use was not infringing; the service provider, because it believed an initial infringer made a bogus claim of authorized use; or the alleged initial infringer, because his or her material was removed by a service provider in response to a false claim of infringement by the copyright owner. See pp. 240–241.

▶ Some copyright owners may abuse the additional enforcement tools, such as the subpoena power. Supported by recent case law, a service provider such as a university may use the statute to recover damages from disingenuous copyright owners that make material and false representations. As a result, libraries, schools, colleges, and universities should not be intimidated by the receipt of communications such as notices or subpoenas, should evaluate the information and proceed appropriately. See pp. 241–244.

▶ The statute also provides a safe harbor for damages based on harms not arising from copyright, e.g., from disgruntled users whose access is disabled or whose posted material is removed, or from persons who made the material available initially and have since learned that the service provider is blocking access to it through its network or from its facilities. See pp. 244–245.

▶ To obtain this additional safe harbor, several steps must be followed. The service provider must contact the subscriber patron or student and offer the subscriber a chance to challenge. The statute dictates the contents of the challenge. See pp. 245–247.

▶ Upon receipt of a proper challenge, the service provider must contact the copyright owner from whom it received the initial notice, informing the copyright owner that it will replace the material or restore access in 10 business days unless the copyright owner "has filed an action seeking a court order to restrain the subscriber from engaging in infringing activity relating to the material on the service provider's system or network." If such second notice is not forthcoming from the copyright owner or agent of the copyright owner, then the service provider must "replace[] the removed material and cease[] disabling access to it not less than 10, nor more than 14, business days following receipt of the counter notice." See pp. 247–252.

ENDNOTES

[1] H.R. Rep. No. 105-796, 105th Cong., 2d Sess. 74 (1998) (conf. Rep.).

[2] In criminal law *mens rea*, literally guilty mind, is "The state of mind that the prosecution, to secure a conviction, must prove that a defendant had when committing a crime." BLACK'S LAW DICTIONARY 1006 (8th ed. 2004).

[3] H.R. Rep. No. 105-796, 105th Cong., 2d Sess. 74 (1998) (conf. Rep.) ("This special consideration is embodied in new subsection (e), which provides special rules for determining whether the college or university, in its capacity as a service provider, may or may not be liable for acts of copyright infringement by faculty members or graduate students in certain circumstances").

[4] Peer-to-Peer Piracy on University Campuses, Hearing, Subcommittee on Courts, the Internet, and Intellectual Property, Committee on the Judiciary, U.S. House of Representatives, 108th Congress, 1st Sess., February 26, 2003 ("It [prototype network traffic monitoring tool] monitored the activity of 54 users of only P2P network, Gnutella network, during the university's summer break. The results of the research showed that 89% of the files transferred to and from the university's network were infringing. Furthermore, those 54 monitored users uploaded 4,614 files."), at p. 106. In addition, more than 75 percent of the transferred data was from university users to individuals located outside of the university network, which shows that there is a growing trend toward outside pirates using university resources to download files. (Prepared Statement of Representative Goodlatte, submitted into the record.) (available at *www://commdocs.house.gov/committees/judiciary/hju 85286.000/hju85286_0.htm*).

[5] House (Conference) Report 105-796, 105th Cong., 2d Sess. 74 (1998).

[6] Jay Dratler Jr., Cyberlaw: Intellectual Property in the Digital Millennium § 6.06, at 6-139 (2004) ("A corollary of that premise is that nonprofit educational institutions should have diminished responsibility for copyright infringement on the part of their faculty and graduate students whom, due to laws and tradition of academic freedom and independence or (in the case of students) the lack of an employment relationship, they have no power to control." (Footnote omitted.)).

[7] H.R. Rep. No. 105-796, 105th Cong., 2d Sess. 74 (1998) (conf. Rep.).

[8] Oddly enough, the most closely aligned vicarious liability concept embodied in section 512 is expressed through the language of subsections 512(c)(1)(B) and (d)(2), i.e., the "does not receive a financial benefit directly attributable to the infringing activity, in a case in which the service provider has the right and ability to control such activity" language, not in subsections 512(a) and (b). In other words, the precise vicarious-related qualifying burden (no financial benefit with right and ability to control) that section 512(c) and (d) impose and that section 512(e) would relax appears somewhat mismatched.

[9] JAY DRATLER JR., CYBERLAW: INTELLECTUAL PROPERTY IN THE DIGITAL MIL-LENNIUM §6.06, at 6-142 (2004).

[10] JAY DRATLER JR., CYBERLAW: INTELLECTUAL PROPERTY IN THE DIGITAL MIL-LENNIUM §6.06, at 6-142 (2004).

[11] H.R. Rep. No. 105-796, 105th Cong., 2d Sess. 74 (1998) (conf. Rep.) ("When the faculty member or graduate student employee is performing a function other than teaching or research, this subsection provides no protection against liability for the institution if infringement occurs.").

[12] H.R. Rep. No. 105-796, 105th Cong., 2d Sess. 74 (1998) (conf. Rep.).

[13] H.R. Rep. No. 105-796, 105th Cong., 2d Sess. 74 (1998) (conf. Rep.).

[14] H.R. Rep. No. 105-796, 105th Cong., 2d Sess. 75 (1998) (conf. Rep.) ("The phrase 'required or recommended' is intended to refer to instructional materials that have been formally and specifically identified in a list of course materials that is provided to all students enrolled in the course for credit.").

[15] H.R. Rep. No. 105-796, 105th Cong., 2d Sess. 75 (1998) (conf. Rep.).

[16] 17 U.S.C. § 512(f).

[17] H.R. Rep. No. 105-796, 105th Cong., 2d Sess. 75 (1998) (conf. Rep.).

[18] Section 512(c)(3)(A)(v) imposes the following requirement within its notice provisions: "A statement that the complaining party has a good faith belief that use of the material in the manner complained of is not authorized by the copyright owner, its agent or the law."

[19] H.R. Rep. No. 105-796, 105th Cong., 2d Sess. 75 (1998)(conf. Rep.).

[20] JAY DRATLER JR., CYBERLAW: INTELLECTUAL PROPERTY IN THE DIGITAL MIL-LENNIUM §6.06, at 6-146–6-147 (2004). Professor Dratler does not articulate what this structural relief might be, but, in keeping with the spirit of section 512(e), it might include specific evidence of remedy; short of having the faculty or graduate student write 'I must not infringe copyright' 1,000 times, it might include a more practical solution of having the faculty member or graduate student responsible for an infraction demonstrate knowledge of the law through attendance at seminars or similar remedial sessions, followed by the successful completion of a brief test of copyright proficiency.

[21] JAY DRATLER JR., CYBERLAW: INTELLECTUAL PROPERTY IN THE DIGITAL MIL-LENNIUM § 6.06, at 6-146 (2004).

[22] 17 U.S.C. § 512(f).

[23] BLACK'S LAW DICTIONARY 998 (8th ed. 2004) (Defines *material* as "[o]f such a nature that knowledge of the item would affect a person's decision-making; significant; essential.").

[24] H.R. Rep. No. 551 (Part 2), 105th Cong., 2d Sess. 59 (1998); S. Rep. No. 105-190, 105th Cong., 2d Sess. 49 (1998) (emphasis added).

[25] 17 U.S.C. § 512(f).

[26] *Online Policy Group v. Diebold, Inc.*, 337 F. Supp. 2d 1195, 1197 (N.D. Calif. 2004).

[27] *Online Policy Group v. Diebold, Inc.*, 337 F. Supp. 2d 1195, 1198 (N.D. Calif. 2004).

[28] *Online Policy Group v. Diebold, Inc.*, 337 F. Supp. 2d 1195, 1202 (N.D. Calif. 2004).

[29] *Online Policy Group v. Diebold, Inc.*, 337 F.Supp.2d 1195, 1202 (N.D. Calif. 2004) (footnote omitted).

[30] BLACK'S LAW DICTIONARY 1369 (8th ed. 2004) (States that a *sanction* is a "penalty or coercive measure that results from failure to comply with a law, rule, or order.").

[31] JOHN W. HAZARD, JR. COPYRIGHT LAW IN BUSINESS AND PRACTICE § 9:8, at 9-11 (2002) ("A likelihood of success on the merits of a claim means that a plaintiff is likely to prevail at trial on the most important elements of an infringement case, be they the basic elements of copyrightability or the more complex elements of substantial similarity.").

[32] *Online Policy Group v. Diebold, Inc.*, 337 F. Supp. 2d 1195, 1204 (N.D. Calif. 2004) ("A party is liable if it 'knowingly' and 'materially' misrepresents that copyright infringement has occurred. 'Knowingly' means that a party actually knew, should have known if it acted with reasonable care or diligence, or would have had no substantial doubt had it been acting in good faith, that it was making misrepresentations. *See* Black's Law Dictionary, [888] (8th ed. 2004) (definitions of 'knowledge,' in particular, 'actual' and 'constructive' knowledge). 'Material' means that the misrepresentation affected the ISP's response to a DMCA letter. *See id.*").

[33] *Online Policy Group v. Diebold, Inc.*, 337 F. Supp. 2d 1195, 1204 (N.D. Calif. 2004).

[34] *Online Policy Group v. Diebold, Inc.*, 337 F. Supp. 2d 1195, 1204-1205 (N.D. Calif. 2004).

[35] *Online Policy Group v. Diebold, Inc.*, 337 F. Supp. 2d 1195, 1203 (N.D. Calif. 2004).

[36] *Online Policy Group v. Diebold, Inc.*, 337 F. Supp. 2d 1195, 1203 (N.D. Calif. 2004).

[37] *Online Policy Group v. Diebold, Inc.*, 337 F. Supp. 2d 1195, 1203 (N.D. Calif. 2004).

[38] *Online Policy Group v. Diebold, Inc.*, 337 F. Supp. 2d 1195, 1203 (N.D. Calif. 2004).

[39] *Online Policy Group v. Diebold, Inc.*, 337 F. Supp. 2d 1195, 1203 (N.D. Calif. 2004).

[40] As recent commentators have indicated: "One of the riskiest forms of gambling is attempting to predict the future course of law from a single court decision." R. Thomas Cane and Sheila Sullivan, The Future of the Economic Loss Doctrine in Wisconsin, WISCONSIN LAWYER, May, 2005, a12,13.

[41] 17 U.S.C. § 512(g)(1).

[42] H.R. Rep. No. 551 (Part 2), 105th Cong., 2d Sess. 59 (1998); S. Rep. No. 105-190, 105th Cong., 2d Sess. 50 (1998).

[43] H.R. Rep. No. 551 (Part 2), 105th Cong., 2d Sess. 59 (1998); S. Rep. No. 105-190, 105th Cong., 2d Sess. 49-50 (1998) ("Subsection (f) [enacted as (g)] provides immunity to service providers for taking down infringing material, and establishes a 'put back' procedure under which subscribers may contest a complaining party's notification of infringement provided under new subsection (c)(3). The put-back procedures were added as an amendment to this title in order to address the concerns of several members of the Committee that other provisions of this title established strong incentives for service providers to take down material, but insufficient protections for third parties whose material would be taken down.").

[44] 17 U.S.C. § 512(g)(2).

[45] H.R. Rep. No. 551 (Part 2), 105th Cong., 2d Sess. 59 (1998); S. Rep. No. 105-190, 105th Cong., 2d Sess. 49-50 (1998) (emphasis added) ("Subsection (f) [enacted as (g)] provides immunity to service providers for *taking down* infringing material, and establishes a 'put back' procedure. . . . The put-back procedures were added as . . . other provisions of this title established strong incentives for service providers to *take down* material, but insufficient protections for third parties whose material would be *taken down*.").

[46] H.R. Rep. No. 551 (Part 2), 105th Cong., 2d Sess. 59 (1998); S. Rep. No. 105-190, 105th Cong., 2d Sess. 50 (1998).

[47] H.R. Rep. No. 551 (Part 2), 105th Cong., 2d Sess. 59-60 (1998); S. Rep. No. 105-190, 105th Cong., 2d Sess. 50 (1998).

[48] JAY DRATLER JR., CYBERLAW: INTELLECTUAL PROPERTY IN THE DIGITAL MILLENNIUM § 6.03[2], at 6-86, n. 311 (2004).

[49] 17 U.S.C. § 512(g)(3) ("To be effective under this subsection, a counter notification must be a written communication provided to the service provider's designated agent that includes *substantially* the following:") (emphasis added).

[50] H.R. Rep. No. 551 (Part 2), 105th Cong., 2d Sess. 60 (1998); S. Rep. No. 105-190, 105th Cong., 2d Sess. 50 (1998).

[51] 17 U.S.C. § 512(g)(3)(A)–(D).

[52] H.R. Rep. No. 551 (Part 2), 105th Cong., 2d Sess. 60 (1998); S. Rep. No. 105-190, 105th Cong., 2d Sess. 51 (1998) (emphasis added).

[53] H.R. Rep. No. 551 (Part 2), 105th Cong., 2d Sess. 56 (1998); S. Rep. No. 105-190, 105th Cong., 2d Sess. 47 (1998).

[54] JAY DRATLER JR., CYBERLAW: INTELLECTUAL PROPERTY IN THE DIGITAL MILLENNIUM § 6.03[2], n. 312, 6-86, 6-87, (2004).

[55] H.R. Rep. No. 551 (Part 2), 105th Cong., 2d Sess. 60 (1998); S. Rep. No. 105-190, 105th Cong., 2d Sess. 50 (1998).

[56] 17 U.S.C. § 512(g)(2)(B).

[57] 17 U.S.C. § 512(g)(2)(C).

[58] 17 U.S.C. § 512(g)(2)(C). H.R. Rep. No. 551 (Part 2), 105th Cong., 2d Sess. 60 (1998); S. Rep. No. 105-190, 105th Cong., 2d Sess. 50-51 (1998) ("And third, under new subsection (f)(2)(C) [enacted as (g)(2)(C)], the service provider is to place the subscriber's material back on-line, or cease disabling access to it, between 10 and 14 business days after receiving the counter notification, unless the designated agent receives a further notice from the complaining party that the complaining party has filed an action seeking a court order to restrain the subscriber from engaging in the infringing activity on the service provider's system or network with regard to the material in question.").

[59] 17 U.S.C. § 512(g)(4).

[60] H.R. Rep. No. 551 (Part 2), 105th Cong., 2d Sess. 60 (1998); S. Rep. No. 105-190, 105th Cong., 2d Sess. 51 (1998).

[61] 17 U.S.C. § 512(g)(2)(C).

[62] *Online Policy Group v. Diebold, Inc.*, 337 F. Supp. 2d 1195, 1207 (N.D. Calif. 2004).

►Appendix to Chapter 8

LIABILITY LIMITATION TABLE FOR ONLINE MATERIALS

After considering the many responsibilities service providers now have under section 512 and the expanded rights of copyright owners to engage service providers in those responsibilities, an institution such as a public library or educational entity may come to the conclusion that the security of the safe harbor is not worth the increased cost of compliance with section 512. This increased cost of course requires an understanding the law forming the basis of those responsibilities. Table 1 provides a summary of section 512, and provides a summary of main points to help the reader become familiar with the section 512 mechanisms.

►TABLE 1. Limitations on Liability Relating to Material Online: 17 U.S.C. § 512

Function	Conduit (store and forward)	System Caching	Posting (user storage)	Linking (information location tools)	Takedown
Statutory Authority	*17 U.S.C. § 512(a)*	*17 U.S.C. § 512(b)*	*17 U.S.C. § 512(c)*	*17 U.S.C. § 512(d)*	*17 U.S.C. § 512(g)**
Immunity	Monetary relief: "damages, costs attorneys' fees." § 512(k)(2).	Same.	Same.	Same.	No liability: "good faith disabling of access or removal of material or activity claimed to be infringing." § 512(g)(1).
	Injunctive relief: limited to that provided in § 512(j).	Same.	Same.	Same.	
Relief Service provider must receive notice of order and "opportunity to appear" except for "preservation of evidence" or other orders not affecting operation. § 512(j)(3).	Injunctive relief limited to a restraining order from providing access, i.e., a termination order, and blocking order: "to a specified, identified, online location outside the United States." § 512(j)(B)(i) and (ii).	Injunctive relief limited to: (1) restraining order from providing access, (2) termination order, (3), "injunctive relief as the court may consider necessary to prevent or restrain." § 512(j)(A)(i), (ii) and (iii).	Same.	Same.	None.

(Continued)

▶**TABLE 1.** Limitations on Liability Relating to Material Online: 17 U.S.C. § 512 *(Continued)*

Function	Conduit (store and forward)	System Caching	Posting (user storage)	Linking (information location tools)	Takedown
Statutory Authority	*17 U.S.C. § 512(a)*	*17 U.S.C. § 512(b)*	*17 U.S.C. § 512(c)*	*17 U.S.C. § 512(d)*	*17 U.S.C. § 512(g)**
Nature of Action	Transmission at initiation or direction of third party. Automatic technical process. No selection of recipients. Copy of material subject to access and time limits. No modification of material. § 512(a)(1)-(5).	Material available by third party. Transmission from one third party to another. Automatic technical process: "users of the system or network."** § 512(b)(1)(A)-(C).	"Examples of such storage include providing server space for user's Web site, for a chatroom, or other forum in which material may be posted at the direction of users." H.R. Rep. No 551 (Part 2), at p. 53; S. Rep. No. 105-190, at p. 43.	"The term . . . includes a directory or index of on-line sites or material, such as a search engine that identifies pages by specific criteria; a reference to other on-line material, such as a list of recommended sites; a pointer that stands for an Internet location or address; and a hypertext link which allows users to access material without entering its address. H.R. Rep. No 551 (Part 2), at p. 56-57; S. Rep. No. 105-190, p. 47.	No liability for removal or disabling if reasonable steps to promptly contact subscriber. § 512(g)(2)(A). Subscriber option to offer a counter notice. Notice must conform to § 512(g)(3) (A)-(D): (A) signature, (B) identification of material, (C) statement of good-faith subject to perjury, and (D) contact data and consent to jurisdiction.
Service Provider	Conduit: "offering transmission, routing, or providing connections for digital online communications . . . without modification." § 512(k)(1)(A).	Same as (c).	Conduit, plus: "provider of online services or network access, or the operator of facilities. therefor [sic]." Includes § 512(k)(1)(A) entity. § 512(k)(1)(B).	Same as (c).	Once in receipt of counter notice, service provider must contact sender of initial (c)(1)(C) notice, and offer opportunity to send second notice: sender has filed restraining order against subscriber. § 512(g)(2)(C).

(Continued)

▶**TABLE 1.** Limitations on Liability Relating to Material Online: 17 U.S.C. § 512 *(Continued)*

Function	Conduit (store and forward)	System Caching	Posting (user storage)	Linking (information location tools)	Takedown
Statutory Authority	*17 U.S.C. § 512(a)*	*17 U.S.C. § 512(b)*	*17 U.S.C. § 512(c)*	*17 U.S.C. § 512(d)*	*17 U.S.C. § 512(g)**
General Compliance Requirements	Adopt, reasonably implement a repeat infringer policy: "termination in appropriate circumstances." Accommodates and does not interfere with standard technical measures. § 512(i)(A) and (B).	Same.	Same.	Same.	If second notice not forthcoming, then service provider restores within 10 to 14 business days after receipt of counter notice. § 512(g)(2)(C).
Registered Agent (notice and takedown or disable) Name, address, phone number, and electronic mail address, and other information designated by the Register of Copyrights. § 512(c)(2) (A) and (B). 37 C.F.R. § 201.38 ($30 filing fee, must file notice of change or termination). Registry available at *www.loc.gov. copyright.*	Not Required.	Not required, but recommended. Dratler, 2004, § 6.01, at 6-13. Notice received per (c)(3): expeditiously remove or disable. § 512(b)(2)(E). Removal or disabling of original source material or court order to effect and and statement of same § 512(b)(2)(E) (i) and (ii).	Required. § 512(c)(2). Same. § 512(c)(1)(C). Also receives counter notifications from subscriber under § 512(g)(3)*** and counter-counter notifications from copyright owner under § 512(g)(2)(C).	Not required, but recommended. Dratler, 2004, § 6.01, at 6-13. Same. § 512(d)(3).	Knowingly material misrepresentations subject to damages: material or activity is infringing per (c)(1)(C), or removed or disabled in error per (g)(2) and (3). § 512(f)(1) and (2).
Elements of Notice		Same.	Notice must include "substantially": (i) Physical or e-signature.	Same.	

(Continued)

▶**TABLE 1.** Limitations on Liability Relating to Material Online: 17 U.S.C. § 512 *(Continued)*

Function	Conduit (store and forward)	System Caching	Posting (user storage)	Linking (information location tools)	Takedown
Statutory Authority	*17 U.S.C. § 512(a)*	*17 U.S.C. § 512(b)*	*17 U.S.C. § 512(c)*	*17 U.S.C. § 512(d)*	*17 U.S.C. § 512(g)**
Failed notice does not trigger the knowledge of awareness standard of (c)(1)(A). If three elements (marked ▶ at right) are substantially complied with, then the notice can trigger (c)(1)(A), unless the service provider "promptly attempts to contact" the person making the notice or ("other easonable steps to assist") in perfecting the notice. § 512(c)(3)(B) (i) and (ii).			▶ (ii) Identification of work infringed. ▶ (iii) identification of infringing material. ▶ (iv) Contact information: address, telephone number, e-mail. (v) Good faith belief. (vi) Verification of accuracy. § 512(c)(3)(A) (i)–(vi).		
Special Compliance Requirements			No knowledge or awareness. If so, expeditiously remove or disable. No financial benefit and right and ability to control. § 512(c)(1)(A)–(B).	No knowledge or awareness. If so expeditiously remove or disable. No financial benefit and right and ability to control. § 512(d)(1)–(2).	
Additional Compliance Requirements	********	Under section 512(h) a copyright owner may request a subpoena from a clerk of the federal court "for identification of an alleged infringer." "[T]he clerk *shall expeditiously* issue and sign the proposed subpoena and return it to the requester for delivery to the service provider." § 512(h)(4). All the copyright owner or its designated agent need do is file three documents: a copy of a notification described in subsection (c)(3)(A), a proposed subpoena, and a sworn declaration to the effect that the purpose for which the subpoena is sought is to obtain the identity of an alleged infringer and that such information will only be used for the purpose of protecting rights under this title. § 512(h)(2). "The subpoena shall authorize and order the service provider receiving the notification and the subpoena to *expeditiously disclose* to the copyright owner or person authorized by the copyright owner information sufficient to identify the alleged infringer of the material described in the notification to the extent such information is available to the service provider." § 512(h)(3).			

(Continued)

▶ **TABLE 1.**   **Limitations on Liability Relating to Material Online: 17 U.S.C. § 512** *(Continued)*

Function	Conduit (store and forward)	System Caching	Posting (user storage)	Linking (information location tools)	Takedown
Statutory Authority	*17 U.S.C. § 512(a)*	*17 U.S.C. § 512(b)*	*17 U.S.C. § 512(c)*	*17 U.S.C. § 512(d)*	*17 U.S.C. § 512(g)**
	****	The issuance of the section 512(h) subpoena is designed to be ministerial in nature. H.R. Rep. No 551 (Part 2), atp. (1998); Senate Report 105-190, atp. 51 (1998). The clerk must "expeditiously issue" the subpoena, and the service provider must "expeditiously disclose" the identity of the alleged infringer. This process is far less costly and potentially more expedient that a court-ordered subpoena under typical practices of the federal courts. However, this subpoena, like all subpoenas, may be challenged by a motion to quash.			
Additional Limitations on Liability	Section 512(e) provides additional limitation on liability for institutions of higher education: Section 512(e) allows the institution to treat faculty or teaching students as a third party for conduit and cache provisions, and the knowledge of the infringing faculty member or student shall not be imputed to the institution for the post and link provisions. Three requirements: the institution does not include access to online instructional material within the preceding three years, "full count" clean hands rule (within 3 years-no more than 2 incidents of notification under (c)(3)) regarding the same faculty member, and system-wide informational compliance programs that "accurately describe, and promote compliance with, the laws of the United States relating to copyright" must be in place. § 512(e)(1)(C).				

Notes:

* The immunity extended by § 512(g) (immunity for liability arising from an erroneous takedown) is not immunity for copyright liability, but for defamation or unfair trade or related offenses. In other words, one could not violate another's copyright by removing an infringing work from network display, but one could defame another by suggesting that a posting (the posting that was taken down) was of a dubious (infringing) nature. See, JAY DRATLER JR., CYBERLAW: INTELLECTUAL PROPERTY IN THE DIGITAL MILLENNIUM § 6.03[2][a][iii][C], at 6-88-6-90 (2004). ("Presumably a service provider's liability to its subscriber for a wrongful 'take down' would involve causes of action extraneous to copyright, such as breach of the subscription or account agreement, defamation (for publishing a false claim of copyright infringement), trade libel or disparagement (for similar reasons), or the like." Id. at 6-89.).

** "If this condition is interpreted narrowly as restricting the limitation on remedies to caching by a system or network for its own subscribers or account holders, it would throw a monkey wrench into the flexible and efficient operation of the Internet by discouraging caching in anticipation of requests for material by *other* subscribers—a common and useful practice. If, on the other hand, the phrase . . . covers anyone . . . then the condition is not much of a limitation. . . . The gross overdrafting of Section 512 in general, however, makes it far more reasonable to assume that Congress unintentionally included superfluous language in the statute than to conclude that Congress intended to exclude from its benefit a common practice that may indeed be the predominant caching practice on the Internet." JAY DRATLER JR., CYBERLAW: INTELLECTUAL PROPERTY IN THE DIGITAL MILLENNIUM § 6.03[1][a][i], at 6-46 (2004) (emphasis original and footnote omitted).

*** Counter notification from subscriber must substantially include the following: "(A) A physical or electronic signature of the subscriber. (B) Identification of the material that has been removed or to which access has been disabled and the location at which the material appeared before it was removed or access to it was disabled. (C) A statement under penalty of perjury that the subscriber has a good faith belief that the material was removed or disabled as a result of mistake or misidentification of the material to be removed or disabled. (D) The subscriber's name, address, and telephone number, and a statement that the subscriber consents to the jurisdiction of Federal District Court for the judicial district in which the address is located, or if the subscriber's address is outside of the United States, for any judicial district in which the service provider may be found, and that the subscriber will accept service of process from the person who provided notification under subsection (c)(1)(C) or an agent of such person. § 512(g)(3)(A)–(D).

**** The dissent in *In re Charter Communications, Inc.*, 2005 WL 15416 (8th Cir. 2005), argued for a broader reading of the statute, effecting its overall purpose: "Section 512(h) authorizes a copyright owner or its representative to request a subpoena to a service provider in order to identify infringers, and the statutory definition of 'service provider' in § 512(k) specifically includes conduit service providers such as Charter." "Although Charter contends that the subpoena power in the DMCA is limited by the function of the ISP, such a limitation is not to be found in a plain reading of the DMCA. . . . If Congress had wanted to limit the type of ISP subject to a statutory subpoena, it could have easily specified that in § 512(h), but it did not." (Murphy, J. dissenting). Two appellate decisions have rejected the use of the section 512(h) subpoena power against section 512(a) conduit providers. See, *In re Charter Communications, Inc.*, 2005 WL 15416 (8th Cir. 2005); and *In re Verizon Internet Services, Inc.*, 351 F.3d 1229 (D.C. Cir. 2003), cert. denied 125 S. Ct. 309 (2004).

►9

WHAT ABOUT TECHNOLOGICAL PROTECTIONS ON COPYRIGHT UNDER SECTION 1201?

Read this chapter to learn about copyright situations like:
► Whether a library can get in trouble if an employee creates and distributes a program to get around the password protections on a database or CD-ROM.
► Whether a library can be liable if an employee finds a way to circumvent technologies that prevent the reproduction of computer programs.
► Whether a nonprofit library can temporarily circumvent password protections to determine whether it should subscribe to a program or database.

A final set of civil liability limitations provisions is found in section 1203; these provisions relate to the remission of damages for violations of the anti-circumvention and anti-trafficking rules of section 1201. A related criminal immunity provision is also offered to nonprofit libraries, archives, educational institutions, and public broadcasting entities in section 1204. The section 1203 rules are important, as the anti-circumvention and anti-trafficking penalties imposed are in addition to any penalities awarded for copyright infringement. Having a separate damage remission provision to offset the additional liability these provisions create is consistent with the existing statutory liability mechanism of the copyright law and is, of course, welcome. This statutory relief is all the more welcome, as there is arguably expanded opportunity for plaintiffs within the anti-circumvention and anti-trafficking rules to pursue targets of opportunity in terms of economic recovery of damages. The plaintiff need not be a copyright owner to pursue remedy, merely one who suffered at the hands of those who unlawfully circumvent or traffic. Section 1203 states that "[a]ny person injured by a violation of section 1201 . . . *may bring a civil action* in an appropriate United States district court for such violation"[1]—not just the copyright owner is eligible, as is typical in an infringement suit, but also a third party, such as a person whose livelihood is impacted by the illegal circumvention or trafficking, i.e., a developer of technological protection measures whose products are made useless by unabashed hacking. Thus an actor not staking any copyright claim in the motion pictures in which he or she starred may still in theory have recourse under section 1203 against a Web site operator who maintains a complete pirated log of his or her film repertoire.

Under section 1203, an aggrieved plaintiff can obtain injunctive relief orders, both temporary and permanent, for impoundment or final "remedial modification or the destruction of any device or product involved in the violation," as well as for costs and attorney's fees.[2] Damages for a violation of the section 1201 rules are subject to election of actual or statutory damages by the complainant, in a process similar to that for copyright infringement litigation (election "any time before final judgment is entered"). Calculation of actual damages includes consideration of monetary loss to complainants as well as any "profits of the violator that are attributable to the violation and are not taken into account in computing the actual damages."[3] Likewise statutory damages are set by the court and range "in the sum of not less than $200.00 or more than $2,500.00 per act of circumvention, device, product, component, offer, or performance of service, as the court considers just."[4] Similar to the section 504 enhancement penalty for "willful" violations, section 1203 contains an enhancement for repeat violators. If the defendant is a repeat offender and the injury underlying the current litigation occurred "within 3 years after a final judgment was entered against the person for another such violation" the court may within its discretion use a numerical multiplier no greater than three, i.e., up to triple the damages, in determining the final damage award.[5] Similar to the section 504 enhancement, the injured party "sustains the burden of proving" the repeat violation. This tri-part mechanism of actual-statutory and enhancement is patterned after the "current Copyright Act."[6]

There are two damage remission provisions. As the focus in this chapter is on the damage remission or limitation provisions of the copyright law, a brief introduction to the section 1201 anti-circumvention and anti-trafficking rules is first presented. However, unlike section 512, the purpose of section 1201 is not to establish a safe harbor, but rather to articulate additional liability; thus section 1201 is discussed in far less detail here. In addition, there are numerous exceptions—some contained within the statute,[7] others established by federal regulation as part of a three-year rule-making cycle,[8] with the previous phase concluding in October of 2003.[9]

Unlike the damage remission provision of section 504 discussed earlier, section 1203 offers two circumstances of remission, one permissive ("the court in its discretion may reduce or remit the total award of damages in any case")[10] and the other mandatory ("the court shall remit damages in any case").[11] Fortunately, a qualifying nonprofit library, archives, educational institution, or public broadcasting entity is also subject to the mandatory provision. For other defendants, permissive remission may entail a damage reduction instead of complete remission; the court can within its discretion do either. In either case—general defendants (permissive and variable damage remission) under section 1203(c)(5)(A)[12] or a nonprofit library, archives, educational institution, or public broadcasting defendant (mandatory and complete damage remission) under section 1203(c)(5)(B)(ii)[13]— the court can only remit when the defendant "sustains the burden of proving, and the court finds" that the defendant was "not aware and had no reason to believe that its acts constituted a violation." The defendant would have the burden of demonstrating that it did not have the knowledge of the violation or did not have any reason to suspect that a violation was occurring.

Though not explicit in the statute, the use of a warning notice by the copyright owner that circumventing or trafficking is unlawful would likely preclude a defendant from claiming that it was "not aware and had no reason to believe that its acts constituted a violation." For example, consider a password-protected Web site with the following notice on its home page: "Warning. This site protected by technological measures. Authorized users only. This site contains copyrighted material. Unauthorized access through illicit means is a violation of section 1201(a)(1), title 17, United States Code" or words to that effect. Since most acts of circumvention or trafficking are willful, i.e., not by accident or mistake, copyright owners can secure an important advantage by the use of such awareness-enhancing measures: rendering most acts subject to possible criminal penalties and foreclosing either species of damage remission.

UNDERSTANDING THE ANTI-CIRCUMVENTION AND ANTI-TRAFFICKING RULES

Circumventing an access control that a copyright owner places on his or her work violates section 1201(a)(1). As discussed below, trafficking in the anti-circumvention access or use "device" is also a violation. But what is an access or use control? It might be something as simple as technology that prohibits viewers from fast-forwarding past advertisements on a DVD[14] or from playing the DVD on a PC or platform other than a DVD player.[15] It might be so-called technological handshake protocols[16] and geographic use restriction codes,[17] or even the authentication sequence that occurs between a printer and microchip contained on a toner cartridge.[18] These examples demonstrate the reach of the anti-circumvention and anti-trafficking rules and the controversy inherent in section 1201. "The act of circumventing a technological protection measure put in place by a copyright owner to control access to a copyrighted work is the electronic equivalent of breaking into a locked room in order to obtain a copy of a book."[19] The statute offers a definition of the act of "circumventing a technological measure": "[to] descramble a scrambled work, to decrypt an encrypted work, or otherwise to avoid, bypass, remove, deactivate, or impair a technological measure, without the authority of the copyright owner."[20] Of course the controversy of section 1201 is that although breaking and entering is illegal, reading is not. In other words, section 1201 can be used to prohibit access to an otherwise lawful activity! However, the debate over the appropriateness of the law must be left for another venue. The task here is to help the reader negotiate its waters.

Basics of When Circumvention and Trafficking Rules Apply

In order for any of the section 1201 rules to apply, the subject of the protection must be a work that is subject to copyright protection: "a work protected under this title" or "the right of a copyright owner under this title." Use of encryption technology to protect a reformatted version of a literary work (a novel) that is in the public domain and the act of circumventing the access control should not in theory be a violation of section 1201(a)(1)(A).[21] Thus if the underlying work is not the subject of copyright protection, then circumventing access to it, or trafficking in an access or use control related to it cannot by the plain language of the statute violate the section 1201 rules. This was the result in *Lexmark International, Inc. v. Static ControlComponents, Inc.*,[22] where the appellate court concluded that the patch of computer code limiting its printers to accepting only authorized toner cartridges was not protected by copyright.[23] As a result, the section 1201 rules did not prohibit the circumvention of the toner cartridge lock-out program: "To the extent these alternatives [different constants and equations used, some measure other than torque used to approximate toner level, same equations used in a different sequence] suggest any originality in the Toner Loading Program, at any rate, the quantum of originality may well be de minimis and accordingly insufficient to support the validity of the Lexmark's copyright in the work."[24]

For the section 1201(a)(1) rules to apply, the access control must be effective in preventing unauthorized access.[25] The control need not be perfect to meet this standard, but if it somehow "requires the application of information, or a process or a treatment"[26] it qualifies. In other words, just because circumvention is possible or even easy (e.g., the circumvention that can occur on some digital disks when a black permanent marker is run across its face) that does not preclude the access control from being a "technological measure that effectively controls access to" copyrighted material and from being subject to the anti-circumvention rule of section 1201(a)(1)(A). By the same token, Congress did not anticipate that attempts to remedy so-called "playability" problems should be viewed as an attempt at circumvention.[27]

The access control must be put in place by the copyright owner or with his or her authorization.[28] In other words, an educational institution or library that purchased an item from a retailer who placed such protection on the work without the approval of the copyright owner could circumvent the retailer's access control and not violate section 1201. In addition, the technological access control must not degrade, corrupt, or distort the work; if it does, section 1201 does not apply, as this is not an "effective" control.[29] In such cases, section 1201 does not make illegal the attempts by "a retailer or individual consumer to modify a product or device solely to the extent necessary to mitigate a noticeable adverse effect on the authorized performance or display of a work . . . if that adverse effect is caused by a technological protection measure on the ordinary course of its design and operation."[30] However, if degradation occurred because a consumer tried to circumvent an access control, then there is no right to make a further circumventing "clean up" of the copy, a sort of legal "you broke it, it's yours" philosophy. The sorts of "measures that can be deemed to 'effectively control access to a work' would be those based on encryption, scrambling, authentication, or some other measure which requires the use of a 'key' provided by a copyright owner to gain access to a work."[31] The copyright owner authorization requirement and degradation conditions apply to both the anti-circumvention (section 1201(a)(1)) and anti-trafficking (section 1201(a)(2)) access rules.

AVOIDING THE TRAFFICKING OF CIRCUMVENTION DEVICES

Section 1201(a)(2) prohibits trafficking in an anti-circumvention access control. If a person writes a piece of code that when combined with certain hardware allows access to the information contained in a DVD or CD-ROM, and then the person shares that code with others, the person violates section 1201(a)(2).[32] Trafficking is defined broadly in the statute: "No person shall manufacture, import, offer to the public, provide, or otherwise traffic in any technology, product, service, device, component, or part thereof."[33] This violation is true even if the DVD or CD-ROM was purchased from a legitimate source, i.e., it is a lawfully made copy, or if the eventual use one desires to make of the accessed work is a fair use or is authorized under any of the other provisions of the copyright law. This is because liability separate from copyright infringement exists under section 1201 for trafficking of a "device" that circumvents access.[34] It does not matter that the range of fair uses available to the nonprofit library, archive, or educational institution is more limited because of legally enforceable access controls that a copyright owner may place upon his or her works.

By the same token, the legislative history stresses that the trafficking provisions are "drafted carefully to target 'black boxes,' and to ensure that legitimate multipurpose devices can continue to be made and sold."[35] The Senate Report, rife with analogy offers the following:

> For example, if unauthorized access to a copyrighted work is effectively prevented through use of a password, it would be a violation of this section to defeat or bypass the password and to make the means to do so, as long as the primary purpose of the means was to perform this kind of act. This is roughly analogous to making it illegal to break into a house using a tool, the primary purpose of which is to break into houses.[36]

Working within the analogy, it is obvious that breaking into another's abode is illegal, but what if you used the device (a skeleton key) to break into your own home because you locked your keys inside by mistake? Should the provider of the passkey be liable in that case, should the homeowner be responsible for circumventing the lock on his own home (this is the equivalent of the circumvention of an access device, as opposed to a use device, and the trafficking of it)?

A better analogy that demonstrates the danger and reach of the section 1201 rules is offered by Lipinski and Rice.[37] Consider a parcel of public park that is surrounded by a private parcel on which the landowner erects a fence too high to jump over. A citizen would like to have a picnic in the park, but the only way to make use of the park is to trespass on the owner's property by cutting across the parcel, and perhaps by cutting a hole in the fence as well. In real property law, courts and legislators have responded to the inequities of such a situation and developed concepts of public easements and eminent domain, to allow some level of public access to the parkland. Unfortunately, section 1201 does just the opposite; it offers the landowner the right to foreclose all public easements and refuse any attempts at domain proceedings. Of course, section 1201 protects content that is subject to copyright protection, so the Lipinski and Rice analogy is strained, as the land behind the fence is public domain land whereas in section 1201 it is not. Only content protected by the copyright law is subject to the anti-circumvention and anti-trafficking rules. But what about content that has both protected and unprotected (public domain) elements in it? Going back to the Lipinski and Rice formulation, what if the orchard behind the fence indeed lay on private property, but a clause in the title document to the parcel stated that any apples the trees produce belong to the citizens of the local town. The only way folks could harvest the "public domain" fruit would be to trespass. This is the potential danger of the section 1201 rules and access-restricting use to which the rules can be put. Of course differences between real and intellectual property make such analogies less than perfect tools, but can nonetheless serve as an initial illustration of inquiry. Perhaps a better analogy is a time-share where Tomas and David have the first two weeks in June to access their Riviera villa. However, the owner has changed the locks and left the keys in an envelope marked "New Keys," visible on the front hall table. The window would have to be broken (damaging a property right) in order to reach the keys (circumventing the access control, the new lock) and make an authorized use of the property (Tomas and David's 14-day fair use of the property). Readers will of course think of others; no analogy is perfect!

A second anti-trafficking rule prohibits the trafficking of technologies that circumvent use controls of protected works. Section 1201(b) makes illegal the sale or distribution (trafficking) of a device that allows someone to use a copyrighted work in contravention of the protections placed by an owner: "No person shall manufacture, import, offer to the public, provide, or otherwise traffic in any technology, product, service, device, component, or part thereof."[38] Like the section 1201(a) anti-trafficking rule, this provision targets the manufacturers of so-called black box technologies that systematically remove use restrictions. "As previously stated in the discussion of Section 102(a)(2) [enacted as section 1201(a)(2)], the Committee believes it is very important to emphasize that Section 102(b)(1) [enacted as section 1201(b)(1)] is aimed fundamentally at outlawing so-called 'black boxes' that are expressly intended to facilitate circumvention of technological protection measures for purposes of gaining *access* to a work."[39] ("Access" is an odd choice of word, as section 1201(b)(1) targets trafficking in "devices" that circumvent use, not access.) The Senate Report explains the difference between the two anti-trafficking rules (access and use): "Although sections 1201(a)(2) and 1201(b) of the bill are worded similarly and employ similar tests, they are designed to protect two distinct rights and to target two distinct classes of devices. Subsection 1201(a)(2) is designed to protect access to a copyrighted work. Section 1201(b) is designed to protect the traditional copyrighted rights of the copyright owner."[40] The latter set of rights, use rights, is traditional to copyright owners: the exclusive rights of the copyright owner listed in section 106 (the right to reproduce, make public performance or display, distribute the work to the public, or make a derivative work.)

The most common use controls would be technological measures that control copying.[41] "Subsection (b) applies when a person has obtained authorized access to a copy of a phonorecord of a work, but the copyright owner has put in place technological measures that effectively protect his or her right under Title 17 to control or limit further use of the copyrighted work."[42] It is further odd that, as far as this author can perceive, a common use control on many DVDs that prevents fast-forwarding past coming attractions is not related to any exclusive right of the copyright owner listed in section 106. True enough, it relates to use of the work (the private performance of an audiovisual work in your home), but it does not relate to the reproduction, public display, public performance, or public distribution of the work or to any derivative right.

Identifying and Complying with Additional Trafficking Requirements

Both the section 1201(a)(2) and section 1201(b)(1) anti-trafficking provisions make it unlawful to manufacture, import, offer to the public, provide, or otherwise traffic in a technology, product, service, device, component, or part thereof, that

- ▶ is "primarily designed or produced for the purpose of circumventing protection afforded by a technological measure" (a primary purpose test), or
- ▶ has only a "limited commercially significant purpose or use other than to circumvent protection afforded by a technological protection measure" (secondary purpose test), or
- ▶ is "marketed . . . for use in circumventing protection afforded by a technological protection measure."[43]

Notice the disjunctive. Engaging in trafficking that falls under any of the three conditions violates the anti-trafficking rule. In addition, the "limited commercially significant purpose" test is a higher standard than previously established by courts for contributory infringement technologies under traditional theories of secondary copyright liability. In *Sony Corporation of America v. Universal Studios, Inc.*, the United States Supreme Court concluded that the Betamax machine (then the rival of the VHS VCR) was not an infringing technology as it was capable of substantial noninfringing uses.[44] Yet, under section 1201, trafficking is prohibited if it has only a limited commercially significant purpose. In other words, the technology may not be a contributory infringing technology under *Sony* because it has substantial noninfringing uses, but may be foreclosed under section 1201 because it presents only a limited commercially significant purpose.

According to the House Report: "This provision is not aimed at products that are capable of commercially significant noninfringing uses, such as consumer electronics, telecommunications, and computer products—including videocassette recorders, telecommunications switches, personal computers, and servers—used by business and consumers for perfectly legitimate purposes."[45] Suppose a person markets a product called the "Disk Wizard." The product's only advertised use is to allow purchasers to circumvent use controls and convert and play any CD-ROM, videodisc, or DVD audiovisual programs on a personal computer. Such conduct would violate the anti-trafficking rules of section 1201(b)(1),[46] even if the product never delivered on its promise, because, under the disjunctive of section 1201(a)(2)(A)–(C) or section 1201(b)(1)(A)–(C), all that is required under subproviso (C) is that it be marketed as such a technology.

The Absence of an Anti-Circumvention Use Rule

Notice that there is *no* parallel in section 1201(b) against circumventing use, only against trafficking in a device that would allow that circumventing use: "Unlike subsection (a), which prohibits the circumvention of access control technologies, subsection (b) does not, by itself, prohibit the circumvention of effective technological copyright protection measures."[47] The reason there is no circumventing rule governing uses is that the use might be a fair one under the copyright law.

In other words, you could circumvent a use control, but not the access control needed to use the protected work because section 1201(a)(1) only prohibits the latter action. You could circumvent a use control, but not traffic in the instrument of the use circumvention, i.e., pass it on to the next user, as this is prohibited by section 1201(b). Finally, you could not circumvent an access control (prohibited by section 1201(a)) nor could you traffic in the circumventing access control because section 1201(a)(2) prohibits this action. Once access is obtained, hack away at creating a use control or locate one that someone else has illegally made available, i.e., trafficked. Again, circumventing a use control is not prohibited under section 1201. Of course, the person who supplied the device can be sued for trafficking it! However, you could nevertheless be sued for copyright infringement if your use exceeds that of the fair use or some other provision of the law.

But why the misalignment here? Why is there no provision against circumventing a use control, but only against trafficking of such a "device" under section 1201(b)? "Unlike Section 1201(a), however, Congress did *not* ban the act of circumventing the use restrictions. . . . Congress did not prohibit the act of circumventing because it sought to preserve the fair use rights of persons who had lawfully acquired a work."[48] The legal rub is that copyright owners under section 1201(a)(1) can still control access, even if the work is lawfully acquired, i.e., your purchase of a book now comes with a lock and, like the voice-over on the commercial, says key "sold separately!" According to the legislative history, the concern was copy control measures not necessarily other circumvention of use devices, such as the ability to fast-forward past advertising: "The prohibition in section 1201(b) extends only to devices that circumvent copy control measures. The decision not to prohibit the conduct of circumventing copy controls was made, in part, because it would penalize some noninfringing conduct such as fair use."[49] Moreover, a fair user now needs to obtain, or more accurately create (read "hack"), the circumventing device by his or her own "devices." Courts have made similar observation: "Fair use of a copyrighted work continues to be permitted as does circumventing use restrictions for the purpose of engaging in a fair use, even though engaging in certain fair uses of digital works may be made more difficult if tools to circumvent use restrictions cannot be readily obtained."[50] Section 1201(b) thus turns those interested fair users into hackers. If everyone followed the anti-trafficking rules outlined in the statute, a circumvention device would be unobtainable, as trafficking or marketing it would be prohibited under section 1201. Hacking a use control is acceptable under section 1201, but hacking an access control remains prohibited. This distinction can be a rather fine line to tread. But what if one obtained such a circumventing (use) device from another? This would mean that it was made available as a result of a prohibited trafficking under section 1201. Could one nontheless make use of the trafficked, circumventing device to make a fair use of the content it protects? Or what if one did indeed create his or her own hack, a circumventing device, what fair uses of DVDs exist? Of course the assumption is that a lawful owner of a copy or phonorecord would have at his or her disposal all the fair "use" rights he or she might desire, but this is not case, or as some courts have pointed out the range of fair uses of small portions of DVD films is rather limited.[51]

Another practical result of the absence of anti-circumventing use prohibition in section 1201 might be to cause users of works governed by use controls to become hackers in their own right, and, armed with a new set of use-hacking skills, these users would also be more likely and able to unlawfully hack through the access control. Worse, they might be tempted to traffic in the fruits of these labors.The latter hack, of course, would be illegal under section 1201(a)(1), but the illegality of abusing copyrighted works has done little to impede such abuse in the past.[52] "So, an individual would not be able to circumvent in order to gain unauthorized access to a work, but would be able to do so in order to make fair use of a work which he or she has acquired lawfully."[53] Congress may have unwittingly unleashed a hacking hydra here. So, too, as a practical matter, the lack of an anti-circumvention use rule for individual readers is somewhat illusory. Distributors of unauthorized use codes will be sought out as traffickers: "[U]sers wishing to exercise their fair use rights and copy an encrypted digital work must do so without enlisting the help of others. By virtue of the fact that few consumers possess the necessary skills and willingness to write their own decryption software, fair use is an illusory right under the DMCA."[54] While section 1201 is lengthier than section 512, only an introduction to section 1201 is provided here. Table 1 can serve as a summary.

TABLE 1. The Anti-Circumvention Rule and Anti-Trafficking Rules: 17 U.S.C.Z. 1201

Operation	Anti-Circumvention	Anti-Trafficking	Anti-Trafficking
Section	17 U.S.C. § 1201(a)(1)	17 U.S.C. § 1201(a)(2)	17 U.S.C. § 1201(b)
Character of Control	Access	Access	Use
Prohibition	Prohibits circumvention of a "technological measure that effectively controls access" to a copyrighted work.	Prohibits distribution of technologies that circumvent access to a copyrighted work.	Prohibits distribution of technologies that circumvent use (exclusive rights) in a copyrighted work.
	Circumvention: "descramble a scrambled work, to decrypt an encrypted work, or otherwise to avoid, bypass, remove, deactivate, or impair echnological measure, without the authority of the copyright owner." § 1201(a)(3)(A).	Trafficking: "manufacture, import, offer to the public, provide, or otherwise a traffic in any technology, product, service, device, component, or part thereof." § 1201(a)(2).	Trafficking: same. § 1201(b)(1). Circumvention: same. § 1201(b)(2)(A).
Definition	▶ Effectively controls access to a work: "in the ordinary course of its operation, requires the application of information, or a process or a treatment, with the authority of the copyright owner, to gain access to the work." § 1201(a)(3)(B).	▶ Traffic (function): "[P]rimarily designed or produced for the purpose of circumventing a technological measure that effectively controls access," or has "limited commercially significant purpose or use other than	▶ Traffic (function): Same definition except "effectively protects a right of a copyright owner under this title" replaces "effectively controls access." § 1201(b)(1)(A)–(C).

(Continued)

TABLE 2.   The Anti-Circumvention Rule and Anti-Trafficking Rules: 17 U.S.C.Z. 1201 *(Continued)*

Operation	Anti-Circumvention	Anti-Trafficking	Anti-Trafficking
Section	*17 U.S.C. § 1201(a)(1)*	*17 U.S.C. § 1201(a)(2)*	*17 U.S.C. § 1201(b)*
	"[M]easures that cause noticeable and recurring adverse effects on the authorized display or performance of works should not be deemed to be effective." H.R. Rep. No. 551 (Part 2), atp. 40 (1998).	to circumvent," or "is marketed . . . for use in circumventing a technological measure that effectively controls access." § 1201(a)(2)(A)–(C).	Effectively protects a right of a copyright owner: "in the ordinary course of its operation, prevents, restricts or otherwise limits the exercise of a right of a copyright owner under this title. § 1201(b)(2)(B).

An access or use control "device" might be something as simple as technology that prohibits viewers from fast-forwarding past advertisements on a DVD,[55] from playing the DVD on a PC or platform other than a DVD player,[56] so-called technological handshake protocols,[57] and geographic use restriction codes.[58]

Nonprofit Library, Archives, or Educational Institution: 17 U.S.C. § 1201(d)

▶ Requirements:
- ▶ Limited retention rule, no "longer than necessary," § 1201(d)(1)(A);
- ▶ Sole purpose of circumvention rule, "access to a commercially exploited copyrighted work solely in order to make a good faith determination of whether to acquire a copy of that work," § 1201(d)(1); and
- ▶ Sole purpose of use rule, "good faith determination of whether to acquire," § 1201(d)(1)(B), see below.
- ▶ Under (d)(2), applies only when an "identical copy of that work is not reasonably available in another form."
- ▶ Institution cannot use exception to engage in acts prohibited by anti-trafficking rules of 17 U.S.C. § 1201(a)(2) or (b), i.e., no trafficking!
- ▶ Collections must be open to public or available to researchers (similar to 17 U.S.C. § 108(a)(2)).

Under section 1203(d)(3) a nonprofit library, archives, or educational institution that "willfully for the purpose of commercial advantage or financial gain violates" the section 1201(d)(1) requirements "shall, for the first offense, be subject to the civil remedies under section 1203," lose its right of remission, and under subsection (d)(3)(B) "shall, for repeated or subsequent offenses, in addition to the civil remedies under section 1203, forfeit the exemption provided under paragraph (1)."

Regulatory Exception Pursuant to 17 U.S.C. § 1201(a)(1)(D): 37 C.F.R. 201.40

▶ Four categories of works:
- ▶ "Compilations of lists of Internet locations blocked by commercially marketed filtering software applications that are intended to prevent access to domains, websites or portions of websites, but not including lists of Internet locations blocked by software applications that operate exclusively to protect against damage to a computer or computer network or lists of Internet locations blocked by software applications that operate exclusively to prevent receipt of e-mail."
- ▶ "Computer programs protected by dongles [i.e., electronic devices connected to a computer in order to run certain programs] that prevent access due to malfunctions or damage and which are obsolete."
- ▶ "Computer programs and video games distributed in formats that have become obsolete and which require the original media or hardware as a condition of access."
- ▶ "Literary works distributed in ebook format when all existing ebook editions of the work (including digital test editions made available by authorized entities) contain access controls that prevent the enabling of the ebook's read-aloud function and that prevent the enabling of screen readers to render the text into a 'specialized format.'" 68 Fed. Reg. 62011, 62014 (October 31, 2003), amending 37 C.F.R. § 201.40.

The third category may may be of benefit to digital libraries: "[T]he Register has concluded that to the extent that libraries and archives wish to make preservation copies of published software and video games that were distributed in formats that are obsolete (either because the physical medium on which they were distributed is no longer in use or because the use of an obsolete operating system is required), such activity is a noninfringing

(Continued)

TABLE 2.   The Anti-Circumvention Rule and Anti-Trafficking Rules of Section 1201 *(Continued)*

Operation	Anti-Circumvention	Anti-Trafficking	Anti-Trafficking
Section	*17 U.S.C. § 1201(a)(1)*	*17 U.S.C. § 1201(a)(2)*	*17 U.S.C. § 1201(b)*

use covered by section 108(c) of the Copyright Act. The exempted class is therefore limited to work distributed in such now-obsolete formats." 68 Fed. Reg. 62011, 62014 (October 31, 2003) (amending 37 C.F.R. § 201.40) (exempted class 3, explanation)). However, as discussed in Chapter 1, the major limitation in using section 108(c) in the creation of digital library content is that the content may only be accessed in-house, i.e., "any such copy or phonorecord that is reproduced in digital format is not made available to the public in that format outside the premises of the library or archives in lawful possession of such copy, it may not be made available outside the premises of the library or archive."

The fourth exemption is also somewhat limited in application, depending on the audience of "readers," as it targets the "blind and visually impaired [user] in gaining meaningful access to literary works distributed as ebooks." Id. at 62014. E-books can allow impaired readers to use "read-aloud" or "screen-reader" software that converts e-book text into synthesized speech or Braille. "By using digital rights management tools that implicate access controls, publishers of ebooks can disable the read-aloud function of an ebook and may prevent access to a work in ebook form by means of screen reader software." Id. at 62014 (exempted class 4, explanation). The exemption allows a library serving such readers under section 121 of the Copyright Act to circumvent the protection, e.g., by reactivating those mechanisms. Moreover, the U.S. Copyright Office rejected a general fair use or educational fair use exemption for technical reasons. The proposals failed to specify a particular class of work as required by the terms of the exemption provision under section 1201. In other words the U.S. Copyright Office cannot create an exemption for certain uses, only for certain classes of works. Id. at 62014-62015 (proposed classes 1 and 2). Such exemption would swallow the rule whole if it could be argued and as the U.S. Copyright Office observed: "The statutory text and the legislative history provide no evidence that Congress intended this rule-making to second-guess congressional determinations." Id. at 62014-62015 (proposed class 2, explanation). As with other proposed exemptions, the importance is not so much in what was proposed but what the Register rejected. For example, circumvention of controls that prohibit fast-forwarding of advertising on DVDs was also rejected. Id. at 62015-62016 (proposed class 9).

QUALIFYING FOR THE RIGHT TO CIRCUMVENT IN LIBRARIES AND EDUCATIONAL SETTINGS

Section 1201(d) provides a specific exception for qualifying nonprofit libraries, archives, or educational institutions to circumvent an access control in order to make a bona fide determination of whether to purchase an item for its collection or curriculum: "access to a commercially exploited copyrighted work solely in order to make a good faith determination of whether to acquire a copy of that work for the sole purpose of engaging in conduct permitted under this title shall not be in violation of subsection (a)(1)(A)."[59] Notice that this exception operates with respect to the section 1201(a)(1)(A) anti-circumvention of access control provision; it does not allow qualifying nonprofit libraries, archives, or educational institutions to traffic in either an access or use control.[60] Such entities are still prohibited from engaging in conduct that remains a section 1201(a)(2) or section 1201(b) trafficking violation.

Similar to section 108(a)(2), discussed in Chapter 5, section 1201(d)(5) contains an open access proviso: "the collections of that *library or archives* shall be open to the public or available not only to researchers affiliated with the library or archives or with the institution of which it is a part, but also to other persons doing research in a specialized field."[61] This requirement applies only to a library or archives, not to an educational institution.

There are several other requirements. First, under section 1201(d)(1)(A), access to the work "circumvented" may not be "retained longer than necessary to make such good faith determination for purposes of collection acquisition or curriculum adoption.[62] Second, not only must the circumvention be made with the sole purpose of a section 1201(d) collection assessment or curriculum evaluation,[63] but once accessed, the work "may not be used for any other purpose,"[64] even if it that subsequent use would otherwise qualify as a fair use under section 107 or be authorized by some other provision of copyright law, such as a classroom performance under section 110(1) or (2). Third, the eventual use the library, archives, or educational institution will make of the acquired copy or copies (though purchase, loan, etc.) must also be in conformity with the copyright law: "for the sole purpose of engaging in conduct permitted under this title." Not that any such entity would by design obtain copyrighted material with the intent to make an unlawful use of it beyond the bounds of the copyright law, but the statute nonetheless establishes a prerequisite of behavior. For example, if a library intends to obtain a number of copyrighted DVDs in order to create an intranet of film excerpts or clippings (similar to the intranet use of copyrighted newsletters found unlawful in *Lowry's Reports, Inc. v. Mason, Inc.*) beyond the boundaries of fair use (as suggested by the *Universal Studios, Inc. v. Corley* dicta regarding student use of DVD excerpts), or a school district desires a number of media products to use as entertainment or reward, beyond the scope of section 110(1) and likely an unfair use as well, then not only might the library face possible copyright infringement proceedings, but it may also face liability under section 1201 for a "failed" (and thus unauthorized) subsection (d) access circumvention.

If the subsequent copy eventually purchased is used unlawfully in terms of the copyright law, then the section 1201(d) circumvention privilege is denied as well. This is the effect of the (d)(1) proviso: "in order to make a good faith determination of whether to acquire a copy of that work for the *sole purpose of engaging in conduct permitted under this title* [i.e., title 17 of the United States Code, the copyright law]."[65] The practical result is the that the section 1201(d) entity might be subject to copyright infringement as well as violation of the anti-circumvention rule and face penalties under section 1203, as discussed below.

"Not Reasonably Available in Another Form": Interpreting the Meaning

Finally, the section 1201(d) exemption operates "only [] with respect to a work when an identical copy of that work is not reasonably available in another form."[66]

It is unclear how strict a court would read the "identical copy" rule. Would holding an available but earlier VHS or print edition of a work disqualify a nonprofit library, archives, or educational institution from circumventing an access control on a newer DVD or e-book version of the original audiovisual or literary work? The e-versions might contain bonus features or additional material, such that one could argue that the two works are not identical. On the one hand, while this would not appear to violate the letter of the law, it might arguably violate its spirit, as the focus of a collection or curriculum decision is more likely to be an evaluation, for example, of the original 119-minute theatrical film *Blade Runner*, not the "bonus features" that accompany it and so many DVDs released today. By the same token, an institution might not be able to make that collection acquisition or curriculum adoption without assessing the new material precisely, because the digital version offers the sought-after different or altered content, or, as is often the case with audiovisual works, a restored, remastered, or enhanced version. This might be the case with the recent DVD of Carol Reed's classic post-war European tale of intrigue, *The Third Man*.[67] The only existing prints contain many scratches and other blemishes; thus when VHS copies are made for commercial release the blemishes transfer as well. Is the new DVD restoration really better than the original, justifying the purchase of yet another copy for the library? In that case, although the two versions are of the same 104-minute film and the same 1949 audiovisual work, the new version is nonetheless different. Moreover the difference is the precise reason for the library's desire to view it. This example might indeed represent a "good faith" need to make an acquisition "determination" as to whether a restored version is worth the purchase price.

Arguably, in a director's cut, the two works are indeed distinct. In the *Blade Runner* example the voice-over narrative is missing, additional footage is added and "happy" ending deleted.[68] A library would likely have a DVD player that would easily play a DVD without problem. Under section 1201(d), however, the library could circumvent the content scramble system (CSS) access control if it only has computers and not a DVD player on which to view the contents—the library "cannot obtain a copy of an identical work by other means."[69] Notice that nothing in section 1201(d) requires the qualifying nonprofit library, archives, or educational institution to purchase the bona fide technology (a DVD player in the present examples) or obtain the proper technological key. This is the precise sort of circumvention, for collection development or curriculum purposes, that section 1201(d)(1) allows. Of course, section 1201(d)(1) would not allow the library to also use the DeCSS version, that is, an unlicensed or pirated copy, at its monthly film night, even if a public performance license was obtained—such a showing would violate the "solely in order to make a good faith determination" proviso as well as the "may not be used for any other purpose" restriction of section 1201(d)(1)(B). Again, this example assumes that the library does not have a DVD player, but instead wants to view the movie through a PC platform. In reality, the library may need to circumvent access for a few works in order to have a look see, ultimately undermining the usefulness of subsection (d) exemption.

Recall that the section 1201(d) privilege applies only to conduct under section 1201(a)(1)(A), circumvention of an access control; it does not offer any assistance to trafficking conduct under section 1201(a)(2), trafficking of an access device, or section 1201(b), trafficking of a use device. Thus, if the library discovered (hacked) its own CSS access decryption code it could not share the code with other libraries within its consortium, as this would violate the section 1201(a)(2) anti-trafficking prohibition.

This is the examination or review and adoption or acquisition pattern of review of new or revised editions in the analog world of schools and libraries, and it is hoped a court would accept a parallel practice in the digital world of section 1201. Just as a library, school district, or faculty is not able to make a collection or adoption decision based on an older edition of a book, likewise it is necessary to have the ability to examine and consider the new e-version of the work. This is the privilege that section 1201(d) was designed to offer. Therefore, an argument could be made that the older VHS movie or print textbook is not "an identical copy of that work" even though it might indeed be "reasonably available in another form"—"an *identical copy* [of the new and improved copy] of that work is *not* reasonably available in another form."

While the privilege of section 1201(d) might be a welcome tool in the collection development arsenal of the qualifying nonprofit library, archives, or educational institution, it seems an odd privilege to offer in light of the trend of Congressional initiatives engaging the library and educational intermediary in compliance-oriented measures. It is wonderful to allow qualifying nonprofit libraries, archives, or educational institutions the right to circumvent use controls for this limited purpose, but it at the same time legitimizes what would otherwise be an unlawful activity under section 1201(a)(1). Without an understanding of the context and limits of section 1201(d), such privileged activity may send the wrong signal to others within the institution, misleading staff and students to believe that circumvention of access controls in other contexts is lawful, when in fact it remains subject to the section 1201 prohibitions.

Penalties for Willfully "Violating" the Section 1201(d)(1) Exception

Section 1201(d) also contains an odd penalty provision of sorts. Odd for its statutory placement, as subsection (d) is designed (as are subsections (e), (f), (g), and (j)) as an exception to the basic anti-circumvention and anti-trafficking rules of subsections (a) and (b), and not as a liability enhancement provision. Moreover, none have the "enhancement" structure of subsection (d). Nonetheless, under section

1203(d)(3) a nonprofit library, archives, or educational institution that "willfully for the purpose of commercial advantage or financial gain *violates*" the section 1201(d)(1) requirements (the requirements of which include the sole purpose of circumvention and no subsequent unlawful use of purchased copy under (d)(1), retention no longer than necessary under (d)(1)(A), and sole purpose of use under (d)(1)(B)) "shall, for the first offense, be subject to the civil remedies under section 1203" and "shall, for repeated or subsequent offenses, in addition to the civil remedies under section 1203, forfeit the exemption provided under paragraph (1).[70]

It is also an odd construction for a statutory provision to create an exception to a prohibition, the anti-circumvention and anti-trafficking rules, and then to use that same language to trigger a "violation." The House Report appears to support use of the provision as a "prohibition" provision—the requirements of which can be violated—along with an exception provision listing the conditions under which circumvention can occur: "Section 102(d)(3) [17 U.S.C. § 1201(d)(3)] seeks to protect the legitimate interest of copyright owners by providing a civil remedy against a library, archive or educational institution that violates Section 102(d)(1) [17 U.S.C. § 1201(d)(1)]."[71] The Senate Report echoes the same sentiment:

> Paragraph (3) seeks to protect the legitimate interest of copyright owners by providing a civil remedy against a library, archive or educational institution that violates section 1201(a) by gaining access to a commercially exploited copyrighted work and willfully and for purposes of commercial advantage or financial gain failing to comply with the provisions of paragraph (1)(A) . . . or paragraph (1)(B).[72]

Perhaps it is poor drafting, or it is more likely that Congress wanted to ensure that damages would be imposed and not remitted for "willful violations"—it might be considered an attempt to create a statutory structure somewhat parallel to the 504(c)(2) statutory damage enhancement penalty for willful infringements. For example, an institution that, once circumvention under section 1201(d) took place, made a fair use of material in order to avoid the cost of licensing that material would arguably trigger the section 1201(d)(3) "willful" proviso[73] ("willfully" used it for another purpose, violating the sole purpose of use under (d)(1)(B), and for "purpose[s] of commercial advantage or financial gain") and "be subject to the civil remedies under section 1203." However, if, for example, the material along with its decryption key made its way by accident onto the e-reserve system or a course Web site, the institution would not face any additional penalty under section 1203 via section 1201(d)(3), as its conduct would arguably *not* be "willful." Nonetheless, it still might face penalty under section 1203 as it made a nonqualifying trafficking of the access device related to the work. The important distinction here is that in the latter, accidental noncompliance with section 1201(d) instance, the library or educational institution might still qualify for damage remission under section 1203(5) as discussed below.

Understanding the Concept of Commercial Advantage or Financial Gain

The term of commercial advantage or financial gain is not defined in the statute, though it used elsewhere, e.g., section 108(a)(1). Undertaking circumvention of an access instead of obtaining authorized access when that access would come with some cost, an access fee for example, would logically be a direct financial gain; or circumventing access in order to make a more informed collection or curriculum decision and thus forego an unnecessary purchase might represent an indirect advantage or gain. Further, it is not logical to read the use of the words "commercial" or "financial" as indicative of Congress's intent to have the provision reach only profit-making entities (such as Texaco, Kinko's or Michigan Document Services, or Legg Mason), as subsection 1201(d) is designed to target nonprofit libraries, archives, or educational institutions in the first instance and the subproviso (d)(3) again uses the qualifier "nonprofit." Thus the terms "commercial advantage or financial gain" cannot refer to the general nature of the organization but to its individual acts of circumvention. In addition, the willfulness provision of section 1204, defining criminal circumvention and trafficking, inserts the modifier "private" into its operational phrase, "commercial advantage or *private* financial gain," to indicate that the criminal rules can apply to individual as well as to organizational gains. Thus, a court could interpret the provision with rather harsh results, finding that most if not all circumventions are done for some direct or indirect (the statute does not specify) commercial advantage or financial gain. Moreover, as discussed below, unless the circumvention occurred by accident or mistake, any volitional act would be deemed made willful; thus, a majority of circumventions could trigger the section 1201(d)(3) proviso and, as discussed below, section 1204, the criminal sanctions provision! Fortunately such result is foreclosed from applying to nonprofit libraries, archives, and educational institutions under section 1204(b).

If this "violation" is made "willfully for the purpose of commercial advantage or financial gain," the nonprofit library, archives, or educational institution loses its remission privileges under section 1203.[74] There is no discussion in the legislative report history of the DMCA regarding what conduct constitutes "commercial advantage or financial gain." It would seem a stretch for a copyright owner to use the section 1201(d)(3) mechanism in a negative collection decision, to claim that because the library failed to waste precious collection monies on the purchase of a lousy product that that decision to save money was somehow one of "commercial advantage or financial gain." The more likely case is that the circumvented copy is then purposely used within the institution in lieu of purchase, thus conserving those precious collection development monies for other purchases. Such conduct would not meet the requirements of section 1201(d)(1) and (2); moreover, it would suggest a willful failure to meet the requirements for the purpose of "commercial advantage or financial gain."

Additional Immunity from Criminal Liability

Complicating this analysis somewhat is the fact that a violation of section 1201 made "willfully and for purposes of commercial advantage or *private* financial gain" is subject to harsh criminal penalties.[75] The criminal provision of section 1204(a) uses the "private financial gain" phrasing, while the section 1201(d)(3) civil damage imposition uses the broader unqualified "financial gain," as the financial gain could be either public or private. There is a presumption that when statutory language is different, that difference must be given legal significance. However, this difference is of little consequence for a nonprofit library, archives, educational institution, or public broadcasting entity since section 1204(b) states that the "willfully and for purposes of commercial advantage or private financial gain" criminal provision of section 1204(a) "shall *not* apply to a nonprofit library, archive, educational institution, or public broadcasting entity." This provision is valuable, as it confers complete immunity for criminal liability upon the qualifying nonprofit library, archives, or educational institution. As Professor Dratler points out, without it, one would be hard pressed to imagine an actionable circumvention or trafficking under section 1201 that is subject to civil penalties (i.e., done by accident, thus no remission is available) but not also subject to criminal sanctions. As a result, any remediable civil infractions (read "damages") will likely qualify for the imposition of criminal penalties as well.[76] However, the employees, patrons, or students do not share in the section 1204(b) immunity from criminal penalties.

The purpose of the section 1201(d)(3) proviso is best considered in light of the criminal anti-circumvention and anti-trafficking penalty and its nonprofit library, archives, and educational institution immunity provision. Using almost identical language to section 1201(d)(3), section 1204 states that any person who violates section 1201 (circumvention or trafficking) "willfully and for purposes of commercial advantage or *private* financial gain" is subject to criminal sanctions (up to $500,000 for the first offense and $1,000,000 for subsequent (repeat) offenses, and up to five years of imprisonment for the first offense and up to ten years for a repeat offenses).[77]

Triggering a Loss of Damage Remission for Nonprofit Institutions

Section 1201(d)(3) in essence pulls back the damage remission for a nonprofit library, archives, or educational institution that "gains access to a commercially exploited copyright" under certain circumstances: "willfully for the purpose commercial advantage or financial gain violates paragraph (1), the paragraph in section 1201(d) that outlines a lawful collection or curriculum circumvention. The problem is that a library, archives or educational entity that "violates paragraph (1) [of subsection (d)]" is not committing the same act as a section 1201(a)(1) violation: The former circumvention of access being for purposes of a collection acquisition or curriculum adoption decision, the latter being any circumvention of an access control for any purpose whatsoever, or of course a trafficking offense, which section 1201(d) does not excuse either.

In addition and as stated above, section 1201(d)(1) is an exception provision, not a liability provision. Applying it as such, according to the command of section 1201(d)(3), dictates that liability should apply to the same set of circumstances to which the exemption applies, i.e., those of paragraph (d)(1): "a good faith determination of whether to acquire a copy of that work for the sole purpose of engaging in conduct permitted under this title." If a subsection 1201(d)(3) "violation" then occurs willfully, Congress softens the blow; such violations are *not* tied to restoration of criminal sanctions (as the statute could have been structured) but rather are now subject to restoration of civil remedies alone, and for repeat willful offenses (per the instruction of section 1201(d)(3)(B)), loss of subsequent subsection exemption, even in circumstances that would otherwise constitute a lawful gain of access, i.e., a circumvention that met the requirements of section 1201(d)(1), (2), and (5).

Thus section 1201(d)(3) rewrites the law of violations made "willfully and for purposes of commercial advantage or private financial gain" for nonprofit libraries, archives, and educational institutions; they "shall, for the first offense, be subject to the civil remedies under section 1203." Such violations pull back the benefit offered by section 1203(c)(5)(B)(ii) (i.e., mandatory remission of damages discussed in detail below), which might otherwise be available in a case where the violation was willful (i.e., not by accident or mistake yet done without knowledge of the intricacies of section 1201), as that immunity-remission applies when the "entity was not aware and had no reason to believe that its acts constituted a violation." Of course, the pullback, i.e., the possibility of statutory damages, relates only to offenses in 1201(d) scenarios, not to all 1201 violations, damage remission is preserved there. The point is that willfulness is not the same as lack of knowledge in the law; one can act purposefully yet have no awareness that one's actions constitute an unlawful act, such as a violation of the anti-circumvention or anti-trafficking rules.

At first glance it might appear inconsistent that a defendant could have available the civil damage remission provision (where the qualifying standard is lack of knowledge—"not aware and had no reason to believe") yet face criminal penalties (where the standard is willfulness—not by accident or mistake), i.e., for a willful act done without an understanding of the section 1201 rules. However, recall that for nonprofit libraries, archives, and educational entities there can be no criminal liability whatsoever, though for other entities and individuals civil damage remission is discretionary under section 1201(c)(5)(A) and criminal penalties remain a possibility.

Moreover, willfulness in section 1204 must also occur "for purposes of commercial advantage or *private* financial gain" however low this standard might be, whereas the section 1201(d)(3) loss of remission is triggered by those violations of paragraph (2) of the subsection done "for the purposes of commercial advantage or financial gain." The presence of the word "private" in the criminal provisions indicates that an individual could be the target of criminal penalties. This is quite logical, whereas the section 1201(d) circumvention privilege, as well as its damage restoration and loss of future privilege, can by the plain text of the statute apply only to an entity: "nonprofit libraries, archives and educational institutions." Congress chose restoration of civil damages in instance of subsection (d)(1) violations committed willfully instead of the criminal penalties normally attributable to willful violations under section 1201, per operation of section 1204(a) but also foreclosed by section 1204(b) immunity. The obvious results that remission is foreclosed in section 1201(d)(3) scenarios: "shall, for the first offense, *be subject to the civil remedies* under section 1203" and "shall, for repeated or subsequent offenses, *in addition to the civil remedies* under section 1203 forefit exemption provided under paragraph (1)."

Repercussions of Repeat "Violations" Under Section 1201(d)

If a nonprofit library, archives, or educational institution repeats this willful conduct then, in addition to losing its damage remission privilege under section 1203(c)(5), the entity will lose the benefit of the section 1201(d) exception for future collection or curriculum decisions where it might desire to circumvent an access control, even if those future decisions are not made "willfully for the purpose of commercial advantage or financial gain."[78]

Second, repeat violators, in addition to general damages (actual or statutory), are now met with loss of future use of the section 1201(d) collection acquisition or curriculum adoption circumvention privilege, instead of the section 1203(c)(4) treble damage enhancement, as would be the case for other repeat violators—at least that is the shifting-replacement of liability that the author believes Congress intended to build into section 1201(d). Though perhaps a bit of legislative drafting oversight, there is no three-year counting rule for repeat violations as in the treble damage rule; rather in section 1201(d)(3) repeat violation will foreclose future use of the section 1201(d) circumvention privilege, regardless of how long ago the initial offense occurred. Remember that in spite of any damage remission provision, costs and reasonable attorney's fees are still available to the prevailing party under section 1203(c)(4) and (5), respectively!

Recall, too, that in the absence of section 1201(d), discretionary remission as well as mandatory remission for nonprofit libraries, archives, and educational institutions occurs only when "the violator was not aware and had no reason to believe that its acts constituted a violation." A repeat violator would surely not meet this standard; moreover, such a violator would be subject to the possibility of treble damage enhancement.

Third, in order for restoration of section 1203 damages and loss of future use of section 1201(d) to occur, the violation must, by operation the statute (section 1201(d)(3(B)), be a repeat "violation." Observe also that repeat violations are subject to treble damage enhancement under section 1203(c)(4) if made "within 3 years after a final judgment was entered against the [institution] for another such violation." Of course, such enhancement is at the discretion of the court (or jury), i.e., "as the court considers just." In yet another example of statutory misalignment, however, the loss of exemption occurs anytime there is a repeat violation of the section 1201(d) rules. This time the misalignment could favor of the nonprofit library, archive, and educational institution, leaving the enhancement penalty subject to an unmodified three-year rule. Thus, in year one, a qualifying nonprofit library could trigger a "violation" of the (d)(3) rule, and in year two, it could make a repeat violation of the same rule. Come year six, a circumvention conforming to section 1201(d)(1) would not be exempt, as section 1201(d)(3)(B) forecloses the exemption from ever applying again. Moreover, the repeat violation might be subject to treble damage enhancement! Suppose the repeat violation occurs in year four, with the same result that the section 1201(d) exemption is not available; however, since the violation is beyond the three-year enhancement window, there can be no treble damages awarded.

Liability for Employees and Other Individuals

Observe that the operation of remission and immunity may apply differently to the institution versus individuals, such as librarians or instructors. Some subsections of sections 1203 and 1204 use the word "violator" and others use the word "person," yet, perhaps as a result of poor drafting, both words appear to cover the same concept: individual and entity. The actual damage provision of section 1203(c)(2) uses the word "violator," as does the general discretionary remission provision of section 1203(c)(5)(A), whereas the treble enhancement provision of section 1203(c)(4) and the section 1204 criminal provision uses the word "person." Second, entities alone ("nonprofit library, archives, educational institution, or public broadcasting entity") are listed in the mandatory remission and criminal immunity provisos of sections 1203(c)(5)(B) and 1204(b), respectively. Thus employees would remain liable. This distinction is given some merit by the fact that the remission provision in the basic copyright law, section 504(c)(2), is drafted to make clear that employees are included:

> *The court shall remit statutory damages in any case where an infringer believed and had reasonable grounds for believing that his or her use of the copyrighted work was a fair use under section 107, if the infringer was an employee or agent of a nonprofit educational institution, library, or archives acting within the scope of his or her employment who, or such institution, library, or archives itself . . .*

This provision is unlike the section 1203(c)(5)(B)(ii) damage remission, which uses similar language but makes no mention of employees. Is this an example of drafting oversight, or exclusion of employees by design? Likewise, the criminal immunity provision of section 1204(b) excludes any mention of employees. On the other hand, perhaps the more intuitive position is that Congress intended the employees of nonprofit libraries, archives, and educational institutions to share in criminal immunity and mandatory damage remission. However that is not what the statute states and, in light of the existing remission provision in the copyright law specifically including employees as well as the parent institution, a court would be justified in coming to the same conclusion: employees of the institutions are excluded by design. Even if this exclusion is the result, there is no language excluding employees or other individuals from qualifying for the discretionary damage reduction or remission of section 1203(c)(5)(A). Hopefully, a court would use its discretionary authority under the statute to nonetheless "reduce or remit the total award of damages" in the case of an employee who is left holding the monetary liability bag because the damages owed by the employing entity were remitted by the statute.

Summary of Liability and Remission

In other words, there are two species of 1201 violations for the nonprofit library, archives, or educational institution. First there are those that violate section 1201 (circumvention and trafficking), subject to section 1203 damages, whereby if repeat infractions occur may be enhanced to triple the award per subsection (c)(4) but subject to mandatory remission in any case where the "entity was not aware and had no reason to believe that its acts constituted a violation" under section 1201(c)(6)(B)(ii). Costs and attorney's fees remain recoverable in all cases. Violations committed willfully that would normally be subject to criminal penalties under section 1204(a) for other violators are foreclosed by section 1204(b) when the subject is a "nonprofit library, archive[], educational institution, or public broadcasting entity."

A second species of circumvention penalties relates to collection acquisition or curriculum adoption. This circumvention is allowed under the general exception of section 1201(d). If made "willfully [other than by accident or mistake] for the purpose of commercial advantage or financial gain," actual or statutory damages are now available (the subsection (c)(5)(B) remission is lost) but are not subject to enhancement for repeat violations, unless repeat violations occur within the initial three-year statutory window; instead they are subject merely to loss of the future use of section 1201(d). Of course, the repeat violations must also be willful. Criminal penalties remain foreclosed.

Finally, the pullback of remission is not tied to circumvention or trafficking in general under section 1201(a) or (b), only to collection acquisition or curriculum adoption under section 1201(d); thus the statute can be construed to preserve damage remission for nonprofit libraries, archives, and educational institutions that "willfully for the purpose of commercial advantage or financial gain" circumvent access in instances other than section 1201(d). This conclusion is reinforced by the previous discussion differentiating between circumvention that is "willful" (triggering criminal penalty for other defendants and loss of remission for nonprofit libraries, archives, and educational institutions) versus that which is made in ignorance of the law (preserving actual and statutory damage remission but not foreclosing award of costs or attorney's fees).

REAL-WORLD EXAMPLES

▶ Real-World Example I

Situation: A technically proficient employee of a university library creates a patch of computer code to circumvent a copyright owner's password protection. The copyright owner uses the password protection to limit access to a CD-ROM after a certain date, unless the subscription is renewed. The library uses this computer code to allow faculty and students continued access to the CD-ROM content. The librarian shares this code with other libraries in its lending consortium.

Legal Analysis: Notwithstanding the terms and conditions of the licensing agreement that may govern use of the CD-ROM, the act of "hacking" around the password expiration mechanism (an access control) is a violation of the anti-circumvention rule of section 1201(a)(1). Sharing the code is a violation of the anti-trafficking rule of section 1201(a)(2).

▶ Real-World Example II

Situation: The situation is similar to Real-World Example I, but here a technically proficient employee of a university library creates a patch of computer code that allows students to circumvent a reproduction and display password protection a copyright owner uses to limit uses of CD-ROM content after a certain date, unless the subscription is renewed. The copyright owner also restricts, through a similar technological key, the amount of copying that can be made from the CD-ROM in a given month. The library uses this code to allow faculty and students continued use without the text being scrambled or images subject to watermarking. The librarian creates a second hack that allows faculty and patrons to make unlimited copies of the CD-ROM content. The librarian shares this code with other libraries in its lending consortium.

Legal Analysis: The act of circumventing a use control ("effectively protecting the right of a copyright owner under this title" (i.e., the copyright law)—in other words, an exclusive right of the copyright owner), in this case limiting the copying or the exclusive right of reproduction, is not a violation of section 1201, as there is no anti-circumvention rule regarding uses. Section 1201(b)(1) nonetheless prohibits trafficking in an anti-circumventing use device (in this case, posting the patch on the librarian's home page or otherwise sharing copying hack code with other libraries).

▶ Real-World Example III

Situation: The situation is similar to Real-World Examples I and II, except that the university library does not currently subscribe to the CD-ROM. The same savvy librarian circumvents the password protection in order to make a "good faith determination of whether to" subscribe ("acquire a copy of that work"). The library also shares the password with other librarians within the consortium considering subscription to the same database.

Legal Analysis: Circumventing the password (an access control) would otherwise be prohibited, but section 1201(d) allows for such circumvention if access to the database is not "retained longer than necessary to make such good faith determination" for purposes of collection acquisition or curriculum adoption, if the access is circumvented "solely" for the purpose of making an acquisition decision and the contemplated use is lawful as well, and if no other use is made of the circumvented material. The statute makes clear that the acquisition or curriculum circumvention privilege does not apply to either form of trafficking, in access or use controls. In addition, the section 1201(d) exemption operates "only . . . with respect to a work when an identical copy of that work is not reasonably available in another form." Finally, the collections of that library or archives shall be open to the public or available not only to researchers affiliated with the library or archives or with the institution of which it is a part, but also to other persons doing research in a specialized field.

▶ Real-World Example IV

Situation: The situation is the same as Real-World Examples I and II, with the addition that the librarian has not kept up his professional reading and knows nothing about the DMCA or its controversial provisions, such as section 1201.

Legal Analysis: If the librarian can claim ignorance in his or her circumvention of the access control (hacking the extension and copying passwords), that the librarian was "not aware and had no reason to believe that its acts constituted a violation" then the court must remit statutory damages under section 1203(c)(5)(B)(ii). However, costs and attorney's fees are nonetheless recoverable by the prevailing party. Unlike the section 504 remission provision in the copyright law's general articulation of remedies for infringement that specifically include "employee" in the remission privilege, the section 1203 provision does not use the word "employee," but refer only to entities such as a nonprofit library, archives, or educational institution. Thus, a court could interpret this absence as intentional and subject the librarian to discretionary damage reduction or remission provision alone, with perhaps the same result.

▶ Real-World Example V

Situation: The situation is the same as Real-World Example IV, and the librarian succeeds in obtaining damage remission. However, the following year the librarian hacks another copyright owner's CD-ROM product in a similar way.

Legal Analysis: Violations of section 1201 "within three years after a final judgment" may result in the imposition of up to triple damages, or some lesser enhancement as the court considers just. The act of hacking by the librarian was no accident; it is willful. Thus under section 1201(d)(3) remission is foreclosed. Also, if the librarian undertakes a similar act (commits "repeated or subsequent offenses" under subsection (d)(3)(B)), not only is remission foreclosed, but use of the section 1201(d) circumvention privilege is prohibited in the future.

▶ Real-World Example VI

Situation: The librarian now familiar with the DMCA, especially section 1201, hacks an access code in a scenario similar to Real-World Example III, in order to make a "good faith determination of whether to" subscribe to a product ("acquire a copy of that work"). However, in reckless disregard for the requirements of section 1201(d)(1), the librarian places a fair use portion of the CD-ROM on e-reserve.

Legal Analysis: Under section 1201(d)(3), the institution is precluded from seeking remission of damages under section 1203. If this happens again, the library may not use the section 1201(d) acquisitions privilege ever again!

KEY POINTS FOR YOUR INSTITUTION'S POLICY AND PRACTICE

▶ Additional liability separate and distinct from copyright infringement exists, known as the anti-circumvention and anti-trafficking rules. Under section 1201(a)(1) a technological measure that controls access to a copyrighted work cannot be circumvented. The rules protect copyrighted material. See pp. 265–267.

▶ In order to be protected, the technological measure must be "effective." To be considered effective, the access control must be put in place by the copyright owner or with his or her authorization, and the technological access control must not degrade, corrupt, or distort the work; if it does degrade, corrupt, or distort the work, section 1201 does not apply, as this is not an "effective" control. See pp. 267–269.

▶ The statute prohibits trafficking in the anti-circumvention access control. Trafficking is defined broadly in the statute: "No person shall manufacture, import, offer to the public, provide, or otherwise traffic in any technology, product, service, device, component, or part thereof." See pp. 269–271.

▶ In addition, the statute makes illegal the sale or distribution (trafficking) of a device that allows someone to circumvent technological protections on copyrighted works, i.e., trafficking of an anti-circumvention use control is prohibited. See pp. 271–276.

▶ Both anti-trafficking provisions make it unlawful to manufacture, import, offer to the public, provide, or otherwise traffic in a technology, product, service, device, component, or part thereof, that is "primarily designed or produced for the purpose of circumventing protection afforded by a technological measure," or that has only a "limited commercially significant purpose or use other than to circumvent protection afforded by a technological protection measure," or that is "marketed . . . for use in circumventing protection afforded by a technological protection measure." See pp. 271–272.

▶ Remedies similar to those available for plaintiff in a general copyright infringement are available to copyright owners in instances of section 1201 violations: injunctive relief orders (both temporary and permanent) for impoundment or final "remedial modification or the destruction of any device or product involved in the violation" are available, as well as costs and attorney's fees. Damages for a violation of the rules are subject to a similar election of actual or statutory damages. Statutory damages are set by the court and are "in the sum of not less than $200.00 or more than $2,500.00 per act of circumvention, device, product, component, offer, or performance of service, as the court considers just." See pp. 265–267.

▶ If repeat violations occur within a three-year period after final judgment, the court may, within its discretion, multiply the damages award by use, up to three times the original award. Similar to the burden of proof for remission in general, copyright infringement action, the injured party "sustains the burden of proving" the repeat violation. See pp. 285–287.

▶ There are two damage remission provisions, one permissive ("the court in its discretion may reduce or remit the total award of damages in any case") and the other mandatory ("the court shall remit damages in any case"). Qualifying non-profit libraries, archives, educational institutions, or public broadcasting entities are subject to the mandatory provision. For other defendants, permissive remission may entail a damage reduction instead of complete remission; the court can within its discretion do either. In either case, the court can only remit when the defendant "sustains the burden of proving, and the court finds" that the defendant was "not aware and had no reason to believe that its acts constituted a violation." See pp. 285–286.

▶ In any case where damage remission occurs, costs and attorney's fees are still recoverable by the prevailing party. See p. 284.

▶ Criminal sanction exists if the rules (circumvention or trafficking) are violated "willfully and for purposes of commercial advantage or private financial gain": up to $500,000 for the first offense and $1,000,000 for subject offenses, and up to five years of imprisonment for the first offense and up to ten years for repeat offenses. However, this sanction does not apply to a nonprofit library, archives, educational institution, or public broadcasting entity. See p. 282.

▶ A limited exception to the rule prohibiting the circumvention of access exists for qualifying nonprofit libraries, archives, or educational institutions. The exception allows for these entities to circumvent an access control in order to make a bona fide determination of whether to purchase an item for their collection or curriculum.

▶ This exception has several requirements. In a measure similar to section 108(a)(2) discussed in chapter 5, "the collections of that *library or archives* shall be open to the public or available not only to researchers affiliated with the library or archives or with the institution of which it is a part, but also to other persons doing research in a specialized field." See pp. 276–277.

▶ In addition, access to the work "circumvented" may not be "retained longer than necessary to make such good faith determination for purposes of collection acquisition or curriculum adoption. Second, not only must the circumvention be made with the sole purpose of a collection assessment or curriculum evaluation, once accessed it "may not be used for any other purpose," even if that subsequent use would otherwise qualify as a fair use under section 107 or be authorized by some other provision of copyright law, such as a classroom performance under section 110(1) or (2). The subsequent acquisition must be for lawful purposes as well. Finally, the section exemption operates only when an identical copy of that work is not reasonably available in another form. See pp. 276–279.

▶ If a nonprofit library, archives, or educational institution "willfully for the purpose of commercial advantage or financial gain *violates*" the requirements of the exception, then the institution shall be subject to the damage provisions, i.e., remission of damages will not apply. For any repeat violations the institution loses it right to use the collection or curriculum exception in the future. See pp. 279–285.

ENDNOTES

[1] 17 U.S.C. § 1203(a).

[2] 17 U.S.C. § 1203(b).

[3] 17 U.S.C. § 1203(c)(2).

[4] 17 U.S.C. § 1203(c)(3)(A).

[5] 17 U.S.C. § 1203(c)(4).

[6] S. Rep. No. 105-190, 105th Cong., 2d Sess. 17 (1998).

[7] See, 17 U.S.C. § 1201(e)–(j) (law enforcement, intelligence, and other government activities, reverse engineering, encryption research, exceptions regarding minors, protection of personally identifying information, and security testing).

[8] 17 U.S.C. § 1201(a)(1)(C) ("during each succeeding 3-year period, the Librarian of Congress, upon the recommendation of the Register of Copyrights, who shall consult with the Assistant Secretary for Communications and Information of the Department of Commerce and report and comment on his or her views in making such recommendation, shall make the determination in a rulemaking proceeding for purposes of subparagraph (B) of whether persons who are users of a copyrighted work are, or are likely to be in the succeeding 3-year period, adversely affected by the prohibition under subparagraph (A) in their ability to make noninfringing uses under this title of a particular class of copyrighted works.").

[9] Exemption to Prohibition on Circumvention of Copyright Protection Systems for Access Control Technologies, Final Rule, 68 Fed. Reg. 62011, 62013-62014 (October 31, 2003) (amending 37 C.F.R. § 201.40). Four categories of works exempted are (1) "Compilations of lists of Internet locations blocked by commercially marketed filtering software applications that are intended to prevent access to domains, websites or portions of websites, but not including lists of Internet locations blocked by software applications that operate exclusively to protect against damage to a computer or computer network or lists of Internet locations blocked by software applications that operate exclusively to prevent receipt of e-mail." (2) "Computer programs protected by dongles that prevent access due to malfunctions or damage and which are obsolete." (3) "Computer programs and video games distributed in formats that have become obsolete and which require the original media or hardware as a condition of access." (4) "Literary works distributed in ebook format when all existing ebook editions of the work (including digital test editions made available by authorized entities) contain access controls that prevent the enabling of the ebook's read-aloud function and that prevent the enabling of screen readers to render the text into a 'specialized format.'"

[10] 17 U.S.C. § 1203(c)(5)(A).

[11] 17 U.S.C. § 1203(c)(5)(B)(ii).

[12] 17 U.S.C. § 1203(c)(5)(A) ("The court in its discretion may reduce or remit the total award of damages in any case in which the violator sustains the burden of proving, and the court finds, that the violator was not aware and had no reason to believe that its acts constituted a violation.").

[13] 17 U.S.C. § 1203(c)(5)(B)(ii) ("In the case of a nonprofit library, archives, educational institution, or public broadcasting entity, the court shall remit damages in any case in which the library, archives, educational institution, or public broadcasting entity sustains the burden of proving, and the court finds, that the library, archives, educational institution, or public broadcasting entity was not aware and had no reason to believe that its acts constituted a violation.").

[14] See Exemption to Prohibition on Circumvention of Copyright Protection Systems for Access Control Technologies, Final Rule, 68 Fed. Reg. 62011, 62015-62016 (October 31, 2003) (amending 37 C.F.R. § 201.40) (proposed class 9).

[15] *Universal Studios, Inc. v. Corley*, 273 F.3d 429 (2d Cir. 2001) (motion picture studios place CSS encryption technology on DVDs to prevent the unauthorized viewing and copying of motion pictures).

[16] *Real Networks, Inc. v. Streambox, Inc.*, 2000 U.S. Dist. LEXIS 1889 (W.D. Wash. 2000) (preliminary injunction) (Findings of Fact 12: "The Secret Handshake is an authentication sequence which only RealServers and RealPlayers know. By design, unless this authentication sequence takes place, the RealServer does not stream the content it holds." Findings of Fact 14: "Through the use of the Secret Handshake and the Copy Switch, owners of audio and video content can prevent the unauthorized copying of their content if they so choose.").

[17] *Sony Computer Entertainment America Inc. v. Gamemasters, Inc.*, 87 F. Supp. 2d 976, 987 (N.D. Cal. 1999) ("Based upon the declarations before this Court, the Game Enhancer's distinguishing feature appears to be its ability to allow consumers to play import or non-territorial SCEA video games. As discussed above, SCEA specifically designed the PlayStation console to access only those games with data codes that match the geographical location of the game console itself. The Game Enhancer circumvents the mechanism on the PlayStation console that ensures the console operates only when encrypted data is read from an authorized CD-ROM. (Pltf's Reply at 7). Thus, at this stage, the Game Enhancer appears to be a device whose primary function is to circumvent.").

[18] *Lexmark International, Inc. v. Static ControlComponents, Inc.*, 253 F. Supp. 2d 943 (E.D. Ky. 2003) (preliminary injunction), vacated and remanded, 387 F.3d 522 (6th Cir. 2004) ("Generally speaking, 'lock-out' codes fall on the functional-idea rather that the original-expression side of the copyright line." Id at 546. "Just as one would not say that a lock on the back door of a house 'controls access' to a house whose front door does not contain a lock and just as one would not say that a lock on any door of a house 'controls access' to the house after its purchaser receives the key to the lock, it does not make sense to say that this provision of the DMCA applies to otherwise-readily-accessible copyrighted works." Id. at 547.

[19] H.R. Rep. No 551 (Part 1), 105th Cong., 2d Sess. 17 (1998). By an extension of this analogy one would question whether breaking into a room to read a book should be punishable both as to breaking and entering and as to stealing, in essence the application of the anti-circumvention and anti-trafficking rules appears to do both regardless of ultimate purpose!

[20] 17 U.S.C. § 1201(a)(3)(A).

[21] *United States v. Elcom Ltd.*, 203 F. Supp. 2d 1111, 1131-1132 (N.D. Cal. 2002) ("In the same vein, the DMCA does not 'prevent access to matters in the public domain' or allow any publisher to remove from the public domain and acquire rights in any public domain work. Nothing within the DMCA grants any rights to anyone in any public domain work. A public domain work remains in the public domain and no party has any intellectual property right in the expression of that work. A flaw in defendant's argument is that it presumes that the only available version of a public domain work is an electronic, technology-protected, version. If a work is in the public domain, any person may make use of that expression, for whatever purposes desired. To the extent that a publisher has taken a public domain work and made it available in electronic form, and in the course of doing so has also imposed use restrictions on the electronic version, the publisher has not gained any lawfully protected intellectual property interest in the work. The publisher has only gained a technological protection against copying that particular electronic version of the work. The situation is little different than if a publisher printed a new edition of Shakespeare's plays, but chose to publish the book on paper that was difficult to photocopy. Copy protection measures could be employed, similar to what is now commonly done on bank checks, so that the photocopy revealed printing that is otherwise unnoticeable on the original, perhaps rendering the text difficult to read on the photocopy. Would the publisher have thus recaptured Shakespeare's plays from the public domain? No, the publisher has gained no enforceable rights in the works of Shakespeare; all that has happened is that the purchaser of the copy-protected book would be unable to easily make a photocopy of that particular book. Publishing a public domain work in a restricted format does not thereby remove the work from the public domain, even if it does allow the publisher to control that particular electronic copy. If this is an evil in the law, the remedy is for Congress to prohibit use or access restrictions from being imposed upon public domain works. Or perhaps, if left to the market, the consuming public could decline to purchase public domain works packaged with use restrictions.").

[22] *Lexmark International, Inc. v. Static ControlComponents, Inc.*, 387 F.3d 522 (6th Cir. 2004).

[23] *Lexmark International, Inc. v. Static ControlComponents, Inc.*, 387 F.3d 522, 542-543 (6th Cir. 2004) ("In reaching this conclusion, we do not mean to say that brief computer programs [33 program instructions occupying 37 bytes and 45 program commands occupying 5 bytes, shorter than the name of the case in ASCII format] are ineligible for copyright protection. Short programs may reveal high levels of creativity and may present simple, yet unique, solutions to programming quandaries. . . . But unless a creative flair is shown, a very brief program is less likely to be copyrightable because it affords fewer opportunities for original expression.").

[24] *Lexmark International, Inc. v. Static ControlComponents, Inc.*, 387 F.3d 522, 540 (6th Cir. 2004).

[25] 17 U.S.C. § 1201(a)(1)(A) ("effectively controls access").

[26] 17 U.S.C. § 1201(a)(3)(A).

[27] H.R. Rep. No. 105-796, 105th Cong., 2d Sess. 65 (1998) (Conf. Rep.) ("Steps taken by the makers or services of consumer electronics, telecommunications or computing products used for such authorized performances or displays solely to mitigate these adverse effects on product performance (whether or not taken in combination with other lawful product modifications) shall not be deemed a violation of sections 1201(a) or (b).").

[28] 17 U.S.C. § 1201(a)(3)(B) ("with the authority of the copyright owner").

[29] H.R. Rep. No. 551 (Part 2), 105th Cong. 2d Sess. 40 (1998) ("[M]easures that cause noticeable and recurring adverse effects on the authorized display or performance of works should not be deemed to be effective.").

[30] H.R. Rep. No. 551 (Part 2), 105th Cong., 2d Sess. 41 (1998).

[31] H.R. Rep. No. 551 (Part 2), 105th Cong., 2d Sess. 40 (1998).

[32] See, *Universal Studios, Inc. v. Corley*, 273 F.3d 429, 436-437 (2d Cir. 2001) ("In November 1999, Corley posted a copy of the decryption computer program 'DeCSS' on his web site *http://www.2600.com*. DeCSS is designed to circumvent 'CSS,' the encryption technology that motion picture studios place on DVDs to prevent the unauthorized viewing and copying of motion pictures. Corley also posted on his web site links to other web sites where DeCSS could be found.").

[33] 17 U.S.C. § 1201(a)(2).

[34] See 17 U.S.C. § 1203.

[35] H.R. Rep. No. 551 (Part 1), 105th Cong., 2d Sess. 18 (1998). See also H.R. Rep. No. 551 (Part 2), 105th Cong., 2d Sess. 38 (1998) ("'(a)(2) is aimed fundamentally at outlawing so-called 'black boxes' that are expressly intended to facilitate circumvention of technological protection measures for purposes of gaining access to a work.").

[36] S. Rep. No. 105-190, 105th Cong., 2d Sess. 11 (1998).

[37] Tomas A. Lipinski and David A. Rice, Organizational and Individual Responses to Legal Paradigm Shifts in the Ownership of Information in Digital Media: The Impact of WIPO, and other Legal Developments, in Proceedings of ETHICOMP 2002: The Transformation of Organizations in the Information Age: Social and Ethical Implications, 13-15, November, 2002, Universidade Lusiada, Lisbon, Portugal.

[38] 17 U.S.C. § 1201(b)(1).

[39] H.R. Rep. No. 551 (Part 2), 105th Cong., 2d Sess. 39 (1998) (emphasis added). See also, *Real Networks, Inc. v. Streambox, Inc.*, 2000 U.S. Dist. LEXIS 1889 (W.D. Wash. 2000) (preliminary injunction) ("The only reason for the Streambox VCR to circumvent the Secret Handshake and interact with a RealServer is to allow an end-user to access and make copies of content that a copyholder has placed on a RealServer in order to secure it against unauthorized copying. In this way, the Streambox VCR acts like a 'black box' which descrambles cable or satellite broadcasts so that viewers can watch pay programming for free." Finding of Fact 26, at *11. "[T]he Copy Switch is a 'technological measure' that effectively protects the right of a copyright owner to control the unauthorized copying of the work." Conclusion of law 8, Id., at *19.).

[40] S. Rep. No. 105-190, 105th Cong., 2d Sess. 12 (1998).

[41] S. Rep. No. 105-190, 105th Cong., 2d Sess. 12 (1998) ("measures that limit the ability of the copyrighted work to be copied").

[42] H.R. Rep. No. 551 (Part 1), 105th Cong., 2d Sess. 19 (1998).

[43] 17 U.S.C. § 1201(a)(2)(A)–(C) and 17 U.S.C. § 1201(b)(1)(A)–(C).

[44] *Sony Corp. of America, Inc. v. Universal City Studios*, 464 U.S. 417, 442 (1984) ("Accordingly, the sale of copying equipment, like the sale of other articles of commerce, does not constitute contributory infringement if the product is widely used to legitimate, unobjectionable purpose. Indeed, it need merely be capable of substantial noninfringing uses.").

[45] H.R. Rep. No. 551 (Part 2), 105th Cong., 2d Sess. 39-40 (1998).

[46] 17 U.S.C. § 1201(b)(1) (Trafficking of a "technology, product, service, device, component, or part thereof," is prohibited if it meets the "circumventing" act: "primarily designed or produced for the purpose of circumventing protection afforded by a technological measure" (a primary purpose test), or has only a "limited commercially significant purpose or use other than to circumvent protection afforded by a technological protection measure" (secondary purpose test), or is "marketed . . . for use in circumventing protection afforded by a technological protection measure.").

[47] H.R. Rep. No. 551 (Part 2), 105th Cong., 2d Sess. 39 (1998).

[48] *United States v. Elcom Ltd.*, 203 F. Supp. 2d 1111, 1120 (N.D. Cal. 2002).

[49] 65 Fed. Reg. 64556, 64557 (October 27, 2000) (Final Rule: Exemption to Prohibition on Circumvention of Copyright Protection Systems for Access Control Technologies).

[50] *United States v. Elcom Ltd.*, 203 F. Supp. 2d 1111, 1125 (N.D. Cal. 2002).

[51] *Universal Studios, Inc. v. Corley*, 273 F.3d 429 (2d Cir. 2001) ("One example is that of a school child who wishes to copy images from a DVD movie to insert into the student's documentary film. We know of no authority for the proposition that fair use, as protected by the Copyright Act, much less the Constitution, guarantees copying by the optimum method or in the identical format of the original. Although the Appellants insisted at oral argument that they should not be relegated to a 'horse and buggy' technique in making fair use of DVD movies, [footnote omitted] *the DMCA does not impose even an arguable limitation on the opportunity to make a variety of traditional fair uses of DVD movies, such as commenting on their content, quoting excerpts from their screenplays, and even recording portions of the video images and sounds on film or tape by pointing a camera, a camcorder, or a microphone at a monitor as it displays the DVD movie.* The fact that the resulting copy will not be as perfect or as manipulable as a digital copy obtained by having direct access to the DVD movie in its digital form, provides no basis for a claim of unconstitutional limitation of fair use." Id. at 459.); *United States v. Elcom Ltd.*, 203 F. Supp. 2d 1111 (N.D. Cal. 2002) ("For example, nothing in the DMCA prevents anyone from quoting from a work or comparing texts for the purpose of study or criticism. It may be that from a technological perspective, the fair user my [sic] find it more difficult to do so—quoting may have to occur the old fashioned way, *by hand or by retyping*, rather than by 'cutting and pasting' from existing digital media. *Nevertheless, the fair use is still available.* Defendant has cited no authority which guarantees a fair user the right to the most technologically convenient way to engage in fair use." Id.

at 1131. "Publishing the public domain work in an electronic format with technologically imposed restrictions on how that particular copy of the work may be used does not give the publisher any legally enforceable right to the expressive work, even if it allows the publisher to control that particular copy." Id. at 1134.); *321 Studios v. Metro Goldwyn Mayer Studios, Inc.*, 307 F. Supp. 2d 1085 (N.D. Cal. 2004) ("Fair use is still possible under the DMCA, although such copying will not be as easy, as exact, or as digitally manipulable as plaintiff desires. Furthermore, as both *Corley* and *321* itself stated, users can copy DVDs, including any of the material on them that is unavailable elsewhere, by non-digital means." Id. at 1102.).

[52] See, e.g., Hearing, U.S. Senate, Committee on Governmental Affairs, Permanent Subcommittee on Investigations, September 30, 2003, on Privacy and Piracy: The Paradox of Illegal File Sharing on Peer-to-Peer Networks and the Impact of Technology on the Entertainment (Senate Hearing 108-275) ("In the real world, violations of copyright law over the Internet are so widespread and easy to accomplish that may participants seem to consider it equivalent to jaywalking—illegal but no big deal."), no pagination (Opening statement of Senator Levin) (available at *http://www.senate.gov/~gov_affairs/index.cfm?Fuseaction=Hearings.Testimony&TestimonyID=325&HearingID=120*). In re Charter Communication, 393 F.3d 771, 778 (8th Cir. 2005) (Murphy, J. dissenting) ("[T]he repercussions of infringement via the internet are too easily ignored or minimized. Regarded by some as an innocuous form of entertainment, internet piracy co copyrighted sound recordings results in substantial economic and artistic costs."). *In Re Aimster Copyright Litigation*, 334 F.3d 643, 645 (7th Cir. 2003) ("The swappers, who are ignorant or more commonly disdainful of copyright and in any event discount the likelihood of being sued or prosecuted for copyright infringement, are the direct infringers."); and *U.S. v. Elcom Ltd.*, 203 F. Supp. 2d 1111, 1132 (N.D. Cal. 2002) ("Congress certainly could have approached the problem by targeting the infringers, rather than those who traffic in the tools that enable the infringement to occur. However, it is already unlawful to infringe, yet piracy of intellectual property has reached epidemic proportions. Pirates are world-wide, and locating and prosecuting each could be both impossible and ineffective, as new pirates arrive on the scene. But, pirates and other infringers require tools in order to bypass the technological measures that protect against unlawful copying. Thus, targeting the tool sellers is a reasoned, and reasonably tailored, approach to 'remedying the evil' targeted by Congress.").

[53] H.R. Rep. No. 551 (Part 1), 105th Cong., 2d Sess. 18 (1998).

[54] Victor F. Calaba, Quibbles 'n Bits: Making a Digital First Sales Doctrine Feasible, 9 MICHIGAN TELECOMMUNICATIONS AND TECHNOLOGY LAW REVIEW 1, 20 (2002).

[55] Exemption to Prohibition on Circumvention of Copyright Protection Systems for Access Control Technologies, Final Rule, 68 Federal Register 62011, 62015-62016 (October 31, 2003) (amending 37 C.F.R. § 201.40) (proposed class 9: "The technology which deactivates the fast-forward function of DVD players (UOP blocking) does not appear to be an access control. Nor does the record show that the CSS, an access control used on motion pictures on DVDs, prevents the deactivation of UOP blocking. Therefore, an exemption

does not appear warranted since it does not appear that access controls are preventing users from fast-forwarding on DVDs."

[56] *Universal Studios, Inc. v. Corley*, 273 F.3d 429 (2d Cir. 2001) (motion picture studios place CSS encryption technology on DVDs to prevent the unauthorized viewing and copying of motion pictures).

[57] *Real Networks, Inc. v. Streambox, Inc.*, 2000 U.S. Dist. LEXIS 1889 (W.D. Wash. 2000) (preliminary injunction) (Findings of Fact 12: "The Secret Handshake is an authentication sequence which only RealServers and RealPlayers know. By design, unless this authentication sequence takes place, the RealServer does not stream the content it holds." Findings of Fact 14: "Through the use of the Secret Handshake and the Copy Switch, owners of audio and video content can prevent the unauthorized copying of their content if they so choose.").

[58] *Sony Computer Entertainment America Inc. v. Gamemasters, Inc.*, 87 F. Supp. 2d 976, 987 (N.D. Cal. 1999) ("Based upon the declarations before this Court, the Game Enhancer's distinguishing feature appears to be its ability to allow consumers to play import or non-territorial SCEA video games. As discussed above, SCEA specifically designed the PlayStation console to access only those games with data codes that match the geographical location of the game console itself. The Game Enhancer circumvents the mechanism on the PlayStation console that ensures the console operates only when encrypted data is read from an authorized CD-ROM. (Pltf's Reply at 7). Thus, at this stage, the Game Enhancer appears to be a device whose primary function is to circumvent.").

[59] 17 U.S.C. § 1201(d)(1).

[60] See, 17 U.S.C. § 1201(d)(4) ("This subsection may not be used as a defense to a claim under subsection (a)(2) or (b), nor may this subsection permit a nonprofit library, archives, or educational institution to manufacture, import, offer to the public, provide, or otherwise traffic in any technology, product, service, component, or part thereof, which circumvents a technological measure.").

[61] 17 U.S.C. § 1201(d)(5)(A) and (B) (emphasis added).

[62] 17 U.S.C. § 1201(d)(1)(A).

[63] 17 U.S.C. § 1201(d)(1) ("A nonprofit library, archives, or educational institution which gains access to a commercially exploited copyrighted work *solely* in order to make a good faith determination of whether to acquire a copy of that work for the sole purpose of engaging in conduct permitted under this title shall not be in violation of subsection (a)(1)(A)." (emphasis added)).

[64] 17 U.S.C. § 1201(d)(1)(B).

[65] 17 U.S.C. § 1201(d)(1).

[66] 17 U.S.C. § 1201(d)(2).

[67] See, *The Third Man* (50th Anniversary Edition), Criterion Collection (1949).

[68] *Blade Runner* (The Director's Cut) (1993).

[69] Senate Report 105-190, 105th Cong., 2d Sess. 31 (1998).

[70] 17 U.S.C. § 1201(d)(3)(A) and (B).

[71] H.R. Rep. No. 551 (Part 2), 105th Cong. 2d Sess. 42 (1998).

[72] S. Rep. No. 105-190, 105th Cong., 2d Sess. 31 (1998).

[73] But see, JAY DRATLER JR., CYBERLAW: INTELLECTUAL PROPERTY IN THE DIGITAL MILLENNIUM § 5.05[2], at 5-44 (2004) (In discussing the slightly different phrasing of the criminal provision of section 1204: "For all these reasons, the words 'commercial advantage or private financial gain' should be construed as requiring some evidence of business activity or motivation on the defendant's part. They should not be construed as applying simply because the defendant avoiding paying for a single or limited unauthorized use of a copyrighted work.").

[74] 17 U.S.C. § 1201(d)(3)(A).

[75] 17 U.S.C. § 1204(a) (a fine of up to $500,000 or 5 years imprisonment or both for the first offense, and up to $1,000,000 or up to 10 years imprisonment or both for a subsequent offense).

[76] JAY DRATLER, JR., CYBERLAW: INTELLECTUAL PROPERTY IN THE DIGITAL MILLENNIUM § 5.05[2], at 5-42 (2004) ("As a result, in most cases the very act of circumvention that creates civil liability ought, *ipso facto*, to satisfy the standards of acting 'willfully' for purposes of the criminal offense."). Nevertheless Dratler argues emphatically against associating every act of circumvention with a motive of "private financial gain." Id. at § 5.05[2], at 5-42-5-45. The "standard for *mens rea* if construed liberally, are likely to . . . bootstrap[] virtually every civil violation of the anti-circumvention rule into a federal felony." Id. at 5-42 (footnote omitted).

[77] 17 U.S.C. § 1204(a)(1) and (2). Emphasis added.

[78] 17 U.S.C. § 1201(d)(3)(B).

►Part IV

THREE WAYS LIBRARIES AND SCHOOLS CAN LIMIT THEIR EXPOSURE

►10

WHAT MUST BE DONE TO LEGALLY REPRODUCE AND DISTRIBUTE COPYRIGHTED MATERIALS IN THE LIBRARY?

Read this chapter to learn about copyright situations like:
► Whether including a legal warning on the order forms for an academic library's article reproduction service is sufficient to ward off liability.
► Whether knowledge that a copy made in the library will be used illegitimately makes a difference for purposes of immunity from liability.
► Whether a library can place interlibrary loan materials on open reserve.

Chapters 10, 11, and 12 do not discuss immunity or remission provisions per se, but they do pertain to significant elements of an institutional risk-management program in two related but distinct ways. First, these chapters focus on sections 108, 109, and 110 of the copyright law, respectively. These provisions allow uses of copyrighted material that might otherwise be infringing or would need to be qualified by the limits of the fair use privilege, by contract (license), or by permission from the copyright owner. In addition, these provisions, or at least some of the subsections of these provisions, are targeted specifically at the institutions that are the focus of this monograph—libraries, archives, and educational institutions. In exchange for these additional uses, rights, or privileges of use, the qualifying entity must do something in return—Congress seldom grants a copyright privilege for free, and that "something" is a focus of this book as well. That "something," or copyright quid pro quo, is the adoption of some compliance measure—a warning notice, a copyright policy, or a technological protection measure. As a result, the adoption of these measures in conformity with the commands of sections 108, 109, and 110 can contribute to a climate of compliance in the library, archives, or educational institution.

Section 108 is an important provision for the public library, school media center, college or university library or archives, or similar unit within the nonprofit educational organization, as it grants additional reproduction and distribution rights beyond that of fair use found in section 107.[1] Though not an "educator's" provision per se, nonetheless it operates in the educational environment as a significant limitation on the exclusive rights of copyright owners when it applies; faculty and students who use the institutional library often benefit from its privileges. Qualifying library or archives units within the organization can make and distribute copies of copyrighted material subject to the limitations of its operative subsections: preservation and security of unpublished works under 108(b), replacement of published works under 108(c), reproduction and distribution of articles or chapters of copyrighted material under 108(d), and entire or substantial portions of works under 108(e). In the former two subsections the copies become part of the library collection,[2] in the latter two subsections the copies become the property of the library patron.[3] A detailed discussion of these subsections is beyond the scope of this book.

The qualifying library or archives can make a copy of an article under section 108 for a student, faculty member, administrator, or other patron, as section 108(d) authorizes that reproduction, assuming compliance with the general provisions of section 108(a) (discussed in Chapter 5), specific provisions of 108(d) and the additional conditions set forth in (g) and (i). However, if the staff of the central principal's or provost's office made a copy of an article for a student, faculty member, or administrator, the copying would need to conform with the general concepts of fair use, as such copying would not be a library or archive reproduction and distribution contemplated by the plain language of section 108. Again, section 108 is a library and archive provision, *not* an educator's provision, and it is not applicable to the institution in general.

BACKGROUND

In the case of copies provided to patrons under subsections (d)(1) and (e)(1), from the library or archive to the patron, both subsections further require that the library or archives through it employees must exist in a negative state of grace, so to speak; there must be "no notice that the copy or phonorecord would be used for any purpose other than private study, scholarship, or research."[4] The legislative history is silent as to what would constitute such notice. Looking to the concept of knowledge in copyright liability in general might help administrators understand what would be a legitimate absence of that notice under 108(d)(1) or (e)(1), or help them identify what inquiry, if any, is required to satisfy the section 108(d)(1) and (e)(1) notice. As discussed in Chapters 2 and 7, the general "mens rea" or "scienter" of contributory copyright infringement might be characterized as a "know or reason to know" standard; it is not a "should have known" standard, i.e., there is no obligation to ascertain the existence or absence of facts which would tend to prove or disprove the supposition. As discussed below, this concept is woven into the fabric of section 108 as well.

Subsection 108(i) also indicates that the patron copying provision cannot apply to a "musical work, a pictorial, graphic or sculptural work, or a motion picture or other audiovisual work other than an audiovisual work dealing with news."[5] However, "pictorial or graphic works published as illustrations, diagrams, or similar adjuncts" to a work are acceptable. An example would be the separately copyrighted photographs that are reproduced when the qualifying library reproduces the article (and its accompanying photographs) for interlibrary loan or as part of its patron photocopy services.

Subsection 108(i) is also the reason that VHS, DVD, or other audiovisual recordings are not the subject of interlibrary loan (ILL), that is, ILL done through library reproduction of the tape and its subsequent distribution. To be sure, such items can be the subject of circulation or loan by the library, either to the library's own patron or to the patron of another library in an ILL transaction, but these acts do not involve making a copy of the work, rather the work itself is circulated or loaned. In other words, section 108(i) prohibits the library or archive from making a copy (reproduction) of the VHS tape (or any other audiovisual work, as well as any other type of copyrighted listed in the sub (i) proviso) and lending that copy through interlibrary loan (distribution under section 108). The lawful circulation (distribution) of the original tape through ILL mechanisms does not rest in section 108, but rather in section 109, discussed in Chapter 11.

According to a leading judicial interpretation, contributory copyright infringement occurs when "one who, with knowledge of the infringing activity, induces or causes, or materially contributes to the infringement of another."[6] Arguably, direct infringement by patrons is what the section 108 copyright warning notice provisions, discussed below, are trying to prevent. Thus, some burden on the intermediary institutional library or archives not to contribute to the direct infringement of others is a subsidiary goal of section 108. Observe the difference in scienter of "use" or subsequent activity between contributory infringement (a concept of liability) and section 108 (a concept of qualification). Does the library have this notice: "knowledge of the infringing activity" versus knowledge, or a reason to know that works reproduced or distributed under section 108(d)(1) or (e)(1) would be used for purposes "other than [those] of private study, scholarship, or research"? In the latter section 108 scienter scenario, other private uses could indeed be lawful (noninfringing) or public uses of study, scholarship, or research. Why the different, arguably more limiting use standard in section 108(d) and (e)? One possible answer is that because section 108 is not designed as a liability provision it confers additional use rights upon its participants. Therefore it is proper to restrict downstream (from the library's perspective) uses to which a patron may put the work reproduced and distributed to a smaller subset of uses, though nonetheless within a larger set of possible lawful uses.

Library Reserve Systems and the Law

Consider a situation where an instructor tells a librarian of an intended subsequent nonprivate use, beyond the statutory obligation of section 108(d) and (c), where other circumstances suggest that likely possibility ("reason to know")? For example, a physics professor asks how to place some articles on reserve for an upcoming unit on strong and weak forces. The list happens to match exactly a list of recent interlibrary loan requests by that faculty member. The distribution of multiple copies (or even a single copy, for that matter) of the ILL article to a physics class would be a public distribution; that is *not* a use consistent with private study, scholarship, or research. Regardless of whether the use would be fair under section 107, that use would be beyond that contemplated by section 108(d)(1) or (e)(1). When combined with the triggering statutory "notice" on the part of the library, a drastic turn of events can result. If the library had been made aware of this nonprivate use, the reproduction through the interlibrary loan process and the distribution of the items to the faculty member would not have been "authorized" under section 108, as it could be argued that the library through its librarian or staff assistant would have had notice that the interlibrary loan copies made under section 108(d) and distributed to the patron would be for a nonprivate use, i.e., a public distribution or display in the classroom or on e-reserve. Such public distribution or display would be beyond the qualifying language of section 108(d)(1) and (e)(1): "any purpose other than private study, scholarship, or research."

In the electronic age, the production of coursepacks is still a common and lucrative practice, even by some legitimate enterprises.[7] The publishing industry continues to pursue legal action against producers of unauthorized coursepacks.[8] E-coursepacks would fall into the same legal result as traditional coursepacks.[9] The question is whether a reserve or e-reserve system is less or more like a coursepack for which authorization is required. Arguably, a traditional reserve system, whereby students can read copyrighted material and make copies of their own volition, violates no law, as the public distribution of that material through the reserve system is within the section 109 right of public distribution, discussed in Chapter 11. However, the industry believes that an e-reserve system, where electronic materials are substitutes for textbooks and where students have the ability to reproduce the entire set of readings with ease, is little different from the clandestine coursepack of old. As Harvard Law School Professor Zittrain explains: "Creating electronic reserves may seem like only a difference in degree of accessibility, but the publishers will point out that the creation necessarily entails the making of copies, for which fair use is an uncertain defense."[10] Thus far, the industry has taken a hard stance against the use of course packs.

The Association of American Publishers is now taking its fight from the for-profit copy shops and for-profit corporate libraries to the nonprofit universities and questioning the e-reserve practices that many institutions have taken for granted.[11] Mr. Alder, vice president for legal and governmental affairs, Association of American Publishers, stated: "We are finding that far from being supplemental reading or additional reading supplied by the teacher, in many classes now it is becoming the required reading and the only reading."[12] In short, the industry recognizes little difference between e-reserves and coursepacks. The *Kinkos'* and *Michigan Document Services, Inc.* decisions support the illegality of coursepacks when the readings included in the coursepacks represent more than a significant percentage of the total pages of a work from which the excerpt is taken or done without permission or proper authorization from the copyright owner.

In addition, because general concepts of knowledge in copyright law do not impose a should-have-known standard (i.e., a duty to investigate every use), a section 108 library or archives would not typically be required to inquire what patrons plan to do with a copy of material made for them under subsection (d) or (e). Consider this example: a patron of a section 108 library (a college or university library, for example) makes 30 copies of an article received from the library's interlibrary loan or photocopy service. She then distributes them to colleagues at the administrative offices of the provost (arguably an infringing reproduction and distribution). Assume the other notice requirements discussed below are followed, but the patron gave the library no indication ("no notice") of the subsequent multiple copying and distribution nor did any circumstances suggest this result ("reason to know"). There is no limitation on the use of section 108 to support the reproduction and distribution of the initial copy by the library to the patron, say the vice-provost for academic affairs. Of course this does not mean that because the initial copying was acceptable, all later uses (making of the 30 copies) cannot be found infringing; quite the contrary, as discussed in Part I. The patron who made the multiple copies would be the direct infringer and the institution might share in the infringement vicariously; however, the institution's liability would not derive from the library but rather from the patron's status as employee.

However, such repeated practice might eventually come to the attention of the library employee. For example, the articles that a particular administrator requests be acquired through interlibrary loan or copied through the library's photocopying service[13] always seem to appear in multiple forms ("other than private study, scholarship, or research.") In possession of such knowledge, the library copy so reproduced and distributed would no longer meet the section 108(d) or (e) requirements. Either permission should then be sought for such reproduction and a fair-use analysis undertaken to justify the copying, or the administrator should be informed that the campus library is no longer able to obtain copies of articles for use under these circumstances. Again, the provisions under section 108 do not create additional liability or prohibition per se, but operate as a qualification mechanism to grant or deny the additional use rights the statute articulates.[14] In this way, conformity with the section 108(d)(1) and (e)(1) notice proviso can actually assist in limiting the possibility of infringing downstream uses of copyrighted material.

Triggering the "no notice" Proviso

The Section 108(d)(1) and (e)(1) "no notice of other than private study, scholarship or research" rule adds an additional twist to the general knowledge requirement (or more precisely, the lack of knowledge requirement) in contributory infringement, arguably restricting the range of downstream uses that can be made of section 108 copies, and it is arguably a more restrictive rule than would otherwise exist under general concepts of contributory liability. Again, the point is that the copyright law giveth and the law taketh away. While section 108 offers expanded rights of reproduction and distribution to the library of the nonprofit educational institution, it also arguably creates a narrower set of circumstances of use than if the library and its parent institution relied on fair use under section 107 and on basic concepts of responsibility for downstream or subsequent uses and the liability that could result from such a use as the courts have articulated. But this is the legal trade-off, the return for the increased reproduction and distribution rights of section 108. The advantage for the library and the educational institution is the certainty and definiteness built into the section 108 compliance structure rather than the fuzzy, four-factor fair-use test of section 107.[15]

The impact of this restriction (the "had no notice that the copy or phonorecord would be used for any purpose other than private study, scholarship, or research" language) can best be viewed through an example. Suppose a student made a photocopy of a magazine article or videotaped a television show (a so-called off-the-air taping), then proceeded either to make multiple copies of the article for distribution to the class or to show (perform) the video to the class as part of a term paper or project presentation. The initial single article or time-shifted videotape are likely fair uses.[16] Moreover, commentators would like to believe that, under certain circumstances, such multiple reproduction and distribution or public performance would also be lawful.[17] Such use is also suggested by the so-called educational fair use guidelines.[18] However, depending on the circumstances, either subsequent use (multiple copying and distribution in class or performance of off-the-air tape) might also be an infringing use.[19] While these uses are "other than" for "private study, scholarship, or research," section 108 imposes no impediment to the use of copies or the videotape in the classroom by the student because the library was not the source-making entity of the copy; the student made the copies.

Moreover, even if the student went to the school library or media center and made the copies, the library might not be a contributory infringer, as the underlying copying or the subsequent multiple copies for classroom use or public performance in the classroom (the alleged underlying direct infringement) may or may not indeed be infringing, and without a direct infringement there can be no secondary liability. Even if there were a direct infringement in the use of the reproducing equipment, a subsequent provision of section 108, 108(f)(1) discussed in detail in Chapter 5, immunizes the library or its employees from such claims for the use of unsupervised reproducing equipment by third parties.

Observe the difference in analysis when the initial article reproduction is a section 108 reproduction and distribution. (The example of the off-air taping is not used as section 108(1) prohibits subsections (d) and (e) from applying to audiovisual works.)[20] Suppose now that the library reproduced and distributed the article as part of its photocopy service under section 108(d)(1) or (e)(1). Then the "other than private study, scholarship, or research" use clause prevents the library from exercising its privilege under section 108. This is not because of the operation of principles of contributory infringement, as such article distribution or video performance can be a lawful use; rather, the initial reproduction and distribution is precluded because of the "private study, scholarship, or research" proviso of section 108(d)(1) and (e)(1), and as such the initial reproductions would be unsupportable, at least under section 108, though they might be acceptable under section 107. This also, of course, assumes that, in this scenario and the other disqualifying scenarios discussed earlier, the library and its librarian or other staff member had some notice (actual or constructive knowledge, the know or reason to know standard) of the subsequent section 108(d)(1) and (e)(1) prohibited use.

REQUIRED COPYRIGHT WARNING NOTICE IN CONJUNCTION WITH INTERLIBRARY LOAN AND LIBRARY REPRODUCTION SERVICES

A second notice provision is also contained in 108(d)(2) and (e)(2). Recall that these two subsections require that the copies made by the library "become[] the property of the user" and that the reproduction and distribution can be made only if the library has "no notice that the copy would be used for any purpose other than private study, scholarship or research." Again, potential infringing uses made by patrons do not necessarily factor into the analysis. Rather, inquiry is into whether the use falls into one of the three private uses articulated in the statute, regardless of whether it would be a lawful use or not. However, in order to ensure that section 108 libraries do not become the source of material for later infringements, subsections (d)(2) and (e)(2) require that "the library or archives displays prominently, at the place where orders are accepted, and includes on its order form, a warning of copyright in accordance with requirements that the Register of Copyrights shall prescribe by regulation." Such warning must be displayed at the place where "orders are accepted," such as the interlibrary loan office or the photocopy service desk and on any forms such departments use.

The text of the notice is precisely prescribed by regulation:[21]

> NOTICE WARNING CONCERNING COPYRIGHT RESTRICTIONS. The copyright law of the United States (Title 17, United States Code) governs the making of photocopies or other reproductions of copyrighted material. Under certain conditions specified in the law, libraries and archives are authorized to furnish a photocopy or other reproduction. One of these specific conditions is that the photocopy or reproduction is not to be "used for any purpose other than private study, scholarship, or research." If a user makes a request for, or later uses, a photocopy or reproduction for purposes in excess of "fair use," that user may be liable for copyright infringement. This institution reserves the right to refuse to accept a copying order if, in its judgment, fulfillment of the order would involve violation of copyright law.[22]

The form and manner of the notice is also detailed and requires that it be on at least one sign in the service area[23] and on the form itself, highlighted in a box on the front page of the form or near the signature line of the patron-requester.[24] It could be argued that having the patron read and sign the warning notice containing the private use language equates to the library having no notice of "other than private study, scholarship, or research." The notice must appear on all forms used and the patron must use such form; therefore, by logic, patrons should be making such assertion (signature statement) with each request that is made. The implementing regulation indicates that "[a]s required by those sections the 'Order Warning of Copyright' *is to be included* on printed forms supplied by certain libraries and archives *and used by their patrons for* ordering copies or phonorecords."[25]

The author respectfully submits that blind adherence to form (patron's signed assertion) over substance (knowledge to the contrary) goes only so far in the copyright law. Consider the comment of Judge Posner in the *Aimster* litigation: "Willful blindness is knowledge, in copyright law (where indeed it may be enough that the defendant should have known of the direct infringement [citation omitted]), as it is in the law generally."[26] How far could this "no notice" envelope be pushed? What are its logical limits?

It could be argued that the copyright warning notice and patron-requester signature required by section 108(d)(2) and (e)(2) provisos allow the library and its employees to take the patron, faculty member, or student at his or word, that the use would not be for anything "other than private study, scholarship, or research." But that approach would allow the library, its employees, and the institution to hide behind the form (and in this case the actual signed interlibrary loan or photocopying request form) and ignore the substance of the transaction. In a case involving secondary liability though not a section 108 situation, recent precedent has treated this sort of "look the other way" mentality with legal disdain and judicial admonishment.[27] Again, this analysis would apply only in those instances where the library through its employees was aware ("notice" under section 108(d)(1) and (e)(1) standard as explained above) of a subsequent nonprivate use in spite of a signed assertion to the contrary by the patron. However, if, as discussed above, the library was in fact aware (actual or constructive knowledge) of such uses "other than private study, scholarship, or research," patron signature to the contrary, legal logic as well as professional ethics would suggest that the library could not hide behind the subterfuge of such a formalization as a mere signature on a piece of paper. The notice and signature mechanism of section 108(d)(2) and (e)(2) stands for the proposition that, as with the law of contributory liability, there exists no duty to investigate or monitor or otherwise check up on the signed assertion of subsequent use by a faculty member, student, or administrator.

The author's point is that, should the library or its employees become aware of such prohibited downstream uses, the section 108(d)(1) and (e)(1) private use prohibition rule would be triggered, in spite of the signed statement to the contrary. Such awareness might also raise an ethical issue regarding the conduct of the patron, who made an affidavit (signed statement) of intended use contrary to the actual use. (The discussion of ethical issues in copyright, however, is beyond the scope of this monograph.) The library and its employees could not ignore obvious facts and circumstances contrary to such a signature.

REQUIRED COPYRIGHT WARNING NOTICE FOR REPRODUCTION EQUIPMENT: A REVIEW

The reader might be surprised by the minutiae of detail regarding the content and form of the notice imposed by the U.S. Copyright Office under section 108(d)(2) and (e)(2) for interlibrary loan or a library copying service. However, regarding a third and final notice provision of section 108, one that protects the library against copyright infringement that might arise vis-à-vis the direct infringement committed by patrons using unsupervised reproducing equipment, the Copyright Office offers no assistance as to content or form. In the earlier example, what if the student made his multiple copies or off-the-air taping with the library photocopier or library VCR? If it was later found that the reproduction of the articles or taping was unlawful, could the library face a claim of contributory copyright infringement? Though no library staff member made the photocopies or off-the-air tape, the library or archives did provide the means (the photocopier, printer, or VCR, or other reproducing technology, for that matter). Is this problematic in light of secondary copyright principles discussed in Chapter 2? No, because section 108(f)(1) states that "Nothing in this section . . . shall be construed to impose liability for copyright infringement upon a library or archives or its employees for the unsupervised use of reproducing equipment located on its premises: Provided, That such equipment displays a notice that the making of a copy may be subject to the copyright law." This is an important grant of immunity to section 108 libraries against the worries of downstream infringement by library patrons, vis-à-vis the re-production of copyrighted material through the misuse of reproducing equipment. Observe also that section 108(f)(1) says nothing of other employees of the institution. Suppose that the patron is a faculty member or administrator who uses library reproducing equipment to make infringing copies. In theory, the (f)(1) immunity would extend to the "library or archives or its employees," but the institution as a whole would not escape liability, as the principles of vicarious liability would operate to impute liability from the direct infringement of the faculty member or administrator as employee to the institution as a whole. This analysis should remind readers that the library is just one part of an overall risk-management process and program. According to the authors of the infamous White Paper on intellectual property reform, regarding the section 108(f)(1) provision, "no other provider of equipment enjoys any statutory immunity."[28] As no notice-fulfilling section 108(f)(1) posting obligation is offered by the U.S. Copyright Office, use of the following text, adapted from the section 108(d) and (e), 37 C.F.R. § 201.14 notice, is possible:

> NOTICE WARNING CONCERNING COPYRIGHT RESTRICTIONS. The copyright law of the United States (Title 17, United States Code) governs the making of photocopies or other reproductions of copyrighted material. Libraries and archives furnish unsupervised photocopy or other reproduction equipment for the convenience of and use by patrons. Under 17 U.S.C. § 108(f)(2) the provision of unsupervised photocopy or reproduction equipment for use by patrons does not excuse the person who uses the reproduction equipment from liability for copyright infringement for any such act, or for any later use of such copy or phonorecord, if it exceeds fair use as provided by section 107 or any other provision of the copyright law. This institution reserves the right to refuse to make available or provide access to photocopy or other reproduction equipment if, in its judgment, use of such equipment would involve violation of copyright law.

Such a notice should be placed on all pieces of equipment in the library that are patron-accessible and that are capable of reproducing copyrighted material—not just the photocopier but the computer, printer, scanner, sampler, VCR, or any other equipment that has a reproducing capacity. (A generic warning notice, sans the section 108(f)(2) patron language, can be used on other photocopiers and reproduction equipment accessible by staff, as the library is not protected under section 108 for their acts of infringement.[29] Such an employee-oriented warning notice either can be required by other provisions of the copyright law, as discussed in Chapter 12, or can serve a valuable purpose in the overall risk management and compliance endeavors of the institution.[30])

In return for the display of a copyright warning notice, no liability for contributory or other copyright infringement relating to the infringement committed by patrons (students or other members of the public) for the unsupervised use of photocopy or other reproducing equipment shall be imposed upon the library or its employees. It is necessary for the statute to extend this protection to the library because it offers technologies capable of infringement such as the photocopier and to an employee because he or she may engage in conduct that might be infringing under principles of secondary liability as discussed in Chapters 2 and 3 by demonstrating and encouraging students to download pirated music from the Internet, for example. Both activities can "lead to contributory liability []: (i) personal conduct that encourages or assists the infringement; and (ii) provision of machinery or goods that facilitate the infringement."[31]

Section 108(f)(1) does not offer immunity, however, for other acts of infringement unrelated to the use of photocopying or other reproduction equipment, e.g., allowing a public performance of a video in the library to the French Club with the use of the library VCR or DVD player. This would be an issue of the performance right of copyright owners, not the exclusive reproduction or distribution rights that section 108 addresses. Arguably, as noted earlier, section 108 does not apply to a library staff member or other employee as a direct infringer—such infringement is then imputed to the employer-institution under vicarious liability standards. (As discussed in Chapter 5, employees are considered to be supervised and so would not meet the section 108(f)(1) requirement of "unsupervised use of photocopy or other reproducing equipment.") Finally, as incorporated into the sample section 108(f)(1) warning notice discussed above, under section 108(f)(2), the student or other third-party patron such as a community member is not relieved from liability for downstream abuses of the copyright law.[32]

REAL-WORLD EXAMPLES

▶ Real-World Example I

Situation: A library in an educational institution offers an article reproducing service for faculty. Following the instructions provided by the U.S. Copyright Office, the library posts a sign near where copying orders are taken and includes a similar notice on the form patrons fill out when making their requests. Faculty members sign the form attesting that the copy will not be "used for any purpose other than private study, scholarship, or research."

Legal Analysis: While at times this reproduction and distribution of periodical literature might be in excess of fair use, section 108 gives qualifying libraries and archives the right to reproduce and distribute such works without fear of copyright liability.

▶ Real-World Example II

Situation: The situation is the same as in Real-World Example I, except that instead of a reproducing service the library offers a self-service copy area. In one instance an educator proceeds to copy an entire workbook for each student in a particular class, in another instance a student proceeds to make a copy of a companion exercise book for each classmate in a particular class.

Legal Analysis: First, the section 108(f)(1) immunity by statutory limitation applies to the "library or archives or its employees," not to other employees of the institution. Second, even if it could be said that the educator was an employee of the library the immunity would not apply to the reproductions made by the educator as the educator is an employee of the library and as such the educator-employee is supervised, thus subsection (f)(1) does not apply. Under section 108(f)(1) the library is not insulated from the acts of employees, as such conduct is supervised in contravention of the (f)(1) requirement that it be "unsupervised." However, the immunity would apply to the instance of student or other third-party copying. Section 108(f)(2) indicates that individuals such as students or patrons (in the case of public library reproductions) remain liable for any infringement resulting from the reproduction.

▶ **Real-World Example III**

Situation: The situation is the same as in Real-World Example I. One faculty member indicates in no uncertain terms to the librarian at the library service desk where the reproducing request is submitted that she intends to make multiple copies of the article for students or to place a copy of the article on the class Web site for use with an upcoming lecture.

Legal Analysis: Under section 108, in spite of the faculty member's signature attestation to the contrary, use of the material as a source of multiple copies for classroom use (a public distribution under the *Hotaling v. Church of Latter Day Saints*[33] decision) or posting on a Web site (public display) are clearly **not** for purposes of "private study, scholarship, or research." As opposed to use for lesson planning or in the preparation of a literature review for an upcoming project. Therefore the library could not look to section 108 for support in making this reproduction or distribution. This is true in spite of the fact that many uses other than for private study, scholarship or research would indeed be fair use. Section 108(f)(1) offers a higher, more exacting standard. Moreover, under the regulation warning notice, the library would be within its rights to refuse to make and distribute this copy: "This institution reserves the right to refuse to accept a copying order if, in its judgment, fulfillment of the order would involve violation of copyright law."

▶ **Real-World Example IV**

Situation: A library in a college setting receives a request for several reserve items it does not have in its collection. The interlibrary loan (ILL) librarian proceeds to request the articles from another library within its acquisitions consortium and places the items on reserve as each is received.

Legal Analysis: While some reserve use might ultimately be fair under section 107 (the determination depends on application and analysis of the four fair use factors applied to each item), section 108 offers no support for the requested reproduction and eventual distribution and or display. Section 108(d), the provision used to support article reproduction and distribution to patrons (i.e., ILL) does not anticipate collection building, and section 108(b) and (c) address the limited circumstances where reproduced material is added to the collection (i.e., preservation or security and replacement of "damaged, deteriorating, lost, or stolen" items or where "the existing format in which the work is stored has become obsolete"). As with Real-World Example III, the "no notice that the copy or phonorecord would be used for any purpose other than private study, scholarship, or research" section 108(d)(1) proviso would not be met.

KEY POINTS FOR YOUR INSTITUTION'S POLICY AND PRACTICE

▶ When copyrighted material is reproduced by the library or archives and distributed to patrons under section 108, the statute requires that the library or archives must have "had no notice that the copy or phonorecord would be used for any purpose other than private study, scholarship, or research." See pp. 304–309.

▶ The statute also requires that the library or archives displays prominently, at the place where orders are accepted, and includes on its order form, a warning of copyright in accordance with requirements that the Register of Copyrights shall prescribe by regulation. The warning notice must be displayed at the place where "orders are accepted" such as the interlibrary loan office or the photocopy service desk and on any forms such departments use. Federal regulation prescribes the precise text of the notice. Patrons are required to sign an attestation that their use will not be for any other purpose. See pp. 309–311.

▶ The notice and signature mechanism of the statute and regulation does not mean that there exists a duty to investigate or monitor or otherwise check up on the subsequent use by a patron, faculty member, student or administrator. If, however, staff were aware (actual or constructive knowledge) of uses "other than private study, scholarship, or research," both legal logic and professional ethics would suggest that the library could not hide behind the patron's signature. See pp. 309–311.

▶ If the library suspects that a use will be for purposes other than private study, scholarship, or research, the library may refuse to make reproduction and distribution to the patron. The warning notice prescribed by regulation informs the patron of the reservation of this right of refusal. See pp. 309–311.

ENDNOTES

[1] Regardless of the particular provision of the law under discussion, section 107 fair use may always be applied to a given scenario; in fact, section 108(f)(4) codifies this concept in specific for section 108: "Nothing in this section . . . in any way affects the right of fair use as provided by section 107, or any contractual obligations assumed at any time by the library or archives when it obtained a copy or phonorecord of a work in its collections."

[2] There is a three-copy limit on the total number of copies that can be made, digital or otherwise, under 108(b) and (c). Digitalization is allowed but copies must be for in-house use only: under 108(b) "any such copy or phonorecord that is reproduced in digital format is *not otherwise distributed* in that format and is not made available to the public in that format outside the premises of the library or archives" (emphasis added) and under 108(c) "any such copy or phonorecord that is reproduced in digital format is not made available to the public in that format outside the premises of the library or archives in lawful possession of such copy." If a digital copy of an unpublished work is made and then transferred to another university for "deposit or research" under 108(b), the copy cannot be available in a digital format but must be printed out for use by patrons of that library. The print copy could of course circulate, as no such limitation exists. This is the interpretation Dwayne K. Butler and Kenneth D. Crews, have assigned to the "not otherwise distributed in that format" language of 108(b). Dwayne K. Butler and Kenneth D. Crews, Copyright Protection and Technological Reform of Library Services: Digital Change, Practical Application and Congressional Action, in LIBRARIES, MUSEUMS, AND ARCHIVES: LEGAL ISSUES AND ETHICAL CHALLENGES IN THE NEW INFORMATION ERA 257, 268 (Tomas A. Lipinski, ed. 2001) ("This language suggests that the restriction applies to *further* distribution of the digital copy beyond the distribution occurring when it is transferred from one library to another. . . . By this construction, a library could therefore make a transfer of a digital copy to the receiving library. That initial transfer is not an *additional distribution* implied in the work 'otherwise.'" (emphasis original) Arguably, an on-campus limitation whereby the digital material would be accessible on the university LAN or Intranet would not be acceptable either, as this would still be outside the physical premises of the library. The point Butler and Crews make is that in order to facilitate transfer to another library under the section 108(b) "for deposit or research use" proviso, is that a digital copy could be the vehicle of that transfer. A public library or university library, for example, that makes a digital copy for its own collection under either section 108(b) or (c), is faced with the same on-premises limitation as well, due to the "not made available to the public in that format outside the premise of the library or archives" proviso of section 108(b)(2) and 108(c)(2). The legislative history of the digital copying provision of section 108, added by the Digital Millennium Copyright Act, Pub. L. No. 105-304, Title IV, sec.

404, 112 Stat. 2860, 2889-2890 (1998) (codified at 17 U.S.C. § 108), indicates that Congress was concerned with infringement vis-à-vis the proliferation of digital libraries: "Although online interactive digital networks have since given birth to online digital 'libraries' and 'archives' that exist only in the virtual (rather than physical) sense on Web sites, bulletin boards and home pages across the Internet, it is not the Committee's intent that section 108 as revised apply to such collections of information. . . . The extension of the application of Section 108 to all such sites is tantamount to creating an exception to the exclusive rights of copyright holders that would permit any person who has an online Web site, bulletin boards, or a home page to freely reproduce and distribute copyrighted works. Such an exemption would swallow the general rule and severely impair the copyright owner's right and ability to commercially exploit their copyrighted works." Thus an on-premises library or archives use of a section 108(b) or (c) digital copy is the rule.

[3] Section 108(d)(1) and (e)(1) both contain the following requirement on the reproduction and distribution of copyrighted material for patron use: "the copy or phonorecord becomes the property of the user."

[4] 17 U.S.C. § 108(d)(1) and (e)(1).

[5] 17 U.S.C. § 108(i).

[6] *Gershwin Publishing Corp. v. Columbia Artists Management, Inc.*, 443 F.2d 11 59, 1162 (2d Cir. 1971).

[7] See, Kinko's Re-enters Coursepack Market: Copy Shop Vows to Comply with all Copyright Laws, PUBLISHERS WEEKLY, September 22, 2003, at p. 9 ("The 1991 settlement, in which Kinko's paid publishers $1,875,000, prohibited Kinko's from supplying coursepacks for 10 years."); Kinko's Launches New Course Pack Business 10 years After Exiting the Business Behind a Lawsuit, EDUCATIONAL MARKETER, October 6, 2003 ("Course packs are customized compilations of materials the college use to supplement textbooks and are part of the $600 million custom publishing segment, one of the fastest-growing segments in the college market.").

[8] Major Publishers File Copyright Infringement Suit Against Collegiate Copies, BUSINESS WIRE, July 8, 2003 ("Collegiate Copies provides coursepacks to local universities in Indiana, including Indiana University at Bloomington. The contents of a typical coursepack include journal articles, excerpts from books, and other printed materials, selected by the instructor of a course as required reading for that course. The copy shop obtains copies of the books and other material in the syllabus from a library, copies the portions identified by the instructor, and binds large numbers of them for students' use. The copy shop then sells these coursepacks to students at a profit."); Five Major Publishers Announce Settlement in Copyright Infringement Suit Against Collegiate Copies, BUSINESS WIRE, November 3, 2003; Elsevier, MIT Press and John Wiley & Sons Settle Copyright Infringement Suit against Custom Copies, Inc., BUSINESS WIRE, July 14, 2003 ("The publishers' complaint, filed in Gainsville last October, alleged that Custom Copies was producing coursepacks for sale near the University of Florida campus in Gainesville without authorization from the publishers which hold the rights to the coursepack content.").

[9] Publishers Settle Suit Over Course Packs, THE CHRONICLE OF HIGHER EDUCATION, April 9, 2004, at 34 ("Six leading academic publishers hae reached an ou-of-court settlement with a copy-shop owner in Austin, Texas, whom the publishers accused of selling course materials online in violation of copyright law. . . . A service run by Mr. Odunsi created electronic versions of course packs without the permission of the publishers or their licensing agent. . . . The course packs, called NetPaks, were sold to students at the University of Texas at Austin.").

[10] As quoted in Marty Graham, Sides Clash Over Online Library: University's 'Electronic Reserve' Alarms Publishers, THE NATIONAL LAW JOURNAL, April 25, 2005, at 4.

[11] Scott Carlson, Legal Battle Brews Over Text on Electronic Reserve at U of California Libraries, THE CHRONICLE OF HIGHER EDUCATION, April 7, 2005.

[12] As quoted in, Scott Carlson, Legal Battle Brews Over Text on Electronic Reserve at U of California Libraries, THE CHRONICLE OF HIGHER EDUCATION, April 7, 2005. See also, Marty Graham, Sides Clash Over Online Library: University's 'Electronic Reserve' Alarms Publishers, THE NATIONAL LAW JOURNAL, April 25, 2005, at 4 ("When we obtained the university reading list for two terms, we found a number of things that could not be justified under the most extreme definition of fair use." Comment of Allan Adler.).

[13] Subject to the no notice of other uses proviso under discussion, this copying is also allowed by section 108(d) as long as the copy "becomes the property of the user"; the source of the copy can be the library's own collection, or, more typically, it can come from another library through interlibrary loan. As a practical matter, most college and university libraries exercise their section 108 rights in the latter capacity rather than the former for fear that it become a glorified "kinkos," i.e., a photocopying service for faculty and students. Most public or tertiary institutional libraries simply do not want to function as a copying service, though section 108 would allow such reproductions subject to its limitations.

[14] Where the qualification is not made and the benefit denied recourse would need to be made to a general notion of fair use under section 107 or authorization from the copyright owner or secure of reproduction, display, and distribution rights through contract, i.e., a license, or pay for the right to make that additional use.

[15] A discussion of fair use in the library or educational setting is beyond the scope of this article. A brief discussion is found in, KENNETH A. CREWS, COPYRIGHT LAW FOR LIBRARIANS AND EDUCATORS 48-76 (2000); and a detailed account, as applied to the networked environment is found in TOMAS A. LIPINSKI, LIBRARIAN'S GUIDE TO COPYRIGHT FOR SHARED AND NETWORKED RESOURCES, 2002 (American Library Association TechSource: Library Technology Reports. The text of section 107, indicating the four fair use factors, is as follows: "Notwithstanding the provisions of sections 106 and 106A, the fair use of a copyrighted work, including such use by reproduction in copies or phonorecords or by any other means specified by that section, for purposes such as criticism, comment, news reporting, teaching (including multiple copies for classroom use), scholarship, or research, is not an infringement of copyright. In determining whether the use made of a work in any particular case is a fair use the factors to be considered shall

include—(1) the purpose and character of the use, including whether such use is of a commercial nature or is for nonprofit educational purposes; (2) the nature of the copyrighted work; (3) the amount and substantiality of the portion used in relation to the copyrighted work as a whole; and (4) the effect of the use upon the potential market for or value of the copyrighted work. The fact that a work is unpublished shall not itself bar a finding of fair use if such finding is made upon consideration of all the above factors. 17 U.S.C. § 107.

[16] See, *U.S. v. Elcom Ltd.*, 203 F. Supp. 2d 1111, 1135 (N.D. Cal. 2002) ("Making a back-up copy of an ebook, for personal noncommercial use would likely be upheld as a non-infringing use, [however] there is as yet *no generally recognized right to make a copy of a protected work*, regardless of its format, for personal noncommercial use." (emphasis added)). See also, *Sony Corp. of America, Inc. v. Universal City Studios*, 464 U.S. 417, 456 (1984) ("In summary, the record and findings of the District Court lead us to two conclusions. First, Sony demonstrated a significant likelihood that substantial numbers of copyright holders who license their works for broadcast on free television would not object to having their broadcasts time-shifted by private viewers. And second, respondents failed to demonstrate that time-shifting would cause any likelihood of nonminimal harm to the potential market for, or the value of, their copyrighted works. The Betamax is, therefore, capable of substantial noninfringing uses. Sony's sale of such equipment to the general public does not constitute contributory infringement of respondent's copyrights."). See also, Derek J. Schaffner, The Digital Millennium Copyright Act: Overextension Of Copyright 14 CORNELL JOURNAL OF LAW AND PUBLIC POLICY 145, 166 (2004) ("In *Sony*, the Court touched upon the use of a VCR to fast forward through commercials but did not issue a direct opinion on the matter, and instead held that personal 'time-shifting' of commercial network television programs was permissible under fair use.").

[17] See, e.g., MARGARET-ANN F. HOWIE, COPYRIGHT ISSUES IN SCHOOLS (1997), discussing multiple copying in education at 2:6-2:7 and off-air taping at 2:8-2:9, but basing interpretation of law based on the fair use guidelines; and similar interpretation in, CAROL SIMPSON, COPYRIGHT FOR SCHOOLS: A PRACTICAL GUIDE (3rd 2002) discussing multiple copying in education at 25-32 and off-air taping at 54-56, but again basing interpretation of the law on the fair use guidelines, though Simpson adds a list of acceptable and unacceptable multiple copying scenarios at 27-28, and later offers the following Q&A: "Q: Can a library include in its vertical file magazine articles or pictures out of a magazine. A: As long as they are cut from the magazines there is no problem. *What is illegal is making copies* and putting them in the vertical file." Id., at 32 (emphasis added), suggesting that even a single copy for a nonprofit (library or educational) use would not be fair.

[18] Guidelines for Classroom Copying in Not For Profit Educational Institutions with Respect to Books and Periodicals, reprinted in U.S. COPYRIGHT OFFICE, CIRCULAR 21: REPRODUCTION OF COPYRIGHTED WORKS BY EDUCATORS AND LIBRARIANS 10-12 (1993); and Guidelines for Off-Air Recording of Broadcast Programming for Educational Purposes, reprinted in U.S. COPYRIGHT OFFICE, CIRCULAR 21: REPRODUCTION OF COPYRIGHTED WORKS BY EDUCATORS AND LIBRARIANS 26 (1993). But see,

Kenneth D. Crews, The Law of Fair Use and the Illusion of Fair-Use Guidelines, 62 OHIO STATE LAW JOURNAL 599 (2001).

[19] See, e.g., *Marcus v. Rowly,* 695 F.2d 1171 (9th Cir. 1983) (teacher and district sued for reproduction, about half of the book *Cake Decorating Made Easy* and repeat term-to-term distribution not a fair use; in excess of the "classroom" guidelines.); *In Re Copyright Litigation,* 334 F.3d 643, 647-648 (7th Cir. 2003) (interpreting fair uses of off-air taping under *Sony Corp. of America, Inc. v. Universal City Studios,* 464 U.S. 417 (1984) the Seventh Circuit observed the following was a fair use: "Time shifting" a television program for later watching at a convenient time. However, the following was not a fair use: "library building" or making copies of programs to retain permanently and "Skipping" or arguably editing, i.e., "skipping commercials by taping a program before watching it and then, while watching the tape, using the fast-forward button on the recorder to skip over the commercials . . . [c]ommercial skipping amounted to creating an unauthorized derivative work." Id. at 647.

[20] In addition, the reproduction of the movie, VHS or DVD, by the library under section 108(d) or (e), a for-the-patron reproduction and distribution scenario, is prohibited by section 108(i): "The rights of reproduction and distribution under this section do not apply to a musical work, a pictorial, graphic or sculptural work, or a motion picture or other audiovisual work other than an audiovisual work dealing with news, except that no such limitation shall apply with respect to rights granted by subsections (b) and (c), or with respect to pictorial or graphic works published as illustrations, diagrams, or similar adjuncts to works of which copies are reproduced or distributed in accordance with subsections (d) and (e)." 17 U.S.C. 108(i). In other words, the library of a college or university cannot use section 108 to support the making of a copy of an entire audiovisual work, such as a movie or "small part" of it, either as a library duplication service or as part of interlibrary loan, as the rights granted under section 108 do not apply to reproductions and distributions under section 108(d), the "small part" provision or section 108(e), the whole or "substantial part" provision. Section 108(i) does not prohibit the interlibrary loan of a VHS or DVD, if the lending library is willing to loan its copy, but as is typical in interlibrary loan, the lending library makes a copy of the item from its collection, retaining its original copy. A similar result be applied to the reproduction of a music DVD or piece of sheet music, as the section 108(d) and (e) rights do not apply to musical works (the DVD contains in essence two potential copyrights—the copyright of the composer, and a sound recording copyright of the performer. However, a library could copy the VHS or DVD for purposes of a section 108(b) or (c) copy and distribution, for preservation or security under subsection (b) or replacement under subsection (c); this is made clear by the "except that no such limitation shall apply with respect to rights granted by subsections (b) and (c)" of section 108(i), provided of course the other requirements of subsection (b) or (c) are met.

[21] "A Display Warning of Copyright and an Order Warning of Copyright shall consist of a verbatim reproduction of the following notice, printed in such size and form and displayed in such manner as to comply with paragraph (c) of this section." 37 CFR 201.14(b).

[22] 37 CFR 201.14(b).

[23] 37 CFR 201.14(c)(1) provides that "A Display Warning of Copyright shall be printed on heavy paper or other durable material in type at least 18 points in size, and shall be displayed prominently, in such manner and location as to be clearly visible, legible, and comprehensible to a casual observer within the immediate vicinity of the place where orders are accepted."

[24] 37 CFR 201.14(c)(2) provides that "An Order Warning of Copyright shall be printed within a box located prominently on the order form itself, either on the front side of the form or immediately adjacent to the space calling for the name or signature of the person using the form. The notice shall be printed in type size no smaller than that used predominantly throughout the form, and in no case shall the type size be smaller than 8 points. The notice shall be printed in such manner as to be clearly legible, comprehensible, and readily apparent to a casual reader of the form."

[25] 37 C.F.R. § 201.14(a)(2) (all emphasis added).

[26] *In Re Aimster Copyright Litigation*, 334 F.3d 643, 650 (7th Cir. 2003).

[27] *In Re Aimster Copyright Litigation*, 334 F.3d 643, 650 (7th Cir. 2003) ("Willful blindness is knowledge, in copyright law (where indeed it may be enough that the defendant should have known of the direct infringement [citation omitted], as it is in the law generally . . . no more can Deep by using encryption software to prevent himself from learning what surely he strongly suspects to the case: that the users of his services—maybe all the users of his service—are copyright infringers. . . . Our point is only that a service provider that would otherwise be a contributory infringer does not obtain immunity by using encryption to shield itself from actual knowledge of the unlawful purposes for which the service is being used.").

[28] INFORMATION INFRASTRUCTURE TASK FORCE, INTELLECTUAL PROPERTY AND THE NATIONAL INFORMATION INFRASTRUCTURE: THE REPORT OF THE WORKING GROUP ON INTELLECTUAL PROPERTY RIGHTS 111, n. 357 (1995).

[29] It could be argued that section 108(f)(1) protects the library from all subsequent liability flowing from the use of "unsupervised use of reproducing equipment" as the limitation on liability is not modified by the use of "by patron" or similar language. This would mean that an employee could use the photocopier or other equipment to make unlawful reproductions and neither the library nor the employee would be liable. This interpretation would be a rather broad grant of liability limitation indeed. It is also inconsistent with concepts of vicarious liability as employees are deemed to always work under the control or supervision of their employers. As a result, and as to employees' use of such photocopying or other reproducing equipment located on its premises, it would not be "unsupervised" as required by section 108(f)(1), and therefore the immunity offered by that subsection would not apply. See also, Carol Simpson, supra note 16, at 91, "If library staff make the copies, certainly that would mean they are supervising the making of copies, and the library would be liable for any infringements made there." It is more likely that the liability limitation in section 108(f)(1) operates to protect the library and its employees from any

secondary liability due to the infringing uses of photocopying or other reproducing equipment by patrons or from direct liability (section 108(f)(1) does not qualify the sort of "copyright infringement") as would be the result under those odd cases in the developing law where a lack of intervention might rise to a level of direct infringement. Contributory infringement might otherwise occur when the librarian refers a patron to an infringing known source (know or reason to know) of material, offers use of the unsupervised photocopy or other reproduction equipment, and the patrons proceeds to make a copy of it using the library photocopier or other equipment. Vicarious liability might arise from patron conduct when the library charges for a photocopy card or other reproduction equipment access on a per-use fee structure; the more reproductions of copyrighted material made by patrons the more revenue the library accrues. This would establish the financial benefit element of vicarious liability and, under certain circumstances, like the dance hall owner who allows bands under his or her control to perform copyrighted music on premise, the library may also have the requisite control of the photocopying or other reproduction equipment to complete the vicarious liability puzzle.

[30] As Professor Crews points out, "Even though you may be making the copies at a location inside the library section 108 generally applies only to copies made *by* the library, not necessarily all copying *at* the library." KENNETH CREWS, COPYRIGHT ESSENTIALS FOR LIBRARIANS 89 (2000) (emphasis original).

[31] *ITSI T.V. Prods. Inc. v. California Authority of Racing Fairs*, 785 F. Supp. 854, 861 n.13 (E.D. Cal. 1992).

[32] Section 108(f)(2) states that "Nothing in this section . . . excuses a person who uses such reproducing equipment or who requests a copy or phonorecord under subsection (d) from liability for copyright infringement for any such act, or for any later use of such copy or phonorecord, if it exceeds fair use as provided by section 107."

▶11

WHAT ABOUT THE CIRCULATION OF COPYRIGHTED SOFTWARE?

Read this chapter to learn about copyright situations like:
▶ Whether a library can circulate software in its collection to patrons.
▶ Whether a school library can donate software weeded from its collection to other institutions.
▶ Whether software circulation rules differ with regard to for-profit institutions.

The first sale doctrine, codified in section 109, operates to limit the copyright owner's ability to control disposition of the physical embodiment of his or her copyrighted work.[1] For example, when a library purchases a book for its collection, it can place it in its collection for loan to patrons; if the library purchases a video-recording (VHS) or DVD for its collection, it could even rent it, i.e., charge patrons a dollar for each circulation, and once the item is no longer needed it could "weed" it from the collection and either give the book, the VHS videotape, or the DVD to a local day care or sell each at its annual "used book" sale.[2] This concept expresses the legal distinction between the copyright in a work and the transfer of a representation or physical embodiment, whether analog or digital, of that work. The statute uses the phrase "copy or phonorecord" to express the concept of "representation." For example, a given musical or literary work might be protected by copyright. If the copyright owner or publisher sells a copy of the work—a piece of sheet music or a book—the copyright has not been transferred, only the right to possess a copy of that work, i.e., the one purchased by the library in our example.

At one point in the development of the law, copyright owners also had some control of what the holder of a lawfully purchased copy could do with the copy. Because copyright is a property right and property rights entail economic value, the revenue stream continued as well. This concept survives to this day as a public lending right,[3] where each successive transfer of the work, even if not a sale, generates revenue for the author or copyright owner somewhat like a perpetual right to "rental" income from subsequent transfers or users. So, too, copyright developed historically into a public right, rather than a private right, in that if the transfer of the representation of the copyrighted work—the sheet music or book in the example—were subject to private rights, then the transferrer of that representation might be able to control subsequent uses by the purchaser. Contract law, including the law of licensing, is a law essentially between two or more parties; thus it is private.[4]

The first sale doctrine limits the copyrights owner's exclusive right of distribution and "assures the copyright owner that, until she parts with ownership, she has the right to prohibit all others from distributing the work. On the other hand, once a sale has occurred, the first-sale doctrine allows the new owner to treat the object as her own."[5] This expansive right gives the purchaser of the work the right to determine the conditions under which a lawfully obtained copy of a work might be resold, lent, or otherwise distributed.

> The first sale doctrine represents an important balancing of interests. . . . Congress has, in the past resisted proposals to alter the balance achieved in section 109, requiring those seeking amendments to make a compelling case for change. Proposals to reform the first sale doctrine are neither easy nor without controversy. They occur in a shifting legal, technological and economic landscape."[6]

Codification of the first sale concept applies in the copyright arena parallels the legal tenet disfavoring restraints on the alienation of property that exist in more familiar transactions of real property.[7]

Section 109(a) states in part that: "Notwithstanding the provisions of Section 106(3) [the provision granting copyright owners the exclusive right of distribution], the owner of a particular copy or phonorecord lawfully made under this title, or any person authorized by such owner, is entitled, without the authority of the copyright owner, to sell or otherwise dispose of the possession of that copy or phonorecord."[8] This language represents the codification of the first sale right or doctrine. The ownership rights of the copyright owner cease after the first or initial transfer (typically by sale, but it could also be by exchange or gift) of possession of a lawful copy or phonorecord of the work. Said in another way, "this provision has been interpreted to mean that the owner [the library] of a material object embodying the copyright owner's work [a book] can dispose of that object without violating the copyright owner's distribution right."[9] Of course, transfer of a copy of the work is not the same as transfer of the copyright in the work itself. Section 109 offers limitations on two of those rights, distribution, and, to a lesser extent display.[10]

UNDERSTANDING DISTRIBUTION RIGHTS IN THE LIBRARY

The concept of distribution is somewhat elusive as it is not defined in section 101, a section of collected definitions in the copyright law.[11] It is akin to the concept of publication, but somewhat broader, as noncommercial or informal distributions might also constitute a public distribution, triggering an exclusive right. Under section 106, public distribution can include "sale or other transfer of ownership, or by rental, lease, or lending" of "copies or phonorecords of the copyrighted work."[12] In other words, proffering public access to copyrighted material may indeed violate the section 106(3) exclusive copyright owner to make public distribution of a work while not at the same time constitute a publication.[13] A common example would be one-of-a-kind archival material that is nonetheless made available to the public through the circulation or loan policies of the library. It would be illogical to say that simply because a library circulates or loans such items it has published the item. Therefore all traditional publications, such as those through a bookstore, are public distributions, but not all distributions in public settings are in fact publications, as one can distribute unpublished works to the public and nonetheless violate the exclusive right of copyright owners to distribute works to the public.[14] Not all publications require a clear commercial aspect, however. For example, a printed set of Power Point slides distributed to scholars at a conference is most likely not a publication, but leaving a stack of handouts at the information desk of the student union likely is a publication.[15] While the concept of distribution is relevant to a determination of exclusive rights and use of that protected material, i.e., the focus of this monograph, the concept of publication is more important to the potential copyright plaintiff, as registration must occur within three months of publication in order for plaintiffs to secure the full array of copyright damage options.[16] In a recent case, the posting of a Web site was deemed a publication of that material.[17]

The first sale rights possessed by the holder of the copy apply only to that copy of the work in the holder's possession, or in the example above, to the library; the right does not apply to a copy of a particular copy, unless of course it is also "lawfully made under this title [Title 17 of the United States Code]." Without getting too far ahead of the discussion, the impact of an increased reliance on licensing can also be observed at the outset. The critical point here in the first sale distribution rights of libraries, archives, educational institutions, or any party, for that matter, is that the copy or phonorecord of the work distributed must be lawfully made. A copyright chain of events is at play. For example, if the photocopy of the item placed on reserve is not lawful (e.g., it is beyond fair use and violates the copyright owner's exclusive right of reproduction), then circulating the item through the reserve system would violate a second exclusive right of the copyright owner, the right of distribution.

The impact of this "lawfully made" catch is demonstrated in a recent case, *Hotaling v. Church of Latter Day Saints*.[18] The case involved a library that reproduced copies of the plaintiff's work without permission for serveral of the organization's libraries. Although the three year[19] statute of limitation for infringement based on a claim of unauthorized reproduction had passed, plaintiffs claimed an unauthorized public distribution was ongoing as the work was available to members of the public through the church library's holdings. The court agreed: "When a public library adds a work to its collection, lists the work in its index or catalog system, and makes the work available to the borrowing or browsing public, it has completed all the steps necessary for distribution to the public."[20] The dissent argued that distribution should not be equated with the mere access to materials via a library's in-house collections.[21] Section 109 allows for such public distributions if the "particular copy or phonorecord [is] lawfully made under this title, but because the copies in *Hotaling* were not (the copyright owner's exclusive right to reproduce the work was violated even though litigation on that point was foreclosed by the three-year statute of limitation), section 109 no longer authorized the public distribution of the copies.

However, the dissent remained silent on whether the circulation (that which would constitute lending under 17 U.S.C. §106(3), thus triggering the exclusive right of the copyright owner to control public distributions thus triggering the need for the privilege to make those distributions either under section 109 or fair use, section 107) versus mere access to or in-house use of unlawfully reproduced materials would be an illegal distribution. Arguably, if the dissent would have so concluded then in that instance both the majority and the dissent might have agreed that the actual "lending" or circulation of the unlawful copies by the library would be an infringement. The lesson from the *Hotaling* decision is important for understanding the rights that educators or any users of copyrighted material possess. Again the case only represents the opinion of a single circuit court, but in the author's opinion it is consistent with the copyright law. Distribution of unlawfully made copies of copyrighted materials (for example, lending reproduced readers or workbooks to students) by a school, college, or university, or by the library at such an institution is a distribution not authorized by the first sale doctrine, as the reproduction is likely not a fair use under section 107. More important, under the facts of *Hotaling*, this was not a commercial distribution per se (a charge per use) and involved a nonprofit entity as copyright defendant. The implications are important for nonprofit educational institutions and their libraries that distribute copyrighted material in similar fashion or that provide access to in-house collections, such as photocopied vertical files or other resource materials. The majority and dissent disagree, however, as to whether the provision of on-premises access to unlawful copies is an illegal distribution. The legal problem is that, while the statute of limitations in copyright actions is three years, each time the material is distributed (e.g., each semester when the items are again placed on reserve), a new offense is created and the three-year tolling period begins anew. Of course, the case is law only in the Fourth Circuit, but it would likely be cited by plaintiff's counsel in similar circumstances.

Further Restrictions on the Distribution of Sound Recordings and Computer Programs

Unfortunately for copyright users, the story does not end there. Both the recording and the software industry lobbied Congress for an exception to the first sale doctrine and its significant limitation on the exclusive distribution right of copyright owners. In light of the early proliferation of software resale shops, the Computer Software Rental Amendments Act of 1990[22] addressed industry concerns by amending section 109 to provide for an exception to the first sale doctrine with respect to two categories of works:

> Neither the owner of a particular *phonorecord* nor any person in possession of a particular copy of a *computer program* (including any tape, disk, or other medium embodying such program), may, for the purposes of direct or indirect commercial advantage, dispose of, or authorize the disposal of, the possession of that *phonorecord* or *computer program* (including any tape, disk, or other medium embodying such program) by rental, lease, or lending, or by any other act or practice in the nature of rental, lease, or lending.[23]

Thus the right to dispose of a phonorecord or computer program by "rental, lease or lending" again requires the permission of the copyright owner. In other words, the 1990 amendment restored the exclusive right of distribution to copyright owners for these two categories of copyrighted works.

However, section 109(b) provides that this exception to the first sale doctrine "shall [not] apply to the rental, lease, or lending of a phonorecord for nonprofit purposes by a nonprofit library or nonprofit educational institution."[24] In other words, there is an exception to the exception for "nonprofit library and nonprofit educational institutions" for the rental, lease, or lending of phonorecords, like a music CD. The first sale doctrine, the right to make public distributions, remains available to a "nonprofit library or nonprofit educational institution" when those distributions are made "for nonprofit purposes."

With respect to software, section 109(b) also provides that the "transfer of possession of a *lawfully* made copy of a computer program by a nonprofit educational institution to another nonprofit educational institution or to faculty, staff, and students does not constitute rental, lease, or lending for direct or indirect commercial purposes under this subsection." This provision would allow colleges or universities to transfer permanent possession of software among institutions, within a consortium, for example (i.e., beyond the transfer that might occur for purposes of interlibrary loan or other nonpermanent sharing practices), and to not run afoul of the distribution right of copyright owners, as restored by the exception of software programs to the operation of the first sale doctrine. This provision does **not** confer the "transfer of possession" right to nonprofit libraries, only to educational institutions.

Of course, any copies of the program would need to be deleted from hard drives or servers of the disposing institution. This provision would also allow the school to hand out software each year to students as well. Perhaps various software programs are now distributed to students at the start of each academic year in the same fashion as textbooks and workbooks were distributed in years past.

Must the transfer of possession be gratis? Arguably this "transfer of possession" right would allow the nonprofit educational institution to resell the software for a nominal fee rather than give it away. This conclusion is reached for two significant reasons. First, the statute uses the term "transfer of possession," indicating that complete "ownership" must be passed from the giving nonprofit educational institution to the receiving nonprofit educational institution. However, the statute does not indicate how that transfer must occur; there is no limitation on the means of transfer. Second, if only a gratis transfer is contemplated, then it causes a complication. A rule of statutory interpretation instructs that language is not to be interpreted as superfluous where possible.[25] Therefore, if the "transfer of possession" language (last sentence of section 109(b)(1)(A)) means only gratis transfers are allowed, then the provision would appear unnecessary. This is because the only transfers prohibited by the section 109(b)(1)(A) language (first sentence of that paragraph) are those transfers undertaken for "purposes of direct or indirect commercial advantage." While it could be argued that the computer program "transfer of possession" proviso does not apply to permanent dispositions of software, i.e., it cannot be characterized by the statutory language, to "dispose of, or authorize the disposal of, the possession of that phonorecord or computer program (including any tape, disk, or other medium embodying such program) by rental, lease, or lending, or by any other act or practice in the nature of rental, lease, or lending," to apply. The transfer of possession proviso authorizing such transfer use the identical *"rental, lease, or lending"* language. Giving the software away does not fall into this category in the first place; therefore it is not prohibited, and there would be no additional dispensation needed in the statute. As a result, the "transfer of possession" proviso appears superfluous unless it is interpreted to include "transfers of possession" that are for "purposes of direct or indirect commercial advantage." This conclusion is further supported by the language granting the transfer right ("of copy of a computer program by a nonprofit educational institution to another nonprofit educational institution or to faculty, staff, and students"); such transfers, whether or not consisting of a financial component, "do[] not constitute rental, lease, or lending for direct or indirect commercial purposes under this subsection."

REQUIRED COPYRIGHT NOTICE FOR CIRCULATION OF SOFTWARE

The significant portion of section 109 relating to the focus of this monograph consists of a compliance-oriented measure and is found in subsection (b)(2)(A) regarding the lending of software. The provision operates as an exception to the software exception to the first sale doctrine, i.e., as an exception to the exception, so to speak:

> Nothing in this subsection [that is subsection (b), which restores the reach of the copyright owner's right of distribution to dispositions of computer programs] shall apply to the lending of a computer program for nonprofit purposes by a nonprofit library, *if each copy of a computer program which is lent by such library has affixed to the packaging containing the program a warning of copyright in accordance with requirements that the Register of Copyrights shall prescribe by regulation.*[26]

Thus, the first sale right of libraries to distribute software is preserved. However, in an attempt to balance the rights of owners and users, Congress required that libraries remind patrons of their obligation to honor the rights of copyright owners:

> The Committee does not wish, however, to prohibit nonprofit lending by nonprofit libraries and nonprofit educational institutions. Such institutions serve a valuable public purpose by making computer software available to students who would not otherwise have access to it. At the same time, the Committee is aware that the same economic factors that lead to unauthorized copying in a commercial context *may lead library patrons also to engage in such conduct.*"[27]

Thus, in return for the ability to lend software to students and patrons of nonprofit educational institutions and their libraries, libraries must place a warning notice on the software they distribute.

As with section 108(d)(2) and (e)(2), the text of the notice is established by regulation:

> Notice: Warning of Copyright Restrictions. The copyright law of the United States (title 17, United States Code) governs the reproduction, distribution, adaptation, public performance, and public display of copyrighted material. Under certain conditions specified in law, nonprofit libraries are authorized to lend, lease, or rent copies of computer programs to patrons on a nonprofit basis and for nonprofit purposes. Any person who makes an unauthorized copy or adaptation of the computer program, or redistributes the loan copy, or publicly performs or displays the computer program, except as permitted by title 17 of the United States Code, may be liable for copyright infringement. This institution reserves the right to refuse to fulfill a loan request if, in its judgment, fulfillment of the request would lead to violation of the copyright law.[28]

The wording of the notice must conform to the prescribed regulation; it may not deviate from it.[29] The form and manner of notice is articulated with a fair amount of specificity as well:

> A Warning of Copyright for Software Rental shall be affixed to the packaging that contains the copy of the computer program, which is the subject of a library loan to patrons,

by means of a label cemented, gummed, or otherwise durably attached to the copies or to a box, reel, cartridge, cassette, or other container used as a permanent receptacle for the copy of the computer program. The notice shall be printed in such manner as to be clearly legible, comprehensible, and readily apparent to a casual user of the computer program.[30]

Affixing the notice could be facilitated by printing self-adhesive labels (consisting of the text of the warning notice) which library staff can easily attach to the software packaging.

Unlike the section 108 regulation, the size and type of the section 109 notice is not prescribed, as long as the notice is printed "in such manner as to be clearly legible, comprehensible, and readily apparent to a casual user of the computer program." This wording accommodates the many ways software may be commercially packaged, ranging from a simple stand-alone software disk or CD in a jacket or plastic case to comprehensive book and disk course-in-a-box binder.

The final sentence of the notice is similar to that required for use in section 108(d) and (e) reproduction for library and archives patrons; it does not require active intervention by the institution, but indicates that the nonprofit library at a college or university would be within its rights if it chose to enforce the copyright law and regulate downstream copying, i.e., the faculty, student, or other library patron, copying on his or her own initiative. The warning notice preserves instead of requires that "refusal" function. Like the section 108 interlibrary loan or patron photocopying request, the section 109 software circulation warning notice ends with a nearly identical admonition. (The section 108 notice reads: "This institution reserves the right to refuse to *accept* a copying order if, in its judgment, fulfillment of the order would involve violation of copyright law."[31] The section 109 notice reads: "This institution reserves the right to refuse to *fulfill* a loan request if, in its judgment, fulfillment of the request would lead to violation of the copyright law."[32]) This wording suggests at least a permissive obligation to intervene if the nonprofit library believes that the patron's use of the item (the copy of the loaned software) would be infringing. This interpretation is the practical meaning of the phrase "would lead to violation." The phrase cannot by logic refer to a "violation" by the library, as the point of sections 108 and 109 is to allow the library to reproduce or distribute in the first instance, i.e., to place copyrighted works in the hands of patrons.

The purpose of the notices in sections 108 and 109 is to remind the patron that certain uses of copyrighted material can be infringing; the text of the notices indicates as much. So, too, the concept of knowledge in the section 108(d)(2) and (e)(2) "no notice" is not a should know concept obligating a duty to inquire but consistent with the know or reason to know concept of knowledge in the copyright law, both warning notices allow the library to refuse the reproduction or distribution if, in its judgment, fulfillment of the reproduction and or distribution would involve violation of copyright law. The refusal is not mandatory; there is no legal duty to refuse; rather it is permissive. The regulatory language may offer a practical benefit. Being able to point to a federal regulation may offer support in a situation where the reproduction and distribution (section 108) or distribution (section 109) is refused by the library (sections 108 and 109) or archive (section 108) much to the dismay of a patron. However, it can place an additional ethical burden on the library. This is another example of the misalignment or divergence of legal versus ethical responsibilities within the copyright law. (Is there a higher ethical duty to intervene?) At least the permissive language ("reserves the right") suggests that such assessment, intervention, and refusal are within the legal responsibility of the library but not necessarily its obligation. However, such intervention can further the creation of a compliant copyright climate within the institution. Moreover, the exercise of that 'permissive right to refuse' is consistent with Congress's most recent articulation on copyright found in TEACH (the Technology, Education and Copyright Harmonization Act), which amended the distance education provisions of the copyright law found in sections 110 and 112, and which is discussed in detail in Chapter 12.

Finally, the section 109(b)(2)(A) software lending right is limited to nonprofit libraries. (In contrast, section 108 includes nonprofit archives, and other provisions of section 109 include nonprofit educational institutions.) Again the rules of statutory construction suggest that such omission is purposeful and not the result of legislative drafting oversight. Thus, a nonprofit archives cannot circulate software; the right is limited to nonprofit libraries.

REAL-WORLD EXAMPLES

▶ Real-World Example I

Situation: A school library purchases several tutorial packages for its collections. The items are a combination book and software program. The library would like to circulate the program to students for use at home.

Legal Analysis: The first sale doctrine codified in section 109 contains a pullback provision restoring the exclusive right of public distribution to the copyright owner. However, under 17 U.S.C. § 109(b)(2)(A) this restoration does not "apply to the lending of a computer program for nonprofit purposes by a nonprofit library." The library must place a copyright warning notice on the package containing the software. The text of the warning notice is found in 37 C.F.R. §201.24(b). In this example, the warning notice could be secured to the pocket where the software is inserted.

► **Real-World Example II**

Situation: The situation is the same as in Real-World Example I. After a period of time, the school library weeds its software tutorial collection and desires to donate the weeded "sets" to a mission school in South Dakota.

Legal Analysis: The section 109(b) provision for the "transfer of possession of a *lawfully* made copy of a computer program by a nonprofit educational institution to another nonprofit educational institution or to faculty, staff, and students does not constitute rental, lease, or lending for direct or indirect commercial purposes under this subsection." As a result, the transfer of possession does not implicate the restoration of the copyright owner's distribution right found in section 109(b)(1)(A).

► **Real-World Example III**

Situation: A public university library with an extensive music collection would like to circulate its phonorecords (LPs, cassettes, and CDs). A private, for-profit music conservatory would like to do the same.

Legal Analysis: The restoration of distribution rights to copyright owners under section 109(b)(1)(A) applies to sound recordings as well as to computer programs. The phonorecords subsume a sound recording copyright. However, section 109(b)(1)(A) contains an exception to this restoration: "Nothing in the preceding sentence shall apply to the rental, lease, or lending of a phonorecord for nonprofit purposes by a nonprofit library or nonprofit educational institution." In other words, the library in this example need not seek the permission of the copyright owner before it circulates such items. Moreover, the section 109(b)(1)(A) proviso does not contain any specific notice requirement as does the section 109(B)(2)(A) proviso. However, the circulation exception ("rental, lease, or lending") does not apply to for-profit educational institutions, such as conservatories or ballet studios.

KEY POINTS FOR YOUR INSTITUTION'S POLICY AND PRACTICE

► The first sale doctrine limits the copyright owner's exclusive right of distribution. The exclusive right to distribute copyrighted material ends after the first "sale" of that work, the historical link to the concept of commercial exploitation, i.e., publication. This right is codified in the statute and gives the person or entity in possession of a lawfully made copy (such as a library, school, college, or university) the ability to determine the conditions under which a copy of a work might be resold, lent, or otherwise distributed. See pp. 324–326.

► In general, the copyright owner's right of control of all distributions, even those occurring after the first sale, is restored by statute for phonorecords and computer programs (including any tape, disk, or other medium embodying such program). However, an exception to this statutory restoration exists for the rental, lease, or lending of a phonorecord for nonprofit purposes by a nonprofit library or nonprofit educational institution. See pp. 327–328.

▶ A second exception exists for the lending of a computer program for nonprofit purposes by a nonprofit library, if each copy of a computer program which is lent by such library has affixed to the packaging containing the program a warning of copyright. Federal regulation again prescribes the contents of the warning notice. See pp. 328–331.

▶ The statute also indicates that the transfer of possession of a lawfully made copy of a computer program by a nonprofit educational institution to another nonprofit educational institution or to faculty, staff, and students does not constitute rental, lease, or lending for direct or indirect commercial purposes under this subsection. This provision would allow colleges or universities to transfer permanent possession of software among institutions within lending consortia. See pp. 327–328.

ENDNOTES

[1] "Section 109(a) of title 17, United States Code, is structured as an exception to the copyright owner's section 106(3) right of distribution. These sections do not act as a limitation on the other exclusive rights granted copyright owners in section 106, title 17, United States Code. For example, an owner of a lawfully made copy may not, without the permission of the copyright owner (or availability of a statutory defense) [footnote referencing section 117 omitted] reproduce copies of the work, prepare derivative works, or publicly perform the work." H.R. Rep. No 101-735, (1990).

[2] H.R. Rep. No. (1976) U.S.C.C.A.N., reprinted in 5 (conf. Rep.) 5659, 5693 (1976) ("Under this principle . . . the copyright owner's exclusive right of public distribution would have no effect upon anyone who owns 'a particular copy or phonorecord lawfully made under this title' and who wishes to transfer it to someone else or to destroy it. Thus, for example, the outright sale of an authorized copy of a book frees it from any copyright control over its resale price or other conditions of its future disposition. A *library* that has acquired ownership of a copy is entitled to *lend* it under any conditions it chooses to impose.").

[3] See, Jennifer M. Schneck, Note: Closing the Book on the Public Lending Right, 63 NEW YORK UNIVERSITY LAW REVIEW 878 (A88); Daniel Y. Mayer, Literary Copyright and Public Lending Right, 18 CASE WESTERN RESERVE JOURNAL OF INTERNATIONAL LAW 483 (1986).

[4] See, *ProCD v. Zeidenberg*, 86 F.3d 1447, 1454 (7th Cir. 1996) ("Rights 'equivalent to any of the exclusive rights within the general scope of copyright' are rights established *by law*— rights that restrict the options of persons who are strangers to the author. Copyright law forbids duplication, public performance, and so on, unless the person wishing to copy or

perform the work gets permission; silence means a ban on copying. A copyright is a right against the world. Contracts, by contrast, generally affect only their parties; strangers may do as they please, so contracts do not create 'exclusive rights.'"). This is what occurs when a library acquires material through license, because a license is a contract and a contract is an expression of private legal rights between the parties to it. The implications of this distinction for digital content are immense. First, most digital content is licensed, not sold; thus, first sale rights do not apply. Moreover, in those works where acquisition is by purchase, a DVD for example, the need to migrate in the future to new technologies can complicate the first sale right that would exist, as migration entails copying into the new format. In order for first sale rights to apply to the subsequent migrated copy, that copy must be a lawfully made copy; it is not at all clear that the resulting complete copy would be one lawfully made under fair use, the usefulness of the section 109 is limited.

[5] ARTHUR R. MILLER AND MICHAEL H. DAVIS, INTELLECTUAL PROPERTY, PATENTS TRADEMARK, AND COPYRIGHT IN A NUTSHELL 324 (2d ed. 1991).

[6] H.R. Rep. No 101-735, 7 (1990).

[7] An example is the *rule against perpetuities*, discussed in BLACK'S LAW DICTIONARY (8th ed. 2004): "The common-law rule prohibiting a grant of an estate unless the interest must vest, if at all, no later than 21 years (plus a period of gestation to cover a posthumous birth) after the death of some person alive when the interest was created. The purpose of the rule was to limit the time that title to property could be suspended out of commerce because there was no owner who had title to the property and who could sell it or exercise other aspects of ownership. If the terms of the contract or gift exceeded the time limits of the rule, the gift or transaction was void." Id. at 1357–1358.

[8] 17 U.S.C. § 109(a).

[9] Keith Kupferschmid, Lost in Cyberspace: The Digital Demise of the First-Sale Doctrine, 16 JOHN MARSHALL JOURNAL OF COMPUTER & INFORMATION LAW 825, 831 (1998).

[10] Under section 101, to 'display' a work means to show a copy of it, either directly or by means of a film, slide, television image, or any other device or process or, in the case of a motion picture or other audiovisual work, to show individual images nonsequentially." Section 109 again provides an exception, or, perhaps more accurately, a clarification of what is not a display for purposes of the section 106 exclusive display right of the copyright owner: "[N]otwithstanding the provisions of section 106(5), the owner of a particular copy lawfully made under this title, or any person authorized by such owner, is entitled, without the authority of the copyright owner, to display that copy publicly, either directly or by the projection of no more than one image at a time, to viewers present at the place where the copy is located." 17 U.S.C. § 109(c). As the definition of display intimates, display includes the presentation of the work by device or process. Display, then, is akin to a concept of transmission and includes multiple transmissions, such as displaying a particular image on every student's monitor in a computer science classroom laboratory. The 1976 legislative history of section 109(b), now section 109(c), excludes "the simultaneous projection of multiple images of the work . . . where each person in a lecture hall is supplied

with a separate viewing apparatus." H. Rep. No. 94-1476, 94th Cong., 2d Sess. 80 (1976) (conf. Rep.), reprinted in 5 U.S.C.C.A.N. 5659, 5694 (1976). However, the exemption to the exclusive right of display granted by section 110(1) allows educators the right to use an overhead or slide projector, LCD, or other panel display device to present copyrighted material as part of a qualifying classroom display. According to the 1976 legislative history of section 109, "[a]s long as there is no transmission beyond the place where the copy is located, both section 109(b) [now section 109(c)] and section 110(1) would permit the classroom display of a work by means of any sort of projection device or process." H. Rep. No. 94-1476, 94th Cong., 2d Sess. 82 (1976) (conf. rep.), reprinted in 5 U.S.C.C.A.N. 5659, 5696 (1976).

[11] Traditionally, courts have interpreted distribution to require some sort of "commercial" enterprise, tied to the formal publication of the work. The description of distribution in Section 106 is almost identical to the definition of "publication" in section 101 (Publication is the "distribution of copies or phonorecords of a work to the public by sale other transfer of ownership, or by rental, lease, or *lending*" 17 U.S.C. (emphasis added)). In addition, the legislative history refers to the section 106 "distribution" right as "publication." H.R. Rep. No. 94-1476, (1976) (conf. Rep.), reprinted in 1976 U.S.C.C.A.N., 5659, 5674-5675. (1976)

[12] 17 U.S.C. § 106(3).

[13] Numerous copyright cases involved distribution of unpublished or prepublication works. See, *Salinger v. Random House, Inc.*, 881 F.2d 90 (2nd Cir.), cert. denied 493 U.S. 1094 (1987) (unpublished letters of author J. D. Salinger); *Harper & Row Publishers, Inc. v. Nation Enterprises*, 471 U.S. 539 (1985) (prepublication excerpt of President Ford's memoirs); *Estate of Martin Luther King, Jr. v. CBS, Inc.*, 194 F.3d 1121 (11th 1999) ("I Have a Dream" speech of Dr. Martin Luther King, Jr., heard by thousands and broadcast to thousands more was not a publication). Moreover, "[t]here must be multiple copies available for distribution, transfer, rent, lease, or lending. Thus, publication occurs only if the single item is one of many copies available for distribution." JOHN W. HAZARD, JR. COPYRIGHT LAW IN BUSINESS AND PRACTICE § 1:5, at 1-10 (2002). "An offering must also be to a 'group of persons,' not just to a single individual, and the offering must be for the purpose of further distribution. If the manufacturer of the greetings cards I the example above offered to distribute the cards for private display only, no publication would occur, because the offer must be made for further distribution, public performance, or public display." Id., at § 1:7, 1-11–1-12.

[14] See, U.S. COPYRIGHT OFFICE, COMPENDIUM II, U.S. COPYRIGHT OFFICE PRACTICES, § 905.01 (1984) (leaving copies in a public place for anyone to take is a publication, but distributing text at a seminar for use only by the recipients is ordinarily not a publication); and discussion in JOHN W. HAZARD, JR. COPYRIGHT LAW IN BUSINESS AND PRACTICE § 1:5, at 1-8–1-12 (2004) (discussing the concept of publication).

[15] 17 U.S.C. § 412.

[16] *Getaped.com v. Cangemi*, 188 F. Supp. 2d 398 (S.D.N.Y. 2002) (Posting a Web site on the Internet constitutes publication for purposes of triggering ownership rights, i.e., in order to receive statutory damages and attorney's fees, registration must occur before infringement

of unpublished works, or registration must occur within three months of infringement for published works.).

[17] *Hotaling v. Church of Latter Day Saints*, 118 F.3d 199 (4th Cir. 1999).

[18] 17 U.S.C. § 507(b) ("No civil action shall be maintained under the provision of this title unless it is commenced within three years after the claim acrued.")

[19] *Hotaling v. Church of Latter Day Saints*, 118 F.3d 199, 203 (4th Cir. 1999).

[20] *Hotaling v. Church of Latter Day Saints*, 118 F.3d 199, 205 (4th Cir. 1999).

[21] *Hotaling v. Church of Latter Day Saints*, 118 F.3d 199, 205 (4th Cir. 1999) (Hall, J. dissenting).

[22] P.L. No. 101-650 (Title VIII), § 802 and § 803, 104 Stat. 5134, 5135 (1990).

[23] 17 U.S.C. § 109(b)(1) (emphasis added).

[24] 17 U.S.C. § 109(b).

[25] NORMAN J. SINGER, SUTHERLAND STATUTORY CONSTRUCTION § 46:6 (2002) (Each word given effect.) ("A statute should be construed so that effect is given to all its provisions, so that no part will be inoperative or superfluous, void or insignificant, and so that one section will not destroy another unless the provision is the result of obvious mistake or error. No clause sentence or word shall be construed as superfluous, void or insignificant if the construction can be found which will give force to and preserve all the words of the statute. While every word of a statute must be presumed to have been used for a purpose, it is also the case that every word excluded from a statute must be presumed to have been excluded for a purpose. But it has been said that words and clauses which are present in a statute only through inadvertence can be disregarded if they are repugnant to what is found, on the basis of other indicia, to be the legislative intent. There is a presumption that the same words used twice in the same act have the same meaning. Likewise, the courts do not construe different terms within a statute to embody the same meaning. However, it is possible to interpret an imprecise term differently in two separate sections of a statute which have different purposes. Yet when the *legislature uses certain language in one part of the statute and different language in another, the court assumes different meanings were intended.* In like manner, where the legislature has carefully employed a term in one place and excluded it in another, it should not be implied where excluded. The use of different terms within related statutes generally implies that different meanings were intended." (Numerous footnotes to supporting case law excluded.).).

[26] 17 U.S.C. § 109(b)(2)(A) (emphasis added).

[27] H.R. Rep. No 101-735, 101st Cong., 2d Sess. 8 (1990) (emphasis added).

[28] 37 C.F.R. §201.24(b).

[29] The introductory sentence to 37 C.F.R. §201.24(b) provides that "the Warning of Copyright for Software Rental shall consist of a verbatim reproduction of the following notice, printed in such size and form and affixed in such manner as to comply with paragraph (c) of this section."

[30] 37 C.F.R. § 201.24(c) (emphasis added).

[31] 37 C.F.R. 201.14(b) (emphasis added).

[32] 37 C.F.R. §201.24(b).

12

WHAT'S DIFFERENT ABOUT COPYRIGHT COMPLIANCE FOR DISTANCE EDUCATION PROGRAMS?

Read this chapter to learn about copyright situations like:
- ▶ Whether instructors in a distance education program can individually work to conform to copyright law.
- ▶ Whether copyrighted material used in distance education programs can be made available over the Internet.
- ▶ Whether a distance education instructor can screen films to his or her students online.

Unfinished business of the DMCA[1] led eventually to the passage of the TEACH Act.[2] In terms of compliance provisions, this act could be considered the mother lode or jackpot and signifies an important trend in copyright legislation, i.e., requiring the adoption of a sweeping copyright compliance quid pro quo by intermediaries in return for expanded or continued use rights.[3] TEACH contains many requirements that must be met before an educational institution can seek the benefit of its provisions. Consistent with the other sections of the copyright law discussed in previous chapters, of relevance to the topic of this monograph are those provisions in TEACH relating to compliance measures, such as notice requirements, policy formation, informational compliance efforts, and network monitoring and maintenance.[4]

TEACH is a distance education provision in terms of the limitations on exclusive rights of display, performance, and reproduction[5] that it grants qualifying educational institutions, i.e., those that are nonprofit and accredited.[6] However, some of its compliance requirements can apply to the entire educational environment, not just to the delivery of distance education course content. TEACH amended provision of the copyright law relating to distance education, sections 110 and 112, relating to performance and displays of copyrighted works in the remote classroom and reproduction of copyrighted works, the so-called ephemeral recording provisions, respectively. TEACH is not a library provision, but since the library is a focal information resource pivot in many distance education programs, familiarity with the TEACH provisions is logical for the library or school media environment, and a discussion of those provisions fits precisely within the topic of this book. An earlier provision of TEACH, the section 110 immunity provision for transient copies, was discussed previously in Chapter 5.

IDENTIFYING PERMISSIBLE TRANSMISSION OF COPYRIGHT MATERIALS IN DISTANCE EDUCATION

To summarize, TEACH expands the sorts of copyrighted material that can be displayed or performed in the course of a distance education class session. Such performances and displays (more accurately transmissions) would normally require permission from the copyright owner through a performance right, license, or some other mechanism. The concept of distance education is quite broad under the copyright law. An on-campus class where students interact over the campus intranet would be considered "by or in the course of a transmission," and thus would fall under the distance education rules, at least as far as those transmissions are concerned. The instructional component that occurs in the actual campus classroom is not, however, transformed into a distance education class as far as the copyright law is concerned. The practical result of this legal bifurcation is that the "live" or face-to-face teaching portion of the course is governed by one subsection of the statute while the distance or "transmission" portion is governed by another subsection of section 110. Section 110(1) addresses the performance and display of copyrighted material in "live" or face-to-face teaching interactions, while section 110(2) governs the performance and display of copyrighted material in the distance education teaching.

In distance education teaching, under section 110(2)—with respect to the performance of nondramatic literary or musical works, there is no limitation on the portion of the copyrighted work that can be used. All other performances are limited to a reasonable and limited portion of the work. What is reasonable in a given circumstance depends on "both the nature of the market for that type of work and the pedagogical purposes of the performance."[7] However, the use of the conditional "reasonable and *limited* portions" phrasing clearly imposes some restriction on the amount of the work falling into this category, i.e., performances of copyrighted material other than nondramatic literary or musical works, that can be used in a distance education interaction. For example, the use of an entire video can never be used under Section 110(2), such a use would constitute the performance of an audiovisual work, i.e., a work other than a nondramatic or musical one: "The performance of works other than non-dramatic literary or musical works is limited, however, to 'reasonable and limited portions' of *less than* the entire work."[8] Any display of copyrighted material in the distance education environment is limited to "an amount comparable to that which is typically displayed in the course of a live classroom session."[9] Of course, the right to use more than these portions can be secured through license or in appropriate circumstances, fair use, but then the use would not be statutorily authorized under the specific provision of the copyright law designed for distance educators, section 110(2) as amended by TEACH.

There are several other requirements found in section 110(2) as amended by TEACH. The use of copyrighted material must be an "integral part of a class session offered as part of the systematic mediated instructional activities of the . . . nonprofit educational institution."[10] According to the legislative history "it must be part of a class itself, rather than ancillary to it."[11] The use of copyrighted material must also be "directly related and of material assistance to the teaching content of the transmission."[12] According to the TEACH Senate and House Reports, both of which also refer to the Register's Report,[13] and relating it to the pre-TEACH 110(2)(B) requirement, "this test of relevance and materiality connects the copyrighted work to the curriculum, and it means that the portion performed or displayed may not be performed or displayed for the mere entertainment of the students, or as unrelated background material."[14] The material displayed or performed must relate to the oft stated "teaching moment," though it can be can be asynchronous in that the student and instructor need not be logged on to an institution's distance education Web site at the same time.[15]

TEACH, as incorporated into section 110(2), excludes certain material as well. For example, the opening clause of section 110(2) excludes a certain category of statutory-defined curricular materials: "a work produced or marketed primarily for performance or display as part of mediated instructional activities [MIA][16] transmitted via digital networks." The legislative history explains that "[t]he exclusion is not intended to apply generally to all educational material or to all materials having educational value . . . limited to material whose primary market is the digital network environment, not instructional materials developed and marketed for use in the physical classroom."[17] Why the exclusion of material designed explicitly for online instruction from a provision of the copyright law articulating the boundaries of educators' use of copyrighted material? One possibility is that Congress desired to create the requisite statutory breathing room for the nascent online instructional materials industry to develop.

A second significant exclusion is for what might best be called instructional support material:

> The amended exemption is not intended to address other uses of copyrighted works in the course of digital distance education, including student use of supplemental or research materials in digital form, such as electronic course-packs, e-reserves, and digital library resources. Such activities do not involve uses analogous to the performance and displays currently addressed in section 110(2).[18]

The definition of MIA, also supports this inclusion, and is incorporated into section 110(2)(A) as amended by TEACH: "the performance or display is made by, at the direction of, or under the actual supervision of an instructor as an integral part of a class session offered as a regular part of the systematic *mediated instructional activities* of a governmental body or an accredited nonprofit educational institution."[19]

Observe also that the institution must be accredited. The statute indicates that accreditation relates not to a particular program but to the institution in general:

> For purposes of paragraph (2), accreditation with respect to an institution providing post-secondary education, shall be as determined by a regional or national accrediting agency recognized by the Council on Higher Education Accreditation or the United States Department of Education; and with respect to an institution providing elementary or secondary education, shall be as recognized by the applicable state certification or licensing procedures.[20]

Finally, no copyrighted material can be used if the "accredited nonprofit education institution knew or had reason to believe [that the material] was not [a] lawfully made and acquired" copy or phonorecord.[21] Since "educational institutions" cannot actually know anything, as each is made up of the sum of its parts, its faculty, staff, administrators, and employees, any knowledge on their part is imputed to the institution, creating a sort of institutional scienter or mens rea for the purposes of section 110(2) eligibility.

Again, as in other areas of the copyright law that deal with intermediary liability as a contributor of infringing activity, the standard is "know or reason to know," not "should know." However, if any employee, from the distance education staff assistant up to the campus administrator, has some suspicion that the material was an unlawful (bootleg) copy, then the benefits of section 110(2) are not available. While this proviso of section 110(2) does not create any affirmative compliance obligation (such as policy adoption or notice use), it does impose a significant burden to ensure that only lawfully made copies are used in the institution's distance education "classrooms." If unlawful copies are used, the rights of performance and display granted by section 110(2) are not available.

This is an expanded concept from previous law. Before TEACH there was no such section 110(2) requirement; moreover, in section 110(1), governing face-to-face instruction, the lawfully made requirement applied only to audiovisual works, and only to the person responsible for the performance, i.e., the instructor or student.[22] The section 110(2) "lawfully" made proviso imposes a broader qualifier—applying to any work performed or displayed—and assesses its standard based on the mind-set of any employee affiliated with the institution, instructor, staff, etc. but excludes students, whether or not that employee was actually responsible for the performance or display of the work, as is the standard in Section 110(1).

Section 110(2)(C)(i) requires that "to the extent technologically feasible the reception of such transmission is limited to . . . students officially enrolled in the course for which the transmission is made."[23] This is not an absolute test, but allows some technological leakage, as a result of a qualification on the reception limitation, the "to the extent technologically feasible" language. However, it does suggest an affirmative burden for the institution to keep abreast of the developments in network technology and "make it happen," so to speak, assuming the technology is available. Moreover, unlike the definition of standard technical measures in Section 512(i)(a)(c), there is no safety valve factor of "substantial costs on service providers or substantial burdens on their systems or networks" in section 110(2). As a result, a technology that could configure an institution's network to indeed limit reception to "students officially enrolled in the course for which the transmission is made" would need to be adopted, even if it were costly. According to the Conference Report: "This requirement is not intended to impose a general requirement of network security."[24] However, the institution must do something and likely that "something"—would not be without some cost or other administrative burden. While it does not require that the institution employ the use of technology to control copyright infringement or uses of copyrighted material beyond the confines of section 110(2), it does at least require the institution to employ technology that regulates access to that content.

In other words, making a performance or display of copyrighted material as part of a course through the institution's main Web site would not be acceptable, even if it were solely intended for students officially enrolled in the course for which the transmission is made, as opposed to the entire campus community. As the Conference Report points out, "[r]ather, it is intended to require only that the students be identified, and the transmission should be technologically limited to such identified authorized recipients through systems such as password access or other similar measures."[25] This requirement is nonetheless significant as it signals a second increased role for institutions that desire to use copyrighted material in furtherance of their educational mission and in conformity with section 110(2). This is the first hint in TEACH that Congress views technology as the arbiter of the proper balance of rights between owners and users and considers the educational institution to be the facilitator of that arbitration. Technology is the key to limiting the exposure of copyrighted works to both unwarranted uses and, in this instance of section 110(2)(C) phrase, unwarranted users.

COMPLYING WITH NEW ANALOG AND DIGITAL COPYRIGHT COMPLIANCE REQUIREMENTS FOR DISTANCE EDUCATION

New forms of digital communication technology make it much easier for copyrighted works, both those that are lawfully made and those that are not (read pirated or "bootlegged"), to be transferred (or "transmitted" to use the statutory term) across the miles: "As noted in the Register's Report, the purpose of the exclusion is to reduce the likelihood that an exemption intended to cover only the equivalent of traditional concepts of performance and display would result in the proliferation or exploitation of unauthorized copies."[26] Such comments set the stage for the statutorily mandated compliance requirements of TEACH. These compliance-oriented provisions comprise the heart of section 110(2) and represent its significant departure from prior quid pro quo formulations. There are two sets of compliance provisions; an initial set applies whether the transmission of the distance education session is analog or digital while a second set of obligations applies only in case of digital transmission.

First, the statute now requires that the "transmitting . . . institution institutes policies regarding copyright."[27] Again the legislative history does not provide detail as to the contents of the policies. Observe, however, that the statute uses the plural to suggest multiple policy statements or documents. The requirement would be broader than the single "repeat infringer" policy requirement of section 512(i)(1)(A) discussed in Chapter 6. The array of policies could include a policy on photocopying and other reproductions in the library and classroom, performance and display of copyrighted material in the classroom, fair use, copyright and campus computing facilities (section 512 or otherwise) and on and on . . . The statutory command does not relegate policies concerning copyright and distance education alone, but commands the institution of "policies regarding copyright" in general.

Second, as in section 512(e)(1)(C), but also in an expanded articulation, the institution must "provide[] informational materials to faculty, students, and relevant staff members that accurately describe and promote compliance with, the laws of the United States relating to copyright."[28] The section 512(e) command only requires that the "institution provides to all users of its system or network informational material that accurately describe, and promote compliance with the laws of the United States relating to copyright." Under section 110(2) there is no limitation to "users of its system or network" alone, but the information must proceed to reach all "faculty, students, and relevant staff members" whether or not "connected" and whether or not involved in education, online or otherwise. There is a similar purpose-content of material charge as well, i.e., that the material "accurately describe and promote compliance with, the laws of the United States relating to copyright." The goal of this informational outreach is to create a climate where compliance is the rule and infringement the exception. The point is not only to inform but to have a positive effect as well: to promote copyright compliance. Again, the content of the message (the "informational materials") is not limited to copyright and distance education but to the copyright law in all its permutations.

Is a one-line comment in an employee handbook stating that "It is the policy of this institution not to infringe the copyrights of others," or words to that effect, fulfilling the letter of the law? Are a poster and a one-page flyer sufficient "informational material[]"? Frankly, these are the wrong questions to ask. Rather, the institution should be seeking ways, in the language of the Conference Report "to promote an environment of compliance with the law, inform recipients of their responsibilities under copyright law, and decrease the likelihood of unintentional and uninformed acts of infringement."[29] Perhaps a better question to ask is what will it take in your school district or campus to create an environment of compliance? One must recognize that such compliance is built on the incorporation of these attitudes into the infrastructure of the institution through policy adoption and implementation, through informational outreach and generous use of copyright notices and, most important, through practice. Viewed in this way, successful "promot[ion of] compliance with the laws of the United States relating to copyright" results in a environment where the possibility of infringement is greatly reduced.

Finally, the institution must "provide[] notice to students that materials used in connection with *the course* may be subject to copyright protection.[30] The use of the definite article ("the" instead of "a") suggests that notice be required only with respect to the use of copyright material in conjunction with a distance education course, and not all courses offered by the institution. While both the legislative history and the U.S. Copyright Office (at least formally) offer no direction as to the content of the required notice, one could be adapted from the section 108 and 109 regulatory notices.[31] Moreover, the U.S. Copyright Office in its report on distance education offered the following footnote: "In an online course, it would be appropriate and effective to have such notice appear on the screen when the student signs on. *Cf.* Fair Use Guidelines for Educational Multimedia, § 2-6.3 (appendix F) (advising both educators and students to include a notice of use restrictions under copyright law on the opening screen of the multimedia program and any accompanying print material)."[32] According to the legislative history, the purpose of these three requirements (policies, outreach, and notice) is to "promote an environment of compliance with the law, inform recipients of their responsibilities under copyright law, and decrease the likelihood of unintentional and uniformed acts of infringement."[33] This is a significant advance in the struggle to bring schools, universities, and other educational entities into copyright compliance.[34] Institutions will have to plan, adopt, and implement a copyright compliance program that includes copyright policies, develop organizational development programs that seek to inform students and staff of copyright law requirements and responsibilities (not just those issues associated with distance education alone, but a wide array of copyright issues), and post warning notices that at least distance education course material may be subject to copyright law.

LEARNING ABOUT FURTHER DIGITAL COMPLIANCE REQUIREMENTS

A second set of requirements in section 110(2)(D)(ii) represents less traditional compliance mechanisms than those previously discussed, but these requirements nonetheless obligate educational institutions to intervene, though somewhat behind-the-scenes of the educational computing environment and "do their part" once again to curb the proliferation of unlawful copyrighted materials in online distance education environments. Why the additional requirements in digital distance education environments? Simple: "The digital transmission of works to students poses greater risks to copyright owners than transmissions through analog broadcasts. Digital technologies make possible the creation of multiple copies, and their rapid and widespread dissemination around the world. Accordingly, the TEACH Act includes several safeguards not currently present in section 110(2)."[35] Digital is dangerous, throwing off the delicate balance of the copyright law between owners and users of copyrighted material. And so, the argument proceeds, Congress must restore that balance in favor of the copyright owner.

First, under section 110(2)(D)(ii)(I)(aa), the educational institution must use technology to prevent "retention of the work in accessible form by recipients of the transmission from the transmitting body or institution for longer than the class session."[36] According to the legislative history, the variable definition of "class session" is designed to accommodate modern notions of 24/7 distance education: "The duration of a 'class session' in asynchronous distance education would generally be that period during which a student is logged on to the server."[37] However there are limits; the institution cannot merely load copyrighted content and leave it accessible on a course Web site indefinitely, or even for an entire semester or academic year: "It does not mean the duration of a particular course (i.e., a semester or term), but rather is intended to describe the equivalent of an actual face-to-face mediated class session."[38] This wording suggests that, for example, material made available during weeks three and four when the material is covered and then again in weeks 8 and 16, during midterm and finals week, would by logic be within the legislative intent.

In addition, section 110(2)(D)(ii)(I)(bb) requires the use of technology to "reasonably prevent" the "unauthorized further dissemination of the work in accessible form by such recipients to others."[39] The legislative history again softens the apparent harsh language of the statute: "the technological protection measure in subparagraph (2)(D)(ii) refers only to retention of a copy or phonorecord *in the computer of the recipient* of a transmission."[40] Apparently, other retentions not in the "computer of the student," i.e., the "recipient of the transmission," are acceptable. Again digital is the "enemy," since retention in the form of a printout or even retention on a disk separate from the computer would not appear to pose a problem from the perspective of the legislative history.

Second, the required use of "technological measures" (i.e., the adoption of access-only technologies) does not imply that the institution must engage in constant real-time monitoring to ensure that no digital copy is ever made: "Nor does it imply that there is an obligation to monitor recipient conduct."[41] The technology chosen need not be perfect, but it must do something to prevent further retention and dissemination. Moreover, by the words of the statute, it must do it "reasonably" well. As the legislative history explains, "the 'reasonably prevent' standard should not be construed to imply perfect efficacy in stopping retention or further dissemination. The obligation to 'reasonably prevent' contemplates an *objectively reasonable standard* regarding the ability of a technological protection measure to achieve its purpose."[42] Given the facts and circumstances of a particular educational environment, is the technological effort of the institution to prevent retention reasonable? A volatile environment where section 512(c)(3) notices are received on a weekly basis might demand a different response than a pre-K- through third grader setting, where the technological savvy of the students would not be expected to be very great.

So, too, the awareness of the technology's effectiveness is tested under an objective standard of reasonableness. An institution that claims it cannot afford to implement technological protection measures when it apparently has the financial resources to mount a digital distance education program would likely not be making a reasonable argument—according to a third party (the objective component), such as a judge or jury. In addition, the institution may need to monitor general developments of copyright compliance in the field, and take action if a technology ceases to "reasonably" prevent the prohibited retention or dissemination. This obligation is suggested by the following comment from the legislative history: "Further, it is possible that, as times passes, a technological protection measure may cease to reasonably prevent retention of the work in accessible form for longer than the class session and further dissemination of the work either due to the evolution of technology or to the widespread availability of a hack that can be readily used by the public."[43] This statement would further suggest a need for periodic monitoring and review of system performance in general to determine if the technological measures used by the institution are reasonably effective. The constant monitoring of individual network users is not necessarily required.

> Examples of technological protection measures that exist today and would reasonably prevent retention and further dissemination, include measures used in connection with streaming to prevent the copying of streamed material, such as the Real Player "Secret Handshake/Copy Switch" technology discussed in *Real Networks v. Streambox*, 2000 WL 127311 or digital rights management systems that limit access to or use encrypted material downloaded onto a computer.[44]

As a result, TEACH represents an extensive array of compliance requirements, including the use of infringement-inhibiting technologies. While the use of such technologies by copyright owners is given legal support in the anti-circumvention and anti-trafficking rules of section 1201 enacted as part of the DMCA in 1998, TEACH, enacted in fall 2002, represents the first time the use of such technologies is required by intermediaries. Of course this obligation is triggered only in circumstances where the institution desires its educators to have the benefit of section 110(2); the provision requiring adoption of infringement-inhibiting technologies contains no such requirement independent of the grant of performance and display rights. Nonetheless, such requirements were heretofore unheard of in the copyright law.

A final proviso related to the use of technological measures in digital distance education is found in section 110(2)(D)(ii)(II). It admonishes the institution not to "engage in conduct that could reasonably be expected to interfere with technological measures used by copyright owners to prevent such retention or unauthorized further dissemination."[45] Unfortunately, there is no definition of the sorts of technological measures. Could a similar definition found in section 1201 and applied under the section's developing case law be used? The legislative history appears to suggest a negative response: "Nothing in section 110(2) should be construed to affect the application or interpretation of section 1201. Conversely, nothing in section 1201 should be construed to affect the application or interpretation of section 110(2)."[46] In other words, not all section 1201 circumventions would trigger the section 110(2)(D)(ii)(II) proviso. Rather, the statute contemplates a subset of all possible circumventions, i.e., those that "could reasonably be expected to interfere with technological measures used by copyright owners to prevent such retention or unauthorized further dissemination," section 110(2)(D)(ii)(I)(aa) and (bb) technological controls. In other words, if the copyright owner has placed a technological control on the material that prevents further retention or dissemination, then the educational institution cannot engage in any conduct that would impede the proper functioning of that measure. Even if the interference does not actually impede the functioning of the protection measure, it might still trigger the proviso, and the benefits of section 110(2) would not be available to the institution.

The legislative history quoted earlier offers two possibilities: "measures used in connection with streaming to prevent the copying of streamed material" or "digital rights management systems that limit access to or use of encrypted material downloaded onto a computer."[47] Notice that section 110(2)(D)(ii)(I)(aa) and (bb) require the institution to use protection measures to assist copyright owners in preventing the sort of retentions and disseminations that might lead to infringement, whereas section 110(2)(D)(ii)(II) requires that the institution not interfere with those measures already in place. In this way section 110(2)(D)(ii)(I) and section 110(2)(D)(ii)(II) complement each other to an extent, and ensure that all copyrighted materials performed or displayed in the context of a section 110(2)(D) digital transmission will be protected by technological measures—by the copyright owner under 110(2)(D)(ii)(II)—or if none are present, by the institution under 110(2)(D)(ii)(I).

Since the statute prohibits conduct that "could reasonably be expected to interfere" with technological measures used by copyright owners to prevent section 110(2)(D)(ii)(I) retentions and disseminations, it would by logic also prohibit conduct that actually succeeds in interfering with those technological measures. Since these sorts of technological measures by nature apply only to copyrighted material in digital form, the proviso is placed with section 110(2)(D)(ii) regarding those uses: "in the case of digital transmissions." Unlike under section 1201, failure to meet this requirement does not create separate liability. Rather, the provision operates only as an eligibility clause, i.e., if triggered, the educational institution cannot take advantage of the expanded performance and display rights of section 110(2).[48]

REAL-WORLD EXAMPLES

▶ Real-World Example I

Situation: A school of visual and performing arts at an accredited institution of higher education desires to launch a distance education program to supplement its master of fine arts (MFA) degree program. The school chooses a course from its art history department in which to "test" the efficacy of launching such a program. In designing the course, the instructor is careful to comply with the portion limitations relating to the amount of copyrighted material that can be performed or displayed. The course is presented through the state university system's television broadcast network.

Legal Analysis: So far so good, but, in order to comply with the provisions of section 110(2), the institution as a whole must also institute policies regarding copyright; provide informational materials to faculty, students, and relevant staff members that accurately describe, and promote compliance with, the laws of the United States relating to copyright; and provide notice to students that materials used in connection with a distance education course may be subject to copyright protection. 17 U.S.C. § 110(2)(D)(i).

▶ Real-World Example II

Situation: The situation is the same as in Real-World Example I, except that, in order to allow students access to course content and instruction 24/7, the school decides to make the class available over the Internet.

Legal Analysis: In addition to meeting initial qualifying requirements as above, 17 U.S.C. § 110(2)(A)–(C), if the performance of display or copyrighted material is rendered by means of a digital transmission, then the educational institution must also apply technological measures that reasonably prevent retention of the work in accessible form by recipients of the transmission for longer than the class session. The institution also must prevent further dissemination of the work in accessible form by such recipients to others. A flexible concept of class session allows for asynchronous but less than the semester-long access. Concept of "in accessible form" akin to a work is usable form, e.g., an encrypted copy would not be "in accessible form." The technological measures need not be perfect, but efforts will judged under a reasonableness standard. 17 U.S.C. § 110(2)(D)(ii)(I)(aa) and (bb). Second, the educational entity must not engage in conduct that could reasonably be expected to interfere with technological measures used by copyright owners to prevent such retention or unauthorized further dissemination. 17 U.S.C. § 110(2)(D)(ii)(II).

▶ Real-World Example III

Situation: The situation is the same as Real-World Examples I and II: accredited institution offering a Web-based distance education course in art history. In addition, in preparation for teaching an art history course "live on the Web" the instructor is planning to perform an audiovisual work (show a film, i.e., stream it on the Web as it is played) and display portions of a literary work, a comprehensive text on Northern European painting from a CD-ROM resource. The audiovisual work is the recent theatrical release, *Girl with a Pearl Earring*, starring Colin Firth and Scarlett Johansson. The instructor uses the film at the beginning of the unit on the Dutch Primitives. The instructor typically shows the entire film, then focuses on 20 to 30 pages of the treatise to stimulate discussion, and finally critiques many of the comments made by its authors. The instructor would like to use the entire film as usual, but decides to make available several additional chapters of CD-ROM text, since it is already in digital form. Assume that both works are protected by copyright and are not acquired through license.

Legal Analysis: Under the portion limitations contained in section 110(2), the instructor is not allowed to use the entire film, as performances of copyrighted materials other than a "nondramatic literary or musical work" are confined to a "reasonable and limited portion[] of any other work"—even though such use in a face-to-face instructional session under section 110(1) would be allowed. Section 110(2) also limits the use of text to the 20 to 30 pages normally discussed, as the display of a work is limited to an "amount comparable to that which is typically displayed in the course of a live classroom session." A license could be obtained to allow performance of the entire documentary, and fair use might support the display of additional amounts of material; however, section 110(2), the main provision of the copyright law dealing with distance education, would not support the use of these materials in these portions.

▶ **Real-World Example IV**

Situation: The situation is the same as in Real-World Example III, except the instructor after reading section 110(2) observes the statutory limit on use of audiovisual works ("reasonable and limited portions"). After consulting the legislative history, he determines that what is reasonable in a given circumstance depends on "both the nature of the market for that type of work and the pedagogical purposes of the performance."[49] As a result, the instructor limits the portion of the film to those sequences depicting Vermeer in his studio or otherwise having specific reference to his paintings. In addition, the instructor would like to make available background readings (make a "display" of text) to go with each lesson; these would be in the form of an e-coursepack also available on the course Web site.

Legal Analysis: Under section 110(2)(A) the performance or display of any copyrighted material must be "offered as a regular part of the systematic mediated instructional activities" of the institution. The definition of mediated instructional activities found at the end of section 110(2) indicates that "[t]he term does not refer to activities that use, in 1 or more class sessions of a single course, such works as textbooks, course packs, or other material in any media, copies or phonorecords of which are typically purchased or acquired by the students in higher education for their independent use and retention." The legislative history further explains:

> The amended exemption is not intended to address other uses of copyrighted works in the course of digital distance education, including student use of supplemental or research materials in digital form, such as electronic course-packs, e-reserves, and digital library resources. Such activities do not involve uses analogous to the performance and displays currently addressed in section 110(2).[50]

As a result, section 110(2) cannot be used to justify the display of such supplemental material. The instructor must either resort to a fair use analysis or secure the material's use through license or other permission.

KEY POINTS FOR YOUR INSTITUTION'S POLICY AND PRACTICE

▶ There is no limitation on the portion of nondramatic literary or musical works that can be performed in a distance education transmission under section 110(2). The performance of all other works is limited to a reasonable and limited portion of the work. The amount is determined by considering a market test (for that type of work) and pedagogical purpose test, but in any case the amount is less than the entire work. See p. 338.

▶ Display of works in a distance education transmission under section 110(2) is limited to an amount comparable to that which is typically displayed in the course of a live classroom session; it need not be less, but it cannot be more simply because the distance education environment makes it easy to present more materials. See pp. 338–339.

▶ The performance and display of section 110(2) rights do not apply to works produced or marketed primarily for performance or display as part of mediated instructional activities transmitted via digital networks, i.e., instructional or curricular materials designed specifically for use in digital distance education are excluded. See pp. 339–340.

▶ The copy or phonorecord performed or displayed must be lawfully made and acquired under the copyright law, and the educational institution must be accredited. See p. 340.

▶ The performance or display must be made by, at the direction of, or under the actual supervision of an instructor as an integral part of a class session offered as a regular part of the systematic mediated instructional activities, and can include asynchronous as well as synchronous instruction. The performance or display is directly related and of material assistance to the teaching content of the transmission; it cannot be for entertainment or as unrelated background material. See pp. 339–341.

▶ The reception of such transmission is limited, to the extent technologically feasible, to students officially enrolled in the course for which the transmission is made. No rule of general network security is specified, but use of a password or similar measure is suggested. See p. 341.

▶ Regardless of whether the transmission of copyrighted material is analog or digital, the educational entity must undertake three significant compliance-oriented tasks:
  ▶ First, the entity must institute policies regarding copyright.
  ▶ Second, the educational institution must provide informational materials to faculty, students, and relevant staff members that accurately describe, and promote compliance with, the laws of the United States relating to copyright.
  ▶ Finally, the educational entity must provide notice to students that materials used in connection with a distance education course may be subject to copyright protection; use of such notices is recommended for all classes (with placement near the beginning of a course syllabus, outline, or reading list). See pp. 341–343.

▶ If the performance or display is by means of a digital transmission, then the educational entity must apply technological measures that reasonably prevent retention of the work in accessible form by recipients of the transmission from the transmitting school, college, university, or other educational entity for longer than the class session. A flexible concept of class session allows for asynchronous access (but for less than the duration of the semester). The concept of a work "in accessible form" is akin to a work in usable form, e.g., an encrypted copy would not be "in accessible form." The technological measures need not be perfect, but efforts will judged under a reasonableness standard. See pp. 344–346.

▶ If the performance or display is by means of a digital transmission, then the school, college, university, or other educational entity must not engage in conduct that could reasonably be expected to interfere with technological measures used by copyright owners to prevent such retention or further unauthorized dissemination. This requirement creates no new liability, it is only a standard of eligibility for the section 110(2) performance and display rights. See pp. 346–347.

ENDNOTES

[1] Section 403 of the DMCA required that the U.S. Copyright Office make a report and recommendation: "Not later than 6 months after the date of enactment of this Act, the Register of Copyrights, after consultation with representatives of copyright owners, nonprofit educational institutions, and nonprofit libraries and archives, shall submit to the Congress recommendations on how to promote distance education through digital technologies, including interactive digital networks, while maintaining an appropriate balance between the rights of copyright owners and the needs of users of copyrighted works. Such recommendations shall include any legislation the Register of Copyrights considers appropriate to achieve the objective described in the preceding sentence." The report and recommendation formed the basis of legislative reform. See, U.S. COPYRIGHT OFFICE, *REPORT ON COPYRIGHT AND DIGITAL DISTANCE EDUCATION* (Washington D.C.: U.S. Government Printing Office, 1999).

[2] The Technology Education and Copyright Harmonization Act of 2001, S. 487, was incorporated into H.R. 2215, the 21st Century Department of Justice Appropriations Authorization Act, later enacted into law as Pub. L. No. 107-273, 116 Stat. 1758, 1910-1913 (2002).

[3] See, Congressional Developments: Peer-to-Peer Piracy on University Campuses, Hearing, Subcommittee on Courts, the Internet, and Intellectual Property, Committee on the Judiciary, U.S. House of Representatives, 108th Cong., 1st Sess., (February 26, 2003). ("There is no difference if the student takes that same music or movie by downloading it off the Internet while sitting in the dorm. Colleges and universities have a duty to address these crimes aggressively. School presidents and other administrators cannot stand by as taxpayer-funded information systems and tuition dollars are being used to build Internet systems that help facilitate unethical behavior. . . . Some students may feel that downloading music and movies is victimless." Id, at p. 20 (Statement of Representative Keller); ("Unfortunately, colleges play a prominent role in contributing to P2P piracy. . . . [C]olleges

can't expect Congress to continuously help them on intellectual property issues if they do not act as responsible members of the intellectual property system."), at p. 13 (Opening statement of Ranking Member Representative Berman) (available at *http://commdocs.house. gov/committees/judiciary/hju85286.000/hju85286_0.htm*).

[4] A detailed discussion of TEACH is found in TOMAS A. LIPINSKI, COPYRIGHT LAW AND THE DISTANCE EDUCATION CLASSROOM (2005); and a thorough overview is in Tomas A. Lipinski, The Climate of Distance Education in the 21st Century: Understanding and Surviving the Changes Brought by the TEACH (Technology, Education, and Copyright Harmonization) Act of 2002, 29 JOURNAL OF ACADEMIC LIBRARIANSHIP (2003) 362.

[5] TEACH also amended section 112, the ephemeral recording provisions, which limit the copyright owner's exclusive right of reproduction, and grants qualifying users the right to make an ephemeral recording, in essence to reproduce the work as a precursor to a section 110(2) use. Section 112 does not contain any compliance-oriented provisions, thus it is not discussed here. TEACH added subsection (f) to section 112: "Notwithstanding the provisions of section 106, and without limiting the application of subsection (b), it is not an infringement of copyright for a governmental body or other nonprofit educational institution entitled under section 110(2) to transmit a performance or display to make copies or phonorecords of a work that is in digital form and, solely to the extent permitted in paragraph (2), of a work that is in analog form, embodying the performance or display to be used for making transmissions authorized under section 110(2), if—(A) such copies or phonorecords are retained and used solely by the body or institution that made them, and no further copies or phonorecords are reproduced from them, except as authorized under section 110(2); and (B) such copies or phonorecords are used solely for transmissions authorized under section 110(2). (2) This subsection does not authorize the conversion of print or other analog versions of works into digital formats, except that such conversion is permitted hereunder, only with respect to the amount of such works authorized to be performed or displayed under section 110(2), if—(A) no digital version of the work is available to the institution; or (B) the digital version of the work that is available to the institution is subject to technological protection measures that prevent its use for section 110(2)."

[6] TEACH, codified in 17 U.S.C. § 110, contains a definition of the qualifying accreditation: "For purposes of paragraph (2), accreditation—(A) with respect to an institution providing post-secondary education, shall be as determined by a regional or national accrediting agency recognized by the Council on Higher Education Accreditation or the United States Department of Education; and (B) with respect to an institution providing elementary or secondary education, shall be as recognized by the applicable state certification or licensing procedures."

[7] H.R Rep. No. 107-685, 227 (2002) (conf. Rep.).

[8] H.R. Rep. No. 107-685, 227 (2002) (conf. Rep.) (emphasis added).

[9] 17 U.S.C. § 110(2).

[10] 17 U.S.C. § 110(2)(A).

[11] H.R. Rep. No. 107-685, 229 (2002) (conf. Rep.).

[12] 17 U.S.C. § 110(2)(B).

[13] U.S. COPYRIGHT OFFICE, *REPORT ON COPYRIGHT AND DIGITAL DISTANCE EDUCA-TION* 80 (1999).

[14] S. Rep. No. 107-31, (2001); H. Rpt. No. 107-687, 107th Cong., 2nd Sess. 11 (2002). H.R. Rep. No. 107-685, 230 (2002) (conf. Rep.), essentially adopts the language of the House Report.

[15] One of the tragic flaws of the pre-TEACH formulation of section 110(2) was that it envisioned a classroom-to-classroom or teacher-to-classroom distance education environment where students accessed course content from a remote place but were still gathered together in a classroom linked typically by some form of broadcast technology. TEACH expands the concept of remote student. The goal of the Section 110(2) revision in the words of the TEACH Conference Report is to "remove the concept of the physical classroom." Conference Report, H.R. Rep. No. 107-685, 226 (2002) (conf. Rep.).

[16] Section 110(2) defines mediated instructional activities as "activities that use such work as an integral part of the class experience, controlled by or under the actual supervision of the instructor and analogous to the type of performance or display that would take place in a live classroom setting. The term does not refer to activities that use, in 1 or more class sessions of a single course, such works as textbooks, course packs, or their material in any media, copies or phonorecords of which are typically purchased or acquired by the students in higher education for their independent use and retention or are typically purchased or acquired for elementary and secondary students for their possession and independent use." 17 U.S.C. § 110(2).

[17] H.R. Rep. No. 107-685, 227 (2002) (conf. Rep.).

[18] H.R. Rep. No. 107-685, 229 (2002) (conf. Rep.).

[19] 17 U.S.C. § 110(2)(B). The definition of MIA in section 110(2), indicates that "[t]he term does not refer to activities that use, in 1 or more class sessions of a single course, such works as textbooks, course packs, or their material in any media, copies or phonorecords of which are typically purchased or acquired by the students in higher education for their independent use and retention or are typically purchased or acquired for elementary and secondary students for their possession and independent use." 17 U.S.C. § 110(2).

[20] 17 U.S.C. § 110.

[21] 17 U.S.C. § 110(2).

[22] 17 U.S.C. § 110(1) ("in the case of a motion picture or other audiovisual work, the performance, or the display of individual images, is given by means of a copy that was not lawfully made under this title, and that the person responsible for the performance knew or had reason to believe was not lawfully made.").

[23] 17 U.S.C. § 110(2)(C)(i).

[24] H.R. Rep. No. 107-685, 230 (2002) (conf. Rep.).

[25] H.R. Rep. No. 107-685, 230 (2002) (conf. Rep.).

[26] H.R. Rep. No. 107-685, 227-228 (2002) (conf. Rep.), citing, U.S. COPYRIGHT OFFICE, REPORT ON COPYRIGHT AND DIGITAL DISTANCE EDUCATION 159 (1999).

[27] 17 U.S.C. § 110(2)(D)(i).

[28] 17 U.S.C. § 110(2)(D)(i).

[29] H.R. Rep. No. 107-685, 231 (2002) (conf. Rep.).

[30] 17 U.S.C. § 110(2)(D)(i) (emphasis added).

[31] The following notice could be used: "All materials that under United States Copyright law would be considered the normal work product of the instructor, i.e., the class or lecture note exception to the work for hire doctrine, are under the sole ownership of the instructor, this includes but is not limited to exercises, discussion questions, etc. See, *Hays v. Sony Corp of America*, 847 F.2d 412 (7th Cir. 1988); and *Weinstein v. University of Illinois*, 811 F. 2d 1091 (7th Cir. 1987). See also, Georgia Holmes and Daniel A. Levin, Who Owns Course Materials Prepared by a Teacher or Professor? The Application of Copyright Law to Teaching Materials in the Internet Age, 2000 BRIGHAM YOUNG UNIVERSITY EDUCATION & LAW JOURNAL 165 (2000); Sunil R. Kulkarni, All Professors Create Equally: Why Faculty Should Have Complete Control Over the Intellectual Property Rights in Their Creations, 47 HASTINGS LAW JOURNAL 47: 221 (1995); Laura G. Lape, Ownership of Copyrightable Works of University Professors: The Interplay Between the Copyright Act and University Copyright Policies, 37 VILLANOVA LAW REVIEW 223 (1992). The instructor, the university, and the Web site designer share the copyright in the "look and feel" of the site. Underlying copyright in the software generating the Web site is also protected by copyright. Documents and other material appearing on the Web site or by link from the site may also be protected by copyright. This site is maintained for educational purposes only. Your viewing of the material posted here does not imply any right to reproduce, to retransmit, or to redisplay it other than for your own personal or educational use. Links to other sites are provided for the convenience of the site user (staff or student) or visitor and do not imply any affiliation or endorsement of the other site owner nor a guarantee of the quality or veracity of information contained on the linked site. As a student your ability to post or link to copyrighted material is also governed by United States Copyright law. This instructor or other staff of the institution reserves the right delete or disable your post or link if, in its judgment, the post or link would involve violation of copyright law." Depending on the circumstances of the educational environment, the language regarding ownership of the copyrighted curricular materials could be modified to reflect the operation of the work for hire doctrine under copyright that vests ownership of copyrighted materials created in the course of employment with the employer and not with the employee-faculty member. For a discussion of the work for hire concept in higher education and faculty ownership issues see, TOMAS A. LIPINSKI, COPYRIGHT LAW AND THE DISTANCE EDUCATION CLASSROOM 6-16 (2005).

[32] U.S. COPYRIGHT OFFICE, REPORT ON COPYRIGHT AND DIGITAL DISTANCE EDUCATION 151, fn. 362 (1999).

[33] Conference Report, H. Rpt. No. 107-685, 107th Cong., 2nd Sess. 230-231 (2002).

[34] The compliance requirements of legislation such as TEACH are likely not to be the last effort by Congress in this area. See, e.g., Peer-to-Peer Piracy on University Campuses, Hearing, U.S. House of Representatives, Judiciary Committee Subcommittee on Courts, the Internet, and Intellectual Property, February 26, 2003 ("Unfortunately, colleges play a prominent role in contributing to P2P piracy. . . . colleges can't expect Congress to continuously help them on intellectual property issues if they do not act as responsible members of the intellectual property system."), at p. 13 (Opening statement of Ranking Member Howard Berman) (available at *http://commdocs.house.gov/committees/judiciary/hju85286.000/hju85286_0.htm*).

[35] H.R. Rep. No. 107-685, 230 (2002) (conf. Rep.).

[36] 17 U.S.C. § 110(2)(D)(ii)(I)(aa).

[37] H.R. Rep. No. 107-685, 231 (2002) (conf. Rep).

[38] H.R. Rep. No. 107-685, 231 (2002) (conf. Rep.).

[39] 17 U.S.C. § 110(2)(D)(ii)(I)(bb).

[40] H.R. Rep. No. 107-685, (2002) (conf. Rep.) (emphasis added).

[41] H.R. Rep. No. 107-685, 232 (2002) (conf. Rep.).

[42] H.R. Rep. No. 107-685, 232 (2002) (conf. Rep.) (emphasis added).

[43] H.R. Rep. No. 107-685, 232 (2002) (conf. Rep.).

[44] H.R. Rep. No. 107-685, 232 (2002) (conf. Rep.).

[45] 17 U.S.C. § 110(2)(D)(ii)(II).

[46] H.R. Rep. No. 107-685, 232 (2002) (conf. Rep.).

[47] H.R. Rep. No. 107-685, 232 (2002) (conf. Rep.).

[48] H.R. Rep. No. 107-685, 232 (2002) (conf. Rep.) ("Further, like the other provisions under paragraph (2)(D)(ii), the *requirement has no legal effect* other than as a condition of eligibility for the exemption. Thus, *it is not otherwise enforceable* to preclude or prohibit conduct.") (first and second emphasis added).

[49] H.R. Rep. No. 107-685, 227 (2002) (conf. Rep.).

[50] H.R. Rep. No. 107-685, 229 (2002) (conf. Rep.).

►13

AFTERWORD: FINAL THOUGHTS ABOUT LIABILITY, IMMUNITY, AND RISK ASSESSMENT IN COPYRIGHT LAW

The purpose of this monograph was straightforward at the outset: to review those provisions of the copyright law that require the library or educational institution (or its staff, such as librarians, faculty, and network administrators) to do "something." Unfortunately, Congress has added to the list of those "something" provisions since the 1976 Copyright Act. Moreover, that "something" takes the form of what might in general be called the promotion of copyright compliance through awareness, and in specific it is accomplished through the use of copyright warning notices, policies, informational outreach, and in some instances the use of technological measures as a preventative measure and takedown or disabling of access to content as a remedial measure. The section 512 rules also entail an increased role as go-between with respect to copyright owners and users. Under the copyright law, an individual or institution can enjoy the advantages of specific "use" provisions only when that "something" is done. The copyright law then creates a decided and obvious quid pro quo. Understanding when this must (shall) be done and when it is a good idea to do so (should) assists administrators, educators, and librarians in creating, in terms of the copyright law, a compliant environment.

These measures are designed to encourage the intermediary library or educational entity to create and foster a more compliant environment in which its staff and patrons or students operate. Whether the intermediary desires to implement all of these commands is a part of its internal decision-making and risk-management process. The intent of the early chapters is to introduce the concepts of liability and damages and damage reduction or remission so that decision makers can assess the level of risk in a given scenario. On this point, an additional comment can be offered.

First, copyright "decisions" of risk, like all similar decisions in the library or school environment, are often a mix of considering what is legal, what is practical, and what is ethical. For example, certain provisions of the law may allow the intermediary to look the proverbial other way (section 108(f)(1)) or to investigate clear red flags of copyright infringement (section 512(c)(1)(A) or (d)(1)) without the need to engage in constant monitoring of patrons. Yet there may be an ethical obligation in terms of the copyright law to intervene or at least explain to users why such infringing conduct undertaken by third parties does not raise an issue of copyright liability for the institution but nonetheless remains a copyright issue for the patron or student. At the same time, a risk-management decision to require users of an intermediary's network or system to complete a copyright tutorial before account access is given might be met with a resounding guffaw (as it was at the author's institution).

Attempts to curb infringing behavior might be deemed by upper administration, as it was at the author's institution, as unrealistic. (It is also interesting to observe—the author will likely make a few enemies here—that some librarians in the author's experience would rush to intervene if a patron accessed so-called controversial or "pornographic" images, but could not care less whether an infringement of copyright is occurring. To be sure, there is a distinction; accessing material that some might consider pornographic might be a protected activity under the First Amendment, yet engaging in copyright infringement is never a lawful activity!)

The point is that a variety of legal, practical, and ethical considerations, or absence of such considerations, may operate to lead the institution to conclude that a higher level of risk is acceptable in a given situation. It should also be pointed out that achieving 100 percent or perfect compliance with copyright law is, as is the case with any law, likely impossible. However, making sincere attempts to comply with the "shall" and the "should" of the copyright law can go a long way to minimizing the risk should infringement occur. This is true for two reasons.

First, undertaking compliance-oriented measures can create a healthy (in a legal sense) environment among employees and third parties, such as patrons or students, and this environment can greatly reduce the chance that such infringement would occur in the first instance. Second, with the compliance mechanisms and institutional enforcement responses described in the previous chapters in place, risk managers are more likely to be alerted of an infringement and have an opportunity to respond in an appropriate and timely manner. Such a response in turn decreases the likelihood that any discovered infringement would perpetuate in the future and it narrows the window of time during which an infringement might be discovered by copyright owners or their agents. Having little or no response forecloses the opportunity to make these assessments and adjustments. A positive cycle of compliance is fostered where the initiatives work to minimize risk in the first instance and to enhance interventions at the institutional level in the second instance when risk occurs.

In the much larger picture, active and consistent behavior across institutions such as libraries, schools, colleges, and universities may cause copyright owners and Congress to shift their energies to other loci of copyright enforcement problems, with the likely result that no new and additional compliance-oriented measures will be enacted.

If this monograph has succeeded in convincing risk managers at your institution that some response is needed and yet the task appears daunting, the following appendixes can help in getting started. In addition, a review of the "Key Points for Your Institution's Policy and Practice" sections at the end of each chapter may also prove useful.

▶Part V

COMPLIANCE TOOLS FOR SCHOOLS AND LIBRARIES

►Tool 1

A COPYRIGHT COMPLIANCE AUDIT

While the author and publisher would certainly like readers to use this book, neither would like readers to photocopy, scan, or otherwise reproduce and distribute protions of this book in excess of fair use without permission. We do, however, want you to use the following compliance (and notice) audit. Therefore the author and publisher grant any purchaser of this book the right to photocopy, scan, or otherwise reproduce and distribute portions of the copyright compliance (notice) audit for use within their own institutional environment. This permission includes the right to make derivative works (edit, revise, etc.), provided that with any use, proper source credit is given to the author and publisher. Thank you!

Text in boldface indicates possible implementing language.

►TOOL 1 A Copyright Compliance Audit

Purpose	Question	Analysis	Required Notice
1. Required notice of copyright on library reproductions and distributions of copyrighted material	*Does the library reproduce copyrighted material for purposes of "preservation and security or for deposit for research" in the collections of another library, or for purposes of replacement? Alternatively, does the library offer interlibrary loan services or reproduction services whereby copies or phonorecords of legally protected material are made and given to patrons? If so, does the library also reproduce or include a copyright warning notice on the material it reproduces and distributes?*	Section 108(a)(3) requires that any copy made and distributed either in the library collection or to a patron must "include[] a notice of copyright that appears on the copy or phonorecord that is reproduced under the provisions of this section, or include[] a legend stating that the work may be protected by copyright if no such notice can be found on the copy or phonorecord that is reproduced under the provisions of this section." 17 U.S.C. § 108 (a)(3). In 1998, amendments to the copyright law radded a § 108 second notice option, now providing librarians with a choice when copyright status is in doubt.	Either reprint or repeat the copyright notice from the original copy or phonorecord in those cases where knowledge of the work's copyright status is established: **"Warning: this material is protected by the copyright laws of the United States, Title 17, United States Code,"** or similar words. When the status of the work is unknown, include a notice that meets the section 108(a)(3) requirement: **"Warning: this work may be protected by the copyright laws of the United States, Title 17, United States Code,"** or words to that effect.
2. Interlibrary Loan and library reproduction services	*Does the library offer interlibrary loan services or copying services for patrons whereby copies or phono-*	In order to ensure that section 108 libraries do not become the source of material for later infringements	**"NOTICE WARNING CONCERNING COPYRIGHT RESTRICTIONS. The copyright law of the United**

(Continued)

▶TOOL 1   A Copyright Compliance Audit *(Continued)*

Purpose	Question	Analysis	Required Notice
2. Interlibrary loan and library reproduction services *(continued)*	*records of copyrighted material are made and given to patrons? If so, does the library display a copyright warning notice near the location where orders are taken and on the form the patron signs in accordance with the statute and the procedures in 37 C.F.R. § 201.14?*	by patrons, subsections 108(d)(2) and (e)(2) require that "the library or archives displays prominently, at the place where orders are accepted, and includes on its order form, a warning of copyright in accordance with requirements that the Register of Copyrights shall prescribe by regulation." Such a warning must be displayed at the place where "orders are accepted," such as the interlibrary loan office or the photocopy service desk, and on any forms such departments use. The regulation makes clear that "[a]s required by those sections the 'Order Warning of Copyright' *is to be included* on printed forms supplied by certain libraries and archives *and used by their patrons* for ordering copies or phonorecords," suggesting that the notice must appear on all forms and that those forms must be used by patrons, which likewise suggests patrons would fill out the entire form, i.e., including affixing their signature. 37 C.F.R. § 201.14(a)(2) (all emphasis added). Under a strict reading of the law, each reproduction must be predicated upon a patron signature or name. consequently, all patrons requesting copy services must be presented with this notice.	**States (Title 17, United States Code) governs the making of photocopies or other reproductions of copyrighted material. Under certain conditions specified in the law, libraries and archives are authorized to furnish a photocopy or other reproduction. One of these specific conditions is that the photocopy or reproduction is not to be 'used for any purpose other than private study, scholarship, or research.' If a user makes a request for, or later uses, a photocopy or reproduction for purposes in excess of 'fair use,' that user may be liable for copyright infringement. This institution reserves the right to refuse to accept a copying order if, in its judgment, fulfillment of the order would involve violation of copyright law."** 37 C.F.R. § 201.14(b). The regulation reiterates that the notice be posted on at least one sign in the service area and on the form itself, highlighted in a box on the front page of the form or near the signature line of the patron-requester. Federal regulation provides that "A Display Warning of Copyright shall be printed on heavy paper or other durable material in type at least 18 points in size, and shall be displayed prominently, in such manner and location as to be clearly visible, legible, and comprehensible to a casual observer within the immediate vicinity of the place where orders are accepted." 37 C.F.R. § 201.14(c)(1).

(Continued)

▶**TOOL 1   A Copyright Compliance Audit** *(Continued)*

Purpose	Question	Analysis	Required Notice
3. Distributing reproduced materials to patrons for non-research purposes	*Does the library offer interlibrary loan services or a reproducing service whereby copies of copyrighted material are made and given to patrons? If so, does staff have notice that the copy or phonorecord would be used for any purpose other than private study, scholarship, or research?*	If the library (or any of its staff) has had evidence to this effect, then the reproduction and distribution is not authorized by section 108, although a license, fair use. or another provision of the copyright law may nonetheless authorize its use. This provision for the production of scholarly copies is contained in 108(d)(1) and (e)(1). These two subsections offer additional "use" rights: the reproduction of periodical article or a "small part" of a copyrighted work or reproduction of an entire work or a "substantial part" of a copyrighted work also require that the copies made by the library "become[] the property of the user"—and the library or archives has had no notice that the copy or phonorecord would be used for any purpose other than private study, scholarship, or research. 17 U.S.C. § 108(d)(1) and (e)(1). The crucial inquiry in such cases is not into whether the potential uses are infringing, only into whether the reproduced works will be used for private scholarship. Questions of infringement enter only after the fact of section 108(e) and (d) considerations. Infringing private study, scholarship, or research, while meeting the section 108(d)(1) and (e)(1) requirements, might still implicate the library in contributory liability depending on the level of knowledge present. Only those private uses that are at least partially for study, scholarship, or research are authorized.	Reproduction and distribution of materials for patrons must be accompanied by attestation by the patron that the material is for purposes of private study, scholarship, or research. If library staff have notice of use other than private study, scholarship, or research, the library may refuse to reproduce and distribute the material, as section 108 will no longer authorize this use. Material reproduced and distributed must become the property of the patron and may not be used to build the collections of the library.

(Continued)

▶ **TOOL 1**   A Copyright Compliance Audit *(Continued)*

Purpose	Question	Analysis	Required Notice
3. Distributing reproduced materials to patrons for non-research purposes *(continued)*		The patron's signed testament does not absolve the institution from liability: If the library was aware of uses "other than private study, scholarship, or research" regardless of the patron's signed claim, legal logic would suggest that the library could not hide behind the patron's false claims. What the attestation does mean is that the institution has no duty to investigate or monitor or otherwise check up on the subsequent use of copied materials. By contrast, to place a copy of a work on open reserve or e-reserve constitutes a public display according to *Hotaling v. Church of Latter Day Saints*, 118 F.3d 199 (4th Cir. 1997). Accordingly, such actions would not meet the "private study" requirement. Finally, subsection (d) or (e) reproductions cannot be used for purposes of collection building.	
4. Warning notice for patron-accessible photocopiers, computers, scanners, samplers, and other media reproduction technologies	*Does the library provide reproducing equipment (photocopier, computer, printer, scanner, sampler, etc.) for patron use? Is the use of the equipment unsupervised? If so, then does the library display a notice that the making of a copy may be subject to the copyright law?*	Section 108(f)(1) immunizes libraries, archives, and the employees thereof from illegitimate use of reproduction technologies by patrons, so long as the infringing activity is wholly unsupervised. To fulfill this provision's requirements, it is also crucial that the institution's employees neither know nor have reason to know that the activity is infringing. Although employee use of reproduction technologies cannot be considered unsupervised, a warning notice similar to the one at right can be adapted for use on machines to which they have access. Use of this notice does not guarantee institutional immunity, but it can be an important part of overall risk	While no notice fulfilling the section 108(f)(1) posting obligation is offered by the U.S. Copyright Office, use of the following text, adapted from the section 108(d) and (e), 37 C.F.R. § 201.14 notice, is possible: "**NOTICE WARNING CONCERNING COPYRIGHT RESTRICTIONS. The copyright law of the United States (Title 17, United States Code) governs the making of photocopies or other reproductions of copyrighted material. Libraries and archives furnish unsupervised photocopy or other reproduction equipment for the convenience of and use by**

(Continued)

▶**TOOL 1   A Copyright Compliance Audit** *(Continued)*

Purpose	Question	Analysis	Required Notice
4. Warning notice for patron-accessible photocopiers, computers, scanners, samplers, and other media reproduction technologies *(continued)*		management and compliance efforts. Note that section 108(f)(1) does not offer immunity for other acts of infringement unrelated to the use of photo-copying or other reproduction equipment. For example, use of the same technology to make an infringing public per-formance of a video cassette would not be protected.	patrons. Under 17 U.S.C. § 108(f)(2) the provision of unsupervised photocopy or re-production equipment for use by patrons does not excuse the person who uses the re-production equipment from liability for copyright infringe-ment for any such act, or for later use of such copy or phonorecord, if it exceeds fair use as provided by section 107 or any other provision of the copy-right law. This insti-tution reserves the right to refuse to make available or provide access to photocopy or other reproduction equip-ment if, in its judgment, use of such equipment would involve violation of copyright law." A practical matter, such notice should be placed on all patron-accessible reproduc-tion equipment in the library that is capable of reproducing copyrighted material, including photocopiers computers, printers, scanners, samplers, VCRs, and any other technology that has a reproducing capacity.
5. Circulating (distributing) copyrighted material	*Does the library circulate or make copyrighted materials in its collections available to the public, i.e., make a public distribution of copyrighted works? If so, in order to exercise distribution rights under the first sale doctrine, all materials so distributed must be lawfully made.*	All copies of legally protected material circulated by a library must be lawfully made. According to section 109, the owners of a legitimate copy have the right to dispose of it as they wish. This is known as the first sale right. A careful reading of the court's decision in *Hoatling v. Church of Latter Day Saints*, 118 F.3d 199 (4th Cir. 1997), suggests that circulations of unauthorized or illegal repro-ductions of a work would be an infringement.	Public distribution of copyrighted materials by the library must consist of the distribution of lawfully made materials. No specific warning notice is required to circulate (distribute) copyrighted material, except for computer programs (see item 7 below).

(Continued)

▶TOOL 1   A Copyright Compliance Audit *(Continued)*

Purpose	Question	Analysis	Required Notice
6. Library distribution of sound recordings	*Does a nonprofit library or nonprofit educational institution lend sound recordings in the form of phonorecords? If so, the distribution is exempt from the restoration of the copyright owner's first sale rights that were explained in item 5.*	In an exception to the first sale doctrine, the right of public distribution described in item 5 above does not apply to phonorecords or software programs made available by rental or lease for the financial advantage of the owner. Section 109(b), however, provides an exception to this exception, allowing nonprofit libraries to distribute such works, so long as it is done in a manner manner befitting their nonprofit status.	No specific warning notice is required to circulate (distribute) phonorecords, except for computer programs (see item 7 below). Public distribution of phonorecords by the library must consist of the distribution of lawfully made phonorecords.
7. Transfer of possession of software in addition to other distributions	*Does a nonprofit educational institution possess a computer program that it desires to publicly distribute through a transfer of possession to another nonprofit educational institution or to faculty, staff, and students? If so, the right is also exempt from the copyright owner's restoration of first sale, explained in item 5.*	In addition to the provision described in item 6, section 109(b) legitimates the transfer of legally made copies of software between nonprofit educational institutions. This allows schools, colleges, or universities to permanently shift possession of software among institutions (within a consortium, for example), beyond the transfer that might occur for purposes of interlibrary loan or other nonpermanent transfers. This provision recognizes the fact that in some settings the library may not be making such distributions, but that such distributions occur on an institutional level. The "*or to faculty, staff, and students*" proviso allows for distributions, common in some school districts, whereby curricular materials, including software or a workbook and software tutorial, are supplied (distributed) to teachers or students by the district at the beginning of each school year.	No specific warning notice is required to transfer possession of a lawfully made copy of a computer program from one nonprofit educational institution to another or to faculty, staff, and students. The transfer of possession of a copy of a computer program from one nonprofit educational institution to another or to faculty, staff, and students must consist of the transfer of a lawfully made copy.
8. Warning notice for libraries lending software	*Does a nonprofit library desire to lend computer programs in its collection? If so, the computer program restoration right of copyright owners does not apply to such lending "for nonprofit*	In addition to the exception for schools and libraries relating to the restoration of the copyright owner's exclusive right of public distribution, a second exception exists for computer programs: "Nothing in this subsection [that is subsection (b), which restores	As with section 108(d)(2) and (e)(2), the text of the notice is established by federal regulation: "**Notice: Warning of Copyright Restrictions. The copyright law of the United**

(Continued)

▶**TOOL 1   A Copyright Compliance Audit *(Continued)***

Purpose	Question	Analysis	Required Notice
8. Warning notice for libraries lending software *(continued)*	*purposes by a non-profit library" if a copyright warning is used.*	the reach of the copyright owner's exclusive right of distribution, the first sale right, to dispositions of computer programs] shall apply to the lending of a computer program for nonprofit purposes by a nonprofit library, *if each copy of a computer program which is lent by such library has affixed to the packaging containing the program a warning of copyright in accordance with requirements that the Register of Copyrights shall prescribe by regulation."* 17 U.S.C. § 109(b)(2)(A). In an attempt to balance the rights of owners and users, Congress requires that libraries remind patrons of their obligation to honor the rights of copyright owners: "The Committee does not wish, however, to prohibit nonprofit lending by nonprofit libraries and nonprofit educational institutions. Such institutions serve a valuable public purpose by making computer software available to students who would not otherwise have access to it. At the same time, the Committee is aware that the same economic factors that lead to unauthorized copying in a commercial context may lead library patrons also to engage in such conduct." H.R. Rep. No 101-735, (1990). Thus, in return for the ability to lend software to students and patrons of nonprofit educational schools and its libraries, the library must place a warning notice on the software to be distributed.	States (title 17, United States Code) governs the reproduction, distribution, adaptation, public performance, and public display of copyrighted material. Under certain conditions specified in law, nonprofit libraries are authorized to lend, lease, or rent copies of computer programs to patrons on a nonprofit basis and for nonprofit purposes. Any person who makes an unauthorized copy or adaptation of the computer program, or redistributes the loan copy, or publicly performs or displays the computer program, except as permitted by title 17 of the United States Code, may be liable for copyright infringement. This institution reserves the right to refuse to fulfill a loan request if, in its judgment, fulfillment of the request would lead to a violation of the copyright law." 37 C.F.R. § 201.24(b). The wording of the notice must conform to the prescribed regulation; it may not deviate from it. 37 C.F.R. § 201.24(b). The form and manner of notice is articulated in the regulation: "A Warning of Copyright for Software Rental shall be affixed to the packaging that contains the copy of the computer program, which is the subject of a library loan to patrons, by means of a label cemented, gummed, or otherwise durably attached to the copies or to a box, reel, cartridge, cassette, or other container used as a permanent receptacle for the copy of the computer program. The notice shall be printed in such manner as to be clearly

(Continued)

▶ **TOOL 1 A Copyright Compliance Audit** *(Continued)*

Purpose	Question	Analysis	Required Notice
8. Warning notice for libraries lending software *(continued)*			legible, comprehensible, and readily apparent to a casual user of the computer program." 37 C.F.R. § 201.24(c). This could be accomplished by having self-adhesive labels printed with the text of the warning notice so that library staff can easily attach the labels to the software packaging.
9. Instituting a repeat infringer policy	*Does the library, school, college, university, or other service provider desire to obtain the limitations on liability (monetary relief), the so-called safe harbor, that section 512 offers? If so, then the service provider must adopt and reasonably implement a repeat infringer policy.*	In order for libraries or schools to qualify for the "safe harbor" they must first have "adopted and reasonably implemented, and informed subscribers and account holders of the service provider's system or network of, a policy that provides for the termination in appropriate circumstances of subscribers and account holders of the service provider's system or network who are repeat infringers." 17 U.S.C. § 512(i)(1)(A). Logic dictates that "reasonable implementation" means enforcement of the policy consistent with the ways and means with which other policies are enforced within a given institutional structure. The legislative history indicates that the threat of termination should indeed be real. H.R. Rep. No 551 (Part 2), 61 (1998); 105-190, 52 (1998). Case law suggests that the policy must be in place before any wrongdoing occurs in order for policy adoption to offer the institution the protection of the section 512 safe harbor. *Ellison v. Robertson*, 357 F.3d 1072, 1080 (9th Cir. 2004). A similar lesson is demonstrated by the *Napster* case. True, Napster also had a repeat infringer policy. Unfortunately, Napster created its policy after the fact of legal	The following language could be used in an educational environment: **Notice: Warning of Copyright Restrictions. As a student your ability to post or link to copyrighted material is also governed by United States Copyright law. This instructor or other staff of this institution reserves the right to delete or disable your post or link if, in his or her judgment, the post or link would involve violation of copyright law. In accordance with 17 U.S.C. § 512(i)(1)(A), this institution has adopted and shall make all reasonable effort to enforce a policy whereby the instructor or staff reserves the right to terminate in appropriate circumstances the access to the system or network of students who disrespect the intellectual property rights of others or who are otherwise repeat infringers of copyright.** The following language could be used in a public library setting: **Notice: Warning of Copyright Restrictions. As a patron your ability to post or link to**

(Continued)

▶TOOL 1   A Copyright Compliance Audit *(Continued)*

Purpose	Question	Analysis	Required Notice
9. Instituting a repeat infringer policy *(continued)*		proceedings against it by the creording industry, some two months later. *A&M Records, Inc. v. Napster, Inc.*, 2000 WL 573136,at * 9 (N.D. Cal. 2000). The court was not convinced and responded that such *rationalization* "defies the logic of making formal notification to users or subscribers a prerequisite to exemption from monetary liability." Id.	copyrighted material is also governed by United States Copyright law. The librarian or or other staff of the library reserves the right to delete or disable your post or link if, in his or her judgment, the post or link would involve violation of copyright law. In accordance with 17 U.S.C. § 512(i)(1)(A), this library has adopted and shall make all reasonable effort to enforce a policy whereby the librarian or staff reserves the right to terminate in appropriate circumstances the access to the system or network of patrons who disrespect the intellectual property rights of others or who are otherwise repeat infringers of copyright.

These notices could be part of a system or network log-in screen, included in the institution's AUP (acceptable-use policy) to which all users assent before obtaining network access. They could be reprinted in other documentation, such as an institutional copyright policy, and could appear on a network and other technology capable of infringing digital copyright; in the case of students, they could appear on the first page of all course syllabi. |
| 10. Respecting online copyright protections | *Does the library, school, college, university, or other service provider desire to obtain the limitations on liability (monetary relief), the so-called safe harbor, that section 512 offers? If so, then the service provider must also accommodate and not interfere with standard* | A second qualifying requirement for libraries desiring to qualify for the safe harbor operates as an anti-interference provision of sorts: the service provider school or library must "accommodate and [must] not interfere with standard technical measures." 17 U.S.C. § 512(i)(1)(B). Standard technical measures are defined as those ,measures "used by copyright owners owners to identify or protect | No particular warning notice is necessary to comply with the accommodation and non-interference with standard technical measures provision. |

(Continued)

► **TOOL 1   A Copyright Compliance Audit** *(Continued)*

Purpose	Question	Analysis	Required Notice
10. Respecting online copyright protections *(continued)*	*technical measures that are employed to protect copyrighted works in online environments.*	copyrighted works." 17 U.S.C. § 512(i)(2). Section 512(i)(2) offers a three-part test to determine what qualifies as a standard technical measure: industry consensus, availability, and non-burdensome cost. Section 512(i)(2)(A) indicates that a standard technological measure is one that has "been developed pursuant to a broad consensus of copyright owners and service providers in an open, fair, voluntary, multi-industry standards process." Availability occurs when the technology is available to any person on "reasonable and nondiscriminatory terms." 17 U.S.C. § 512(i)(2)(B). This phrasing, coupled with the section 512(i)(1)(B) "accommodates," suggests at least that any affirmative duty to accept and adopt ("accommodates"), i.e., purchase and use, such measures is first conditioned on the chosen technology (the "standard technical measure[]" accepted by "multi-industry" "consensus") being available on "reasonable and nondiscriminatory terms." Finally, the technical measure must be affordable; it must "not impose substantial costs on service providers or substantial burdens on their systems or networks." 17 U.S.C. § 512(i)(2)(C). The standard suggests a relative assessment, perhaps measured against other institutional technology expenditures; thus a technical measure might not come without some cost to the institution. It would only be considered "substantial" if it were out of the ordinary.	
11. Copyright education on campus	*Does the college, university, or educational entity of higher education desire to obtain the additional limitations on liability*	Section 512(e) allows institutions of higher education to gain additional advantage of the safe harbor by treating faculty and graduate students engaged in teaching and research functions as third parties	While the use of a copyright warning notice is not required by either statute or regulation, an additional compliance burden is nonetheless placed upon the tertiary institution.

(Continued)

▶**TOOL 1**   **A Copyright Compliance Audit** *(Continued)*

Purpose	Question	Analysis	Required Notice
11. Copyright education on campus *(continued)*	*(monetary relief) offered by section 512(e)? If so, then the service provider educational entity must, in addition to meeting several qualifying conditions, "provide[] to all users of its system or network informational material that accurately describe, and promote compliance with the laws of the United States relating to copyright."*	(and not as employees) with respect to the conduit and cache provisions, sections 512(a) and (b). In addition, for purposes of the post and link provisions, sections 512(c) and (d), the institution need not impute the knowledge of such employees toward the institutional scienter, triggering what would otherwise be the "red flag" of awareness standard of section 512(c)(1)(A)(i) and (ii) or (d)(1) (A) and (B)." Not all faculty or TA or RA employee duties are covered; teaching and research are covered, but administrative or service duties are not. Section 512(e) will not shield the institution from liability for the infringing activity of teaching and researching faculty and graduate students undertaken in conjunction with "online access to instructional materials." Section 512(e)(1)(B) requires that within the preceding three years the institution must not have received more than two notices of infringement, under the formal notice provisions of 512(c)(3), from copyright owners regarding the behavior of the particular faculty member or graduate student "and such notifications of claimed infringement were not actionable under subsection (f) [dealing with false claims of infringement: 'knowingly materially misrepresents']." 17 U.S.C. § 512(e)(1)(B). Section 512(e)(1)(C) requires that "the institution provide[] to all users of its system or network informational material that accurately describe, and promote compliance with the laws of the United States relating to copyright."	The institution must provide "informational materials" to all users of its system or network, such as students, other patrons, and staff ("provides to all users of its system or network"), and not just to the targets of section 512(e), i.e., the teaching and research faculty and graduate students. The legislative history does not articulate what sort of informational material should be provided, but suggests what could be provided: "The legislation allows, but does not require, the institutions to use relevant informational materials published by the U.S. Copyright Office in satisfying the condition imposed by paragraph (C)." House (Conference) Report 105-796, 105th Cong. 2d Sess. 75 (1998). This suggestion refers to the various copyright circulars available from the Copyright Office Web site, but it could of course include other information in the form of posters, brochures, handouts, and brief articles in various institutional house organs, such as newsletters or magazines. In-service training, workshops, and other methods of instruction would also satisfy this requirement. By command of the statute, materials must not be limited to copyright issues related to section 512 alone, but to all the laws relating to copyright ("laws of the United States relating to copyright").

(Continued)

► **TOOL 1   A Copyright Compliance Audit** *(Continued)*

Purpose	Question	Analysis	Required Notice
12. Compliance tools for use (public performance and display) of copyrighted materials in distance education	*Does the school, college, university, or educational entity of higher education engage in distance education that involves the perform-ance or display of copyrighted material? If so, then, in order to obtain the benefits of section 110(2) the entity must fulfill several compliance-oriented obligations.*	In order for educators to obtain the additional rights in distance education, accredited institutions of education must first "*institute policies* regarding copyright, *provide informational materials to faculty, students, and relevant staff members* that accurately describe, and promote compliance with, the laws of the United States relating to copyright, and *provide[] notice to students* that materials used in connection with the course may be subject to copy-right protection." 17 U.S.C. § 110(2)(D)(i). While the statute does not pro-vide detail as to the contents of the policies, the statute uses the plural to suggest multiple policy statements or documents. It would be broader than the single "repeat infringer" policy requirement of section 512(i)(1)(A) discussed in item 9. Unlike section 512(e), section 110(2) benefits qualifying accredited nonprofit educational entities that engage in distance education, i.e., a transmission of copyrighted material, regardless of level. Second, like section 512(e)(1)(C), but also in an expanded articu-lation, the institution must "pro-vide[] informational materials to faculty, students, and relevant staff members that accurately describe, and promote compliance with, the laws of the United States relating to copyright." The section 512(e) command discussed in item 11 is more limited, as it targets network users alone: the "institution provides to all users of its system or network informa-tional material that accurately describe, and promote compliance with the laws of the United States relating to copyright." Under	The institution must "provide[] notice to students that mate-rials used in connection with *the course* may be subject to copyright protection. 17 U.S.C. § 110(2)(D)(i) (emphasis added). The use of the definite article "the," instead of "a," suggests that notice be in-cluded only with respect to the use of copyright material in conjunction with a distance education course, and not all courses offered by the institu-tion. While both the legislative history and the U.S. Copyright Office offer no direction as to the content of the required notice, one could be adopted from the section 108 and 109 regulatory notices. The following notice could be used to fulfill the notice require-ment; the language included would also satisfy the repeat infringer policy requirement notice of section 512(i)(1)(A): **Notice: Warning of Copyright Restrictions. All materials that under United States Copyright law would be considered the normal work product of the instructor, i.e., the class or lecture note exception to the work-for-hire doctrine,[*] are under the sole ownership of the instructor; this includes but is not limited to assign-ments and exercises, discussion questions and case studies, tests, etc. See, *Hays v. Sony Corp of America*, 847 F.2d 412 (7th Cir. 1988); and *Weinstein v. University of Illinois*, 811 F.2d 1091 (7th Cir. 1987).** **The instructor, the university, and the Web site designer share the copyright in the**

(Continued)

▶**TOOL 1**   **A Copyright Compliance Audit** *(Continued)*

Purpose	Question	Analysis	Required Notice
12. Compliance tools for use (public performance and display) of copyrighted materials in distance education *(continued)*		section 110(2), however, there is no limitation to "users of its system or network" alone, but the information must proceed to reach all "faculty, students, and relevant staff members." As with section 512(e), there is a similar purpose-content of material charge, i.e., that the material "accurately describe and promote compliance with, the laws of the United States relating to copyright." See item 11, Required Notice column for suggestions as to the sort of material that could be provided. According to the legislative history, the purpose of these requirements is to "promote an environment of compliance with the law, inform recipients of their responsibilities under copyright law, and decrease the likelihood of unintentional and uniformed acts of infringement." Conference Report, H. Rpt. No 107-685, 107th Cong. 2nd Sess. 230-231 (2002). Institutions will have to plan, adopt, and implement a copyright compliance program that includes copyright policies and organizational development programs that seek to inform students and staff of copyright law requirements and responsibilities; they must post warning notices that at least distance course material may be subject to copyright law.	"look and feel" of the site. Underlying copyright in the software generating the Web site is also protected by copyright. Documents and other material appearing on the Web site or by link from the site may also be protected by copyright. This site is maintained for educational purposes only. Your viewing of the material posted here does not imply any right to reproduce, to retransmit, or to redisplay it other than for your own personal or educational use. Links to other sites are provided for the convenience of the site user (staff or student) or visitor and do not imply any affiliation or endorsement of the other site owner nor a guarantee of quality or veracity of information on the linked site. As a student your ability to post or link to copyrighted material is also governed by United States Copyright law. The instructor or other staff of the institution reserves the right to delete or disable your post or link if, in his or her judgment, the post or would involve violation of copyright law. In accordance with 17 U.S.C. § 512(i)(1)(A), this institution has adopted and shall make all reasonable effort to enforce a policy whereby the instructor or staff reserves the right to terminate in appropriate circumstances the access to the system or network of students who disrespect the intellectual property rights of others or are otherwise repeat infringers of copyright. *In primary and secondary educational settings the section work-for-hire doctrine vests copyright ownership with the employer-school district.

(Continued)

►TOOL 1   A Copyright Compliance Audit *(Continued)*

Purpose	Question	Analysis	Required Notice
13. Respecting copyright in the use (public performance and display) of copyrighted materials in distance education	*Does the college, university, or educational entity of higher education engage in distance education that involves the performance or display of copyrighted material by means of a digital transmission? If so, then, in order to obtain the benefits of section 110(2), the entity must fulfill several additional compliance-oriented obligations.*	An educational entity that desires to obtain performance and display rights under section 110(2) must use "technological measures that reasonably prevent retention of the work in accessible form by recipients of the transmission from the transmitting body or institution for longer than the class session and unauthorized further dissemination of the work in accessible form by such recipients to others." 17 U.S.C. § 110(2)(D)(ii)(aa) and (bb). This provision is interpreted by the legislative history to require the use of encryption or other technology. Though it need not require actual monitoring, it does require periodic review of the technological measures the educational institution employs. If the copyright owner has placed a technological control on the material that prevents further retention or dissemination, then the educational institution cannot engage in any conduct that would impede the proper functioning of that measure. Since the statute prohibits conduct that "could reasonably be expected to interfere" with technological measures used by copyright owners to prevent section 110(2)(D)(ii)(I) retentions and disseminations, it would by logic also prohibit conduct that actually succeeds in interfering with those technological measures. Failure to meet this requirement does not create separate liability. Rather, the provision operates only as an eligibility clause for section 110(2); however, such interference could also violate the anti-circumvention rules of section 1201(a)(1) as discussed in Chapter 8.	While the use of a copyright warning notice is not required by either statute or regulation, an additional compliance burden is placed on the institution. The institution must use technological measures to prevent retention of a work by recipients. This requirement would suggest a need for at least periodic monitoring to determine if the technological measures used by the institution are reasonably effective; the constant monitoring of individual network users is not necessarily required. "Examples of technological protection measures that exist today and would reasonably prevent retention and further dissemination, include measures used in connection with streaming to prevent the copying of streamed material, such as the Real Player 'Secret Handshake/Copy Switch' technology discussed in *Real Networks v. Streambox*, 2000 WL 127311 or digital rights management systems that limit access to or use encrypted material downloaded onto a computer." Conference Report, H. Rpt. No 107-685, 107th Cong. 2nd Sess. 232 (2002).

►Tool 2

IMPLEMENTATION CHECKLIST FOR SECTION 512 REGISTERED AGENTS

While the author and publisher would certainly like readers to use this book, neither would like readers to photocopy, scan, or otherwise reproduce and distribute portions of this book in excess of fair use without permission. We do, however, want you to use the following checklist for implementation of section 512. Therefore the author and publisher grant any purchaser of this book the right to photocopy, scan, or otherwise reproduce and distribute portions of the checklist for implementation of section 512 for use within their own institutional environment. This permission includes the right to make derivative works (edit, revise, etc.), provided that with any use, proper source credit is given to the author and publisher. Thank you!

Reference is made to page numbers in the text where the measure is discussed in detail.

◄

☐ Institution meets definition of service provider in section 512(k)(1)(A) for conduit functions ("an entity offering the transmission, routing, or providing of connections for digital online communications, between or among points specified by a user, of material of the user's choosing, without modification to the content of the material as sent or received") or section 512(k)(1)(B) for cache, post, or link functions ("a provider of online services or network access, or the operator of facilities therefor, and includes an entity described in subparagraph (A)"). See discussion, pages 143–145.

☐ In addition, to qualify for the conduit function under section 512(a), "by reason of the provider's transmitting, routing, or providing connections for, material through a system or network controlled or operated by or for the service provider, or by reason of the intermediate and transient storage of that material in the course of such transmitting, routing, or providing connections," the following circumstances must exist:

  ☐ the transmission of the material was initiated by or at the direction of a person other than the service provider;

  ☐ the transmission, routing, provision of connections, or storage is carried out through an automatic technical process without selection of the material by the service provider;

  ☐ the service provider does not select the recipients of the material except as an automatic response to the request of another person;

- ☐ no copy of the material made by the service provider in the course of such intermediate or transient storage is maintained on the system or network in a manner ordinarily accessible to anyone other than anticipated recipients, and
- ☐ no such copy is maintained on the system or network in a manner ordinarily accessible to such anticipated recipients for a longer period than is reasonably necessary for the transmission, routing, or provision of connections; and
- ☐ the material is transmitted through the system or network without modification of its content. Section 512(a)(1)–(5).
- ☐ In addition, in cases of caching, the following requirements must exist:
  - ☐ the material is made available online by a person other than the service provider;
  - ☐ the material is transmitted from the person other than the service provider through the system or network to a person other than the service provider at the direction of that other person; and
  - ☐ the storage is carried out through an automatic technical process for the purpose of making the material available to users of the system or network who, after the material is transmitted as described above (previous bullet), request access to the material from the person other than the service provider, Section 512 (b)(1)(A)–(C).
  - ☐ the material results from "the intermediate and temporary storage of material on a system or network controlled by or for the service provider" and which meets the previous three bullets is transmitted to the subsequent users described in previous bullet without modification to its content from the manner in which the material was transmitted from person other than the service provider.
  - ☐ a service provider meeting the requirements complies with rules concerning the refreshing, reloading, or other updating of the material when specified by the person making the material available online in accordance with a generally accepted industry standard data communications protocol for the system or network through which that person makes the material available, except that this subparagraph applies only if those rules are not used by a person other than the service provider to prevent or unreasonably impair the intermediate storage to which this subsection applies;
  - ☐ the service provider does not interfere with the ability of technology associated with the material to return to a person other than the service provider the information that would have been available to that person if the material had been obtained by the subsequent users described in the previous paragraph directly from that person, except that this subparagraph applies only if that technology
    - ☐ does not significantly interfere with the performance of the provider's system or network or with the intermediate storage of the material;

- ☐ is consistent with generally accepted industry standard communications protocols; and
- ☐ does not extract information from the provider's system or network other than the information that would have been available to a person other than the service provider if the subsequent users had gained access to the material directly from that person;
- ☐ if a person other than a service provider has in effect a condition that a person must meet prior to having access to the material, such as a condition based on payment of a fee or provision of a password or other information, the service provider permits access to the stored material in significant part only to users of its system or network that have met those conditions and only in accordance with those conditions." Section 512(b)(1)(A)–(C) and (2)(A)–(D).
- ☐ Institution is operating as conduit for others, or caches ("intermediate or temporary storage") material of others, or allows users (patrons, students, etc.) to post or link material of others. See discussion, pages 142–145.
- ☐ Institution "has adopted and reasonably implemented, and informs subscribers and account holders of the service provider's system or network of, a policy that provides for the termination in appropriate circumstances of subscribers and account holders of the service provider's system or network who are repeat infringers." Section 512(i)(1)(A). See discussion, pages 160–167.
- ☐ Institution "accommodates and does not interfere with standard technical measures." Section 512(i)(1)(B). Standard technical measures are defined in section 512(i)(2). See discussion, pages 167–170.
- ☐ Institution has appointed a designated agent to receive complaints and has filed a notice of such designation with the U.S. Copyright Office. See discussion, pages 188–189.
- ☐ The notice ("Interim Designation of Agent to Receive Notification of Claimed Infringement") is made "available through its service, including on its website in a location accessible to the public, and by providing to the Copyright Office, substantially the following information" (Section 512(c)(2)) and "shall be identified as such by prominent caption or heading, and shall include the following information with respect to a single service provider:
  - ☐ The full legal name and address of the service provider;
  - ☐ All names under which the service provider is doing business;
  - ☐ The name of the agent designated to receive notification of claimed infringement;
  - ☐ The full address, including a specific number and street name or rural route, of the agent designated to receive notification of claimed infringement. A post office box or similar designation will not be sufficient except where it is the only address that can be used in that geographic location;

☐ The telephone number, facsimile number, and electronic mail address of the agent designated to receive notification of claimed infringement." 37 C.F.R. §201.38(c). See discussion, pages 190–193.

☐ Institution has filed an Interim Designation of Agent to Receive Notification of Claimed Infringement with the Public Information Office of the Copyright Office, Room LM-401, James Madison Memorial Building, Library of Congress, 101 Independence Avenue, SE, Washington, DC, during normal business hours, 9 am to 5 pm. If mailed, the Interim Designation should be addressed to: Copyright GC/I & R, PO Box 70400, Southwest Station, Washington, DC 20024. Each designation shall be accompanied by a filing fee of $30. Designations and amendments will be posted online on the Copyright Office's Web site (//www.loc.gov/copyright). 37 C.F.R. § 201.38(e). See discussion, pages 191–192.

☐ Any change of contact information (additional filing fee of $30) or termination of service (notice by certified or registered mail) is also filed with Copyright Office. 37 C.F.R. § 201.38(f) and (g). See discussion, pages 191–192.

☐ If the institution receives notice ("a written communication") from the copyright owner or its agent relating to cache, post, or link scenarios that substantially complies with requirements of (c)(3)(A)(i)–(vi), the institution acts expeditiously to remove or disable access to the material. 17 U.S.C. § 512(c)(1)(C). See discussion, pages 193–194.

☐ To be effective under this subsection, a notification of claimed infringement must be a written communication provided to the designated agent of a service provider, including substantially the following:

▶ (i) A physical or electronic signature of a person authorized to act on behalf of the owner of an exclusive right that is allegedly infringed.

▶ (ii) Identification of the copyrighted work claimed to have been infringed, or, if multiple copyrighted works at a single online site are covered by a single notification, a representative list of such works at that site.

▶ (iii) Identification of the material that is claimed to be infringing or to be the subject of infringing activity and that is to be removed or access to which is to be disabled, and information reasonably sufficient to permit the service provider to locate the material.

▶ (iv) Information reasonably sufficient to permit the service provider to contact the complaining party, such as an address, telephone number, and, if available, an electronic mail address at which the complaining party may be contacted.

▶ (v) A statement that the complaining party has a good-faith belief that use of the material in the manner complained of is not authorized by the copyright owner, its agent, or the law.

▶ (vi) A statement that the information in the notification is accurate, and under penalty of perjury, that the complaining party is authorized to act on behalf of the owner of an exclusive right that is allegedly infringed.

☐ If the institution otherwise possesses actual knowledge or is aware of facts or circumstances from which infringing material or activity is apparent, relating to a post or link scenario, the institution acts expeditiously to remove or disable access to the material. 17 U.S.C. § 512(c)(1)(A). See discussion, pages 202–206.

☐ If the notice from the copyright owner or its agent does not substantially comply with (c)(3)(A)(i)–(vi), but does at least substantially comply with (ii)–(iv) (identification of work infringed, identification of infringing material, and contact information, designated by a "▶" above), then in order for the failed (c)(3) notice not to trigger the general knowledge or awareness and remove or disable of 17 U.S.C. § 512(c)(1)(A), the institution must "promptly attempt to contact the person making the notification or take other reasonable steps to assist in the receipt of notification that substantially complies with all the provisions of subparagraph (A)," i.e., section 512(c)(3)(A)(i)–(vi). 17 U.S.C. § 512(c)(1)(B)(i) and (ii). See discussion, pages 197–200.

☐ The institution does "not receive a financial benefit directly attributable to the infringing activity, in a case in which the service provider has the right and ability to control such activity." 17 U.S.C. § 512(c)(1)(B) and 17 U.S.C. § 512(d)(2). See discussion, pages 206–210.

☐ If the service provider is an institution of higher education, it is allowed to treat faculty and graduate students (when employed by the institution) who perform teaching or research functions as third parties (and not as employees). With respect to the conduit and cache provisions "such faculty member or graduate student shall be considered to be a person other than the institution," and for purposes of the post and link provisions "such faculty member's or graduate student's knowledge or awareness of his or her infringing activities shall not be attributed to the institution," if:

  ☐ (1) the infringing activity of teaching and research faculty and graduate students is not undertaken in conjunction with online education offered within the preceding three-year period. U.S.C. § 512(e)(1)(A).

  ☐ (2) there are no more than two statutory (c)(3) notices of infringement within a three year period relating to that faculty member or graduate student. 17 U.S.C. § 512(e)(1)(B).

  ☐ (3) "the institution provides to all users of its system or network informational material that accurately describe, and promote compliance with the laws of the United States relating to copyright." 17 U.S.C. § 512(e)(1)(C). See discussion, pages 232–239.

☐ Upon receipt of a subpoena from a clerk of the federal court "for identification of an alleged infringer" under section 512(h), an institution, in cache, post, and link scenarios, i.e., the likely scenarios affecting a public library or educational entity, must "expeditiously disclose to the copyright owner or person authorized by the copyright owner information sufficient to identify the alleged infringer of the material described in the notification to the extent such information is available to the service provider." 17 U.S.C. § 512(h)(3). (The clerk must "expeditiously issue" the subpoena and the service provider must "expeditiously disclose" the identity of the alleged infringer.) However, this subpoena, like all subpoenas, may be challenged by a motion to quash. See discussion, pages 210–216.

☐ If the institution removes or disables access under any of the provisions of section 512, in order to obtain additional immunity from damages arising from a claim of improper removal or disabling the institution must:

    ☐ (1) contact the "subscriber" or patron or student whose post was removed or disabled, offering the subscriber a chance to challenge the service providers notification-request to remove or disable. 17 U.S.C. § 512(g)(2)(A).

    ☐ (2) if a challenge occurs, a so-called counter notification, then the service provider must contact the copyright owner or its representative from whom it received the initial subsection (c)(1)(C), informing the copyright owner that it will replace the material or restore access in ten business days unless the copyright owner "has filed an action seeking a court order to restrain the subscriber from engaging in infringing activity relating to the material on the service provider's system or network." 17 U.S.C. § 512(g)(2)(B).

    ☐ (3) if such second notice is not forthcoming from the copyright owner or agent of the copyright owner, then the service provider must "replace[] the removed material and cease[] disabling access to it not less than 10, nor more than 14, business days following receipt of the counter notice." 17 U.S.C. § 512(g)(2)(C). See pages 244–252.

►Tool 3

SIXTEEN SAMPLE COPYRIGHT POLICIES

Note: a model copyright policy for implementing section 110(2) and other provisions related to distance education is found in Tomas A. Lipinski, *Copyright in the Distance Education Classroom*, Appendix B, 201–207. Resources for drafting and implementing copyright policies can also be found in Claire Weber, "Designing, Drafting, and Implementing New Policies," in *Libraries, Museums and Archives: Legal Issues and Challenges in the New Information Era*, 303–319 (Tomas A. Lipinski, editor, 2002), and Donna L. Ferullo, "Struggling with Your Copyright Policy," *The Copyright and New Media Law Newsletter for Librarians and Information Specialists*, 8: 3, at 3 (2004).

The focus of these sample policies reflects the emphasis of this monograph. Additional provisions are possible! However, the suggested language can help the institution begin the process of tailoring a series of copyright statements that reflect its particular compliance environment. As with any institutional policy formulation, there is no cookie-cutter, one size fits all "model" policy. The policies here can be used to fulfill statutory requirements, either that exist specifically in the copyright law regarding the adoption of a policy or policies, the use of specific language as required by regulation or the general commands and requirements that must be adhered to in order to obtain the benefit (particular use of copyrighted material) of a provision of the copyright law.

SAMPLE COPYRIGHT POLICY PROVISIONS: SECTION 108

1. Using a Copyright Notice

In an effort to preserve the rights of reproduction and public distribution granted to qualifying libraries and archives under section 108, any copies reproduced, under this section must include a notice of copyright.

[Include the following if in an educational environment: "The reproduction and distribution rights under section 108 are available to the library or archives not to the institution as a whole, but only to that reproduction and distribution that occurs within the premises of the library or archives."]

[As appropriate, use an illustration from your institutional environment. For example: "This policy covers reproduction of copyrighted material made for purposes of preservation and security or through the library's Reproduction Service Center."]

In instances where the item has an existing copyright notice, it should be reproduced. Such notice can typically be found in the front pages of a book, or at the beginning or end of an article. This notice (e.g., "Copyright © 2005 Tomas A. Lipinski") must be added to the copy that the library reproduces.

If a copyright notice does not appear, a "legend" can be stamped on the copy, saying that the work may be under copyright protection. For example: *"NOTICE: This material may be protected by Copyright Law (Title 17 U.S.C.)."* See, 17 U.S.C. § 108(a)(3).

Any reproduction or distribution made under this section must be without any purpose of direct or indirect commercial advantage; any fees should be on a cost-recovery basis only. Second, the collections of the library or archives must remain open to the public, or be available not only to researchers affiliated with the library or archives, or with the institution of which it is a part, but also to other persons doing research in a specialized field. See, 17 U.S.C. § 108(a)(1)–(3).

2. Copying for the Library or Archives

Reproduction includes copies or phonorecords of unpublished material made for purposes of preservation and security in the library or archives or for deposit for research use in another qualifying library under section 108(b) or 108(c) of published materials in case of damage, deterioration, loss, or theft, or if the existing format in which the work is stored has become obsolete, or copies made for patrons, respectively.

In cases of preservation and security under section 108(b), the copy or copies, phonorecord or phonorecords made (up to three copies or phonorecords may be made) must be from a work in the current collections of the library or archives, and if a digital copy is made, it must not be made available to the public in that format outside the premises of the library or archives, i.e., remote access to the material is not allowed. A copy made under subsection (b) for deposit in another library or archives may be transferred to that library or archives in digital format, but the receiving library or archives must not distribute the material in that format. Likewise, if this institution is the receiving library or archives, staff cannot make the reproduced material available to patrons in digital form in any capacity, whether through in-house or remote access. See, 17 U.S.C. § 108(b).

In cases of damage, deterioration, loss, or theft, or if the existing format in which the work is stored has become obsolete under section 108(c), the copy or copies made (up to three copies may be made) are subject to the same limitation on digital distribution, i.e., remote access to the material is not allowed, and the library or archives must first make a reasonable effort to obtain an unused replacement at a fair price. See, 17 U.S.C. § 108(c).

A "reasonable effort" "will vary according to the circumstances of a particular situation. It will always require recourse to commonly-known trade sources in the United States, and in the normal situation also to the publisher or other copyright owner (if such owner can be located at the address listed in the copyright registration), or an authorized reproducing service." H. Rpt. No. 94-1476, 94th Cong., 2d Sess. 75-76 (1976) reprinted in 5 United States Code Congressional and Administrative News 5659, 5689 (1976).

3. Copying for Patrons

Reproduction of copyrighted material under section 108 includes copies or phonorecords made for patrons, where the library or archives provides a reproducing service, or through interlibrary loan, of no more than one article or other contribution to a copyrighted collection or periodical issue or to a copy of a small part of any other copyrighted work under section 108(d), or of an entire work or to a substantial part of it under section 108(e). Reproduction under section 108(d) and (e) must meet three conditions:

- ▶ The copy must become the property of the user.
- ▶ The library or archives, through its staff, must have no notice that the copy would be used for any purpose other than private study, scholarship, or research, i.e., the copy cannot be used for reserve, e-reserve, or coursepack creation, or for other public distribution, nor for other private uses even if lawful, such as for recreation or entertainment.
- ▶ The library or archives displays prominently at the place where orders are accepted (such as the interlibrary loan office or the reproduction service center) and includes on its order form a warning of copyright in accordance with requirements that the Register of Copyrights shall prescribe by regulation. See, 17 U.S.C. § 108(d)(1) and (2) and 17 U.S.C. § 108(e)(1) and (2).

The text of the notice is precisely prescribed by regulation, 37 C.F.R. § 201.14(b):

NOTICE WARNING CONCERNING COPYRIGHT RESTRICTIONS. The copyright law of the United States (Title 17, United States Code) governs the making of photocopies or other reproductions of copyrighted material. Under certain conditions specified in the law, libraries and archives are authorized to furnish a photocopy or other reproduction. One of these specific conditions is that the photocopy or reproduction is not to be "used for any purpose other than private study, scholarship, or research." If a user makes a request for, or later uses, a photocopy or reproduction for purposes in excess of "fair use," that user may be liable for copyright infringement. This institution reserves the right to refuse to accept a copying order if, in its judgment, fulfillment of the order would involve violation of copyright law.

The notice must be (1) on at least one sign in the service area (reproducing center or interlibrary loan office, or similar station), and (2) on the patron request form itself, highlighted in a box on the front page of the form or near the patron-requester signature line. See, 17 U.S.C. § 108(d)(2) and 17 U.S.C. § 108(e)(2).

The form and manner of the notice is also prescribed by regulation. The notice "shall be printed on heavy paper or other durable material in type at least 18 points in size, and shall be displayed prominently, in such manner and location as to be clearly visible, legible, and comprehensible to a casual observer within the immediate vicinity of the place where orders are accepted." 37 C.F.R. § 201.14(c)(1).

Interlibrary loan or reproducing service request forms must also contain a notice:

printed within a box located prominently on the order form itself, either on the front side of the form or immediately adjacent to the space calling for the name or signature of the person using the form. The notice shall be printed in type size no smaller than that used predominantly throughout the form, and in no case shall the type size be smaller than 8 points. The notice shall be printed in such manner as to be clearly legible, comprehensible, and readily apparent to a casual reader of the form. 37 C.F.R. § 201.14(c)(2).

4. Copying by Patrons

In order to protect the institution from secondary liability for the reproductions made by patrons [use "students or members of the public" as appropriate] a warning notice must be placed on all reproducing equipment located on library or archives premises. See, 17 U.S.C. § 108(f)(1). Such notice should be placed on all photocopiers or other reproduction equipment in the library or archives that is accessible by patrons [use "students or members of the public" as appropriate] and that is capable of reproducing copyrighted material, e.g., photocopier, computer, printer, scanner, sampler, VCR, or any other technology that has a reproducing capacity.

The following notice based on 37 C.F.R. § 201.14, shall be used:

NOTICE WARNING CONCERNING COPYRIGHT RESTRICTIONS. The copyright law of the United States (Title 17, United States Code) governs the making of photocopies or other reproductions of copyrighted material. Libraries and archives furnish unsupervised photocopy or other reproduction equipment for the convenience of and use by patrons. Under 17 U.S.C. § 108(f)(2) the provision of unsupervised photocopy or reproduction equipment for use by patrons does not excuse the person who uses the reproduction equipment from liability for copyright infringement for any such act, or for any later use of such copy or phonorecord, if it exceeds fair use as provided by section 107 or any other provision of the copyright law. This institution reserves the right to refuse to make available or provide access to photocopy or other reproduction equipment if, in its judgment, use of such equipment would involve violation of copyright law.

In order to preserve the immunity from secondary liability, contributory or vicarious, that might result, library or archives staff must make every effort to ensure that the reproducing by patrons [use "students or members of the public" as appropriate] remains unsupervised, otherwise the immunity will not apply. In the absence of the section 108(f)(1) immunity, the library or archives may be subject to liability as a contributory or vicarious infringer.

Under 17 U.S.C. § 108(f)(2), patrons [use "students or members of the public" as appropriate] remain liable for any copying in excess of fair use or that is otherwise infringing.

Additional Requirements

In instances of copies made under section 108(d), library or archives staff must not engage in the systematic reproduction or distribution of single or multiple copies. Interlibrary loan arrangements are acceptable as long as the library or archives receiving the copies for distribution does not copy in such aggregate quantities as to substitute for a subscription to or purchase of such work. See, 17 U.S.C. § 108(g)(2).

[The institution may consider adoption of the CONTU Guidelines on Photocopying under Interlibrary Loan Arrangements, the so-called rule of five, i.e., "filled requests of a library or archives (a 'requesting entity') within any calendar year for a total of six or more copies of an article or articles published in such periodical within five years prior to the date of the request" as constituting reproduction "in such aggregate quantities as to substitute for a subscription to or purchase of such work." H. Rpt. 94-1733, 94th Cong., 2nd Sess. 74 (1976) (Conference Report), reprinted in 5 U.S.C.C.A.N. 5810, 5815 (1976); reprinted in U.S. Copyright Office, Circular 21: Reproduction of Copyrighted Works by Educators and Librarians 22-23 (1993). The author cautions against the use of any so-called guidelines, as they may not be consistent with current legal standards. In specific, a court has never interpreted the interlibrary loan guidelines. One option is to use a statement indicating the limit of interlibrary loan. Alternative options include choosing a number different from that suggested by the guidelines (i.e., a rule of 4 or 6) to indicate that interlibrary loan must be consistent with fair use (potentially the least limiting), or limiting the reproduction to that which falls within the institution's license array (potentially the most limited).]

Finally, no copies can be made under section 108 if any staff member is aware or has substantial reason to believe that it is engaging in the related or concerted reproduction or distribution of multiple copies or phonorecords of the same material, whether made on one occasion or over a period of time, and whether intended for aggregate use by one or more individuals or for separate use by the individual members of a group. See, 17 U.S.C. § 108(g)(1). [Use as appropriate an illustration from your institutional environment, for example: "A prohibited example would be a series of students requesting copies from the library or archives Reproduction Service Center, when all of the students are registered for the same class and request the same article within the first two weeks of the semester and the article is related to the topic of the course, and moreover appears on the reading list prepared by the instructor for the class."]

MODEL COPYRIGHT POLICY PROVISIONS: SECTION 109

5. Distribution of Lawful Copies

In an effort to preserve the right of public distribution granted under section 109, all staff shall make every effort to ensure that any items made available to the patrons [use "students or members of the public" as appropriate] in the collections of the library [use "school," "college," "university," or other institutional designation as appropriate] are lawfully made copies. See, 17 U.S.C. § 109(a).

6. Circulation of Phonorecords

[This provision applies to either a nonprofit library or nonprofit educational institution.]

The library [use alternative institutional designation as appropriate] may circulate phonorecords for nonprofit purposes in the form of rental, lease, or lending. Under this provision a nominal or cost-recovery fee is acceptable. See, 17 U.S.C. § 109(b)(1)(A).

7. Distribution of Computer Programs

[The following provision applies to a nonprofit library.]

The institution may circulate software in its possession if it affixes to the package containing the software the following warning notice (see, 17 U.S.C. § 109(b)(2)(A)):

Notice: Warning of Copyright Restrictions. The copyright law of the United States (title 17, United States Code) governs the reproduction, distribution, adaptation, public performance, and public display of copyrighted material. Under certain conditions specified in law, nonprofit libraries are authorized to lend, lease, or rent copies of computer programs to patrons on a nonprofit basis and for nonprofit purposes. Any person who makes an unauthorized copy or adaptation of the computer program, or redistributes the loan copy, or publicly performs or displays the computer program, except as permitted by title 17 of the United States Code, may be liable for copyright infringement. This institution reserves the right to refuse to fulfill a loan request if, in its judgment, fulfillment of the request would lead to violation of the copyright law. 37 C.F.R. § 210.24(b).

The notice should be affixed by means of a label cemented, gummed, or otherwise durably attached to the copies or to a box, reel, cartridge, cassette, or other container used as a permanent receptacle for the copy of the computer program. The notice shall be printed in such manner as to be clearly legible, comprehensible, and readily apparent to a casual user of the computer program. 37 C.F.R. § 210.24(c).

[If the institution is a nonprofit educational institution (or library within such institution), the following provision may also be included.] The following provision does not apply to a freestanding library such as a public library or historical society archive, i.e., the sort of entity targeted by section 108.

8. Transfer of Computer Program

The institution may transfer the possession of a lawfully made copy of a computer program to another nonprofit educational institution or to faculty, staff, and students under any conditions, but it must ensure that no copy remains on any computer or any place on its network or system. See, 17 U.S.C. § 109(b)(1)(A).

MODEL COPYRIGHT POLICY PROVISIONS: SECTION 512

9. Initial Requirements: Repeat Infringer Policy and Noninterference

The "safe harbor" provisions of section 512 operate to remit all monetary damages relating to copyright infringement in networked digital environments, including actual or statutory damages, costs, attorney's fees, or any other form of monetary payment. See, 17 U.S.C. § 512(k)(2). It is the goal of this institution to manage its copyright risk such that monetary loss is limited as much as possible.

In order to obtain the "safe harbor" of section 512 for all monetary liability that might arise from the infringing conduct of library [use "school," "college," "university" or other institutional designation as appropriate] patrons [use "students or other members of the public" as appropriate], the library shall "adopt and reasonably implement . . . a policy that provides for the termination in appropriate circumstances of subscribers and account holders of the service provider's system or network who are repeat infringers." 17 U.S.C. § 512(i)(1)(A).

The following statement shall be disseminated through appropriate institutional mechanisms:

[For use by schools, colleges, universities or other educational settings.]

> *As a student your ability to post (including storage) or link to copyrighted material is also governed by United States copyright law. This instructor or other staff of the institution reserves the right delete or disable any post or link if, in its judgment, the post or link would involve violation of copyright law. In accordance with 17 U.S.C. § 512(i)(1)(A), the institution adopts and shall make all reasonable effort to enforce a policy whereby the instructor or staff reserves the right to terminate in appropriate circumstances the access to the system or network of students who disrespect the intellectual property rights of others and are repeat infringers."*

[For use in public library settings.]

> *As a student your ability to post (including storage) or link to copyrighted material is also governed by United States copyright law. This institution or its staff reserves the right delete or disable access to any post or link if, in its judgment, the post or link would involve violation of copyright law. In accordance with 17 U.S.C. § 512(i)(1)(A), the institution adopts and shall make all reasonable effort to enforce a policy whereby the institution or staff reserves the right to terminate in appropriate circumstances the access to the system or network who disrespect the intellectual property rights of others and are repeat infringers.*

Subscribers must be informed of the policy through appropriate institutional mechanisms, such as a system or network log-in screen, the institution's AUP (acceptable-use policy), and the Patron Code of Conduct to which all users assent before obtaining network access. It should be reprinted in other documentation such as an institutional copyright policy, and should appear on on any technological equipment capable of infringing digital copyright. In the case of students, the policy should also appear on the first page of all course syllabi [use an alternative mechanism as appropriate].

This policy shall be enforced in a manner consistent with the implementation of other policies within the library, such as the AUP and the Patron Code of Conduct, and the other institutional policies relating to copyright [use an alternative mechanism as appropriate]. 17 U.S.C. § 512(i)(1)(A).

Optional provision: "Any patron [use "students or members of the public" as appropriate] whose system or network access is terminated may have his or her access restored after demonstration of the ability to respect the intellectual property rights of others.

[Use an illustration from your institutional environment as appropriate. For example: "Such respect may be demonstrated by completion of an online copyright tutorial, copyright workshop, or course 540-825, Legal Issues for the Library and Information Manager."]

While constant monitoring of patron conduct is not required of "suspect" patrons, it is not prohibited. However, before such monitoring is undertaken, supervisor approval is required.

Staff must accommodate (i.e., adopt) where reasonably feasible standard technical measures, and not interfere with those standard technical measures used by copyright owners to identify or protect copyrighted works. See, 17 U.S.C. § 512(i)(1)(B) and 17 U.S.C. § 512(i)(2) (defining standard technical measures). Standard technical measures that "do not impose substantial costs on service providers or substantial burdens on their systems or networks" must be adopted. 17 U.S.C. § 512(i)(2)(C).

[Use an illustration from your institutional environment as appropriate. For example: "Technology, the annual cost of which represents less than 5% of the fiscal operating budget of the I&MT (Information & Media Technologies) Department dedicated to network or system software, programs or related technologies, shall not be considered 'substantial' for the purposes of this policy; nor shall service burden, such as stoppage, degradation, or other impact similar to or within tolerances for other network or system software, programs, or related technologies, be considered 'substantial' for purposes of this policy."]

10. Adoption and Use of the Registered Agent Mechanism Under Section 512(c)

The Director [use other institutional title as appropriate] shall designate a Copyright Compliance Officer [use other institutional title as appropriate] to receive complaints from copyright owners relating to infringing material or activity on its system or network and arising from caching, posting, or linking. The Copyright Compliance Officer [use other institutional title as appropriate] shall file a notice of such designation with the U.S. Copyright Office.

The notice must be identified with the following heading: "Interim Designation of Agent to Receive Notification of Claimed Infringement." The notice shall include the following information: (1) the full legal name and address of the service provider, (2) all names under which the service provider is doing business, (3) the name of the agent (i.e., the Copyright Compliance Officer, designated to receive notification of claimed infringement), (4) the full address, including a specific number and street name or rural route, of the agent (a post office box or similar designation will not be sufficient except where it is the only address that can be used in that geographic location), and (5) the telephone number, facsimile number, and electronic mail address of the agent. 37 C.F.R. § 201.38(c).

The notice shall be filed with the Public Information Office of the Copyright Office, Room LM-401, James Madison Memorial Building, Library of Congress, 101 Independence Avenue, SE, Washington, DC, during normal business hours, 9 a.m. to 5 p.m. If mailed, the Interim Designation should be addressed to: Copyright

GC/I & R, PO Box 70400, Southwest Station, Washington, DC 20024. Each designation shall be accompanied by a filing fee of $30. Designations and amendments will be posted online on the Copyright Office's Web site (*www.loc.gov/copyright*). 37 C.F.R. § 201.38(e).

The Copyright Compliance Officer shall file any change of contact information (additional filing fee of $30) or termination of service (notice by certified or registered mail) with Copyright Office. 37 C.F.R. § 201.38(f) and (g).

Once the registered agent, i.e., the Copyright Compliance Officer, receives proper notice ("a written communication") from the copyright owner or its agent relating to cache, post, or link scenarios, the Copyright Compliance Officer must act expeditiously to remove or disable access to the alleged infringing material. 17 U.S.C. § 512(c)(1)(C). A proper notice is one that substantially complies with requirements of (c)(3)(A)(i)–(vi):

(i) A physical or electronic signature of a person authorized to act on behalf of the owner of an exclusive right that is allegedly infringed.

► (ii) Identification of the copyrighted work claimed to have been infringed, or, if multiple copyrighted works at a single online site are covered by a single notification, a representative list of such works at that site.

► (iii) Identification of the material that is claimed to be infringing or to be the subject of infringing activity and that is to be removed or access to which is to be disabled, and information reasonably sufficient to permit the service provider to locate the material.

► (iv) Information reasonably sufficient to permit the service provider to contact the complaining party, such as an address, telephone number, and, if available, an electronic mail address at which the complaining party may be contacted.

(v) A statement that the complaining party has a good-faith belief that use of the material in the manner complained of is not authorized by the copyright owner, its agent, or the law.

(vi) A statement that the information in the notification is accurate, and under penalty of perjury, that the complaining party is authorized to act on behalf of the owner of an exclusive right that is allegedly infringed.

In order for a notice to be valid in instances of caching, the notice must also contain a statement that the material has been removed or access to it disabled, or that a court has ordered such occurrence. See, 17 U.S.C. § 512(b)(E)(i) and (ii).

In instances where the failed notice under section 512(c)(3) substantially complies with notice sub-provisos (ii), (iii), and (iv) (the identification of the work, identification of infringing material, and contact information, marked with a "►" above), then this partial notice can still trigger the removal or disabling obligation (see "Knowledge or Awareness and Appropriate Response Mechanisms" below), unless the Copyright Compliance Officer "promptly attempts to contact the person making the notification or takes other reasonable steps to assist in the receipt of notification that substantially complies with all the provisions of subparagraph (A)." 17 U.S.C. § 512(c)(3)(B)(ii). As a result, in these circumstances, the Copyright Compliance Officer must contact the issuer of the notice and attempt to facilitate receipt of a perfected notice, i.e., one that substantially complies with all of the (i)–(vi) provisos of section 512 (c)(3)(A).

11. Knowledge or Awareness and Appropriate Response Mechanisms

In instances of posting and linking by patrons [use "students or members of the public" as appropriate], if any staff member possesses knowledge or is aware of facts or circumstances from which infringing activity is apparent, then that staff member shall contact the Copyright Compliance Officer who shall then act expeditiously to remove, or disable access to, the alleged infringing material. See, 17 U.S.C. § 512(c)(1)(A) and 17 U.S.C. § 512(d)(1).

For purposes of this policy, "knowledge" means actual knowledge and "awareness" is the equivalent of a "red flag" test.

> The "red flag" test has both a subjective and an objective element. In determining whether the service provider was aware of a "red flag," the subjective awareness of the service provider of the facts or circumstances must be determined. However, in deciding whether those facts or circumstances constitute a "red flag"—in other words whether infringing activity would have been apparent to a reasonable person operating under the same or similar circumstances-an objective standard should be used. H.R. Rep. No 551 (Part 2), 105th Cong., 2d Sess. 53 (1998); Senate Report 105-190, 105th Cong., 2d Sess. 44 (1998).

The red flag standard "imposes no obligation on a provider to seek out such red flags. Once a provider becomes aware of a red flag, however, it ceases to qualify for the exemption" unless it responds in the appropriate fashion. H.R. Rep. No 551 (Part 1), 105th Cong., 2d Sess. 25 (1998).

The following can assist staff in determining when the requisite "awareness" is raised:

▶ "[O]nline editors and catalogers would not be required to make discriminating judgments about potential copyright infringement. If, however, an Internet site is obviously pirate, then seeing it may be all that is needed for the service provider to encounter a 'red flag.'" H.R. Rep. No 551 (Part 2), 105th Cong., 2d Sess. 58 (1998); Senate Report 105-190, 105th Cong., 2d Sess. 49 (1998).

▶ For example, in a information location tool scenario, "if the copyright owner could prove that the location was clearly, at the time the directory provider viewed it, a 'pirate' site of the type described below where sounds recordings, software, movies or books were available for unauthorized downloading, public performance or public display" the red flag would be raised. H.R. Rep.

No 551 (Part 2), 105th Cong., 2d Sess. 57 (1998); Senate Report 105-190, 105th Cong., 2d Sess. 48 (1998).

▶ "[A] directory provider would not be similarly aware merely because it saw one or more well known photographs of a celebrity at a site devoted to that person. The provider could not be expected, during a brief cataloging visit, to determine whether the photograph was still protected by copyright or was in the public domain; if the photograph was still protected by copyright, whether the use was licensed; and if the use was not licensed, whether it was permitted under the fair use doctrine." H.R. Rep. No 551 (Part 2), 105th Cong., 2d Sess. 57-58 (1998); Senate Report 105-190, 105th Cong., 2d Sess. 48 (1998).

If the infringing nature of the post or link is apparent it should be removed or disabled. If staff is in doubt, consultation with the Copyright Compliance Officer, Office of Legal Counsel representative or other appropriate staff member [use alternative institutional title as appropriate] should be sought.

12. Additional Requirements: No Financial Benefit

In order to secure the safe harbor, the library [use alternative institutional designation as appropriate] must not receive a financial benefit directly attributable to the infringing activity. However, a one-time set-up fee or flat periodic payments from patrons [use "students or members of the public" as appropriate] for access to the library [use alternative institutional designation as appropriate] system or network is permissible, as well as a fee structure based on the length of the message (e.g., per number of bytes) or by connect time. See, H.R. Rep. No 551 (Part 2), 105th Cong., 2d Sess. 54 (1998); Senate Report 105-190, 105th Cong., 2d Sess. 44-45 (1998).

Receipt of a "financial benefit directly attributable to the infringing activity" would exist "where the *value of the service lies in providing access* to infringing material." H.R. Rep. No 551 (Part 2), 105th Cong., 2d Sess. 54 (1998); Senate Report 105-190, 105th Cong., 2d Sess. 45 (1998) (emphasis added). See also, *Marobie-FL, Inc. v. National Association of Firefighter Equipment Distributors*, 983 F. Supp. 1167, 1179 (N.D. Ill. 1997).

[Note: state statutes regarding "free" public libraries may preclude the use of a fee mechanism for system or network access (Internet use), regardless of how it is structured. Thus, appropriate state statute and interpreting documents (such as a state attorney general opinion) should be consulted before initiating a fee mechanism.]

13. Follow-Up Procedures for the Removal or Disabling of Infringing Material

At times it may be difficult to judge whether material is infringing or to know whether a notice provided by a copyright owner or its agent is in error. The default should be in favor of removal or disabling.

Section 512(g) provides immunity for erroneous removal or disabling made in good faith by or at the direction of the Copyright Compliance Officer. In instances of removal or disabling in response to a subsection 512(c)(1)(C) notice, and in order to protect the library [use alternative institutional title as appropriate] for claims that may arise from a good-faith removal or disabling made in error, the following procedures shall be followed.

The Copyright Compliance Officer (i.e., the registered agent of the library [use alternative institutional title as appropriate) shall "take[] reasonable steps promptly to notify" the subscriber or patron [use "students or members of the public" as appropriate] whose post or link was removed or disabled "that it has removed or disabled access to the material" and offer the subscriber the opportunity to challenge the service provider's removal or disabling. See, 17 U.S.C. § 512(g)(2)(A).

For purposes of this policy "promptly to notify" shall mean within three to five (3 to 5) business days [use other designation of time limit as appropriate] within receipt of a section 512(c)(1)(C) notice from a copyright owner or his or her representative.

The Copyright Compliance Officer shall conduct a search of the library's registration and circulation records to obtain the appropriate contact information. [Use alternative formulation if in an educational environment. For example: "The Copyright Compliance Officer shall conduct a search of the school's [use "college" or "university" as appropriate] student registration records to identify the appropriate contact information."] Once the contact information is retrieved, the Copyright Compliance Officer shall notify the patron of the removal or disabling and include in the notification to the subscriber patron [use "student or other member of the public" as appropriate] a copy of the following materials:

- ▶ the notice received from copyright owner,
- ▶ section 512(g), highlighting the subsection (g)(3) counternotification requirements
- ▶ the relevant institution policy relating to section 512(g) implementation.

To be effective, the challenge be in writing and must include substantially the following:

1. A physical or electronic signature.
2. Identification of the material that has been removed or to which access has been disabled, and the location at which the material appeared before it was removed or access to it was disabled.
3. A statement under penalty of perjury that the subscriber has a good-faith belief that the material was removed or disabled as a result of mistake or misidentification of the material to be removed or disabled.
4. Contact information including the name, address, and telephone number of the subscriber, and a statement that the subscriber consents to the jurisdiction of Federal District Court for the judicial district in which the address is located,

or, if the subscriber's address is outside of the United States, for any judicial district in which the service provider may be found, and indication that the subscriber will accept service of process from the person who provided notification under subsection (c)(1)(C) or an agent of such person. See, 17 U.S.C. § 512(g)(3)(A)–(D).

For purposes of this policy "substantially" shall mean the inclusion of at least items 2 and 4.

If a challenge occurs by a subscriber, a so-called counter notification, then the Copyright Compliance Officer shall contact the copyright owner (or its agent) from whom it received the initial subsection 512(c)(1)(C), within three (3) business days after receipt of an effective counter notification from the subscriber. The Copyright Compliance Officer must inform the copyright owner (or its agent) that it will replace the material or restore access in ten (10) business days from the receipt date of the subscriber's counter notification unless the copyright owner (or its agent) responds to the officer indicating that the owner has filed an action seeking a court order to restrain the subscriber from engaging in infringing activity relating to the material on the library's system or network. The Copyright Compliance Officer shall request that the owner include with the second notice appropriate documentation such as a court issued receipt of filing or a stamped copy. See, 17 U.S.C. § 512(g)(2)(B).

This copyright owner contact must include two items:

▶ a copy of the subscriber's counter notification or challenge
▶ a statement that the service provider will "replace the removed material or cease disabling access to it in 10 business days" 17 U.S.C. § 512(g)(2)(B).

If such second notice is not forthcoming from the copyright owner (or its agent), then the Copyright Compliance Officer shall replace the removed material or cease disabling access to it not less than ten (10), nor more than fourteen (14), business days following receipt of the subscriber counter notification. See, 17 U.S.C. § 512(g)(2)(C).

14. Responding to Section 512(h) Subpoena Powers

Upon receipt of a subpoena issued by a clerk of the federal court "for identification of an alleged infringer" under section 512(h), the Copyright Compliance Officer shall "expeditiously disclose" the identity of the alleged infringer to the copyright owner (or its agent). Any staff member in receipt of any such subpoena issued under section 512(h) or under any other provision of the law for release of patron [use "student or other member of the public" as appropriate] identity information shall refer the matter to the Copyright Compliance Officer, or Office of Legal Counsel representative, or other appropriate staff member [use alternative institutional title as appropriate].

[An additional statement may be added. For example: "A court-ordered subpoena is subject to challenge, known as a motion to quash. An administrative subpoena issued without court authority may in fact have no legal effect. In addition, state confidentiality statutes may regulate the disclosure of library patron information. Federal law may also regulate the disclosure of student information."]

15. Compliance-Oriented Measures

[If the library or setting is that of an institution of higher education, then the following section may also be included.]

In order to obtain the additional safe harbor under section 512(e), whereby the institution may treat faculty and graduate students (when employed by the institution) and perform teaching or research functions as third parties (and not as employees). The result is that with respect to conduit and cache activities and similarly for post and link activities, the knowledge of qualifying employees to the institutional scienter of the knowledge or "red flag" awareness of 512(c)(1)(A)(i) and (ii) and (d)(1)(A) and (B). The Copyright Compliance Officer [use other title or committee as appropriate] shall develop and distribute informational materials to faculty, students, and relevant staff members (including administrators) that accurately describe, and promote compliance with, the copyright laws of the United States. [List appropriate mechanisms as appropriate and consistent with institutional environment, e.g., in-service training, newsletter, e-mail, employee or student handbook.]

The additional safe harbor of section 512(e) does not apply to other duties (such as administration) of faculty or graduate students.

Section 512(e) does not shield the institution from liability for the infringing activity of teaching and research faculty and graduate students undertaken within the past three years in conjunction with online education. 17 U.S.C. § 512(e)(1)(A).

If the Copyright Compliance Officer has received more than two complaints regarding the faculty member or graduate student in accordance with subsection (c)(3) within the last three years, then the additional protections section 512(e) are not available to the institution. 17 U.S.C. § 512(e)(1)(B).

16. Model Copyright Policy Provisions: Section 1201

Staff must not circumvent a technological measure that effectively controls access to copyrighted material, i.e., an access control. See, 17 U.S.C. § 1201(a)(1).

Staff may circumvent a technological measure that effectively controls the exercise of an exclusive right of a copyright owner, i.e., a use control. See, 17 U.S.C. § 1201(b).

Staff must not "traffic" or distribute or otherwise make available a "device" that circumvents either an access or use control. See, 17 U.S.C. § 1201(a)(2) and (b).

An example, would be a patch of code that allows an individual to hack past a technological protection measure, the DeCSS code that allows individuals to crack the CSS code on a DVD in order to port it onto a computer or other technology.

Anti-circumventing technology or such a "device" is one that meets any of the following conditions:

▶ Is primarily designed or produced for the purpose of circumventing the protection afforded by a technological measure that effectively protects a right of a copyright owner under the copyright law or the protection afforded by a technological measure that protects a right of a copyright owner under the copyright law. See, 17 U.S.C. § 1201(a)(2)(A) and (b)(1)(A).

▶ Has only limited commercially significant purpose or use other than to circumvent either a technological measure that effectively controls a work protected under law or protection afforded by a technological measure that effectively protects a right of a copyright owner under the copyright law in a work or a portion thereof. See, 17 U.S.C. § 1201(a)(2)(B) and (b)(1)(B).

▶ Is marketed by the actual person or another acting in concert with trafficker with the trafficker's knowledge for use in circumventing either a technological measure that effectively controls access to a work protected under the copyright law or protection afforded by a technological measure that effectively protects a right of a copyright owner under the copyright law in a work. See, 17 U.S.C. § 1201(a)(2)(C) and (b)(1)(C).

Examples would include patches of computer code or other technologies that allow patrons [use "students or other members of the public" as appropriate] to fast-forward past advertisements on a DVD (see, Exemption to Prohibition on Circumvention of Copyright Protection Systems for Access Control Technologies, Final Rule, 68 Fed. Reg. 62011, 62015-62016 (October 31, 2003)), play a DVD on a PC or platform other than a DVD player (see, *Universal Studios, Inc. v. Corley*, 273 F.3d 429 (2d Cir. 2001)), disable so-called technological handshake protocols (see, *Real Networks, Inc. v. Streambox, Inc.*, 2000 U.S. Dist. LEXIS 1889 (W.D. Wash. 2000)), and disable or alter geographic use restriction codes (see, *Sony Computer Entertainment America Inc. v. Gamemasters, Inc.*, 87 F. Supp. 2d 976, 987 (N.D. Cal. 1999)).

General Exceptions

As provided by federal regulation, it is not a violation of the anti-circumvention rule to circumvent a technological measure that controls access to:

▶ Lists of Internet locations blocked by commercially marketed filtering software applications that are intended to prevent access to domains, Web sites, or portions of Web sites. (Note that lists of Internet locations blocked by software applications that operate exclusively to protect against damage to a computer or computer network and lists of Internet locations blocked by software applications that operate exclusively to prevent receipt of e-mail are not included.)

▶ Computer programs protected by dongles that prevent access due to malfunctions or damage. Obsolete dongles are those that are "no longer manufactured or reasonably available in the commercial marketplace."

▶ Computer programs and video games distributed in formats that have become obsolete and which require the original media or hardware as a condition of access.

▶ Literary works distributed in e-book format when all existing e-book editions of the work (including digital text editions made available by authorized entities) contain access controls that prevent the enabling of the e-book's read-aloud function and that prevent the enabling of screen readers to render the text into a "specialized format." See, 68 Federal Register 62011, 62014 (October 31, 2003), amending 37 C.F.R. § 201.40.

Specific Exception for Nonprofit Libraries, Archives, and Educational Institutions

In addition, if the following conditions are met, it is not a violation of the anti-circumvention rule to circumvent a technological measure that controls access to a copyrighted work when:

▶ The purpose of the access is to make a good-faith determination of whether to acquire a copy of that work for a lawful purpose. See, 17 U.S.C. § 1201(d)(1).

▶ The work so accessed must not be retained longer than necessary to make such good-faith determination. See, 17 U.S.C. § 1201(d)(1)(A).

▶ The work so accessed must not be used for any other purpose. See, 17 U.S.C. § 1201(d)(1)(B).

▶ An identical copy of the work must not be reasonably available in another form. See, 17 U.S.C. § 1201(d)(2).

In order for this institution to take advantage of this privilege for purposes of its library or archives, the collections of that library or archives shall be either open to the public or available not only to researchers affiliated with the library or archives or with the institution of which it is a part, but also to other persons doing research in a specialized field. See, 17 U.S.C. § 1201(d)(3).

Staff of the institution shall not "willfully for the purpose of commercial advantage or financial gain violate[]" the requirements of the specific exemption. If such violation occurs, the institution will lose the benefit of mandatory damage remission provided by section 1203 ("entity sustains the burden of proving, and the court finds, that the library, archives, educational institution, or public broadcasting entity was not aware and had no reason to believe that its acts constituted a violation," see, 17 U.S.C. § 1203(c)(5)(B)(ii)), and shall be subject to civil penalties under section 1203(c)(2) and (3)(A) (actual or statutory damages of "not less than $ 200 or more than $ 2,500 per act of circumvention, device, product, component, offer, or performance of service, as the court considers just."). See, 17 U.S.C. § 1201(d)(3)(A).

Staff of the institution must not repeat a violation of the specific exemption requirements "willfully for the purpose of commercial advantage or financial gain." If such violation occurs, then the institution may not avail itself of the specific exemption in the future; in addition to being subject to civil penalties under section 1203(c)(2) and (3)(A), the institution may face the potential for treble damage enhancement under section 1203(c)(4) for repeat violations that occur "within 3 years after a final judgment was entered against the [institution] . . . as the court considers just." See, 17 U.S.C. § 1201(d)(3)(B).

►Index

CASES

▶Index

SUBJECT

▶About the Author

Tomas A. Lipinski, a native of Milwaukee, Wisconsin, completed his Juris Doctor (J.D.) at Marquette University Law School, Milwaukee, Wisconsin. He received his Master of Laws (LL.M.) from The John Marshall Law School, Chicago, Illinois, and his Ph.D. from the University of Illinois at Urbana-Champaign.

Lipinski has worked in a variety of legal settings, including the private, public, and nonprofit sectors. He taught at the American Institute for Paralegal Studies and at Syracuse University College of Law. He is a visiting associate professor at the Graduate School of Library and Information Science, University of Illinois at Urbana-Champaign. From 1999 to 2003, he taught at the Department of Information Science, School of Information Technology at the University of Pretoria, Pretoria, South Africa.

Lipinski currently teaches and speaks frequently on various topics within the areas of information law and policy, especially copyright, privacy, and free speech issues in schools and libraries, and he continues to counsel libraries and schools in these areas. In addition, he serves as co-director of the Center for Information Policy Research at the University of Wisconsin-Milwaukee. Recent publications include:

▶ THE LIBRARY LEGAL ANSWER BOOK (ALA 2003) co-authored with Mary Minow.

▶ "The Decreasing Impact of Technological Neutrality in Copyright Law and Its Impact on Institutional Users," in the *Journal of the American Society for Information Science and Technology* with Lee S. Strickland and Mary Minow.

▶ "Patriot in the Library: Management Approaches When Demands for Information are Received from Law Enforcement and Intelligence Agents," in *Notre Dame Journal of College and University Law.*

▶ COPYRIGHT LAW IN THE DISTANCE EDUCATION CLASSROOM, with Thomas Gould and Elizabeth Buchanan.

▶ "Copyright Policies and the Deciphering of Fair Use in the Creation of Reserves at Major University Libraries," in the *Journal of Academic Librarianship.*